Also by Robert Kimball

COLE
(editor)

REMINISCING WITH SISSLE AND BLAKE
(co-author)

THE GERSHWINS
(co-author)

THE UNPUBLISHED COLE PORTER
(editor)

THE COMPLETE LYRICS OF COLE PORTER
(editor)

THE COMPLETE LYRICS OF LORENZ HART
(co-editor)

CATALOG OF THE AMERICAN MUSICAL
(co-author)

THE COMPLETE LYRICS OF IRA GERSHWIN
(editor)

READING LYRICS
(co-editor)

THE COMPLETE LYRICS OF IRVING BERLIN
(co-editor)

Also by Steve Nelson

ONLY A PAPER MOON:
THE THEATRE OF BILLY ROSE

GOWER CHAMPION:
DANCE AND AMERICAN MUSICAL THEATRE
(co-editor)

The Complete Lyrics of

FRANK LOESSER

ALFRED A. KNOPF   NEW YORK   2003

The Complete Lyrics of

FRANK LOESSER

Edited by

ROBERT KIMBALL and STEVE NELSON

THIS IS A BORZOI BOOK PUBLISHED BY ALFRED A. KNOPF

Copyright © 2003 by Frank Loesser Enterprises, Robert Kimball, and Steve Nelson

All rights reserved under International and Pan-American Copyright Conventions. Published in the United States by Alfred A. Knopf, a division of Random House, Inc., New York, and simultaneously in Canada by Random House of Canada Limited, Toronto. Distributed by Random House, Inc., New York.

www.aaknopf.com

Knopf, Borzoi Books, and the colophon are registered trademarks of Random House, Inc.

Copyright information on the lyrics of Frank Loesser appears on the first page of the index.

ISBN 0-679-45059-9

LC 2003109481

Manufactured in the United Kingdom

FIRST EDITION

Photographic Credits

Courtesy of the Academy of Motion Picture Arts and Sciences: 125; Frank Loesser Enterprises: xii, xvii, 1, 17, 40, 66, 94, 106, 136, 156, 169, 196, 204, 214; Photofest: vi, 78, 146, 176 (bottom); Margo Feiden Galleries: following 157; Time-Life Publications: 176 (top)

To Frank Loesser's children:

SUSAN, JOHN, HANNAH, and EMILY

Contents

Left: *Frank Loesser and Abe Burrows.* Below: *Frank
Loesser, Cole Porter, and Louis Lipstone.*

Contents

Contents

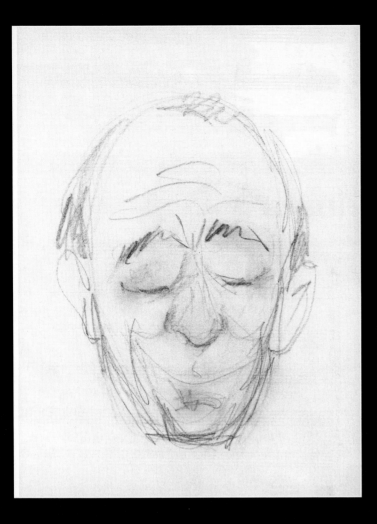

Introduction

The morning after the triumphant opening night of the musical fable *Guys and Dolls,* Irving Berlin placed a phone call to Richard Rodgers. "Dick, what are we going to do about the kid?" The kid was Frank Loesser, the composer-lyricist of *Guys and Dolls.*

If Loesser "arrived" that stellar night of November 24, 1950, he was no new kid on the block. Forty years old at the time, he had honed his craft and served his apprenticeship by writing songs for more than two decades. He had worked with almost one hundred different composers and lyricists, fashioning songs for nearly one hundred films. He had started as a lyricist but began writing music with the title song for the 1940 film *Seventeen,* and followed that up with such songs as the huge wartime hit "Praise the Lord and Pass the Ammunition" (he served as a private in the army from 1942 to 1945) and the exquisite 1944 "Spring Will Be a Little Late This Year." He had a major success with "On a Slow Boat to China" in 1948 and won the Academy Award for Best Song with the amazing conversation duet "Baby, It's Cold Outside" for the 1949 Esther Williams film *Neptune's Daughter.* Two years before *Guys and Dolls,* he had made his Broadway debut with a successful, richly varied score for *Where's Charley?,* starring Ray Bolger.

While Berlin and Rodgers had been aware of Loesser by 1950, there is no doubt Loesser had long admired and actually modeled himself after these two musical-theater titans. With Berlin's example in mind, he was aware of the importance of retaining his own song copyrights and establish-

ing his own music publishing company, which he did in 1948. According to his longtime friend, attorney, and business partner Harold Orenstein, he had even picked as his attorneys Francis Gilbert of New York and Irving Cohen of Los Angeles precisely because they were Berlin's lawyers. (Four years after the opening of *Guys and Dolls,* at ASCAP's fortieth-anniversary dinner, Berlin tipped his hat to Loesser in a humorous goodbye to "the little colored boy" who some people believed had written Berlin's songs: "A few years ago he left me / Like one of those temp'ramental molls / It was just around that certain time / Frank Loesser wrote *Guys and Dolls.*")

From Rodgers's example, Loesser noted how important it was for each movie or theater project to be a unique musical adventure, a goal he would pursue with rare distinction in the varied scores that came from his pen. Also with Rodgers as his model, he saw the value of setting up a full-service organization of his own, including a show production company and a dramatic licensing agency. (Rodgers and Oscar Hammerstein II had produced Berlin's *Annie Get Your Gun.*) In the early 1950s, Loesser acquired and developed Music Theater International, which would license his shows as well as those of other musical-theater creators. Rodgers, for his part, recalled that when he first heard "Baby, It's Cold Outside," "I listened to it and jumped up from the chair to phone Frank in California and say I thought it was one of the finest pieces of song writing I had ever heard."

. . .

Frank Henry Loesser was born in New York City on June 29, 1910, the second child of Henry and Julia Ehrlich Loesser.

Above: *Frank Loesser, self portrait.* Right: *Frank Loesser and daughter Hannah*

Julia's older sister, Bertha, had been Henry's first wife, and they had had a son, Arthur, who was twelve in 1906 when Bertha died. The following year Henry and Julia were married. Frank's sister, Grace, was born that December.

Frank's parents had come to the United States from Germany—Henry in the 1880s, Julia the following decade at seventeen. Henry found work as a grocer and supplemented his income by teaching piano, a vocation he later pursued full-time. Arthur, who became well known as a pianist and musicologist (he wrote the entertaining book *Men, Women, and Pianos: A Social History*), observed of his family, "The atmosphere of our modest home was acutely intellectual. . . . During my early youth I used to hear the words Art and Philosophy pronounced in a tone of reverence that few Americans could comprehend. . . . In our household German was the vehicle of culture and loftier thought, English was the suitable medium for purchasing vegetables."

The withering disdain with which Henry, Julia, and Arthur Loesser viewed American popular culture was no small factor in Frank Loesser's drive to be a songwriter. While his need to please and impress his family never waned, he was determined to do it on his terms and in an arena they utterly loathed. Harold Orenstein, in his brief unpublished memoir of Loesser, noted that "there was something essentially sad about Frank, not pervasive but an underlying overcast," which Orenstein attributed to the early death of Loesser's father in the summer of 1926, when Frank was sixteen, and his mother's failure to show him much appreciation or affection. "From time to time," Orenstein wrote, "Frank would leave home. He slept on park benches. . . . Even with his successes she never understood what Frank stood for."

Surrounded by music and other intellectual activities, young Frank rebelled by refusing to speak German and struggling as a student. His penchant for practical jokes was one of the reasons he was expelled from the prestigious Townsend Harris High School (which Ira Gershwin and Yip Harburg, among many other luminaries, had attended) before graduating from DeWitt Clinton High, at age fifteen. In her biography of her father, *A Most Remarkable Fella*, Susan Loesser reports that he was also expelled from City College of New York "shortly after entering—for failing every subject but English and gym, and for polishing the nose of a bronze statue."

Loesser started writing song lyrics in his teens, not long after his father's sudden death. When Henry died, the family income vanished, and there were no savings. To help support the family, Frank took on a series of jobs. He was by turns waiter, restaurant "checker" (he monitored the quality of food and service), process server, seller of classified newspaper ads, factory worker (he screwed lids on insecticide cans), press agent, newspaper reporter, and editor of a short-lived paper in New Rochelle.

One of the earliest of Loesser's long list of collaborators was William Schuman, later a Pulitzer Prize–winning "serious" composer, music administrator, and first president of New York's Lincoln Center for the Performing Arts. "Everyone else wrote hits with Frank," Schuman recalled. "I only managed flops." Actually, Loesser's first published composition was a Schuman/Loesser ballad, "In Love with a Memory of You," which appeared in 1931.

Although much of Loesser's early work is uneven, there are occasional glimpses of the songwriter to come. In "Doing the Dishes" and "Where the Grass Grows Green," two light romantic comedy songs written with Schuman (page 3) around 1930, Loesser's talent for inventive song settings begins to emerge, as does a gift for character, situation, and novelty. In "The Traffic Was Terrific" (page 13), Loesser spins a romantic encounter from the idea of two people stuck in a traffic jam:

> The traffic was terrific
> And she was caught between
> A truck that had no conscience
> And a reckless limousine.

The song concludes with the happy couple managing a different sort of automotive chaos:

> It's just a noisy cottage,
> As noisy as the street,
> But we can hear our love song
> In the tramp of tiny feet.
> The kiddie cars and scooters

Have the right of way,
'Cause the traffic was terrific that day.

His ability to fit an original story, situation, and character into the format of a popular song was beginning to blossom. In the mid-1930s, Loesser started working with a piano player named Irving Actman, who was then accompanist for Lita Grey (the former Mrs. Charlie) Chaplin. While also writing specialty vaudeville numbers, Loesser and Actman plied their songs at a club on West Fifty-second Street called the Back Drop. One day in 1935 an aspiring young singer named Mary Alice Blankenbaker (professionally known as Lynn Garland) walked into the club. As Susan Loesser reports in *A Most Remarkable Fella*, Lynn, her mother recalled,

> [There were] two young men at an old upright piano that matched the antiquity of the potbellied stove at the back of the room. The one at the piano was of medium height, rather solidly build, wearing eyeglasses and a genial, benign expression on his face. The other young man was leaning on the lid of the old upright, his right elbow and hand supporting the weight of his head. He was short, slim and dark; his expression was intense, challenging, sardonic. His brown eyes commanded attention as they audaciously scanned the audience. "All I did was look at you, you gorgeous thing, and bang, the bell rang!" sang the short, dark, intense young man looking straight into *my* eyes.

On October 19, 1936, Lynn Garland became Mrs. Frank Loesser.

In the meantime, "Bang–The Bell Rang!" along with some other Loesser and Actman numbers (and a song by a young Viennese composer named Frederick Loewe), got a hearing in a revue called *The Illustrators' Show*. While the revue closed in less than a week, a favorable mention of the songs in *The Hollywood Reporter* garnered Loesser and Actman a contract at Universal Studios, where they wrote for various B pictures and several early cartoons by animator Walter Lantz, who would later create Woody Woodpecker. In 1937 Loesser's

lyrics came to the attention of composer Burton Lane, who secured the young lyricist a job at Paramount Pictures, a considerable step up the Hollywood pecking order from Universal. (Irving Actman returned to New York, where, twelve years later, he would join forces with his former collaborator as music director and conductor of *Guys and Dolls*.)

As Lane told the editors of this collection, Loesser's great talent was apparent from the start. But Lane knew all too well that the comic spontaneity and brilliant imagination also masked a fiery temper. The short, dark, intense young man who caught Lynn Garland's eye in the Back Drop could be an equally intense collaborator. "He'd put a complete lyric on the piano in his awful handwriting," recalled Lane, "and say 'Now play it!' I couldn't make it out and he'd scream, 'Goddamnit, you stupid son of a bitch, can't you READ?' " Still, Lane remembered how Loesser's ease with fresh conversational vernacular helped make many of their collaborations in 1938 into hits. "He knew how people talked and how to fit that into a song. He was good, he knew it, and from then on, he was off and running."

Loesser's first song to register strongly in Hollywood was "The Moon of Manakoora" (music by Alfred Newman) for the Dorothy Lamour film *The Hurricane* (1937), which also starred Jon Hall, Mary Astor, and Raymond Massey. Lamour recorded the number, but ultimately it was used only as underscoring and not sung onscreen. Others who introduced Loesser film songs were Betty Hutton, Bob Hope, Shirley Ross, Bing Crosby, Mary Martin, Marlene Dietrich, Dick Powell, Bette Davis, Deanna Durbin, and Danny Kaye.

Loesser's most successful Hollywood collaborations were with composers Burton Lane ("Moments Like This," "The Lady's in Love with You," "I Hear Music"), Hoagy Carmichael ("Two Sleepy People," "Small Fry," "Heart and Soul"), Jimmy McHugh ("Murder, He Says," "Say It [Over and Over Again]," "Let's Get Lost"), Victor Schertzinger ("Sand in My Shoes," "Kiss the Boys Goodbye"), Jule Styne ("I Don't Want to Walk Without You"), Louis Alter ("Dolores"), Frederick Hollander ("The Boys in the Backroom"), Joseph J. Lilley ("Jingle, Jangle, Jingle"), and Arthur Schwartz ("They're Either Too Young or Too Old").

• • •

Loesser's debut as a Broadway composer-lyricist in 1948 was the result of one of those curiously familiar show-business breaks that frequently launch careers. Harold Arlen had been asked to write the music for producers Cy Feuer and Ernest Martin's first Broadway show, *Where's Charley?*, the musical version of Brandon Thomas's 1892 farce *Charley's Aunt*. Loesser was to write the lyrics. Feuer, who had known Loesser during his years as head of the music department at Republic Pictures, told Susan Loesser, "I didn't even consider Frank for the music." When Arlen bowed out of the project, Loesser auditioned for the show's director-librettist, George Abbott, who then hired him to write the music as well as the lyrics. Ray Bolger was the star; George Balanchine, the choreographer.

After a troubled tryout, the show became a hit when Bolger turned his soft-shoe number "Once in Love with Amy" into an audience-participation sing-along. The score also boasted two soaring ballads, "My Darling, My Darling" and "Lovelier Than Ever," the lively Latin-flavored ensemble dance number "Pernambuco," and the rousing march "The New Ashmolean Marching Society and Students' Conservatory Band." Arguably the best song in the score—one that Stephen Sondheim has said he wished he'd written—was "Make a Miracle," which employed the overlapping conversation style of "Baby, It's Cold Outside" and transformed a mildly comic romantic moment into a delightfully inventive discourse on the modern world disguised as a marriage proposal. *Where's Charley?* ran for two years, toured, and returned briefly to Broadway, but, sadly, because of a recording strike at the time, no original cast album with Bolger and his colleagues was made.

In his next Broadway outing, Loesser gave the world *Guys and Dolls*, that merry, tough yet tender romp through Damon Runyonland with its crapshooters, Hot Box girls, and "Save-a-Soul" missionaries. It won numerous Tony Awards and established Loesser at the peak of his profession.

By then Loesser had two children—Susan, born in 1944; John, in 1950—and an increasingly troubled marriage, which ended in divorce in 1956.

A lilting film score for *Hans Christian Andersen* in 1952, starring Danny Kaye, was followed four years later by the Broadway musical *The Most Happy Fella*, a boldly ambitious, bountifully melodic adaptation of Sidney Howard's play *They Knew What They Wanted*, for which Loesser wrote both the score and libretto. According to Abba Bogin, Loesser's musical associate from *Happy Fella* on, Loesser

never really had a thorough musical training—he was almost completely self-taught. His father and brother, Arthur, performed music in their home when Frank was growing up and music absorbed him. He knew so much of the literature. I remember being in his office one day when he was listening on the radio to an obscure Haydn string quartet, which he knew. He had an unbelievable retentive memory for what he heard and unbelievable instincts. He had great ears and always knew how he wanted his music to sound.

In 1959, Loesser married *The Most Happy Fella*'s leading lady, Jo Sullivan, and they had two daughters, Hannah, born in 1962, and Emily, in 1965.

During the rest of his too-brief career, Loesser wrote the fantasy *Greenwillow* (1960) and, a year later, the Pulitzer Prize–winning *How to Succeed in Business Without Really Trying*. He kept at his craft throughout the 1960s, but his *Pleasures and Palaces* opened and closed in Detroit in 1965, and *Señor Discretion Himself*, which he worked on from 1965 through 1968, was left unfinished at his death, in July 1969, of lung cancer. He was fifty-nine.

During most of his career, Loesser applied himself tirelessly on behalf of others. No one in the American musical theater since George Gershwin did more than Loesser to foster and encourage the work of his colleagues. In the late 1940s he had started his own music company, which he called Susan Publications after his daughter. Following the opening of *Guys and Dolls*, he renamed it Frank Music, and before long Loesser's new company was launching hits by other writers, such as "Unchained Melody" and "Cry Me a River." Later he formed a dramatic licensing agency, Music

Theater International, and, in 1960, Frank Productions. He became the publisher and chief cheerleader for Robert Wright and George Forrest ("the boys," as he called them) from their musical *Kismet* (1953) until the end of his life. He guided Richard Adler and Jerry Ross literally and figuratively from "Rags to Riches" (their hit song of 1953) to their two blockbuster shows, *The Pajama Game* (1954) and *Damn Yankees* (1955), and coaxed Meredith Willson through the writing of *The Music Man* (1957). He gave Jerry Herman important early encouragement, spending half a day listening to Herman's songs and offering him sound, practical ideas on songwriting. He even found an attorney for a young Stephen Sondheim.

How to describe Loesser? Generous, curious, warm-hearted and hot-tempered, restlessly energetic, a first-rate businessman, and an early riser who seldom slept more than four hours a night. (His first wife, Lynn, describing how he worked, said, "He gets up early, drinks a pot of strong coffee, and digs.") He was also a dedicated cabinetmaker and caricaturist (he dubbed himself a "Ball-Pointilliste") and amazingly well informed on a range of subjects.

"Knowing Frank Loesser," recalled his friend, writer Cynthia Lindsay, "was a rare and rewarding experience for many reasons, but the most important was that no matter who and what you were, he made you better. Whether it was your talent, your humor, your confidence in yourself, you came away from him more creative, funnier, more perceptive about yourself, and lighter in spirit; a prettier woman, a stronger man—in fact, crazy about yourself, because he made you the best of what you were."

• • •

The nearly seven hundred lyrics in this book, more than half of which are being published for the first time, are arranged chronologically. The lyrics not written for shows or films are presented in the order in which they were registered for copyright. The rest appear with the films and shows for which they were written and in the sequence in which they were first performed. Deleted and unused songs for each production appear after the material that was actually performed.

Each film or stage production is introduced with pertinent information (creative credits, release/opening date, length of run, tryout data, cast albums). Headnotes precede each lyric. They include collaborator credits and the publication date or, for unpublished songs, the date of copyright registration. In films with multiple songs, the collaborator information is given in the headnote for the film and is not repeated in the headnotes for the individual songs. Sources and/or dates are cited for unregistered lyrics. Alternate or earlier titles are listed, as are the names of the artists who introduced the songs. For well-known numbers there is a selective list of recordings and, where it survives, commentary by Loesser, his collaborators, or others closely connected with his work. We also have noted if the music for a lyric is not known to exist.

The lyrics were gathered from various sources, including manuscripts, typed lyric sheets, scripts, conductors' scores, sheet music, recordings (cast, commercial, private and film studio tapes and acetates, radio broadcasts and interviews, and World War II V-Discs), film soundtracks, and the personal files of Frank Loesser and his collaborators. Other sources include the Music Division of the Library of Congress in Washington, D.C.; the New York Public Library for the Performing Arts at Lincoln Center; the Shubert Archive, Famous Music, and Frank Music in New York City; and the Academy of Motion Picture Arts and Sciences Library, Paramount Pictures, and Universal Studios in Los Angeles.

This book could not have been undertaken and completed without the work of those family members, close associates, and dedicated professionals who preserved and promoted Frank Loesser's legacy from his death in 1969 to the time this project began in 1996. In fact, the foundation for this book was laid by Loesser himself in 1948 when he started Susan Publications. Two years later, with the assistance and oversight of Harold Orenstein, Frank Music was begun. It became not only the repository for Loesser's published songs, but also a base for the many production-related activities that bore his stamp during the 1950s and 1960s.

After Loesser died, Frank Music was managed by his

widow, Jo Sullivan Loesser, until its sale to CBS in 1976. In 1979, it became a part of MPL Communications, the Paul McCartney music publishing operation. In 1997, Jo Sullivan Loesser established Frank Loesser Enterprises to manage and oversee the Loesser archives and the activities of the Loesser catalogue and to serve as a clearinghouse and information base for all Loesser-related projects. The original Rosabella in the 1956 production of *The Most Happy Fella*, Mrs. Loesser has also kept her husband's songs before the public through her own performances and through various revues and revivals of his stage shows. Frank Loesser's children—Susan, John, Hannah, and Emily—have also been tireless in supporting their father's legacy and this project in particular.

Many of the lyrics appearing here for the first time were first catalogued by Abba Bogin. Much of the previously unknown material came from the soundtracks and production records of both the well-remembered and the long-forgotten films, as well as from demo recordings and so-called censorship files at Paramount Music, where Loesser worked from 1938 to 1950. (Few contemporary filmgoers recall that all Hollywood film lyrics and dialogue were subject to censorship during most of the 1930s and 1940s.) In cases where the only source for a lyric was a soundtrack or demonstration recording, several sets of ears were sometimes needed. The editors were ably assisted in this by Loesser copyright and catalogue specialist Joseph Weiss, who labored tirelessly on this book. Less traditional written sources were also of immense help. On one occasion, a "lost" lyric was found on a film studio publicity photograph in which Frank Loesser holds a clipboard with a typed lyric sheet. After carefully enlarging the photograph, we were able to read the lyric.

—Robert Kimball and Steve Nelson

Frank Loesser

Chronology

1910

JUNE 29   Frank Loesser born in New York City to Henry Loesser and the former Julia Ehrlich. Siblings: Arthur Loesser (child of Henry's marriage to Julia's elder sister Bertha, who died in 1907), 1898–1969, and Grace Loesser, 1907–1986.

1914

Henry Loesser writes that young Frank "plays any tune he's heard and can spend an enormous amount of time at the piano. Always he wants attention and an audience."

1923

Frank Loesser enrolls in the Townsend Harris School. He is expelled prior to graduation.

1925

Loesser is accepted at City College without a high school diploma and expelled soon thereafter for polishing the nose of a bronze statue. He fails every subject except English.

1926

JULY 20   Henry Loesser dies suddenly. To help support the family, Arthur Loesser abandons his career as a concert pianist and accepts a teaching position at the Cleveland Institute of Music.

1927

Frank Loesser works a variety of odd jobs—a time he later describes as his "rendezvous with failure." These include process serving, screwing lids on insecticide cans, writing political cartoons for the *Tuckahoe Record*, and a stint as knit-goods editor at *Women's Wear*.

1928

Loesser becomes city editor for the short-lived *New Rochelle News* and begins writing song lyrics with friends at the Old Algiers restaurant. In collaboration with Joe Brandfonbrenner, Loesser signs a $100-a-week contract with Leo Feist. Feist never publishes any of their songs, and no lyrics are known to survive from this period.

1929

First three Loesser songs registered for copyright (music by Carl Rice).

1930

First collaboration with William Schuman.

1931

First published Loesser song, "In Love with a Memory of You" (music by William Schuman).

1933

Loesser writes the libretto for a comic operetta about Leonardo da Vinci with music by William Schuman, and a vaudeville routine with Jean Herbert entitled *Hollywood Be Thy Name* for Mary Nolan.

1934

First Loesser hit song, "I Wish I Were Twins" (music by Joseph Meyer), recorded by Thomas "Fats" Waller.

"Junk Man" (music by Joseph Meyer) recorded by Benny Goodman.

Loesser meets and begins collaboration with Irving Actman.

1935

JANUARY   Irving Actman and Loesser perform their songs at the Back Drop Club on West Fifty-second Street. Broadway press agent Tom Weatherly promises to hire them for an upcoming show.

SPRING   Loesser meets his future first wife, Lynn Garland, at the Back Drop Club. She had recently abandoned her given name, Mary Alice Blankenbaker, and had come to New York seeking a singing career.

Poetic Gems published (music by Louis Herscher).

Loesser and Actman write songs and vaudeville routines for Lita Grey Chaplin.

1936

JANUARY 20   *The Illustrator's Show* opens at the Forty-eighth Street Theatre, with six songs by Loesser and Actman. Five performances.

APRIL   Loesser and Actman sign six-month contract with Universal Studios.

AUGUST   *Postal Inspector* and *Yellowstone* released by Universal.

SEPTEMBER   Loesser's Universal contract expires.

OCTOBER   *The Man I Marry* released by Universal.

OCTOBER 19   Loesser marries Lynn Garland in Hollywood.

WINTER   Loesser collaborates with Manning Sherwin.

1937

JANUARY–MARCH   *Three Smart Girls, The Golfers, Mysterious Crossing, Everybody Sing,* and *The Duck Hunt,* released by Universal.

SPRING–SUMMER   Loesser writes for Universal, RKO, and United Artists on a per-song basis.

JULY   Burton Lane hears Loesser/Sherwin songs and helps secure them a ten-week contract with Paramount Pictures.

AUGUST   *Walter Wanger's Vogues of 1938* released by United Artists.

OCTOBER 1   Loesser and Sherwin renew contract with Paramount Pictures.

NOVEMBER   *Fight for Your Lady* released by RKO Radio. *The Hurricane*, a Goldwyn Film starring Dorothy Lamour, is released by United Artists. "The Moon of Manakoora," music by Alfred Newman and recorded by Lamour but not sung in the film, becomes Loesser's first Hollywood hit song.

DECEMBER   *Blossoms on Broadway* released by Paramount.

1938

APRIL   *College Swing* released by Paramount. Score includes first collaborations with Hoagy Carmichael and Burton Lane, notably the Lane/Loesser "Moments Like This" and How'dja Like to Love Me?"

MAY–JULY   *Stolen Heaven*, *Cocoanut Grove*, and *The Texans* released by Paramount. *Cocoanut Grove* includes Lane and Loesser's "Says My Heart," which became the first Loesser song to reach number one on the popular music charts. Red Norvo and His Orchestra's recording was the top seller.

AUGUST   *Sing You Sinners*, with the Loesser/Carmichael song "Small Fry," released by Paramount.

AUGUST 24   "Heart and Soul," music by Hoagy Carmichael, registered for copyright. The Bea Wain–Larry Clinton recording reaches number one on the popular music charts; Wain introduces the song in the Paramount short film *A Song Is Born*, released in December 1938.

AUGUST–OCTOBER   *Give Me a Sailor*, *Spawn of the North*, and *Men with Wings* released by Paramount.

SEPTEMBER   *Freshman Year* released by Universal.

DECEMBER   *Thanks for the Memory*, with Bob Hope and Shirley Ross introducing Loesser and Carmichael's "Two Sleepy People," is released by Paramount. Fats Waller's recording of "Two Sleepy People" is number one on the popular music charts.

1939

JANUARY–FEBRUARY   *Zaza*, *St. Louis Blues*, and *Café Society* released by Paramount.

MAY   *Some Like It Hot* released by Paramount. Songs include Loesser and Lane's "The Lady's in Love with You." Glenn Miller's recording is number two on the popular music charts.

JUNE   *The Gracie Allen Murder Case*, *Heritage of The Desert*, *Man About Town*, and *Invitation to Happiness* released by Paramount.

AUGUST–OCTOBER   *Beau Geste*, *Island of Lost Men*, *The Star Maker* and *$1,000 a Touchdown* released by Paramount. *Hawaiian Nights* released by Universal.

NOVEMBER   *Destry Rides Again*, starring Marlene Dietrich and James Stewart, with songs by Loesser and Frederick Hollander, released by Universal. Songs include "The Boys in the Back Room."

DECEMBER   *The Llano Kid* and *The Great Victor Herbert* released by Paramount. The title song of *Seventeen* is the first song published—one month prior to the film's release—with both music and lyrics by Loesser.

1940

JANUARY–MARCH   *All Women Have Secrets*, *Seventeen*, and *The Farmer's Daughter* are released by Paramount.

APRIL–MAY   *Adventure in Diamonds*, *Buck Benny Rides Again*, and *Typhoon* are released by Paramount. "Say It (Over and Over Again)" from *Buck Benny Rides Again*, with music by Jimmy McHugh, scores a major success, with Glenn Miller's recording reaching number two on the popular music charts. The film *Johnny Apollo* is released by 20th Century–Fox.

JULY   *Those Were the Days* released by Paramount.

JULY–AUGUST   Loesser and Hoagy Carmichael travel to Florida to write songs for the cartoon feature *Mr. Bug Goes to Town*.

OCTOBER–DECEMBER   *The Quarterback*, *Moon Over Burma*, and *Dancing on a Dime* are released by Paramount. The song, "I Hear Music" from *Dancing on a Dime*, music by Lane, achieves popularity.

NOVEMBER   *Seven Sinners* is released by Universal. *Youth Will Be Served* is released by 20th Century–Fox.

DECEMBER   Loesser and John Steinbeck meet and begin their lifelong friendship.

1941

JANUARY–MARCH   *A Night at Earl Carroll's*, *Arizona Sketches*, and *Las Vegas Nights* are released by Paramount. "Dolores," from *Las Vegas Nights*, with music by Louis Alter, is nominated for an Academy Award. The recording by Tommy Dorsey with vocal by Frank Sinatra is number one on the popular music charts.

APRIL   *Sis Hopkins* is released by Republic.

JUNE   *There's Magic in Music* and *Caught in the Draft* are released by Paramount.

JULY   *Manpower* is released by Warner Bros.

AUGUST   *Kiss the Boys Goodbye*, *World Premiere*, and *Aloma of the South Seas* are released by Paramount. The title song and "Sand in My Shoes" from *Kiss the Boys Goodbye*, music by Victor Schertzinger, achieve popularity.

SEPTEMBER–OCTOBER   *Hold Back the Dawn* and *Henry Aldrich for President* are released by Paramount. *Sailors on Leave* is released by Republic.

DECEMBER   *Birth of the Blues* and *Glamour Boy* are released by Paramount.

1942

FEBRUARY–MARCH   *Mr. Bug Goes to Town* and *Reap the Wild Wind* are released by Paramount.

MAY–JUNE   *This Gun's for Hire*, *Tortilla Flat*, *True to the Army*, and *Beyond the Blue Horizon* are released by Paramount.

JULY   *Sweater Girl* and *Priorities on Parade* are released by Paramount. Harry James and Helen Forrest's recording of Loesser and Jule Styne's "I Don't Want to Walk Without You" from *Sweater Girl* becomes the number one hit on the popular music charts.

AUGUST 8   Loesser copyrights "Praise the Lord and Pass the Ammunition," for which he wrote the music and lyrics. It becomes one of the biggest hits of World War II. Kay Kyser's recording reaches number one on the popular music charts.

OCTOBER   *The Forest Rangers* is released by Paramount. Kay Kyser's recording of Loesser and Joseph J. Lilley's "Jingle Jangle, Jingle" is number one on the popular music charts.

FALL   Loesser enlists in the army and is assigned to the Radio Productions Unit at the Army Air Force base in Santa Ana, California.

DECEMBER *Seven Days' Leave* is released by Paramount. Includes "Can't Get out of This Mood" (music by Jimmy McHugh), which achieves popularity.

1943

MARCH *Happy Go Lucky* is released by Paramount. Its songs, with music by Jimmy McHugh, include "Sing a Tropical Song," "Murder, He Says," and "Let's Get Lost." The Vaughn Monroe recording of "Let's Get Lost" reaches number one on the popular music charts.

SPRING Loesser is transferred to Army Special Services Division in New York.

AUGUST *Tornado* is released by Paramount.

OCTOBER *Thank Your Lucky Stars*, with an all-star cast and songs by Loesser and Arthur Schwartz, is released by Paramount. Numbers include "They're Either Too Young or Too Old," which is nominated for an Academy Award.

FALL Short-subject film *Army Show* is released by Warner Bros.

NOVEMBER *Riding High* is released by Paramount.

1944

JANUARY Loesser begins writing songs for army's "Blueprint Special" soldier shows.

FEBRUARY 4 Army Special Services show *Skirts* opens in London. Title song is by Loesser.

MARCH Film *See Here, Private Hargrove* is released by Paramount.

MAY *The Road to Victory* is released by Warner Bros.

MAY 26 "Blueprint Special" show *About Face!* opens.

JUNE 30 *Christmas Holiday* with Loesser's song "Spring Will Be a Little Late This Year," is released by Universal.

AUGUST 7 "Blueprint Special" show *Hi, Yank!* opens.

OCTOBER 5 Daughter Susan Loesser is born.

OCTOBER The Loessers move into three suites in the Navarro Hotel in New York.

NOVEMBER *Pfc. Mary Brown* (A WAC Musical Revue) opens.

1945

FEBRUARY 19 Loesser copyrights his song "Rodger Young," an infantry ballad memorializing a Medal of Honor recipient.

MARCH 11 "Rodger Young" performed at "Rodger Young Day" in Los Angeles. Audience includes Governor Earl Warren of California and Mayor Fletcher Bowron of Los Angeles.

JUNE "Blueprint Special" show *Okay U.S.A.* performed.

SUMMER Loesser writes nine animal songs.

NOVEMBER *It's the Goods*, an unproduced Quartermaster Corps show, is copyrighted by collaborators David Mann, Frank Provo, and John Pickard. It includes several Loesser songs, music mostly by David Mann.

1946

JANUARY The Loessers return to California and buy Veronica Lake's house in Beverly Hills.

FALL Loesser writes songs for the unproduced film *The Day Before Spring* (music by Johnny Green).

1947

JUNE 11 Loesser publishes his song "Bloop, Bleep."

JULY 11 Loesser publishes his song "What Are You Doing New Year's Eve."

JULY Film *The Perils of Pauline* is released by Paramount. Music and lyrics are by Loesser. Songs include "Rumble, Rumble, Rumble" and the Academy Award nominee "I Wish I Didn't Love You So."

OCTOBER Film *Variety Girl* is released by Paramount. Music and lyrics are by Loesser.

FALL Loesser writes songs for the unproduced film *Lady from Lariat Loop*.

1948

SPRING Loesser forms the first of his music publishing companies, Susan Publications Inc.

APRIL–MAY Loesser begins working on a stage musical version of the play *Charley's Aunt*.

MAY 7 "On a Slow Boat to China," one of Loesser's biggest song hits, is registered for copyright.

JUNE *On Our Merry Way* is released by United Artists.

SEPTEMBER 13 World premiere of *Where's Charley?* at the Forrest Theatre in Philadelphia.

OCTOBER 11 *Where's Charley?* opens at the St. James Theatre, New York City; 792 performances. A recording of one of its songs, "My Darling, My Darling," by Jo Stafford and Gordon MacRae reaches number one on the popular music charts.

1949

JUNE *Neptune's Daughter* is released by MGM. "Baby, It's Cold Outside," introduced by Esther Williams and Ricardo Montalban, wins the Academy Award for Best Song.

AUGUST 20 The Goldwyn film *Roseanna McCoy* is released by RKO Radio.

NOVEMBER The film *Red, Hot and Blue* is released by Paramount. Loesser appears in the film in the role of a gangster.

1950

APRIL 3 Publication of the song "Hoop-Dee-Doo" (music by Milton DeLugg). A recording of it by Perry Como is number one on the popular music charts.

SPRING–SUMMER Loesser works on songs for *Guys and Dolls*.

SEPTEMBER 19 Son John Loesser is born.

OCTOBER 14–28 World premiere of *Guys and Dolls* at Shubert Theatre, Philadelphia.

OCTOBER 31–NOVEMBER 11 *Guys and Dolls* continues Philadelphia tryout at the Forrest Theatre.

NOVEMBER Film *Let's Dance* is released by Paramount. Includes the song "Why Fight the Feeling?"

NOVEMBER 24 *Guys and Dolls* opens at the Forty-sixth Street Theatre in New York City; 1,194 performances.

1951

Frank Music Corp. founded.

MARCH Loesser writes theme song for television show *The College Bowl*, starring Chico Marx.

JUNE Loesser receives Tony Award as composer and lyricist for *Guys and Dolls*. The show receives seven other Tonys including the award for Best Musical.

FALL   Loesser begins writing songs for Samuel Goldwyn's film *Hans Christian Andersen*.

WINTER   Loesser begins work on "Project 3," the score and libretto for a musical version of Sidney Howard's play *They Knew What They Wanted*, which becomes *The Most Happy Fella*.

1952

AUGUST   Film *Where's Charley?* is released by Warner Bros. Artists in film include Ray Bolger and Allyn Ann McLerie of original Broadway cast.

NOVEMBER   The Goldwyn film *Hans Christian Andersen* is released by RKO Radio.

1955

NOVEMBER   Samuel Goldwyn's film *Guys and Dolls* is released by MGM. Five songs from the Broadway production are cut; three new numbers are written for the film.

1956

MARCH 13   World premiere of *The Most Happy Fella* at the Shubert Theatre, Boston.

APRIL 10   *The Most Happy Fella* begins a run at the Shubert Theatre, Philadelphia.

MAY 3   *The Most Happy Fella* opens at the Imperial Theatre, New York; 676 performances.

LATE MAY   Loesser family moves from Beverly Hills to New York.

SEPTEMBER   Loesser begins work with Garson Kanin on a musical version of Kanin's play *A Touch of the Moon*, tentatively titled *Dream People*.

1957

MARCH 7   Frank and Lynn Loesser divorce.

OCTOBER   Loesser abandons work on *Dream People*.

FALL   Loesser begins work on a musical version of B. J. Chute's novel *Greenwillow*.

1958

MAY   Loesser writes Piels Beer commercial.

1959

APRIL 29   Jo Sullivan and Frank Loesser marry.

1960

JANUARY 30   World premiere of *Greenwillow* at the Shubert Theatre, Philadelphia.

MARCH 8   *Greenwillow* opens at the Alvin Theatre New York; 97 performances.

SUMMER   The Loessers vacation in Europe.

SEPTEMBER.   Loesser returns from Europe and begins work on *How to Succeed in Business Without Really Trying*.

1961

SEPTEMBER 4   World premiere of *How to Succeed in Business*, at the Shubert Theatre, Philadelphia.

OCTOBER 14   *How to Succeed in Business* opens at the Forty-sixth Street Theatre, New York; 1,417 performances.

1962

MARCH–AUGUST   Loesser works on and then abandons musical adaptation of *Time Remembered* by Jean Anouilh.

MAY 7   Loesser and Abe Burrows win the Pulitzer Prize for Drama for *How to Succeed in Business*.

OCTOBER 22   Daughter Hannah Loesser is born.

1963

FALL   Loesser begins work on musical version of the Sam Spewack play *Once There Was a Russian*, which becomes *Pleasures and Palaces*.

1965

MARCH   World premiere of *Pleasures and Palaces* at the Fisher Theatre in Detroit. Show closes in Detroit after a four-week run before reaching New York.

JUNE 2   Daughter Emily Loesser is born.

SEPTEMBER   The Loessers buy a house in Remsenburg, Long Island, on Moriches Bay.

NOVEMBER   Loesser begins work on *Señor Discretion Himself*, a musical adaptation of a short story by Budd Schulberg.

1967

MARCH   The Mirisch film *How to Succeed in Business Without Really Trying* is released by United Artists.

1968

MARCH   Loesser abandons work on *Señor Discretion Himself.*

FALL   Loesser hospitalized twice for tests.

DECEMBER 20   John Steinbeck dies.

1969

JANUARY 5   Brother Arthur Loesser dies.

JULY 28   Frank Loesser dies at age 59 in New York City.

Acknowledgments

The compilation, annotation, and publication of the lyrics of Frank Loesser has taken many years, and we would like to acknowledge the extensive help we have received and extend gratitude to the many people who made the project possible.

Thanks first and foremost to Jo Sullivan Loesser, without whose tireless support and encouragement this book would not exist; to Susan Loesser, for her scrupulous review of the manuscript and permission to quote liberally from her book about her father, *A Most Remarkable Fella;* and to all the members of the Loesser family for generously sharing memories of their father; and to the late Harold Orenstein, Frank Loesser's longtime friend and attorney, for providing temporary workspace for the project, memories of Frank Loesser, and counsel on song copyrights.

Thanks also go to Joseph Weiss of Frank Loesser Enterprises and Miles Kreuger of the Institute of the American Musical for their careful readings of this manuscript and invaluable help with film-related material; to Andrew Davis and Sharon Lehner, who assisted in researching and compiling lyrics and production information and screened rare film and audio source materials; to the Kimball and Nelson families for their assistance and patience at all stages of the project; to Cynthia Lyndsay for

permission to quote from her interviews with Frank Loesser's collaborators; to Irwin Robinson, Eldridge Walker and Mary Beth Roberts of Famous Music and John Eastman and Dave Bogart of Frank Music for help with copyright listings; to Mark Horowitz of the Music Division of the Library of Congress; to Brooks McNamara and Mary Ann Chach of the Shubert Archive; to Bob Taylor and George Bozowick of the New York Public Library Theatre and Music Collections; to Ron Mandelbaum at Photofest; to Jeanne Newlin of the Harvard Theatre Collection for her timely assistance and professionalism.

Thanks also to: John Actman, Isabel Bigley, Abba Bogin, Ken Bloom, Jim and Laurie Burrows, Alvin Colt, Cy Feuer, Michael Kidd, Hilary Knight, Burton and Lynn Lane, Elliot Lawrence, Ernest Martin, Allyn Ann McLerie, Larry Moore, Stuart Ostrow, Jack Raymond, Colin Romoff, Arthur Rubin, Tony Schuman, and Steve Suskin.

And finally, our deepest appreciation to Alfred A. Knopf, especially our editors Robert Gottlieb and Katherine Hourigan, and to Kevin Bourke, Patrick Dillon, Eric Bliss, Cassandra Pappas, and Roméo Enriquez.

The Complete Lyrics of

FRANK LOESSER

Oh! What A Beautiful Baby
(YOU TURNED OUT TO BE)

Words by
FRANK LOESSER

Music by
J. FRED COOTS

Little Jack Little

MILLS MUSIC

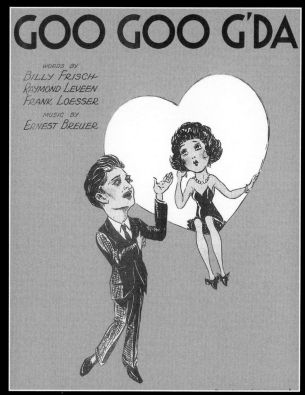

GOO GOO G'DA

WORDS BY
BILLY FRISCH
RAYMOND LEVEEN
FRANK LOESSER

MUSIC BY
ERNEST BREUER

In Love With A Memory Of You

BALLAD

Lyric by
FRANK LOESSER
Music by
WILLIAM H. SCHUMAN

MORTON
DOWNEY

THE TRAFFIC WAS TERRIFIC

Lyric by Frank Loesser
and
Buddy Bernier

Music by Otto Motzan

Songs of 1929–1935

ALONE IN YOUR CLASS (LITTLE GIRL)

Music by Carl Rice. Registered for copyright as an unpublished song April 12, 1929. Loesser's collaborations with Rice were his first copyrighted songs. Nothing (not even his birth and death dates) is known about the composer. Very little information remains about Loesser's first attempts at songwriting, and even less on his collaborators prior to William Schuman in 1929 or 1930. We do know that his turn to songwriting began shortly after his father's death on July 20, 1926, at which point supporting the family became a necessity for Frank and his halfbrother Arthur. In her biography of her father, *A Most Remarkable Fella*, Susan Loesser discusses his initial forays into lyric writing:

> His earliest collaborators were a group of friends who hung out at the Old Algiers restaurant on upper Broadway and tossed song ideas around while they socialized. One of these was a kid named Joe Brandfonbrenner, and he and my father took some songs they wrote down to Leo Feist [a major music publisher of the period], where they managed to come away with a year's $100 a week contract for all the songs they could write. Little Frankie had his $100 advance changed into singles, burst into the house, and merrily scattered bills all over the living room to the raised eyebrows of his mother. . . .

A year later they had written dozens of songs, none of which Feist wanted to publish. Not a lyric survives from this earliest work. The three lyrics that follow are the earliest surviving examples of Frank Loesser's work.

VERSE

HE: You're so charming,
 It's quite alarming,
 You're my idea of the best.
 It's appalling,
 I can't help falling,
 It's true.
 No debating
 What I've been stating,
 You're way ahead of the rest.
 Here's a notion
 Of my devotion
 To you.

REFRAIN 1

You're just divine,
You've got the features,
Wonderful line,
No girl can beat yours.
You're a departure,
Pretty and smart, you're
Alone in your class,
Little girl.
You set the pace,
Girls emulate
Your beautiful grace,
Marvelous nature.
That combination
Wins you a station,
Alone in your class,
Little girl.
Now I wonder who in thunder ever
Was so cute and also was so clever?
You are your own
Reason for being,
Just you alone,
Something worth seeing.
Nobody's second,
You're to be reckoned
Alone in your class,
Little girl.

REFRAIN 2

SHE: You're such a dear,
 Man in a million,
 Not just a mere
 Handsome civilian.
 Few men could rake up
 Such perfect makeup,
 Alone in your class,
 Little boy.
 You've got a lot,
 Loving and gentle,
 Although you're not
 Too sentimental.
 So consequently,
 You're evidently
 Alone in your class,
 Little boy.
 Now I wonder who in thunder ever
 Was so cute and also was so clever?
 You've got the mind,
 Sex appeal also,
 You strike 'em blind,
 That's why they fall so.
 Girls are demanding
 Something outstanding,
 Alone in your class,
 Little boy.

LET'S INCORPORATE

Music by Carl Rice. Registered for copyright as an unpublished song April 12, 1929.

VERSE

Once at the close of day
Down on old Wall Street way,
When brokers were at home in bed,
Two well-known stocks were spied
Lovemaking side by side,
And this is what they softly said:

REFRAIN 1

Look me over if you please,
I've no liabilities,
We're two sep'rate companies,
So let's incorporate.
You've got assets back of you,
And I'd fail for lack of you,
If I don't keep track of you,
So let's incorporate.
Here's a bond that won't mature
Till death do us part.
I can't rest till you put
Your mortgage on my heart.
Both of us are on the verge
Of a most exciting splurge,
With success we ought to merge,
So let's incorporate.

REFRAIN 2

Though you seem to stay at par,
I know what your prospects are:
You will lead all stocks by far
If we incorporate.
See my proposition through,
For I'm bound to rise with you.
We will cause a panic too
If we incorporate.
I'm in such financial shape,
I can't help but please.
Proof is on the ticker tape,
We're affinities.
Soon of margin we'll be rid
When we get together, kid.
I have asked and you have bid
So let's incorporate.

REFRAIN 3

When we're spliced we'll be preferred
To the lowly common herd.

We'll be Wall Street's latest word
When we incorporate.
My maternal sword I'll wield
On the high financial field,
Seven bucks per annum yield
When we incorporate.
Free of all misogyny,
I shall love you well.
You'll produce that progeny
When we start to sell.
We'll catch Wall Street unawares
With a brood of baby shares.
We'll control the board's affairs,
So let's incorporate.

MELANCHOLY ME

Music by Carl Rice. Registered for copyright as an unpublished song April 12, 1929.

VERSE

How I yearn for love's return,
For all my time, it's spent.
I've been taught with,
Tightly caught with,
Disillusionment.
Things that charmed me
Now have harm'd me,
I've been prey to fate.
Though there's call for
Girls to fall for,
This time love's too late.

REFRAIN

Nights like these cause memories,
'Cause stars shine peacefully.
Never known someone so lonesome,
Melancholy me.
I've been waiting,
Meditating,
Sentimentally.
I've been jilted,
Love boat tilted,
Melancholy me.
All night long
My sad song
Tells a tale of despair.
My poor heart
Must impart
Blue notes into the air.
I'm dejected,
So neglected,

Lonely as can be.
I'm lovesick
And sorrow-stricken,
Melancholy me.

DOING THE DISHES

Music by William Schuman (1910–1992). Recorded to Speak-O-Phone disc, probably in 1930, by Frank Loesser and William Schuman. This recording appears on the compact disc *Frank Sings Loesser* (Koch). Schuman gave the following spoken introduction to the recording: "This record was made by Masters Frank Loesser and William Schuman of New York City."

Schuman, who went on to prominence as a Pulitzer Prize–winning "serious" composer and the first president of the Lincoln Center for the Performing Arts, later remarked of his early collaborations with Loesser, "Everybody else wrote hits with Frank. I only managed flops."

Who's that singing in the kitchen,
Drumming on the tub with a knife?
My sweetie and me in close harmony,
Having the time of our lives.
Some fun, dum de dum de dum,
Helping my sweetie along.
Doing the dishes,
Harmonizing a song.
Some tune all about the moon,
A rhythm that never goes wrong.
Doing the dishes,
Harmonizing a song.

She likes to wash,
I like to dry;
I'm singing low,
She's singing high.
I go to her house,
She goes to my house;
We'll go to our house
By and by
And

Someday, hooray, hooray, hooray,
A baby boy chiming in strong.
Doing the dishes,
Harmonizing a song.
Hey, hey, hey,
After dinner every day,
Ho, ho, ho,
Juliet and Romeo,
Ha, ha, ha,

Still a lot of dishes coming.
Dum, dum, dum,
Love to do aluminum.
Damn, damn, damn,
Hate to do the frying pan.
Da, da, da,
Listen to the song we're humming:
"Old Black Joe," "Auld Lang Syne,"
"Sweet and Low," "Sweet Adeline."
Clink, clink clink,
Glasses in the kitchen sink,
Up, up, up,
Ashes in the coffee cup,
Rah, rah, rah,
Blues are running down the plumbing.
Someday, hooray, hooray, hooray,
A baby boy chiming in strong.
Doing the dishes,
Harmonizing a song.

WHERE THE GRASS GROWS GREEN

Music by William Schuman. Recorded to Speak-O-Phone disc, probably in 1930, by Frank Loesser and William Schuman. This recording appears on the compact disc *Frank Sings Loesser* (Koch).

VERSE

Girlfriends, boyfriends
Going to the movies or a dance.
Girlfriends, boyfriends
Going where the gang goes for romance.
My sweetie and I aren't proud,
But why should we follow the crowd?
Yesterday we found a hideaway
Where nobody else is allowed.

REFRAIN

I got a sweet little spot by the river
To take the sweet little gal in the flivver.
And it's a great place for running out of gasoline,
Where the grass grows green.
We never stay in the car for a minute,
Because the cop comes around looking in it.
And so we're out sittin' pretty on a magazine
Where the grass grows green,
Just two miles away from the city skies of gray,
Where the big avenue ends,
Where stars twinkle down like they never do in
    town

And you don't bump into friends.
I'm going to trade in the sweet little flivver
And get a house and a lot by the river
Where I can be with the sweetest gal you've ever
    seen,
Where the grass grows green.

TICKER TAPE TAP

Music by Carl Rice. Registered for copyright as an un-published song May 24, 1930.

Dance down to Wall Street,
Take a chance in the rise-and-fall street,
Do the Ticker Tape Tap.
Make speculations,
Watch and wait for the day's quotations,
Do the Ticker Tape Tap.
Bull or bear,
You'll wonder where
All your hard-earned cash is
When you feel
One of those real
High-financial crashes.
You can't go wrong now,
Take a good tip and tape along now,
Do the Ticker Tape Tap.

SATAN

Music by Carl Rice. Registered for copyright as an un-published song August 3, 1931.

VERSE

When the wind moans,
Horrible groans,
Devil is prowlin' around.
When the owl hoots,
Shivr'n your boots,
Get on your knees on the ground.
Swing low,
To and fro,
Tell that devil to go:

REFRAIN

Satan, get away—
Cloudin' up my day—

Don't come anymore,
Darkening my doorway,
Satan.
When a darky croons
Hallelujah tunes,
That's the end of you,
That'll spoil your hoodoo,
Satan.
Lord musta forgotten,
Can't wait till the morn,
Spooks hauntin' the cotton,
Ghosts wavin' the corn.
Satan, say goodbye—
Clear away the sky—
All your work is through,
Hocus-pocus too,
Oh, Satan.

IN LOVE WITH A MEMORY OF YOU

Music by William Schuman. Published. Copyrighted December 28, 1931. Previously registered for copyright as an unpublished song November 17, 1931. This was Loesser's first published song. It was performed by the noted tenor Morton Downey, but no recordings are known to survive.

VERSE 1

I don't know what you've been doing
Since we've been apart,
I don't know what song you're singing
Deep down in your heart.
Can our love still be
In your memory?
I don't know what dreams you're dreaming,
But as for me:

REFRAIN

I'm still walking in the moonlight
Where sweet honeysuckles grew,
Just me walking in the moonlight
In love with a memory of you.
I'm still singing little love songs
With no one to sing them to,
Just me singing little love songs,
In love with a memory of you.
The sun always shines to remind me,
The wind always whispers your name;
I know that the past is behind me,
You'll never find me, but just the same:

I'm still living in a daydream,
A dream never to come true,
Just me living in a daydream,
In love with a memory of you.

VERSE 2

I don't know if moonlight beams
Wherever you may be,
I don't know if you've had dreams
Of Lovers' Lane and me.
Did our romance die
When we said goodbye?
I don't know if you've forgotten,
But here am I:

REPEAT REFRAIN

I'LL SEE YOU IN THE MORNING

Music by Percy Wenrich (1887–1952). Registered for copyright as an unpublished song March 31, 1932. Wenrich (born in Joplin, Missouri) also composed "Put On Your Old Gray Bonnet" and "Moonlight Bay."

VERSE

Back home from Lovers' Lane,
Back to your door again.
Sweetheart, the evening is through.
I hate to see you go.
There's consolation, though—
Something to look forward to.

REFRAIN

I'll see you in the morning,
What a happy way to say good night.
I'll see you in the morning,
Though we're far apart while stars are bright.
One kiss goodbye, from now till dawning,
And then the night won't seem so blue.
Until I see you in the morning,
I'll be dreaming dreams, sweet dreams, of you.

LIBRETTO FOR AN OPERETTA

Music by William Schuman. Lyrics by Frank Loesser. Libretto by Loesser and Schuman. Copy of typescript deposited at the Music Division of the Library of Congress April 13, 1965, as a gift of William Schuman. Probably written between the summer of 1932 and the spring of 1933. The influence of Gilbert and Sullivan and the Marx Brothers is apparent throughout. No music is known to survive, although William Schuman remembered using some of it years later and recounted one of the lost lyrics to Susan Loesser in *A Most Remarkable Fella:*

> We once started on an operetta based on the life of da Vinci and Frank had some wonderful lyrics. Then a few years ago I wrote a choral work, in which I wanted to bring in some old American tunes. I felt I ought to have a waltz, and suddenly a waltz tune I had written with Frank for the da Vinci show came to mind. The work was first performed by the New York Philharmonic. There they were playing the waltz—a rousing tune—and I'll tell you what the real words were: "Here comes that drunken da Vinci again, all filled with highballs, stewed to the eyeballs."

These additional titles appeared in the libretto. No lyrics were found:

Act I, scene 1　"You're a Bounder, You're a
　　　　　　　　Blighter"
　　　　　　　　"I've Lived for This Moment"
Act I, scene 2　"Here Comes a Patron of the
　　　　　　　　Arts"
Act I, scene 3　"Here's to It, Whatever It Is"
Act I, scene 4　"One Word from You"
Act I, scene 5　"Dirty Work at the Crossroads"
　　　　　　　　"I'd Love to Push the Plow with
　　　　　　　　You"
　　　　　　　　"Love Is One of Those Things"*
Act II, scene 1　"Bravo"
　　　　　　　　"Unaccustomed As I Am to
　　　　　　　　Public Speaking"

------

* *Also listed in Loesser's 1936 Universal Studios contract as by Loesser and Irving Actman. No music or lyrics found.*

THINGS HAVE COME TO A PRETTY PASS

FATHER:　Things have come to a pretty pass
　　　　In the old da Vinci home.
　　　　He stays out with a pretty lass
　　　　Till the bells have rung for the
　　　　　　morning mass.
LEONARDO:　Things have come to an awful state
　　　　When a man is slandered so.
　　　　I stayed out with a heavy date,
　　　　But I didn't go to the hippodrome,
　　　　'Twas a burlesque show.
ENSEMBLE:　'Twas a burlesque show. Oh!

Note: This number was to segue into a song for which no lyrics survive, "You're a Bounder, You're a Blighter," which after a dialogue interlude was reprised by Leonardo as:

I'M A GENTLEMAN

LEONARDO:　I'm a gentleman, a scholar
　　　　And a versatile young lad.
　　　　I'm a painter and a poet
　　　　And I'm not half bad.
　　　　I'm an author and a writer
　　　　And a most accomplished gent—
　　　　Why, you ought to see the fairy tales
　　　　That I invent.

OH HEAVEN, GIVE ME STRENGTH TONIGHT

TOMASO:　[*spoken*] She looked kind of hard to get.
LEONARDO:　That's what I'm afraid of.
TOMASO:　You know what little girls are made of.
LEONARDO:　Yes, but this one's made of sterner
　　　　stuff.
BENITO:　She said she would meet you.
TOMASO:　I wonder how that gal will treat you.
LEONARDO:　I've a hunch the going will be tough.

Oh heaven, give me strength tonight—
I must have the breeze that murmurs
　low,
I must have the moon that shines
　just so
Upon a new romance.
Oh heaven, give me strength tonight,
The wildrose perfume must hover
　near,
For good old romantic atmosphere,
And I'll have half a chance.
For the lady is a lady,
The lady isn't weak—
I'll need more charms than lips
　and arms
And all my good technique.
So heaven, give me strength tonight,
And sweet mother nature, show your
　love
And make ev'rything suggestive of
A new romance tonight.

EGGS

COLUMBO:　Eggs! Eggs!
I've a subconscious craving for eggs.
So I steal them, conceal them, for
　future use
And I risk the police and the
　hangman's noose,
For if I can have goose eggs direct
　from the goose,
Give me
Eggs! Eggs!
My libido is on its last legs.
So I hook eggs and crook eggs from all
　the farms,
The policemen from Florence are up
　in arms,
But my heart is immune to the fear of
　alarms.
How it
Begs! Begs!
For an adequate diet of eggs.
So I nab them and grab them. These
　eggs I stole,
Indispensable balm for my tortured
　soul,
For the world is a henhouse, and life's
　just a bowl
Of
Eggs! Eggs! Eggs!

I REGARD YOU WITH SUSPICION

CEZAR: I regard you with suspicion,
For I'm tracking down a crook.
With your very kind permission
I shall circumspectly look.
LEONARDO: He's tracking down a crook.
BOYS: He's tracking down a crook.
LEONARDO: Allow him just a look,
For he's tracking down a crook.
CEZAR: [*calling cops forward to search*]
O'Reillio! Mulrooneyo!
LEONARDO: [*spoken*] What does this criminal
look like?
CEZAR: [*sung*] He's a most neurotic nature
And his mind's a single track.
And in legal nomenclature
He's an eggomaniac.
LEONARDO: An eggomaniac.
BOYS: An eggomaniac.
LEONARDO: The cops are on his track
For he's an eggomaniac.
CEZAR: O'Reillio! Mulrooneyo!
[*spoken*] Have you seen the man we
are looking for?
LEONARDO: [*sung*] Does he mutter, does he
mumble,
Does he kick his bandy legs?
Does he passionately grumble
For his daily dozen eggs?
CEZAR: That's the very man.
COPS: That's the very man.
Just tell me where he ran,
For that's the very man.
LEONARDO: [*spoken*] I never saw him in my life.

[*Scene interlude*]

CEZAR: [*sung*] O'Reillio! Mulrooneyo!
I regard him with suspicion,
Though I haven't made a pinch,
But I have an intuition
That the robber is da Vinch.
O'REILLIO: The robber is da Vinch?
MULROONEYO: The robber is da Vinch?
BOTH: Let's go and make a pinch
Because the robber is da Vinch.
CEZAR: O'Reillio! Mulrooneyo!
We must wait until we're certain
That he's criminally bent.
In this meantime draw the curtain
On this profitless event.

[*End of scene 2*]

IF THAT'S WHAT YOU'RE LOOKING FOR

LEONARDO: I've had ladies from floozies to lilies
And other types for models.
Not that I turn up my nose
At the lovely way you pose,
But
Mona darling, you give me the willies.
I hate a girl who toddles.

There's a lovely keg of beer
On the table over here,
If you find that sitting still is such a
bore.
You may drink until you're drunk,
Here's a pretzel you may dunk,
If that's what you're looking for.

There's the *Florentine Gazette*,
If you haven't read it yet,
With its narrow editorials galore.
Or the narrow *Daily News*
With its somewhat broader views,
If that's what you're looking for.

Though you fidget and you squirm
With that odd neurotic strut,
I am adamant and firm
That the damn doors shall stay shut.
But

There's a tiny little shack
In the woods around the back
With a crescent neatly carved upon
the door.
I beseech you, help yourself,
And there's papyrus on the shelf,
If that's what you're looking for.

WHEN ISABELLA LIKES A FELLA

[*Scene: Queen Isabella's castle in Madrid*]

COLUMBO: When Isabella likes a fella,
She shells out,
She practic'lly sells out,
The King.
Poor Ferdinando,
He has to hand-o

Very cold cash.
Her Majesty's new pash
Gets ev'rything.
Then Isabella shows her fella
The time of his life,
And Ferdy
Gets the birdie
From his loyal royal wife.
But don't count your chickens till
they're hatched,
Wait till you see the strings attached.
When Isabella likes a fella,
The deal goes through,
When Isabella likes a fella
Like you.

[*Fanfares for entrance of* KING, QUEEN, *and* JESTER]

LEONARDO: Your Majesty, Your Majesty,
I'm da Vinch,
Ev'ry inch
An explorer.
Get a load of my exploring suit.
QUEEN: I suppose you are just another
schnorer,
But you're pretty darn cute.
KING: [*querulously*] Izzy!
QUEEN: Shut up. I'm busy.

[*She socks him down with scepter.*]

LEONARDO: I've found
The world is round.
The world is round,
Or I'll eat my hat.
But I'm in no condition
To finance an expedition,
So I beg your kind permission
To reiterate that:
I've found
The world is round
But I am flat!
QUEEN: Da Vinci boy, da Vinci boy,
I am so
In the dough
It's a pleasure.

[*Holds up money bag*]

But we'll have to have a rendezvous.
LEONARDO: It's a date, with a weekend for good
measure,
When my voyage is through.
KING: Izzy!
QUEEN: Shut up, I'm busy.
LEONARDO: I've found,
The world is round.
The world is round,

But it's funds I lack.
QUEEN: Then take my proposition.
There can be no intermission,
For I have a premonition
That you'll never come back.
You hound,
You may get drowned
With all my jack.

[LEONARDO *signals to* COLUMBO, *who steps forward.*]

LEONARDO: Your Majesty, Your Majesty,
Meet my mate,
He's a great
Little seaman.
He will tell Your Majesty what's what.
QUEEN: I suppose he's a clever little demon
But he isn't so hot.
LEONARDO: Oh, you'll like him a lot.
QUEEN: What the hell has he got?
KING: You're no beauty, old pot.
QUEEN: Rot!

[*Socks him again*]

COLUMBO: Da Vinci's a guy
That's nuts about geography—
It's always on his mind.
He's got a gal
That's nuts about geography,
For she is just his kind.
They go exploring ev'ry day
On the road to Mandalay.
When he brings her home,
They've had too much
Geography
To tear themselves away.
They try and try—
But they never say goodbye—

Abyssinia? Abyssinia, Abyssinia, says
she—
I Bolivia, I Bolivia, but I'm leavin' ya,
says he
Well, Oolong! I Moscow.
Afghanistan around all night and say:
Abyssinia, I'm not kiddin' ya—
Abyssinia, someday!
LEONARDO: Your Majesty, Your Majesty!
Trust in me
And you'll see
That I'll make it
And I'll settle with you bye and bye.
QUEEN: I suppose that I shouldn't let you
take it,
But you're such a sweet guy.

[*Gives him money*]

KING: Izzy!
QUEEN: Shut up, I'm busy.

[CREW *enters.*]

CREW: We've found
The world is round.
We're westward bound with a rah,
rah, rah.
QUEEN: The *Nina* and the *Pinta*
Are all ready to get inta.
And in case of heavy winta
There's the Santa *Maria.*
ALL: She's found
The ships are sound,
So there you are!
LEONARDO: Your Majesty, Your Majesty,
Thank you lots
For the yachts
And Mazuma.
And when I return to Spain—oh
well—
QUEEN: I'm afraid it will start an ugly rumor,
But it's gonna be swell.
KING: Izzy!
QUEEN: Shut up. I'm busy.

[LEONARDO *kisses* QUEEN *lightly on the cheek. He
starts to leave.*]

QUEEN: Oh, please stick around
And play some more geography—
It's only half past ten.
If that's what you mean,
I'm nuts about geography,
So let's start in again.
Let's go exploring all around,
Let the king go take a nap.
And you can prove you're
Nuts about geography
By mussing up my map.
LEONARDO: Let's shake, just shake,
'Cause I have to make a break . . .
QUEEN: Tiajuana stay, Tiajuana stay,
Tiajuana stay, baby?
LEONARDO: Nicaragua, Nicaragua, Nicaragua
with me.
QUEEN: But I want Samoa, I won't Havana fun
while Uruguay.
LEONARDO: Abyssinia, I'll bump India, Abyssinia,
someday.

[KING *laughs at* QUEEN, *who once more socks him
down.*]

ALL: We've found
The world is round,
The world is round as a derby hat.

And now we're in position
To finance the expedition,
It's a crazy supposition,
But we're gonna stand pat.
We've found
The world is round
And that is that!

ABYSSINIA

No music is known to survive. From a typed lyric sheet,
probably 1933. A slightly different version of this lyric
also appeared in "When Isabella Likes a Fella" from *Libretto for an Operetta.*

VERSE 1

I know a guy
That's nuts about geography—
It's always on his mind.
He's got a gal,
She's nuts about geography—
She's just his kind.
They go exploring every day
On the road to Mandalay.
When they get home,
They've had too much
Geography
To tear themselves away.
They try and try
But they never say goodbye.

REFRAIN 1

Abyssinia, Abyssinia, Abyssinia, says she.
I Bolivia, I Bolivia, but I'm leavin' ya, says he.
Well Oolong, I Moscow,
Afghanistan around all night and say:
Abyssinia, I'm not kiddin' ya,
Abyssinia someday.

VERSE 2

Then she says to him,
I'm nuts about geography
And it's only half past ten.
And he says to her,
Let's play some more geography,
So they start in again.
Well, the way that guy explores around
Makes Columbus look like a sap.
And just to show
She's nuts about

Geography,
She musses up his map.
They shake and shake,
But they never make a break.

REFRAIN 2

Tiajuana stay, Tiajuana stay, Tiajuana stay? says
  she.
Aw, Nicaragua, Nicaragua, Nicaragua with me.
But I want Samoa,
I don't Havana fun while Uruguay—
Abyssinia, I'll bump India,
Abyssinia some day.

ACROBATS
(The Hiccough Song)

No music is known to survive. From a typed lyric sheet,
probably 1933. Two capital letters at the start of a word
indicate a hiccough.

VERSE

Everybody's got a little weakness,
Everybody's got his pet disease.
There's athlete's foot and liver pains,
Halitosis, softened brains,
Or a touch of housemaid's knees.
Now some folks can't eat oysters at a party
And some can't drink before they go to bed.
Now I am never feeling ill,
But when I work in vaudeville,
I feel something going to my head:

REFRAIN

It's those
ACrobats, they get me so darn nervous,
ACrobats'll drive me nertz.
Every time I watch them I go crazy,
They go higher, higher, higher, UPsadaisy.
Radishes don't give me gases,
But ACrobats make me drop my OPraglasses.
When they're on the high trapezes,
I just holler, Holy—! ACcidents are bound to
    happen
And ACcidents always hurts.
Those ACrobats, they get me so darn nervous.
ACrobats'll drive me,
EXcuse me,
ACrobats'll drive me
ABsolutely—!

HOLLYWOOD BE
THY NAME

A vaudeville act written for Mary Nolan by Frank Loesser and Jean Herbert (b. 1905). Registered for copyright
as an unpublished dramatic work September 15, 1933.
The New York–born Herbert also collaborated with
Billy Rose, Sammy Fain, Irving Caesar, and James Han-
ley. Mary Nolan (real name Mary Imogene Robertson,
1906–1948) had a checkered career that included a stint
with the *Follies* in the early 1920s, at which point Flo-
renz Ziegfeld called her "the most beautiful girl I ever
glorified." Performing under the name Imogene "Bubbles" Wilson, she was involved in a destructive liaison
with Broadway comic Frank Tinney, which led to a front-
page scandal that ruined both their careers. She married
a wealthy financier, lost him and the money in the crash
of 1929, and attempted a comeback in film, vaudeville,
and nightclubs as Mary Nolan in the 1930s.

IF I CAN'T GET THE MAN
I WANT

HE: Will you hold that pose?
SHE: May I powder my nose?
HE: Yes, but hurry, we're shooting a scene.
SHE: Oh, I'm the heroine!
HE: Yes, you're the heroine,
    Register love—you know what I mean.
SHE: But where's my hero?
    My wonderful hero?
    My passionate love affair?
HE: I'll play the part,
    I'll get in your heart.
SHE: Say, listen, you get in my hair!
HE: How about Georgie Raft?
SHE: Ah, don't make me laugh,
    He's not a great sensation.
HE: Joe E. Brown?
SHE: Thumbs down.

[*opens her mouth*]

    What an excavation!
HE: Try Jack Oakie?
SHE: He's too hokey-pokey,
    He doesn't know what class is.
HE: Harold Lloyd?
SHE: Oh, I can't be annoyed,
    One look and I'd break his glasses.

HE: Richard Arlen?
SHE: No, he's mama's darlin'.
    He couldn't give me a thrill.
HE: How about Leslie Howard?
SHE: He's not high-powered;
    Remember, I've been through the mill.
HE: What star can I get
    To play opposite you?
    Can you suggest any others?
SHE: I want a man that's worth four of you.
HE: Alright, I'll send for the Marx Brothers!

[HE *then exits.*]

REFRAIN

SHE: If I can't get the man I want,
    God help the man I get!
    My next leading man will have to be hotter
    Than the lovers I have met.
    I'm sick and tired of being admired
    By amateurs like Clark Gable.
    And as for Tom Mix, I'll tell him nix,
    If he tries to park Tony in my stable.
    If I can't land the fish I want,
    God help the shrimp I catch.
    If I land Gary Cooper and he's not
        super-super,
    He'll land in the booby hatch.
    I'm looking for nature in the raw,
    Not one of those soft sweethearts;
    A he-man actor, a big sex attractor,
    Who can handle the prominent parts.

    I pity the mug that gets into my hug,
    'Cause when I make love I make it.
    It's rumored about that when I dish it out
    There's not many men that can take it.
    So if I can't get the man I want,
    God help the man I get.
    Edmund Lowe won't do it for a beau.
    Besides, Lilyan Tashman's not through with
        him yet.
    I know the guy who'll qualify—
    He makes John Barrymore look all wet.
    Yes sir, if I can't have Schnozzle Durante,
    God help the palooka I get!

HE WENT LIKE THIS, SO I WENT LIKE THAT

VERSE

They say you can tell a man by his talk;
If he says "dees" and "dose" he comes from New
York.
If he says "cheerio" he's a duke or an earl;
If he says "Vos you dare, Sharlie?"—don't give
your right name!
But I find the talkative kind are the easiest to
learn about.
It's the strong silent he-man type that's hard to
figure out.
For instance—

REFRAIN

I was driving alone in a limousine
That I borrowed from a friend named Jim.
He had the car on time,
But of course I had something on him.
As I drove along the boulevard
I was full of deviltry.
In a well-tailored suit
I saw a handsome brute
Making a peculiar motion to me:
He went like this—
[*Hitchhiker's signal*]
As he tipped his hat;
I went like this—
[*Winking and nodding head*]
And I went like that—
[*Beckoning to him with fingers*]
He sat in the car beside me,
And I admired his handsome physique.
I had picked him up,
Now would he let me down?
I wondered about his technique.
'Cause he went like this—
[*Resting her chin in hand, bored*]
And I went like that—
[*Haughty, with hands on steering wheel*]
Was this stranger giving me the high hat?
Then I slowed down and stopped the car
At a dark, secluded spot,
So the motor would have a chance to cool off,
And so he'd have a chance to get hot.
But he went like this—
[*Fixing a tie*]
With his silk cravat;
He went like this—
[*Then putting hand to hair as if brushing*]
So I went like that—

[*Powdering her nose and touching sides of her face*]
I waited for something to happen;
He was shy for a guy on the make.
I kept shooting him glances,
But he made no advances,
So I thought I'd make the first break.
I went like this—
[*Pinching his cheek*]
And he went like that—
[*Looking goofy, twirling her thumbs*]
I went like this—
[*Puckering her lips*]
Then he went like that—
[*Shaking her index finger from left to right, indicating no*]
That strong silent man was as cold as ice,
But I was as warm as could be.
He just wouldn't melt;
I don't know how he felt,
But he certainly didn't feel me!
I went like this—
[*Yanking him toward her, grabbing around neck*]
He went like that—
[*Slapping her wrist*]
Then I went like this—
[*Does a snake-hips*]
And he went like that—
[*Slapping her face*]
For a minute I was in doubt,
But then the truth came out
As he blushed when I rushed for a kiss.
Then he rushed for the door,
And the last thing I saw,
He was running away, like this—
[*Prancing off like a pansy*]

MY FOOTBALL HERO!

VERSE

There's more than one good reason
Why I love the football season,
'Cause I got a special interest in the game.
When I wave this blue-and-yellow
I'm rootin' for my fellow,
And incidentally good old Notre Dame.
My halfback Larry, the pride of the team,
He's the answer to this coed's dream.

REFRAIN

My football hero,
He wins every time
For alma mater and me.

I'm cheering for him
With the crowd,
Only twice as loud,
'Cause I'm mighty proud
Of my football hero.
He breaks through the line
Till every battle is done:
Block that tackle!
Get that pass!
Run down the field!
Faster! Faster!
My football hero,
Even if he scores a zero,
My heart he's won!

[*Monologue indicated in text, but missing.*]

Block that tackle!
Get that pass!
Run, run, down the field. . . !
Faster, faster!
My football hero,
Even if your score is zero
My heart you've won!

LOOKING OUT THE WINDOW AT THE RAIN

VERSE

It's been raining,
It's been pouring,
It's been thundering!
We've been sitting in the parlor
Kinda wondering
What party we'll go to,
What picture we'll see,
And it just occurs to me:

REFRAIN

Oh, ain't you glad we stayed home tonight,
Looking out the window at the rain?
And when it thunders I'll hold you tight,
Looking out the window at the rain.
We could go out to dinner, I guess,
But let's stay high and dry,
And I'll call up the delicatess'
For a ham on white and a Swiss on rye.
If we'd gone walking we'd look a sight;
It's drenchin' ev'ry bench in Lovers' Lane.
I've got a million love words to write
Here upon the foggy windowpane.

Let's hope it showers ev'ry twenty-four hours
So we can be alone again.
Oh, ain't you glad we stayed home tonight,
Looking out the window at the rain?

I'VE GOT SO MUCH TO FORGET

Music and lyrics by Frank Loesser and Jean Herbert. From undated typed lyric and lead sheet. Probably late 1933 or early 1934.

VERSE

It seemed too easy to say goodbye;
You took it bravely, and so did I,
For love was a thing of the past.
It seemed so simple to say farewell;
It seemed so simple, how could I tell
Those memories always would last?

REFRAIN

When I loved you,
Ev'ry sky was bright and blue,
That's why I can't see blue skies now
Without remembering you.
Love ended, and yet
I've got so much to forget.
When I loved you,
All the earth was green and new;
That's why I can't hear robins sing
Without remembering you.
That springtime we met,
I've got so much to forget.

Ev'ry breeze that blows
Keeps whisp'ring your name to me
Ever since the day we parted.
Romance comes and goes,
But it's just a game to me,
Just a game I play half-hearted.
For I loved you,
And your kiss was warm and true.
Now I can't feel a kiss somehow
Without imagining you
Embracing me yet.
I've got so much to forget.

SPAGHETTI

Music by Otto Motzan (1880–1937). Lyrics by Billy Frisch (1882–1968) and Frank Loesser. Registered for copyright as an unpublished song October 5, 1933. Motzan, a composer, conductor, and violinist, was music director for Belle Baker. Frisch was a composer, author, and vaudevillian from Philadelphia who frequently collaborated with Motzan. Among his song hits was "I'd Like to See the Kaiser with a Lily in His Hand."

VERSE

Over in Venice and Naples and Rome
There's an op'ra they show at the old hippodrome.
They call it *Gorgonzola*
By Tony Raviola,
Oh, what a show, what a piece, what a play!
What an audience comes there to see it each day!
They're wild about the music,
The tenors and the baritones.
When they come out, tune their mandolins and
    shout:

REFRAIN

Spaghetti!
I feed-a da kids,
I feed-a da wife,
I feed-a da family alla my life-a
Spaghetti! Spaghetti!
Spaghetti!
And add-a da sauce,
You live-a da long,
You add-a da garlic,
She make-a you strong.
Spaghetti! Spaghetti!
When my marioocha take a steamboat,
She come back and what-a you think
She bring-a da me
For-a da big-a surprise-a?
Spaghetti!
No get-a da love,
No get-a da kiss,
'Cause my marioocha,
She give me so mooch-a
Spaghetti! Spaghetti!
Spaghetti!
If I get-a sick,
If I gonna die,
No bring-a me flower,
Just bring-a me my
Spaghetti! Spaghetti!

JUNK MAN

Music by Joseph Meyer (1894–1987). Published. Copyrighted January 12, 1934. Recorded by Benny Goodman, vocal by Mildred Bailey (Bluebird)—one of the first successful commercial recordings of a Loesser song. Meyer had a hit earlier with "California, Here I Come" (lyrics by B. G. DeSylva and Al Jolson). He also collaborated on "If You Knew Susie" and "Crazy Rhythm."

VERSE 1

Junk man, junk man,
Moochin' roun' Harlem town
When all the lights are dim.
Junk man, junk man,
Moochin' roun' Harlem town,
I've got a big job for him.

REFRAIN 1

I'm gonna give that junk man my broken heart,
The broken heart I got from you.
I'm gonna give that junk man my broken heart
For a loaded thirty-two.
I'm gonna give that junk man my old glad rags,
I'm gonna wear a gown of black.
You better pack your trunk, man, and pack your
    bags,
'Cause I'm gettin' on your track.

Now I ain't braggin', no! no!
But you can't throw me down.
I'm gonna fix your wagon, yeah! man,
So you can't go to town!
I'm gonna do you right, 'cause you done me
    wrong,
I'm gonna do you black and blue.
And then I'll tell that junk man to come along
And pick up what's left of you!

VERSE 2

Junk man, junk man,
Where is that junk man at,
Him and his old gray nag?
I've got souvenirs, salty tears,
To fill his big rag bag.

REFRAIN 2

I'm gonna give that junk man my broken heart,
The broken heart I got from you.
I'm gonna give that junk man my broken heart,
For a loaded thirty-two.
I'm gonna give that junk man my old glad rags,

I'm gonna wear a gown of black.
You better pack your trunk, man, and pack your
    bags
'Cause I'm gettin' on your track.

Now I ain't braggin', no! no!
But you can't throw me down.
You thought you fixed my wagon, yeah! man,
But watch me go to town!
I'm gonna do you right, 'cause you done me
    wrong,
I'm gonna do you black and blue.
And then I'll tell that junk man to come along
And pick up what's left of you!

THE OLD OAK TREE

Music by Joseph Meyer. Published. Copyrighted March 27, 1934. Introduced by Ted Fiorito and His Orchestra, but not recorded. Fiorito and Loesser collaborated in 1939 on "I'm All A-Tremble Over You" (page 53).

VERSE 1

I don't need the fam'ly album
To picture the joys of yesteryear.
I don't need an old love letter;
I have a better souvenir.

REFRAIN

There's an old oak tree
Full of memories for me
Of a sweetheart long ago.
After school we'd stroll till the close of day,
And that old oak tree was our hideaway.
There are two hearts there
That we carved with tender care
For the whole wide world to see.
And our schoolday love
Lingers like the moon above
On the old oak tree.

VERSE 2

Somewhere in the shady woodland,
There's one of my sweetest souvenirs.
Just a little old love token,
A charm unbroken through the years.

REPEAT REFRAIN

GOO GOO G'DA

Music by Ernest Breuer (1886–1981). Lyrics by Frank Loesser, Billy Frisch, and Raymond Leveen (1899–1984). Published. Copyrighted April 26, 1934. Composer-pianist Breuer, born in Augsburg, Germany, served as entertainment director for the United States Army of Occupation under General Pershing at the end of World War I. Leveen, a lyricist from Newark, New Jersey, co-wrote the World War II hit "I Wonder."

VERSE

Newlyweds go off their heads about babies,
All the neighbors' babies,
But wait till a year or more:
Now they've got theirs—
It's got three hairs
And a teething ring—
Yours and mine don't mean a thing,
Since that blessed event next door.

REFRAIN

Ev'ry mama's child is the cutest thing,
Just the cutest thing
That the stork could bring.
Baby, show your pa how smart you are—
And all the baby says is "Goo goo g'da."
Ev'ry papa's boy is heaven-sent,
Just another future president,
And his proud papa knows he'll go far—
Why, all he has to say is "Goo goo g'da."
Parents are uncertain
Just the kind of a name for their darling son;
Looks just like Ben Turpin,
So they up and call him George Washington.
Ev'ry mama's child is the cutest thing,
How he keeps the fam'ly arguing:
Does he look like Ma?
No, he looks like Pa—
And all the baby says is "Goo goo g'da."

I WISH I WERE TWINS

Music by Joseph Meyer. Lyrics by Edgar De Lange (1904–1949) and Frank Loesser. Published. Copyrighted May 3, 1934. Leading recording by Thomas "Fats" Waller (Bluebird). Frank Loesser's recording appears on the compact disc *Frank Sings Loesser* (Koch). Edgar De Lange (better known as Eddie) was a composer, lyricist, and conductor whose best-known songs include "Darn That Dream," "Solitude," and "Moonglow."

VERSE

When I'm with you I feel so small,
Right in my shell I want to crawl,
I wonder why I had to fall for you.
Why do you make my life so tough?
It seems I can't love you enough—
You're so heavenly,
Much too much for me.

REFRAIN

I wish that I were twins,
You great big babykins,
So I could love you twice as much as I do.
I'd have four loving arms to embrace you,
Four eyes to idolize you
Each time I face you.
With two hearts twice as true
What couldn't four lips do?
When four ears hear you saying "I'm yours!,"
You great big babykins,
I wish that I were twins,
So I could love you twice as much as I do!

Alternate refrain (recorded by Frank Loesser in late 1940s)

I wish that I were twins,
You great big babykins,
So I could love you twice as much as I do.
I'd have four loving arms to embrace you,
Four eyes to idolize you
Each time I face you.
I'd feel no jealousy
If you kissed both of me,
'Cause both of me would only want you
To double your pleasure.
You great big babykins,
I wish that I were twins,
So I could love you twice as much as I do.

STARS ON THE HIGHWAY

Music by Joseph Meyer. Probably spring–summer 1934. Loesser tried to revive this song during World War II but was unable to interest any music publishers.

VERSE

Nightfall, nightfall, cold and gray,
Still my mem'ries glow;
Nightfall comes, but come what may
In my heart I know—

REFRAIN

There'll be stars on the highway,
There'll be wine on the wind,
There'll be warm arms of welcome at my door.
And I'll sing to the world that I'm home again,
I'm home again . . . once more.
There are clouds on the highway,
There's a chill in the wind,
As I stand on a strange and distant shore.
But there's peace in my mind,
For tomorrow I'll find
Shining stars on the highway,
Fragrant wine on the wind,
And the warm arms of welcome at my door!

OH! WHAT A BEAUTIFUL BABY YOU TURNED OUT TO BE

Music by J. Fred Coots (1897–1985). Published. Copyrighted June 28, 1934. Coots is known as the composer of "Santa Claus Is Coming to Town" and "You Go to My Head" (lyrics by Haven Gillespie).

VERSE 1

Here comes a beautiful baby,
Walking down the street my way.
I guess I'll take a chance and say hello.
Here I go: Hello.
What's that you're calling me, baby?
How'dja come to know my name?
Well, I'll be jiggered, it's the same old pal
From the days when we were boy and gal.

REFRAIN

You had freckles and two teeth missing
In nineteen twenty-three,
But oh! what a beautiful baby
You turned out to be.
All the kids called you Skinny Minnie,
It fit you to a T—
But oh! what a beautiful baby
You turned out to be.

You're the one at Sunday school
Hung around me like a fool.
I'm the fool who treated you cool,
Never dreaming how cute ya
Would be in the future.
You had freckles and two teeth missing,
But now the joke's on me,
For oh! what a beautiful baby
You turned out to be.

VERSE 2

I never dreamed of you, baby,
Growing up the way you did,
Oh, you were such a funny kid!
Oh gee, me oh my, oh me,
I never dreamed of you, baby.
Now that we have met by fate,
I guess I'm just a bit too late to say:
"How the devil did you get that way?"

REPEAT REFRAIN

HOME TIES

Music and lyrics by Charles Tobias (1898–1970), Samuel Pokrass (c. 1893–1939), and Frank Loesser. Published. Copyrighted November 30, 1934. Previously registered for copyright as an unpublished song November 9, 1934. Charles, one of the Tobias brothers, is remembered for such hits as "Don't Sit Under the Apple Tree" and "Comes Love." Pokrass was a collaborator of E. Y. Harburg's on songs for *Ziegfeld Follies of 1934* and wrote music for 20th Century–Fox musicals of the late 1930s.

VERSE 1

Here in the gloaming I long to stray,
Back on the highway of yesterday.
Slowly my dreams unfold,
Scenes that will never grow old.

REFRAIN

Home ties cling to me,
They still mean ev'rything to me,
What memories they bring to me
Of the long ago!
Home ties hold me tight—
I heard an organ through the night,
An angel in the candlelight
Singing soft and low.
Those I love seem near to me

Though we may be far apart.
Silver threads so dear to me
Are bound around my heart.
Home ties, through the years,
How sweetly they renew the years,
With smiles and tears for souvenirs
Of the long ago!

VERSE 2

Each open doorway I chance to see
Brings back a doorway so dear to me.
That door, I realize,
Opened to my Paradise.

REPEAT REFRAIN

DOESN'T THAT MEAN ANYTHING TO YOU?

Music by Bob Emmerich (1904–1988). Published. Copyrighted December 17, 1934. Emmerich, a singer in vaudeville, radio, and nightclubs, was accompanist to the Yacht Club Boys. He worked extensively with Buddy Bernier and had hits which included "Our Love" and "The Big Apple."

VERSE

Bees got roses, dogs got noses,
You and I got these and thoses.
We've got all it takes,
But for goodness sakes, oh!

REFRAIN

Don'tcha know? Can'tcha see?
Here you are alone with only moonlight and me,
List'ning to the love birdies bill and coo,
Now, doesn't that mean anything to you?
Don'tcha know wrong from right?
When I say I'm feeling kinda chilly tonight,
Do I have to tell you to hold me tight?
Oh, doesn't that mean anything to you?
Oh, listen to the naughty autumn breeze
Give all the willow trees a kiss!
I wouldn't want as cold a kiss as that,
But what I'm driving at is this, oh!
Don'tcha know what I mean?
Might as well be sitting reading some magazine.
Don'tcha know that I'm over seventeen?
And doesn't that mean anything to you?

SUNDAY AT SUNDOWN

Music by Otto Motzan. Published. Copyrighted January 1, 1935. Featured by Don Pedro and His Orchestra. No recordings are known to survive.

VERSE

In all my dreams I see a scene so dear to me:
A little church in an old country lane.
And someone's voice I hear:
She's singing soft and clear
Our song of sweet love again.

REFRAIN

Meet me by the chapel door,
Sunday at sundown.
For all week long I'm living for
Sunday at sundown.
I find you there,
We stroll away,
After ev'ning pray'r
Ends the day, dear,
Wand'ring to the wishing well,
Sunday at sundown.
I wish we'd hear that old church bell
Telling the whole town
To meet us by the chapel door
And sing our wedding tune,
Some happy Sunday in June
At sundown.

THE TRAFFIC WAS TERRIFIC

Music by Otto Motzan. Lyrics by Buddy Bernier (1910–1983) and Frank Loesser. Published. Copyrighted May 31, 1935. Previously registered for copyright as an unpublished song February 20, 1935. Bernier, who frequently collaborated with Bob Emmerich, also wrote lyrics for "Poinciana" and "The Night Has a Thousand Eyes."

VERSE

A taxi might have hit me,
For I was in a trance.
I ran before a jitney,
I took an awful chance;
But the only thing that hit me
Was such a sweet romance
That I'll tell my story here and now,

What and when and where and why
And how!

REFRAIN

The traffic was terrific
And she was caught between
A truck that had no conscience
And a reckless limousine.
She asked me for assistance;
I helped her cross the way—
Oh! The traffic was terrific that day.

My heart felt sort of funny;
She leaned against my arm,
And then she turned her eyes to me,
And that's what did the harm.
We both got kind of giddy
And started in to sway—
Oh! The traffic was terrific that day.

A cab went zooming by.
I heard her cry;
She squeezed my arm so tight.
And so I asked if I could see her
Safely to her home.
Now safely to her home
I see her ev'ry single night!

It's just a noisy cottage,
As noisy as the street,
But we can hear our love song
In the tramp of tiny feet.
The kiddie cars and scooters
Have the right of way,
'Cause the traffic was terrific that day.

I JUST CAME BACK TO HAUNT YOU (BOOGY BOOGY BOOGY BOO!)

Words and music by Frank Loesser, Billy Hueston (1896–1957), and Bob Emmerich. Published. Copyrighted June 22, 1935. A sometime songwriter, Hueston owned a booking agency and produced shows for radio and nightclubs.

VERSE

You broke my heart; you said "Let's part,"
But I've gotten over that somehow.
We're all through, but keep your door shut;
This is why I'm calling on you now.

REFRAIN 1

Oh, I just came back to haunt you—
Boogy boogy boogy boo!
Yes, I just came back to haunt you,
'Cause you killed my love for you.
Baby, I don't really want you,
Since you found somebody new,
But I just came back to haunt you—
Boogy boogy boogy boo!
You're dreaming a brand-new dream of love,
But you can't forget me yet.
'Cause I'm gonna change your dream of love
To a nightmare of regret.
So I'm knocking at your doorway,
Like I always used to do.
But I just came back to haunt you—
Boogy boogy boogy boo!

REFRAIN 2

Oh, I just came back to haunt you—
Boogy boogy boogy boo!
Yes, I just came back to haunt you,
Just to keep you feeling blue.
Baby, I don't really want you
Like I thought I used to do,
So I just came back to haunt you—
Boogy boogy boogy boo!
I'm scheming a lot of things to do,
And you'll wish we'd never met.
You're laughing at me right now, it's true,
But I'll do some laughing yet.
All your wishes will be wasted,
'Cause I know a trick or two,
And I just came back to haunt you—
Boogy boogy boogy boo!

POETIC GEMS

Music by Louis Herscher (1894–1974). Published. Copyrighted September 18, 1935. Thirteen songs inspired by the poems of Edgar A. Guest (1881–1959), for a planned series of musical film short subjects entitled *Edgar A. Guest's Poetic Gems*, supervised by Nathan Cy Braunstein. There is no evidence that these films were ever made or released. Edgar Guest enjoyed considerable popularity from the mid-teens through the 1930s. The reach of his syndicated poetry and radio appearances led Warner Bros. to hire him in 1935. Herscher was a composer, lyricist, conductor, author, and publisher from Philadelphia, whose books include *Practical Songwriting* and *Successful Songwriting*.

In a 1962 memo to his attorneys, Loesser recalled the circumstances surrounding the composition of *Poetic Gems*:

> This collection of songs represents all my collaborations with Herscher. They were written at the request of a man named Pizor (spelling?) who seemed to be a film manufacturer on 9th Avenue. I seem to recall that they made a series of short scenic films based on Edgar Guest's poetry and Herscher and I were required to adapt Guest's subjects to song form. I remember that I did not use any of Guest's actual titles or poetic lines, but simply adapted his subjects. I believe the songs were used in the films mentioned, but there was also a reading of the original Guest poetry. . . . I simply sat down with Herscher and Herscher paid me in hand $5 cash for each completed work . . . Somewhere in my gederum I have the feeling that the $5 he gave me was out of the $100 they gave him, and in those years the gederum had a lot of wrinkles in it. My opinion of the series of pieces is as low as my calorie count was in those days.

EV'RYBODY'S SHIP COMES IN (BUT MINE)

Based on Edgar A. Guest's poem "Sea Dreams."

VERSE

The sea rolls in, and the sea rolls out,
But the sea doesn't know what I'm sighing about.
Standing alone on the shore,
Must I be alone forevermore?

REFRAIN

Why is it dreams come true
For you and you and you?
Why is it ev'rybody's ship comes in but mine?
Why do the tides of fate
Just make me wait and wait?
I'm watching ev'rybody's ship come in but mine.
Why do I see a horizon that always is gray
With mem'ries of old casting driftwood my way?
They say that love returns
For ev'ry heart that yearns.
Why is it ev'rybody's ship comes in but mine?

A SYMPHONY IN GREEN

Based on Edgar A. Guest's poem "Early in the Mornin'."

VERSE

Noonday was made for the laughter of children,
Twilight for gossips at tea,
Ev'ning for romance and music and moonlight;
But dawn's early ray,
At the birth of each day,
Must have been made for me.

REFRAIN

Wake me early in the morning,
Let me gaze upon the scene
Of the treetops in the dewy dawning,
A symphony in green.
Wake me early in the morning,
Let me wander from my bed,
With the weeping willow for an awning,
A-hanging overhead.
Here for a cool fragrant hour,
Cradle me close to the sod;
Here in a heavenly bower,
High on a hillside, nearer to God.
Wake me early in the morning,
Let me gaze upon the scene
Of the treetops in the dewy dawning,
A symphony in green.

TAKE ME HOME TO THE MOUNTAINS

Based on Edgar A. Guest's poem "The Old Prospector Talks."

VERSE

Take me home to the mountains,
Back with those grub-staking men,
To the hills that were mine
Back in old 'forty-nine,
Take me home to the mountains again.

REFRAIN

Now I've grown old and gray,
And I'll go any day
For the longest journey of all;
So I'm dreaming tonight
Of my campfire light
In the hills where the timber grows tall.

INDIAN MOON

Based on Edgar A. Guest's poem "When Redskins Bit the Dust."

VERSE

I see lovers;
Night is falling.
I hear lovers
Softly calling.

REFRAIN

Indian moon
Shining above,
Indian trail,
Lead me to love.
Indian moon
Weaving a spell,
Indian call
I know so well.
Leave your little tepee,
Come with me where sleepy breezes blow.
Ooh-oo-oo-oo-oo-oo-oo-oo-oo-oo-oo,
I love you so.
Meet me tonight by the lagoon,
Under the bright Indian moon.

LITTLE MISS MISCHIEF

Based on Edgar A. Guest's poem "Worn Out."

VERSE

My trouble is a little one,
But I love her just the same.
Tho' folks all call her Sally Lou,
I've given her another name. And—

REFRAIN 1

I call her Little Miss Mischief,
At the tender age of three.
She's always so full of mischief,
But she means the world to me.
The other day she ran away
And hid Grandfather's hat.
She poured molasses on the doorstep
And pinched the neighbor's cat.
[*spoken*] Meow.

REFRAIN 2

I call her Little Miss Mischief,
Never wants to go to bed.
I just can't give her the mischief,
I forgive the kid instead.
Now don't suggest a spankin's best,
For that's something you couldn't do
If Little Miss Mischief,
My Little Miss Mischief,
Belonged to you.

DOWN THE LANE TO YESTERDAY

Based on Edgar A. Guest's poem "Boyhood."

VERSE

Some folks dream of riches,
Others dream of fame,
And some folks have no dreams at all.
I have little rev'ries,
All of them the same:
Mem'ries of my youth I recall.

REFRAIN

Roaming thru the wildwood,
Back to days of childhood,
Thru my dreams of long ago.
The golden rods that nod hello,
They seem to call me yonder,
Down the lane to yesterday.
Neath a mossy pillow,
By a weeping willow,
There's the fishing pole I hid
When I was just a barefoot kid.
Oh, how I'd love to wander
Down the lane to yesterday!
I wonder if the village smithy's there,
Still standing by his door.
The smithy had a daughter fair,
I wonder if she still waits for me
Somewhere in the wildwood,
Sweetheart of my childhood.
She was so demure and shy;
I dream of her and wake and sigh.
Oh, how I'd love to wander
Down the lane to yesterday!

BY A SILVERY STREAM

Based on Edgar A. Guest's poem "Bill and I Went Fishing."

VERSE

People say I'm wrong
'Scaping from the throng,
Sittin' by a stream
Where it's shady and cool.
Ev'rybody says I'm a lazy old fool,
Fishin' all day long.

REFRAIN

By a silvery stream
Neath a summery sky,
Let me go right on fishin'
Till the waters run dry.
By a silvery stream,
Where the world is all mine,
I just got no ambition
But to throw in my line.
Oh, let me smoke my pipe in peace,
Waitin' for the trout to run,
Long as I can smoke in peace,
What do I care if I don't catch one?
It's a lazy old day,

Made for dreamers to dream—
Don't you wish you were fishin'
By a silvery stream?

THE SNOWFLAKES

Based on Edgar A. Guest's poems "Call of the Woods" and "Silence of the Snow."

VERSE

I'm looking out of my window
At the deep white snow on the lawn.
I'm looking out of my window,
Dreaming of a night bygone.

REFRAIN

How I love the merry dancing of
The sparkling flakes when they fall!
Then, it seems,
I'm back again in dreams,
A happy winter I recall,
When the woodland was white
On a cold December night
And you loved me best of all.
That's why I love
The merry dancing of
The sparkling snowflakes when they fall.

DON'T GROW ANY OLDER (MY LITTLE BOY BLUE)

Based on Edgar A. Guest's poem "Couldn't Live Without You."

VERSE

Childhood is sweet,
Childhood is free,
But somehow it doesn't last long.
We live and we learn,
Grow up and yearn
Once more to sing youth's happy song.
You little shaver,
So busy at play—
To you, little shaver,
I tenderly say:

REFRAIN

Don't grow any older,
My little boy blue.
Don't grow any older,
Whatever you do.
For the world is your playground,
You're carefree today,
With no butcher, or baker, or piper to pay.
So don't grow any older,
My little boy blue,
Solving grown-up problems
Like your pa.
Now you're seven, and it's heaven,
My little boy blue,
So don't grow any older than you are.

HERE'S TO THE BUILDER

Based on Edgar A. Guest's poem "Song of the Builder."

VERSE

A man among men is he,
Molder in granite and brick and lime.
A man among men is he,
Leading the way in the march of time.

REFRAIN

Here's to the builder, the man of steel;
Here's to the mansions tow'ring high!
Sing his praise to the clang of the anvil,
The sound of rivets thund'ring in the sky.
He is a builder of dreams come true,
Everlastingly designed.
Sing his praise in your hearts always,
For his monuments to mankind.

GET UNDER THE SUN

Based on Edgar A. Guest's poems "After the Storm"
and "When We Were Kids."

VERSE

Oh, what a feeling when the rain stops,
When the raindrops disappear!
Oh, what a feeling when the rain stops,
Then it makes you want to cheer!

REFRAIN

Get under the sun,
Get under the sun,
Ev'ry robin's singing to you,
Get under the sun.
Come on, ev'ry one,
The thunder is done,
Clouds are rolling out of the blue,
Get under the sun.
Come out, come out
From behind your windowpane.
There's a rainbow in the sky above,
And there ain't gonna be no rain.
Get under the sun,
Start having your fun,
All the world is smiling anew—
Get under the sun.

A REAL TRUE PAL

Based on Edgar A. Guest's poem "Scout Master."

VERSE

Life is only what you make it,
Lose or win.
You need someone to help you take it
On the chin.

REFRAIN

For it never rains and it never pours,
And the sky is blue and the world is yours,
When you're strolling along with
A real true pal.
You share your troubles and you share your dreams,
And it's twice as easy to smile, it seems,
When you're singing a song with
A real true pal.
When the dark clouds are in the sky,

Fair-weather playmates all say goodbye;
But good as gold, as the sun above,
Is the helping hand of a friend you love,
And you'll never go wrong with
A real true pal.

BACKSEAT DRIVERS

Based on Edgar A. Guest's poem "Ma and the Auto." Refrain based on earlier lyric for "Acrobats" (see page 8).

VERSE

I'm gonna sell my car.
The axle isn't broken,
The engine isn't smokin',
But I'm gonna sell my car.
The tires aren't tired,
The batteries are wired,
But I'm gonna sell my car.
The carburetor's perfect,
And the cylinders don't miss.
Ask me why I'm through with it,
The reason is this:

REFRAIN

Oh, those backseat drivers,
They're driving me crazy,
Backseat drivers get me wild.
Uncle Charlie's nervous
And so is Aunt Daisy,
And Oscar, their angel child.
You should hear them in the rear,
When I'm trying to steer,
How they scream and holler and squawk!
Oh, those backseat drivers,
Those scared of their livers,
Why don't they get out and walk?

Top: Nan Grey, Deanna Durbin, and Barbara Read in the film Three Smart Girls. *Bottom: Irving Actman, Frank Loesser, and unidentified actress at Universal Studios, 1936*

Songs of 1936–1937

THE ILLUSTRATORS' SHOW

New York run: Forty-eighth Street Theatre, January 22–25, 1936. Five performances. Music and lyrics mostly by Frank Loesser and Irving Actman (1907–1967). Actman, who had been Lita Grey Chaplin's rehearsal pianist, would later work with Loesser as music director for *Guys and Dolls*. Additional songs by Charlotte Kent (words and music); Milton Pascal (words) and Edgar Fairchild (music); Earle Crooker (words) and Frederick Loewe (music); Nat and Max Lief (words) and Michael H. Cleary (music); Carl Randall (words) and Bernece Kazounoff (music). Produced by Tom Weatherly. Sketches by Harry Evans, Fred Cooper and Frank Goodwin, Donald Blackwell, Max Liebman and Hi Alexander, Kenneth Webb, Will Glickman, Napier Moore, and Otto Soglow. Production supervised by Tom Weatherly. Dances and musical numbers staged by Carl Randall. Sketches staged by Allen Delano. Settings by Arne Lundborg from designs by the Society of Illustrators. Costumes designed by Carl Sidney. Orchestra under the direction of Gene Salzer. Cast featured Helen Lynd, Earl Oxford, Niela Goodelle, and Gomez and Winona, and included Dan Harden, Fred Cooper, Norman Lind, William Houston, Elizabeth Houston, Otto Soglow, Davenie Watson, O. Z. Whitehead, Joe Donatello, Robert Berry, Edward Mowen, and the Fourteen American Beauties. Soglow, the cartoonist who created the comic strip *The Little King*, performed the part of the Little King in this production.

No lyrics available for the following Loesser/Actman songs listed in the program:

"If You Didn't Love Me." Lyrics by Frank Loesser, music by Irving Actman. Introduced by Niela Goodelle and Earl Oxford.
"I Like to Go Strange Places." Lyrics by Frank Loesser, music by Irving Actman. Introduced by Helen Lynd.
"I'm You." Lyrics by Frank Loesser, music by Irving Actman. Introduced by Elizabeth Houston, Dan Harden, and the Girls.
"Finale." Lyrics by Frank Loesser and Carl Randall, music by Irving Actman. Introduced by entire company.

Although Loesser's first Broadway show closed after only five performances, the *Hollywood Reporter* wrote favorably about the Loesser/Actman songs. This helped Loesser and Actman secure a six-month, $200-a-week contract with Universal Studios in April 1936.

BANG—THE BELL RANG!

Music by Irving Actman. Published. Copyrighted January 18, 1936. Introduced by Niela Goodelle and Earl Oxford. The song was also used in the 1936 Universal film *Flying Hostess*, where it was performed by Ella Logan. Loesser and Actman had performed this song for some months prior to the show at the Back Drop Club on West Fifty-second Street. It was here that Loesser met his first wife, Lynn Garland; they were married in October 1936.

VERSE

You didn't have to lure me into romance,
You didn't even have to ask me "Let's dance,"
You didn't have to drop your handkerchief,
You didn't have to tote that
Potent whiff of perfume rare,
For I stood here and you stood there,
And oh, oh!

REFRAIN

All you did was look at me,
You gorgeous thing,
And bang! The bell rang!
And bing! Did I swing!
All I did was look at you.
I couldn't stop,
'Cause bang! The bell rang!
And bop! Did I flop!
When your eyes said come hither,
There was I in a dither.
I've been pushed over with a
Dance or a drink or a genuine mink,*
But all you did was look at me,
To seal my doom,
And boy! Was that joy?
And boom! Did I zoom!
Oh, pardon my slang, but
Bang! The bell rang!

* *Alternate line for male voice:*
  Drink or a dance or a kick in the pants,

WILD TRUMPETS AND CRAZY PIANO (GOT A GAL TO FORGET)

Music by Irving Actman. Published. Copyrighted March 5, 1936. Introduced by Niela Goodelle. Listed in program as "Give Me Wild Trumpets."

VERSE

Don't you play that melancholy fiddle,
And don't you sing that sentimental song;
Put away your melancholy fiddle,
And don't remind me that my love went wrong.

REFRAIN

Tell me not in mournful numbers,
Numbers all about sad goodbye,
Give me wild trumpets and crazy piano.
Wild trumpets,
I don't want my poor heart to cry.
Tell me not in mournful numbers,
"Stormy Weather" and "Am I Blue,"
Give me wild trumpets and crazy piano.
Wild trumpets,
Come and drown my sorrow
All night through.
Give me brass jam,
Let me shim-sham,
Let me shout tra la la la la la la,
Feeling low as I am,
Tell me not in mournful numbers,
Got a gal to forget about,
Give me wild trumpets and crazy piano.
Wild trumpets,
Here's my torch light,
Blow my torch right out.

POSTAL INSPECTOR

A film produced by George Owen for Universal Pictures. Released in August 1936. Music by Irving Actman. Screenplay by Horace McCoy, adapted from an original story by Robert Presnell and Horace McCoy. Directed by Otto Brower. Cast featured Ricardo Cortez, Patricia Ellis, Hattie McDaniel, Bela Lugosi, and Michael Loring.

In the summer of 1936, Loesser wrote to Lynn Loesser about his first film assignment at Universal (quoted by Susan Loesser in *A Most Remarkable Fella*):

> Right now Irving and I are in the throes, trying to knock off a hit out of a situation where the producer orders a certain title, the musical director orders a certain rhythm, the dance director orders a certain number of bars and the composers order a certain number of aspirins. . . .
>
> The first picture of ours to be released [*Postal Inspector*] is an utter stinker. The only redeeming feature is the orchestrations and recording of the music, which we watched like hawks at every step. "Don't Let Me Love You" is in it at every possible moment, during bank robberies, flood scenes, dance hall sequences and a long shot of the Bronx Zoo. It is also sung by a guy and Pat Ellis, very mournfully indeed, while they dance. God, why didn't I stay in the process serving business?

The vocal performances of "Don't Let Me Love You" were later cut from the film, and no lyrics are currently available. It was registered for copyright as an unpublished song April 5, 1937.

LET'S HAVE BLUEBIRDS

Registered for copyright as an unpublished song April 5, 1937. Introduced by Patricia Ellis.

VERSE

Here we are together, flying high.
We're up in heaven, you and I!
We'll be coming down to earth someday,
But in the meantime, let's be gay!

REFRAIN

Let's have bluebirds
On all our wallpaper,
Decorating our dreams.
Shy little rosebuds on the chinaware,

Murmurs of love from the Frigidaire!
Let's have carpets
With clover all over,
Neath a lamp of moonbeams.
We'll have showers, lots of showers, that's certain,
So let's paint a rainbow on the shower curtain
And bluebirds on all our wallpaper,
Decorating our dreams!

HOT TOWEL

Registered for copyright as an unpublished song April 5, 1937. Introduced by Patricia Ellis and Hattie McDaniel.

VERSE

ELLIS: When you're through with your shower,
Do you shiver?
Do you quiver?
Well, you're wrong!
When you're through with your shower,
You should treat it,
You should heat it,
With a song
And a—

REFRAIN

MCDANIEL: Hot towel—
Get out of your tub and rub-a-dub-dub,
Just like a hot number
To the rhythm of a rhumba.
Hot towel, get hold of a hot towel.
Let ev'rything fly and shake yourself
    dry,
Oh, how can you slumber
To the rhythm of a rhumba!

Oh yes, you might look silly,*
But you don't get chilly!
Oh, if you do it Spanish,
Ev'ry drop will vanish
In your hot towel.
Get hold of a hot towel—
You're going to town by rubbing
    it down
Just like a hot number
To the rhythm of a rhumba.

_____

* *Last stanza not sung in film.*

YELLOWSTONE

Produced by Val Paul for Universal Pictures. Released in August 1936. Music by Irving Actman. Screenplay by Jefferson Parker, Stuart Palmer, and Houston Branch, adapted from a story by Arthur Phillips. Directed by Arthur Lubin. Cast featured Judith Barrett, Ralph Morgan, Andy Devine, Henry Hunter, and Monroe Owsley.

JOGGIN' ALONG

Registered for copyright as an unpublished song April 1, 1937. Introduced by unidentified cowboy quartet and soloist. This lyric anticipated another Loesser cowboy song, "Jingle, Jangle, Jingle," which became a hit in 1942.

VERSE

COWBOY
QUARTET: I'm an old Yellowstone ranger,
And I rode this trail since back in
    'eighty-three.
And if you're asking me, stranger,
It's the only life for me.

REFRAIN

SOLO: Just joggin' along,
Spurs on my heels,
Jingling a song.
Just Broomtail and me,
Riding the range,
High, wide, and free.
Old Faithful spoutin' to the western
    sky—
He's in his glory now, and so am I.
Just joggin' along,
Spurs on my heels,
Jingling a song,
Jingling a song.

THE MAN I MARRY

Produced by Charles Rogers for Universal Pictures. Released in October 1936. Music by Irving Actman. Screenplay by Harry Clork, based on an original story by M. Coates Webster. Directed by Ralph Murphy. Cast starred Doris Nolan and featured Michael Whalen, Charles "Chic" Sale, Nigel Bruce, and Skeets Gallagher.

OLD HOMESTEAD

Registered for copyright as an unpublished song April 29, 1937. Introduced by ensemble.

ALL: Old homestead, old homestead,
　　Soon I'll be at your door,
　　Down where the stars always shine.
MEN: Where the stars are shining . . .
ALL: Old homestead, old homestead,
　　You're what I'm heading for,
　　Deep in that southland of mine.

I KNOW I'M IN HARLEM

Registered for copyright as an unpublished song April 29, 1937. Introduced by ensemble.

VERSE

If I dance when I walk,
If I sing when I talk,
Then I know I'm in Harlem,
Harlem town, New York.
If my heart gets that beat
From those feet in the street,
Then I know I'm in Harlem,
And suddenly life is sweet.

REFRAIN

When I go to work downtown,
Skies are gray and I'm draggin' mah heels all day.
But at night when I cross that great divide,
Hundred and Twenty-fifth Street and Morningside,
I dance when I walk and I sing when I talk,
'Cause I know I'm in Harlem,
Harlem town, New York.

THREE SMART GIRLS

Produced by Joe Pasternak for Universal Pictures. Released in January 1937. Music by Irving Actman. Screenplay by Adele Comandini and Austin Parker. Directed by Henry Koster. Cast starred Deanna Durbin in her screen debut and featured Binnie Barnes, Alice Brady, Charles Winninger, Ray Milland, Nan Grey, and Barbara Read. Other songs in the film included "My Heart Is Singing" and "Someone to Care for Me" by Gus Kahn (lyrics) and Bronislau Kaper and Walter Jurmann (music). "I Think You Have Got Something There" was registered for copyright as an unpublished song May 25, 1937. No lyrics currently available. Not used in film.

YOU'RE MY HEART

Registered for copyright as an unpublished song May 25, 1937. Used instrumentally only.

You're my heart,
My reason for living,
Not just my darling,
Not just my love.
You're the song
I'm constantly singing,
Not just a someone
To daydream of.
You're my heart,
You're my undying flame.
How can I call you
By any sweeter name?
You're such a precious part
Of this life I'm living,
Not just my darling,
Not just my love—
What are you?
You're my heart!

LIFE IS PEACHES AND CREAM

Registered for copyright as an unpublished song May 25, 1937. Used instrumentally only.

Hi-ho the merry-o!
What's the diff'rence how the breezes blow?

Long as you can dream a dream,
Your life is peaches and cream.

So, hi-ho the merry-o,
Make believe you're with your Romeo,
Sailing on a silver stream,
Where life is peaches and cream!

Now you don't need a bench for two
Or a cottage small.
'Cause you can build them all,
And when they fall,
Wake up, singing—

Hi-ho the merry-o!
What's the diff'rence where your dreams all go,
Long as they can make it seem
That life is peaches and cream!

SINCE WHEN

Registered for copyright as an unpublished song May 25, 1937. Used instrumentally only.

Since when does lamplight look like moonlight?
Since when does water taste like wine?
Since when is the air like a sweet perfume rare?
Now you never heard of anything so divine,
Now did you?

Since when does thunder sound like music?
And stormy winter feel like spring?
Since when? Since when?
Baby, ask me again.
Since you told me that you love me!
Since when?
Since then!

HEART OF HARLEM

Registered for copyright as an unpublished song May 25, 1937. Used instrumentally only.

Lenox Avenue is the heart of Harlem,
Lenox Avenue, neath the open sky!
Not the hot spots, not the sniff-sniff cellars
Full of high-high yellers,

But the heat of the feet on the street called Lenox Avenue,
That's the heart of Harlem.

White folks come on up just to truck on down,
And they don't have to hire a hall
For a darktown strutter's ball,
'Cause the avenue is the heart of Harlem town!

THE GOLFERS

A Meany, Miny, Moe cartoon produced by Walter Lantz for Universal Pictures. Released in January 1937. Music by Irving Actman. Story by Walter Lantz and Victor McLeod. Animation by LaVerne Harding, Ed Benedict, and Leo Salkin.

In late 1936 and early 1937, Loesser and composer Irving Actman worked on a number of early Walter Lantz cartoons at Universal. With the exception of this theme song for the Meany, Miny, Moe series, the cartoon *Everybody Sing*, and Loesser's rewrite of "A-Hunting We Will Go" in *The Duck Hunt*, these cartoons were scored without lyrics.

MEANY, MINY, MOE

Registered for copyright as an unpublished song May 24, 1937.

Just three monkeys from the sticks,
Nothing more than jungle hicks,
But they know a lot of tricks,
That's Meany, Miny, Moe.

They've got personality,
Crazy nuts as they can be.
Are they on your family tree?
Meany, Miny, Moe.

MYSTERIOUS CROSSING

Produced by Charles R. Rogers for Universal Pictures. Released in February 1937. Music by Irving Actman. Screenplay by Jefferson Parker and John Grey, based on a story by Fred MacIsaacs. Directed by Arthur Lubin. Cast featured James Dunn, Jean Rogers, and Andy Devine.

THE RAILROAD THAT RAN THROUGH OUR LAND

Registered for copyright as an unpublished song July 22, 1937.

Oh, sorrow and mis'ry have come over me,
And gone are all the pleasures I planned.
And the cause of all my sorrow
To you I now will tell:
'Twas the railroad that ran through our land.

Right through my pasture they built the right of way,
That's one thing my cattle could not understand.
So I got ten days in jail
For obstructing U.S. mail
On the railroad that ran through our land.

My dear old grandmother was healthy as a bull,
But that whistle was more than she could stand.
In the state institution now
She screams in all her dreams,
Like the railroad that ran through our land.

Esmeralda Johnson, she married me one day
And my solid-gold ring was on her hand.
But for a souvenir
She gave it to the engineer
Of the railroad that ran through our land.

My faithful horse Matilda, she slipped and broke her neck,
When blindly in a gopher hole she ran.
Neath the prairie sand she lies
Since smoke got in her eyes
From the railroad that ran through our land.

My poor honest father, the Lord rest his soul,
He killed rattlesnakes and Indians by hand.
But the rattlesnakes came back
Since we scraped him off the track
Of the railroad that ran through our land.

EVERYBODY SING

An Oswald Rabbit cartoon produced by Walter Lantz for Universal Pictures. Released in February 1937. Music by Irving Actman. Story by Walter Lantz and Victor McLeod. Animation by Ray Abrams and Bill Mason.

EVERYBODY SINGS

Registered for copyright as an unpublished song May 12, 1937. Performed by Oswald Rabbit & His Rhythm Birds. Verse taken from photo of typed lyric sheet; other lyrics transcribed from cartoon soundtrack.

VERSE (NOT SUNG IN FILM)

Far be it from me to hand out radical
    propaganda—
Maybe you'll call it slander
After I get through.
Far be it from me to weep in your demitasses,
Calling those lower classes
Just as good as you.
But maybe you'll agree when I proclaim
The reason why we're all of us the same . . .

CHORUS
GULLS: Everybody sings,
    Society matrons and beanery patrons,
    Ya-da-ya, ya-da-ya,
    Everybody sings, everybody sings.
    The prince and the piker,
    The boss and the striker,
    Ya-da-ya, ya-da-ya,
    Everybody sings.
OWL: Everybody's got a right to croon sharp or
    flat.
PARROT: 'Cause there's no tax on that anywhere.
OWL: What did Abe Lincoln declare?
PARROT: Everybody's free.
OWL: He made them all equal,
    And here is the sequel.
PARROT: Ya-da-ya, ya-da-ya.
OWL: Ya-da-ya, ya-da-ya.
CHORUS
GULLS: People do
    Lots of different things,
    Yet everybody sings.

Preacher's Sermon

PREACHER: Brothers and sisters,
The sermon for today.
CHOIR: Hallelujah, what are you going
to say?
PREACHER: Lily white or black as night,
We all look much the same,
And this is what the Good Book
done proclaim.
CHOIR: Hallelujah!
PREACHER: Everybody sings.
CHOIR: Da-ya-ya-ya-ya-ya da-dum.
MAMMY: Ya-da-ya, ya-da-ya.
CHOIR: Everybody sings,
Everybody sings.
PREACHER: The saints and the sinners,
The losers and winners.
BABY BIRDS: Ya-da-ya, ya-da-ya,
Everybody sings.
PREACHER: Everybody's got a right to croon
Any tune neath the moon.
Doodle-oodle-oodle-oodle-oo-
doo-doo.
NIGHTINGALE: Everybody swings, tweedle-deedle-
dee,
Everybody sings a melody.
SANDPIPER: Every lassie sings,
Every laddie sings because it's
free.
HUMMINGBIRDS: You can hum, I can hum,
Anyone can dum-dum-dum,
Oo-oo-oo-oo-ooo.

Song of the Sparrow

ENGLISH
SPARROW: [spoken] My word, what's all this?
Everybody sings,
I say, it's a bit of all right.
ALL: [sung] Everybody sings,
We're getting the habit
From Oswald Rabbit
Ya-da-ya, ya-da-ya,
Ya-da-ya, ya-da-ya.
People do lots of different things,
But everybody sings.

Three Black Crows

CROWS: Oh, we're the three black crows,
We're the toughest boids in town.
We was hard-boiled eggs
When we was born.
If we see a hunk of jewelry,
We don't stand for no tomfool'ry.
We will take it if we like it,
And we like it, so we'll take it right away.

We will take it if we like it,
And we like it, so we'll take it right away.

CHORUS: Won't someone help us?
Won't someone come to our rescue?

CROWS: Even if it's zero weather,
And you're down to your last feather,
We will take it if we like it,
And we like it, so we'll take it right away.

If you've got a little honey,
We can call for ransom money,
We will take her if we like her,
And we like her, so—

Everybody Sings reprise

ALL: Everybody sings.
The prince and the piker,
The boss and the striker.
Made them all equal,
And here is the sequel.
He brought independence
And now his descendants
WOMEN: Ya-da-ya, ya-da-ya.
MEN: Ya-da-ya, ya-da-ya.
ALL: People do lots of different things,
But everybody sings.
Fa-la-la-la-la,
Fa-la-la-la-la,
Everybody sings a melody.

Lyrics not sung in film

Everybody sings.
The boys in Atlanta
Are rivaling Cantor,
Ya-da-ya, ya-da-ya.
Everybody sings,
Everybody sings.
Republican rallies,
Bing Crosbys and Vallees,
Ya-da-ya, ya-da-ya.
Everybody sings.
Everybody's got a right to croon sweet or hot—
Is it wrong? It is not, when you're gay.
What did George Washington say? Hey!
Everybody's free.
He brought independence,
And now his descendants,
Ya-da-ya, ya-da-ya,
Ya-da-ya, ya-da-ya.
Sure we are, Communists and kings,
For everybody sings!

THE DUCK HUNT

An Oswald Rabbit cartoon produced by Walter Lantz for Universal Pictures. Released in March 1937. Music by Irving Actman. Story by Walter Lantz and Victor McLeod.

A-HUNTING WE WILL GO

Registered for copyright as an unpublished song October 1, 1937. Performed by Oswald Rabbit and Elmore the Dog.

OSWALD: A-hunting we will go,
A-hunting we will go,
We're gonna get a duck,
A-hunting we will go.
ELMORE: Yip, yip.
OSWALD: A-hunting we will go.
ELMORE: Yip, yip.
OSWALD: A-hunting we will go.

WALTER WANGER'S VOGUES OF 1938

Produced by Walter Wanger for United Artists. Released in August 1937. Screenplay by Bella and Sam Spewack. Directed by Irving Cummings. Cast starred Warner Baxter and Joan Bennett and featured Helen Vinson, Mischa Auer, Alan Mowbray, Jerome Cowan, Alma Kruger, Marjorie Gateson, Dorothy McNulty (Penny Singleton), Polly Rowles, Georgie Tapps, Virginia Verrill, Fred Lawrence, Gloria Gilbert, Olympic Trio, Wiere Brothers, (Maurice) Rocco and (Dotty) Salter, The Four Hot Shots, and Victor Young and His Orchestra. Other songs in this film include "That Old Feeling" by Lew Brown (lyrics) and Sammy Fain (music) and "Turn On the Red Hot Heat" by Paul Francis Webster (lyrics) and Louis Alter (music).

LOVELY ONE

Music by Manning Sherwin (1902–1974). Published. Copyrighted June 14, 1937. Previously registered for copyright as an unpublished song April 26, 1937. Introduced by Fred Lawrence, Virginia Verrill, girls' chorus, and Wiere Brothers. Composer Sherwin's most famous song is "A Nightingale Sang in Berkeley Square."

VERSE 1

BOY: I should have known
All the starlight that shone in your eyes
Was just a charming disguise.
I should have seen
In the soft golden sheen of your hair
That I was in danger there.
Now it's too late to beware;
It isn't fair.

REFRAIN

Lovely one, sweet as a breeze in May,
Stealing my heart away,
Why do I let you?
Lovely one, give me my heart again,
Give me my heart and then
Let me forget you.
I should go and find romance
In eyes not quite so bright,
In lips not quite so magical
As your lips are tonight. But
It's begun, sweet as the charm of spring,
I'm just a helpless thing
Now that I've met you,
Lovely one.

VERSE 2

GIRL: Picture a man so enchanted by some lady fair
That it's too late to beware.
Picture the scene as she smiles like an angel serene:
He can't escape, though he tries,
And with that look in his eyes
He sadly sighs—

REPEAT REFRAIN

Film version

MAN: Lovely one, sweet as a breeze in May,
Stealing my heart away,
Why do I let you?
WOMAN: Dearest one, I feel the urge of love,
I'm on the verge of love,
Now that I've met you.
MODEL 1: Lovely damsel in distress,
Be careful with your love.
MODEL 2: Think twice before you answer yes,
Or you'll be last year's glove.
MAN: Oh, lovely one, sweet as a charm
of spring.
WOMAN: I'm just a helpless thing,
Now that I've met you.
BOTH: Lovely one.
MODEL 3: Boy meets girl,
Takes the hand of helpless thing—
MODEL 4: Does she get a diamond ring?
She's not so helpless.
MAN: Lovely one, deep in the heart of me—
WOMAN: You are a part of me,
I'll never leave you.
WIERE
BROTHERS: Voices of experience
Advise you how to stick,
If you want to hold your girl,
Amuse her with a trick.
MAN: I won't need a trick for you.
WOMAN: Hear my heart tick-tick for you.
BOTH: Can't you see, you'll always be
My only one.
WIERE
BROTHERS: Women like the Tarzan type,
Musclebound and strong.
Watch this little feat of strength
And you can't go wrong.
MAN: Can it be the magic of,
The miracle of June?
WOMAN: Blame it on that thing called love,
Don't blame it on the moon.
MAN: Lovely one, you are the song I sing.
WOMAN: You are my everything,
I'll never leave you—
BOTH: Lovely one.

FIGHT FOR YOUR LADY

Produced by Albert Lewis for RKO Radio Pictures. Released in November 1937. Screenplay by Ernest Pagano, Harry Segall, and Harold Kussell, adapted from a story by Isabel Leighton and Jean Negulesco. Directed by Ben Stoloff. Cast starred John Boles and Jack Oakie and featured Ida Lupino, Margot Grahame, Gordon Jones, and Erik Rhodes.

BLAME IT ON THE DANUBE

Words and music by Frank Loesser and Harry Akst (1894–1963). Published. Copyrighted September 7, 1937. Introduced by a ventriloquist's dummy handled by Ida Lupino; reprised by John Boles. Akst had previously written the music for such hits as "Baby Face," "Am I Blue?" and "Dinah." The title was originally "Blame It on Vienna," as Frank Loesser related at the time in a letter to his wife, Lynn (quoted in Susan Loesser's *A Most Remarkable Fella*):

> Going off the lot we ran into Dave Dreyer, who asked in his usual high tension hurry-up manner whether we have a continental type of waltz for Ida Lupino and John Boles—a melody that is easy enough for Lupino to yawp, and good enough to sound all right with Boles singing it. We said we would whip one up, which we proceeded to do this afternoon at Akst's house. This is about it:
>
> > If we should kiss
> > While dancing like this
> > Let's blame it on Vienna
> >
> > If muted strings
> > Say heavenly things
> > Let's blame it on Vienna
> >
> > If I get gay
> > On too much Tokay
> > And foolishly say:
> > "Be mine!"
> >
> > And if you answer yes
> > Let's blame it on Vienna
> > For making this night so divine!
>
> I get home and call Akst. They don't like Vienna. . . . For fun, I sing the old Vienna lyric, which wasn't bad. They love it! Only we're to change the locale from Vienna to the Danube. Half conscious from my lack of sleep and their lack of taste and brains, I make a few highly unsubtle changes to the Danube of all things and up we go to Briskin, who okays the song, and that's that.

VERSE (NOT SUNG IN FILM)

Gypsy atmosphere fills the night!
Violins, pale moonlight.
Gypsy atmosphere full of charms
Can carry you into someone's arms, and so—

REFRAIN

If we should kiss while waltzing like this,
Let's blame it on the Danube.

If muted strings say heavenly things,
Let's blame it on the Danube.
If I get gay on too much Tokay*
And recklessly say "Be mine,"
Who knows if this is love,
Or just the magic of the music
And sparkle of wine?
Don't blame it on my heart,
But blame it on the Danube,
For making this night so divine.

THE HURRICANE

Produced by Samuel Goldwyn and distributed by United Artists. Released in November 1937. Music by Alfred Newman. Screenplay by Dudley Nichols and Oliver H. P. Garrett, adapted from a novel by Charles Nordhoff and James Norman Hall. Directed by John Ford. Cast featured Dorothy Lamour, Jon Hall, Mary Astor, C. Aubrey Smith, Thomas Mitchell, Raymond Massey, John Carradine, and Jerome Cowan.

Alfred Newman (1901–1970) was one of Hollywood's foremost composers, receiving nine film-scoring Oscars and more than forty nominations.

The Hurricane was wildly popular and launched a genre of steamy tropical romance pictures featuring Dorothy Lamour and other stars in scanty island garb. Loesser wrote lyrics for many of these post-*Hurricane* palm-tree epics, including *Typhoon* (page 59), *Moon Over Burma* (page 65), and *Aloma of the South Seas* (page 75). "One hundred and fifty million people in this country," he remarked. "How many of them have a lagoon?" He later spoofed these films in a song entitled "Queen of the Hollywood Islands," which Lamour herself sang in *On Our Merry Way* (page 147).

THE MOON OF MANAKOORA

Copyrighted December 13, 1937. Used instrumentally only. Leading recordings by Bing Crosby (Decca) and Ray Noble and His Orchestra, vocal by Tony Martin (Brunswick). Dorothy Lamour never sang the song in the film, but recorded it with Cy Feuer and His Orchestra in November 1937. (Feuer later produced *Where's*

---

* *Sheet music version:*
  If I get gay while violins play,

Charley?, *Guys and Dolls*, and *How to Succeed in Business Without Really Trying* with Ernest Martin.) This recording was used for promotion.

Although a few of his earlier works enjoyed modest success as recordings, this was Loesser's first big hit. Newman's melody was written first, and they were given the name of the island to write the lyric to once production began. Newman found out the particulars and called Loesser on the telephone. After learning that the island was to be called "Manakoora," Loesser called Newman back ten minutes later and dictated the lyrics over the phone.

Here we stand once more upon the sand of
    Manakoora,
Moon-enchanted isle.
Darling, here we kiss—
Do you remember this,
The paradise we dreamed a little while?

REFRAIN

The moon of Manakoora filled the night
With magic Polynesian charms;
The moon of Manakoora came in sight
And brought you to my eager arms.

The moon of Manakoora soon will rise
Again above the island shore;
Then I'll behold it in your dusky eyes
And you'll be in my arms once more.

BLOSSOMS ON BROADWAY

Produced by B. P. Schulberg for Paramount Pictures. Released in December 1937. Screenplay by Theodore Reeves. Directed by Richard Wallace. Cast starred Edward Arnold, Shirley Ross, John Trent, Rufe Davis, Joe Weber and Lew Fields, William Frawley, and Frank Craven. Other songs in this film include "Blossoms on Broadway" by Leo Robin (lyrics) and Ralph Rainger (music).

This was Loesser's first picture for Paramount. His initial ten-week contract began a relationship that would last thirteen years and involve work on more than ninety films. Composer Burton Lane, who was instrumental in securing Loesser his job with the studio, told the story to the editors in an interview in October 1996, shortly before his death:

I was at Paramount working with Ralph Freed, who was Arthur Freed's brother. Our first year's contract was coming up and I didn't know if they were going to renew or not. My agent called up and said, "I've got a couple of songwriters and I'd like to get your opinion of them." So he brings over two writers, one is Frank Loesser and the other is Manning Sherwin. I was just floored by Frank's lyrics. I thought he was a sensational writer. I was so excited that I went down to the front office and spoke to the head of the studio. Frank and Sherwin each got a ten-week contract. . . .

Just prior to his signing with Paramount, I learned that Frank wanted to get rid of Manning Sherwin. He called me and asked me to come to his apartment. He wanted to show me some lyrics. It was around 8:30 in the evening and he and his wife Lynn asked me if I wanted dinner . . . which consisted of one apple and a can of baked beans. I was shocked. One apple and they were going to share it with me.

Right after Frank was signed, he used my office. I came in one day and there was a guy in my office measuring him for suits, shirts, the whole bit. A week earlier it was baked beans and an apple. He was off and running.

YOU CAN'T TELL A MAN BY HIS HAT

Music by Manning Sherwin. Published. Copyrighted October 25, 1937. Previously registered for copyright as an unpublished song August 26, 1937. Introduced by Shirley Ross.

VERSE

Once upon a time before the world had gone
    informal,
Things were normal, and a girl could figure out
By a man's fedora, or his skull cap, or his panama,
Exactly what that man was all about.
Bankers were conservative in black.
Actors were extravagant in green.
You could always recognize
The carriage trade from poolroom guys,
But now just look what's happened to the scene:

REFRAIN 1

Lowbrows in high hats, and highbrows in no hats,
Oh, what is this world coming to?
Zulus in earlaps, and crooks in police caps,
The day of discretion is through!
There was a time when you could tell a sailor

By his sailor chapeau.
Brown derby was a symbol democratic,
Most emphatic'lly so!
But now all gobs have new Dobbs,
While Roosevelts wear old felts
Like something dragged in by the cat.
That man in the blue beret may be none other
Than Wallace Beery or Whistler's mother.
You can't tell a man by his hat!

PATTER

The Daniel Boone in beaver
Is a boy from Singapore.
The fellow in the dusty cap
Sells brushes door-to-door.
MacTavish is the Santa Claus
In Cohn's department store.
Oh, you can't tell a man by his hat!

A fireman saved a lady*
When the flames were all about.
The spark of love he kindled
In her heart without a doubt.
You'd think from his red helmet
He'd be putting fires out.
But you can't tell a man by his hat.

REFRAIN 2

You'll see Texas sombreros on Bronx caballeros
And that, my dear children, is that!
The bare-headed hobo may be Jolson's Mammy
Or next year's version of Uncle Sammy.
You can't tell a man, by his hat!

NO RING ON HER FINGER

Music by Manning Sherwin. Published. Copyrighted October 25, 1937. Previously registered for copyright as an unpublished song August 26, 1937. Introduced by Rufe Davis, Edward Arnold, Shirley Ross, and William Frawley.

* *Second stanza of patter originally:*
  A jealous husband left his home
  At nine o'clock, and then
  He dressed up like the iceman
  And he came back home at ten.
  And as the judge in Reno said,
  "That proves the fact again
  That you can't tell a man by his hat!"

VERSE

In a homemade white gown with a hand-picked
    bouquet
Stands poor little Daisy McGee.
And she watches and waits by the church ev'ry day
And if you look sharp, you can see—

REFRAIN

There's *no* ring on her finger.
Her rings are all under her eyes.
For she gave her heart to a hosiery drummer,
Who vowed by the stars that he'd come back next
    summer.
There's no ring on her finger,
Not even a ring on her phone.
For just like his stockings, he ran,
And she's all alone—

With *no* ring on her finger
And nothing but time on her hands
She soon fell in love with a man from the city
Who sold her some cold cream and swore she'd
    look pretty.
But no ring on her finger,*
Not even a half-carat stone,
For just like his cold cream, he vanished,
And she's all alone—

With *no* ring on her finger,
And fingers were pointing in scorn,
She next found romance with a gas-meter reader,
Who promised that right to the altar he'd lead her.
But no ring on her finger,
No plain golden band does she own.
For just like the gas, he escaped her,
And she's all alone!

* *Lines 13–20 not sung in film.*

MISCELLANEOUS SONGS OF 1936–1937

A TREE IN TIPPERARY

Music by Irving Actman. Published. Copyrighted February 19, 1936.

VERSE 1

Strolling the lane
Among these heather hills of mine,
Here once again
I find a sweet old valentine.
Dear souvenir,
For all the world to see
That I love you
And you love me.

REFRAIN

There's your heart and my heart,
Just a schoolboy's work of art,
We carved them together
On a tree in Tipperary.
Your life and my life,
Blended by an old jackknife
When I used to meet you
By a tree in Tipperary.
Now you've gone
From the little school,
From the shady lawn,
But love lingers on
In your heart and my heart,
Though they're beating miles apart,
They're still close together
On a tree in Tipperary.

VERSE 2

Strolling the lane,
The lane that is so dear to me,
Here once again
I stand beneath a shady tree.
Here are my dreams,
The dreams I used to know,
The same today
As long ago.

REPEAT REFRAIN

CHILE MOONLIGHT

Music by Otto Motzan. Registered for copyright as an unpublished song March 16, 1936.

Oh!
Mariana, Mariana, Mariana, Mariana,
Don't go out tonight
When the moon's aglow.
Oh!
Mariana, Mariana, Mariana, Mariana,
Hold your lover tight
In your patio.
High above the Andes range,
A new moon rises,
Bringing danger.
Whispering, "Mister,
Change her for a stranger."
So,
Mariana, Mariana, Mariana, Mariana,
Keep him safe at home,
Don't you let him roam.
Beware, señorita!
He's bound to deceive,
For that midsummer eve
Has something up its sleeve!
There's a thief in the mighty Chile moonlight
Stealing your love away.
Cling to your caballero!
He might get a bee
In his sombrero.
Under the bright Chile moonlight
He'd find a new love soon.
Don't let your caballero
Dally-dilly neath the Chile moon.

HERE COMES TOMORROW (GIMME ANOTHER KISS GOODNIGHT)

Music by Irving Actman. Published. Copyrighted May 14, 1937.

VERSE 1

He brought her home at midnight,
He kissed her at the door,
And then they lingered, making love,
Until the clock struck four.
They couldn't seem to tear themselves away;
At five o'clock I still could hear them say:

REFRAIN

Here comes tomorrow,
By the dawn's early light.
Oh! never mind tomorrow,
Just gimme another kiss good night.
Here comes tomorrow—
Does your father sleep tight?
Oh! never bother Father,
Just gimme another kiss goodnight.
There's lipstick all over my face,
And darling, your hair's a disgrace.
Let's make this the final embrace,
For there goes yesterday
And here comes tomorrow.
Was the last kiss all right?
Oh! never mind the last one,
Just gimme another kiss good night.

VERSE 2

They hung around the doorway,
They couldn't say goodbye,
They never noticed all the stars
Were fading in the sky.
The sun was up, and so was every bird,
And here's the conversation that they heard:

REPEAT REFRAIN

KISS AT MIDNIGHT

Music and lyrics by Dailey Paskman (1897–1979), Frank Loesser, and Irving Actman. Registered for copyright as an unpublished song July 24, 1970. From undated lyric sheet. Probably 1937. Paskman, a lyricist and producer, also worked with composers Rudolf Friml, Peter De Rose, and Victor Young. He was a pioneer in radio broadcasting and an authority on American minstrel shows.

VERSE

Beneath a starry sky
You heard my lonely sigh;
It was midnight when I danced with you.
My heart is dancing still
As I recall the thrill
Of that moment of romance we knew.

REFRAIN

I never can forget
That kiss at midnight

When your heart was dancing close to mine.
I never can forget
That gleam of starlight
In the skies and in your eyes divine.
Now ev'ry lonesome ev'ning I've been spending
Has a happy ending when twelve o'clock comes due.
For we're close together and
We kiss at midnight,
Ev'ry midnight, in my dreams of you.

STRIVER'S ROW TO SUGAR HILL

Music by Harry Akst. Probably 1937.

Way down low in Striver's Row,
Sittin' by the windowsill,
There's a woman known as Sadie.
She used to be a lady,
She used to live on top of Sugar Hill.
Long ago, so long ago,
She was Harlem's Di'mond Lil.
She had di'monds by the fistful,
That's why she looks so wistful,
A-sittin' gazin' up at Sugar Hill.

Oh! Oh! Sadie,
Sittin' by the windowsill.
Oh, it takes a lot of hustle and bustle and muscle
To get from Striver's Row to
Sugar Hill, Sugar Hill, Sugar Hill.

She came round to Harlem town,
Came in from the Deep Deep South,
And she met up with a sweet man
A-drivin' in a sedan,
With fifty-cent Coronas in his mouth.
Sadie climbed, she climbed and climbed;
Sugar Poppa paid the bill.
She said, "Though his love offends me,
The thing that really sends me
Is livin' here in style on Sugar Hill."

Oh! Oh! Sadie,
Sadie from the cotton mill.
Oh, it takes a lot of hustle and bustle and muscle
To get from Striver's Row to
Sugar Hill, Sugar Hill, Sugar Hill.

But Sadie had a hometown lad
Waitin' in the Deep Deep South,

And he heard about the sweet man
A-drivin' in the sedan
With fifty-cent Coronas in his mouth.
Full of junk he packed his trunk,
Came up from the Deep Deep South.
Now he wasn't such a sweet man,
He didn't have no sedan,
And nothin' but a reefer in his mouth.

Oh! Oh! Sadie,
Sadie had to get that thrill.
Oh, it takes a lot of strivin', connivin', and
    jivin',
But gossip travels fast on
Sugar Hill, Sugar Hill, Sugar Hill.

Knock, knock, knock, it's three o'clock,
In the door the sweet man stands.
When he sees the situation,
He's black with indignation
And tears the di'mond rings from Sadie's
    hands.
Sadie cries and alibis,
"Don't shoot him—he's my cousin Phil!"
But the sweet man says to Sadie,
"You call yourself a lady?
Get down, you dirty dog, from Sugar Hill."

Oh! Oh! Sadie,
Sadie never could sit still.
After carefully connivin' and strivin' and
    jivin',
She's back in Striver's Row from
Sugar Hill, Sugar Hill, Sugar Hill.

So, my friends, the story ends,
Life is just a bitter pill.
What a mis'rable finale,
To wind up in the alley.
She's back in Striver's Row from Sugar Hill.

Old and gray, she's had her day,
But she keeps a-dreamin' still.
When the Harlem night is fallin',
She hears a voice a-callin';
It seems to come from up on Sugar Hill.

Old broken-down Sadie,
Sittin' by the windowsill.
Oh, it takes a lot of hustle and bustle and
    muscle
To get from Striver's Row to
Sugar Hill, Sugar Hill, Sugar Hill.

FOREVERMORE

Music by Manning Sherwin. Probably late 1937.

Here we are in love;
Never dreamed we'd fall,
Simply overcome
By the wonder of it all.
Here we are in love,
And who would ever know
That this was mere flirtation an hour ago?

I'm holding you tight forevermore.
Not just for tonight, forevermore.
I thought I could resist you,
And then you smiled at me,
And carelessly I kissed you,
And now I'm caring constantly.
Keep your lips to mine forevermore.
Sweet angel divine that I adore.
You're not the passing fancy I mistook you for,
You're mine tonight, tomorrow, and
    forevermore.

SHIM-SHAM RUMBA

Music by Manning Sherwin. From undated lyric sheet. Probably late 1937.

VERSE

Down around a Hundred and Sixteenth Street,
Where Harlem and the Latin Quarter meet,
Stands the Black and White Café.
And if you should pass that way,
You can hear the music play
And learn a new beat, beat, beat—

REFRAIN

It's the Shim-Sham Rumba,
Oh, that Shim-Sham Rumba,
It's the "Peanuts" of Harlem town!
Castanets keep clicking,
Though the band's hot-licking,
And they croon a Spanish tune while truckin' on
    down.
The pale Puerto Ricans
Mix with dark Southern deacons,
And their señoritas are just a little bit brown.
So their fav'rite numba
Is the Shim-Sham Rumba
It's the "Peanuts" of Harlem town!

DREAM TONIGHT

Music and lyrics by Frank Loesser and Jackson Swales II (no dates known). Registered for copyright as an unpublished song May 17, 1937. No lyrics currently available.

Songs of 1938

COLLEGE SWING

Produced by Lewis E. Gensler for Paramount Pictures. Released in April 1938. Screenplay by Walter DeLeon and Francis Martin, based on a story by Frederick Hazlitt Brennan. Directed by Raoul Walsh. Cast starred George Burns and Gracie Allen, Martha Raye, and Bob Hope, and featured Edward Everett Horton, Florence George, Ben Blue, Betty Grable, Jackie Coogan, John Payne, Cecil Cunningham, Robert Cummings, Skinnay Ennis, the Slate Brothers, Bob Mitchell and St. Brendan's Choristers, and Jerry Colonna.

THE OLD SCHOOL BELL

Music by Manning Sherwin. Studio Ozalid copy of music and lyrics dated November 4, 1937. Introduced by St. Brendan's Choristers.

The old school bell has a tale to tell,
Ding, dong, down in the dell.
I kissed my love such a sweet farewell,
Ding, dong, down in the dell.
I kissed my love on a Sunday morn
When all seemed peaceful and still.
The good townsfolk to the church had gone,
Ding, dong, high on the hill.
But above our heads hung the old school bell
When we kissed not wisely but all too well.
Now the old school bell has a tale to tell,
Ding, dong, down in the dell.

COLLEGE SWING

Music by Hoagy Carmichael (1899–1981). Published. Copyrighted February 3, 1938. Previously registered for copyright as an unpublished song January 7, 1938. Lyrics dated November 11, 1937. Introduced by Betty Grable and Skinnay Ennis. Reprised by Martha Raye.

Loesser's collaboration with Hoagy Carmichael (from 1937 to 1941), one of America's greatest songwriters, was his first with an established composer of hits. Carmichael's first impressions of the headstrong young lyricist were recalled to Cynthia Lindsay in a 1973 interview:

Bob Hope with Martha Raye (top) and Shirley Ross (bottom)

I was looking out a window in the music department at Paramount. I asked the head man "who's that little character swinging his coat tails and whistling—acting so self assured?" He said, "A new kid came on the lot at somebody's request—probably some new director—I don't even know his name." The manner of his walk got me. The cockiness of the kid impressed me. I found out later where he was going in the middle of the afternoon—to the commissary for his 10th or 11th cup of coffee of the day.

Somebody said, "He writes pretty good lyrics, I'm told. That's his tune writer with him." Since I didn't really have a lyricist other than writing with whoever was assigned to me by the studio, I suddenly felt jealous of that other boy. They were a team. And the team is the thing—you could accomplish so much more if you just pal around, exchange ideas and not wait for an assignment.

You can well understand my enthusiasm when the head of the music department deposited Frank in my crib. But he shook me up a little bit on first meeting. His exuberance and zany talk was too much for an older man who took composing seriously. All of a sudden I felt as if I wasn't adequate in spite of the hits I'd written. He just didn't seem serious enough about this serious matter of writing songs.

VERSE

Teacher, teacher,
I'm a swingin' creature,
Oh, ho, look-a me go,
When I do the College Swing.
Teacher, teacher,
Here's my special feature,
Yi, yi, look-a me fly,
Listen to the College Swing.

REFRAIN 1

I ain't such a killer diller yet,
But I'm gonna be the teacher's pet,
'Cause I'm gonna practice till I get
College Swing.
[*spoken*] What did you call it?
[*sung*] College Swing.
They don't serve the jam at Notre Dame,
Or down at the Army–Navy game,
But it's education all the same,
College Swing.

REPEAT VERSE

REFRAIN 2

Ba-deep-dip-n-ditty, hoop-de-yay,
Be-deep-dip-n-ditty, hoop-de-yay,
College Swing.
[*spoken*] What did you call it?
[*sung*] College Swing.
Now you've heard the way I sing and shout,
You know what the lesson's all about,
So strike up the band and give it out,
College Swing.

CODA

Ha, ha, ho, ho,
Ha, ha, ho, ho,
Ha, ha, ho, ho,
Listen to the College Swing.
Listen to the College Swing.

WHAT DID ROMEO SAY TO JULIET?

Music by Burton Lane (1912–1997). Published. Copyrighted April 4, 1938. Previously registered for copyright as an unpublished song December 8, 1937. Introduced by John Payne and Florence George, with Skinnay Ennis and ensemble.

This was the first result of Loesser's collaboration with Burton Lane, a brilliant composer and pianist who later worked with E. Y. "Yip" Harburg on *Finian's Rainbow* and Alan Jay Lerner on *On a Clear Day You Can See Forever*. Loesser and Lane worked together only twice; in 1938 and again in 1944, when Loesser provided uncredited assistance to Lane on the Olsen and Johnson revue *Laffing Room Only*.

VERSE

Yoo-hoo-hoo!
Come out from behind your windowpane.
Come out for a stroll in Lovers' Lane,
I want to quote poetry.
Yoo-hoo-hoo!
You're smiling at me from up above,
And suddenly all those words of love,
The words I had plenty of, have failed me.

REFRAIN

What did Romeo say to Juliet?
You thrill me so that I forget.
What did Juliet say to Romeo?
I'm so bewitched I just don't know.

Oh, I wish I'd studied Shakespeare for occasions
  like this.
And I wish that I'd rehearsed a scene or two,
'Cause what did Romeo say to Juliet
That I couldn't say to you?

Film version

VERSE

PAYNE: Yoo-hoo-hoo!
  Come out from behind your
    windowpane.
  Yoo-hoo-hoo!
  Come out for a stroll in Lovers' Lane,
  Lady fair, I would a word with thee!
GEORGE: [spoken] You would a word with me?
PAYNE: [sung] With thee!
  There you stand so radiant!
  So Quelques Fleurs! So Toujours Moi!
  So Nuit de Noël! Number Five Chanel!
  So terrific!
  Lady fair, I feel the need to quote
  Ev'rything Shakespeare wrote,
  But oh!
  I can't remember a single thing.
  Oh, what is so rare as a ding-de-ding
  To be, to be, or not to be.
  The Merchant of Venice is up a tree,
  Friends, Romans, and boys in blue
  Alas, poor Yorick, I've lost my cue.
  Oh, what am I trying to do?
GEORGE: [spoken] I don't know. Do you?

REFRAIN 1

PAYNE: [sung] What did Romeo say to Juliet?
  You thrill me so that I forget.
  What did Juliet say to Romeo?
  I'm so bewitched, I just don't know.
  Oh, I wish I'd studied Shakespeare
  For occasions like this.
  And I wish that I'd rehearsed a scene
    or two!
  'Cause what did Romeo say to Juliet
  That I couldn't say to you?

REFRAIN 2

PAYNE: What did Romeo say to Juliet?
GEORGE: [spoken] Oh, speak again, speak again,
    bright angel!
PAYNE: [spoken] Can't you hear me? Listen!
  [sung] What did Juliet say to Romeo?
GEORGE: [spoken] Oh, Romeo, Romeo, wherefore
    art thou Romeo?
PAYNE: [spoken] Over here!

GEORGE: [sung] Oh, a tender little sonnet goes as
    far as a kiss,
  So you might go home and study two
    or three!
  'Cause what did Romeo say to Juliet
  That you couldn't say to me?

HOW'DJA LIKE TO LOVE ME?

Music by Burton Lane. Published. Copyrighted February 9, 1938. Previously registered for copyright as an unpublished song December 8, 1937. Introduced by Martha Raye and Bob Hope. Burton Lane told film historian Miles Kreuger that "How'dja Like to Love Me" was written for Lyda Roberti, who was originally cast in the film, to utilize her Polish accent singing words like "how'dja." When Roberti died in 1938, she was replaced by Martha Raye. Leading recordings by Jimmy Dorsey and His Orchestra, vocal by Don Mattison (Decca); Dolly Dawn (Vocalion); Larry Clinton and His Orchestra, vocal by Bea Wain (Victor); Horace Heidt and His Orchestra (Brunswick); and Abe Lyman and His Orchestra (Bluebird).

VERSE

RAYE: You're just a quick romancer,
  You're just a fly-by-night.
  But I'm a take-a-chancer,
  So come on and hold me tight.
  You've got the same old answer
  For every girl you've met.
  But here is one, my pet,
  You haven't answered yet.

REFRAIN 1

How'dja like to love me?
How'dja like it?
How'dja like to kiss me?
How'dja like it?
Could'ja kinda care,
Could'ja learn to part your hair my way?
How'dja like to love me
On the level?
How'dja like to miss me
Like the devil?
Wouldja be so kind
As to keep me on your mind
All day?
I told my doctor, my lawyer, to see what they think.
The moment they saw ya, were they tickled pink!

So, how'dja like to love me, and no other?
How'dja like to drop in, meet my mother?
How'dja like your toothbrush
A-hangin' right alongside mine?
How'dja like it?
As for me, I'd like it fine.

REFRAIN 2

HOPE: How'dja like to love me?
  There's a question.
  How'dja like to work on
  My digestion?
  Would'ja be so bold
  As to nurse me through a cold next May?
  How'dja like to love me?
  That's a honey.
  Pick me out my neckties,
  Save my money?
  Would'ja rise in wrath
  If I beat you to the bath each day?
  I need a doctor, a lawyer, a keeper of
    books,
  A bridge partner, nursemaid, an angel
    who cooks.
  So how'dja like to love me?
  There's a notion.
  How'dja like a cottage
  By the ocean?
  I could let my hair down
  And you could let your cold cream shine.
  How'dja like it?
  As for me, I'd like it fine!

REFRAIN 3

RAYE: How'dja like to love me?
HOPE: Does she mean it?
RAYE: How'dja like to kiss me?
HOPE: What a racket.
RAYE: Could'ja kinda fall,
  Hang my picture on your wall
  To stay?
HOPE: How'dja like to love me?
RAYE: Oh, boy!
HOPE: How'dja like to miss me?
RAYE: Oh, joy!
HOPE: Would'ja go so far
  As to be my guiding star
  Each day?
RAYE: I'll say!
  I told my doctor, my lawyer to see what
    they think
  The moment they saw ya were they
    tickled pink!
HOPE: So how'dja like to love me?
  Are you list'ning?

RAYE: How'dja like a license
     And a christ'ning?
HOPE: A baby boy with my brains—
RAYE: A daughter with a mouth like mine!
BOTH: How'dja like it?
     As for me, I'd like it fine!

I FALL IN LOVE WITH YOU EVERY DAY

Music by Manning Sherwin and Arthur Altman (1910–1994). Altman's other well-known song was "All or Nothing at All." Published. Copyrighted February 7, 1938. Previously registered for copyright as an unpublished song December 8, 1937. Introduced by Florence George and John Payne. Leading recording by Jimmy Dorsey and His Orchestra, vocal by Bob Eberly. Other recordings by Larry Clinton and His Orchestra, vocal by Bea Wain (Victor); Dolly Dawn with George Hall's Orchestra (Vocalion); Horace Heidt and His Orchestra (Brunswick); and Abe Lyman and His Orchestra (Bluebird). Also used in Paramount Pictures' *Sing You Sinners* (1938).

VERSE (NOT USED IN FILM)

The day we fell in love was simply rapturous,
I never thought that spell could quite recapture us.
Yet each time we meet it's all the same again,
And this eager heart bursts into flame again.

REFRAIN

I fall in love with you ev'ry day.
I fall in love with you, same old way.
Just like that first great moment long ago,
Same old thrill, same old glow.
I always find your kiss just like new
And rediscover this charm of you.
And ev'ry day like our first rendezvous,
I fall in love with you.

YOU'RE A NATURAL

Music by Manning Sherwin. Published. Copyrighted March 29, 1938. Previously registered for copyright as an unpublished song December 8, 1937. Introduced by Gracie Allen.

VERSE (NOT SUNG IN FILM)

All my life this heart of mine's
Been beating in terror.
Ev'ry old romance had broken it,
Would the next one break it more?
But now I've canned that system
Known as trial and error.
'Cause there can't be any mistake
About the one I adore,
For—

REFRAIN

You're a nat'ral,
Positively nat'ral,
In a world of Clark Gables I found you.*
Fresh from heaven,
Like a lucky seven,
In a world full of fables you came true.†
Why, the moment you passed me by
I said to myself,
I said, said I,
There's the thrill
That fills the bill,
Hits the spot,
Cops the pot!
'Cause you're a nat'ral,
Absolutely nat'ral.
So nat'rally I'd love to amble
Down the aisle for one last gamble,
Nat'rally with you.

MOMENTS LIKE THIS

Music by Burton Lane. Published. Copyrighted February 9, 1938. Previously registered for copyright as an unpublished song December 8, 1937. Used in film as an instrumental. Recordings by Maxine Sullivan (Victor); Dick Stabile and His Orchestra, featuring Teddy Wilson (Bluebird); Nan Wynn (Brunswick). More recent recordings by Tony Bennett (Columbia); Peggy Lee (Capitol); Dinah Shore (RCA Victor); Johnny Mathis (Columbia); Bobby Short (Elektra); Michael Feinstein and Burton Lane (Elektra Nonesuch); among others. Also sung by Phil Regan in *Las Vegas Nights* (1941) with Tommy Dorsey and His Orchestra, and by Dean Martin in the Martin and Jerry Lewis picture *Money from Home* (1953).

---

* *Sheet music version:*
    In a world full of phonies I found you.

† *Sheet music version:*
    Like a hunch on the ponies that came true.

VERSE

Here is my casual smile, playing its part,
Keeping the two of us good friends.
Here is my cigarette smoke, hiding my heart,
But here's where the masquerade ends.

REFRAIN

Moments like this make me thrill through and
    through,
Careless moments like this close to you.
Nonchalantly we dine and we dance,
Yet my heart seems to melt in your glance.
Sweet moments like this, with the soft lights
    aglow,
Make me long for your kiss, though I know
I'd be just one of all your affairs.
But at moments like this, who cares?

WHAT A RUMBA DOES TO ROMANCE

Music by Manning Sherwin. Published. Copyrighted September 27, 1938. Previously registered for copyright as an unpublished song December 8, 1937. Introduced by Martha Raye. Danced by Raye and Ben Blue.

VERSE

We used to be the coziest pair;
We danced with such an intimate air.
But ever since we fell for that thing called
    rumba,
I've lost you somehow.
I knew the very moment that rhythm started
That soon we'd be parted;
Just look at us now.

REFRAIN

I'm over here,
You're over there,
You never hold me tight for a minute.
Why did the Cubans ever begin it?
Look what a rumba does to romance.
I'm going north,
You're going south
And don't forget to write, "How's the weather?"
I understand we're dancing together—
Look what a rumba does to romance!
Oh, why can't they play us a fox trot,
Good old reliable fox trot?
This is the loneliest dance.

I'm over here,
You're over there,
We have to yell sweet things to each other.
You might well be my little brother,
I might as well be somewhere in France—
That's what a rumba does to romance.

BEANS

Music by Manning Sherwin. Not used in film.

VERSE

They say a working girl's life can be a happy
      one—
Well, do you see a smile on this map?
Most girls can play
With a three-hour day,
Or twiddle their thumbs
While the boss is away,
But me!
Me, I'm just a poor sap!
They say a working girl's life can be a merry one,
But me, I'm caught in a trap.
Most girls get by
Though their pay isn't high,
And they step out at night
With a gleam in their eye;
But me!
Me, I'm just a poor yap!
I thought that all the slaves were free
In eighteen sixty-one,
But here's a weary, dreary drudge
Whose work is never done.
What's to the left of me?
What's to the right of me?

REFRAIN 1

Beans, beans,
Marching up and down again.
Beans, beans,
Served with Boston brown again.
Lima beans, kidney beans,
Butter beans and soy beans,
For the special benefit
Of people who enjoy beans.
You may spend a thousand days
And nights to study botany,
Or you may play a saxophone
Until your brain gets cottony,
And you may think you know the
Meaning of the word "monotony,"

But ah, my friends, and ah, my foes,
You don't know what it means
To be raised from the cradle
With a ladle in your hand.
To fish 'em up and dish 'em up
For all the world to swish 'em up—
It's more than any mortal man can stand.
That gooey, sticky, icky,
Picky family of greens
Known as beans, beans, beans.

INTERLUDE 1

Oh, I wish I'd run off with that millionaire
Who used to drop in here for tea.
Then I fed him a plate
Of dinner number eight,
And he went and died on me!
[spoken] I might have been rich by now and in
      society.
Ah! Society—
Champagne and caviar,
Di'monds and aquamarines,
Six maids and a yacht;
But what have I got?

REFRAIN 2

[sung] Beans, beans,
Marching up and down again.
Beans, beans,
Mister Beans goes to town again.
Pork and beans, ham and beans,
Wet beans and dry beans.
Why oh why oh why oh why
Oh why oh why oh why beans?
A million years I've stood the smell
Of this delightful beanery;
A million years I've prayed and prayed
For just a change of scenery.
You see before you now a hunk
Of broken-down machinery,
But ah, my friends, and ah, my foes,
My soul is in its teens.
I meet men by the thousands,
Why, they drop in ev'ry day!
They haunt me and they taunt me,
And the reason why they want me,
A decent girl would be ashamed to say!
Not for dancing, or romancing,
Or for rides in limousines,
But for beans, beans, beans!!!

INTERLUDE 2

Oh, I wish I'd eloped with that picture man
Who told me as a movie queen I'd reign.

Till he suddenly tore
Into lunch number four
And ran away mildly insane.
[spoken] I might have had a star now in Hollywood.
Ah, Hollywood!
With Bing Crosby, dancing in the moonlight,
With Fred MacMurray, walking and talking,
With George Raft, making love,
With Gary Cooper, truckin'—
Look, I'm truckin'!
I can do the Big Apple, too.
So what?
She's even got rhythm,
But what have I got?

REFRAIN 3

[sung] Beans, beans,
Marching up and down again.
Beans, beans,
Just a common noun again.
Army beans, navy beans,
Chili beans and black beans,
I'd like to meet the sons of guns
Who plant and grow and pack beans.
From nine to ten I sit me down,
From nine to ten I'm stringin' 'em.
From ten to twelve I stand me up,
And in the pot I'm flingin' 'em.
From twelve to one, till day is done,
I'm on my toes and bringin' 'em.
And ah, my friends, and ah, my foes,
Of all the dull routines,
To be raised from the cradle
With a ladle in your hand
To fish 'em up and dish 'em up,
For all the world to swish 'em up—
It's more than any mortal man can stand.
Those tootin', tootin', hootin',
Shootin', nasty little fiends
Known as beans! Beans! Beans!

STOLEN HEAVEN

Produced by Andrew L. Stone for Paramount Pictures. Released May 1938. Screenplay by Eve Greene and Frederick Jackson, adapted from a story by Andrew L. Stone. Directed by Andrew L. Stone. Cast starred Gene Raymond and Olympe Bradna and featured Glenda Farrell and Lewis Stone. Other songs in the film include "Stolen Heaven" by Ralph Freed (lyrics) and Frederick Hollander (music).

BOYS IN THE BAND

Music by Manning Sherwin. Registered for copyright as an unpublished song May 14, 1938. Introduced by Olympe Bradna, Gene Raymond, and ensemble.

BRADNA: Oh—
Somebody stole the drum from the band.
Oh, somebody stole the drum from the band.
So the band played on without the drum,
And just where the drummer's part should come,
Dum-diddle-um-dum-dum went the boys in the band.

BRADNA
AND CHORUS: Dum-diddle-um-dum-dum went the boys in the band.
Oh—

BRADNA: Oh, somebody stole the fiddle from the band.

BRADNA
AND CHORUS: Somebody stole the fiddle from the band.

BRADNA: So the band played on without the fiddle,
And just when they got to the spot in the middle,
Fiddle-diddle-diddle-diddle-dee
Went the boys in the band.
Fiddle-diddle-diddle-diddle-dee
Dum-diddle-um-dum-dum
Went the boys in the band.
Oh, somebody stole the bass from the band.

BRADNA
AND CHORUS: Somebody stole the bass from the band.

BRADNA: So the band played on without the bass,
And just when the leader got red in the face—

CHORUS: Zum! Zum! Zum!

BRADNA
AND CHORUS: Went the boys in the band.

CHORUS: Zum! Zum! Zum!

BRADNA: Fiddle-diddle-diddle-diddle-dee.

CHORUS: Zum! Zum! Zum!

BRADNA: Fiddle-diddle-diddle-diddle-dee
Went the boys in the band.

MAN 1: Now somebody shteals der moosic from der bandt.

CHORUS: Now somebody shteals der moosic from der bandt.

BRADNA: So der boys can't blay vitoudt der notes,

MAN 2: Budt vee make sounds like der billy goats.

CHORUS: Baa-baa-baa goes der boys in der bandt.
[*whistle*] Went the boys in the band.
Oh—

MAN 3: Somebody in the band stole my ha-ha-ha-ha.

CHORUS: Somebody in the band stole his ha! ha! ha! ha!

BRADNA: Now he can't laugh anymore—

MAN 3: Cause my ha-ha's lying on the floor.

ALL: [*laughter—ha-ha etc.*]
Went the boys in the band!

COCOANUT GROVE

Produced by George M. Arthur for Paramount Pictures. Released in June 1938. Screenplay and story by Sy Bartlett and Olive Cooper. Directed by Alfred Santell. Cast starred Fred MacMurray and featured Harriet Hilliard, The Yacht Club Boys, Ben Blue, Eve Arden, Rufe Davis, and Billy Lee. Other songs in this film include "Cocoanut Grove" and "Dreamy Hawaiian Moon," lyrics and music by Harry Owens, and "You Leave Me Breathless" by Ralph Freed (lyrics) and Frederick Hollander (music).

SAYS MY HEART

Music by Burton Lane. Published. Copyrighted February 25, 1938. Introduced by Harriet Hilliard and Harry Owens and His Royal Hawaiian Orchestra. Reprised by Harriet Hilliard and The Yacht Club Boys. This was the first of Loesser's songs to reach the number-one spot on the popular music charts. The top recording was by Red Norvo and His Orchestra (Brunswick). Other leading recordings were by Ozzie Nelson and His Orchestra, vocal by Harriet Hilliard (Bluebird); Tommy Dorsey and His Orchestra, vocal by Edythe Wright (Victor); and the Andrews Sisters (Decca).

Composer Burton Lane, whose recommendation got Loesser his first contract at Paramount, recalled the circumstances surrounding "Says My Heart" to the editors shortly before his death:

I came in one morning and Frank was sitting outside my office with two men—a producer and a director of a film that was just about to be made at Paramount [*Cocoanut Grove*]. They wanted a new tune to this lyric, one that Frank and Manning Sherwin had played for me when my agent first called me about them. I asked, "When do you want this tune?" and they said, "We're going to wait out here." They were going to sit there till I got it. So, I said all right and went into my office, putzed around for a couple minutes, and came out with this tune. I called Frank in, he said it was a pretty good tune, so I made a piano part of it and turned it in. . . . I lost track of it until one day when I turned on the *Hit Parade* program on the radio. I didn't even know the goddamn picture had been released and suddenly "Says My Heart" is number two on the *Hit Parade*. Next week it's number one and stays there for eighteen weeks.

VERSE (NOT SUNG IN FILM)

You've got me on the brink of a new affair,
And though I'm in the pink for a new affair,
I don't know what to think of a new affair with you.
Oh! What can I do?

REFRAIN

"Fall in love, fall in love," says my heart,
"It's romance, take a chance," says my heart.
But each time that I'm almost in your arms,
This old schoolteacher brain of mine
Keeps ringing in false alarms.
Then my head rules instead, and I'm wise
To the scheme of that gleam in your eyes.
So I kiss and run,
But the moment we're apart,
"Oh you fool, that was love!"
Says my heart.

TEN EASY LESSONS

Music by Burton Lane. Introduced by Rufe Davis, and Harry Owens and His Royal Hawaiian Orchestra.

VERSE

Anyone can look at me and guess (two, three, four)
How I became a musical success (two, three, four).
I used to go to parties and just sit (two, three, four)
And sit (two, three four)
And sit (two three, four)
But now (two, three, four)
I'm a hit (two, three)!

REFRAIN 1

For I learned it in ten easy lessons,
Yes, I learned how to play a hot cornet.
That correspondence school
Said I'd knock 'em for a gool,
And by airmail, I became the teacher's pet.
[*Toot, toot, toot, etc.*]
Why, I never could do that ten weeks ago.
But I guess I must be
The life of the party,
'Cause all they ever say to me is "Blow."
[*Toot, toot, toot, etc.*]

REFRAIN 2

Oh, I learned it in ten easy lessons,
Yes, I learned how to play a bass viol.
At parties now I shine
When I slap that bass of mine,
Though I couldn't slap a bass to save my soul.
[*Slap, slap, slap, etc.*]
You'll excuse me if I seem to be conceited,
But I guess I must be
The life of the party,
'Cause all they ever say to me is "Beat it."
[*Slap, slap, slap, etc.*]

REFRAIN 3 (NOT SUNG IN FILM)

Oh, I learned it in ten easy lessons,
Yes, I learned how to play the steel guitar.
I twang it round the yard,
I pick it good and hard,
And all the neighbors say I should go far.
[*Twang, twang, twang, etc.*]
You can ask my many friends just what they
    think.
Yes, I'm sure I must be
The life of the party,
'Cause all they ever say to me is [*holds nose*]
[*Twang, twang, twang, etc.*] [*String breaks.*]

REFRAIN 4

Oh, I learned it in ten easy lessons.
Yes, I learned the bazooka that-a way.
That instrument I found
Kind of buried in the ground,
Now the cellar gets all flooded when I play.
[*Poop, poop, poop, etc.*]
On the radio I sure would be a bear.
Oh, I know I must be the life of the party,
'Cause everybody tells me, "Take the air."
[*Poop, poop, poop, etc.*]

THE TEXANS

Produced by Lucien Hubbard for Paramount Pictures. Released in July 1938. Screenplay by Bertram Millhauser, Paul Sloane, and William Wister Haines, based on the novel *North of 36* by Emerson Hough. Directed by James P. Hogan. Cast starred Joan Bennett and Randolph Scott and featured May Robson, Walter Brennan, and Robert Cummings. Other songs in this film included "Silver on the Sage" by Leo Robin (lyrics) and Ralph Rainger (music).

I'LL COME TO THE WEDDING

To the tune of "Buffalo Gals." Introduced by unidentified trio.

VERSE 1

There's gonna be a weddin' in town,
Weddin' in town, weddin' in town.
There's gonna be a weddin' in town,
And don't the bride look grand.

REFRAIN

Bet your boots I'll come to the weddin',
Come to the weddin', come to the weddin',
Bet your boots I'll come to the weddin',
If she will hold my hand.

VERSE 2

She bought herself a long white gown,
Long white gown, long white gown.
She bought herself a long white gown,
In which to say "I do."

REPEAT REFRAIN

VERSE 3 (NOT SUNG IN FILM)

The lady's name is Susie Brown,
Susie Brown, Susie Brown.
The lady's name is Susie Brown,
But who's the groom to be?

REPEAT REFRAIN

OPTIONAL CODA (NOT SUNG IN FILM)

If she will marry me,
If she will marry me,

Bet your boots I'll come to the weddin',
If she will marry me.

GIVE ME A SAILOR

Produced by Jeff Lazarus for Paramount Pictures. Released in August 1938. Screenplay by Doris Anderson and Frank Butler, based on the musical *Linger Longer Letty* by Anne Nichols. Directed by Elliott Nugent. Cast starred Martha Raye and Bob Hope and featured Betty Grable and Jack Whiting. Other songs in this film include "It Don't Make Sense," "A Little Kiss at Twilight," "The U.S.A. and You," and "What Goes on Here in My Head" by Leo Robin (lyrics) and Ralph Rainger (music).

GIVE ME A SAILOR

Music by Hoagy Carmichael. Not used in film.

Said the girl to the boy:
"Yo-heave-ho, let the winter wind blow!"

"Give me a sailor
Fresh from the salty sea.
Give me a sailor
Fresher than fresh can be.
With a cute white cap
Over half his map
And trouser legs
That flap-flap-flap.
One phone call
And I'd grab my shawl
To dance with him down the Roseland hall."

Said the girl to the boy:
"Yo-heave-ho, I don't want a rich beau,
Gable and Taylor ain't worth the dreaming of.
Give me a sailor with gobs and gobs of love."

"Ship ahoy! Ship ahoy!"
Said the girl to the boy.

I'M IN DREAMLAND

Music by Burton Lane. Intended for Rufe Davis and Martha Raye. Not used in film.

DAVIS: [*Snore, whistle*]
I'm in Dreamland.
It's a land of bliss
Where the early birds
Get up too late for worms
And kinda blink their eyes
And sing a song like this.
[*Snore, whistle*]
I'm in Dreamland.
Dreaming through the day,
Where the busy bees
Get busy when they please,
And like the busy bees
I buzz around this way.
[*Snore, whistle, whistle*]
[*Snore, whistle, whistle*]
I ain't doing dishes,
I ain't chopping wood,
I ain't so ambitious—
Ain't that good?
[*Snore, whistle*]
I'm in Dreamland,
Wishing you was here.
Now I'll say so long,
So let me end my song
With a [*snore, whistle*]
Oh, dear!
[*Snore, whistle*]

RAYE: Oh dear.

DAVIS: [*Snore, whistle*]
I'm in Dreamland,
It's a land of bliss.

RAYE: Oh, you lazy dog,
You're in a constant fog.
You're like a useless bump
Upon a useless log.

DAVIS: [*Snore, whistle*]
I'm in Dreamland,
Getting nice and fat.

RAYE: And I cook your grub,
You let me wash and scrub,
You good-for-nothing dub,
What do you say to that?

DAVIS: [*Snore, whistle, whistle*]
[*Snore, whistle, whistle*]

RAYE: You won't do the dishes,
You won't chop the wood,
You won't get ambitious—

DAVIS: Ain't that good?
[*Snore, whistle*]
I'm in Dreamland,
Kindly dim the light.
Now I'll say so long,
So let me end my song
With a [*snore, whistle*]
Good night
[*Snore, whistle*]

Good night
[*Snore, whistle*]

RAYE: Good night!

SING YOU SINNERS

Produced by Wesley Ruggles for Paramount Pictures. Released in August 1938. Screenplay and story by Claude Binyon. Directed by Wesley Ruggles. Cast starred Bing Crosby and Fred MacMurray and featured Donald O'Connor, Elizabeth Patterson, and Ellen Drew. Other songs from this film include W. Franke Harling (music) and Sam Coslow's (lyrics) 1930 hit "Sing You Sinners," and "Don't Let the Moon Get Away," "I've Got a Pocketful of Dreams," and "Laugh and Call It Love" by Johnny Burke (lyrics) and James Monaco (music).

SMALL FRY

Music by Hoagy Carmichael. Published. Copyrighted June 29, 1938. Previously registered for copyright as an unpublished song May 10, 1938. Introduced by Bing Crosby, with Fred MacMurray and Donald O'Connor. Leading recordings by Bing Crosby and Johnny Mercer (Decca) and Mildred Bailey (Vocalion). In 1973 Hoagy Carmichael told Cynthia Lindsay this story of how he and Loesser wrote the song:

> He used so many jokes to keep me alive and happy—he said, "let's write a song called 'Small Fry,'"—that sounded like him. Before he had reeled off a few stanzas, it was quite evident that he was the lyricist I hoped he would be. It only took us a day and a half to write the whole thing. The music department decided we should record it ourselves for the library. I can still hear myself being the papa singing my part and Frank singing in the high pitched voice of a 12 year-old kid. I think Frank really enjoyed this song. . . . You've heard the expression in show business, "Be there at the right place and the right time?" Frank's timing came up again the very same week. Wesley Ruggles made a picture using a 12 year-old boy. Somebody said, "Take your record over to his office and see if he likes it and can use it." Frank and I entered Ruggles' office that Saturday. There was a boy sitting there. Frank ran over and put the record on the Victrola. Ruggles listened, looked at the boy, listened to the record, back at the boy. The record never finished. He said, "That's it,

gentlemen. Meet Donald O'Connor. He, Bing Crosby and Fred MacMurray will sing your song in the picture."

VERSE (NOT SUNG IN FILM)*

Here comes that good-for-nothin' brat of a boy.
He's such a devil I could whip him with joy.
He's been carousin' at the burleycue—
Just watch me teach him with the sole of my shoe!

REFRAIN

CROSBY: Small fry,
Struttin' by the poolroom.
Small fry,
Should be in the schoolroom.
My! My! Now you put down that
    cigarette—
You ain't a grown-up high-and-
    mighty yet.
Small fry,
Dancin' for a penny.
Small fry,
Countin' up how many.
My! My! Just listen here to me—
You ain't the biggest catfish in the
    sea.
You practice peckin' all day long
To some old radio song.

MACMURRAY: Oh, yes! Oh, yes! Oh, yes!
You better listen to your pa
And someday practice the law.

CROSBY: And then you'll be a real success.
Small fry,
Now you kissed the neighbor's
    daughter.
Small fry,
Stay in shallow water.
Seems I should take you cross my
    knee,
You ain't the biggest catfish in
    the sea.
You've got your feet all soakin' wet.

MACMURRAY: You'll be the death of me yet.

CROSBY: Oh me!

MACMURRAY: Oh my!

CROSBY: Small fry.

O'CONNOR: [*spoken*] You call me small fry?

CROSBY: [*sung*] You is most infinitesimal—
Too big for your britches.

O'CONNOR: [*spoken*] You call me small fry?

CROSBY: You look a here, shorter than me.
I wonder where that switch is?

---

* *The verse was later used in the Paramount cartoon* Small Fry.

O'CONNOR: [*spoken*] My! My! My! I never heard
such carryin' on—
Better look in the closet, Ma, I bet
the gin's all gone.*
MACMURRAY: [*sung*] Oh, yes! Oh, yes!
CROSBY: Small fry—you was bettin' on the
ponies.
O'CONNOR: [*spoken*] Aw, you're just burned
'cause I was winning.
Some guy—he picks all the phonies.
CROSBY: [*sung*] My! My! Just listen here to me.
O'CONNOR: I know, I know, I know.
I ain't the biggest catfish in the sea.
[*spoken*] Let's hear something new.
CROSBY: [*sung double time*] You've got a
pinochle deck in your pocket.
O'CONNOR: What became of Ma's wedding
ring, did you hock it?
MACMURRAY: Oh, yes! Oh, yes! Oh, yes!
CROSBY: [*double time*] You signed your own
report card last night.
O'CONNOR: [*spoken*] Well, why don't you learn
how to write?
And then you'll be a real success.
CROSBY: [*spoken*] Yes?
O'CONNOR: [*spoken*] Yes!
CROSBY: [*sung*] Small fry, you kissed the
neighbor's daughter.
O'CONNOR: [*spoken*] Sure I gave her a little
smackeroo, but
Wiseguy, you're the one who
taught her.
CROSBY: [*sung*] Seems I should take you
cross my knee,
Now you ain't the biggest catfish in
the sea.
[*spoken*] Ma, I think I know what to
do with this boy.
Is that castor oil around here?
MACMURRAY: [*spoken*] Why, he just slipped it in
your beer!
CROSBY: [*sung*] Oh, me!
MACMURRAY: Oh, my!
O'CONNOR: Small fry.

Tall Fry

Special lyrics from private recording by Bob Crosby and
son, 1950s. From undated typed lyric sheet.

SON: Now, tall fry?
DAD: Yes, small fry

---

* *Earlier version:*
My, my, just listen how he shrieks—
He hasn't changed his underwear in weeks and
weeks and weeks.

SON: Uh, how come you ain't workin'?
DAD: Workin'!
SON: Tall fry?
DAD: Yes?
SON: Seems to me you're shirkin'.
DAD: Fiddlesticks, boy, fiddlesticks.
SON: My, my, what's Momma gonna say?
DAD: Momma!
SON: When I tell her where I saw you today.
DAD: I beg your pardon?
SON: Oh, tall fry?
DAD: I'm innocent!
SON: You been playin' poker.
DAD: Wow!
SON: Tall fry?
DAD: You been goin' around a bit.
SON: Isn't that the joker?
DAD: Get your hand outta my pocket, boy.
SON: My, my, I got you by the hook.
Why, Pa, you haven't got a good lie in your
book!
DAD: Well, give me time, boy, I'm thinkin'.
SON: I'll make a bargain with you, Pa,
I'll promise not to tell Ma.
DAD: Will you?
SON: Oh, yes.
DAD: Oh, yes!
Look, son, my winnings weren't really a lot.
SON: Well, I'll only take all you got.
DAD: Can't I bargain?
Seems to me, boy, like you gonna be a real
success.
SON: Yes, tall fry.
DAD: Small fry.
SON: Did my message reach you?
DAD: Pigeon carrier.
SON: Tall fry?
DAD: Mmmm?
SON: When I grow up, what will I be?
DAD: Now look here, son.
You'll be the biggest catfish in the sea.
Unless you just happen to tell your mother,
son.
SON: Then I'll be the deadest one.
DAD: Smart guy.
SON: Oh, my.
BOTH: Small fry.
DAD: Bye, bye.
SON: Bye, bye.
BOTH: Small fry.

FRESHMAN YEAR

Produced by George R. Bilson for Universal Productions. Released in August 1938. Screenplay by Charles Grayson, from a story by Thomas Ahearn and F. Maury Grossman. Directed by Frank MacDonald. Cast starred Dixie Dunbar, William Lundigan, Constance Moore, and Ernest Truex and featured Stanley Hughes, The Diamond Brothers, the Murtah Sisters, The Lucky Seven Choir, and Alan Ladd. Other songs from the film include "Ain't That Marvelous" and "Swing That Cheer" by Joe McCarthy and Harry Barris.

CHASING YOU AROUND

Music and lyrics by Irving Actman and Frank Loesser. Registered for copyright as an unpublished song October 26, 1938. Introduced by Dixie Dunbar and The Lucky Seven Choir.

VERSE

I hang around your neck,
I hang around your door,
I know I make you feel like a fugitive of war,
But oh! What a thrill for me!
I phone you ev'ry night,
I phone you ev'ry day;
I know I make you feel like an animal at bay,
But oh! oh! oh! What a novelty for me.

REFRAIN

I've chased many, many foxes
In a red coat, with a hound;
But I've let them go,
'Cause I get a brighter glow
Out of chasing you around.
I've chased fame all over Broadway,
In the spotlight, smartly gowned;
But I'm off that gang,
'Cause I get a nicer bang
Out of chasing you around.

Why do I pursue you from here to there?
It's going to get me nowhere.
Still I'm clinging to you—
It must be love.
It must be, on account of
I've chased many dukes and princes,
I've had offers to be crowned,
I could get rich quick,

But I get a bigger kick
Out of chasing you around.

SPAWN OF THE NORTH

Produced by Albert Lewin for Paramount Pictures. Released in September 1938. Incidental music and underscore by Dimitri Tiomkin. Screenplay by Jules Furthman and Talbot Jennings, based on the novel by Florence Barrett Willoughby. Directed by Henry Hathaway. Cast starred George Raft, Henry Fonda, and Dorothy Lamour and featured Akim Tamiroff, John Barrymore, Louise Platt, Lynne Overman, and Fuzzy Knight.

I WISH I WAS THE WILLOW

Music by Burton Lane. Published. Copyrighted April 12, 1938. Introduced by George Raft and Henry Fonda.

VERSE (NOT SUNG IN FILM)

It's a busy world and I'm in it,
It's a struggle 'gainst the tide,
It's a dizzy pace ev'ry minute,
But I'm dreamin' deep inside.

REFRAIN

Oh, I wish I was the willow on the river bank,
'Cause I'd never have to make a livin' then,
Hustlin' up the stream and down the stream
And up the stream again.*

Oh, I wish I was the willow on the river bank,
Then I'd find the peace of mind I'm lookin' for,
'Stead of up the stream and down the stream
And up the stream once more.

Oh, the starlight is dancin' on the ripples,
And the soft ev'nin' breeze will soon begin.
Oh, I wish I had the time to watch the ripples,
The time to settle down and take it all in.

---

* Only the first four lines of refrain are sung in film.

But I wasn't born a willow on the river bank,
I'm just one of Mother Nature's little men,
Hustlin' up the stream and down the stream
And up the stream again!

I LIKE HUMPED-BACKED SALMON

Music by Burton Lane. Based on an Alaskan folk song. Registered for copyright as an unpublished song April 12, 1938. Introduced by Fuzzy Knight, John Barrymore, Lynne Overman, and ensemble.

Twenty-seven years after the film was released, orchestra leader Skitch Henderson used this song during the "stump the band" segment on Johnny Carson's *Tonight Show* on NBC television, which prompted the following response from Loesser:

Dear Mr. Carson:

You may tell Skitch Henderson that . . . I take very special umbrage at his lofty dismissal of a very fine contribution to musical literature called "I Like Humped-Backed Salmon." In addition to his outrageous taste in clothing, he is now displaying a profound ignorance of a gem among the great American compositions—a piece that is absolutely undying in its sheer loveliness.

For him to be seen and heard publicly dismissing "I Like Humped-Backed Salmon" as obscure, if not indeed some sort of hoax—seems to me to be an insult to the American public and its treasured sentiments.

I cannot write this letter of rebuke directly to Mr. Henderson as the morning mail might find him not properly dressed (in his opinion) for reading. Further, no doubt he would probably find my stationery to be not at room temperature and therefore not decently negotiable—and would forthwith toss the whole thing into his flowered chintz wastebasket. Therefore I am addressing this to you in the hope that you will transmit the following information to him toward his cultural betterment: "I Like Humped-Backed Salmon," beloved by millions and ever on the lips of young and old alike, was first performed in a Paramount picture called *Spawn of the North*, starring George Raft, Henry Fonda and Dorothy Lamour, in 1938. Only shut-ins . . . and a few feeble minded missed seeing this great cinema classic. But nobody, absolutely nobody, failed to hear the enchanting sound of the song via radio, night clubs, organ grinders, and strolling minstrels.

I thank you in advance for transmitting this bit of elementary education to Mr. Henderson

who cannot have been too young to go to the movies in 1938 . . . and therefore must have been one of the feeble-minded.

Very sincerely,
Frank Loesser

P.S. Oh. I forgot to tell you. *I* wrote the lyrics of "ILHBS."

ENSEMBLE: I like humped-backed salmon,
Good old humped-backed salmon,
Caught by a Norskie fisherman.
KNIGHT: Way up stream swam a great big whale,
Far from the salty ocean.
I told him, That's the place to swim.
He said, Promise me on your life,
You won't tell my wife:
ENSEMBLE: I like humped-backed salmon,
Good old humped-backed salmon,
Caught by a Norskie fisherman.
BARRYMORE: I don't care who's the President,
Still gotta pay the taxes.
I don't mix into politics,
But the coming Election Day
You will hear me say:
ENSEMBLE: I like humped-backed salmon,
Good old humped-backed salmon,
Caught by a Norskie fisherman.
OVERMAN: My wife just had a baby boy,
Can't feed him from a bottle;
'Tain't no use, with this new papoose,
'Cause his mother and I we tried,
But the kid replied:
ENSEMBLE: I like humped-backed salmon,
Good old humped-backed salmon,
Caught by a Norskie fisherman.

CUT VERSES

I don't care for a T-bone steak
Cut from a steer from Texas.
I don't cry for a chicken pie,
And I wouldn't know what to do
With an Irish stew:

Cleopatra from Egypt land,
She had a Roman boyfriend.
Take a look in your history book—
When she threw him into the Nile,
It was worth his while:

Old man Jones is a millionaire,
Last week I met his daughter.
She asked me could I learn to care,

So I gave her a little kiss
And I must say this:

Don't like gals wearin' sweet perfume,
Can't stand the smell of roses.
I'll take life with an old fishwife,
'Cause I never could spend a day
Sniffing new-mown hay.

MEN WITH WINGS

Produced by William A. Wellman for Paramount Pictures. Released in October 1938. Screenplay by Robert Carson. Directed by William A. Wellman. Cast featured Fred MacMurray, Ray Milland, Louise Campbell, Andy Devine, Walter Abel, and Lynne Overman.

MEN WITH WINGS

Music by Hoagy Carmichael. Published. Copyrighted September 21, 1938. Previously registered for copyright as an unpublished song June 4, 1938. Used instrumentally only.

VERSE

Mister and Missus America,
We introduce you to the Old Air Corps.
Mister and Missus America,
We guard the sky for you from shore to shore.
We fly and we sing,
We sing and we fly,
But flying is all we know.
We give her the gun
And into the sun
We go!

REFRAIN

Oh! We are the men with wings,
Yours truly, men with wings,
Roaring a song to the sky,
Soaring along till we die.
When trouble is in the air,
Who'll beat the devil there?
No sir! Not angels,
Just men with wings.

THANKS FOR THE MEMORY

Produced by Mel Shauer for Paramount Pictures. Released in December 1938. Screenplay by Lynn Starling from the play *Up Pops the Devil* by Albert Hackett and Frances Goodrich. Directed by George Archainbaud. Cast featured Bob Hope, Shirley Ross, Charles Butterworth, Otto Kruger, and Hedda Hopper.

TWO SLEEPY PEOPLE

Music by Hoagy Carmichael. Published. Copyrighted September 29, 1938. Previously registered for copyright as an unpublished song September 10, 1938. Introduced by Shirley Ross and Bob Hope, who also recorded it with Harry Sosnik's Orchestra (Decca). Fats Waller's recording (Bluebird) achieved the top spot on the popular music charts. Other leading recordings: Sammy Kaye and His Orchestra (Victor); Kay Kyser and His Orchestra (Brunswick); Bob Crosby and His Orchestra, vocals by Bob Crosby and Marian Mann (Decca); Hoagy Carmichael and Ella Logan (Brunswick); and Lawrence Welk and His Orchestra (Vocalion). There are two versions of the song's birth. The first is offered by Susan Loesser in *A Most Remarkable Fella*:

> The Carmichaels had been entertaining the Loessers and Hoagy and my father had been trying unsuccessfully all evening to come up with a new song. Finally, around three in the morning, the exhausted foursome decided to call it a night. At the door my mother said, "Look at us: four sleepy people." My father and Hoagy looked at each other, said, "That's it!" and went back into the house. When the song was published the sheet music noted, "Title suggested by Lynn Garland."

Hoagy Carmichael gave his version to Cynthia Lindsay in 1973:

> My wife Ruth and I used to go back and forth to Frank and Lynn's for spaghetti or something. . . . I sat at the old upright piano he had in the rented cottage, just fiddling around, Frank with a beer in his hand. The girls yelled, "Write something, you bums." At that moment Frank was trying to find a cigarette and I was too. We both smoked too much and were frantic. So Frank's first reaction to writing a song was his line, "Here we are, out of cigarettes" and I followed with my next melody line to match his words . . . and he sang "Holding hands and yawning." By that time, we could both see that here was the song situation. . . . Words of Frank's like "by dawn's early light" were the type of things only great lyric writers come up with— "Picking on a wishbone from the Frigidaire." I knew then that Frank had not only found his pace as a big songwriter, but also the confidence I felt when I first saw him strutting down the lot at Paramount was justified.

VERSE

I guess we haven't got a sense
Of responsibility.
Our young romance is so intense,
We're close to imbecility.
Tick, tock! Cuckoo!

REFRAIN

Here we are, out of cigarettes,
Holding hands and yawning,
Look how late it gets.
Two sleepy people, by dawn's early light,
And too much in love to say good night.
Here we are, in the cozy chair,
Picking on a wishbone
From the Frigidaire.
Two sleepy people with nothing to say
And too much in love to break away.
Do you remember the nights we used to linger in the hall?
Father didn't like you at all.
Do your remember the reason why we married in the fall?
To rent this little nest
And get a bit of rest.
Well, here we are,
Just about the same,
Foggy little fella,
Drowsy little dame.
Two sleepy people, by dawn's early light,
And too much in love to say good night.

Film version

HOPE: Two sleepy people, by dawn's early light,
        Too much in love to say good night.
ROSS: Here we are, out of cigarettes,
HOPE: Holding hands and yawning,
        Look how late it gets.
ROSS: Two sleepy people, with nothing to say
        And too much in love to break away.
HOPE: Do you remember the nights we had to linger in the hall?

ROSS: [*spoken*] Father didn't like you at all.

HOPE: [*spoken*] Whatever happened to him?

ROSS: [*sung*] Remember the reason why we
        married in the fall?

HOPE: To rent this little nest
    And get a bit of rest.
    But here we are
    Just about the same:

ROSS: Foggy little fella,

HOPE: Drowsy little dame.

ROSS: Two sleepy people, by dawn's early light,

HOPE: Too much in love to say good night.

ROSS: Here we are, don't we look a mess?

HOPE: Lipstick on my collar,
    Wrinkles in your dress.

ROSS: Two sleepy people, who know very well
    They're too much in love to break the spell.

HOPE: Here we are, crazy in the head.
    [*spoken*] Gee, your eyes are gorgeous,
    Even when they're red!

[*Two bars whistled; crash of bottles.*]

ROSS: [*spoken*] Is that the milkman?

HOPE: [*spoken*] No, that's dawn breaking!
    [*sung*] Do you remember the nights
        we used to cuddle in the car,
    Watching every last fading star?

ROSS: Remember the doctor said your health
        was under par?

HOPE: And you, my little snooks, were ruining
        your looks.

ROSS: Here we are, keeping up the pace,

HOPE: Letting each tomorrow
    Slap us in the face.

BOTH: Two sleepy people, by dawn's early light,
    And too much in love to say . . .

[*They kiss.*]

A SONG IS BORN

Paramount-Headliner short released in December 1938. Cast featured Leo Baruch, Bea Wain, Ford Leary, and Larry Clinton and His Orchestra. Cameo appearances by songwriters Ralph Freed and Burton Lane, Ralph Rainger and Leo Robin, and Hoagy Carmichael and Frank Loesser. Songs included "Love Doesn't Grow on Trees" (Freed and Lane), "I Fell Up to Heaven" (Rainger and Robin), "Heart and Soul" (Carmichael and Loesser), and "The Devil with the Devil" (Clinton).

HEART AND SOUL

Music by Hoagy Carmichael. Published. Copyrighted September 8, 1938. Previously registered for copyright as an unpublished song August 24, 1938. Introduced by Bea Wain. The recording by Larry Clinton and His Orchestra, vocal by Bea Wain, reached the number-one spot on the popular music charts in October 1938. Other leading recordings: Eddy Duchin and His Orchestra (Brunswick) and Al Donahue and His Orchestra (Vocalion); and, later, The Four Aces (Decca), Johnny Maddox (Dot), Floyd Cramer (RCA Victor), The Cleftones (Gee), and Jan and Dean (Challenge). Hoagy Carmichael noted in an interview with Cynthia Lindsay that the song was heard quite frequently at Paramount before it became a hit:

> For a while, before Paramount gave it to Clinton, the best use the song got was by the vocal coach, a man named Siegal who used it to test the vocal cords of aspiring contract players. Anthony Quinn was on the lot then, and Frank and I heard him sing it so many times before it was even published that by the time it was a hit, we were sick of it.

Another take on the song's ubiquity comes from Susan Loesser:

> When I was a kid my friends and I would play the piano at parties—easy things like "Chopsticks" and "Heart and Soul." I never knew my father wrote "Heart and Soul." I thought whoever wrote "Chopsticks" had written it.

In 1988 the song was performed in the film *Big*.

VERSE (NOT USED IN FILM)

I've let a pair of arms enslave me
Ofttimes before.
But more than just a thrill you gave me,
Yes, more, much more.

REFRAIN

Heart and soul,
I fell in love with you,
Heart and soul,
The way a fool would do,
Madly,
Because you held me tight
And stole a kiss in the night.
Heart and soul,
I begged to be adored,
Lost control
And tumbled overboard,
Gladly,
That magic night we kissed
There in the moon mist.
Oh! but your lips were thrilling,

Much too thrilling;
Never before were mine so
Strangely willing.
But now I see
What one embrace can do,
Look at me,
It's got me loving you
Madly,
That little kiss you stole
Held all my heart and soul.

MISCELLANEOUS SONGS OF 1938

ENCHANTED

Music by Burton Lane. From 1938 Paramount demo record performed by Lane.

Enchanted, enchanted,
The night is enchanted
When I'm near you.
No starlight, no moonrise,
But somehow in your eyes
It all shines true.
When we dance to the music
Of muted strings,
Every step has wings,
Every beat of my heart sings.
If my wish were granted,
You'd keep me enchanted
Forevermore.

WALLPAPER ROSES

Music by Hoagy Carmichael. From 1938 demo record performed by Martha Mears.

Wallpaper roses are all in bloom,
The wallpaper roses around my room.
Strange how things change when you fall in love.
I'm in love.
You brought the magic of
Lamplight that looms like a bright new moon,
A broken Victrola that plays in tune,
Warmly inviting all the world to see
Wallpaper roses in bloom for me.

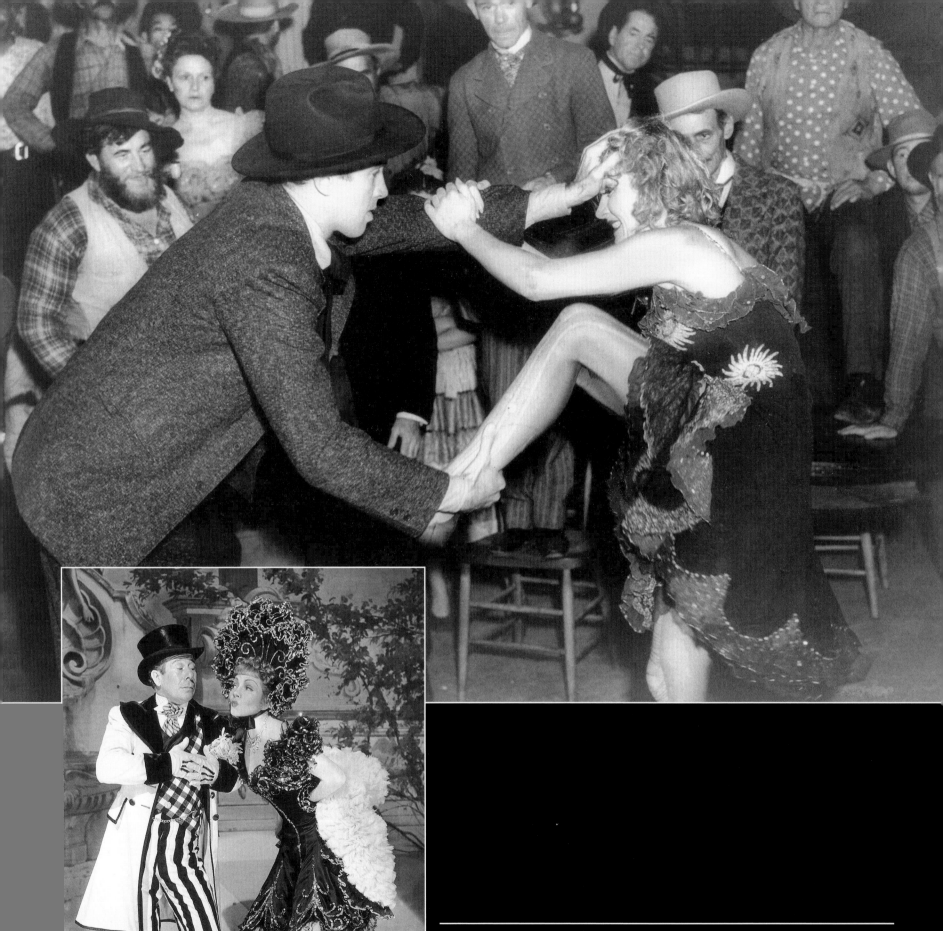

Songs of 1939

ZAZA

Produced by Albert Lewin for Paramount Pictures. Released in January 1939. Music by Frederick Hollander (1896–1976). Screenplay by Zoe Akins, based on the play *Zaza* by Pierre Berton and Charles Simon. Directed by George Cukor. Cast starred Claudette Colbert and Herbert Marshall and featured Bert Lahr, Helen Westley, Constance Collier, and Genevieve Tobin. Hollander wrote music for many of Marlene Dietrich's hits, including her theme song, "Falling in Love Again."

ZAZA

Registered for copyright as an unpublished song October 13, 1938. Introduced by Bert Lahr and Claudette Colbert.

VERSE

LAHR: Little man, little man,
When you're visiting the music hall,*
If your eyes ever chance to roam,
Give a thought to your happy home.
Little man, little man,
There's a lady at the music hall,†
With a smile and big hello—
COLBERT: Hello.
LAHR: But the answer is no-no-no . . .
Tsk-tsk-tsk . . .
Ah-ah-ah . . .

REFRAIN 1

LAHR: Don't fall in love with that one,
Not that one—
She'll break your heart.
COLBERT: It'll cost you a string of pearls.
There are plenty of other girls.
LAHR: If she smiles at you sweetly,
Discreetly, my friend, depart—
COLBERT: Or the rest of your natural life,
You're a problem to your wife.

---

* *Alternate line:*
  When you're walking on the avenue

† *Alternate line:*
  There's a lady on the avenue

Top: *James Stewart and Marlene Dietrich in* Destry Rides Again. *Bottom:* Bert Lahr and Claudette Colbert *in* Zaza.

LAHR: Try someone not quite so gay.
COLBERT: Little man, little man.
LAHR: Go have your fun.
COLBERT: Little man, little man.
LAHR: But on my knees I pray
Don't fall in love with that one,
Not that one—
She'll break your heart.
If it must be the next in line,
Will you wait till she's through with
mine?

REFRAIN 2

LAHR: Don't fall in love with that one.
COLBERT: Not this one!
She'll break your heart.
BOTH: She's too wise—she's too smart.
COLBERT: If I smile at you sweetly,
LAHR: Discreetly I'll turn my eyes.
BOTH: She's too smart, she's too wise.
COLBERT: My darling, I must be loved.
LAHR: It's a lie—it's a lie.
COLBERT: I must be kissed—
LAHR: Oh, me! Oh, my!
I must be on your list.
COLBERT: Oh, don't say that to Zaza,
For Zaza loves only one.
LAHR: Only one made your life sublime?
COLBERT: Only one at a time!
BOTH: No-no-no!
Ah-ah-ah!
Tsk-tsk-tsk!
No-no-no!
Ah-ah-ah!
Tsk-tsk-tsk!

HELLO, MY DARLING

Published. Copyrighted December 5, 1938. Previously registered for copyright as an unpublished song August 3, 1938. Introduced by Genevieve Tobin, Bert Lahr, and Claudette Colbert. Reprised by Colbert (dubbed by Martha Mears).

VERSE (NOT SUNG IN FILM)

Never let it be said that I've missed you,
Never let it be told how you cried.
Never let it be known
Since the last time I kissed you
Something within me has died.
This is a matter of pride.

REFRAIN

I'll forget your tender kiss,
I'll be brave after this.
I'll say "Hello, my darling"
If we should meet again.
You'll forbid the tears to slip,
You'll behave, bite your lip,
And say, "Hello, my darling"
If we should meet again.
If we do meet again,
How can that moment of delight
Be sweet again?
Oh, my love,
Though it's a bitter word,
I know, my love,*
Go, my love,
Please remember not to sigh
Over this last goodbye.
Just say, "Hello, my darling"
If we should meet again,
If we should meet again!

FORGET ME

Registered for copyright as an unpublished song June 4, 1938. Not used in film.

REFRAIN

Forget me, forget me,
Loved one of yesterday,
Forget me!
Don't bring to life the old smile that bored you;
Stop making me recall I adored you.
Forget me, forget me . . .
And should I dream of you,
Don't let me.
Find other arms to fly to,
And I too
Will try to
Forget yesterday's love!

---

* *Originally:*
  Though it's a bitter pill
  I know, my love

HE DIED OF LOVE

Not used in film.

VERSE 1

Read the paper, read the paper,
You'll see all about it in the paper.
They found the body of a man upon the street;
A little knife had made his history complete.
It was murder, it was murder;
The police discovered all the signs.
[spoken] Thief steals dead man's ring. No money
    missing.
[sung] But you can read between the lines.

REFRAIN 1

He died of love, of too much love.
He swore he'd always be mine,
But her kiss was a fine work of art.
But in the morgue,
The dreary morgue,
There lies the light of my life,
With two loves and a knife in his heart.

VERSE 2

Read the paper, read the paper,
There's a murder story in the paper.
They found his body on the street and that was all,
Perhaps the victim of a crazy drunken brawl.
It was murder, it was murder;
The police are searching high and low.
[spoken] Victim notorious gambler. Had dangerous
    enemies.
[sung] But this they'll never, never know.

REFRAIN 2

He died of love, of too much love;
That other woman came by—
What a shame he and I had to part!
But in the morgue,
The dreary morgue,
There lies the light of my life,
With two loves and a knife in his heart.

I'M THE STUPIDEST GIRL IN THE CLASS

Not used in film.

VERSE

I'm not like the other girls at all,
For when I was very, very small,
By an accident, it's said,
I was dropped upon my head;
It must have been a very nasty fall,
For—

REFRAIN 1

Alas, alas,
I'm the stupidest girl in the class.
My hist'ry professor was careful to mention
That though it's not quite an established
    convention
He could give me personal, private attention,
And possibly then I might pass.
I'm the stupidest girl in the class.

REFRAIN 2

Alas, alas,
Just the stupidest girl in the class.
My botany teacher remains after hours
To teach me regarding the plants and the flowers.
Now, why should a man waste his time and his
    powers
On someone as green as the grass?
I'm the stupidest girl in the class.

REFRAIN 3

Alas, alas,
Just the stupidest girl in the class.
Now this is the trinket my art teacher bought me,
And somewhere at home is the candy he brought me
For learning those lessons in art that he taught me.
I also take algebra, Latin, and Greek,
But I cannot remember one rule—
I'm the stupidest girl in the school.
A mule! A fool!*
She's the stupidest, stupidest, stupidest,
    stupidest,
Stupidest girl in the school.

---

* Last three lines sung by chorus of other girls.

STREET SONG

Not used in film.

Come to your window, my love,
And hear my tender song.
Come to your window, my love,
And bring your pennies along.

ST. LOUIS BLUES

Produced by Jeff Lazarus for Paramount Pictures. Released in February 1939. Screenplay by John C. Moffitt and Malcolm S. Boylan, based on an adaptation by Frederich Hazlitt Brennan of a story by Eleanore Griffin and William Rankin. Directed by Raoul Walsh. Cast starred Dorothy Lamour and Lloyd Nolan and featured Tito Guizar, Jerome Cowan, William Frawley, Jessie Ralph, Maxine Sullivan, Hall Johnson Choir, The King's Men, and Matty Malneck and His Orchestra. In addition to W. C. Handy's classic "St. Louis Blues," written in 1914, this score also included "Kinda Lonesome" by Leo Robin, Sam Coslow, and Hoagy Carmichael and "Let's Dream in the Moonlight" by Raoul Walsh and Matty Malneck.

OH, YOU MISSISSIPPI

Music by Burton Lane. Introduced by Hall Johnson Choir.

Oh, Mississippi,
You Mississippi,
Muddy waters all aroun'.
Oh, Mississippi,
Look at what you've been doin'.
Look at Dixie lan' a-layin' in ruin
While you're sweepin' on your way,
On your reckless way.
Don't you hear the darkies pray?
Muddy waters dark and deep,
Why do ya rise up out of bed and go carousin'?
Why do ya get that yeller fever in the spring?
Why are ya sweepin' on your way,
On your reckless way,
Makin' me a homeless thing?
Desolation over the lan'—
Oh, Mississippi

Yo' Mississippi,
Look what you've done!

I GO FOR THAT

Music by Matty Malneck (1903–1981). Published. Copyrighted November 21, 1938. Previously registered for copyright as an unpublished song August 13, 1938. Introduced by the King's Men. Reprised by Dorothy Lamour. Recorded by Dorothy Lamour (Brunswick). Malneck (better known as "Matty") was a successful composer, conductor, violinist, and arranger whose noteworthy songs include "Goody Goody," "I'll Never Be the Same," and "I'm Through with Love."

VERSE (NOT USED IN FILM)

Some people simply love to eat raw fish
And pay high rent and dance on broken glass.
Some people simply love to kill themselves,
And, sad to say, I think I'm in that class, alas!

REFRAIN

Your dopey walk,
Your double talk,
I go for that.
Your corny jokes,
Your dizzy folks,
I go for that.
Your kiss just misses,
Your dancing is rough,
But I love that stuff.
I guess I don't get around quite enough.
You play the uke,
You're from Dubuque,
I go for that.
And furthermore,
I just adore
Your fuzzy hair,
Your vacant stare.
To Mister Cupid I take off my hat;
You can't account for silly taste.
Of all the hearts I could have chased,
I look at you, and ooh,
I go for that,

JUNIOR

Music by Burton Lane. Published. Copyrighted November 21, 1938. Previously registered for copyright as an unpublished song August 31, 1938. Introduced by Dorothy Lamour, The King's Men, and Matty Malneck and His Orchestra. Recorded by Lamour with Jerry Joyce and His Orchestra (Brunswick).

VERSE (NOT USED IN FILM)

Maybe my imagination gets the better of me,
But in your smile my future I can see.
Maybe I won't rule the nation or be noble and
  great,
But in your smile I see my lovely fate;

REFRAIN*

Junior,
Sweet little daydream for two.
You with your arms around Junior,
Me with me arms around you.
That's what I see
Each time your eyes meet mine,
Deep in your eyes that shine
Pictures of us beside our pride,
Junior,
Making an awful to-do.
You feeding oatmeal to Junior,
Me singing love songs to you.
That's all I see,
That fam'ly portrait of
Our love and Junior,
Sweet little daydream for two.

BLUE NIGHTFALL

Music by Burton Lane. Published. Copyrighted December 22, 1938. Previously registered for copyright as an unpublished song August 13, 1938. Introduced by Dorothy Lamour and Lloyd Nolan. Reprised by Lamour. Recorded by Dorothy Lamour (Caliban).

VERSE (NOT USED IN FILM)

Another lonely day is ending;
Blue shadows gather in the sky.
Once more I see the night descending
And greet it with a sigh.

---

* *Lines 5–12 not used in film.*

REFRAIN

Nightfall, blue nightfall above me,
Nightfall, bring someone to love me.
Night wind, so gentle and tender,
Teach him your song of surrender.
Oh, tropical charms, lend us your loveliness,
Then deep in my arms, what can he say but yes?
That's all, blue nightfall above me.
Nightfall, bring me that someone to love me.

THE SONG IN MY HEART IS A RUMBA

Music by Burton Lane. Registered for copyright as an unpublished song August 13, 1938. Originally titled "The Beat of My Heart Is a Rumba." Not used in film.

VERSE

I have listened to trombones in Harlem
And piano concertos in France.
I have heard all the bagpipes in Scotland,
But the music did not bring romance.
I've been dancing to thousands of waltzes,
But they've never made me reminisce.
Oh, I guess I don't care much for music,
But the wonder of wonders is this:

REFRAIN

The song in my heart is a rumba,
It's going clickety-click ta-da-da-da-boom.
The doctor tells me I caught it in a ballroom.
The song in my heart is a rumba,
It's going clickety-click ta-da-da-da-boom,
And I'm a blankety-blank if I know why.
It might be that lady at the Cuban café
That night we were dancing in a very unusual way.
I don't know her name or her number,
But every night when I see her in my slumber,
I hear the song in my heart and it's a rumba!

CAFÉ SOCIETY

Produced by Jeff Lazarus for Paramount Pictures. Released in February 1939. Screenplay by Virginia Van Upp. Directed by Edward H. Griffith. Cast starred Madeleine Carroll, Fred MacMurray, Shirley Ross, and Allyn Joslyn.

KISS ME WITH YOUR EYES

Music by Burton Lane. Published. Copyrighted January 27, 1939. Previously registered for copyright as an unpublished song November 29, 1938. Introduced by Shirley Ross.

VERSE (NOT USED IN FILM)

They kiss so madly,
They sigh so sadly,
Lovers, lovers,
Showing the world they care.
They dance so closely
That people stare,
So, my darling,
Let's be that diff'rent pair.

REFRAIN

Kiss me with your eyes, and I'll know you love me.
Kiss me with your eyes, a secret embrace.
No need to hold my hand or to speak,
Just that look that leaves me weak.
Thrill me with your glance,
I'll know you've caressed me,
Need we shout romance all over the place?
Let's keep this one affair in disguise,
Darling, kiss me with your eyes.

PARK AVENUE GIMP

Music by Leo Shuken (1906–1976). Registered for copyright as an unpublished song February 21, 1939. Previously registered for copyright with lyrics by Jock Rock, December 30, 1938. Danced by Madeleine Carroll and Allyn Joslyn. Composer Shuken wrote many film and television scores. He won an Academy Award in 1939 for *Stagecoach*.

VERSE

There's something new
In the book of etiquette now.
It got there
I don't know how,
But—

REFRAIN

You'll try it, as sure's you're born!
You'll try it, from dark till dawn!
You're gonna join the line and limp,
It's the Park Avenue Gimp!
You'll get it, of course, of course,
You'll bet it's a charley horse.
You'll holler for a tacit timp
And the Park Avenue Gimp.
Must dress—white tie,
You can't get in unless your brow is high.
Must dress—to try
The latest passion of the world of fashion!
You'll love it, oh yessiree,
Above it though you may be—
You're gonna give your style a crimp
With the Park Avenue Gimp!

SOME LIKE IT HOT

Produced by William C. Thomas for Paramount Pictures. Released in May 1939. Screenplay by Lewis R. Foster and Wilkie C. Mahoney based on the play *The Great Magoo* by Ben Hecht and Gene Fowler. Directed by George Archainbaud. Cast featured Bob Hope, Shirley Ross, Una Merkel, Rufus Davis, William "Tiny" Whitt, Harry Barris, and the Gene Krupa Band.

SOME LIKE IT HOT

Music by Gene Krupa (1909–1973) and Remo Biondi (1905–1981). Published. Copyrighted April 21, 1939. Previously registered for copyright as an unpublished song March 3, 1939. Introduced by Rufus Davis, William "Tiny" Whitt, Harry Barris, and the Gene Krupa Band. Reprised by Shirley Ross. Recordings include Red Norvo (Vocalion) and Mel Tormé (Verve). Krupa gained fame as Benny Goodman's drummer from 1935 to 1938 and went on to lead his own big band. Biondi was a guitarist and violinist who appeared on many Chicago blues and jazz records.

VERSE (NOT USED IN FILM)

I believe in reincarnation;
When a thing's really good it cannot die.
I believe in hot swingcopation,
And for your information here is why:

REFRAIN

Long ago swung a young gorilla
Through the trees—what a killa-dilla!
Ever since, thanks to that gorilla,
Some like it hot.
Later on, fiddled Mister Nero
Down in Rome, he was quite a hero,
Ever since, thanks to Mister Nero,
Some like it hot.
When a rooster first went peck-peck,
The community bent his neck,
But did rhythm perish with him?
No, no, no, no, no, I should say not.
Ev'rywhere you can find survivors,
Nowadays people call them jivers—
Thanks to those senders and arrivers,
Some like it hot.

THE LADY'S IN LOVE WITH YOU

Music by Burton Lane. Published. Copyrighted March 30, 1939. Previously registered for copyright as an unpublished song January 24, 1939. Introduced by Bob Hope and Shirley Ross with the Gene Krupa Band. Hope and Ross recorded the song (Decca) as did Krupa, vocal by Irene Daye (Brunswick). The best-selling recording, number two in the popular music charts, was by Glenn Miller and His Orchestra, vocal by Tex Beneke (Bluebird). Other leading recordings by Bob Crosby and His Orchestra (Decca); Benny Goodman and His Orchestra (Victor); Doris Day (Columbia); Mel Tormé (Atlantic); and Sarah Vaughan (Roulette).

VERSE (NOT USED IN FILM)

Have you ever seen the dawn of love?
Little things that mean the dawn of love?
Why wait for her to say that she adores you?
Long before the first kiss,
Have you ever seen this?

REFRAIN 1

HOPE: If there's a gleam in her eye
ROSS: Each time she straightens your tie,

HOPE: You'll know the lady's in love with you.
    If she can dress for a date
ROSS: Without that waiting you hate,
    It means the lady's in love with you.
HOPE: And when your friends ask you over to
        join their table,
    But she picks that faraway booth for two,
    Well, sir, here's just how it stands:
    You've got romance on your hands,
    Because the lady's in love with you.

REFRAIN 2 (SECOND STANZA NOT USED IN FILM)

HOPE: If you've been traveling by plane
ROSS: And she says, "Please take the train,"
HOPE: Betcha three to one the lady's in love
        with you.*
ROSS: And if she writes you every day
HOPE: Though she hasn't got a darn thing to say,
ROSS: You're a cinch, the lady's in love.
    How true!
    And if she phones, but she doesn't reverse
        the charges,
    Like all kinds of lady friends often do.
    Well, sir, here's just how it stands:
    You've got romance on your hands,
    Because the lady's in love with you.

REFRAIN 3 (NOT USED IN FILM)

If she goes deaf, dumb, and blind
While you've got things on your mind,
You'll know the lady's in love with you.
If she has met your old flames
And she remembers their names,
It means the lady's in love with you.
And Sunday night when you take her to that
    movie,
And she says, "The balcony seats will do,"
Well, sir, here's just how it stands:
You've got romance on your hands,
Because the lady's in love with you.†

REFRAIN 4†

If you've been traveling by plane
And she begs you to please take the train,
Betcha three to one the lady's in love with you.
How true!
And if she wires you each day
Though there isn't a darn thing to say,
It's a cinch the little lady's in love with you.

---

* Sheet music version reads:
    You'll know the lady's in love with you.

† First four lines not used in film.

HOPE: And Sunday night when you take her to see
        that movie—
    [spoken] Two loges, please.
ROSS: [spoken] Darling, the balcony seats will do.
HOPE: [sung] Well, sir, that's just how they act.
ROSS: You might as well face the fact.
BOTH: Yes sir, the lady's in love with you.

WHODUNIT?

Music by Hoagy Carmichael. Registered for copyright as an unpublished song January 24, 1939. Not used in film.

VERSE

Oh, you can't fool an eagle eye like me.
No you can't, no you can't.
Don't you dare say you're keeping company
With someone's aunt,
Or maybe General Grant.

REFRAIN

You've got a great big box of candy there,
And here's a new dent in my favorite chair.
What a blow! I'd like to know
Whodunit?
You've got a bunch of posies wet with dew,
And here's a card that says: "I'm crazy for you."
'Twasn't me! I'd like to see
Whodunit?
There's a blue sedan outside
Where'd you get the key to run it?
Honey, I'm not satisfied
That you went to the movies and won it!
The other night you said,
"I love you, Jake"—
The trouble is my name is Joe.
Whodunit? Doggonit!
Whodunit? I'd like to know!

Female version

REFRAIN

You've got a whiff of Number Five Chanel*
And there's a new pink powder on your lapel.
What a blow! I'd like to know
Whodunit?
You get a shave and shoeshine every day,

---

* Alternate line:
    You've got a strange gardenia kind of smell

It wasn't Em'ly Post that got you that way.*
Pardon me! I'd like to see
Whodunit?
There's a program from a show
And a pair of opera glasses.
Honey, I don't care to know
That a friend of the family had passes!
The other night you said,
"I love you, Jane"—
The trouble is my name is Flo.
Whodunit? Dawgonit!
Whodunit? I'd love to know!

THE GRACIE ALLEN MURDER CASE

Produced by George Arthur for Paramount Pictures. Released in June 1939. Screenplay by Nat Perrin based on the novel *The Gracie Allen Murder Case* by S. S. Van Dine. Directed by Alfred E. Green. Cast featured Gracie Allen, Warren William, Ellen Drew, and Kent Taylor.

SNUG AS A BUG IN A RUG

Music by Matty Malneck. Published. Copyrighted March 24, 1939. Previously registered for copyright as an unpublished song February 11, 1939. Introduced by Gracie Allen. Recordings include Artie Shaw and His Orchestra, vocal by Tony Pastor (Bluebird).

VERSE (NOT SUNG IN FILM)

Never in all my days
Have I found a pair of arms so ideal.
What is that well-known phrase
That describes the way your arms make me feel?

REFRAIN

Snug as a bug in a rug,
Whenever you hold me tight.
Cozy and warm
On the chilliest night.
Snug as a bug in a rug
Whenever I feel your kiss.

---

* Alternate line:
    It isn't this romance that got you that way.

Talk about home,
Home was never like this.
First your arms come stealing,
And my heart goes on a roller coaster;
Then I get that feeling
Like a little piece of toast in a toaster.
My, but my life would be cold
Without your delicious hug
Keeping me snug
As a bug in a rug.

HERITAGE OF THE DESERT

Produced by Harry Sherman for Paramount Pictures. Released in June 1939. Music by Victor Young. Screenplay by Norman Houston and Harrison Jacobs from the novel by Zane Grey. Directed by Lesley Selander. Cast featured Donald Woods and Evelyn Venable.

HERE'S A HEART

Music by Victor Young (1900–1956). Registered for copyright as an unpublished song, March 3, 1939. Not used in film. The multitalented Young won an Academy Award posthumously for his score for *Around the World in Eighty Days* (1956). His best-known songs include "Sweet Sue," "When I Fall in Love," and "My Foolish Heart."

VERSE

I've never begged you to love me,
Held your hand, whispered low.
You've always seemed above me;
Still I know,
Yes, I know:

REFRAIN

Here's a heart and there's a heart,
Your lonely heart and mine.
Here's a dream and there's a dream,
The very same design.
If I should call you "darling,"
Some blue night, by moonlight,
I know you'd answer "darling,"
I know you'd hold me tight.
For you've that look and I've that look

That tells a tale so true:
That there's a heart for me
And here's a heart for you.

MAN ABOUT TOWN

Produced by Arthur Hornblow for Paramount Pictures. Released in June 1939. Screenplay by Morrie Ryskind, based on a story by Ryskind, Allan Scott, and Z. Myers. Directed by Mark Sandrich. Cast starred Jack Benny, Dorothy Lamour, and Edward Arnold and featured Binnie Barnes, Phil Harris, Betty Grable, Monty Woolley, Eddie "Rochester" Anderson, and Matty Malneck and His Orchestra.

THAT SENTIMENTAL SANDWICH

Music by Frederick Hollander. Published. Copyrighted March 20, 1939. Previously registered for copyright as an unpublished song March 1, 1939. Introduced by Dorothy Lamour, with Phil Harris and Eddie "Rochester" Anderson. Recorded by Dorothy Lamour (Brunswick).

VERSE (NOT SUNG IN FILM)

You haven't even touched your Lobster Newburg,
I haven't even sipped my dry champagne.
It isn't loss of appetite,
But somehow on this lovely night
We're suff'ring a tender and nostalgic pain.

REFRAIN 1

LAMOUR: I'm hungry for something,
But it seems so far away—
That sentimental sandwich
That we shared one day.
You're hungry for something,
Nothing fancy, nothing new—
One sentimental sandwich
Coming up, for two.
Gee! We were poor,
And though fate has changed our scenery,
Gee! The allure
Of that broken-down old beanery!
We're hungry for something,
Not for lobster, not for wine—
That sentimental sandwich
That was yours and mine.

REFRAIN 2

LAMOUR: [*spoken*] You know, I'm hungry for
something . . . like one of those
dinners at the Ritz.
HARRIS: Two coffees and one sandwich—
We've only got two bits.
I'm hungry for something,
A big filet mignon aux champignons,
and a bit of Escoffier too . . .
ROCHESTER: One ham on white.
ORDER COOK: Coming up!
HARRIS: Look, cut it in half, it's for two.
LAMOUR: [*sung*] Broke though we are, there's
a charm that sees us through,
dear.
HARRIS: Broke though we are, I can feast my
eyes on you, dear.
LAMOUR: [*spoken*] Someday we'll remember—
HARRIS: When we're wealthy—
LAMOUR: And doing fine—
[*sung*] That sentimental sandwich
That was yours and mine!

[LAMOUR *reprises last eight lines of refrain 1.*]

FIDGETY JOE

Music by Matty Malneck. Published. Copyrighted March 30, 1939. Previously registered for copyright as an unpublished song February 23, 1939. Introduced by Betty Grable, Phil Harris, and Matty Malneck and His Orchestra.

VERSE

There's a man that hangs around
The bandstand all night long.
He's wacky, he's goofy, he's dizzy;
He goes slightly crazy
When they play his fav'rite song.
Who is he, I ask you,
Who is he?

REFRAIN

Fidgety Joe,
He doesn't care to dance or sing,
But when those swing cats start to swing,
He's beating out the rhythm blow by blow.
That's Fidgety Joe.
He shakes his head from side to side
When Mister Trumpet takes a ride;
Don't ask him what he's doing,

He don't know.
He says music sends him,
Sends him out of his head,
But there's nothing that sends him
Home to bed.
He's the whole show.
He can't read notes,
He's not that smart,
But he knows ev'ry lick by heart,
The Paganini* of the second row.
There he sits,
Throwing fits
Over all the latest hits,
Whoa-ho, Fidgety Joe.

STRANGE ENCHANTMENT

Music by Frederick Hollander. Published. Copyrighted March 24, 1939. Previously registered for copyright as an unpublished song January 24, 1939. Introduced by Dorothy Lamour. Recordings include Lamour with Lou Bring and His Orchestra. (Brunswick) and Vic Damone (Capitol).

VERSE (NOT USED IN FILM)

How can I but remember this delight
Wherever I go,
Whatever I do?
The magic of this oriental night and you?

REFRAIN

Strange enchantment fills the moonrise;
There's a breeze like sandalwood and wine.
Strange enchantment lies in your eyes,
Saying, "Please, oh please, tonight be mine."
When the moon has gone
In the blue dawn
And we go wandering apart,
Darling, I'll be dreaming of this moment
With a strange enchantment in my heart.

---
* *Alternately:*
  Toscanini or great Stokowski

MAN ABOUT TOWN

Music by Frederick Hollander. Published. Copyright April 24, 1939. Previously registered for copyright as an unpublished song March 1, 1939. Not used in film.

VERSE

You're the kind that flits
From El Morocco to the Ritz,
My busy friend,
And you never seem
To spare a moment for a dream,
My busy friend—
And it'll get you in the end!

REFRAIN

Man about town,
Dapper and smart,
Where do you hide your heart?
Man about town,
Neath your white tie
Is there a real true guy?
Whom do you love, if any?
You've been seen out at the races
And the op'ra with so very many.
Man about town,
Playing your part,
Where do you hide your heart?

PETTY GIRL ROUTINE

Music by Frederick Hollander. Intended for Betty Grable and girls. Not used in film. George Petty was a preeminent creator of risqué "girlie" illustrations. His voluptuous airbrushed style typically featured buxom young girls in coy but highly suggestive poses and settings.

GRABLE: Gentlemen, gentlemen, I thank you so much
For the fanfare, applause, and confetti.
Gentlemen, gentlemen, I give you the works
Of that brilliant young artist—George Petty!
Up in Park Avenue, down on the farm,
Doing the eyes of the nation such harm,
That subtle designer of feminine charm—

George Petty!
He paints, he paints,
And he doesn't exactly paint saints.
We're not real live creatures,
Just magazine features.
FIRST GIRL: I haven't had any complaints.
GRABLE: We're flat, yes, flat,
For we're just paper dolls,
And that's that.
Yet somehow or other,
We shock your grandmother.
SECOND GIRL: Well, what are you staring at?

[*Instrumental passage*]

GRABLE: Be kind, be kind,
Mister Petty is really refined.
THIRD GIRL: So if you grow dreamy,
Whenever you see me,
I'm sure that it's all in your mind.
ALL GIRLS: Gentlemen, gentlemen, we are the art
Upon which your fancy may roam;
But gentlemen, gentlemen, now we must part—
GRABLE: Hello, Mother, I'll be right home.

A LOVE LETTER

Music by Frederick Hollander. Not used in film.

REFRAIN

I adore you,
I simply adore you, Missus Brown—
You're married, yes, married
And nicely settled down.
But darling, I long for your kiss,
Though your children might frown upon this—
I beseech you,
If this note should reach you, Missus Brown,
Would you dare,
Could we share,
Some weekend out of town?
Oh, darling, please don't let me down—
Yours forever, Mister Brown.

INVITATION TO HAPPINESS

A Paramount Picture produced by Wesley Ruggles. Released in June 1939. Screenplay by Claude Binyon, based on a story by Mark Jerome. Directed by Wesley Ruggles. Cast starred Irene Dunne and Fred MacMurray, and featured Charles Ruggles, Billy Cook, William Collier, Sr., Eddie Hogan, and Marion Martin.

INVITATION TO HAPPINESS

Music by Frederick Hollander. Registered for copyright as an unpublished song March 21, 1939. Not used in film.

Here's an invitation to happiness
Any fool could find.
Don't you see the dreamy look?
Darling, are you blind?

Here's an invitation to happiness,
Yet you pass it by.
This is not a yawn, my love;
This is a sigh.

I suppose while we dance I could kiss you;
Reach for your hand when we dine.
But I'd rather be careful and kiss you
With these eyes of mine.

Here's an invitation to happiness
In my tender glance;
Speaking for a foolish heart
Full of romance.

BEAU GESTE

Produced by William A. Wellman for Paramount Pictures. Released in August 1939. Screenplay by Robert Carson, based on the novel by Percival Christopher Wren. Directed by William A. Wellman. Cast featured Gary Cooper, Ray Milland, and Robert Preston.

THE LEGIONNAIRE'S SONG

Special lyrics by Loesser. Music from "Foreign Legion March" by Troy Sanders (1901–1959). Introduced by male ensemble. Sanders was active in Hollywood as an arranger and music director.

VERSE 1 (NOT USED IN FILM)

Foe, beware,
Our song is in the air,
We are the law of the region.
One for all,
We'll fight until we fall,
Brave, loyal men of the Legion.

REFRAIN

For France we march together,
For France, beneath Sahara's sky.
For France, no matter whether
We live or we die.

VERSE 2 (NOT USED IN FILM)

Noble birth
Or beggars of the earth,
Men of disgrace and of glory,
Low or great,
We share an equal fate,
No legionnaire tells his story.

ISLAND OF LOST MEN

Produced by Eugene Zukor for Paramount Pictures. Released in August 1939. Screenplay by William R. Lipman and Horace McCoy based on the play *Hangman's Whip* by Norman Reilly Raine and Frank Butler. Directed by Kurt Neumann. Cast featured Anna May Wong, J. Carrol Naish, Anthony Quinn, Eric Blore, and Broderick Crawford.

MUSIC ON THE SHORE

Music by Frederick Hollander. Published. Copyrighted June 27, 1939. Introduced by Anna May Wong.

VERSE (NOT USED IN FILM)

Somewhere in the back of my mind I see
Just the kind of jumping-off place for me.

REFRAIN

With a beach for my bed
And the palms overhead
And the waves making music on the shore.
Leave me there, leave me there,
Getting sand in my hair,
Watching boats drifting by from Singapore.
I'll leave this crazy world to fight things out,
And I'll never shout "What's the score?"*
With a beach for my bed
And the palms overhead
And the waves making music on the shore.

THE STAR MAKER

Produced by Charles R. Rogers for Paramount Pictures. Released in August 1939. Screenplay by Arthur Caesar, Frank Butler, and Don Hartman from a story by Arthur Caesar and William A. Pierce. Directed by Roy Del Ruth. Cast featured Bing Crosby, Louise Campbell, Linda Ware, Ned Sparks, and Walter Damrosch and the Los Angeles Philharmonic Orchestra.

---

* *Alternate lyric for lines 10 and 11 of refrain:*
I'll trade this crazy world of storm and strife
For a lazy life evermore

VALSE DES FLEURS

Special lyrics by Frank Loesser to Tchaikovsky's "Waltz of the Flowers" from his ballet *The Nutcracker*. Introduced by Linda Ware with Walter Damrosch conducting the Los Angeles Philharmonic Orchestra. Lyrics were transcribed from film soundtrack. Missing lyrics indicated by ellipses.

Why is my heart aglow?
Why is my heart ever dancing?
Why is everything
Like a breath of spring
In a garden so entrancing?
Gone is the winter snow,
Gone are the raindrops of April.
All the world is in love once again.
Summer breezes playing,
Flowers gently swaying,
Hear them softly saying,
"Love is yours and love is mine."
Ah-ah-ah-ah etc.
All too soon there will be
Autumn leaves a-falling.
Ah, but this lovely moment of June
I'll always be recalling.
Ah-ah-ah-ah etc.
Melody in the air,
Roses in bloom everywhere
Ah-ah-ah-ah etc.
Over and over and over
The flowers are calling
To us [. . .]
Ah-ah-ah-ah etc.

HAWAIIAN NIGHTS

Produced by Max H. Golden for Universal Pictures. Released in September 1939. Screenplay by Charles Grayson and Lee Loeb, based on an original story by John Grey. Directed by Albert S. Rogell. Cast featured Johnny Downs, Mary Carlisle, Constance Moore, Eddie Quillan, and Princess Luana.

HAWAII SANG ME TO SLEEP

Music by Matty Malneck. Published. Copyrighted August 23, 1939. Introduced by Princess Luana.

VERSE

Tenderly stole the night over the island shore,
Bringing its tropic charm into my heart.
It seemed that you and I were no longer apart.

REFRAIN

Oh, the warm wind blew and Hawaii sang me to
   sleep;
A guitar or two, making mem'ries always to keep.
Then the sea kissed the sand,
And that lullaby so gentle and deep
Made me dream of you,
When Hawaii sang me to sleep.

THEN I WROTE THE MINUET IN G

Special lyrics by Frank Loesser to the Minuet in G by Ludwig van Beethoven. Adaptation by Matty Malneck. Published. Copyrighted August 23, 1939. Introduced by Mary Carlisle, Johnny Downs, Milton DeLugg, Eddie Quillan, and Matty Malneck and His Orchestra.

VERSE

I was a cad,
My ways were bad,
I never knew what kind of talent I had.

REFRAIN

Then I wrote the Minuet in G,
What's the words? Let me see,
Yes, I wrote the Minuet in G,
And Beethoven helped me pick the key.
Now you've heard the Minuet in G,
Yes, of course, certainly,
Well, I wrote the Minuet in G,
And my mother's very proud of me.
I was a chambermaid, I was a ribbon clerk,*
And in the summertime I was a soda jerk,
But now I'm a diff'rent kind—
What a terrific mind!
For I wrote the Minuet in G
That was my Reverie,
Now I'm working on his Symphony,
Pardon me—
Pardon me.

----
* *Alternate line for male voice:*
   I was a butcher boy, I was a groc'ry clerk,

HEY, GOOD-LOOKING

Music by Matty Malneck. Published. Copyrighted August 23, 1939. Introduced by Mary Carlisle and Matty Malneck and His Orchestra.

VERSE

Once there was a musician,
And his love life was just a long intermission,
'Cause he never knew the proper thing to say.
Oh, that lonely musician,
He could play hot sax but was doomed to perdition
By the fact that he would greet strange ladies this
   way:

REFRAIN

Hey, good-looking,
You with the dental plates,
Hey, good-looking,
Who's booking all your dates?
Hey, good-looking,
You with the curly nose,
Hey, good-looking, what goes?
Are you young?
Are you old?
Are you single?
Does your money fold
Or does it jingle?
Do you mingle?
Hey, good-looking,
You with the purple hair.
Hey, good-looking,
What's cooking over there?

$1,000 A TOUCHDOWN

Produced by William C. Thomas for Paramount Pictures. Released in October 1939. Story and screenplay by Delmar Daves. Directed by James Hogan. Cast starred Joe E. Brown and Martha Raye and featured Eric Blore, Susan Hayward, Tom Dugan, and Dewey Robinson.

FIGHT ON FOR MADISON

Music by Victor Young. Introduced by Martha Raye and ensemble.

Fight on for Madison,
Grit your teeth and face the foe.
Brother, let 'em know*
You'll fight on for Madison.
Let them know their doom is sealed,
Chase 'em down the field.
We're off, we're off to victory
For the good old pink and blue,
Woo! Woo!
Fight on for Madison,
And Madison will fight for you.
Who does your laundry?†
Madison will fight for you.

DESTRY RIDES AGAIN

Produced by Joseph Pasternak for Universal Pictures. Released in November 1939. Screenplay by Felix Jackson, Gertrude Purcell, and Henry Myers from the novel by Max Brand. Directed by George Marshall. Cast featured Marlene Dietrich, James Stewart, Mischa Auer, Charles Winninger, Brian Donlevy, and Una Merkel.

LITTLE JOE, THE WRANGLER

Lyrics for anonymous Western song revised by Frank Loesser. Music arranged by Frederick Hollander. Published. Copyrighted December 11, 1939. Introduced by Marlene Dietrich, Charles Winninger, and ensemble. Reprised at the end of the film by unidentified children.

VERSE

ENSEMBLE: It was Little Joe the Wrangler,
He will wrangle nevermore,

---

* Original line:
  Let the sissies know

† Original line:
  Are we from hunger?

For his days with the roundup they
are o'er.
'Twas a year ago last April when he
rode up to our camp,
Just a little Texas stray and nothin' more.

REFRAIN

DIETRICH: Little Joe.
ENSEMBLE: Little Joe.
DIETRICH: Little Joe.
ENSEMBLE: Little Joe.
DIETRICH: Oh, whatever become of him, I
don't know.
ENSEMBLE: She don't know.
DIETRICH: Oh, he sure did like his liquor,
And it would have got his ticker,
But the sheriff got him quicker—*
Eeeeeeeyuhoooo!

DIETRICH: Little Joe.
ENSEMBLE: Little Joe.
DIETRICH: Little Joe.
ENSEMBLE: Little Joe.
DIETRICH: Oh, wherever his body lies, I
don't know.
ENSEMBLE: She don't know.
DIETRICH: When the yellow moon was beamin'
He could wrangle like a demon,
And you'd always hear him screamin'
Eeeeeeeyuhoooo!

DIETRICH: Little Joe.
ENSEMBLE: Little Joe.
DIETRICH: Little Joe.
ENSEMBLE: Little Joe.
DIETRICH: Oh, wherever his body lies, I
don't know.
ENSEMBLE: She don't know.
DIETRICH: Oh, whatever he's doing now, I
don't know.
He had women by the dozens
And he swore they was his cousins
Till he met up with their husbands—
Eeeeeeeyuhoooo!

REPRISE

WINNINGER: Little Joe,
Little Joe.
Whatever happened to him, I
don't know.
But I sure do like my liquor,
But I see you got it quicker,

---

* Sheet music version:
  But the sheriff acted quicker

And I hope it makes you sick, you
buffalo.

UNUSED LYRICS

DIETRICH: Little Joe.
ENSEMBLE: Little Joe.
DIETRICH: Little Joe.
ENSEMBLE: Little Joe.
DIETRICH: Oh, wherever his body lies, I
don't know.
ENSEMBLE: She don't know.
Oh, from place to place he floated
Till he got hisself railroaded
For them loaded dice he toted—
Eeeeeeeyuhoooo!

YOU'VE GOT THAT LOOK (THAT LEAVES ME WEAK!)

Music by Frederick Hollander. Published. Copyrighted December 8, 1939. Introduced by Marlene Dietrich. Song also used in Universal Pictures' *Burma Convoy* (1941).

VERSE*

All I do is dine with them
And split a pint of wine with them,
Respectable as can be.
Yet here's what they say to me:

REFRAIN

You've got that look,
That look that leaves me weak,
You with your eyes-across-the-table technique.
You've got that look,
That look between the lines,
You with your let's-get-more-than-friendly designs.
I should be brave and say
Let's have no more of it.
But oh, what's the use when you know I love it?!
You'll only kill my will before I speak.
So turn on that low left hook,
That look that leaves me weak.

---

* Sheet music version:
  All I do is dine with you
  And split a pint of wine with you,
  Respectable as can be.
  Yet here's what you do to me.

THE BOYS IN THE BACKROOM

Music by Frederick Hollander. Published. Copyrighted December 11, 1939. Introduced by Marlene Dietrich.

VERSE

See what the boys in the backroom will have,
And tell them I'm having the same.
Go see what the boys in the backroom will have,
And give them the poison they name.

REFRAIN

And when I die,
Don't spend my money on flowers
Or my pictures in a frame.
Just see what the boys in the backroom will have,
And tell them I sighed
And tell them I cried
And tell them I died of the same!

And when I die,
Don't buy a casket of silver
With the candles all aflame.
Just see what the boys in the backroom will have,
And tell them I sighed
And tell them I cried
And tell them I died of the same!

And when I die,
Don't pay the preacher for speaking
Of my glory and my fame.
Just see what the boys in the backroom will have,
And tell them I sighed
And tell them I cried
And tell them I died of the same!

THE LLANO KID

Produced by Harry Sherman for Paramount Pictures. Released in December 1939. Screenplay by Wanda Tuchock, after O. Henry's story "A Double-Dyed Deceiver." Directed by Edward D. Venturini. Cast starred Tito Guizar and featured Gale Sondergaard, Alan Mowbray, and Jane (also Jan) Clayton.

EL HUAPANGO

Music by Troy Sanders. Possibly co-composed with Ralph Rainger and James J. Reina (no dates or other information known). Introduced by Tito Guizar. First and last stanzas not sung in film.

The dove is so lovely in flight
As she looks for a place to alight.
And her song is a song of delight,
But she isn't exactly polite—
Oh, the dove, oh, the dove
Is a very remarkable bird.

The gambler is no man of danger,
For he's only a small-time conniver,
He tries to take over a stranger,
But he complains when he loses a fiver—*
Oh, the gambler, the gambler
Is a very remarkable man,
Ay-yi-yi-yi, is a very remarkable man.

The girl from the dance hall is nice,
And of beauty and charm she has plenty.
See that faraway look in her eyes?
Well, she's dreaming of when she was twenty—
Dancing lady, dancing lady,
She's a very remarkable girl,
Muchacha a que sabe querer
Ay-yi-yi-yi.

The sheriff's the man of high station,
Though a little bit big in the figger;
He's all full of fast conversation,
Though he's not very quick on the trigger—
Oh, the sheriff, the sheriff
Is a very remarkable man.

The bartender's life is a pity,
For his own drinks someday will destroy him.
Oh, he's ever so jolly and witty,
But you've got to be drunk to enjoy him—
The bartender, the bartender
Is a very remarkable man.

* Original line:
  But he squawks when he loses a fiver—

POSADA

Special lyrics by Frank Loesser to traditional Mexican folk song. Introduced by Jane Clayton and Tito Guizar.

CLAYTON: Pilgrims are we and we come to your door.
  Please give us lodgings, we humbly implore.
  Long have we traveled our tortuous way—
  Open the door and tonight let us stay.
GUIZAR: Strangers, I welcome you not in my home,
  So on your way I command you to roam.
  I have no lodgings or shelter for you.
  My door is bolted and you may not pass through.

  Ah, but this woman is in a sad plight.*
  She has no more strength to journey tonight.
  Once more we beg you to let us within,
  Journeying on for nine days he and I have been.

  This is no tavern, you may not remain—
  Take her along on her travels again.
  I cannot shelter you even one day.
  I am no innkeeper, so be on your way.

MALE VOICE: Open the portals and let this woman enter—
  She is a queen and heaven has sent her.
  Open the door—she is Mary, none other—
  She is to be the Savior's holy mother.
GUIZAR: Mary and Joseph, I knew you not,
  Wandering here to this desolate spot.
  Enter, poor pilgrims, to my humble home—
  Mary and Joseph, no more will you roam.
CHORUS: Enter, pilgrims, poor tired pilgrims,
  Come to my fireside—it will be my heart's delight.
  Enter, pilgrims, holy pilgrims—
  Come to my fireside and remain here for the night.

* Lines 9–16 not sung in film.

STARRY EYES

Music by Troy Sanders and James J. Reina. Used instrumentally only.

VERSE

Ah, but it's lovely to wander
On such a beautiful night,
Knowing that somewhere out yonder
Is waiting my heart's delight.

REFRAIN

Starry eyes,
Oh, summer evening with the starry eyes,
Smile down on me,
Until my lover comes along.*
Angels there,
If there are really any angels there,
Watch over me
Until I hear her tender song,
Until I hear her tender song,
Until I see her
Starry eyes,
And then I'm sure I'll get along
Without the beauty of the skies—
In the meantime,
Starry eyes,
Oh, summer evening with the starry eyes,
Watch over me
Until my lover comes along,*
Until I see her starry eyes,
Until I hear her tender song.

THE GREAT VICTOR HERBERT

Produced by Andrew L. Stone for Paramount Pictures. Released in December 1939. Screenplay by Russel Crouse and Robert Lively, from a story by Lively and Stone. Directed by Andrew L. Stone. Cast featured Allan Jones, Mary Martin, Walter Connolly (as Victor Herbert), Lee Bowman, Susanna Foster, and Jerome Cowan. This fictionalized period love story (which featured many Victor Herbert songs but few details of his life), was Mary Martin's first starring film role.

---

* Alternate line:
    Until my loved one comes along

HAPPY DAY

Lyrics by Frank Loesser and Phil Boutelje (1895–1979). Based on "Punchinello" by Victor Herbert. Originally titled "Happy Days." Introduced by ensemble. Boutelje was a pianist and arranger for the Paul Whiteman Orchestra. Later he was a music director for Paramount and United Artists.

VERSE (NOT SUNG IN FILM)

Happy day, happy day, happy day
To you, good fellow, everlasting
Happiness and health—
May all your little troubles
Vanish in the air like bubbles.
Happy day, happy day, happy day—
May fairest weather be with you until eternity,
All the very best we drink to
Happiness and health to you.

REFRAIN

Bottoms up, bottoms up, bottoms up,
Raise your glasses high
And we will toast His Royal Highness—
Bottoms up, bottoms up, bottoms up
To a fellow artist
Whom we love for all his fineness—
Greet him with a Hallelujah Chorus,
There's a night of revelry before us.
Let the party ring with laughter,
Never mind the morning after.
La, la, la, la, la
La, la, la, la, la, la, la, la.*
DUET: ⎡For you—
    ⎢Happy day!
    ⎣Ah! To you.
    ⎡To you—
    ⎢Happy day!
    ⎣Happy, happy birthday.
Happy day, happy day, happy day,
In celebration and congratulations once again.
Hail to you,
Hail to you†
Happy day, happy day, happy day—
May fairest weather be with you until eternity.
So now may the future hold in store
Each happy day forevermore.

---

* Lines not sung in film:
    While the music plays,
    Keep drinking to his happy days.

† Lines not sung in film:
    May all your little troubles
    Vanish in the air like bubbles

WONDERFUL DREAMS

Lyrics by Frank Loesser and Phil Boutelje. Based on melody "Yesterthoughts" by Victor Herbert. Introduced by Mary Martin and Allan Jones. Originally titled "Beautiful Dreams."

MARTIN: Wonderful dreams*
    I dream each day,
    Wond'ring if they'll come true.
    Wonderful dreams*
    That seem to say,
    "Do you dream too?"
JONES: My heart is longing
    For that wonderful hour—
MARTIN: When in your arms
    I'll hear you say—
BOTH: I love you.

YOU ARE BEAUTIFUL

Lyrics by Frank Loesser and Phil Boutelje. Based on melody "Al Fresco" by Victor Herbert. Introduced by Mary Martin.

So he told me I was beautiful,
Yes, he told me I was beautiful.
Was it romance when he tried to kiss my hand,
Or was he just appraising diamonds?
But he said, "You are so lovely, dear,"†
As he gazed upon my lavaliere.
Now my diamonds all are gone—and so is he—
He writes to me—that I am beautiful.‡

---

* Original line:
    Beautiful dreams

† Originally:
    Anyway—he told me, "You are lovely, dear,"

‡ Lines 7–8 originally:
    Though my diamonds are all gone—and so is he—
    He writes from jail—that I am beautiful.

MISCELLANEOUS SONGS OF 1939

IF I'D NEVER BEEN IN LOVE BEFORE

Music by Ted Fiorito (1900–1971). Typed lyric from Paramount censorship copy dated February 22, 1939. Fiorito, a performer, composer, and conductor, co-wrote "Toot, Toot, Tootsie, Goodbye" and "No, No, Nora."

VERSE

I've been around,
Yes, I've been around.
And many's the fly-by-night romance
I've found.
And every one has taught me something new—
That's why I'm telling this to you:

REFRAIN

If I'd never been in love before,
How could I waltz you like I waltz you round this
     floor?
If I'd never been in love last year,
How could I whisper like I whisper in your ear?
So don't you worry and cry
About affairs of my past.
You should be glad you're not my first
But my last—my very last.
'Cause if I'd never been in love before,
How could I tell it's you for me for evermore?

WHEN YOU'RE DRESSED IN BLUE

Music by Ted Fiorito. Typed lyric from Paramount censorship copy dated February 22, 1939.

REFRAIN

My love, I love you best
When you're dressed in blue.
My dream, you're so supreme
When you're dressed in blue.
When I met you, that color of heaven you wore,
Never been so close to heaven before.

And so I love you best
When you're dressed that way,
The way I found you on that beautiful day.
Though you're charming, quite charming
In gray or green, it's true,
My love, I love you best
When you're dressed in blue.

FRAGRANT NIGHT

Music by Louis Alter (1902–1980). Registered for copyright as an unpublished song March 31, 1939. Alter was accompanist to Nora Bayes, Irene Bordoni, and Helen Morgan, among others. In addition to his hit "Dolores" with Loesser (page 68), Alter wrote the instrumental "Manhattan Serenade."

VERSE

If you could only come and share
This intoxicating, lilac-scented air!
It's so hard to bear alone, alone,
The lilac-scented air,
Sweet atmosphere that once was all our own.

REFRAIN

Fragrant night,
It was such a very fragrant night.
There was magic in the breeze on high,
And you and I were breathing in romance.
Fragrant night,
Full of blossoms that fell from up above,
This delight
Is my everlasting memory of your love.
Starry skies,
I don't know if there were starry skies.
Can't remember what I said to you
Or if your eyes were brown or gray or blue.
All I know
Is whenever April comes,
And blossoms are white,
Dreams return me to you
And that fragrant night.

BUBBLES IN THE WINE

Words and music by Frank Loesser, Bob Calame (no dates or other information known), and Lawrence Welk (1903–1992). Published. Copyrighted May 31, 1939. In-

troduced in Paramount short film *The Champagne Music of Lawrence Welk*. Theme song of Lawrence Welk. Besides the version by Welk and his orchestra (Vocalion), leading recordings include Nelson Riddle (Capitol), Spike Jones and His City Slickers (Bluebird), and "Weird Al" Yankovic (Rock 'n' Roll). A successful conductor and accordianist from North Dakota, Welk later became famous for his long-running television show on the ABC network. The *Famous Music Song Guide* tells the story:

> In 1938 Welk read a fan letter describing his band as "sparkly and bubbly like champagne." He decided to call his style "champagne music" and perfected a way of popping his cheek on the air in imitation of an exploding cork. "Bubbles in the Wine" became a hit single for his orchestra in the summer of 1939.

My heart gets a little gay,
Like bubbles in the wine,
Ev'ry time I dance with you.
Your arms take me far away,
Like bubbles in wine,
Just as if I'd had a few.
Oh, maybe it's that moon,
Or maybe it's that tune,
Playing as we gently sway,
Or maybe it's the fact that I love you.
Can't really say
How I get this way.

My heart whispers a refrain,
Like bubbles in the wine,
Ev'ry time you're close to me.
I needn't drink champagne;
A feeling quite insane
Lights me up and sets me free.
Someday I may lose you,
But no matter how fate may go,
Apart or together, when I think of tonight,
I know I'll hear in this heart of mine
Music like the pretty bubbles in the wine.

I'M ALL A-TREMBLE OVER YOU

Music by Ted Fiorito. Published. Copyrighted June 30, 1939. Recorded by Dorothy Lamour with Lou Bring and His Orchestra (Brunswick).

VERSE

I've looked into plenty of starry eyes,
I've listened to lots of romantic sighs,
And never got weak in the knees.
But now will you look at me, please?

REFRAIN

Ooh hoo hoo hoo,
Hoo hoo hoo, hoo hoo hoo,
I'm all atremble over you.
Got my heart on a string,
It's a fluttery thing—
Ooh hoo hoo hoo,
Hoo hoo hoo, hoo hoo hoo,
I'm all atremble over you.
Can't remember a kiss
With a wallop like this;
How come I stumble when I walk?
How come I stutter when I talk
To you on the telephone?
I used to think I had a heart made of stone,
But ooh hoo hoo hoo,
Hoo hoo hoo, hoo hoo hoo,
This is a nice how-do-you-do—
I'm all atremble over you.

I KINDA DREAM

Music by Bernie Kane (b. 1907). Published. Copyrighted September 11, 1939. Kane, born Frank Joseph Aquino in Buffalo in 1907, later led a band closely associated with the *Mickey Mouse Club* television program.

I kinda dream when I dance with you,
And so
I'm no good at conversation.
I kinda dream a romance for two,
And oh,
What a sweet intoxication!
You and your two arms, suddenly all my own.
Crowded though the floor may be, we're alone.
So if I seem half asleep, say boo!
'Cause I kinda dream whenever I dance with you.

OLD FASHIONED LOVE

Music by Fritz Miller (no dates known). Published. Copyrighted September 11, 1939. Theme song of Fritz Miller and His Orchestra.

VERSE

Never want to see Park Avenue,
Through with all the Broadway lights.
Never want to hear that ballyhoo
From a million cute fly-by-nights.

REFRAIN

Old-fashioned love, for my next romance,
That's all that I've got to give.
It's time my heart met some sweet sensation
Without that smart-set sophistication,
Someone simple who's satisfied
To cuddle up by a cozy fireside
With that old-fashioned love long as we live,
'Cause that's all I've got to give.

HERE COMES THE NIGHT

Music by Hilly Edelstein and Carl Hohengarten. Published. Copyrighted September 25, 1939. Recorded by Frank Sinatra and Harry James (Columbia). Little is known about the two composers.

VERSE

Faithful to you only,
I'm faithful to you only.
And yet it seems
I have my dreams
To keep from being lonely.

REFRAIN

Here comes the night,
My cloak of blue.
Here comes the night
With dreams of you.
Somewhere up there
I'll see your face;
The breeze will be
Your warm embrace.
Here comes the night
To thrill my heart,
My one delight

While we're apart.
And now I'll keep that rendezvous.
Here comes the night,
Holding me tight
For you.

THAT MOONLIGHT FROM LAST NIGHT

Music by Matty Malneck. Probably late 1939. Typed lyric from undated Paramount censorship copy.

That moonlight from last night
Is still in my eyes,
That moonlight from last night
That fell from the skies.
You thrilled me, but thrilled me,
You've got me this way,
So I thought I'd phone you to say:

I'm all right from last night,
I slept well, I guess,
But somehow this morning
I've got to confess;
I looked in the mirror,
And it never lies:
That moonlight from last night
Is still in my eyes.

NIGHT-BLOOMING JASMINE

Music by Matty Malneck. Probably late 1939. Registered for copyright as an unpublished song, April 21, 1958.

The wind was wearing jasmine,
Fragrant night-blooming jasmine.
And as our hearts began to melt,
The magic that we felt
Was jasmine, only night-blooming jasmine,
But we called it love.
And now it's ended,
All the magic has ended,
And we are strangers once again,
With mem'ries, now and then,
Of jasmine, fragrant night-blooming jasmine,
Illusion of love,
Illusion of love.

HER BEAUTY...
made them beasts!

Tearing at each other like beasts of the jungle ... forgetting their friendship, forgetting everything but their mad desire to have this woman praise their might ... Bob Preston and Preston Foster battling for the love of Lamour in the thrill picture of the year.

DOROTHY LAMOUR · ROBERT PRESTON · PRESTON FOSTER

in

"MOON OVER BURMA"

A Paramount Picture with
DORIS NOLAN
ALBERT BASSERMAN

Directed by LOUIS KING · Screen Play by Frank Wead, W. P. Lipscomb and Harry Clork · Based on a Story by Wilson Collison

Songs of 1940

ALL WOMEN HAVE SECRETS

Produced by William LeBaron for Paramount Pictures. Released in February 1940. Originally titled *Campus Wives*. Screenplay by Agnes Christine Johnston, based on a story by Dale Eunson. Directed by Kurt Neumann. Cast featured Virginia Dale, Joseph Allen, Jr., Jeanne Cagney, Peter Lind Hayes, Betty Moran, John Arledge, Janet Waldo, and Lawrence Grossmith.

ROCKABYE BABY— INTERRUPTION

Special lyrics by Frank Loesser to traditional tune. Arrangement by Loesser and Johnny Cascales. Introduced by Jeanne Cagney and unidentified male singer. Loesser's lyrics are bracketed by Jeanne Cagney's performance of the traditional lullaby.

CAGNEY: [*traditional*] Rockabye baby in the treetop,
BOY: [*interrupting*] Now that's very pretty
         music for a good-night kiss,
         But modern kids appreciate this—

Rockabye rhythm—swing, baby, swing—
Rockabye rhythm, rhythm is the thing.
The sandman's a bandman, land sakes alive!
Hold tight, baby, and he'll make you jive!
CAGNEY: Well, all right—well, okay,
         But I'll take mine the old-fashioned way.
         [*traditional*] Rockabye baby, maybe you'll
            fall,
         Then down will come baby, cradle and all.

THE FARMER'S DAUGHTER

Produced by William C. Thomas for Paramount Pictures. Released in February 1940. Screenplay by Lewis R. Foster from story by Delmer Daves. Directed by James Hogan. Cast featured Martha Raye, Charlie Ruggles, Richard Denning, Gertrude Michael, William Frawley, Inez Courtney, William Demarest, Jack Norton, and Betty McLaughlin (Sheila Ryan).

JUNGLE JINGLE

Music by Frederick Hollander. Introduced by Martha Raye.

Just a jungle jingle
By the native ladies—
It'll make you tingle
Through and through
With the beat, beat, beat, beat, ooh ha hoo!

It's a jungle jingle
By the native ladies—
Makes you want to mingle
With a few
When they beat, beat, beat, beat, ooh ha hoo!
And no matter how much it aches them,
They dance all night long—
It's the coconut milk that makes them
Big and strong.

Sing a jungle jingle
To the native ladies—
You'll be glad you're single when you do,
With a beat, beat, beat, beat, ooh ha!
Beat, beat, beat, beat, ooh ha!
Beat, beat, beat, beat, ooh ha hoo!
Just between us monkeys, that means "I love you,"
With a beat, beat, beat, beat, ooh ha hoo!

SEVENTEEN

Produced by Stuart Walker for Paramount Pictures. Released March 1940. Screenplay by Agnes Christine Johnston and Stuart Palmer, based on the novel by Booth Tarkington and the play of the same name by Stuart Walker, Hugh Stanislaus Stange, and Stannard Mears. Directed by Louis King. Cast starred Jackie Cooper and Betty Field and featured Otto Kruger and Betty Nelson.

SEVENTEEN

Published. This is the first published song for which Frank Loesser wrote the music. Copyrighted September 11, 1939. Introduced by off-camera chorus during opening credits. Recorded by Ozzie Nelson (Bluebird).

VERSE (NOT SUNG IN FILM)

Young man with your hair so neatly parted,
Young man with your beard as soft as down,
Young man with your life so happy-hearted,
Young man, you're the envy of the town.

REFRAIN

When you're seventeen and you're in love
With some seventeen-year-old angel from above.
How she cuddles oh-so-close as you sail away,
In your good old nineteen twenty-nine Model A.
When you're seventeen, you're in a trance
And the cut of your first tuxedo spells romance.
There'll be nothing half as sweet in your life as
   the mem'ry
Of when you're seventeen and you're in love.

ADVENTURE IN DIAMONDS

Produced by A. M. Botsford for Paramount Pictures. Released in April 1940. Originally titled *Diamonds Are Dangerous*; later titled *Portrait in Diamonds*. Screenplay by Leonard Lee and Franz Schulz, from a story by Frank O'Connor. Directed by George Fitzmaurice. Cast starred George Brent and Isa Miranda and featured John Loder, Nigel Bruce, Elizabeth Patterson, Matthew Boulton, Rex Evans, Cecil Kellaway, Walter Kingsford, and Ernest Truex.

THE WHISTLER'S DITTIES

Introduced by Rex Evans. Written in July 1939.

There was a young fellow called Tony
Who put all his dough on one pony.
Oh, the horse ran that day,
And his time was okay,
But his sense of direction was phony.

[*"A Flea Flew in My Flute," which follows, was sung between the two verses of "The Whistler's Ditties."*]

Oh, what are you doing at midnight?
Why don't you and I get together?

Neath the rain I get cold,
Neath the moon I get bold,
So it all depends on the weather.

A FLEA FLEW IN MY FLUTE

Music by Phil Boutelje. Introduced by Rex Evans. Originally intended for *The Gracie Allen Murder Case.*

A flea flew in my flute [*trill*],
It just wouldn't play.
A flea flew in my flute [*trill*]
And ruined my day.
Right in the middle of my serenade
The lady was smiling at me.
And oh, what a mess
Of my romance he made!
Caramba! Caramba!
That flea!
The lady was a beaut [*trill*],
My heart will not mend.
A flea flew in my flute [*trill*]
And that was the end!

LOVE IN BLOOM
(Special Lyrics)

Special lyrics by Frank Loesser. Music and original lyrics by Ralph Rainger (1901–1942) and Leo Robin (1895–1984). Introduced by Rex Evans. The songwriting team of Rainger and Robin also wrote "June in January," and the Academy Award–winning "Thanks for the Memory." Rainger died tragically in an airplane crash. Robin went on to work with other songwriters, including Jule Styne and Harold Arlen. This lyric addition refers to the characters of Mr. Perrins (Ralph Forbes) and Captain Stephen Dennett (George Brent).

Can it be a strange and magic change
In Perrins' family tree?
Oh, no! It's not Mister P,
It's Captain D.

JOHNNY APOLLO

Produced by Harry Joe Brown and Darryl F. Zanuck for 20th Century–Fox Pictures. Released in April 1940. Originally titled *Dance with the Devil.* Screenplay by Philip Dunne and Rowland Brown based on an original story by Samuel G. Engel and Hal Long. Directed by Henry Hathaway. Cast starred Tyrone Power and Dorothy Lamour and featured Edward Arnold, Lloyd Nolan, Charley Grapewin, and Lionel Atwill.

DANCING FOR NICKELS AND DIMES

Music by Lionel Newman (1916–1989). Published. Copyrighted April 29, 1940. Introduced by Dorothy Lamour. Lionel Newman was long associated with 20th Century–Fox as a composer, conductor, and musical supervisor. He was the brother of Alfred Newman and the uncle of Randy Newman, who said that Lionel described working at the studio as "better than pipe fitting, but the gap is closing."

VERSE

They say that Fred Astaire
Gets a grand a minute,
Just tappin' his feet.
And Isadora Duncan
Made a million in it—
Oh, isn't that sweet?
But far beneath the notice
Of the noble Ballet Russe
Lies the germ of revolution
That will someday cook its goose.
For a dime a dozen now you get
Arabesque, pirouette, buck and wing,
Lindy hop, hep hep, chicky the cop.

REFRAIN

Dancing for nickels and dimes—
What a show you'll see
Under each marquee
Along about eleven-thirty!
Dancing for nickels and dimes—
Those Nijinskys from ev'ry low-down slum,
They're ragamuffin and they're dirty.*
You saw *Hamlet,* but what did you see?

* Published lyric:
They're absolutely filthy dirty.

Nothing that's worth your five-fifty.
You heard *Tosca,* but what did you hear?
It may be uplifty, but couldn't be nifty
As down round that square known as Times.
When you've done the Met and the Theatre Guild,
You find as yet that you ain't been thrilled,
Just watch those urchins, urchins dancin',
Dancing for nickels and dimes.

Request your number,
Or will you have a hunk of rumba?
Who said a minuet?
Well, there's your minuet.
It's the Minuet in G,
Or is it in the key of C?
Whatever key it happens to be,
They're dancing for nickels and dimes,
Alley-cattin' around that square known as Times
In Manhattan.
So get yourself a ringside seat
Out in the middle of the street,
And watch those urchins,
Watch those toughies, those ragamuffies,
Dancing for nickels and dimes.

YOUR KISS

Music by Alfred Newman. Published. Copyrighted February 13, 1940. Intended for *Johnny Apollo.* Not sung in film. Recorded by Dorothy Lamour (Brunswick). Later used in the 1946 film *Strange Triangle.*

My dreams are full of you,
The you that once embraced me.
My dreams are full of you
Without a pause
And all because,

REFRAIN

Your kiss is like a melody,
It's gone, and yet it sings to me,
Your kiss, a tender song
That fills the chilly night with such a warm delight.

Your kiss is like a crimson flame,
It's gone, and still I feel the same bright glow
Within my heart,
Although our lips are far apart.

Each dream brings the sight of your lovely face,
Each dream brings you to me through time and space,

Then we embrace, and love becomes a living
    thing,
Our love that I'm remembering.*
You're gone; still I have this,
The sweet enchantment of your kiss.

BUCK BENNY RIDES AGAIN

Produced by Mark Sandrich for Paramount Pictures. Released in April 1940. Screenplay by William Morrow and Edmund Beloin, based on an adaptation by Zion Myers of a story by Arthur Stringer. Directed by Mark Sandrich. Cast starred Jack Benny and featured Ellen Drew, Eddie "Rochester" Anderson, Andy Devine, Phil Harris, Dennis Day, Virginia Dale, Lillian Cornell, and Theresa Harris.

SAY IT (OVER AND OVER AGAIN)

Music by Jimmy McHugh (1893–1969). Published. Copyrighted March 15, 1940. Introduced by Lillian Cornell, Ellen Drew (dubbed by either Martha or Liz Tilton), and Virginia Dale. Leading recordings by Glenn Miller and His Orchestra (Bluebird) and Tommy Dorsey and His Orchestra, vocal by Frank Sinatra (Victor). Instrumental recording by John Coltrane (Verve). McHugh, a master songwriter, also collaborated with Dorothy Fields and Harold Adamson, among others. His hits include "I'm in the Mood for Love," "On the Sunny Side of the Street," and "I Can't Give You Anything But Love, Baby."

VERSE (NOT SUNG IN FILM)

Never you mind the flowers and candy;
They'll only wind up way up on the shelf.
Never you mind the tokens so handy;
Just make your mind up to speak for yourself.

REFRAIN

Say it, over and over again,
Over and over again,

---

*Alternate line:
    Our love, that dim remembering.

Never stop saying you're mine.
Say it, ever and ever so sweet,
Ever and ever so sweet,
Just like an old Valentine.
When you say "I love you,"
The same old "I love you"
They whisper in stories and plays,
You can change "I love you,"
The same old "I love you"
To oh, such a heavenly phrase!
Say it, softly and gently, and then
Over and over again,
Never stop saying you're mine.

MY! MY!

Music by Jimmy McHugh. Published. Copyrighted March 15, 1940. Introduced by Eddie "Rochester" Anderson and Theresa Harris. Leading recordings by Tommy Dorsey and His Orchestra (Victor), Eddie "Rochester" Anderson (Columbia), and Glenn Miller and His Orchestra (Bluebird).

VERSE (NOT SUNG IN FILM)

My talk was tricky and clever,
My line was sharp as a tack.
But ever since I met you
Ev'rything's gone black.

REFRAIN 1

ROCHESTER: I want to shout a poem about
    How I dream of that gleam in
        your eye.
    I want to shout, but all that
        comes out
    Is "My! My!"
    I want to sing of flowers in spring,
    But oh dear, when you're near, I
        just die.
    I want to sing and can't sing a thing
    But "My! My!"
    I should say, "Oh, how lovely!"
    I should say: "Ah, how sweet!"
    I should have Shakespeare at the tip
        of my tongue,
    But ev'ry time we meet,
    I look at you, and what do I do?
    I get weak—I can't speak—I
        just sigh;
    And though I try, the best I can
        sigh
    Is "My! My!"

REFRAIN 2

HARRIS: Come to think about it,
    You're sorta sweet, strictly elite,
    Not too bold, not too cold, but so shy.
    You're sorta sweet, the way you repeat
    "My! My!"
    You're kinda smart,
    The way you're capturing my heart
    With that line, you divine little guy.
    You're kinda smart to make a
        fine art
    Of "My! My!"
    You could say, "How intriguing!"
    Or you could say, "How petite!"
ROCHESTER: I could have Webster in the palm of
        my hand,
    But ev'ry time we meet—dead
        pigeon!
HARRIS: You don't do bad—in fact I
        might add,
    You're my type, and time's ripe,
        sugar pie.
ROCHESTER: Why, Josephine!
    That's just what I mean
    By "My! My!"

MY KIND OF COUNTRY

Music by Jimmy McHugh. Published. Copyrighted March 15, 1940. Introduced by Dennis Day and chorus. Song also used in Paramount Pictures' *Stick to Your Guns* (1941). Recording by Clint Walker (Warner Bros.).

VERSE

Yonder sky bright and clear,
Shining for me.
Heaven is near—
Say, can you see?

REFRAIN

There lies my kind of country,
Round that last bend we're headin' for.
Old-timer, stay with me
And tonight we'll see
My kind of country once more.

There lives my kind of people,
Where that sundown smiles bright and red.
Old-timer, I'll strike gold
When these eyes behold
My kind of country ahead.

Travel home, travel home,
Maybe five more miles, maybe ten.
May I ever grieve if I ever leave
My kind of country again!

DRUMS IN THE NIGHT

Music by Jimmy McHugh. Published. Copyrighted March 15, 1940. Introduced by Lillian Cornell with Virginia Dale and Ellen Drew dubbed by either Martha or Liz Tilton.

VERSE (NOT SUNG IN FILM)

There it is again,
My song of many moons ago.
There it is again,
The strangest melody I know.
Tom-toms are in my heartbeats,
Tom-toms that thrill me through.
There it is again,
The song that brings me close to you.

REFRAIN

I fell under the spell of drums in the night,
Song of primitive love that comes in the night.*
You came, set me aflame, and now we're apart—
Can't fight drums in the night that pound in the heart.
Though you're gone, the magic spell remains
When the moon rides high above the plains.
I'm still deep in that thrill of pagan delight,
One mad moment we had from drums in the night.

ROSES ROUND MY ROOM

Music by Jimmy McHugh. Not used in film.

Roses round my room,
Casting a spell—
Shabby old room,
Don't you look swell?
Roses round my room,

___
* *Original line:*
  Song of Cherokee love that comes in the night.

Fragrant and bright—
Shabby old room,
Now you're all right.
You faded carpet, how'd you get so gay?
Broken-down Victrola, oh, how sweet you play!
Magic round my room,
All because of roses from someone I love!

TYPHOON

Produced by Anthony Veiller for Paramount Pictures. Released in May 1940. Screenplay by Allen Rivkin from a story by Steve Fisher. Directed by Louis King. Cast featured Dorothy Lamour, Robert Preston, Lynne Overman, and J. Carrol Naish.

PALMS OF PARADISE

Music by Frederick Hollander. Published. Copyrighted February 23, 1940. Introduced by Dorothy Lamour. Leading recording by Henry King and His Orchestra, vocal by Bob Carroll (Decca). Other recordings include Lamour with Lou Bring and His Orchestra (Bluebird) and Harry James (Columbia).

VERSE (NOT SUNG IN FILM)

The tropical trees, they breathe their melody!
That tropical tune that brought you close to me!

REFRAIN 1

The palms of paradise,
They sing high above,
Caressed by the breeze,
Sweet music of love.
These palms of paradise,
With stars gleaming through,
Will you dream of me
As I dreamed of you?*
Someday we may sail far away
From this magic island shore,
And yet we will keep in our hearts
One song forevermore.
These palms of paradise

___
* *Lines 7–8 originally:*
  Made you dream of me,
  Made me dream of you

That sing high above,
Caressed by the breeze,
Sweet music of love.*

REFRAIN 2

The palms of paradise,
They murmur above
That here is my heart,
But where is my love?
The palms of paradise
With stars gleaming through,
They sigh in the wind,
As I sigh for you.
Ah, so lovely,
But oh, so lonely,
This moonlit tropical shore,
Without the one I adore!
Only the palms of paradise
That murmur above—
And here is my heart,
But where is my love?

THOSE WERE THE DAYS

Produced by Jay Theodore Reed for Paramount Pictures. Released in July 1940. Also released as *At Good Old Siwash*. Screenplay by Don Hartman, based on the novel *At Good Old Siwash* by George Fitch. Directed by Jay Theodore Reed. Cast starred William Holden and featured Bonita Granville, Ezra Stone, William Frawley, Alan Ladd, Richard Denning, and Vaughan Glaser.

ALPHA RHO SONG

Special lyrics by Frank Loesser to the tune of "When Johnny Comes Marching Home." Introduced by male chorus.

___

You gotta belong to Alpha Rho,
You do, you do.
You gotta belong to Alpha Rho,
It's good for you.
Oh, you'll never get up to heaven,

___
* *Remainder of lyrics not sung in film.*

But you know the place you'll go
If you don't belong to wonderful Alpha Rho.

You gotta belong to Alpha Rho
To live, to live.
You gotta decide to Alpha Rho
Your soul you'll give.
For you never will get a self-respecting worm
To say hello
If you don't belong to marvelous Alpha Rho,
If you don't belong to marvelous Alpha Rho.*

You gotta belong to Alpha Rho
To gain success.
You gotta belong to Alpha Rho
Your life to bless.
When you're trying to reach the gutter,
You'll be standing much too low
If you don't belong to beautiful Alpha Rho.

ANY MINUTE NOW

Introduced by male chorus.

Any minute now, any minute now,
You're gonna take the pledge,
You're gonna make the vow.
Just you wait and see,*
Just you wait and see,
We'll stick you with the pin
Of this fraternity.
We'll stick you with the pin,
We'll stick you with the pin,
And you'll be stuck for life,
Boy, once we let you in.
So take a little bow,
Let us show you how;
Here you go for Alpha Rho,
Any minute now.

SIWASH ALMA MATER

Special lyrics by Frank Loesser to the tune of Beethoven's "Ode to Joy" from the fourth movement of his
Ninth Symphony. Sung by chorus during closing credits.

_____
* *Remainder of lyrics not sung in film.*

Alma Mater, proudly we will hail thy glory
    evermore.
May thy spirit guide us through the path of life
    that lies in store.*
May tomorrow, as today, be full of all thy wisdom,
And thy voice go ringing through the twilight of
    the years to come.
May chapel bells a-tolling
Fondly to our hearts recall
Our beloved Alma Mater,
Dearest, fairest place of all.
Thy name will ever invoke
All the love for thee we bore,
Alma Mater, proudly we will hail thy glory evermore.

WE'RE ALL HERE AT SIWASH

Special lyrics by Frank Loesser to music by Johannes
Brahms from the fourth movement of his First Symphony. Not used in film.

We're all here at Siwash;
Hello, old friend, hello.
We're all here at Siwash
To learn what there is to know.
To grab a degree
For you and for me
And root for Siwash teams,
And maybe to find us the girl of our dreams.
For life, love, and knowledge
We all go to Siwash College.

SIWASH SPRING SONG

Special lyrics by Frank Loesser to unspecified music by
Beethoven. Not used in film.

Will we return when spring is here
With starry eyes and voices clear?
Arm in arm, will we be strolling
Lanes all fragrant, green, and rolling
While soft and gentle and sentimental
Sweet words of love echo in each ear?
And yes they will,
Soft and gentle,
Oh yes, they will,

_____
* *Remainder of lyrics not sung in film.*

Surely they will,
In the springtime of the year.

La, la, la, etc.

Will I find you young and gay as ever?
Will I find you in my two arms once more?
Will you carry me away as ever
With that smile I found so lovely before?
Yes, I'll be here and so will you,
And we'll be strolling two by two.
Sure as April lies before us,
We'll have magic moonlight o'er us.
And ever after, the joy and laughter
Will be a gay echo in our ears.
Oh yes it will,
Joy and laughter,
Oh yes it will,
Surely it will,
Ev'ry springtime,
All through the years!

THE QUARTERBACK

Produced by Anthony Veiller for Paramount Pictures.
Released in October 1940. Story and screenplay by
Robert Pirosh. Directed by H. Bruce Humberstone.
Cast featured Wayne Morris, Virginia Dale, Lillian Cor-
nell, Edgar Kennedy, Alan Mowbray, Jerome Cowan,
Rod Cameron, and William Frawley. The score also in-
cluded "Sentimental Me" by Jack Lawrence (lyrics) and
Paul Mann and Stephen Weiss (music).

OUT WITH YOUR CHEST (AND UP WITH YOUR CHIN)

Music by Matty Malneck. Published. Copyrighted September 11, 1940. Introduced by Lillian Cornell.

VERSE

"Faint heart never won fair lady,"
That's just how the saying goes;
In other words, young Romeo,
Get on your toes.
Sad face never looked romantic,
So if you're depressed and blue,
Take this advice, young Romeo,
It's good for you.

REFRAIN

So, out with your chest and up with your chin
And fight for your lady fair.
You can't lose, you might win,
So, out with your chest and up with your chin.
Of course you can make her care.

SEVEN SINNERS

Produced by Joe Pasternak for Universal Pictures. Released in November 1940. Screenplay by Jon Meehan and Harry Tugend from a story by Ladislaus Fodor and Laslo Vadnai. Directed by Tay Garnett. Cast starred Marlene Dietrich and featured John Wayne, Albert Dekker, Broderick Crawford, Anna Lee, Mischa Auer, and Billy Gilbert.

THE MAN'S IN THE NAVY

Music by Frederick Hollander. Published. Copyrighted September 27, 1940. Introduced by Marlene Dietrich. Leading recording by Marlene Dietrich with Victor Young and His Orchestra (Decca).

VERSE (NOT SUNG IN FILM)

Here we are at Pier Twenty-two.
Yes sir, the fleet is in!
Wait and see who strolls into view,
Sharp as a tack, slick as a pin.

REFRAIN

See those shoulders broad and glorious?
See that smile? That smile's notorious.
You can bet your life the man's in the navy.
See those nice blue trousers walk about?
That's that salty walk they talk about.
Mister, watch your wife, the man's in the navy!

Now lots of men stand six foot seven,
And lots of men have arms like heaven,
And lots of men have hair all golden and wavy.
But when ten thousand gorgeous women'll
Chase him like some hunted criminal,
You can bet your life the man's in the navy!

See those shoulders broad and glorious?
See that smile? That smile's notorious.
You can bet your life the man's in the navy.

See those nice blue trousers walk about?
That's that salty walk they talk about.
Mister, watch your wife, the man's in the navy!

Now lots of men just can't remember
That big romance from last November
And leave a lady as cold as yesterday's gravy.
But when he says, "I love you, Bessie,"
To some poor kid whose name is Jesse,
You can bet your life the man's in the navy!

I FALL OVERBOARD

Music by Frederick Hollander. Copyrighted September 16, 1940. Used instrumentally only.

VERSE

Better not get chicken-hearted—
If you ever get me started
Falling for you,
Gonna have me on your hands if you do!

REFRAIN

For I fall overboard,
Ev'ry time I fall, it's overboard!
So, you gorgeous thing, beware—
When I care, I care!
No halfway affair there!
I fall overboard,
Just the kind of love you can't afford.
So, you gorgeous thing,
Careful how you play,
For I fall overboard that way.

I'VE BEEN IN LOVE BEFORE

Music by Frederick Hollander. Published. Copyrighted September 16, 1940. Introduced by Marlene Dietrich. Recordings include Marlene Dietrich with Victor Young and His Orchestra (Decca); Frank Sinatra (Reprise); and Benny Carter and His Orchestra (Decca). Loesser added a different twist to this title ten years later in *Guys and Dolls* with "I've Never Been in Love Before."

VERSE (NOT SUNG IN FILM)

You understand,
Don't you,

Why I'm sure I'm yours forever and a day?
You'll understand,
Won't you, darling,
When I say:

REFRAIN

I've been in love before,
It's true.
Been learning to adore
Just you.
Some old romance taught me how to kiss,
To smile like that and sigh like this.
I've been in love before,
You see.
Or, darling what a bore I'd be.*
A heart that's lived a bit
Can tell when it beats true.
I've been in love before,
Haven't you?

DANCING ON A DIME

Produced by A. M. Botsford for Paramount Pictures. Released in November 1940. Screenplay by Maurice Rapf, Anne Morrison Chapin, and Allen Rivkin. Directed by Joseph Santley. Cast featured Robert Paige, Peter Lind Hayes, Eddie Quillan, Frank Jenks, Grace McDonald, Virginia Dale, Carol Adams, Lillian Cornell, and William Frawley.

MAÑANA

Music by Burton Lane. Published. Copyrighted September 5, 1940. Introduced by Virginia Dale, Carol Adams, Peter Lind Hayes, Eddie Quillan, Frank Jenks, and chorus.

Mañana—
The indolent word that you say with a smile—
It's your way of saying "Forget for a while."
Mañana, mañana—
The sleepy old word with a promising twist—

_____
* *Sheet music version:*
   So you mean all the more to me!

I wanna kiss now but I'm gonna get kissed
Mañana, mañana—
You're gonna get kissed, kissed mañana.

You! You! You! You!
Alibi all day.
Oh, why do you,
Why do you alibi this way?
Mañana, mañana—
You promise me candy, you promise me beans,
I'll get them mañana, mañana, which means
Tomorrow!
Tomorrow!
You'll play me a rumba,
You'll dance and you'll sing,
You'll even get married,
Or any old thing I wanna
Mañana—
Oh . . .

[Interlude]

BOYS: We wanna.
GIRLS: Mañana.
　The sleepy old word with a promising
　　twist:
　I wanna kiss now,
BOYS: And you're gonna get kissed
ALL: Mañana!

Earlier version (dated April 4, 1940)

Mañana—
The Mexican word that you say with a smile—
It's your way of saying "Forget it a while."
Mañana, mañana—
The Mexican word with the Mexican twist—
I wanna kiss now, but I'm gonna get kissed
Mañana.
You! You! You! You!
Alibi all day.
Oh, why do you alibi this way?
Mañana, you promise me chili,
You promise me beans,
I'll get them mañana,
Mañana, which means
Tomorrow!
Tomorrow you'll play me a rumba,
You'll dance and you'll sing,
You'll even get married,
Or any old thing I wanna—
Mañana!

I HEAR MUSIC

Music by Burton Lane. Copyrighted September 5, 1940. Introduced by Peter Lind Hayes, Eddie Quillan, Frank Jenks, and Robert Paige. Recordings include Billie Holiday (Columbia), Ella Fitzgerald (Verve), Nat "King" Cole (Capitol), Peggy Lee (Capitol), George Shearing (MGM), and Anita O'Day (Polydor).

VERSE (NOT SUNG IN FILM)

Not that I'm a Punchinello,
Just an optimistic fellow
With a lot of very mellow
Music in my soul.
Not that I'm a Pollyanna,
Shoutin' out a loud Hosanna—
It's my singing heart I can't control.

REFRAIN

HAYES: I hear music,
　Mighty fine music.
　The murmur of a morning breeze
　　up there,
　The rattle of the milkman on the
　　stair—
　Sure that's music,
　Mighty fine music.
　The singing of a sparrow in the sky,
　The perking of the coffee right nearby,
　Laughing children down the street—
　Where is there a tune so sweet?*
　I hear music,
　Mighty fine music,
　And any time I think my world is
　　wrong,
　I get me out of bed and sing this song.

QUILLAN: I hear music,
　Mighty fine music.
　A symphony of lovely, lovely tones,
　The creaking of my lazy, lazy bones.
HAYES: Sure that's music,
　Operatic music.
　Once I sang to Carmen, oh so sweet—
　I'm the guy who knocked her off
　　her feet.
　Laughing children down the street,
　Where is there a tune so sweet?
JENKS: I hear music,

* Lines 9–10 originally:
　There's my fav'rite melody,
　You, my angel, phoning me.

　Magnifique music.
　The crackling of the bacon in the pan.
OTHERS: There isn't any bacon, my good man.
ALL: Laughing children, running down
　　the street—
　Where, oh where is there a tune so
　　sweet?
PAIGE: I hear music,
　Sweet romantic music,
　A song of love to someone you adore—
　If you like my song I'll sing you more.
　Laughing children down the street—
　Where is there a tune so sweet?
ALL: I hear music,
　Mighty, mighty fine music.
　And any time I think the world is
　　wrong,
　I get me out of bed and sing this song.

OPERATIC PROLOGUE TO "I HEAR MUSIC" REPRISE

Additional music by Jule Styne.

BOYS: Ladies and gentlemen,
　We present to you—
　Ha ha ha ha ha ha ha ha!
HAYES: Ladies and gentlemen,
　Listen to my melodramatic,
　　operatic play—
BOYS: Hey, pal, where do you get that stuff?
QUILLAN: Enough is enough.
HAYES: It's opening night.
BOYS: Let's keep it light.
JENKS: Let's keep it light.
SOLO: For you—
BOYS: You'll feel rhythm.
　You'll see action.
　Laughs all fresh and new.
　Girls, mmmm!
　Beautiful girls, mmmm!
GIRLS: And you'll see a lot of us too.
ENSEMBLE: And you'll hear music, mighty
　　fine music.
　It's only the beginning of the show,
　But what's the use of talking? Here
　　we go!

[Segue into dance number and "I Hear Music" reprise.]

LOVABLE SORT OF PERSON

Music by Victor Young. Published. Copyrighted September 5, 1940. Introduced by Grace McDonald.

VERSE (NOT SUNG IN FILM)

I wouldn't describe you as an angel
Or a super-super-glamorous thing.
I wouldn't describe you as an angel,
But this I'll say, this I'll sing:

REFRAIN

You—you're a lovable sort of person.
Ooh—I could love you without rehearsin'.
Poor me, I'd just nat'rally fall,
Wouldn't feel like a stranger at all,
Holding you oh so tight—
Just name the night.
Yes, you
With those lovable eyes a-flashin',
Two
That will never go out of fashion.
Poor me,
I can see myself in love a lifetime through
With a lovable sort of person like you.

DANCING ON A DIME

Music by Burton Lane. Published. Copyrighted September 5, 1940. Introduced by Robert Paige and Grace McDonald. Recordings include Larry Clinton and His Orchestra (Victor), Russ Morgan and His Orchestra (Decca), and Michael Feinstein and Burton Lane (Elektra).

VERSE

PAIGE: Now, I'd never dream of making love
        With so many people near.
MCDONALD: Now, I'd never dream of making love,
        But love is here.

REFRAIN

PAIGE: Oh, isn't this sublime?
        We're dancing on a dime.
        The crowded floor
        Is perfect for
        A nice romantic time.
        Oh, how can I help but hold you tight
        Here in a warm embrace?

MCDONALD: There isn't an inch of space
        For being discreet,
        So I repeat:
        Isn't this sublime,
        This dancing on a dime?
PAIGE: We're hand in glove,
        The picture of
        A romance in its prime.
        Now, darling, I guess
        I'd better confess—
MCDONALD: Shh, I knew it all the time,*
        That I'd be close to you—
BOTH: Dancing on a dime.

[Dance interlude]

MCDONALD: Isn't this sublime,
PAIGE: This dancing on a dime?
        We're hand in glove,
        The picture of
        A romance in its prime.
MCDONALD: Now, darling, I guess
        I better confess—
PAIGE: [spoken] Why, I knew it all the time!
MCDONALD: [spoken] You did?
PAIGE: [sung] That I'd be close to you—
MCDONALD: Dancing on a dime.

DEBUTANTE NUMBER ONE

Music by Victor Young. Introduced by Lillian Cornell and ensemble.

CORNELL: Night falls over Manhattan,
        With its bored and jaded eyes,
        Till a sudden touch of moonlight
        For a moment lingers there and
            then dies.
        Comes an angel over Manhattan
        To the bored and jaded throng,
        Just a sudden touch of moonlight
        For a moment filling hearts with
            a song.
        She's Debutante Number One,
        Until the next one comes along.
GIRLS: Look! Isn't she sweet?
        Isn't she perfectly wonderful, beautiful?
ENSEMBLE: Isn't she sweet?
        Isn't she sweet?

_____

* *Alternate line:*
    For I knew it all the time—

Isn't she perfectly wonderful, beautiful,
    beautiful?
CORNELL: Here comes Debutante Number One.
        She's a front-page story,
        And her night of glory
        Has just begun.
        Debutante Number One!
        That baby face of hers
        To the photographers
        Is bread and wine.
        All over old New York
        Where ev'ry champagne cork
        Is a salute to her form divine.
        For all the crowded nights
        A dozen satellites
        Are near at hand,
        And through the hectic days
        A dozen more always
        At her command.
        Here's to Debutante Number One!
CHORUS: Isn't she sweet?
        Isn't she perfectly wonderful, beautiful?
CORNELL: She dances
        Through a series of empty romances
        And smiles for the press,
        And she loves it, I guess.
        And she races
        Past an ocean of curious faces,
        And smiles for them all,
        Never dreaming she'll fall.

[Interlude]

CORNELL: [spoken] She's tasted delicious applause;
        She can't do without it somehow.
        She can't do without it because
        She's much too used to it now.

        She'll be nineteen tomorrow,
        And how can she survive?
        When all this is gone tomorrow,
        She'll feel like ninety-five

        The public finds a new love;
        They always do.
        They find a new love,
        And her dance is through!
        [sung] Ah———
MEN: Here's to Debutante Number One.
CORNELL: In a blaze of glory.
MEN: One glorious night.
CORNELL: It's the same old story.
MEN: Then fades out of sight, once more
            begun—
CORNELL: Debutante Number One!
MEN: Ah———One!

YOUTH WILL BE SERVED

Produced by Lucien Hubbard for 20th Century–Fox. Released in November 1940. Screenplay by Wanda Tuchock from a story by Ruth Fasken and Hilda Vincent. Directed by Otto Brower. Cast starred Jane Withers and featured Jane Darwell, Robert Conway, Elyse Knox, Joe Brown Jr., John Qualen, and Charles Holland.

WITH A BANJO ON MY KNEE

Special lyrics by Frank Loesser to "Oh! Susannah" by Stephen Foster. Introduced by Jane Withers with Mildred Gover and Joe Brown Jr.

VERSE

I never done a lick of work;
I never even tried.
My pappy got so sick of work
That he just up and died.

REFRAIN

Ohhhh—let it rain,
Let it pour,
Nothin' worries me—
'Cause I just go on singin'
With a banjo on my knee
Ohhhh—let it rain,
Let it pour,
Nothin' worries me—
'Cause I go right on singin'
With a banjo on my knee.

YOUTH WILL BE SERVED

Music by Louis Alter. Introduced by a chorus featuring Jane Withers.

Youth will be served—
Keep that well-known phrase preserved.
And remember, friend, when you're lookin' at the future,
You're lookin' at the young ones of the land.

We're singing, youth will be served—
That's no more than we deserve.
So remember, friend, when you need a little action,
You'll get it from the young ones of the land.

We're not the smart set,
The à la carte set,
But we have our hearts set
On being heard.

So listen—youth will be served.
Yes, we've got our place reserved.
So remember, friend, when you're counting on the nation,
You're counting on the people,
Brave, strong, tomorrow's people,
You're counting on the young ones of the land.

HOT CATFISH AND CORN DODGERS

Music by Louis Alter. Published. Copyrighted May 19, 1941. Introduced by Charles Holland and Jane Withers with children's chorus.

HOLLAND: "Hot catfish and corn dodgers.
    Hot catfish a nickel and a dime today."

I nebber been down de river to be baptized,
So I dunno what religion's all about.
I nebber been down de river to be baptized,
And still de Lord fo'give me when I shout,
"Hot catfish and corn dodgers.
Hot catfish a nickel and a dime today."

I nebber go down de river wi' de washbo'd,
I nebber did see a washbo'd ketch a thing.
I nebber go down de river wi' de washbo'd,
And still my wife fo'give me when I sing,
"Hot catfish and corn dodgers.
Hot catfish for washin' all your sins away!"

Neighbor, neighbor, stop yo' worryin' 'bout de nation,

Neighbor, neighbor, stop yo' figgerin' out inflation!
Aggravation! Tribulation!
Neighbor, take a look in my fryin' pan,
Is sorrow and woe inside of you?
Neighbor, take a sniff at my fryin' pan
And fill up your soul with one or two
Hot catfish and corn dodgers,
Hot catfish, dey's plenty of 'em right dis way.

I nebber go down de river in de moonlight,
I nebber get time to stroll aroun' and sigh.
I nebber go down de river in de moonlight,
And still my gal fo'give me when I cry,
"Hot catfish and corn dodgers.
Hot catfish a nickel and a dime today,
A nickel and a dime today!"

WITHERS: Gather round, little chil'n,
    For a down-South afternoon tea.
    Ain't exactly what you'd call tea and crumpets,
    Oh, but it's heaven for you and me.

Ohhhh—gather round, little chil'n,
For a down-South piece of advice.
When the fish'man comes along and you're hungry—
KIDS: Yeah!
WITHERS: If you're hungry—
KIDS: Yeah!
WITHERS: Then treat him nice,
    And you'll get
    Hot catfish and corn dodgers!
    Hot catfish—what he can't sell he gives away!
KIDS: Away!
WITHERS: He's never been baptized.
KIDS: Ain't he baptized?
WITHERS: Don't know what that's about.
KIDS: How don't he?
WITHERS: He's never been baptized.
KIDS: Oh, what a sinner!
WITHERS: But the old folks heed him when he shouts,
    "Hot catfish and corn dodgers!"
    He never pushed a washbo'd—
KIDS: Oh, he's lazy!
WITHERS: It wouldn't catch a thing.
KIDS: He's not crazy!
WITHERS: He'd never pushed a washbo'd—
KIDS: Down by the river!
WITHERS: But the white folks heed him when he sings,
    "Hot catfish a nickel and a dime today."

So neighbor, neighbor,
Stop your worryin' 'bout the nation!
KIDS: Stop your worry, worry, worry.
WITHERS: Ohhh—neighbor, neighbor,
Stop your figgerin' out inflation!
KIDS: What's that?
WITHERS: Here comes a man that's low on dollars,
But he says a mouthful when he
hollers:
HOLLAND: "Hot catfish and corn dodgers!
Hot catfish a nickel and a dime today!"
WITHERS
AND KIDS: A nickel and a dime today,
You've only got a dime to pay
For chasin' all the blues away—
A nickel and a dime today!

MOON OVER BURMA

Produced by A. M. Botsford for Paramount Pictures. Released in December 1940. Screenplay by Frank Wead, W. P. Lipscomb, and Harry Clork, based on a story by Wilson Collison. Directed by Louis King. Cast starred Dorothy Lamour, Robert Preston, and Preston Foster and featured Doris Nolan and Albert Basserman.

MEXICAN MAGIC

Music by Harry Revel (1905–1958). Published. Copyrighted September 17, 1940. Introduced by Dorothy Lamour. Recorded by Lamour with Lou Bring and His Orchestra (Bluebird). The English-born Revel collaborated successfully with lyricist Mack Gordon on such hits as "Stay as Sweet as You Are," "There's a Lull in My Life," and "Did You Ever See a Dream Walking?"

VERSE (NOT SUNG IN FILM)

You must have charmed Chihuahua,
You must have wowed Juarez.

And though you speak no Americano,
I have a hunch that it says:

REFRAIN

You've got a bit of the Mexican magic,
You've got a bit of it there in your eyes.
You've got a bit of the Mexican magic,
A little touch of the tropical skies.
You've got a lot of the Mexican flavor,
You've got a lot of it there on your lips.
So could you do me a Mexican favor
And maybe give me a couple of sips?
Ay, sí, sí, sí!
That's all I knew in Spanish.
Ah, sí, sí, sí!
But now I know much more.
Ay, sí, sí, sí!
You're making my cares vanish,
So close to me upon a dancing floor.
For I was right in the mood to get tragic,
But then we happened to rumba by chance.
I got a bit of the Mexican magic,
And now I'm right in the mood for romance.

MOON OVER BURMA

Music by Frederick Hollander. Published. Copyrighted September 17, 1940. Introduced by Dorothy Lamour. Leading recordings by Shep Fields and His Rippling Rhythm, vocal by Dorothy Allen (Bluebird), and Gene Krupa and His Orchestra (Okeh). Also recorded by Lamour with Lou Bring and His Orchestra (Bluebird).

VERSE (NOT SUNG IN FILM)

Moon, high in the beautiful eastern sky,
Moon, when will you answer my lonely cry?

REFRAIN

Moon over Burma, smiling above,
They say that you are the wonderful Goddess of
Love.
Moon over Burma, heavenly light,
Couldn't you smile

In the eyes of my loved one tonight—tonight?
Steal into the song of the temple bell.
Steal into his heart like a spell.
Moon over Burma, power divine,
Couldn't you go where my loved one is dreaming
And shine?
And, moon over Burma, tell him he's mine!

MISCELLANEOUS SONGS OF 1940

BY THE BY

Music by "By" Woodbury (no dates known). Published. Loesser wrote this lyric for bandleader Woodbury's theme song.

By the by,
Have you been dreaming lately?
By the by,
I'd sure appreciate it greatly
If you could dream a dream of me.
By the by,
Have you that lonely feeling?
Or would my embrace be just as appealing?
Or would it never come to be?

I thrill with delight
'Cause you're so darn sweet,
And still we're polite
Ev'ry time we meet
With "By the by."
Although I know I bore you,
In my shy and tender heart
A message for you says, "I adore you,"
By the by.

Songs of 1941

A NIGHT AT EARL CARROLL'S

Produced by Earl Carroll for Paramount Pictures. Released in January 1941. Screenplay and story by Lynn Starling. Directed by Kurt Neumann. Cast featured Ken Murray, Rose Hobart, Blanche Stewart, Elvia Allman, J. Carrol Naish, and Lillian Cornell. Other songs in this film include "Caliconga," lyrics by Earl Carroll and Dorcas Cochran, music by Nino Menendez, and "One Look at You," lyrics by Ned Washington and Earl Carroll, music by Victor Young.

LI'L BOY LOVE

Music by Frederick Hollander. Published. Copyrighted June 19, 1940. Introduced by Lillian Cornell and chorus girls. Recordings include Benny Goodman and His Orchestra, Helen Forrest, vocal (Columbia), and Ray Herbeck (Okeh).

VERSE (NOT SUNG IN FILM)

Just because I happened to meet
Someone very charming and sweet
Doesn't necessarily spell romance.
So, Mister Cupid, let me say this to you in advance.

REFRAIN

CORNELL: Li'l Boy Love, don't get cute
In your dimpled birthday suit.
Li'l Boy Love, you can't shoot this
old heart.
Li'l Boy Love, get along
With your safety-pin sarong—
Don't you know I'm too wise, I'm
too smart?
Zing! Ouch! What was that?
Cupid knocked me flat
With his li'l bow-'n'-arry.
Watch me marry,
Watch me weaken and fall,
'Cause I'm human after all,
Just one more victim of
Li'l Boy Love.

Mary Martin and members of the ensemble in the film
Kiss the Boys Goodbye

FIRST GIRL: [*spoken*] Now suppose you hold my
parasol
While I sit upon your knee,
And leave the rest to Cupid,
'Cause he's watching you and me.
SECOND GIRL: [*spoken*] And then suppose you
whisper
Pretty nothings in my ear,
And the tiny little fellow
With the arrows might appear.
THIRD GIRL: [*spoken*] Zing! Ouch! What was that?
Cupid knocked me flat
With his li'l bow-'n'-arry.
Watch me marry—
ALL GIRLS: [*sung*] Watch me weaken and fall,
'Cause I'm human after all,
Just one more victim of
Li'l Boy Love!

I WANNA MAKE WITH THE HAPPY TIMES

Words and music by Frank Loesser and Gertrude Niesen (1911–1975). Published. Copyrighted June 19, 1940. Introduced by Debutante Trio. Only the first refrain was sung in the film. Niesen was better known as a ballad singer and recording artist. She appeared in several Broadway musicals and films and introduced "Where Are You?" in the 1937 film *Top of the Town* and the saucy "I Wanna Get Married" in the 1944 musical *Follow the Girls*, a show that also featured Jackie Gleason as the comic Goofy Gale.

VERSE (NOT SUNG IN FILM)

Hoorah! Hooray!
I don't know which to say.
Hoorah! Hooray!
I guess I'll say them both anyway.

REFRAIN 1

I wanna make with the happy times,
I wanna give out with songs and rhymes,
I feel like whistling, tweet, tweet, tweet, tweet,
And ringing bells, all the bells on the street.
Don't need no di'monds or sweet perfume,
But let me blow up paper bags and make them
boom.
Ain't got no nickels, don't get no dimes,
Just wanna make with the happy times!

REFRAIN 2 (NOT SUNG IN FILM)

I wanna make with the slide trombones,
I wanna lap up ten ice cream cones,
I feel like dancing around the block
And tearing the hands off the grandfather
clock.
Don't need no orchids or marble halls,
But let me shut my eyes and walk right into
walls.
Ain't got no nickels, can't lose no dimes,
Just wanna make with the happy times!

REFRAIN 3 (NOT SUNG IN FILM)

I wanna make with the big bass drum,
I wanna beat it till kingdom come,
I feel like singing a hunk of song,
So if I'm flat, so I'm flat, so I'm wrong.
Don't need no sables, can't use no mink,
I'm floating paper boats around the kitchen sink.
Ain't got no nickels, don't know from dimes,
Just wanna make with the happy times!

I'VE WALKED THROUGH WONDERLAND

Music by Frederick Hollander. Not used in film.

I've walked through wonderland,
I know its charms,
For I've looked in your eyes,
And I've been in your arms.
I've walked through wonderland
And lingered there
To taste your lovely lips
And see stars in your hair.
So I'll never sigh, complain, or cry
If by and by you're gone,
For the mem'ry of that land of love
Will live on!
I've known the only one my heart beats for—
I've walked through wonderland,
Could a heart ask for more?

ARIZONA SKETCHES

A Paramount Pictures short subject. Released in January 1941.

PRAIRIELAND LULLABY

Music by Victor Young. Published. Copyrighted January 13, 1941. Recorded by Bing Crosby (Decca) and Glenn Miller (Bluebird).

My prairieland lullaby,
The sweetest tune that I know,
The wind out there singin' high
And prairie doves hummin' low.

It's in my soul
Like the dusty tumbleweeds that roll
And purple hills that rise way up to the sky,
The sweetest tune that I know,
My prairieland lullaby.

It's in my veins,
All the music of these lonely plains,
And now I lay me down and peacefully sigh,
The sweetest tune that I know,
My prairieland lullaby.

LAS VEGAS NIGHTS

Produced by William LeBaron for Paramount Pictures. Released in March 1941. Screenplay by Ernest Pagano and Harry Clork. Directed by Ralph Murphy. Cast featured Constance Moore, Bert Wheeler, Phil Regan, Lillian Cornell, Virginia Dale, and Tommy Dorsey and His Orchestra, with Frank Sinatra in his film debut. Other songs in this film included "On Miami Shore" by William LeBaron (lyrics) and Victor Jacobi (music).

I GOTTA RIDE

Music by Burton Lane. Published. Copyrighted March 19, 1941. Introduced by male trio that included Phil Regan. Featuring Tommy Dorsey and His Orchestra.

VERSE (NOT SUNG IN FILM)

Hand me my Stetson and necktie,
I'm on a Saturday spree.
If you see dynamite flash by,
Well, pardner, that's me.

REFRAIN

I gotta ride
Out where the prairie opens wide.
With that Nevada wind a-moanin' and sighin',
Gotta go tryin' my stride.
There ain't a durn canoe I could paddle,
I couldn't take the bumps on a bus—
I gotta spend my nights in the saddle
Or I'm the most unhappiest cuss.

I gotta ride—
This ain't no night to sit inside.
That feel of hoofs beneath me poundin' like
thunder
Kinda gets under my hide
And I decide
I gotta ride!
Yippie-i-ay!

ADDITIONAL VERSE (NOT SUNG IN FILM)

They've been a-ridin' since mornin',
Calf-ropin' all the day long.
Ought to be weary and yawnin',
But still goin' strong.

MARY, MARY, QUITE CONTRARY

Music by Burton Lane. Published. March 19, 1941. Introduced by Lillian Cornell, Constance Moore, and Virginia Dale with Tommy Dorsey and His Orchestra. Recorded by Blossom Dearie (Painted Smiles). Originally intended for *Dancing on a Dime* (page 61).

VERSE (NOT SUNG IN FILM)

Here's a little story ev'ry girl should know,
And the moral is: Don't be dumb.
Just a little story told me long ago,
A tale that you might learn a lesson from.

REFRAIN

ALL: Shh—shh!
We're letting you in on a little secret about
Mary, Mary, quite contrary.
CORNELL: Tasty little sugar cake.
MOORE: Sweet as honey.
ALL: Mary, Mary, quite contrary—
CORNELL: Never gave the boys a break.
MOORE: But still they tried—
DALE: And tried.
CORNELL: Still the lady could not be kissed.
ALL: Oh, no.
CORNELL: For years and years—
ALL: Till they called it a "case dismissed."
Oh, Mary, Mary, quite contrary—
CORNELL: Waited for the one true love—
DALE: She wanted lovin'.
ALL: For that extraordinary angel
From the sky above.
CORNELL: He came! He saw!
ALL: Then he started once more to roam.
For he found Mary, still contrary,
Sittin' in the Old Maids' Home!
Sittin' in the Old Maids' Home!

DOLORES

Music by Lou Alter. Published. Copyrighted February 17, 1941. Sung first in Spanish by Nick Moro, Frank Yoconelli, and Earl Douglas. Reprised in English by Bert Wheeler, Nick Moro, Frank Yoconelli, Earl Douglas, Mark Ladd, Tommy Dorsey and His Orchestra. Nominated for an Academy Award as Best Song. Top recordings by Tommy Dorsey and His Orchestra, vocal by Frank Sinatra (Victor—number one in America) and Bing Crosby, with the Merry Macs and Bob Crosby's Orchestra (Decca—number two in America). Other recordings include Lawrence Welk (Coral) and Russ Morgan (Decca).

VERSE (NOT SUNG IN FILM)

It was a sunny little, funny little border town
Where on a moonlit night I rode,
And all the local guys were vocalizing up and
down

Before a certain girl's abode.
And from a hundred lips the melody came,
Crooning her name:

REFRAIN

WHEELER: How I love the kisses of Dolores!
ENSEMBLE: Ay-ay-ay, Dolores!
WHEELER: Not Marie or Dorothy or Doris,
Only my Dolores.
From a balcony above me,
She whispers "Love me"
And throws a rose.
Ah, but she is twice as lovely
As the rose she throws!
I would die to be with my Dolores.*
ENSEMBLE: Ay-ay-ay, Dolores!
WHEELER: I was made to serenade Dolores,
Chorus after chorus.
Just imagine eyes like moonrise,
A voice like music,
And lips like wine!
What a break if I could make Dolores
Mine, all mine!

NATIVES' VERSES (NOT SUNG IN FILM)

Ah, señor, how I adore Dolores!
Ay-ay-ay, Dolores.
In the spring I always bring las flores
Just for my Dolores.
Listen to my song, amigo, I am Rodrigo,
My love is true.
Any place Dolores she go,
Rodrigo he go too.
Ah, señor, you're looking for Dolores?
Ay-ay-ay, Dolores.
Sí, sí, sí, so Dorothy Lamourus,
She is my Dolores.
Listen to my song, amigo, I am Rodrigo,
I tell no lie.
Que placer, ay, mi querer, Dolores.
Ay-ay-ay!

Ah, señor, how I adore Dolores!
Ay-ay-ay, Dolores.
In the spring I always bring las flores
Just for my Dolores.
Listen to my song, young fellow,
I am Marcelo, my love is true.
Any time Dolores mellow,
Marcelo mellow too.
Por favor, mírame mi amor Dolores.
Ay-ay-ay, Dolores.
Que placer, oy, mi querer, Dolores.

* Alternate line:
  I would like to die with my Dolores

Ay-ay-ay, Dolores.
Listen to my song, young fellow,
I am Marcelo, I tell no lie.
Por favor, mírame mi amor Dolores
Ay-ay-ay!

ON MIAMI SHORE PROLOGUE

Music by Victor Young. Loesser lyrics are the lead-in to "On Miami Shore" by Victor Jacobi and William LeBaron (words) and Victor Young (music). Introduced by Lillian Cornell, The Pied Pipers and Tommy Dorsey and His Orchestra.

I tried to find romance on the beach at Waikiki,
But Waikiki was not for me.
Then I strolled on the boardwalk at Coney,
Took a ride on a carousel pony.
Then I tried Coronado, Rosarita, Ensenada—
They left me cold.
But way down yonder in the southland,
My heart discovered gold:
There's a lure in Miami
That never grows old.

SIS HOPKINS

Produced by Robert North for Republic Pictures. Released in April 1941. Screenplay by Jack Townley, Milt Gross, and Edward Eliscu from the play by Carroll Fleming and George A. Nichols. Directed by Joseph Santley. Cast starred Judy Canova and featured Bob Crosby and His Band, Charles Butterworth, Jerry Colonna, and Susan Hayward. A silent film version was made in 1919 by Samuel Goldwyn with Mabel Normand in the title role.

LOOK AT YOU, LOOK AT ME

Music by Jule Styne. Published. Copyrighted April 16, 1941. Introduced by Bob Crosby and Susan Hayward. Styne (1905–1994) went on from Republic to a distinguished songwriting career. His Broadway musicals include High Button Shoes, Gentlemen Prefer Blondes, Bells Are Ringing, Gypsy, and Funny Girl. Loesser was

loaned to Republic at Styne's request (with some lobbying by music director Cy Feuer, who would later co-produce Where's Charley? and produce Guys and Dolls and How to Succeed in Business Without Really Trying). In exchange for Loesser, Republic got John Wayne from Paramount.

VERSE

CROSBY: This could have been a glorious night,
But it isn't.
HAYWARD: You could have been embracing me tight,
But you aren't.
CROSBY: You're in your room, I'm in mine,
And this is the usual half past nine,
and—

REFRAIN

CROSBY: Look at you, look at me—
You're so unhappy, I'm all at sea.
And yesterday we bravely said goodbye,
Because we're sensible, that's why.

HAYWARD: Look at you, look at me—
You've smoked up two packs, I've poured me three.
CROSBY: And yesterday we thought we'd break the spell,
With just a little word, "farewell."
But all the lovely visions we decided we'd erase,
Back to this lonely room they came.
I'm looking in the mirror at a very foolish face,
And I suppose you're doing the same.

HAYWARD: Where's that smile? Where's that kiss?
What are we proving?
CROSBY: We're proving this:
You can't just take a heart and set it free.
BOTH: Look at you, look at me.

THAT AIN'T HAY (THAT'S THE U.S.A.)

Music by Jule Styne. Published. Copyrighted April 16, 1941. Introduced by Judy Canova, Bob Crosby and the Bobcats.

VERSE

CANOVA: [*spoken*] When you sit down to your
    dinner,
    Do you ever happen to think
    [*sung*] Who raised the chicken, who
    baked the biscuit,
    And who grew the wine that you drink?

    'Twas a great big army of little people,
    From California to Maine;
    'Twas a great big army of little people,
    And maybe this will explain:

REFRAIN

    See that man with the hoe
    Making fields of taters grow?*
    Well, that poor old hired hand
    Put potatoes all over the land.
    And that ain't hay!
    That's the U.S.A.!

    See that man with the drill?
    Round the wells they call him Bill.
    Well, that rough-and-ready guy
    Gets the gas for those planes in the sky.†
    And that ain't hay!
    That's the U.S.A.!

    Hooray, hooray, for the little guy!
    He's what this country is living by.
    He's more a hero than you and I,
    Singing a song,
    While he's diggin' it all the day long.

    He's the man on the street,
    And he's making both ends meet.
    Just a plain old Jack or Jim,
    But there's millions and millions
    like him.
    And that ain't hay!
    That's the U.S.A.!

ENSEMBLE: Hooray, hooray, for the little guy!
    He's what this country is living by.
    He's more a hero than you and I,
    Singing a song—
CANOVA: While he's a-buildin' it all the day long.

---

* Sheet music version:
    Making fields of cabbage grow?

† Sheet music version of lines 8–10 of refrain:
    Down the mines they call him Bill.
    Well, that rough old dirty face
    Gets the coal for your old fireplace.

See those men marchin' by
With their chins away up high?
They're a mighty big expense,
But they're part of our nation's
    defense.
And that ain't hay!
That's the U.S.A.!
ENSEMBLE: Hooray, hooray, for the little guy!
    He's what this country is living by.
    Hooray, hooray! That's the U.S.A.!

WELL! WELL!

Music by Jule Styne. Published. Copyrighted April 16,
1941. Introduced by Judy Canova and Bob Crosby and
His Band. Recording by Bob Crosby and His Orchestra
(Decca).

VERSE

CROSBY: I never saw Cupid pull the bow,
    Never saw the arrow fly.
    All I know is that there stood you
    And there stood I.

REFRAIN

CANOVA: (And) well! well!
    I went and fell!
    I fell into your terrific spell,
    And well! well!
    I went and fell for you!

    Well! well!
    You rang the bell!
    You did so right by our Little Nell,
    That well! well!
    I hope to yell "I do!"

    You tried to kiss me;
    I hollered "Don't,
    Don't you dare to kiss me!"
    I hollered "Don't!"
    I hollered "Stop!"
    I hollered "Don't! Stop! Don't stop!
    Don't ya dare stop!"

    Well! well!
    You fixed me swell!
    You hit my heart like a William Tell,
    And well! well!
    I went and fell for you!

IF YOU'RE IN LOVE

Music by Jule Styne. Published. Copyrighted April 16,
1941. Introduced by Judy Canova, Jerry Colona, and
Bob Crosby and His Band.

VERSE

Treasure each hug and cherish each kiss—
The moral of my story is this:

REFRAIN

If you're in love, you're lucky;
If you're in love, don't lose it;
If you're in love, you're doing all right;
If you're in love, that's ducky—
Only poor saps refuse it.
If you're in love, hold on to it tight.
Oh, you may not have a dollar down in your jeans,
Or the wherewithal to make a local call
Or buy her one highball or even beans.
But if you're in love, you're lucky;
If you're in love, don't lose it;
If you're in love, then shout "Hooray!"
Once you get it, keep it—
Don't you ever throw it away.

CRACKER BARREL COUNTY

Music by Jule Styne. Published. Copyrighted April 16,
1941. Not used in film. Used for promotion only.

VERSE

Oh, you city slicker
With the fickle ticker,
The toil and the trouble
And the seventy-five-cent liquor!

REFRAIN

Come to Cracker Barrel County
If you need a change of pace,
Get acquainted with the lazy summer breeze,
For it's Cracker Barrel County
Where you join the human race
And you gallivant exactly as you please,
Where you can yodel when you want to yodel, lady,
Yodel lady, yodel lady,
Or you can whistle out a whistle where it's shady
Or just slumber all day in the newly mown hay.

When you've made your second million
And you've figured out the tax,
And the strain has got you dropping in your
    tracks,
Come to Cracker Barrel County and relax.

THERE'S MAGIC IN MUSIC

Produced by Andrew L. Stone for Paramount Pictures. Initially released as *The Hard-Boiled Canary*. Released in June 1941. Screenplay by Frederick Jackson, based on a story by Andrew L. Stone and Robert Lively from an idea by Ann Ronell. Directed by Andrew L. Stone. Cast featured Allan Jones, Susanna Foster, Margaret Lindsay, and Lynne Overman. The film also featured the song "Fireflies on Parade" by Ann Ronell.

THE STUTTERING SONG

Not used in film.

C-c-can't h-h-help
T-t-talking like I do,
'C-c-cause I'm so c-c-c
    c-c-c
    c-c-crazy over you.
C-c-can't h-h-help
S-s-stuttering like this,
'C-c-cause I'm so n-n-n
    n-n-n
    n-n-nervous when we kiss.

But I swear by the stars above you
That I'll always—l-l-l
    l-l-l
    l-l-let me say
What I want to say.

Can't h-h-help
T-t-talking like I do,
'C-c-cause I'm so c-c-c
    c-c-c
    c-c-c—
Cut it out, will ya!

Version 2

B-b-b-boy, I'm dizzy,
I g-g-guess it's love,
'Cause it gets me n-n-n
    n-n-n
    n-n-nervous as can be.

B-b-b-boy, I'm flying
In h-h-heaven above,
Why, I'm p-p-p
    p-p-p
    p-p-positively up a tree.

He p-p-p-p-puts me
In a trance.
This must be r-r-r
    r-r-r
    r-r-romance,
Pants, ten cents a dance.

'Cause b-b-b-b-boy I'm dizzy
From e-e-ev'ry kiss,
Otherwise I'd never t-t-t
    t-t-t
    t-t-talk like this!

WHAT SORT OF MUSIC DOES THE PUBLIC LIKE?

Music by Phil Boutelje, with fragments of four pop songs as indicated. Not used in film.

What sort of music does the public like?
What kind of singing will it be?
What sort of music does the public like?
Don't ask me.
For I've gone to movies just to find that out,
But in the movies all they sing about is—

[*Sings "Falling in Love Again"*]

If that's what the people really clamor for
Why do they crowd around a nightclub floor
    for—

[*Sings "Oh! Johnny! Oh!"*]

But though that young lady may be the rage,
There's still such a thing as the vaud'ville
    stage.
Millions of tickets are bought every year
By millions of people who just want to hear—

[*Sings "You Tell 'Er, I S-t-u-t-t-e-r"*]

Nobody seems to be the public choice;
They're always listening to another voice,
    like—

[*Sings "You Made Me Love You," leading into quick medley*]

Now after looking for a style to swipe,
I have decided on one thing:
Susanna Foster would be more my type,
So I'll sing—

[*Sings coloratura to finish*]

CAUGHT IN THE DRAFT

Produced by B. G. DeSylva for Paramount Pictures. Released in June 1941. Screenplay and story by Harry Tugend. Directed by David Butler. Cast starred Bob Hope and Dorothy Lamour and featured Lynne Overman, Eddie Bracken, Clarence Kolb, and Paul Hurst.

LOVE ME AS I AM

Music by Louis Alter. Published. Copyrighted April 30, 1941. Used instrumentally only. Intended for Bob Hope and Dorothy Lamour. Recorded by Frank Sinatra with Tommy Dorsey and His Orchestra (Victor).

VERSE

You'll find ev'rything out, my love,
When you know me a little bit better.
You'll find out somehow,
So I might as well tell you now.

REFRAIN 1

HOPE: I snore in my sleep,
    I'm always late for dinner,
    And my tablecloth doodling is notorious.
    Ah, but lovely one, keep this romance
        glorious,
    And love me as I am.

I dream while I drive,*
I linger in the shower,
And there isn't much rhythm in that waltz
    of mine.
Ah, but lovely one, skip those little faults
    of mine,
And love me as I am.

And don't try to make any changes;
It wouldn't be worth your tears.
Don't try to make any changes—
My mother's been trying for years!

I sing when I drink,
I never cap the toothpaste,†
And my company manners are deplorable.
Ah, but lovely one, tell me I'm adorable,
And love me as I am.

REFRAIN 2

LAMOUR: I wear the wrong hats,
    I make the strangest coffee,
    And my repartee isn't so spectacular.
    Ah, but honey boy, in your own vernacular,
    Just love me as I am.

    I let the phone ring,
    I park my gum all over,‡
    And when playing bridge, I can't put my
        mind to it.
    Ah, but honey boy, get yourself resigned
        to it,
    And love me as I am.
    So what if my lip rouge annoys you
    By messing you up this way?
    What if my lip rouge annoys you,
    As long as my kiss is okay?

    I talk a blue streak,
    I'm awf'lly fond of onions,§
    And I sing like some baritone from
        China might.
    Ah, but honey boy, otherwise I'm
        dynamite!
    So love me as I am.

---

* Alternate line:
    I talk to myself,

† Alternate line:
    I'm awfully fond of onions,

‡ Alternate line:
    I never cap the toothpaste,

§ Alternate line:
    The jokes I tell have whiskers,

MANPOWER

Produced by Mark Hellinger for Warner Bros.–First National. Released in July 1941. Story and screenplay by Richard Macaulay and Jerry Wald. Directed by Raoul Walsh. Cast starred Edward G. Robinson, Marlene Dietrich, and George Raft and featured Alan Hale, Frank McHugh, Eve Arden, Barton MacLaine, Ward Bond, Walter Catlett, Joyce Compton, and Egan Brechor.

HE LIED AND I LISTENED

Music by Frederick Hollander. Introduced by Marlene Dietrich. No written lyric available. The song is sung mostly in the background during a noisy club scene. The following lyrics were taken from film soundtrack. Missing lyrics indicated by ellipses.

He lied and I listened;
That's how my simple story goes.
Yes, he lied and I listened
And asked me what [. . .]

He lied and I listened
[. . . . .]
I lied and he listened
[. . .] too too divine.

KISS THE BOYS GOODBYE

Produced by William LeBaron for Paramount Pictures. Released in August 1941. Music by Victor Schertzinger. Screenplay by Harry Tugend and Dwight Taylor based on the play by Clare Boothe Luce. Directed by Victor Schertzinger. Cast featured Don Ameche, Mary Martin, Oscar Levant, Virginia Dale, Barbara Allen, Raymond Walburn, Elizabeth Patterson, Jerome Cowan, Connee (here billed as Connie) Boswell, and Eddie "Rochester" Anderson. The versatile Schertzinger (1890–1941), a composer as well as a film director, also wrote the brilliant score to *The Fleet's In* with Johnny Mercer, which featured such standards as "Tangerine" and "I Remember You."

KISS THE BOYS GOODBYE

Published. Copyrighted June 6, 1941. Introduced by Mary Martin and the girls' chorus. Reprised by Don Ameche. Leading recordings by Tommy Dorsey and His Orchestra, vocal by Connie Haines (Victor), and Bea Wain (Victor). Other recordings include Mary Martin (Decca) and Rhonda Fleming (Painted Smiles).

VERSE (NOT SUNG IN FILM)

We're such a happy pair,
That it isn't right, no, it isn't fair
To all those other boys I gave the air,
So—

REFRAIN

MARTIN: Daddy, let me stay out late,
    For tomorrow is our wedding date—
    Let the baby kinda celebrate,
    Kiss the boys goodbye.
    Daddy, let me wear the mink—
    What's the diff'rence what the
        neighbors think?
CHORUS: Let the baby linger on the brink,
    Kiss the boys goodbye.
    And while I'm kissing them
        sentiment'ly,
    Keep the liberal point of view,
    Because I'm breaking it to them
        gently—
CHORUS
AND MARTIN: That my heart belongs to you.
CHORUS: So, Daddy, please remember this,
    That tomorrow starts a life of bliss.
GIRL: Let me show them what they're
        gonna miss.
CHORUS: Kiss the boys goodbye.

REPRISE

MARTIN: Oh, Daddy, let me stay out late,
    Can't the baby kinda celebrate?
    Beat me, Daddy, with an old whisk
        broom—
    Kiss the boys goodbye.
    Oh, Daddy, let me wear the mink—
    I don't know the words, but I think
    We'll stick around and go to town—
    Kiss the boys goodbye.

FIND YOURSELF A MELODY

Published. Copyrighted June 17, 1941. Introduced by Mary Martin and African-American chorus.

VERSE

MARTIN: Why start chasing rainbows?
Get them off your mind.*
Honey, that's for the other fellows;
You be content to—

REFRAIN

Find yourself a melody
And take it to your heart,
Just a simple melody,
No classic work of art.
You may borrow from the whippoorwill,
Or better still,
Compose one all your own.
But find yourself a melody
And you will never be alone.
CHORUS: Say it, say it with a song.
Find yourself a melody
And take it to your heart.
MARTIN: The old familiar voices singin' through
the air.
CHORUS: Just a simple melody,
No classic work of art.
MARTIN: An' for a Dixie lullaby,
It's only fair to borrow from the
whippoorwill,
Or better still—compose one.
With a tra-la-la-la-la, ah-ah-ah-ah-ah-
ah-ah-ah-ah,
Like this—

[ENSEMBLE launches into "Joshua Fit de Battle of
Jericho," followed by "Mah Curly Headed Baby."]

CHILDREN: Oh, Miss Cindy Lou, Oh, Miss Cindy
Lou,
How can anybody jive with you?
Ya don' dig—
MARTIN: I don' dig?
CHILDREN: Ya don' dig—
MARTIN: I don' dig?
CHILDREN: Ya don' dig—ya don' dig—ya don'
dig—
MARTIN: I don' dig? I dig big!

---

* Sheet music version:
  All the gold's been mined.

Go find myself a melody,
Take it high, take it low,
Take it right into your heart.
Just a simple kinda melody,
Unbutton your coat and just pick out
a note,
An' then start to whistle.
CHORUS: Borrow from the whippoorwill
Or better still—
MARTIN: Here's one to call your own.
But find yourself a melody
And you will never—
CHORUS: No, you'll never—
MARTIN: You will never be alone.
CHORUS: You will never find yo'self alone.

SAND IN MY SHOES

Published. Copyrighted June 6, 1941. Introduced by Connee Boswell and Eddie "Rochester" Anderson. Leading recording by Connee Boswell, accompanied by Victor Young's Orchestra (Decca). Other recordings include Bobby Short (Atlantic), Tito Puente and His Orchestra (Victor), and Gwen Verdon (Victor).

VERSE (NOT USED IN FILM)

Out of sight, out of mind,
That's what I told myself.
So I left you behind
And I controlled myself.
Yet some mysterious thing
Makes every memory cling.
It makes me want to take wing again tonight
And know the delight of holding you tight.

REFRAIN 1

BOSWELL: Sand in my shoes,
Sand from Havana,
Calling me to that ever-so-heavenly
shore,
Calling me back to you once more.
Dreams in the night,
Dreams of Havana,
Dreams of a love I haven't the
strength to refuse.
Darling, the sand is in my shoes.
Deep in my veins,
The sensuous strains of the soft
guitars.
Deep in my soul,
The thundering roll of a tropic sea
under the stars.

That was Havana,
You are the moonlit mem'ry I can't
seem to lose.
That's why my life's an aimless
cruise.
All that is real is the feel
Of that sand in my shoes!

REFRAIN 2

ROCHESTER: Sand in my shoes,
But not from Havana.
It's from the Harlem River that flows
way uptown.
That's why I'm feelin' so low-down.
Dreams in the night,
Boogie piana
Calling me to the Cotton Club and
the Savoy.
That's why I'm such a lonesome
boy.
Deep in my veins,
The sepia stains of a hot guitar.
Deep in my soul,
The thundering roll of a pair of
dice.
Eight to the bar,
That was my Harlem,
That was the place that gave me this
case of the blues.
That's why my life's an aimless
cruise.
Play me some jive with that band—
I've got sand in my shoes.

I'LL NEVER LET A DAY PASS BY

Published. Copyrighted June 6, 1941. Introduced by Don Ameche and Mary Martin. Recorded by Tommy Dorsey and His Orchestra, vocal by Frank Sinatra (Victor), and Harry James and His Orchestra, vocal by Dick Haymes (Columbia).

VERSE (NOT SUNG IN FILM)

Another day gone by, but that can't discourage me.
There's still the night left to dream in,
And I know what that dream will be.
And when I waken, just as sure as the sun will
break through,
My day will start and end with thoughts of you.

REFRAIN

AMECHE: I never let a day pass by
Without a pray'r or two
That heaven find a way so I
Might just run into you.
Just to be near you
And to hear you say hello
Would give an ordinary day a lovely glow.

I'll never let a day pass by
But that I'll see your face
And thrill to ev'ry tender sigh
While you're in my embrace.
I know it's all a dream,
But, darling, if it were true,
I'd never let a day pass by
Without my loving you.

[*Refrain repeated by* MARTIN.]

THAT'S HOW I GOT MY START

Published. Copyrighted June 17, 1941. Previously titled "My Start" and "Once I Met." Introduced by Mary Martin.

VERSE

Once I had a stamp collection;
Then I switched to autographs.
And some of them were on the nicest letters
I forgot to save, just for laughs.
Now I'm older and I'm wiser,
Still my hobby never ends,
And now I have the loveliest collection
Of things that I can show my friends.

REFRAIN 1 (NOT SUNG IN FILM)

Once I met a cloak-and-suiter,
Never was a suitor cuter.
My wardrobe got more ample
With each sample.
And that's how I got my start.

Then I met a famous flyer,
Goodness, was that guy a liar!
He loved me like a brother—
That's another.
But that's how I got my start.

Nobody has a string on me,
Let people talk as they do.
Nobody has a thing on me,
Except a mink and a bracelet or two.

Prove it by my rich banker,
How I made that banker hanker!
So let this be a lesson:
Keep 'em guessin',
'Cause that's how I got my start.*

REFRAIN 2

Once I met a famous painter,
Never was a painter quainter.
I got this bit of knitting
Merely sitting.
That's how I got my start.

Once I met a dry-goods drummer,
Never was a drummer dumber.
But now my wardrobe's ample—
Here's a sample.
That's how I got my start.

Nobody has a string on me,
I'm just as free as the air.
There's still an age of chivalry,
If the truth of it all were laid bare.

Once I met an old gold miner,
Practically a forty-niner.
You see this little nugget?
Well, I dug it.
That's how I got my start.

REFRAIN 3

Once I met a desperate bandit,
Lordy, how that bandit planned it!
With a look of wild desire
He said, "Give or I'll fire!"

Started dancing with a bubble,
Then developed bubble trouble.
The pink one that I trusted
[*sound of balloon losing air*] busted.
That's how I got my start.

_____

* *Earlier version:*
  Prove it by my rich banker,
  Never was a banker franker.
  His interest was gigantic,
  Isn't this romantic?
  Well, that's how I got my start.

Why is it they're so kind to me,
Men who have all made a mint?
Why do they act so gallantly?
Couldn't somebody drop me a hint?

There you have my whole life story,
Struggling on the road to glory.
So let this be a lesson:
Keep 'em guessin',
'Cause that's how I got my start.

ALTERNATE FINAL STANZA (NOT SUNG IN FILM)

Once I met a wealthy broker,
And I played that broker poker.
I wouldn't say he gypped me,
But with one hand he stripped me.
That's how I got my start.

WE'VE MET SOMEWHERE BEFORE

Not used in film.

VERSE

Call it reincarnation,
Call it what you will,
But the moment I set eyes on you
My heart stood still.

REFRAIN

We've met somewhere before.
I could never forget you,
But how did I let you
Escape from me then?
Your smile brings back once more
A moment of rapture
I've tried to recapture
Since heaven knows when.
I heard your name and still
My heart didn't thrill to its sound.
But when your hand touched mine,
My feet wouldn't stay on the ground.
We've met somewhere before.
How could I be mistaken?
You've come to awaken
A love I once knew—
It's always been you.

WORLD PREMIERE

Produced by Sol C. Siegel for Paramount Pictures. Released in August 1941. Screenplay by Earl Felton, from a story by Earl Felton and Gordon Kahn. Directed by Ted Tetzlaff. Cast featured John Barrymore, Frances Farmer, Eugene Pallette, Virginia Dale, Ricardo Cortez, Don Castle, and Fritz Feld.

DON'T CRY, LITTLE CLOUD

Music by Burton Lane. Used instrumentally only.

VERSE

It's a perfect night,
And the moon is bright,
But I notice a cloud in the sky.
So I ups to the cloud and I says, says I:

REFRAIN

Don't cry, little cloud,
Roll by, little cloud,
Don't cry, little cloud up above,
'Cause I'm all dressed up tonight
For someone I love.
Don't cry little cloud,
No weeping aloud.
Keep dry, little cloud,
Won't you please?
Or you'll turn the sweetest kisses
Into a sneeze.
You wouldn't drizzle, would ya,
On a lovely romance?
Give a fellow a chance,
Thanking you in advance.
Don't cry, little cloud,
Roll by, little cloud,
Make way for that moon up above,
'Cause I'm all dressed up tonight
For someone I love.

ALOMA OF THE SOUTH SEAS

Produced by B. G. DeSylva for Paramount Pictures. Released in August 1941. Screenplay by Seena Owen, Frank Butler, and Lillie Hayward, based on a story by Kurt Siodmak and Seena Owen. Directed by Alfred Santell. Cast starred Dorothy Lamour and Jon Hall and featured Philip Reed, Katherine deMille, Lynne Overman, Fritz Leiber, and Dona Drake.

THE WHITE BLOSSOMS OF TAH-NI

Music by Frederick Hollander. Published. Copyrighted July 3, 1941. Introduced by Dorothy Lamour. Recordings include Frances Langford with Victor Young and His Orchestra (Decca) and Ray Kinney and His Hawaiian Serenaders (Victor).

VERSE (NOT USED IN FILM)

When the zephyrs blow warm through the
    mangrove trees,
There's a magical scent in the air,
And it's time to set sail for the tropic seas,
For romance is there.

REFRAIN

The white blossoms of Tah-ni
Keep weaving their fragrant spell.
And young lovers of Tah-ni
Have an old tale of the islands to tell.

They say when your heart's lonely,
Try twining them in your hair,
And those white blossoms of Tah-ni
Will soon bring your loved one there.

HOLD BACK THE DAWN

Produced by Arthur Hornblow Jr. for Paramount Pictures. Released in October 1941. Screenplay by Charles Brackett and Billy Wilder, based on a novel by Ketti

Frings. Directed by Mitchell Leisen. Cast starred Charles Boyer, Olivia de Havilland, and Paulette Goddard and featured Veronica Lake, Brian Donlevy, Victor Francen, Walter Abel, Rosemary De Camp, and Mitchell Leisen. Other songs in this score include "Hold Back the Dawn," music and lyrics by Richard Loring and Steven Cross, and "A Sinner Kissed an Angel" by Mack David (lyrics) and Ray Joseph (music).

MY BOY, MY BOY

Words by Frank Loesser, Jimmy Berg, and Frank Jacobson. Music by Fritz Spielman (1906–1977). Published. Copyrighted November 7, 1941. Used instrumentally only. Austrian-born composer-pianist Spielman's biggest hits were "Paper Roses" and "It Only Hurts for a Little While."

VERSE 1

Not long ago a man came to this country.
He brought an accent and his little Frau.
And in his furnished room he sits around and
    schemes.
He says he is so happy in this country,
He is so proud, he's got first papers now.
And with a smile he tells me what he dreams.

REFRAIN 1

My boy, my boy will be an American boy.
My son, my son will be such a son of a gun.
And he won't need a passport for his
    immigration,
He'll need only Pop and Mom.
He'll have no troubles with his visa application,
He'll say only "Here I am."
My boy will say in English "Oh, Daddy" to me,
One day, one day.
Maybe he'll reside in D.C.
To ev'ry meal he'll drink a double ice-cream
    soda,
And ev'ry day he will enjoy,
Because my boy will be an American boy!

VERSE 2

I listened to the song the greenhorn chanted.
A greenhorn knows how other countries are,
And so he loves the little things that we don't see.
We people here, we take too much for granted.
We all, we all should thank our lucky star,
And you and I, we all should sing like he.

REFRAIN 2

My boy, my boy will be an American boy.
My son, my son will be such a son of a gun.
He'll talk the Yankee Doodle Dandy kind of lingo.
He'll be Harvard's quarterback.
He'll win a hundred thousand dollars playing
    bingo.
Yes, I guess we'll call him Jack.
My boy, my boy will lead an American life.
My pride and joy,
He'll have an American wife,
For I have just received that extra quota
    number—
Now there's a dream they can't destroy!
My boy, my boy will be an American,
Real American, strictly American boy!

SAILORS ON LEAVE

Produced by Albert J. Cohen for Republic Pictures. Previously titled *Sailor Be Good*. Released in October 1941. Screenplay by Art Arthur and Malcolm Stuart Boylan, from a story by Herbert Dalmas. Directed by Albert S. Rogell. Cast featured William Lundigan, Shirley Ross, and Chick Chandler. Other Loesser songs attributed to the film include "How'ya, Sailor?" "When a Sailor Goes Ashore," "I'm Proud I'm a Navy Man," and "Finale." Lyrics currently unavailable.

SINCE YOU

Music by Jule Styne. Published. Copyrighted October 17, 1941. Introduced by Shirley Ross.

VERSE

It may seem a little ridiculous,
Impossible,
Preposterous,
But oh!
This is what I want to know.

REFRAIN

Hasn't been anyone else in my heart since you.
Hasn't been anyone tear it apart since you.
Though I've been free to choose
A new affair,
If someone stepped in your shoes,

I know he could never compare.
Hasn't been anyone thrill me that way since you.
Maybe it gives you a laugh when I say I'm through,
But it's true.
That's why I tell them "No dice,"
'Cause that lightning could never strike twice.
Hasn't been anyone else and there never will be,
Since you loved me.

SENTIMENTAL FOLKS

Music by Jule Styne. Registered for copyright as an unpublished song October 18, 1941. Introduced by William Lundigan and Shirley Ross.

VERSE

Look at those couples, strolling along,
Sighing a sigh or humming a song.
Most of those couples haven't a dime,
But they're having a beautiful time.

REFRAIN

Oh, what a night for sentimental folks,
For sentimental folks like you and me.
Oh, what a night for drifting on a stream
Or dreaming up a dream beneath a tree.
A silver moon on high
And starlight in the sky
That a smart sophisticated guy
Wouldn't bother to see—
But darling, what a night
For John and Mary Doakes
And all the sentimental folks
Like you and me.

HENRY ALDRICH FOR PRESIDENT

Produced by Sol C. Siegel for Paramount Pictures. Released in October 1941. Screenplay by Val Burton as a sequel to Clifford Goldsmith's "Henry Aldrich" stories. Directed by Hugh Bennett. Cast starred Jimmy Lydon and featured June Preisser, Mary Anderson, and Charles Smith.

JOHNNY JONES

Music by Harry Barris (1905–1962). Introduced by June Preisser. Barris was a member of the Paul Whiteman Rhythm Boys with Bing Crosby and Al Rinker. His songs include "Mississippi Mud," "I Surrender, Dear," and "Wrap Your Troubles in Dreams."

Johnny Jones hasn't got a nickel,*
And Johnny Jones hasn't got a dime.
Johnny Jones has himself a wonderful time!
Just watch that Johnny Jones—hasn't got a
    quarter,
And Johnny Jones hasn't got a half.
Bless my bones!
Johnny has the very last laugh!

And when the band plays—ra-da-da-da-da—
He sways—ra-da-da-da-da—
Always close to that Mary Smith
That you wish you were with!
Oh, Johnny Jones doesn't need a dollar,
And Johnny Jones doesn't need a sou,
Johnny Jones cuts a better carpet
Than you, or you, or you!

Why, Sammy Green, you're looking mighty
    snazzy!
Oh, Sammy Green, you're looking mighty gay!
Now, Sammy Green, vote for Barrett on the big
    day!
Why, hello, Bobby Lee, you're dancing like a
    demon!
Oh, Bobby Lee, how you feeling, Bob?
B'lieve you me, Barrett is the man for the job!

And when the band plays—ra-da-da-da-da—
I'll gaze—ra-da-da-da-da—
Always, into your eyes of blue—
And I really mean you.
Oh, Johnny Jones doesn't need a dollar,
And Johnny Jones doesn't need a sou,
Johnny Jones digs a ditty cuter
Than you and you and you.
Vote for Barrett!
You and you and you!

_____
* *First stanza not sung in film.*

BIRTH OF THE BLUES

Produced by B. G. DeSylva and Monta Bell for Paramount Pictures. Released December 1941. Screenplay by Harry Tugend and Walter DeLeon from an original story by Tugend. Directed by Victor Schertzinger. Cast featured Bing Crosby, Mary Martin, Brian Donlevy, Carolyn Lee, Eddie "Rochester" Anderson, and Jack Teagarden. Many well-known songs were used in this film.

MEMPHIS BLUES
(Special Lyrics)

Music by W. C. Handy (1873–1958) and George A. Norton (1880–1923). Introduced by Bing Crosby. The legendary blues pioneer Handy also wrote "St. Louis Blues" and "Beale Street Blues." Norton co-wrote "My Melancholy Baby" with Ernie Burnett.

Now, brother, just stand pat
While I see where we're at.
Uh-oh, we're a little short right now,
But we're gonna beat that jail,
Raise a bit of bail somehow.
And when we raise that coin,
You polish up your horn and join
The Memphis Blues.

GLAMOUR BOY

Produced by Sol C. Siegal and Colbert Clark for Paramount Pictures. Released in December 1941. Screenplay by Bradford Ropes and Val Burton. Directed by Ralph Murphy. Cast featured Jackie Cooper, Susanna Foster, Walter Abel, and Darryl Hickman.

THE MAGIC OF MAGNOLIAS

Music by Victor Schertzinger. Published. Copyrighted September 22, 1941. Introduced by Susanna Foster and chorus. Earlier title: "Magnolias in the Night."

VERSE (NOT SUNG IN FILM)

Wherever you may be,
What dreams do you dream?
And if you dream of me,
How near do I seem?
Have you this memory supreme?

REFRAIN

FOSTER: We felt the magic of
Magnolias in the night.
It made us fall in love,
Magnolias in the night.
For you and I were together,
Strolling under the trees;
It came, it saw, it conquered all,
That heavenly breeze.
And now that we're apart,
Magnolias in the air
Still whisper to my heart
That you will soon be there,
And once again we'll share
That fragrant delight
Of sweet magnolias in the night.

[CHORUS *whistles first line.*]

FOSTER: Magnolias in the night.
CHORUS: It made us fall in love—
ALL: Magnolias in the night.
FOSTER: For you and I were together,
Strolling under the trees.
CHORUS: Strolling under the trees.
It came, it saw, it conquered all,
That heavenly breeze.
FOSTER: And now that we're apart—
CHORUS: Magnolias in the air—
FOSTER: Still whisper to my heart that you—
CHORUS: Will soon be there.
FOSTER: And once again we'll share
That fragrant delight—
CHORUS: Of sweet magnolias—
FOSTER: In the night.

LOVE IS SUCH AN OLD-FASHIONED THING

Music by Victor Schertzinger. Published. Copyrighted September 22, 1941. Introduced by Susanna Foster.

VERSE (NOT USED IN FILM)

Styles may come and styles may go,
With fashions new and strange;
But when romance appears by chance,
Why, it never seems to change.

REFRAIN

Love is such an old-fashioned thing,
But it all seems new:
The frail bouquet, the old-fashioned ring,
And the bride saying "I do."

Though ev'ry new embrace may seem
A newfangled dream,
This always is true:
Love is such an old-fashioned thing,
But it's new when it happens to you!

Though ev'ry new embrace may seem
A newfangled dream,
This always is true:
Love is such an old-fashioned thing,
But it's new when it happens to you!

Styles may come and styles may go,
But it's new when it happens to you.

MISCELLANEOUS SONGS OF 1941

AHOY, MINNIE

Music and lyrics by Jule Styne and Frank Loesser. Lyric taken from a taped interview of Jule Styne by Susan Loesser, who recorded his performance of it shortly before Styne's death.

During their stint together in Hollywood, Styne and Loesser wrote and sang sea chanties to break the tedium of studio work at Paramount and Republic. According to Styne, this was their favorite. "No one in the world was as sophisticated as the two of us sitting there singing 'Ahoy, Minnie' like a couple of Peck's Bad Boys."

Oh, whatever became of Minnie—Ahoy, Minnie!
Oh, whatever became of Minnie J. McGee?
Oh, the Admiral married Minnie—Ahoy, Minnie!
And I hope she did for him what she did for me!

Praise The Lord And Pass The Ammunition!!

Words and Music by FRANK LOESSER

BUY WAR BONDS AND STAMPS FOR VICTORY

Songs of 1942

MR. BUG GOES TO TOWN

A Max Fleischer cartoon feature produced for Paramount Pictures. Released in February 1942. Later released under the title *Hoppity Goes to Town*. Screenplay and story by Dave Fleischer, Dan Gordon, and Ted Pierce. Directed by Dave Fleischer. Other songs in this film included "Be My Little Baby Bumble Bee" by Stanley Murphy (lyrics) and Henry Marshall (music).

KATY-DID, KATY-DIDN'T

Music by Hoagy Carmichael. Published. Copyrighted November 24, 1941. Introduced by Stan Freed, Pauline Loth, and the Four Marshalls.

VERSE (NOT USED IN FILM)

There's a burning, burning question
Concerning Katy Brown;
Here's a bit of a suggestion
Of the way they talk in town:

REFRAIN

ALL: Say, who came to Sunday school
With cherries on her lid?
Katy did, Katy didn't,
Katy did, Katy didn't,
Katy did, Katy didn't, Katy did!

And who kissed the banker's boy
And ran away and hid?
Katy did, Katy didn't,
Katy did, Katy didn't,
Katy did, Katy didn't, Katy did!

Gracious, what a scandal!
Ev'ry other girl would cry.
She can't hold a candle
To somebody such as I.
But who got the banker's boy
And fifty thousand quid?
Katy did, Katy didn't,
Katy did, Katy didn't,
MALE: You can bet your life she did.

ALL: Say, who came to Sunday school
Wearing cherries on her lid?
Katy dom-dom, Katy dom-dom,
Katy didn't, da-da-da-da-da-da.
LOTH: And who kissed the banker's boy
And ran away and hid?
ALL: Katy did, did-did-did, Katy, Katy did.
FREED: Katy's hard to handle,
And as far as I can see,
She can't hold a candle
To a certain honeybee.
ALL: But who got the banker's boy
And fifty thousand quid?
Katy did, Ka-Ka-Katy
You can bet your life she did!

UNUSED LYRICS

Say, who made the football team
Break training in the spring?
Katy did, Katy didn't,
Katy did, Katy didn't,
Katy did, Katy didn't do a thing!

And who dug the candy man
For candy all the time?
Katy did, Katy didn't,
Katy did, Katy didn't,
Katy did, Katy didn't need a dime.

Gracious, ain't it awful?
All the other girls would wail.
Really it's unlawful—
Why, she ought to go to jail!
But who got the banker's boy,
That tall and handsome kid?
Katy did, Katy didn't,
Katy did, Katy didn't,
You can bet your life she did.

BOY, OH BOY!

Music by Sammy Timberg (1903–1992). Published. Copyrighted November 24, 1941. Introduced by Stan Freed, Pauline Loth, and Jack Mercer. Recordings by Frankie Masters and His Orchestra (Okeh) and Bob Houston (Decca). Sammy Timberg wrote songs for Popeye, Betty Boop, and Little Lulu cartoons and other novelties.

VERSE (NOT SUNG IN FILM)

Sure there's taxes, sure there's trouble,
Sure the price of beans is double.
Yes, sir! The skies are gray.
Though it's tough and getting tougher,
Are you gonna sit and suffer?
No sir! get up and say:

REFRAIN

Boy, oh boy, oh boy, oh boy!
We've got fun, we've got freedom, we've got joy.
Oh boy, oh boy, oh boy, oh boy!
Got a rainbow, and it's the real McCoy.

There are bumps, bumps, bumps in the road,
And we're totin' a darn heavy load.
But boy, oh boy, oh boy, oh boy!
We've got fun, we've got freedom, we've got joy.

ADDITIONAL REFRAIN (NOT SUNG IN FILM)

Boy, oh boy, oh boy, oh boy!
Got a feeling that nothing can destroy.
Boy, oh boy, oh boy, oh boy!
Here's a country a fellow can enjoy.
With the whole world going to pot,
Brother, look round and see what we've got.
Oh boy, oh boy, oh boy, oh boy!
We've got fun, we've got freedom, we've got joy.

WE'RE THE COUPLE IN THE CASTLE

Music by Hoagy Carmichael. Published. Copyrighted November 24, 1941. Introduced by Kenny Gardner. Reprised at finale by chorus. Leading recording by Glenn Miller and His Orchestra, vocal by Ray Eberle (Bluebird). Other recordings include the Four King Sisters (Bluebird) and Claude Thornhill and His Orchestra (Columbia).

VERSE (NOT SUNG IN FILM)

Do drop in any time you're passing by where we live.
Spend a day where the Milky Way meets Rainbow Road.
Do drop in any time you're passing through,
And you'll find heaven in our heavenly abode.

REFRAIN

We're at nineteen Moonbeam Terrace,
Overlooking Starlight Square.
We're the couple in the castle

Way up high in the air!
On the corner there's a cloud bank,
And we bank our millions there.
We're the couple in the castle
In the air!

One day a daydream came a-stealing
Through the gloomy part of town.
Well, that daydream brought us way up here,
And we'll never come down!
Call us Lord and Lady Stardust,
Call us crazy, we don't care.
We're the couple in the castle
In the air.

I'LL DANCE AT YOUR WEDDING (HONEY DEAR)

Music by Sammy Timberg. Published. Copyrighted November 24, 1941. Introduced by ensemble. Recorded by Buddy Clark (Columbia).

Honey, marry money in the spring of the year,
And I'll dance at your wedding, honey dear.
Honey, marry money and I may shed a tear,
But I'll dance at your wedding, never fear.

Chimes will ring, the choir will sing,
And I'll try to be smiling.
Maybe then you'll kiss me as a sweet souvenir,
When I dance at your wedding, honey dear.

You'll be such a honey, such a honey of a bride—
What a lucky fellow is the fellow at your side!
But within my heart,
Deep within my heart,
Here's hoping you and your love never part.

Honey, marry money in the spring of the year,
And I'll dance at your wedding, honey dear.
Oh yes, we'll dance at your wedding,
Your lovely, lovely wedding
In the spring of the year.

[ENSEMBLE *then repeats song, with the following lyrics in place of the last stanza:*]

So, honey, marry money and your diamonds will
    shine,
And I'll dance at your wedding,
Dance at your wedding,
Wishing your lovely wedding could be mine!

UNUSED LYRICS

I'll wear something borrowed,
You'll wear something nice and new.
Sweetly I'll congratulate
The one who borrowed you.
But within my heart,
This is from the heart:
Here's hoping you'll soon be drifting apart.

REAP THE WILD WIND

Produced by Cecil B. DeMille for Paramount Pictures. Released in March 1942. Screenplay by Alan Le May, Charles Bennett, and Jesse Lasky Jr. from a novel by Thelma Strabel. Directed by Cecil B. DeMille. Cast starred Ray Milland, John Wayne, and Paulette Goddard and featured Raymond Massey, Robert Preston, Lynne Overman, Susan Hayward, Charles Bickford, Walter Hampden, and Louise Beavers.

SEA CHANTY

Music by Victor Young. First stanza introduced by Lynne Overman. Entire song (minus second stanza) performed later in the film by Paulette Goddard.

Oh, the *Nellie B*'s your packet,
And you're far away from home,
And it breaks your back to tack it
O'er the briny, shiny foam.
But heave-ho, haul away,
Just the same as me,
For you're just another packet rat
Aboard the *Nellie B*.

Oh, her timbers are so rotten,*
That she'll soon be in her grave,
And her name will be forgotten
Neath the briny, shiny wave.
But heave-ho, haul away,
Just the same as me,
For you're just another packet rat
Aboard the *Nellie B*.

___
* *Second stanza not used in film*

Bread and water for your suppers
When you board the *Nellie B*,
And your blood runs from her scuppers
In the briny, shiny sea.
But heave-ho, haul away,
Just the same as me,
For you're just another packet rat
Aboard the *Nellie B*.

Oh, the mate, he'll talk so civil,
But he'll rob you in your sleep.
There's no uglier a devil
On the briny, shiny deep.
But heave-ho, haul away,
Just the same as me,
For you're just another packet rat
Aboard the *Nellie B*.

Oh, it's lashes nine and thirty
For the galley-growling crew,
For the bos'n is a dirty
Son of the shiny, briny blue.
But heave-ho, haul away,
Just the same as me,
For you're just another packet rat
Aboard the *Nellie B*.

THIS GUN FOR HIRE

Produced by Richard Blumenthal for Paramount Pictures. Released in May 1942. Screenplay by Albert Maltz and W. R. Burnett, based on a novel by Graham Greene. Directed by Frank Tuttle. Cast starred Veronica Lake and Robert Preston and featured Laird Cregar, Alan Ladd, Tully Marshall, and Marc Lawrence.

NOW YOU SEE IT, NOW YOU DON'T

Music by Jacques Press (1903–1985). Introduced by Veronica Lake. Dubbed by Martha Mears. Press was a Russian émigré composer/arranger for "Roxy" (Samuel L. Rothafel), the Capitol Theatre, and Radio City Music Hall.

VERSE

Have you ever seen the lovelight in a lady's eyes
And then suddenly watched it vanish away?
If there's trouble in your love life,
Well, my friend, get wise.
For as we magicians would say—

REFRAIN

Now you see it, now you don't;
It goes hocus pocus alakazam!
That's love, that's love.
Try to kiss her, first she won't,
And then presto change-o, fiddle-dee-dee,
You're hand in glove.
One moment she's making you see
Canaries in the air.
Next moment instead of her heart
The ace of spades is there.
Now you see it, now you don't,
Because hocus pocus, lo and behold,
You get blinded by that moon of bright gold
    above—
That's love.

I'VE GOT YOU

Music by Jacques Press. Introduced by Veronica Lake. Dubbed by Martha Mears.

I've got you
Right where I wanted you,
Dangling on my line.
I've got you
And I'm enjoying it fine.
You had me
Right where you wanted me;
That's the way I learned.
You had me,
Ah, but the tables have turned.
I was one out of fifty in your address book,
Oh, what a spot you had me in!
But today you're the sucker for the shiny hook
And you'll never wriggle off.
You can bet your bottom fin
That I've got you
Right where I wanted you,
Dangling on my line.
I've got you
And I'm enjoying it fine,
'Cause I'm not yours anymore,
You're mine—

'Cause I'm not yours,
You're mine.

I'M AMAZED AT YOU

Music by Harold Spina (1906–1997). Not used in film. Spina's hits include "Annie Doesn't Live Here Anymore" and "My Very Good Friend, the Milkman," both written with Johnny Burke. Not used in film.

VERSE

You seem to believe there's a magic spell
Way down deep in these innocent eyes of mine,
A strange unbelievable charm that changes
Ordinary water into wine.
I guess you suppose when I smile at you
That canaries go fluttering through the air.
Now, how can you dream that I've captured your
    heart
When really there's nothing there?

REFRAIN

I'm amazed at you
For believing in love at first sight.
Got an eyebrow raised at you,
Why, you've only just met me tonight!
I'm amazed at you—
Did you think such a romance could be?
Well, it's time you knew
I think so too—
Now aren't you amazed at me?

TORTILLA FLAT

Produced by Sam Zimbalist for MGM. Released in May 1942. Screenplay by John Lee Mahin and Benjamin Glazer, based on the novel by John Steinbeck. Directed by Victor Fleming. Cast starred Spencer Tracy, Hedy Lamarr, John Garfield, and Frank Morgan and featured Akim Tamiroff, Sheldon Leonard, and John Qualen.

AI-PAISANO

Based on a Mexican folk tune, arranged by Franz Waxman (1906–1967). Registered for copyright as an unpublished song January 27, 1942. Introduced by John Garfield, Spencer Tracy, Akim Tamiroff, and Sheldon Leonard. Waxman won Academy Awards for his scores for *Sunset Boulevard* and *A Place in the Sun*.

ALL: Ai, ai-paisano,
　　Whoop, la vita necessi!
GARFIELD: I love Torelli, he is a friend of mine.
　　I love Torelli, I love him for his wine.
　　He's got my watch, his wine is in my
　　　belly,
　　If it wasn't for his wine, I would not
　　　love Torelli.
ALL: Ai, ai-paisano,
　　Whoop, la vita necessi!
TRACY: You love Torelli, that's a funny joke.
　　If Torelli were on fire, he wouldn't give
　　　you smoke.
　　Not that I'm so handsome, but my eyes
　　　they are ashine,
　　If it wasn't for his wife, we wouldn't
　　　get much wine.
ALL: Ai, ai-paisano,
　　Whoop, la vita necessi!
TAMIROFF: Listen, amigos, I will ask you this.
　　Why is a glass just like a woman's kiss?
　　When it's full of wine, it makes you
　　　blind a little bit.
　　When the wine is gone, you can see
　　　through it.
ALL: Ai, ai-paisano,
　　Whoop, la vita necessi!
LEONARD: I know a lady named Arabella Gross.
　　You know her, and *you* know her, but I
　　　know her the most.
　　Every little drink I drink, I drink a
　　　little toast
　　To your friend and my friend Arabella
　　　Gross.
ALL: Ai, ai-paisano,
　　Whoop, la vita necessi!
TRACY: Mrs. Morelli has chickens in her yard.
　　If you want to catch one, it is not very
　　　hard.
　　Smile at the señora, you'll get a chicken
　　　free—
　　If Danny feels like smiling, he gets two
　　　or three.
ALL: Ai, ai-paisano,
　　Whoop, la vita necessi!

OH, HOW I LOVE A WEDDING

Music by Franz Waxman (1906–1967). Registered for copyright as an unpublished song January 10, 1942. Introduced by John Qualen.

Oh, how I love a wedding
With plenty of food and wine!
Oh, how I love a wedding—
As long as it is not mine!

TRUE TO THE ARMY

Produced by Jules Schermer and Sol C. Siegel for Paramount Pictures. Released June 1942. Screenplay by Bradford Ropes and Art Arthur, adaptation by Edmund Hartmann and Val Burton, based on the novel *She Loves Me Not* by Edward Hope and the play of the same title by Howard Lindsay. Directed by Albert S. Rogell. Musical direction by Victor Young. Cast featured Judy Canova, Allan Jones, Ann Miller and Jerry Colonna, and featured William Demarest.

IN THE ARMY

Music by Harold Spina. Main title version introduced by ensemble. Finale introduced by Allan Jones, Ann Miller, Jerry Colonna, Judy Canova, and ensemble.

Main title version

You'll find me in the Army
And having quite a time.
It won't get me a famous name,
It won't get me a dime,
But brother, you can bet your boots
I'm mighty proud that I'm
In the Army,
In the Army!
I'm a son of a gun if I didn't get
In the Army,
In the Army,
In the A-R-M-Y.

Finale

JONES: I used to think a soldier
          Would grumble all the time
          And march in mud and peel a spud
          And hardly earn a dime.
          I beg to state I'm feeling great
          And mighty glad that I'm—
CHORUS: In the Army, in the Army, in the Army.
COLONNA: I'm a son of a gun if I didn't get in the Army.
CHORUS: In the Army, in the A-R-M-Y.

ADDITIONAL VERSES (NOT USED IN FILM)

I used to be a tailor,
I'd sew a seam and sit;
I always thought it would be nice to stretch my
    legs a bit.
And now I have a feeling that I'm overdoing it
In the Army, in the Army, in the Army.
I'm a son of a gun if I didn't get in the A-R-M-Y.

I used to like adventure;
I thought it would be grand
To dig for buried treasure in a strange and tropic
    land.
So just to make me smile, they put a shovel in my
    hand
In the Army, in the Army, in the Army.
I'm a son of a gun if I didn't get in the A-R-M-Y.

I used to care for music;
I loved to roll and rock.
To hear a trumpet solo I would put my life in hock.
Well, now I give that solo ev'ry morn at five
    o'clock
In the Army, in the Army, in the Army.
I'm a son of a gun if I didn't get in the A-R-M-Y.

I used to be a copper,
And oh, it was a shame:*
For every traffic ticket I was called a dirty name.
Now I'm a second looie, which is just about the
    same
In the Army, in the Army, in the Army.
I'm a son of a gun if I didn't get in the A-R-M-Y.

I once was a magician;
I used to charge a fin
To make a lady vanish from a padlocked iron bin.
But I can't get my Daisy out of what I got her in
In the Army, in the Army, in the Army.
I'm a son of a gun if I didn't get in the A-R-M-Y.

---

* *Alternate lines:*
    And when you're on the road, boy,
    It's quite a different game

I used to be a lady,
But something's mighty queer:
I'm sure I'm still a lady, but nobody calls me
    "dear."
I wish somebody'd tell me what a lady's doing here
In the Army, in the Army, in the Army.
I'm a son of a gun if I didn't get in the A-R-M-Y.

I used to be in trouble,
Forever in a jam,
But then I got acquainted with a guy called Uncle
    Sam.
Now all is peace and quiet since they put me
    where I am
In the Army, in the Army, in the Army.
I'm a son of a gun if I didn't get in the A-R-M-Y.

And if you're fond of strolling,
You'll never sigh and sit;
In fact you're gonna get a chance to stretch your
    legs a bit.
And soon you're gonna find you're kind of
    overdoing it
In the Army, in the Army, in the A-R-M-Y.

SPANGLES ON MY TIGHTS

Music by Harold Spina. Introduced by Judy Canova.

I was born down in the Ozarks,
Where they never stay up nights,
But I knew someday I'd wind up
With spangles on my tights.

So I up and ran away
Just to see the city lights,
And I swapped my old red flannels
For these spangles on my tights.

Spangles on my tights,
Spangles on my tights.
If you want to find me in the dark,
Put spangles on my tights.

And if I should go to heaven,
Which a good girl should by rights,
Please don't give me wings to fly on,
Give me spangles on my tights.

I go in the lion's cage,
But the lion never bites,
'Cause what ruins his digestion
Is the spangles on my tights.

I can rassle with the python*
And the python never fights,
'Cause he can't stand being tickled
By the spangles on my tights.

Spangles on my tights,
Spangles on my tights—
No, I did not fall in broken glass,
That's spangles on my tights.

And if I should go to heaven,
Which a good girl should by rights,
Please don't give me wings to fly on,
Give me spangles on my tights.

NEED I SPEAK?

Music by Harold Spina. Published. Copyrighted April 20, 1942. Introduced by Allan Jones.

VERSE (NOT USED IN FILM)

Day after day, little by little,
I'll tell you why and how
I first came to adore you.
But please don't ask me now,
Please not now.

REFRAIN

Need I speak,
When I'm looking at you this way?
Need I speak,
When my heart has so much to say?
I'm oh so sure you understand
From just the mere touch of my hand.
Need I add,
Something magic is taking place?
Aren't you glad
Just to feel it in my embrace?
One kiss from you leaves me so weak,
Oh, lovely one, need I speak?

_____
* *Stanza not sung in film.*

SWING IN LINE

Music by Joseph J. Lilley (1913–1978). Introduced by men's military chorus. Mostly sung under dialogue. Lilley's biggest hit, also written with Loesser, was "Jingle, Jangle, Jingle" (see page 88).

Swing in line
And life will seem easier.
Swing in line, soldier man.
For as long as they're making you step,
Well, you might as well step a little bit hep
And learn to swing in line.
Your smile will be breezier;
Rise and shine, soldier man.
For as long as they're telling you to shoulder arms,
Just remember that music has charms,
So learn to dig a military jive like mine
And swing in line.

JITTERBUG'S LULLABY

Music by Harold Spina. Published. Copyrighted May 8, 1942. Introduced by Ann Miller with chorus and Conrad Wiedel.

VERSE 1

There's a pretty little girl next door with many a date;
She goes out lots but never out late.
She's home by ten right there at the gate
With her feller, her feller, her feller, her feller.
With the gum-soled shoes and baggy old pants,
He brings her home from many a dance
And then begins this song of romance,
A jitterbug's lullaby.

REFRAIN

WIEDEL: Good night, sleep tight,
           Your dancin' sure was dynamite,
           Now good night, sleep tight, my baby.
MILLER: Good night, sleep tight,
           We should have won the cup all right,
           But not quite.
WIEDEL: Great fight, my baby.
MILLER: I was so proud, that Palladium crowd,
           They thought you were really cute.
WIEDEL: You murdered them, kid,
           Why, by diggin' you did,

Made all of the other creatures look as
           square as a root!
MILLER: Well, good night, sleep tight—
WIEDEL: We'll try again tomorrow night.
BOTH: Now good night, sleep tight, my baby.

[*Dance interlude*]

VERSE 2

CHORUS: Then they kiss and then she climbs
           upstairs and tumbles in bed,
           And oh what dreams go pop in her head!
           "We jump tomorrow," that's what he said,
           Her feller, her feller, her feller, her feller,
           With the gum-soled shoes and the baggy
           old pants,
           Who brings her home from many a dance,
           The boy who sings a song of romance,
           A jitterbug's lullaby.

WACKY FOR KHAKI

Music by Harold Spina. Introduced by Judy Canova and male ensemble. Loesser's brief stint with *Women's Wear Daily* in 1927 came in handy for this song, especially the unused lyrics for Canova and the female chorus.

CANOVA: I just came to this fashion show
           To see the latest styles,
           To watch the gorgeous models
           Parade around for miles
           In silks and satins and velveteen and
           wool,
           In polka dots and stripes and prints
           And all that kind of thing.
           But I don't see a sample of the very
           latest fashion
           That fills my heart with a (tsk, tsk)
           patriotic passion.*

           I'm, wacky for khaki and Sam Browne
           belts.
           When I meet a soldier my heart just melts.
           I'm one of those gluttons for buttons
           that shine.
           Oh, Captain, Captain, Captain, be my
           Valentine,

_____
* *Lines 7–9 originally:*
   And all that kind of bull.
   But I didn't see a sample of a certain kind of goods
   That turns me into just a little babe in the woods.

'Cause I'm wacky for khaki, I'll say that
    twice.
It scratches a little, but it scratches so
    nice.
Oh, Captain, Captain, Captain,
Just look out or I'll fall,
'Cause I'm wacky for khaki, that's all.

[*Interlude*]

CHORUS: She's wacky for khaki.
CANOVA: Not tweed, not serge.
    It's khaki by cracky that gives me the
        urge.
    The stripes on the shoulders, they set me
        aflame.
    Why, sure I'll marry you, Lieutenant—
        oh, what's your name?
BOYS: She's wacky for khaki.
CANOVA: And that means you.
    I've gone with Marines and with sailors
        in blue.
    But don't you worry, I'll be true
    To Company B.
BOYS: 'Cause she's wacky for khaki.
CANOVA: That's me!

ADDITIONAL LYRICS (INTENDED FOR CANOVA
AND FEMALE CHORUS; NOT USED IN FILM)

FIRST GIRL: Girls, girls, do you like this shade?
    The skirt is blue velvet, trimmed
        with braid.
SECOND GIRL: How delightful!
THIRD GIRL: Sweet!
FOURTH GIRL: So becoming, my dear!
    But I prefer the foulard print on
        Elsie over here.
THIRD GIRL: Oh, *I* made this old rag myself,
    ninety cents a yard.
FIRST GIRL: She picked it up at Katzenmeyer's
    on the boulevard.
SECOND GIRL: Why, Alice, you're exquisite in that
    taffeta creation!
FOURTH GIRL: I really wanted muslin—with a
    floral decoration.
FIRST GIRL: I'm going to get a suit this fall in
    purple virgin wool,
    With the skirt cut on the bias and
        the shoulders rather full.
    And then I'll get a blouse of silk—
CANOVA: Wait a minute!
    I guess you get a thrill about your
        silks and velveteens,
    Your cashmere and your satins from
        the ladies' magazines.
    But as for me, I'm crazy for the very
        latest fashion,

And if you girls will gather round,
    I'll spill my secret passion.

I'm wacky for khaki, it feels so warm.
Just give me romance in a uniform.
It thrills me, it chills me, it fills me
    with pride,
Why, I don't even care if it's got
    you inside!
Because I'm wacky for khaki, that's
    what I mean,
And you can have muslin and crepe
    de chine.
I wouldn't turn my nose up at a
    cavalry guy
'Cause I'm wacky for khaki, that's
    why.

OPHELIA

Music by Harold Spina. Intended for Jerry Colonna to sing to a carrier pigeon. Not used in film.

VERSE

Time to go to sleep, my little ones;
Into your cages on the shelf.
And when I got you all tucked in,
I join the boys and play some gin,
For I'm quite a pigeon myself.
It's time to go to sleep, my precious ones;
Off to your little beds you go.
And now in parting let me say,
You've all been very good today,
Except one little lady I know.

REFRAIN 1

Ophelia, my darlin', Ophelia my dove,
Ophelia, oh feel ya no feeling of love?
The finest of crumbs I have crumbled for thee,
But oh what a crumb thou has turned out to be!
Ophelia, Ophelia, don't laugh in my face.
Ophelia, oh feel ya no shame and disgrace?
Ophelia, Ophelia, Ophelia, be nice,
Or I'll be filled with wild notions
And you'll be filled with wild rice.

REFRAIN 2

Ophelia, Ophelia, obey me, I beg.
I've known you since you were a dear little egg.
The finest birdcage I have built you, it's true,
But oh what a bird I've been getting from you!

Oh, don't you recall, to your rescue I came
Last time you got caught in a badminton game?
Ophelia, my pigeon, get back on the job,
Or I'll become very angry
And you'll become roast squab.

WE'RE BUILDING MEN

Music by Harold Spina. Not used in film.

Lend an ear
And an eye
For the nation's defense,
For Paramount Presents!
See that gun?
There's a man behind that gun.
A straighter-shooting guy you'll never find,
For we're building men like we're building guns—
They're all-American designed!

See that tank?
There's a man inside that tank.
He's rugged and he's regular, he's real,
For we're building men like we're building
    tanks—
As true and trusty as the steel!

See that plane?
Doesn't it give you a kick?
Well, off with your hats to the fellow at the
    stick!
Be it plane, tank, gun,
There's a man for ev'ryone,
A soldier in his heart and in his mind.
Yes, we're building men, and we want the world to
    know
That they're all-American designed.

BEYOND THE BLUE HORIZON

Produced by Monta Bell for Paramount Pictures. Released in June 1942. Screenplay by Frank Butler and Harry Tugend from a story by E. Lloyd Sheldon and Jack DeWitt. Directed by Alfred Santell. Cast starred Dorothy Lamour and featured Richard Denning, Jack Haley, Walter Abel, and Patricia Morison. Earlier titles: *Malay*, *Pagan Lullaby*, and *Her Jungle Mate*.

MALAY LOVE SONG

Music by Jule Styne, based on Malay folk song. Not used in film.

Oh, that Malay love call,
That Malay love call,
Oh, why did it start
On this moonlit night of splendor?
It says, "Surrender,
Surrender your heart."
On every tropic wind it comes;
It's in the jungle drums.
It won't let me be.
Oh, that haunting Malay love call,
Why must it sing your name to me?

PAGAN LULLABY

Music by Jule Styne. Registered for copyright as an unpublished song February 25, 1942. Not used in film.

I knew a pagan lullaby,
A pagan lullaby,
A long time ago,
When the wind sang through the jungle,
The dreamy music,
So tender and low.
Tonight I hear that song again;
It came along again
From out of the sky.
That's the music of the night wind
I call my pagan lullaby.

SWEATER GIRL

Produced by Sol C. Siegel for Paramount Pictures. Released in July 1942. Previously titled *Sing a Song of Homicide*. Music by Jule Styne. Incidental music by Victor Young, Charles Bradshaw, Gerard Carbonara, and Gil Grau, respectively. Screenplay by Eve Greene and Robert Blees. Directed by William Clemens. Cast starred Eddie Bracken, June Preisser, Betty Jane Rhodes, and Johnnie Johnston.

SWEATER GIRL

Copyrighted. Lyrics published in *Song Hits* December 25, 1941. Introduced by Eddie Bracken and chorus.

When the sweater girls parade around the campus,
Talk about your heavenly scenes:
Why, they get a better hand
Than a big brass band
Or a company of Marines!
I don't wanna look at shiny, shiny medals
Or at twenty-one guns ablaze;
But when the sweater girls parade around the
    campus,
Mama,
Gimme those,
Gimme those,
Gimme those college days!

When the sweater girls parade around the campus,
All the student body is there;
For the university
Scrambles out to see—
And they not only see, they stare.
Why, the statues of the noble founding fathers
Seem to open their eyes and gaze,*
And then they sing the Alma Mater of the campus,
Which goes:
Gimme those,
Gimme those,
Gimme those college days!

When the sweater girls parade around the campus,
Shoot the education to me.
(All the seniors and the juniors
And the sophomores and frosh)
And so did the faculty.
Oh someday I'll see the angels up in heaven,

* *Following 12 lines not sung in film.*

With those wings that the poets praise;
But when the sweater girls parade around the
    campus,
Mama,
Gimme those,
Gimme those,
Gimme those college days!

I SAID NO

Published. Copyrighted December 10, 1941. Introduced by Betty Jane Rhodes. Leading recordings by Alvino Rey and His Orchestra (Bluebird) and Jimmy Dorsey and His Orchestra (Decca). Also recorded by Lena Horne (Victor) and Ella Fitzgerald (Polygram).

VERSE

There he stood in my doorway so boldly,
And he whispered of pleasures I'd missed.
Though at first I refused very coldly,
How long can a lady resist?
How long can a lady resist?

REFRAIN

I said, "No."
He said, "Please."
I said, "No."
He said, "Please."
I said, "No."
He said, "Please,
Pretty baby."

I said, "No."
He said, "Why?"
I said, "No."
He said, "Why?"
I said, "Uh-uh."
He said, "Try."
I said, "Maybe."

He said, "Now."
I said, "Well . . ."
He said, "Ah, this is swell!
And you'll never know how much it will mean!"
So at last, I confess,
I said, "Yes-yes-yes-yes-yes."
That's how I subscribed to *Liberty* magazine.

UNUSED LYRICS

And the moonlight in his eyes was sublime.
So at last, I confess,

I said, "Yes-yes-yes-yes-yes."
That's the word I really meant to say all the time.

I DON'T WANT TO WALK WITHOUT YOU

Published. Copyrighted December 16, 1941, and May 24, 1948. Introduced by Johnnie Johnston (refrain only) and Betty Jane Rhodes (with verse). The number-one-selling recording in America was by Harry James and His Orchestra (Columbia). Other leading recordings included Bing Crosby (Decca), Dinah Shore (Bluebird), Glenn Miller (Victor), Helen Forrest (Warner), and Jo Stafford (Columbia).

Susan Loesser recalled the song's origins in *A Most Remarkable Fella:*

My father met Jule Styne in 1940. . . . At their first session at Republic, Jule played my father the tune to "I Don't Want to Walk Without You, Baby," a song he had been working on with another lyricist. "I play about eight bars of it, and he says, 'Sh! Don't ever play that around here again. We'll take it to Paramount and write it over there.' " Which they did.

After it became a hit, Loesser received a visit from a fellow songwriter: "Irving Berlin came in today and spent a solid hour telling me that 'Walk' is the best song he ever heard. I was flattered. He played and sang it over, bar by bar, explaining *why* it's the best song he ever heard. I was flattered like crazy, then. Maybe he'll take an ad in *Variety* about it."

VERSE

All our friends keep knocking at the door;
They've asked me out a hundred times or more.
But all I say is "Leave me in the gloom,"
And here I stay within my lonely room,
'Cause—

REFRAIN

I don't want to walk without you, baby,
Walk without my arm about you, baby.
I thought the day you left me behind,
I'd take a stroll and get you right off my mind,
But now I find that
I don't want to walk without the sunshine.
Why'd you have to turn off all that sunshine?
Oh, baby, please come back,
Or you'll break my heart for me,

'Cause I don't want to walk without you,
No siree.

WHAT GIVES OUT NOW?

Published. Copyrighted December 25, 1941. Introduced by June Preisser and Eddie Bracken.

VERSE

PREISSER: Well, my precious, I'm waiting,
Waiting for the next move.
And by that look in your eye
I have a feeling, have I,
The situation's about to improve.

REFRAIN 1

What gives out now,
Now that we're under the moon?
What gives out now?
How's about making it soon?
What happens now that we've found
This nice romantic spot
And you've asked me to be seated
And have I refused?
I have not!
So what gives out now,
Now that you're holding my hand—
What makes romance take command?
Here's hoping it's something
My mother would never allow.
So, far, so good,
So what gives out now?

REFRAIN 2

BRACKEN: What gives out now,
Now that you've got me alone?
What gives out now?
Why can't my life be my own?
What happens now that you've got me
Neath the starry skies
With that blitzkrieg in your tactics
And that sabotage in your eyes?

UNUSED REFRAINS

What gives out now?
Gee, but I feel like a dope.
I'm at the end of my rope.
You're planning on something

Your mother would never allow.
So far, so good,
So what gives out now?
What gives out now?

What gives out now?
What does psychology teach?
What gives out now?
Why does he keep out of reach?
What gives out now?
What does psychology prove?
Who's gonna make the next move?
Who started on something
You're not gonna finish nohow?
So far, ha, ha,
So what gives out now?

ADDITIONAL REFRAIN

HE: What gives out now,
Now that you've got me alone?
SHE: What gives out now?
HE: I gotta answer the phone.
SHE: What gives out now
That we've found this nice romantic spot
And you've asked me to be seated?
HE: And do I feel safe?
I do not!
SHE: What gives out now?
HE: Maybe I'll whistle a tune. [*whistles melody*]
SHE: What gives out now neath that moon?
HE: [*spoken*] Did you know the Chicago fire
Was started by Mrs. O'Leary's cow?
SHE: [*sung*] So what?
HE: It was quite hot!
SHE: So what gives out now?

TAG

HE: And now I must leave you,
And so I respectfully bow.
SHE: So far, so good—
BOTH: So what gives out now?

BOOKER T. WASHINGTON BRIGADE

Not used in film.

VERSE

My man is on his way;
He's gonna leave me

Some time today.
Packin' his belongin's
And leavin' me and Harlem.
Don't you worry, little lady,
Same as ev'ry man alive,
He's just leaving, little lady,
To get hep
To that patriotic jive.
Booker T.—Booker T.T.T.
Booker T.—Booker T.T.T.
Tr———boom boom.

REFRAIN

Booker T.
Booker T.
Booker T.T.T.
Tr-r-r-r-r-r-r-r boom boom!
They're on the march!
They're on the march!
They're under Lenox Avenue Arch.
Oh, brother, who said Harlem's afraid?
Here comes the Book-Book-Booker T. Washington
    Brigade!

They're coming near,
They're coming near,
Look out your window, sister, and cheer—
And when you see that sepia shade,
Well, that's the Book-Book-Booker T. Washington
    Brigade!

There's Lunceford's trombone man—
There's half of Fletcher's clan—
There's the Duke's old drummer boy,
Recently caught in the draft
In the middle of a riff at the Old Savoy!

They're on the move,
They're on the move,
And not a Jackson out of the groove!
For all the darktown strutters have strayed
Into the Book-Book-Booker T. Washington
    Brigade!

Booker T.
Booker T.
Booker T.T.T.
Tr-r-r-r-r-r-r boom boom!
I said the Book-Book-Booker T. Washington
    Brigade!

PRIORITIES ON PARADE

Produced by Sol C. Siegel for Paramount Pictures. Released in July 1942. Screenplay by Art Arthur and Frank Loesser. Directed by Albert S. Rogell. Cast featured Ann Miller, Johnnie Johnston, Jerry Colonna, Betty Jane Rhodes, Vera Vague (Barbara Jo Allen), Harry Barris, and Eddie Quillan.

JOHNNY'S PATTER

Credited to Frank Loesser, Art Arthur (1911–1985), and Troy Sanders. Recited by Johnny Johnston. Missing lyrics indicated by ellipses.

We're just what you need—
The greatest group of entertainers this side of
    Broadway.

[*Interlude*]

Like when a man is working, working on a drill,
That when he hears a beat
It gives him a thrill.
And then he hears another and another,
And pretty soon he's steamin' like a demon, brother.
When his hand is sore or his neck is stiff,
Don't send him to a doctor . . . wrist.
Give him a ride, give him . . . rackie sackie . . .
Turn the wheels faster for the boys in khaki.

HERE COMES KATRINKA

Music by Jule Styne. Introduced by Johnnie Johnston and His Band.

Oh, here comes Katrinka,
The powerful Katrinka,
The biggest attraction of the year.
Oh, here comes Katrinka,
She's not much of a thinker,
But brother, get that cauliflower ear!
Three chairs for Katrinka—
Ask any young fellow who's followed 'er,

There is no citizen solider.*
Here comes Katrinka,
No battleship could sink 'er,
That tackle from the old assembly line.†
Oh, let's drink a drink-a
To the powerful Katrinka—
She's a great big weakness of mine.

YOU'RE IN LOVE WITH SOMEONE ELSE (BUT I'M IN LOVE WITH YOU)

Music by Jule Styne. Published. Copyrighted June 16, 1942. Introduced by Johnnie Johnston and Betty Jane Rhodes. Reprised by Johnston and Rhodes. Recordings include Harry James and His Orchestra, vocal by Helen Forrest (Columbia), and Glen Gray and the Casa Loma Orchestra (Decca).

VERSE

Lately, I'm singing a blue song,
Feeling as mean as can be.
I can't help thinking that you're to blame
For all of this mis'ry in me.

REFRAIN

You're in love with someone else,
But I'm in love with you.
Night and day I hope and pray
That he'll find someone new.
Then you'll burn, and then you'll learn
To sing this torch song too,
Entitled "You're in Love with Someone Else
(But I'm in Love with You)."

---

* *Earlier version of lines 8–9:*
    What you may think is bustle
    Is nothing else but muscle.

† *Earlier version:*
    Gentlemen . . . the female Frankenstein!

PAYDAY

Music by Jule Styne. Introduced by Jerry Colonna and Johnnie Johnston, with Dave Willock, Eddie Quillan, Vera Vague, Betty Jane Rhodes, Ann Miller, and Harry Barris. The verse owes much to a comical Christmas poem Loesser submitted (unsuccessfully) some years earlier to the *Saturday Evening Post* (see "No Sales Slip Necessary," page 256).

VERSE 1

COLONNA: I am the cabbage department,
A sociological rarity,
A thin little fellow left over from*
The thing we once called prosperity.
Allow me to introduce myself,
Paymaster Moe O'Flaherty.

I am the cabbage department,
I hand out the weekly simoleons
To millions of boys and millions of girls*
From Maine to Dubuque to New
Orleans,
To the folks who are building and
welding and drilling
To knock off the would-be Napoleons.

Oh, I'm not important anymore,
Though I can't say my day is done;
But the fellow who really counts
today—well, there's one,
The man behind the man behind the
gun! Hiya, son!

REFRAIN

JOHNSTON: It's payday, payday,
Payday at the plant.
I'm the feller who keeps 'em rolling—
Tell the feller who says I can't
That I'm glad that Sam's my uncle
And Miss Liberty is my aunt,
Or there never would be a payday,
Payday at the plant.

A lot of it goes for taxes,
A lot of it goes for a bond,
A little bit goes to me and my wife,
Of whom I'm awful fond.
But as long as our kids can go to school
(Where they don't learn Japanese)
WILLOCK: Then I'll go right on
Welding those wings—

QUILLAN: Riveting rivets—
VAGUE: Doing those things.
ALL: I'd go right on fighting this fight—
JOHNSTON: If none of it goes to me.
ALL: Payday.
RHODES: It's payday, payday, in more ways than
one.
Got another big bomber flying,
Build another big long-range gun,
And I'll bet my right rear tire,
Brother, it'll mean more than dough
When we get to that great big payday
over Tokyo.
ALL: It's payday, payday,
Hooray!
BARRIS: I'm taking me down to Chauncey's
To buy me a beer or two,
And if it's okay, allow me to say
I'll buy a beer for you.
But as long as the soldiers over there
Need the soldiers over here,
Then I'd go right on
Rushing those props—
WILLOCK: Moving those motors—
QUILLAN: Madder than hops.
HARVEY: I'd go right on fighting this fight
If never was no more beer.

VERSE 2

VAGUE: I'm going to buy a bonnet,
A dollar and ninety-eight,
A pair of new shoes and a lipstick too,
And I might get a date.
But if ever I hear from Uncle Sam
That it's too much luxury,
Then I'll go right on
Looking like this,
Tough to go out with,
Tougher to kiss.
I'll go right on fighting this fight
If nobody goes for me.

MILLER: It's payday, payday all along the line.
Did you notice those new P-40's?
Did you know they were yours and mine?
Well, be glad that Sam's your uncle
And Miss Liberty likes you fine,
For those babies up there mean payday
All along the line.
JOHNSTON: I'm going to see a newsreel,
At twenty-five cents, to watch all our
bombs
And see just where they go.
But as long as I know they're dropping
down
On a certain black moustache,
Well, I'll go right on seeking that steel—

ENSEMBLE: Building that bomber,
Turning that wheel.
JOHNSTON: I'll go right on fighting this fight
If nobody pays me cash.

THE FOREST RANGERS

Produced by Robert Sisk for Paramount Pictures. Released in October 1942. Screenplay by Harold Shumate from a story by Thelma Strabel. Directed by George Marshall. Cast starred Fred MacMurray, Paulette Goddard, and Susan Hayward and featured Lynne Overman, Albert Dekker, Eugene Pallette, and Regis Toomey.

JINGLE, JANGLE, JINGLE

Music by Joseph J. Lilley. Published. Copyrighted May 26, 1942. Introduced by Fred MacMurray and ensemble. Leading recordings by Kay Kyser and His Orchestra (Columbia—number one on pop charts in summer of 1942), the Merry Macs (Decca), and Gene Autry (Okeh). Other recordings include Tex Ritter (Capitol), Glenn Miller (Bluebird), Roger Williams (MCA), and Burl Ives (Decca).

The lyrics were performed in the film by a young groom who had just learned that his wedding was canceled. Loesser dedicated the words to the Pico Stables in Burbank, from whom he would often rent a horse for a ride in the Burbank hills. It was here that he learned of the attack on Pearl Harbor: "I heard about it on the bridle path yesterday. A lot of soldiers on leave were riding. I got up on a trail overlooking the whole section—and *watched* the news spread—and could see the soldiers turning their horses around and making for the stables" (quoted by Susan Loesser in *A Most Remarkable Fella*).

INTRODUCTION

Yippeeay!
There'll be no weddin' bells,
For today:

REFRAIN*

I got spurs that jingle, jangle, jingle
As I go ridin' merrily along.

---

* Lines 3–4 and lines 9–10 in verse 1 are not sung in film.

* *Only the refrain lyrics were sung in the film; no verses were sung.*

And they sing, "Oh, ain't you glad you're single!"
And that song ain't so very far from wrong.

VERSE 1

Oh, Lillie Belle, oh, Lillie Belle,
Though I may have done some foolin',
Here is why I never fell:

REPEAT REFRAIN

VERSE 2

Oh, Mary Ann, oh Mary Ann,
Though we done some moonlight walkin',
This is why I up and ran:

REPEAT REFRAIN

VERSE 3

Oh, Sally Jane, oh Sally Jane,
Though I'd love to stay forever,
This is why I can't remain:

REPEAT REFRAIN

VERSE 4

Oh, Bessie Lou, oh, Bessie Lou,
Though we done a heap of dreamin',
This is why it won't come true:

REPEAT REFRAIN

VERSE 5

Oh, Celia dear, oh, Celia dear,
Though it's mighty pretty music,
That ain't wedding bells you hear:

TALL GROWS THE TIMBER

Music by Frederick Hollander. Published. Copyrighted June 2, 1942. Introduced by Fred MacMurray and ensemble. Recordings include Glen Gray and the Casa Loma Orchestra (Decca).

VERSE (NOT SUNG IN FILM)

Last little road,
Last little bridge,
Last little trail,
Then over the ridge,

REFRAIN

MACMURRAY: Tall grows the timber
    And mellow shines the moon.
ENSEMBLE: I'm high, I'm happy, I'm home.
MACMURRAY: There's my sweetheart waiting there
    With the moonlight in her hair—
    Makes me wonder, why did I decide
        to roam?
MACMURRAY: Tall grows the timber
    And mellow shines the moon.
ALL: I'm home, I'm happy, I'm high.
    And I'll never shed a tear
    If I never stray from here,
    Where tall grows the timber to the sky.

SEVEN DAYS' LEAVE

Produced by Tim Whelan for RKO Radio Pictures. Released in December 1942. Screenplay by William Bowers, Ralph Spence, Kenneth Earl, and Curtis Kenyon. Directed by Tim Whelan. Cast starred Victor Mature and Lucille Ball and featured Harold "the Great Gildersleeve" Peary, Mapy Cortés, Ginny Simms, Marcy McGuire, Peter Lind Hayes, Arnold Stang, Buddy Clark, Les Brown and His Orchestra, and Freddy Martin and His Orchestra. A film with the same title was released by Paramount in 1930.

PLEASE, WON'T YOU LEAVE MY GIRL ALONE?

Music by Jimmy McHugh. Published. Copyrighted October 5, 1942. Introduced by Victor Mature (dubbed by Ben Gage), Peter Lind Hayes, Buddy Clark, Arnold Stang, and male ensemble. Reprised by male and female ensembles.

Please, won't you leave my girl alone?
Please, won't you leave my girl alone?
She hasn't got a heart of stone.
She wrote she misses my kisses
On lonely summer nights.
She might be giving her kisses
To hungry parasites.
Now though she isn't the missus,
And you're still within your rights,
Please, won't you leave my girl alone?

Please, won't you leave my girl alone?
Go out and get one of your own.

She used to love to go dancing—
What evenings we would spend!
She still would love to go dancing,
But there it's got to end.
For dancing leads to romancing,
So I ask you as a friend,

Please, won't you leave my girl alone?*
Don't even call her on the phone.
She's awful crazy for candy,
And that's what makes me blue:
Now don't be buying her candy
The way I used to do—
She's awful crazy for candy,
And she might get sweet on you.

Please, won't you leave my girl alone?
Please, note my very gentle tone.
She's mighty full of devotion,
'Cause I'm the only one.
Now don't be getting the notion
That something can be done—
Remember when I come marching,
I'm coming with my gun.
Now will you leave my girl alone?

Reprise

MEN: Please, won't you leave my girl alone?
    Please, won't you leave my girl alone?
    I'm far away in the Army,
    And she is all I've got.
    I'm far away in the Army,
    And though she cares a lot,
    I'm far away in the Army
    And you're Johnny on the spot!
    Please, won't you leave my girl alone?
    Every time I forward march,
    I march another mile away.
    So, buddy, if you're a buddy of mine,
    All that I can say is:

WOMEN: Please, won't you leave my man alone?
    Please, won't you leave my man alone?
    You ladies up in Alaska,
    If he should stop to chat,
    Be sure to show him Alaska
    And not your furnished flat.
    It's awful cold in Alaska,
    But it's not as cold as that.
    Please, won't you leave my man alone?
    Every time they forward march,
    They march another mile away.
    So, sister, if you're a sister of mine,
    All that I can say is:

---

* *Third stanza not sung in film.*

Please, won't you leave my man alone?
He hasn't got a heart of stone.
You ladies down in Australia,
You know how soldiers are.
If he should happen to hail ya,
Don't carry things too far.
Remember he's in Australia
Thanks to me and FDR.
ALL: Please, won't you leave my girl [man] alone?

YOU SPEAK MY LANGUAGE

Music by Jimmy McHugh. Published. Copyrighted October 5, 1942. Introduced by Mapy Cortés and Victor Mature (dubbed by Ben Gage). Played by Les Brown and His Orchestra.

VERSE

CORTES: I just arrived in the U.S.A.,
I just arrived and I'm happy to say,
I'm happy to say what it says right here,
What it says right here,
What it says right here—
What it says right here is a mystery—
I wish someone would come along and
rescue me!

REFRAIN

You speak my language—
What a big surprise!
You speak my language,
And my heart replies.
Each time you play*
That's what I can tell—
You speak my language,
Speak it very well.
I am a Latin,
You're a Yankee Doodle.
When you talk, it's double-talk
I can't get through my noodle.
But when it comes to making with the love,
You speak my language,
And we're hand in glove!
MATURE: You speak my language
When you dance like that.
You speak my language;
How's about a chat?

* Sheet music version, lines 4–5:
Speak it with your eyes.
Each time I kiss you

You speak my language;
What do you say we spoon?
CORTES: Who needs a language
Underneath the moon?
MATURE: You are a Latin;
I'm from Alabama.
You don't know my adjectives
And I don't know your grammar.
But when it comes to—
CORTES: Making with the love.
MATURE: You speak my language.
BOTH: And we're hand in glove.

A TOUCH OF TEXAS

Music by Jimmy McHugh. Published. Copyrighted October 2, 1942. Introduced by Marcy McGuire with Harold Peary, Peter Lind Hayes, and Victor Mature (dubbed by Ben Gage) with Freddy Martin and His Orchestra. Leading recording by Freddy Martin and His Orchestra, vocal by Eddie Stone and Glen Hughes (Victor).

MCGUIRE: Headin' for that depot,
Goodbye, goodbye, goodbye;
Headin' for that depot,
And here's the reason why:
ENSEMBLE: Why, gal why?

MCGUIRE: Got a touch of Texas in my talk,
I got too much of Texas in my talk;
Oh, this place will be my ruin,
Ki-yi-yip-pin' and wahooin',
Oh, take me back to Noo Yawk!
Got a touch of Texas in my hair,
Got too much of Texas in my hair.
Yes, the sand from Amarillo
Keeps a scratchin' on my pillow,
Oh, take me back to Times Square!
For I've seen ev'ry part of,
Ev'ry part of
What I'm deep in the heart of.

Got a touch of Texas in my walk,
Got too much of Texas in my walk.
Oh, the sage may be a-bloomin',
But for miles there's nothin' human,
Take me back to Noo Yawk!

Headin' for that depot,
Goodbye, goodbye, goodbye;
Headin' for that depot,
And here's the reason why:

HAYES: Now wait a minute si,*
You've got a touch of Texas in your
walk—
PEARY: Got too much of Texas in your walk.
MCGUIRE: I rode a bronco down in Dallas
So be careful of my callus,
Take me back to Noo Yawk!
PEARY: [spoken] Hold on, chum, you got Texas
on your brain, yeah.
HAYES: [sung] Yeah, too much Texas on your
brain,
MCGUIRE: Oh, the brush that's full of rabbits
Got me in these jumpin' habits—
Put me back on that train!
For I've seen ev'ry part of

[Clap-clap-clap-clap]

Just what I'm deep in the heart of.
That's why I'm headin' for the depot,
Goodbye, goodbye, goodbye.
MATURE: You'll never make the depot,
And here's the reason why:
You got too much of Texas in you, gal.
MCGUIRE: And that's too much of Texas for me,
pal.
HAYES: I reckon I will have to stop you.
If'n you move, I'll have to drop you.
PEARY: Get back in your corral.
MATURE: You got too much Texas in your talk.
MCGUIRE: I got too much of Texas in my walk.
But the funny part about it
Is that I can do without it.
Don't take me back, don't take me back,
Oh, please don't
Take me back to New York!

UNUSED LYRICS

Got a touch of Texas in my face,
Got too much of Texas in my face.
Oh, that sunshine in Laredo,
Got it like a ripe tomato.
Oh, take me out of this place!

* He says "si" (pronounced "sigh"), which is his slang
for "sister."

I GET THE NECK OF THE CHICKEN

Music by Jimmy McHugh. Published. Copyrighted August 27, 1942. Introduced by Marcy McGuire. Leading recording by Freddy Martin and His Orchestra, vocal by Eddie Stone (Victor).

VERSE (NOT SUNG IN FILM)

There's always one in ev'ry fam'ly,
And nobody loves her one bit;
There's always one in ev'ry fam'ly,
And in my fam'ly I'm it!

REFRAIN*

I get the neck of the chicken,
I get the rumble-seat ride,
I get the leaky umbrella,
Ev'ryone shoves me aside.
When I jump in my shower each morn,
Sure as fate,
I'm too late,
All the hot water is gone!

I get the neck of the chicken,
I get the hand-me-down shawl,
And when there's company weekends,
I get the couch in the hall.
That's why I can't get over
This dream that came true:
If I get the neck of the chicken,
Well, how did I ever get you?

I get the neck of the chicken,
I get the burnt piece of toast,
I get the seat in the movies
Smack in the back of a post.
When morning papers come to the door,
Sure as fate,
I'm too late
And they're mine 'long about four.

I get the neck of the chicken,
I get the plate with the cracks,
I get those evenings with Grandma,
Ev'ryone else can relax.
That's why I can't get over
This bolt from the blue:
If I get the neck of the chicken,
Well, how did I ever get you?

* Lyrics sung in film include the first stanza of refrain,
the first four lines of the second stanza, and the last
three lines of the final stanza.

I get the neck of the chicken,
That's how they give me the bird,
And in the family snapshots
Mine is the face that's all blurred.
The phone bell rings: "Who's calling?" It's Jim.
Sure as fate,
I'm too late,
And my big sister gets him.
I get the guy with the glasses,
Wearing an awful toupee,
Somebody else gets a Victor Mature,
Mine's always strictly 4-A.
That's why I can't get over
This fine "how-de-do":
If I get the neck of the chicken,
I'm a cinch to get you.

CAN'T GET OUT OF THIS MOOD

Music by Jimmy McHugh. Published. Copyrighted August 27, 1942. Introduced by Ginny Simms, with Freddy Martin and His Orchestra. Reprised by Marcy McGuire. Leading recordings by Kay Kyser and His Orchestra, vocal by Harry Babbitt (Columbia), and by Johnny Long and His Orchestra, vocal by the Four Teens (Decca).

VERSE 1 (NOT SUNG IN FILM)

All day long, before my eyes
Come little visions of you;
They shouldn't, they mustn't,
But they do.

REFRAIN

Can't get out of this mood,
Can't get over this feeling.
Can't get out of this mood,
Last night your lips were too appealing.
The thrill should have been all gone by today,
In the usual way,
But it's only your arms I'm out of;
Can't get out of this dream,
What a fool to dream of you;
'Twasn't part of my scheme
To sigh and tell you that I love you.
But I'm saying it,
I'm playing it dumb.
Can't get out of this mood—
Heartbreak, here I come!

VERSE 2

The lonely hours, the dreamy days,
The moments away from you.
That voice inside
That cries and cries
"You're through,
You're through,
You're through!"

REPRISE

Can't get out of this mood,
Can't get over this feeling;
Can't get out of this mood,
Your face is too appealing.
The thrill should have been all gone by today,
But it won't go away,
So, baby, I'm all set to get you.
I can't get out of this dream
That I'm forever dreaming of you.
'Twasn't part of my scheme
To want to tell you that I love you.
But I'm saying it,
You're still playing it dumb.
Why don't you get in the mood?
You heartbreaker, here I come!

SOFT HEARTED

Music by Jimmy McHugh. Published. Copyrighted October 2, 1942. Played by Les Brown and His Orchestra. Used instrumentally only.

VERSE

What stories I told myself!
I should have controlled myself.
I thought you were gone on me;
Why didn't it dawn on me that—

REFRAIN

You don't really love me,
You're just soft hearted,
You're soft hearted with fools like me.
You don't really kiss me,
You're just soft hearted;
It all started from sympathy.
I was so blind
With you on my mind,
And you were so kind,
You couldn't say no, darling,
You don't really love me,

You're just soft hearted—
My heart should have told me so.

PUERTO RICO

Music by Jimmy McHugh. Published. Copyrighted October 5, 1942. Introduced by Mapy Cortés with Les Brown and His Orchestra. Used in foreign prints of film only.

VERSE

The balmy climate will make that heart of yours
    soften,
To native rhythms you'll move as never before.
You see it once, and you want to see it more often,
My very beautiful bit of tropical shore,

REFRAIN

Puerto Rico!
You won't know wrong from right
With those drums in the night
Going br-rr-rr boom, br-rr-rr boom, br-rr-rr boom.
Puerto Rico!
You're a cinch for romance,
From the moment you dance
To that br-rr-rr boom, br-rr-rr boom, br-rr-rr boom.
Señor Chico teaches br-rr-rr boom, br-rr-rr boom,
Cheek to Chico.
You'll get that way
From Puerto Rico.
You may up and depart,
But the song in your heart
Will be br-rr-rr boom, br-rr-rr boom,
Br-rr-rr boom, br-rr-rr boom,
Br-rr-rr boom, br-rr-rr boom,
Night and day.

BABY

Music by Jimmy McHugh. Published. Copyrighted October 5, 1942. Not used in film.

VERSE

Some people like Tchaikovsky;
Well, let them like Tchaikovsky,
And I won't stand in their way.
But as for me, let me say:

REFRAIN

My kind of tune is the popular tune with the word
"Baby."
Sing me a song and I'm happy as long as I've heard
"Baby."
There are songs all about mothers,
And a few about sisters and brothers,
And there's "Trees,"
And there's "Please,"
And "Louise,"
And a hundred and fifty million others.
But I'll take the same old reliable dame with the
    name
"Baby."
Rhyme her with "maybe,"
It sounds so divine.
May her charm never diminish,
May my ear always hear that dynamite finish;
The finish that finishes me,
"Baby mine."

RECITATION (SPOKEN AGAINST FIRST SIXTEEN
MEASURES OF REFRAIN.)

There's the "Melancholy Baby" that you've heard
    most everyplace,
"Rock-a-bye My Baby," "Baby Shoes," and "Baby
    Face."
There's "Baby, Won't You Please Come Home,"
    you know it well, no doubt,
And then the famous "Baby, I Don't Wanna Walk
    Without."
There's "I Can't Give You Anything but Love,"
    they play each minute—
That song became a hit because it's got a "baby" in it.
There's "Everybody Loves My Baby," "Pretty
    Baby," too,
And "When My Baby Smiles at Me," that thrills
    me through and through.

MISCELLANEOUS SONGS OF 1942

PRAISE THE LORD AND PASS THE AMMUNITION

Published. Copyrighted August 21, 1942. Leading recordings by Kay Kyser and His Orchestra (Columbia—

number one on the pop charts in January 1943) and the Merry Macs (Decca).

Frank Loesser's second published song for which he wrote both music and lyrics became one of the biggest hits of World War II, with 2.5 million records and more than 750,000 copies of sheet music sold. The song was so popular that the Army asked radio stations not to play it more than once every four hours. Although many versions of this story have circulated, the editors have been able to determine the following: Loesser's inspiration for the song came from a newspaper clipping crediting the famous title line to a Chaplain McGuire, who declined to take credit for it. The official Navy account finally attributed it to Chaplain Howell E. Forgy of the U.S.S. *New Orleans*. Arthur Loesser recalled the song in his article "My Brother Frank" in *Notes*, published by the Music Library Association in March 1950:

> In August [1942] my mother showed me a letter from Frank explaining that he was writing a song on the alleged Pearl Harbor outburst. . . . The nature of the tune reveals a great canniness. It refrains from modern, urban, musical slang; it avoids any suggestion that anyone might consider disreputable, anything Negroid, jazzy, Jewish, Broadwayish, or night clubby. Instead the melody has an affinity for that of "The Battle Hymn of the Republic;" it tastes like school, church, grandma, and biscuits; a master-stroke of diplomacy, aptness, and good business.

VERSE

Down went the gunner; a bullet was his fate.
Down went the gunner, and then the gunner's
    mate.
Up jumped the sky pilot, gave the boys a look
And manned the gun himself as he laid aside the
    Book,
Shouting—

REFRAIN

"Praise the Lord and pass the ammunition!
Praise the Lord and pass the ammunition!
Praise the Lord and pass the ammunition
And we'll all stay free!"

"Praise the Lord and swing into position,
Can't afford to sit around a-wishin'.
Praise the Lord, we're all between perdition
And the deep blue sea!"

Yes, the sky pilot said it.
You've got to give him credit,
For a son-of-a-gun of a gunner was he,
Shouting, "Praise the Lord, we're on a mighty
    mission!

All aboard! We're not a-goin' fishin'.
Praise the Lord and pass the ammunition
And we'll all stay free!"

THE MOON IS DOWN

Music by Arthur Schwartz (1900–1984). Written in April 1942. Schwartz was a great Broadway composer (his shows include *The Band Wagon*) whose most notable collaborators were Howard Dietz, Dorothy Fields, and Ira Gershwin. He wrote music for "Dancing in the Dark," "That's Entertainment," and "I Guess I'll Have to Change My Plan," among others.

On April 30, 1942, Loesser wrote to William Schuman:

This is a poem written by me and set to music by Arthur Schwartz. It was inspired by the book [about the war in Norway] and Steinbeck gave me permission to use the title. This piece of work is soon to be highly publicized by the government itself. Its ultimate function is to reach people of the conquered countries via short wave. . . .

It is an example, not of the form, but of the language that you and I discussed in our breakaway plans for the great American oratorio and that dream about an opera. Am I in the right groove for you? If "The Moon Is Down" is successful, will it help my stock with those opera people?

People of Norway, listen,
People of Holland, listen,
People of France,
People of Java, listen:

Your nights of despair are not without number;
You live without life, you sleep without slumber;
But nights of despair are not without number!
People of Poland, listen,
People of Belgium, listen, listen:

The moon is down,
The moon that was life in our eyes;
Now the wind that was full of our song only cries.

Yet even so,
There is light from the moon that is down,
There is fear in the conqueror's heart,
There is death in the streets of the town,
That the music of freedom may start.

And the song will be whispered along,
From the doomed and the dead to the young.
And the young will be mighty and strong,
And the song once again will be sung,
Will be sung,
In the light will be sung.

The moon is down,
The moon that gave promise of day.
Now the night will be endlessly long on the way,
On its ominous way.

Yet even so,
There is light from the moon that is fled,
In the sparks where the barracks have burned,
In the blood that is gleaming so red,
On the knife in a back that was turned.

And the song will be whispered along,
From the doomed and the dead to the young.
And the young will be mighty and strong,
And the song once again will be sung,
Will be sung,
In the light will be sung.

The moon is down,
The moon that was life in our eyes.
The moon is down,
Yet even so,
The moon will rise!

SONG OF THE WINDSHIELD WIPER

Music and lyrics by Frank Loesser from a title and idea by Peter Lind Hayes. Probably late 1942.

I go driving to work through the rain
To the plant where I'm building a plane,
With my windshield wiper singing gaily through the trip.
Singing, "Flip-flap, flip-flap, flip-flap,
Pitter-patter, pitter-patter, flip-flap flip-flap flip."

There's a beautiful girl by my side,
She's a welder who's sharing the ride,
And my windshield wiper seems to know that she's a pip,
Singing, "Flip-flap, flip-flap, flip-flap,
Pitter-patter, pitter-patter, flip-flap flip-flap flip."

And that busy little song of the windshield wiper
Will become a song of love when the time is riper.
When we're off to Niagara someday,
I don't mind if it rains all the way,
With my windshield wiper giving ev'ry care the slip,
Singing, "Flip-flap, flip-flap, flip-flap,
Pitter-patter, pitter-patter, flip-flap flip-flap flip."

Songs of 1943

HAPPY GO LUCKY

Produced by Harold Wilson for Paramount Pictures. Released in March 1943. Screenplay by Norman Panama, Melvin Frank, Walter DeLeon. Directed by Curtis Bernhardt. Choreography by Paul Oscard. Cast starred Mary Martin, Dick Powell, Eddie Bracken, Betty Hutton, and Rudy Vallee.

SING A TROPICAL SONG

Music by Jimmy McHugh. Published. Copyrighted December 30, 1942. Introduced by Sir Lancelot (Lancelot Pinard) and His Calypso Song, with Dick Powell and Eddie Bracken. Recorded by the Andrews Sisters (Decca) and Frank Loesser (MGM). The Loesser recording is also on the compact disc *Frank Sings Loesser* (Koch). The word "syllable" is here sung as "syl-LA-ble."

LANCELOT: Upon the island from which we come,
We have a national characteristic
which is very strong.
Because we put the accent upon the
wrong syllable
And we sing a tropical song.

Upon the island from which we come,
The point of interest, besides the
coconut and the sarong,
Is that we put the accent upon the
wrong syllable
And we sing a tropical song.

We could show the natural wonders of
the scenery
To you.
We could show the native birds
And perhaps give two or three
To you.
And describe the climate and also tell
the elevation.
We could very hastily introduce the
population
To you.
ENSEMBLE: Upon the island from which we come,
The point of interest, beside the
coconut and the sarong,

Is that we put the accent upon the
wrong syllable
And we sing a tropical song.
POWELL: We could show you the hotel
And many of the fascinating places.
We could take you to the bar
Where visitors may fall upon their
faces.*
BRACKEN: If we only had a track,
We could probably take you to the
races.
But we prefer to acquaint you
With the following interesting fact:
ENSEMBLE: That upon the island from which we
come—
LANCELOT: We have a national characteristic
which is very strong,
And if you should remain,
You will discover one
Peculiar thing
Before very long.
ENSEMBLE: That you have put the accent upon the
wrong syllable
And you sing a tropical song.
And so we say wel-come
To you!†

HAPPY GO LUCKY

Music by Jimmy McHugh. Published. Copyrighted January 18, 1943. Introduced by Mary Martin and Dick Powell.

VERSE

MARTIN: I don't care what time it is,
What time it is, or what the climate is,
Or if my shoes are shined,
Or if the rent's behind.
What's happening to my poor old heart
and mind?

REFRAIN 1

MARTIN: Can this be me feeling so happy-go-lucky,
Looking in your happy-go-lucky eyes?
Can this be me feeling so—
POWELL: Feeling so—

MARTIN: Happy-go-lucky?
POWELL: Happy-go-lucky—
BOTH: Me—
MARTIN: What's always acted so smart and wise?!
Can this be me singing "Oh—
POWELL: Oh-ho-ho-hummm—
MARTIN: Ev'rything's ducky,"
Following you on your happy-go-lucky
way?
POWELL: Could be, could be.
MARTIN: Well, if it's me feeling so happy-go-lucky,
Pardon me while I skip a beat* to say,
Heaven bless this happy-go-lucky day!

REFRAIN 2

POWELL: Can this be you feeling so happy-go-
lucky?
MARTIN: I'm looking in your happy-go-lucky eyes.
POWELL: Can this be me feeling so happy-go-
lucky?
MARTIN: La la la la.
POWELL: Me what's always acted so smart and wise?!
MARTIN: Can this be me feeling so happy-go-lucky,†
Following you on your happy-go-lucky
way?
POWELL: Could be, could be.
BOTH: Well, if it's me—
MARTIN: Feeling so—
POWELL: Feeling so—
MARTIN: Happy-go-lucky—
POWELL: Happy-go-lucky—
MARTIN: Pardon me—
POWELL: Hmmm—
MARTIN: While I skip a beat* to say—
BOTH: Heaven bless this happy-go-lucky day!

MURDER, HE SAYS

Music by Jimmy McHugh. Published. Copyrighted January 18, 1943. Introduced by Betty Hutton. Leading recording by Dinah Shore accompanied by the Gordon Jenkins Orchestra (Victor). Other recordings include Betty Hutton (Victor); Jimmy Dorsey and His Orchestra, vocal by Helen O'Connell (Decca); Gene Krupa and His Orchestra, vocal by Anita O'Day (Columbia); and Roy Eldridge (Columbia).

Eddie Cantor and cast members in the film Thank Your Lucky Stars

---

* Line originally read:
   Where Americans fall upon their faces,

† *Last two lines not sung in film.*

---

* *Sheet music version:*
   "Kiss" instead of "beat."

† *Sheet music version:*
   Can this be me singing, "Oh, ev'rything's ducky."

VERSE

Finally found a fellow
Almost completely divine,
But his vocabulary
Is killing this romance of mine!
We get into an intimate situation
And then begins this Romeo's conversation:

REFRAIN 1

He says, "Murder," he says,
Ev'ry time we kiss,
He says, "Murder," he says,
At a time like this.
He says, "Murder," he says—
Is that the language of love?

He says, "Solid," he says,
Takes me in his arms,
And says, "Solid," he says,
Meaning all my charms.
He says, "Solid," he says—
Is that the language of love?

He says, "Chick Chick, you torture me,
Zoot! Are we livin'!"
I'm thinking of leaving him flat.
He says, "Dig, dig, the jumps the old ticker is givin'!"
Now, he can talk plainer than that!

He says, "Murder," he says,
Ev'ry time we kiss,
He says, "Murder," he says—
Keep it up like this
And that "Murder" he says,
In that impossible tone,
Will bring on nobody's murder but his own.

REFRAIN 2

He says, "Jackson," he says,
And my name's Marie.
He says, "Jackson," he says,
"Shoot the snoot to me."
He says, "Jackson," he says—
Is that the language of love?
He says, "Woof, woof," he says,
When he likes my hat,
He says, "Tsk, tsk," he says—
What the heck is that?
He says, "Woo, woo," he says—
Is that the language of love?

He says, "Hep hep, with helium,
Now, babe, we're cookin'!"
And other expressions, to wit:
He says, "We're in the groove

And the groove is good-lookin'."
He sounds like his uppers don't fit.

He says, "Murder," he says,*
Ev'ry time we kiss,
He says, "Murder," he says—
Keep it up like this
And that "Murder" he says,
In that impossible tone,
Will bring on nobody's murder but his own.

He says, "Murder,"
He says, "Murder,"
And the way he says "Murder" in that impossible tone,
I've told him over and over and over again,
It'll be nobody else's murder but his own.

LET'S GET LOST

Music by Jimmy McHugh. Published. Copyrighted January 18, 1943. Introduced by Mary Martin. The orchestra that appears in the film is billed as the "Loesser-McHugh Orchestra." The recording by Vaughn Monroe and His Orchestra with the Four Lee Sisters (Victor) reached the number-one spot on the popular music charts. Other leading recordings by Kay Kyser and His Orchestra, vocals by Julie Conway, Max Williams, Harry Babbitt, and Jack Martin (Columbia), and by Jimmy Dorsey and His Orchestra, vocal by Bob Eberly (Decca).

VERSE (NOT SUNG IN FILM)

The party's rather dull,
Isn't it?
We'd love to steal away,
Wouldn't we?
So let's not even ask
Should we or shouldn't we.

REFRAIN

Let's get lost,
Lost in each other's arms.
Let's get lost,
Let them send out alarms.
And though they'll think us rather rude,
Let's tell the world we're in that crazy mood.
Let's defrost in a romantic mist,
Let's get crossed off ev'rybody's list.
To celebrate this night we found each other,
Mmmm, let's get lost.

---

* *Stanza not sung in film.*

THE FUDDY-DUDDY WATCHMAKER

Music by Jimmy McHugh. Published. Copyrighted January 18, 1943. Introduced by Betty Hutton and the Sportsmen. Leading recording by Kay Kyser and His Orchestra, vocal by Julie Conway (Columbia).

VERSE 1

I broke my watch the other night,
I broke my watch 'cause I wound it too tight.
I broke my watch round a quarter to nine,
So I took it down the corner to a friend of mine.

REFRAIN 1

Well, I don't know how he does it, but he does it,
I don't know how he does it, but he does it,
I don't know how he does it, but he does it,
The fuddy-duddy watchmaker at the joolery store.

I don't know how he does it, but he does it,
I don't know how he does it, but he does it,
I don't know how he does it, but he does it,
He got it on the beam, steadier than ever before.

Look-a the old man go!
He's a hundred and three and that's no lie.
Look-a the old man go!
When he raises that glass up to his eye.

Well, I don't know how he does it, but he does it,
I don't know how he does it, but he does it,
I don't know how he does it, but he does it,
The fuddy-duddy watchmaker at the joolery store.

VERSE 2

He fixed my watch, he fixed it quick,
And mighty soon he was makin' it tick.
He made it tick with a beautiful beat,
And I watched him through the window from
    outside on the street.

REFRAIN 2

Well, I don't know how he shook it, but he shook
    it,
I don't know how he shook it, but he shook it,
I don't know how he shook it, but he shook it,
The fuddy-duddy watchmaker with the glass in his
    eye.

I don't know where he dug it, but he dug it,
I don't know where he dug it, but he dug it,

I don't know where he dug it, but he dug it,
To fuddy-duddy watchmakers it's as easy as pie.

Look-a the old man go!
He's a hundred and three and maybe more.
Look-a the old man go!
Let me say it again just like before:

That I don't know how he does it, but he does it,
I don't know how he does it, but he does it,
I don't know how he does it, but he does it,
The fuddy-duddy watchmaker at the joolery store.

JERRY OR JOE

Music by Jimmy McHugh. Used instrumentally only.

Somehow or other I've gotten my dates mixed;
Where I'll be tonight I don't know.
Should I go to the ball with Jerry
Or go to the brawl with Joe? Oh, Mother,
Oh, Mother, it's almost eight-thirty;
I should have been dressed long ago.
Should I wear my hair up for Jerry
Or let my hair down with Joe?

Oh, how I've worried for hours and hours—
They both are so handsome and tall!
Jerry, sweet boy, sends me beautiful flowers,
But Joe, he just sends me, that's all.
Somehow or other I've gotten my dates mixed,
Two gentlemen waiting to know.
Should I join the old set with Jerry
Or upset the old joint with Joe?

Jerry loves his Bach cantatas and concertos and
    sonatas,
And through twenty *Traviatas* we have sat.
But my Joe, he wears a derby, he's the Barrelhouse
    Iturbi,
Known as Jumpin' Joseph Kirby, solid cat.
Ah—[*classical music phrase*]—that's Jerry.
Ra-dah-dah ra-dah-dah—that's Joe.

Now my Jerry's in society,
The model of propriety,
How passionately quiet he can be!
Whereas Joseph is notorious,
For being so uproarious,
The glow he gets is glorious to see.
[*legitimate dance*]—That's Jerry.
[*barrelhouse dance*]—That's Joe.

How shall I dress when we're making the
    rounds—
Is it tails or Tenth Avenue togs?
Jerry, sweet boy, takes me riding to hounds,
But with Joe I got to go to the dogs.
Somehow or other I've gotten my dates mixed,
Should my brow be highbrow or low?
Should I get myself in with Jerry,
Or knock myself out with Joe?

TORNADO

Produced by William H. Pine and William Thomas for Paramount Pictures. Released in August 1943. Screenplay by Maxwell Shane based on the novel by John Guedel. Directed by William Berke. Cast starred Chester Morris and Nancy Kelly. The film score also included "I'm Afraid of You" by Ralph Freed (lyrics) and Frederick Hollander (music).

THERE GOES MY DREAM

Music by Frederick Hollander. Published. Copyrighted January 3, 1944. Originally written for *A Night at Earl Carroll's*. Introduced by Nancy Kelly.

There goes my dream,
My lovely young dream,
But he doesn't know I exist.
Why without so much as glancing my way
Those blue eyes just ruined my day.

There goes my dream,
My heart's only seam,
With lips that were meant to be kissed.
And I stand here in my sorrow supreme
Sighing, "There goes my dream."

ARMY SHOW

Two-reel short produced by Warner Bros. Released in September 1943. Directed by Jean Negulesco. A concert film featuring the Army Air Force Orchestra under the direction of Captain Eddie Dunstedter. Based on the radio program *Soldiers with Wings*. Other songs performed included "Song of the Bombardier," music by Richard Rodgers, lyrics by Lorenz Hart, and "Glide, Glider, Glide" by Cole Porter.

HELLO, MOM

Music by Captain Eddie Dunstedter (1897–1974). Lyrics by Captain Arthur V. Jones and Frank Loesser. Published. Copyrighted August 17, 1942. In film, lyrics spoken, not sung. Leading recording by Bing Crosby. Dunstedter was a composer, organist, and bandleader who worked on film and television scores; nothing currently is known about Jones.

VERSE

FIRST
SERVICEMAN: Hello! Long distance?
    I want to place a call,
    A person-to-person call to my best
        girl,
    The grandest girl of all.

REFRAIN

    Hello, Mom, I thought I'd phone
        tonight.
    Gee, I've got so much to tell!
    I passed my solo flight,
    Yeah, they say I'm doing swell.
    Gee, I wish that you were here to
        see!
    Listen, Mom, remember Sally Lou,
    The girl who lives next door?
    Could you find out exactly who
    She's really waiting for?
    I kinda sorta hope it's me.
    Sure, Mom, the food is mighty good,
    And lately we got a raise in pay.
    Oh, listen, those bonds that you're
        buying,
    They're sure keeping us flying,
    Makes the whole darn thing okay.
    So long, Mom, I do a lot of things
        you really don't expect.

I hope that Dad won't mind I called
collect,
But I just had to say
Hello, Mom.

SECOND
SERVICEMAN: Hello, Mom, yeah, well I just called
up to say
That everything's gonna be all right.
I'll soon be on my way—
Yep, I'm really in the fight.
Well, I kinda thought you'd want to
know.
Say, listen, Mom, remember Mary
Jane?
That's right, the one with eyes of blue.
Will you please explain
That I'm thinking of her, too.
I haven't time to tell her so—
That'd be swell.
Sure, Mom, it's not so very far
away—
Just listen, listen, and hear those
motors roar.
You'll be proud that I'm in it,
You'll be proud every minute,
'Cause it's you that I'm fighting for.
So long, Ma!
What? Youwant to see me soon?
Yeah, yeah, yeah, I know, I know, I
know.
First I've got a date with Tokyo,
And then I'll come back to say,
Hello, Mom.

THANK YOUR LUCKY STARS

Produced by Mark Hellinger for Warner Bros. Released in October 1943. Music by Arthur Schwartz. Screenplay by Norman Panama, Melvin Frank, and James V. Kern, based on a story by Everett Freeman and Arthur Schwartz. Directed by David Butler. Cast starred Humphrey Bogart, Eddie Cantor, Bette Davis, Olivia de Havilland, Errol Flynn, John Garfield, Joan Leslie, Ida Lupino, Dennis Morgan, Ann Sheridan, Dinah Shore, Alexis Smith, Jack Carson, Alan Hale, George Tobias, Edward Everett Horton, S. Z. Sakall, Hattie McDaniel, Ruth Donnelly, Don Wilson, Spike Jones and His City Slickers with Joyce Reynolds, Willie Best, Jess Lee Brooks, and Rita Christiani. The film score also included "Blues in the Night" by Harold Arlen and Johnny Mercer and "Now's the Time to Fall in Love" by Al Sherman and Al Lewis.

THANK YOUR LUCKY STARS

Published. Copyrighted March 5, 1943. Introduced by Dinah Shore and Edgar Fairchild and His Orchestra.

How's your love life?
Well, thank your lucky stars,
Yes, thank your lucky stars,
It's doing fine.
Keep your love life
As sweet as candy bars,
And thank your lucky stars
Like I thank mine.

Ev'rybody's living on less and less,
But you're okay,
You big success.
You've got your love life,
And that's the only thing
They won't be rationing.
They don't know how,
So, thank your lucky stars right now.
Thank your lucky stars right now.

I'M RIDIN' FOR A FALL

Published. Copyrighted March 5, 1943. Introduced by Dennis Morgan and Joan Leslie and ensemble, with Spike Jones and His Orchestra.

VERSE

MORGAN: Sprinkle me with perfume rare
And I'll be on my way.
Stick some slickum on my hair—
I may be gone all day;

REFRAIN

Oh! I'm ridin' for a fall,
Dudin' up, dudin' up in my shirts
and ties,
For the gal with the big blue eyes.
Oh! I'm ridin' for a fall,
Dudin' up, dudin' up in my two-tone
shoes,
For the gal with the baby blues.

Oh, yes, I know, she's a dangerous
critter,
I know, she's a dangerous critter,
I know, she's a dangerous critter,

I know, but I can't quit her.
I'm ridin' for a fall,
Dudin' up, dudin' up like I wasn't
wise
To the gal with the big blue eyes.

ENSEMBLE: Oh, yes, I know, she's a witch of a
woman,
I know, she's a witch of a woman,
I know, she's a witch of a woman—
MORGAN: I know, but I'm so human.
I'm ridin' for a fall,
Dudin' up, dudin' up like I wasn't
wise
To the gal with the big blue eyes.

ENSEMBLE: Oh, yes, I know, people died of her
cookin',
I know, people died of her cookin',
I know, people died of her cookin'—
MORGAN: But oh, she's so good-lookin'!
I'm ridin' for a fall,
Dudin' up, dudin' up like I wasn't wise
To the gal with the big blue eyes.

LESLIE: Oh yes, I know, she's a-quick on the
trigger,
I know, she's a-quick on the trigger,
I know, she's a-quick on the trigger,
MORGAN: I know, but oh that figger!
ENSEMBLE: I'm ridin' for a fall,
Dudin' up, dudin' up like I wasn't
wise
To the gal with the big blue eyes.
ENSEMBLE: Oh yes, I know.
MORGAN: She'll be spending my sugar.
ENSEMBLE: I know.
MORGAN: She'll be spending my sugar.
ENSEMBLE: I know.
MORGAN: She'll be spending my sugar.
ENSEMBLE: But oh—
LESLIE: You can't rhyme sugar.
ENSEMBLE: I'm riding for a fall,
Dudin' up, dudin' up like I wasn't
wise
To the gal with the big blue eyes.
MORGAN
AND LESLIE: Yes, I'm riding for a fall,
Dudin' up, dudin' up like I wasn't
wise
To the gal with the big blue eyes.
Dudin' up, dudin' up like I wasn't
wise
To the gal with the big blue eyes.
Dudin' up, dudin' up like I wasn't wise
To the gal with the big blue eyes.

WE'RE STAYING HOME TONIGHT (MY BABY AND ME)

Introduced by Eddie Cantor.

Thank you for your cordial invitation, Mrs. Jones,
But with nightclub life we're through.
Nonessential spending brings inflation, Mrs.
    Jones,
So here's what we're planning to do.

We're staying home tonight, my baby and me,
Doing the patriotic thing.
I've got my income tax return to hurdle,
And she'll be saving mileage on her girdle.

Don't want to roam tonight, we're snug as can be,
Hoping the phone will never ring.
The landlord never told us when we moved in this
    flat
That you can use the fireside for more than a chat.
We're staying home tonight, my baby and me,
Doing the patriotic thing.

We're staying home tonight, my baby and me,
Having a patriotic time.
It's not that Mommy doesn't trust her poppy,
It's just that we don't trust our old jalopy.
Don't want to roam tonight,
We're snug as can be.
Being alone is just sublime.

While I sit in my slippers and munch a piece of
    fruit,
She'll iron out the wrinkles in my victory suit.
We're staying home tonight, my baby and me,
Having a patriotic time.

We'll play a game of rummy,
It's cheaper than the Ritz.
The winner wins a kiss and just in case of a blitz.
We're staying home tonight, my baby and me,
Having a patriotic time.

Her coffee could be sweeter, but I'm not in the
    dumps,
'Cause every time she hugs me, it's like two extra
    lumps.
We're staying home tonight, my baby and me,
Having a patriotic time.

I'M GOIN' NORTH

Registered for copyright as an unpublished song June 25, 1943. Studio ozalid dated November 18, 1942. Prologue dated December 9, 1942. Introduced by Jack Carson and Alan Hale.

CARSON: Weren't you on the bill with me in Dallas,
    Or was it the Palace,
    Or was it the Strand?
HALE: Didn't you have a blonde with you named
    Alice?
CARSON: Yes, that was in Dallas,
    And wasn't she grand?
HALE: I know your face, it's a face in a million!
BOTH: Shake, brother, shake with a brother
    vaudevillian!
CARSON: Hello.
HALE: Hello.
CARSON: Hello.
HALE: Hello.
CARSON: You look all ready to go.
    But where are you going to go?
    I certainly wish you'd let me know.
HALE: Goodbye.
CARSON: Goodbye.
HALE: Goodbye.
CARSON: Goodbye.
HALE: A happy fella am I,
    And though you'll call me an awful sap—
CARSON: Who, me?
HALE: I found a wonderful spot on the map.

HALE: I'm going north.
CARSON: He's going north.
HALE: Not talking about south.
CARSON: Not talking about south.
HALE: Not talking about west.
CARSON: One place he loves best.
HALE: I'm shouting
    I don't want to live without the—
CARSON: Why don't they write a song about the—
HALE: North.
CARSON: You heard him say north.
HALE: Not talking about east.
CARSON: He never mentioned east,
HALE: I just want to feast—
CARSON: Oh, boy, what a feast!
HALE: —these eyes on Syracuse and Albany—
CARSON: And Buffalo and Schenectady.
HALE: North is my favorite direction,
    Pointing to the state of Maine.
BOTH: Pardon me, boy, if that's the
    Chattanooga Choo-Choo,
    Well, I guess I must be on the wrong train,
    Because I'm heading—

HALE: North.
CARSON: I think you mean it.
HALE: I've been back and forth.
CARSON: You've really seen it.
HALE: Oh, Mother, you can take a rock and
    slam me
    If I should ever call you Mammy.
BOTH: Way up north.

[*Soft shoe*]

    Two, three, four—

[*Soft shoe*]

    —six, seven, eight—
    Stop!
HALE: I'm going north.
CARSON: He's still going north.
HALE: Too lazy down south.
CARSON: Hates the sugar cane in his mouth.
HALE: Too lonely out west.
CARSON: Pardner, get it off your chest.
HALE: I can't begin to tell you how I love the—
CARSON: Cities and states and counties of the—
HALE: North.
CARSON: He knows his own mind.
HALE: Northeast will not do.
CARSON: He's quite particular.
HALE: Northwest gets me blue.
CARSON: He's perpendicular.
HALE: Head straight for Saskatoon,
    Saskatchewan.
CARSON: Labrador and on and on.
BOTH: To the north.
HALE: That's my favorite direction,
    Pointing up to Hudson Bay.
BOTH: Pardon me, boy, but when the midnight
    choo-choo leaves for Alabam,
    I won't be going your way,
    Because I'm headin'—
HALE: North.
CARSON: He'll never have a famine.
HALE: I've been back and forth.
CARSON: He lives on Nova Scotia salmon.
HALE: You'll find me where there is no cotton
    pickin',
    Never again to fry a chicken—
BOTH: Way up north.

[*Dance interlude*]

BOTH: Stop!
    The north,
    Is my favorite direction.
    Pointing to the Arctic Sea—brrr!
    Pardon me, boy, is this the road to
    Mandalay?

Well, you can go to Mandalay, but not me!
Because we're headin'—
HALE: North.
CARSON: Is that your attitude?
HALE: I've been back and forth.
CARSON: In every latitude?
BOTH: We are the only act in vaudeville
That never will be content until
We're way up—
CARSON: Mush!
BOTH: Way up—
We're not from Dixie.
Way up—
We are from hunger.
Way up north!

LOVE ISN'T BORN (IT'S MADE)

Published. Copyrighted June 25, 1943. Introduced by Ann Sheridan, Joyce Reynolds, and girls' chorus. Chorus parts are of uncertain authorship and were omitted.

VERSE

Oh, my precious young dove,
If you're dreaming of love,
You've got to join in the chase yourself,
And here's my story, so brace yourself:

REFRAIN 1

Love isn't born
On a beautiful April morn,
Love isn't born,
It's made.
And that's why ev'ry window has a window shade.
Love can't do much
For a couple who don't quite touch,
Love can't advance by chance.
And that's why folks who never cared for dancing
dance.
So, my precious young dove,
If you're waiting for love,
Better make the most of your charms,
For the feeling won't start
In the gentleman's heart
Till you're in the gentleman's arms.
Love isn't born,
That's a fable to treat with scorn.
Let's call a spade a spade:

And don't keep crying wolf at ev'ry gay young blade.*
Remember, love isn't born,
It's made.

REFRAIN 2

Love has to climb,
It can't suddenly ring that chime.
Climb, sister, time is short.
You'll find there's no partition in a davenport.
Love doesn't act
Till the cards are discreetly stacked,
Here is a fact to face:
A man won't take a taxi just to get no place.
So, my precious young dove,
If you're dreaming of love,
Better lead him into the trap;
For you'll never remain
On the gentleman's brain—
Till you're on the gentleman's lap.
Love won't exist—
If you constantly slap that wrist—
Right off his list you'll fade—
Those Elks don't come to town for just the Elks
Parade.†
So when you walk—
Alone and forlorn—
And then you hear—
A Cadillac horn—
Remember, love isn't born,
It's made.

NO YOU, NO ME

Introduced by Dennis Morgan and Joan Leslie.

VERSE

MORGAN: Without you I'll never be much,
Without you my plans will fall through.
So I have prepared this reliable
Collection of facts undeniable
To point out how much I depend on you.

REFRAIN

No sunny little sunbeam,
No springtime,

* Film version:
    When he says, "Dear, come up and see my antique
    jade."

† Film version:
    So don't keep crying wolf at ev'ry gay young blade.

No tasty little apple,
No pie.
No tricky little trombone,
No swing time,
No one and one, no two.
LESLIE: Nothing could be more true.

No rainy little raindrop,
No ocean.
MORGAN: No lovely one to sigh for,
No sigh.
And there's my little song of
devotion,
Which all adds up, so obviously,
No you, no me.

No sixty little minutes.
LESLIE: No hour.
No happy little moo cow.
MORGAN: No cream.
No alternating current.
LESLIE: No power.
MORGAN: No great Tchaikovsky tunes.
LESLIE: No hit parade moons and Junes.

MORGAN: No pretty little mirror.
LESLIE: No reflection.
No pretty little dream girl.
MORGAN: No dream.
Plus lots of other terms of affection—
BOTH: Which all add up, more personally.
No you, no me.
MORGAN: In other words, I'm hot on your trail.
LESLIE: Mm-huh.
CASH
REGISTER: [picture and sound of] NO SALE

THE DREAMER

Published. Copyrighted March 5, 1943. Introduced by Dinah Shore. Reprised later in film in a swing version by Ida Lupino, Olivia de Havilland (dubbed by Lynn Martin), and George Tobias. Leading recording by Kay Armen with the Balladeers (Decca).

VERSE

The early birdie used to sing,
Go to work, go to work, better go to work,
And a day was a busy thing.
But now without you, you,
That birdie sings another tune,
Stay asleep, stay asleep, better stay asleep
All morning, night, and noon.

REFRAIN

The dreamer, the dreamer,
I reckon that's my name,
Since you're gone away.
But how'm I gonna see you
'Less I dream all day,
All the long and mis'rable day?
They call me the dreamer,
They tell me it's a shame
How lazy I seem.
But how'm I gonna hold you
'Less I dream, dream, dream?

So I stroll among the trees
Like I didn't have a chore to do,
And I let the summer breeze
Come and kiss me like a real and true kiss from
    you.
The dreamer, the dreamer,
I reckon that's my name.
Why change it? What for?
I wanna stay a dreamer
Till you're home once more.

So I stroll among the trees
Like I didn't have a chore to do,
And I let the summer breeze
Come and kiss me like a real and true kiss from
    you.
The dreamer, the dreamer,
I reckon that's my name.
Why change it? What for?
I wanna stay a dreamer
Till you're home once more,
Till you're home and wakin' me up once more.

ICE COLD KATY

Published. Copyrighted June 25, 1943. Introduced by
Hattie McDaniel, Willie Best, Jess Lee Brooks, Rita
Christiani, and ensemble.

MCDANIEL: Private Jones is camping on the
    doorstep of Miss Katy Brown.
    She must be the very, very
        coldest creature in this town.
    He's been there for seven days
        and nights,
    And now his leave is through—
TWO WOMEN: And still she won't, still she
        won't, still she won't say
MCDANIEL: I do. Brrrr!

MCDANIEL: Ice cold Katy, won't you marry
    the soldier?
    Ice cold Katy, won't you do it
        today?
FIRST WOMAN: Ice cold Katy, won't you marry
    the soldier?
TRIO: Soon he'll march away.
ENSEMBLE: Ice cold Katy, he's a-dyin' to
    hold ya.
MCDANIEL: Keep that date he came
    a-hurrying for.
ENSEMBLE: Ice cold Katy, won't you marry
    the soldier?
TRIO: Soon he's off to war.
JONES: Here I am outside ringin',
    ringin',
    Ringin' on your bell.
MCDANIEL: Ringin' so long he's gonna be
    A–double U–O–L.
ENSEMBLE: No! Ice cold Katy, why'doncha
    do what I told ya!
SECOND WOMAN: Ice cold Katy you're the talk of
    the town.
THIRD WOMAN: Ice cold Katy, please marry the
    soldier.
MCDANIEL: Melt, melt, melt on down—
ENSEMBLE: Ice cold Katy Brown.

MEN: Here comes the justice—
WOMEN: Yon comes the justice—
ALL: Here comes the justice now.

[Dance interlude]

JUSTICE: I was here at seven,
    I was here at ten,
    I was here at eleven,
    And I positively won't be back
        again.
JONES: I don't blame you.
JUSTICE: Is the ring all ready?
MCDANIEL: [spoken] Ask him.
JUSTICE: [sung] Did the bride get sense?
MCDANIEL: [spoken] No.
JUSTICE: [sung] Is the groom feeling steady
    After all the matrimonial
        suspense?
ENSEMBLE: Is there cake and candy?
MCDANIEL: Is the choir in tune?
JUSTICE: Is the fee handy?
    The private may be leaving
        mighty soon.
ENSEMBLE: Ka-ka-ka-ka-Katy,
    Won't you step outside?
    Everything is ready for the bride.
    Ice cold Katy, won't you marry
        the soldier?
    Ice cold Katy, won't you do it

today?
MCDANIEL: Ice cold Katy, won't you marry
    the soldier?
ENSEMBLE: Soon he'll march away.
JUSTICE: Ice cold Katy, he's just dying to
    hold you.
ENSEMBLE: Ice cold Katy, how he grumbles
    and groans.
    Ice cold Katy, won't you marry
        the soldier?
FIRST SOLDIER: [whistle] Private Jones,
    Don't you know you ain't got no,
        got no,
    Got no time to spare?
SOLDIERS: Don't you know we're all sailing,
        sailing,
    Sailing over there?

ENSEMBLE: Ice cold Katy, won't you do what
    I told you?
    Ice cold Katy, ain't a moment to
        lose!
    Ice cold Katy, won't you marry
        the soldier?
SOLDIERS: Looks like rice and shoes.
ENSEMBLE: Spread, spread, spread the news.

[Dance]

ENSEMBLE: Here goes the justice—
    Just watch the justice—
    Here goes the justice now.
JUSTICE: Do you take this woman?
MCDANIEL: [spoken] Of course.
JUSTICE: [sung] Do you take this man?
MCDANIEL: [spoken] Go ahead.
JUSTICE: [sung] Well, young man and
        young woman,
    You better get a little loving
        while you can.
MCDANIEL: [spoken] That's right.
JUSTICE: [spoken] I now pronounce you
        man and wife.
MCDANIEL: [spoken] That's over.
JUSTICE: [sung] I never had such trouble in
    my life.

[Dance interlude]

SECOND
SOLDIER: Private Jones, don't you know
        you ain't
    Got no time to spare?
ENSEMBLE: Don't you know they are sailing,
        sailing,
    Sailing over there?
    Ice cold Katy went and married
        the soldier,

Ice cold Katy in her silvery gown.
Ice cold Katy went and married
   the soldier,
Cold, cold Katy Brown.
GROUP 1: Got a man.
GROUP 2: Oh, Katy did.
GROUP 1: Got a man.
GROUP 2: Oh, Katy did.
GROUP 1: Got a man.
GROUP 2: Oh, Katy did.
ALL: Oo-ooh, Katy Brown.

HOW SWEET YOU ARE

Published. Copyrighted March 5, 1943. Introduced by Dinah Shore and chorus. Leading recordings by Kay Armen with the Balladeers (Decca) and Jo Stafford (Capitol).

VERSE (NOT SUNG IN FILM)

Once I walked in the darkness,
Through the gloom of the night.
Then I found you beside me,
Close beside me.
Now I'm out of the darkness,
My horizon is bright,
For I know so well,
Yes, I know so well—

REFRAIN

How sweet you are,
How sweet you are,
How dear your tenderly smiling face.
Through days all bitter and gray and grim,
Through nights when even the stars are dim,
How sweet to know
My heart can glow
From just the warmth of our first embrace.
The world's a lovelier world by far
When I remember how sweet you are.

THAT'S WHAT YOU JOLLY WELL GET

Introduced by Errol Flynn and ensemble.

FLYNN: I can see the question in your eyes,
I can see the twitching of your ears.
Now it's not to be repeated,
But gentlemen, be seated
And I'll tell you where I've been for
   all these years.
ENSEMBLE: If he's very nicely treated,
And we have his toddy heated,
He'll tell us where he's been for all
   these years.

FLYNN: I was out on the blue Pacific
With a cruiser of the fleet.
I'd been over the side for my
   Saturday dip—
FIRST MAN: [spoken] Go on, go on!
FLYNN: [sung] When I noticed a Jap torpedo
Whizzing by beneath my feet,
Coming lickety-split and headed for
   our ship.
SECOND MAN: [spoken] Fancy that.
FLYNN: [sung] I stuffed her with me left
And turned her with me right,
And I aimed her very careful,
And I shoved with all me might.
And I sank the sub what sent her,
And I roared with righteous wrath:
That's what you jolly well get,
That's what you jolly well get,
Disturbing me Saturday evening
   bath!

ENSEMBLE: Hooray, he's won the war,
He's won the war!
FLYNN: But I'm modest to the core.
ENSEMBLE: Hooray, he's won the war,
And though he's rather shy—
FLYNN: I'm terribly, terribly shy.
ENSEMBLE: He will admit he's won the war.

FLYNN: I was captured around Bengazi
By a Nazi regiment
After polishing off half a thousand
   or more.
THIRD MAN: [spoken] He's balmy.
[sung] And it took them two pairs of
   tanks
To drag me into the general's tent,
Where they started to search the
   uniform I wore.
FOURTH MAN: [spoken] My word!
FLYNN: [sung] When they took away my
   gun,
I was pleasant as could be,
But then they took a letter
What my sweetheart wrote to me.
So I bashed their bloomin'
   brains in,

And I lived to tell the tale:
That's what they jolly well get,
That's what they jolly well get,
For reading a gentleman's private
   mail!

ENSEMBLE: Hooray, he's won the war,
He's won the war!
FLYNN: And I won the one before.
ENSEMBLE: Hooray, he's won the war!
FLYNN: I hates to tell the tale.
ENSEMBLE: But give him a barrel of ale
And he'll admit he's won the war.

FLYNN: I was having me leave in London,
Back in nineteen forty-one,
Having breakfast in bed at a fancy
   address—
FIRST MAN: [spoken] Oh, yes.
FLYNN: [spoken] When a Jerry come by and
   dropped a bomb
What must have weighed a ton.
It was difficult to collect myself, I
   guess.
FIRST MAN: [spoken] I should think.
FLYNN: [sung] So to Croydon Field I ran,
And I hopped a plane from there.
Now, I couldn't tell the one who
   done it—
There were thousands in the air—
So I shot down all the blighters
And I told them all, you see,
That's what you jolly well get—
ALL: That's what you jolly well get—
FLYNN: For splashing a gentleman's cup of
   tea!

ENSEMBLE: Hooray, he saved the day,
He saved the day!
FLYNN: In my own quiet way.
ENSEMBLE: Hooray, he saved the day!
FLYNN: I always zips me lips.
ENSEMBLE: But treat him to fish and chips,
And he's convinced he saved the day.
Hooray, he's won the war,
He's won the war,
He's won the war,
This mighty conqueror!
Hooray, he's won the war!
So to this most heroic gent
We all erect a monument—
MEN: And put it in Trafalgar Square,
Where he can enjoy the open air.
Hooray!

THEY'RE EITHER TOO YOUNG OR TOO OLD

Published. Copyrighted June 25, 1943. Introduced by Bette Davis. Leading recording, which reached number two on the charts, by Jimmy Dorsey and His Orchestra, vocal by Kitty Kallen (Decca). Nominated for an Academy Award as Best Song of the Year.

VERSE

You marched away and left this town as empty as
    can be.
And I am like the driftwood in a deadly calm
    at sea.*
I can't sit under the apple tree with anyone else
    but me.
For there is no secret lover
That the draft board didn't discover.

REFRAIN 1

They're either too young or too old;
They're either too gray or too grassy green.
The pickins are poor and the crop is lean;
What's good is in the Army—
What's left will never harm me.

They're either too old or too young,
So, darling, you'll never get stung.
Tomorrow I'll go hiking with that Eagle Scout,
    unless
I get a call from Grandpa for a snappy game of
    chess.
I'm finding it easy to stay good as gold—
They're either too young or too old.

REFRAIN 2

They're either too warm or too cold;
They're either too fast or too fast asleep.
So, darling, believe me, I'm yours to keep;
There isn't any gravy—
The gravy's in the Navy.

They're either too fresh or too stale;
There is no available male.
I will confess to one romance I'm sure you will
    allow:
He tries to serenade me, but his voice is changing
    now.
I'm finding it easy to keep things controlled—
They're either too young or too old.

_____
* *Line not sung in film.*

REFRAIN 3

They're either too bald or too bold.
I'm down to the wheelchair and bassinet;
My heart just refuses to get upset—
I simply can't compel it to
With no Marines to tell it to.

I'm either their first breath of spring
Or else I'm their last little fling.
I either get a fossil or an adolescent pup;
I either have to hold him off or have to hold him
    up.
The battle is on, but the fortress will hold—
They're either too young or too old.

[*Interlude*]

I'll never, never fail ya
When you are in Australia,
Or out in the Aleutians
Or off among the Rooshans.
And flying over Egypt,
Your heart will never be gypped.
And when you get to India,
I'll still be what I been t'ya.
I've looked the field over
And lo and behold—
They're either too young or too old.

GOOD NIGHT, GOOD NEIGHBOR

Published. Copyrighted June 25, 1943. Introduced by Dennis Morgan and chorus. Danced by Alexis Smith and dancers.

VERSE

The lady came from South America,
And she was lovely to see.
When she arrived in North America,
They introduced her to me.
And so I showed her the town,
And I was such a gallant guide,
And when the moon had gone down,
I sighed:

REFRAIN

Good night, good neighbor,
This evening with you has charmed me so.
Tomorrow those Latin eyes aglow
Will haunt me all day.

Good night, good neighbor,
We're back at your door and now we kiss;
Though down in Brazil you'd frown at this,
You'll soon learn our way.

I know you're dreaming of a homeland
So very dear,
Land of many charms.
But oh, you'll find another homeland
Right over here,
Right over here in my arms!

Good night, good neighbor,
Though I have no soft guitar to play,
Come close to my heart and hear it say:
Good neighbor, good night.

[*Dance interlude*]

Good night, good neighbor,
Though I have no soft guitar to play,
Come close to my heart and hear it say:
Good neighbor, good night.
Good night, good neighbor,
Good neighbor, good night.

CLOSING MEDLEY

Introduced by Eddie Cantor, Alan Hale, Jack Carson, Dinah Shore, Ida Lupino, George Tobias, Olivia de Havilland (dubbed by Lynn Martin), Dennis Morgan, Joan Leslie, Ann Sheridan, Errol Flynn, Bette Davis, Hattie McDaniel, and ensemble. This number features new lyrics for songs introduced earlier in the film.

We're Staying Home Tonight

CANTOR: We're staying home tonight, my baby
    and me,
    Having a patriotic time.
    No ballroom floor the jitterbugs all
      pile on,
    Those jitterbugs are murder on your
      nylon.
    No brush and comb tonight, no people
      to see,
    Being alone is so sublime.
    We've bought a big bologna,
    And though it's hard to take,
    We'll turn out all the lights
    And make believe it's a steak.
    We're staying home tonight, my baby
    and me,
    Having a patriotic time.

How Sweet You Are

WOMEN'S
CHORUS: How sweet you are,
How sweet you are,
How dear your tenderly smiling face!

I'm Going North

HALE: We're way up north.
CARSON: And still together.
HALE: No trips back and forth.
CARSON: We like the weather.
BOTH: And if you happen to be wondering still
Whatever became of vaudeville,
It's way up north.

The Dreamer

SHORE: The dreamer, the dreamer,
I reckon that's my name.
Why change it? What for?
I wanna stay a dreamer
Till you're home once more,
Till you're home and wakin' me up once
more.

I'm Riding for a Fall

ENSEMBLE: Oh yes, I know—
MORGAN: Every gal in the city.
ENSEMBLE: I know—
LESLIE: Every gal in the city?
ENSEMBLE: I know—
MORGAN: Every gal in the city.
ENSEMBLE: But, oh—
MORGAN: They ain't this pretty.
ENSEMBLE: I'm ridin' for a fall,
Dudin' up, dudin' up like I wasn't wise
To the gal with the big blue eyes.

Love Isn't Born

SHERIDAN: Love isn't born—
That's a bit of old-fashioned corn.
Let's call a spade a spade:
When you find more than lemon in
your lemonade,
You'll know that love isn't born,
It's made.

That's What You Jolly Well Get

MALE
CHORUS: Hooray—
[operatic tenor dubbing for Flynn:]
Ahhh—

MALE
CHORUS: He's won the war,
He's won the war,
This mighty conqueror!
FLYNN: [spoken] Oh, that voice is so divine!
I'm sorry it isn't mine.
[operatic tenor dubbing for Flynn:] Ahh—
MALE
CHORUS: [sung] But he'll admit he won the war.

Good Night, Good Neighbor

MORGAN: Good night, good neighbor,
Though I have no soft guitar to play,
Come close to my heart and hear it say:
Good neighbor, good night.
Good night, good neighbor,
Good neighbor, good night.

They're Either Too Young or Too Old

DAVIS: You marched away and knew so well our
love would stay alive;
I'm stuck with either sweet sixteen or kids
of sixty-five.
You must have known it the day you
enrolled—
They're either too young or too old.

Ice Cold Katy

CANTOR: Ice cold Katy, won't you marry the
soldier?
MCDANIEL: Ice cold Katy, you're the talk of the
town.
CANTOR: Ice cold Katy, won't you marry the
soldier?
MCDANIEL: Melt, melt, melt on down.
BOTH: Ice cold Katy Brown.

Thank Your Lucky Stars

CHORUS: How's your love life?
Well, thank your lucky stars,
Yes, thank your lucky stars,
It's doing fine.
Keep your love life
As sweet as candy bars,
And thank your lucky stars
Like I thank mine.

Ev'rybody's living on less and less,
But you're okay,
You big success.
You've got your love life,
And that's the only thing
They won't be rationing.
They don't know how.

So, thank your lucky stars right now.
Thank your lucky stars right now.

RIDING HIGH

Produced by Fred Kohlmar for Paramount Pictures. Released December 1943. Screenplay by Walter DeLeon, Arthur Phillips, and Art Arthur, based on the play *Ready Money* by James Montgomery. Directed by George Marshall. Cast starred Dorothy Lamour, Dick Powell, and Victor Moore and featured Gil Lamb, Cass Daley, and the Milt Britton Band. The songs in this film included "He Loved Me Till the All Clear Came" by Johnny Mercer (lyrics) and Harold Arlen (music); "Injun Gal Heap Hep" by Leo Robin and Joe Lilley (lyrics) and Ralph Rainger (music); "Mister Five by Five," lyrics and music by Don Raye and Gene DePaul; "Whistling in the Light" and "You're the Rainbow" by Leo Robin (lyrics) and Ralph Rainger (music). The film's working titles were *Calgary Stampede* and *Canadian Capers*. It was released internationally as *Melody Inn*. In 1950, Paramount released another film titled *Riding High*, directed by Frank Capra and starring Bing Crosby.

MUSIC FROM PARADISE

Originally set to music by Manning Sherwin circa 1937–38. Lyrics reset to music by Jimmy McHugh. Not used in film.

VERSE

I wouldn't mind if the saxophone stopped,
If the fiddlers went home,
If the trumpeter dropped.
I wouldn't care if the orchestra just wasn't there,
For that's not the music I hear,
When I hold you close in my arms, dear.

REFRAIN

Music from paradise is playing
When I waltz with you.
Music from paradise, conveying
A love song for two.
Your heart and my heart are dancing in a world apart,
Although the floor is crowded as can be,
And any old tune the band is playing
Is music from paradise to me.

MISCELLANEOUS SONGS OF 1943

WHAT DO YOU DO IN THE INFANTRY?

Published. Copyrighted July 22, 1943. Official marching song of the 264th Infantry Regiment. Recorded by the Glenn Miller Army Air Force Band (RCA Victor), among others.

What do you do in the infantry?
You march, you march, you march.
What do you do when your pack has got
Your back as stiff as starch?
There's many a fall in the cavalry,
But never a fallen arch.
And what do you do in the infantry?
You march, you march, you march!

What do you do in the infantry?
You hike, you hike, you hike.
What do you do in the infantry?
A left and right oblique.*
The son of a gun in the Signal Corps
Is traveling on a bike.
And what do you do in the infantry?
You hike, you hike, you hike!
The hard way, the hard way—
Sweat till you get there the hard way!

What do you do in the infantry?
You win, you win, you win.
What do you do for the victory?

---

* Pronounced "oh-blike."

You move into Berlin.
The rest of the Army are riding,
Riding through a triumphal arch.
And what do you do in the infantry?
You march (two, three, four)!

HAVE I STAYED AWAY TOO LONG?

Published. Copyrighted October 21, 1943. Recorded by Tex Ritter (Richmond), Glen Campbell (Capitol), Perry Como (Victor), and Willie Nelson (Justice), among others.

Have I stayed away too long?
Have I stayed away too long?
If I came home tonight,
Would you still be my darlin',
Or have I stayed away too long?

The love light that shone so strong,
Sweet love light that shone so strong,
If I came home tonight,
Would that same light be shinin',
Or have I stayed away too long?

I'm just outside of town,
I'll soon be at your door,
But maybe I'd be wrong to hurry there.
I'd best keep out of town
And worry you no more,
For maybe someone else has made you care.

Have all of my dreams gone wrong?
My beautiful dreams gone wrong?
If I came home tonight,
Would you still be my darlin',
Or have I stayed away too long?

YOU HAVEN'T GOT CHEEKS LIKE ROSES

Probably 1943–44. Music and lyrics by Frank Loesser and Abe Burrows (1910–1985). This was one of Loesser's first collaborations with Burrows. The two would later work together on *Guys and Dolls* (1950) and *How to Succeed in Business Without Really Trying* (1961). Burrows's Broadway credits as writer/director include *Can-Can* and *Silk Stockings*.

VERSE

I get a feeling of sweet contentment
Ev'ry time I find you by my side.
Don't need you in my arms
To analyze your charms—
Believe me, I'm completely satisfied.

REFRAIN

You haven't got cheeks like roses;
You haven't got eyes like stars.
Your sigh doesn't sound like music,
The music of soft guitars.
You haven't got lips like rubies;
Your hair doesn't even curl.
But baby, it makes no diff'rence to me,
'Cause you're not my girl.

SKIRTS

An All-American Musical Adventure in 15 Scenes

Premiere: Cambridge Theater, London, England, on January 25, 1944. Music by Pfc. Frank Loesser, Pfc. Harold Rome, Leslie Stuart, Val Guest, and others. Words by Lt. Arthur G. Brest, Pfc. Frank Loesser, Pfc. Leslie Weiner, Ben Begnal, Sam Locke, Pfc. Harold Rome, Leslie Stuart, G. Gabrielson, Cliff Gordon, Eric Spear, and others. Produced and directed by Lt. Arthur G. Brest for Special Services, Eighth Air Force. Sets designed by Capt. Tom Lee. Dances directed and musical numbers staged by Wendy Toye. Music provided by 739th U.S. Army Band, "The Flying Yanks," under the direction of T/Sgt. Charles L. Cleaver. Additional songs included "Little Brown Suit My Uncle Bought Me," "Passing the Buck," "Pin Up Girl," and "Juke Box Girl," music and lyrics by Pfc. Harold Rome.

SKIRTS

Introduced by Pfc. Richard E. Taylor, Sgt. Melville Zollicoffer, and Capt. John G. McCutcheon. Leading recording by Johnny Denis and His Novelty Quartet (English Decca).

VERSE

Night after night in the Army,
I dream such a lonely dream.
It's not that I miss the World Series,
Or hot dogs, or choc'late ice cream.
It isn't my old Buick Roadster,
Or stars on the Texas plain.
It isn't the bright lights of Broadway;
So maybe I should explain
What's on my brain:
I keep dreaming of—

REFRAIN 1

Skirts, skirts,
Lovely ladies in skirts,
But the same old OD trousers keep marching by.
I've been dreaming of skirts, skirts,
Through a thousand alerts,

Bottom: *Frank Loesser, Bing Crosby, unidentified soldier, and Peter Lind Hayes*

But there is no silk or satin to greet the eye.
So if you'd like to send me something for my birthday
And you can't decide between a cake or a pie,
Make it something in skirts, skirts,
That's the shortage that hurts,
As the same old OD trousers go marching by!

INTERLUDE

I don't mean a plaid kilted colonel from the Highlands.
I don't mean a grass-covered chieftain from the islands.
I mean something in—

REFRAIN 2

Skirts, skirts,
Gorgeous women in skirts,
But it's plain old GI khaki I see all day.
I mean something that's sleek, chic,
And a little bit weak,
But the government won't issue a dream that way.
So if you'd like to send me something for my birthday
And you can't decide between a pipe or a tie,
Make it something in skirts, skirts,
That's the shortage that hurts,
As the same old OD trousers go marching by!

SEE HERE, PRIVATE HARGROVE

Produced by George Haight for MGM. Released in March 1944. Screenplay by Harry Kurnitz, based on the book by Marion Hargrove. Directed by Wesley Ruggles. Cast featured Robert Walker, Donna Reed, Keenan Wynn, Robert Benchley, Ray Collins, Chill Wills, and Bob Crosby.

IN MY ARMS

Music by Ted Grouya (1910–2000). Published. Copyrighted May 5, 1943. Previously registered for copyright as unpublished song April 10, 1943. Introduced by ensemble. Recordings include Frank Loesser with Mitch Miller's Orchestra (Columbia). Grouya was born in Rumania and studied in France with Nadia Boulanger and

Alfred Cortot. His other songs include "Flamingo" and "I Heard You Cried Last Night."

VERSE 1 (NOT USED IN FILM)

His cousin had sent him a sweater,
And his sister wrote a letter,
But he wanted something much better,
This boy who was sailing away.
For his buddies were there with their sweethearts,
All around him with their sweethearts;
Now, he'd never had any sweethearts,
And over and over he'd say:

REFRAIN 1

In my arms, in my arms,
Ain't I never gonna have a girl in my arms?
In my arms, in my arms,
Ain't I never gonna get a bundle of charms?
Comes the dawn, I'll be gone,
I just gotta have a honey holdin' me tight.
You can keep your knittin' and your purlin',
If I'm gonna go to Berlin,
Gimme a girl in my arms tonight.

VERSE 2 (NOT USED IN FILM)

His grandma had sent him some candy,
And as he chewed on the candy,
He said, "My morale is just dandy,
And still there's a tear in my eye."
For his buddies were there with their sweethearts,
Kissing bye-bye with their sweethearts;
Now, he'd never had any sweethearts,
And over and over he'd cry:

REFRAIN 2 (NOT USED IN FILM)

In my arms, in my arms,
Ain't I never gonna have a girl in my arms?
In my arms, in my arms,
Ain't I never gonna get a bundle of charms?
Comes the dawn, I'll be gone,
And I thank you for the many letters you'll write.
As for something nice and cute and female,
I'll never get it in the V-Mail,
Gimme a girl in my arms tonight.

ADDITIONAL REFRAINS

In my arms, in my arms,
Ain't I never gonna have a girl in my arms?
In my arms, in my arms,
Ain't I never gonna get a bundle of charms?
Comes the dawn, I'll be gone,

I'll be headin' for the very thick of the fight.
You can wine and dine and cigarette me,
But if you really wanna get me,
Gimme a girl in my arms tonight.

In my arms, in my arms,
Ain't I never gonna have a girl in my arms?
In my arms, in my arms,
Ain't I never gonna get a bundle of charms?
Comes the dawn, I'll be gone,
Now does anybody wanna please treat me right?
You can keep your shavin' cream and lotion,
If I'm a-gonna cross the ocean,
Give me a girl in my arms tonight.

Lines sung by Loesser on his recording with Mitch Miller

I ain't in the army for the pastime,
Don't knit me nothin' like the last time—
Give me a girl in my arms tonight.

Dear old Veterans Administration,
Take back my college education—
Give me a girl in my arms tonight.

Please don't bake another batch of cookies,
Go shove your cookies at the rookies—
Give me a girl in my arms tonight.

ABOUT FACE!

Premiere: Camp Shanks of the New York Port of Embarkation, May 26, 1944. Music and lyrics by Pvt. Frank Loesser, Pvt. Hy Zaret, T/Sgt. Peter Lind Hayes, Pvt. Jerry Livingston, and Lou Singer. Sketches by Pvt. Arnold Auerbach, Mort Lewis, Howard Harris, Sid Zelinka, and Dave Schwartz. Additional dialogue by T/3 Bob Lieb, Pvt. Lester Lewis, and Cpl. William Stein. Music arranged by Sgt. Walter Gross, Pvt. Sidney Green, Pvt. Wilbur Beitel, and Pvt. George Leeman. Directed by Robert H. Gordon. Production supervised by Maj. Harry Salter. Cast included 1st Lt. Lawrence Rhodes, 2nd Lt. Thomas Massey, T/3 Robert Lieb, Sgt. Luke Glennon, Sgt. Sidney Black, Sgt. David Dolling, T/4 Norman Green, Cpl. Edgar Camp, Pfc. Thomas Leonard, Pfc. Leon Gray, Pvt. Lenny Kent, Pvt. Jules Munshin, Pvt. Vincent Gomez, Pvt. Lester Lewis, Pvt. Nat Donato, Pvt. Nate Ackerman, WAC Sgt. Lynn Durkin, T/4 Bonnie Vaughan, T/5 Margaret Snider, T/5 Winifred Waters, T/5 Sarah Schlossberg, Pfc. Alice McLaughlin, and Pfc. Tillamac Hendel.

About Face! was the first in a series of "Blueprint Specials," so called because their working scripts and scores were complete in all details for speedy and simple production by soldier entertainers.

The Special Services Division, Army Service Forces, acknowledged the following in preparation of *About Face!*: Robert S. Gordon, Howard Harris, Al Hirschfeld, George S. Kaufman, Mort Lewis, Jerry Livingston, Dave Schwartz, Lou Singer, and Sid Zelinka.

Hy Zaret (b. 1907) and Lou Singer (1912–1968) had a huge hit with "One Meat Ball," which sold a million records for the Andrews Sisters. Zaret also co-wrote "Unchained Melody" with Alex North. In addition to his work in film and television, Peter Lind Hayes (1915–1998) hosted a successful radio show with his wife, singer Mary Healy. Colorado native Jerry Livingston (1909–1987) had a storied songwriting career that included such hits as "Mairzy Doats," "A Dream Is a Wish Your Heart Makes," and "It's the Talk of the Town."

DOG FACE

Music and lyrics by Pvt. Frank Loesser, Pvt. Hy Zaret, T/Sgt. Peter Lind Hayes, Pvt. Jerry Livingston, and Lou Singer.

[*Twelve men with white beards, wearing various American military uniforms of past wars, run onstage and sing.*]

ALL: Dog face, dog face,
Where did you get that dog face?
Is it from the diet of Army stew,
Or is it from the top kick barking at you?
(Woof.)
Dog face, dog face,
Why don't you come smiling through?
Would you like to learn how grand the Army life can be?
Would you like to learn to wear a smile that's fancy free?
Would you like to learn the trick—well why ask me?
I'm a dog face too.
JOE: [*spoken*] Remove beards, one—two—three—four!
[*sung*] You look familiar, and you look familiar,
And I remember you from way back.
You were Jolly Jim Brown
Back in your hometown,
But now you're a sad-looking sack—
you're a—

ALL: Dog face, dog face,
You're just a GI dog face.
Is it from those little bones dogs love most?
Or are you just a wolf that can't leave the post?
Dog face, dog face,
Who says your dreams can't come true?
Would you like a three-day pass and come in four years late
And then tell a big MP to blow it out the gate?
If you think I know the trick—you're a Section Eight.
I'm a dog face too.

ALL: Dog face, dog face,
You're just a sad-eyed dog face.
Is it that the Army shoes pinch a bit,
Or is it from a detail shoveling it? (Whew!)
Dog face, dog face,
Why, you don't have to be blue.
Would you like to sleep all morning when it's ten below?
Would you like to tell the second louie where to go?
Would you like to learn the trick? Well, how the heck would I know?
I'm a dog face too.

GEE, BUT IT'S GREAT

Music and Lyrics by Pvt. Frank Loesser, Pvt. Hy Zaret, T/Sgt. Peter Lind Hayes, Pvt. Jerry Livingston, and Lou Singer.

ALL: Gee, but it's great to be in the Army,
Great to wake up in the night and hear the bugle blow.
Gee, but it's great to be in the Army,
Great to do some easy work and rake in all the dough.
There's lots of time for fun and play,
That's why we say "Hip hip hooray."
Gee, but it's great to be in the Army,
Doing a job the Army way.
SAM: The marksmen medals they give out,
We never try to win 'em.
We're always getting Maggie's drawers,
And Maggie's always in 'em.
MIKE: Each time we break a fingernail,
A nurse repairs the harm.
We get a kiss for a broken nail—
Oh boy, for a broken arm!
HANK: We mustn't let a word of this
Get out to the civilians.

'Cause if they do, I'm warning you,
They'll join us by the millions.
ALL: Gee, but it's great to be in the Army,
Great to have a buddy there to touch you
for a few.
Gee, but it's great to be in the Army,
Great to know he'll pay you back in
nineteen eighty-two.
We let the sergeants do the work,
And we just sit around and smirk—
Gee, but it's great to be in the Army.

There's lots of time for fun and play,
That's why we say "Hip hip hooray."
Gee, but it's great to be in the Army,
Doing a job the Army way.

FIRST CLASS PRIVATE MARY BROWN

Music and lyrics by Frank Loesser. Published. Copyrighted June 16, 1944. Introduced by Pfc. Leon Gray.

VERSE

I carry around a heavy old rifle
And a heavy old pack.
But I don't seem to feel how much they weigh,
'Cause I carry around a dream all day.

REFRAIN 1

First Class Private Mary Brown,
She wore that uniform like a million-dollar gown.
And my heart would leap when she drove that jeep
With the one big stripe on her arm,
For it seemed to me that a P F C
Stood for Perfect Feminine Charm.
First Class Private Mary Brown,
Oh, how she smiled goodbye when they shipped
me out of town!
Let the big guns roar, let me win this war,
'Cause I want to hurry right back (on the double)
To First Class Private Mary Brown,
My wonderful WAC.

REFRAIN 2

First Class Private Mary Brown,
I've got her Army serial number written down.
She was all GI but when she passed by,
I just had to look at her twice.
And it struck me then that the A S N

Meant an Angel Specially Nice.
First Class Private Mary Brown,
Could make the PX seem like the Ritz in New
York town.
Let the big guns roar, let me win this war,
'Cause I want to hurry right back (hubba hubba)
To First Class Private Mary Brown,
My wonderful WAC.

PX PARADE

Music and lyrics by Pvt. Frank Loesser, Pvt. Hy Zaret, T/Sgt. Peter Lind Hayes, Pvt. Jerry Livingston, and Lou Singer.

There's a jumpin' situation at the PX,
Where there is no sign of Army braid or brass.
You may get yourself a night out,
And for town you think you'll light out,
But you tear in there and suddenly tear up your pass.
'Cause the scene is really solid at the PX,
When the long and lonely evening shadows fade.
It's a chain store worth the tryin',
Where the yardbirds do their flyin'—
Brother, get in the PX parade.

It's a jumpin' situation at the PX,
Where the Army life becomes a life of ease.
With the jukebox really goin',
And the GI beer a-flowin',
And the only kind of shootin' is shootin' the breeze.
Sellin' cigarettes and toothpaste at the PX,
Is a sweet delicious date that should be made.
Brother, don't stand there just lookin',
Askin' everyone what's cookin',
Brother, get in the PX parade.

WHY DO THEY CALL A PRIVATE A PRIVATE?

Music and lyrics by Pvt. Frank Loesser and T/Sgt. Peter Lind Hayes. Published. Copyrighted June 19, 1944. Introduced by Pvt. Lenny Kent. Recorded by Ethel Merman (V-Disc).

VERSE

I know why they call a corporal a corporal—
Because he's got two stripes.
And I know why they call a sergeant a sergeant—

Because he always gripes.
Yes, I know about all the military types,
But—

REFRAIN 1

Why do they call a private a private
When each night is a public event?
The Pennsylvania Station,
That crossroads of the nation,
Has nothing on a regular Army tent.
They snore and snore and snore all night,
They drop their shoes, they light the light.
Or did you ever smell a regiment?
(Have you been marching?)*
Why do they call a private a private,
When each night is a public event?

REFRAIN 2

Why do they call a private a private
When there's nothing more public on earth?
Take military travel,
It makes your nerves unravel—
The Army's really getting its money's worth.
In any other walk of life,
You'd think that you were man and wife,
The way you've got to share a lower berth.
(Your feet are icy!)
Why do they call a private a private,
When there's nothing more public on earth?

REFRAIN 3

Why do they call a private a private
When his life is a public affair?
A hundred other rookies
Enjoying his mother's cookies,
And read his mail and borrow his underwear.
And when a fellow's gotta go†
A fellow's gotta go, you know
There's seven other fellows sitting there
[spoken] Good morning, good morning, good morning.
[sung] (Who's got my Colliers?)
Why do they call a private a private?
(The joint is crowded!)
His life is a public affair.

---

* Sheet music version of lines 8–9 of refrain 1:
You find that you're the only perfect gent
(The rest are sergeants!)

† Sheet music version of lines 6–10 of refrain 3:
And in the morning when he wakes,
With every shower that he takes
There's seven other fellows standing there.
(I'm so embarrassed!)

THE ROAD TO VICTORY

A one-reel short film produced by Jack Warner for Warner Bros. Released in May 1944. Screenplay by James Bloodworth after a story by Mannie Manheim. Directed by LeRoy Prinz. Cast featured Frank Sinatra, Cary Grant, Bing Crosby, Irene Manning, and Dennis Morgan. It was originally released as a two-reel picture entitled *The Shining Future*, a promotional film for Canada's Sixth Victory Loan. Deanna Durbin and Benny Goodman appeared in this longer version.

THE ROAD TO VICTORY

Introduced by Bing Crosby and ensemble.

CROSBY: Get on, get on,
Get on the road to victory.
Get off, get off,
Get off the rusty dusty
And get on, get on,
Get on the road to victory,
And buy another bond today.

Get in, get in,*
Get in your weekly envelope.
Get out, get out,
Get out some ever-lovin'
And get on, get on,
Get on the road to victory,
And buy another bond today.

Get up, get up,
Get up tomorrow morning,
Get down, get down,
Get down and give another pint of blood.
Get one, get ten,
Get fifty victory bonds again,
For you can win the war that way.

When you're safe at home this evening
from the factory,
You can write that lonely soldier overseas.
You can tell him that you're working at
the factory,

But compared to him you live a life of
ease.
So you better—

Get on, get on,
Get on the road to victory.
Get off, get off,
Get off the rusty dusty
And get on, get on,
Get on the road to victory,
And buy another bond today.
CHORUS: And buy another bond today!

[CROSBY *does pitch for war bonds.*]

CHORUS: Get on, get on,
Get on the road to victory.
Get off, get off,
Get off the rusty dusty
And get on, get on,
Get on the road to victory,
And buy another bond today.
CROSBY: Sure, I know you bought a few of them
the last time,*
Thinking that was all you'd ever need
to get.
Well, the army has been fighting since
the last time,†
And they haven't laid a rifle down as yet!
So you better get on, get on,
Get on the road to victory,
Get off, get off,
Get off the rusty dusty
And get on, get on,
Get on the road to victory,
And buy another bond today!

---

* Second stanza not used in film.

---

* Sheet music reads:
Sure, I know you bought a bunch of them in April,

† Sheet music reads:
Well, the boys were fighting for you back in April,

CHRISTMAS HOLIDAY

Produced by Felix Jackson for Universal Pictures. Released in June 1944. Screenplay by Herman Mankiewicz after the novel by Somerset Maughan. Directed by Robert Siodmak. Cast starred Deanna Durbin and Gene Kelly and featured Gale Sondergaard, Gladys George, and Richard Whorf.

SPRING WILL BE A LITTLE LATE THIS YEAR

Published. Copyrighted January 10, 1944. Introduced by Deanna Durbin. Recorded by Durban (Decca), Ella Fitzgerald (Verve), Sarah Vaughn (Columbia), Jo Sullivan Loesser (DRG), and Ray Charles (MGM), among others.

VERSE (NOT SUNG IN FILM)

January and February were never so empty and
gray.
Tragic'lly I feel like crying,
"Without you, my darling, I'm dying."
But let's rather put it this way:

REFRAIN

Spring will be a little late this year,
A little late arriving in my lonely world over
here.
For you have left me, and where is our April of
old?
You have left me, and winter continues cold,
As if to say,
Spring will be a little slow to start,
A little slow reviving that music it made in my
heart.
Yes, time heals all things, so I needn't cling to this
fear;
It's merely that
Spring will be a little late this year.

AND THE ANGELS SING

Produced by E. D. Leshin for Paramount Pictures. Released in July 1944. Screenplay by Norman Panama and Melvin Frank. Directed by George Marshall. Cast featured Fred MacMurray, Dorothy Lamour, Betty Hutton, and Diana Lynn. Other songs included "It Could Happen to You," music by James Van Heusen, lyrics by Johnny Burke, and the title song, music by Ziggy Elman, lyrics by Johnny Mercer.

SHAKE HANDS WITH YOUR NEIGHBOR

Music by Victor Young. Not used in film.

Shake hands with your neighbor ev'ry day,
Shake hands with your neighbor ev'ry day,
Shake hands, shake hands ev'ry day
With ev'ryone who comes your way.
If you want your reward,
You can certainly afford
To shake hands with your neighbor ev'ry day.

Be kind when your neighbor is in need,
Be kind when your neighbor is in need.
Though you haven't a lot,
Give him half of what you've got,
And the Lord will reward you for your deed.
Be kind, be kind ev'ry day
To ev'ryone who comes your way.
Let him drink from your cup,
And those gates will open up:
Shake hands with your neighbor ev'ry day.

HI, YANK!

Premiere: War Department Theatre No. 5, Fort Dix, New Jersey, August 7, 1944. Music and lyrics Pvt. Frank Loesser, Lt. Alex North (1910–1991), Lt. Jack Hill, and Sgt. Jesse Berkman. Produced by Capt. Hy Gardner. Sketches by Lt. Ben Eastright, Lt. Jack Hill, T/4 Ed Milk, Pfc. Martin Weldon, Pvt. Arnold Auerbach. Directed by Cpl. David E. Fitzgibbon. Choreographed by Pvt. José Limón, N.Y.P.E. Costumes and scenery by Robert T. Stevenson and Sgt. Al Hamilton. Orchestra under the direction of Sgt. Ronald Snyder. Orchestrations by T/5 Bernard Landes, T/5 George Leeman, T/5 Robert Williams, Pvt. Herbert Bourne, Pvt. Bert Buhrman, and Pvt. Lee Montgomery. Cast featured Cpl. David Fitzgibbon, Cpl. Bobby Faye, Sgt. Bobby Evants, Cpl. Sam Alessi, T/4 John Fostini, Sgt. C. R. Bixel, Pfc. Joshua Shelley, Sgt. Jay Lundy, Pvt. Sam Ostrow, Sgt. David Brooks, Pfc. John Reesman, Pfc. Raymond Swenson, Pvt. James Speed, Pvt. Stanley Solomon, Sgt. Jerry Tomann, and Cpl. James Boxwill.

Although the Blueprint Special script credits all songs to Pvt. Frank Loesser, Lt. Alex North, Lt. Jack Hill, and Sgt. Jesse Berkman, the program from the original show indicates the following credits: "Report from the Caribbean," music by Lt. Alex North and lyrics by Lt. Jack Hill; music by Pvt. Frank Loesser and lyrics by Lt. Jack Hill; "Saga of the Sack," music by Frank Loesser and lyrics by Pvt. Hy Zaret. All other original music and lyrics are credited to Pvt. Frank Loesser.

Alex North received fifteen Oscar nominations for his film background scores. In addition to "Unchained Melody," his song hits include "I'll Cry Tomorrow" with lyrics by Johnny Mercer.

YANK, YANK, YANK

Music and lyrics by Pvt. Frank Loesser, Lt. Alex North, Lt. Jack Hill, and Sgt. Jesse Berkman. Introduced by ensemble.

Yank! Yank! Yank!
The latest copy of *Yank!*
Everything from the cartoon strip
To a big long story 'bout a submarine we sank—

In *Yank! Yank! Yank!*
But let's be perfectly frank:
A magazine can't really put you wise;
You want the news before your very eyes.

So here's a show to bring it to you guys,
Called *Yank! Yank! Yank!*

We're selling
Yank! Yank! Yank!
Oh, get your copy of *Yank!*
Everything from the mail call page,
To an interview with a General Sherman tank—

In *Yank! Yank! Yank!*
But let's be perfectly frank:
We print the words but never show the deed.
So on this stage we bring you what you need—
For you Sad Sacks who don't know how to read,
Here's *Yank! Yank! Yank!*

THE SAGA OF THE SACK

Music and lyrics by Pvt. Frank Loesser, Lt. Alex North, Lt. Jack Hill, and Sgt. Jesse Berkman. Introduced by Bobby Faye and ensemble.

SACK: When I was born my mother took one look
And sighed "Alack."
My dad ran to the roof and yelled,
"Hey, stork, please take it back!"
My cousin Sal said to her pal,
"It smells to me like sap."
My uncle Joe from Borneo said,
"Turn it in for scrap."
The laundry starched my diapers
When I was a little tot.
The day I fell and broke a leg,
They almost had me shot.
I grew up and was drafted,
But my bad luck never fails.
A Sad Sack's army life is just
A mess of sad details.

CHORUS: Anything can happen to a Sad Sack,
The Army's unluckiest guy.
A Sad Sack is a Sad Sack, and a Sad Sack
Never can understand why.
I wouldn't care what happens to a Sad Sack,
No matter how sad it might be.
No, I wouldn't care what happens to a Sad Sack,
But the Sad Sack happens to be me.

SACK: Last night I staggered into bed,
All knocked out from KP.

I fell asleep; my sleep was deep;
A storm came suddenly.
Our tent had just a little hole—
That hole was over me,
And was I dripping.

CHORUS: Anything can happen to a Sad Sack,
The Army's unluckiest guy.
SACK: I had so much romance in me,
I thought that I would burst.
I hurried off to see my gal;
My line was all rehearsed.
I rang the bell—she said, "So sorry,
The Marines have landed first."
With full equipment—

CHORUS: Anything can happen to a Sad Sack,
The Army's unluckiest guy.
SACK: One night my girlfriend said to me,
"See here, my little flower,
Now you can scrub a pot so clean,
You'd thrill Ike Eisenhower.
But when it comes to lovin',
You're a reg'lar Tyrone Power—
Without the power.

CHORUS: Anything can happen to a Sad Sack,
The Army's unluckiest guy.
A Sad Sack is a Sad Sack, and a Sad Sack
Never can understand why.
We wouldn't care what happens to a Sad
Sack,
Nor worry if he should feel blue.
No, we wouldn't care what happens to a
Sad Sack
When the Sad Sack happens to be you.

MY GAL AND I

Music and Lyrics by Pvt. Frank Loesser, Lt. Alex North, Lt. Jack Hill, and Sgt. Jesse Berkman. Revised as "My Gal's Working at Lockheed," with music by Matt Dennis. Introduced by Cpl. Samuel Alessi.

My gal and I were once together;
I used to see her ev'ry night and more.
And though we're apart, I can't help feeling
She's closer than ever before.

My gal and I were once together,
And now I fly a plane in this man's war.
And each time I reach that blue, blue ceiling,
She's closer than ever before.

Once I used to worry about her
Every time we parted for a while.
Now I'm really never without her,
Flying with a proud and happy smile
To think that—

My gal and I were once together,
Yet she's beside me when the engines roar.
And though we're apart, I can't help feeling
She's closer than ever before.

MY GAL'S WORKING AT LOCKHEED

Copyrighted September 18, 1944. Music by Matt Dennis (1914–2002). Lyrics by Frank Loesser. Singer and composer Dennis teamed with lyricist Tom Adair to write such notable songs as "Let's Get Away from It All," "Violets for Your Furs," and "Everything Happens to Me."

My gal's workin' at Lockheed,
Building those bomber planes for this man's war.
And though we're apart, I can't help feelin'
We're closer than ever before.

My gal's workin' at Lockheed:
She drove the rivets in my bomb-bay door.
So each time I reach that blue, blue ceilin',
We're closer than ever before.

Once I used to worry about her
Every time we parted for a while.
Now I'm never really without her,
Flyin' with a proud and happy smile,
To think that—

My gal's workin' at Lockheed,
She's right behind me in that old air corps.
And though we're apart, I can't help feelin'
We're closer than ever before.

GENERAL ORDERS

Music and lyrics by Pvt. Frank Loesser, Lt. Alex North, Lt. Jack Hill, and Sgt. Jesse Berkman. With the exception of the last three lines, these are essentially the Army's General Orders set to music.

To take charge of this post and all Government
property in view
To walk my post in a military manner, keeping
always on the alert and observing
Ev'rything that takes place within sight or
hearing.
To report all violations of orders I am instructed
to enforce.
To repeat all calls from posts more distant from
the guardhouse than my own.
To quit my post only when properly relieved.
To receive, obey, and pass on to the sentinel who
relieves me all orders from the commanding
officer, officer of the day, and officers and non-
commissioned officers of the guard only.
To talk to no one except in line of duty.
To give the alarm in case of fire or disorder.
To call the corp'ral of the guard in any case not
covered by instructions.
To salute all officers and all colors and standards
not cased.
To be especially watchful at night and, during the
time for challenging, to challenge all persons
on or near my post, and to allow no one to pass
without proper authority.

These are the Gen'ral Orders
Ev'ry soldier must obey
In the Army, in the Army of the U.S.A.

CLASSIFICATION BLUES

Music and lyrics by Pvt. Frank Loesser, Lt. Alex North, Lt. Jack Hill, and Sgt. Jesse Berkman. Introduced by Pvt. Stanley Solomon, Pfc. Joshua Shelley, Sgt. Jerry Tomann, and Pfc. Raymond Swenson.

VERSE 1

I used to handle shirts and pants and blouses,
The owner of a famous clothing store.
So naturally the Quartermaster Corps is where
they put me,
Where they put me—
Scrubbing the floor!

REFRAIN

I got the Classification Blues,
The Classification Blues.
If they ever classified me right,
That would be news.
The somebody else's occupation,

Living a life of aggravation—
Oh, what a lousy Classification Blues!

VERSE 2

I used to be a pro at golf and tennis,
A pro who had a record long and bright.
So naturally the pro department's just the place
    they put me,
Where they put me—
By the green light!

REPEAT REFRAIN

VERSE 3

I used to play the horses at Jamaica;
I made a million bucks before I quit.
So naturally the Cavalry is exactly where they put me,
Where they put me—
Shovelin' it!

REPEAT REFRAIN

VERSE 4

I used to be the city health inspector;
I knew the cure for every rare disease.
So naturally the Medics is exactly where they put me,
Where they put me—
Bend over, please!

LITTLE RED ROOFTOPS

Music and lyrics by Pvt. Frank Loesser, Lt. Alex North,
Lt. Jack Hill, and Sgt. Jesse Berkman. Introduced by
Cpl. Samuel Alessi.

Little red rooftops
By a little green hillside
'Neath a pretty blue sky—
That's a picture of my hometown.

Little red rooftops
Shining out in the sunlight—
'Bout the very best bet
For a couple to settle down.

I got a postal card this morning
From you can imagine whom.
See where she sends love and kisses,
See where the X marks my room
Among the—

Little red rooftops,
On the little green hillside—
Not the pride of the States
Or a city of great renown,
But you're feasting your eyes on a picture
Of my hometown.

THE MOST IMPORTANT JOB

Music and lyrics by Pvt. Frank Loesser, Lt. Alex North,
Lt. Jack Hill, and Sgt. Jesse Berkman.

MP: This is the biggest, the toughest,
The ruggedest and the roughest,
The most important job I ever had.
I used to hold a job in a groc'ry store,
But now I've turned it over to my dad.
Now I could gripe more and brood more
And holler about the food more,
But what's the diff'rence when you're
    fighting mad?
This is the biggest, the toughest,
The ruggedest and the roughest,
The most important job I ever had.

ALL: This is the biggest, the hardest,
The battle-'em-yard-by-yardest,
The most important job I ever did.
I used to keep the books in the National
    Bank;
Now that's done by a fourteen-year-old kid.
Now I could sleep more and shave more
And get me the dames I crave more,
But what's the diff'rence when you're
    fighting mad?
This is the biggest, the toughest,
The ruggedest and the roughest,
The most important job I ever had.

This is the biggest, the strongest,
The rottenest and the wrongest,
The most important enemy I've met.
I once was in the ring fighting heavyweights,
But that was just a sissy minuet.
I could be cleaner and neater
And temperament'lly sweeter,
But what's the diff'rence when you're
    fighting mad?
This is the biggest, the toughest,
The ruggedest and the roughest,
The most important job I ever had.

P.F.C. MARY BROWN

Music and lyrics by Capt. Ruby Jane Douglass (b. 1919),
Pvt. Frank Loesser, Pvt. Hy Zaret, and Arthur Altman.
A Soldier Show Production of a WAC Musical Revue.
No performance dates established. Book by Pvt. Arnold
Auerbach, Lt. Bob Eastright, and Lt. Jack Hill. Scenic
designs by T/5 Edward E. Wolf. Costume designs by
Mary Schenck. Orchestrations by Pvt. Herbert Bourne,
T/5 Bernard Landes, and T/5 George Leeman. Ruby
Jane Douglass (real name Jane Douglass White) later be-
came assistant producer of *Name That Tune*. Arthur
Altman wrote "All or Nothing at All" with lyricist Jack
Lawrence. Although Loesser is credited in all of these
songs, his involvement may well have been minimal.

SOMETHING NEW HAS BEEN ADDED

WACS: There's a sound of marching feet
And my heart skips a beat—
Something new has been added to the
    Army.
Right along with khaki shirts
Comes the sight of khaki skirts—
Something new has been added to the
    Army.
In ev'ry town and state,
In ev'ry village green,
The girls will say it's great,
The greatest thing they've ever seen.
Forward march! Right about!
Something new beyond a doubt,
Something new has been added to the
    Army.

[*Dance routine*]

In ev'ry town and state,
In ev'ry village green,
The girls all say it's great,
The greatest thing they've ever seen.
Forward march! Right about!
Something new beyond a doubt,
Something new has been added to the
    Army.
SERGEANT: Pla——toon! Atten-hut!

[*The girls snap to attention in military fashion.*]

SERGEANT: Ri——ght! Hh——aace!

[*The girls snap right.*]

SERGEANT: For'erd! Hh——arch!

[*The girls continue to sing last eight bars as they march off left.*]

IN TWENTY-FIVE WORDS OR LESS

Oh, twenty-five words or less,
That's what they always say.
And twenty-five words or less
Is all we need to say today, so—

In twenty-five words or less
Why did you join the WAC?
In twenty-five words or less
Tell me the reason why you joined.

[*Dialogue*]

In twenty-five words or less
Why did you join the WAC?
In twenty-five words or less
Tell me the reason why you joined.

[*Dialogue*]

For the Red, White, and Blue,
To make this world a better place for you.
For the Red, White, and Blue,
To make this world a better place for you.

NEW-STYLE BONNET

Back in grandmother's day,
She bought a bonnet for Easter,
She picked it out with care.
Today her grandchildren all agree
Her choice was okay.

In the spring
There'll be a new-style bonnet
In the Easter Parade,
And you'll see
There will be ribbons on it
When it's made in the old-fashioned way.
For each girl wears a hat that is smart and new

And some wear a bonnet of Navy blue.
All the girls come out in a hat that's okay,
Though they were not designed by Lily Daché.
And the men
Will sport a new-style bonnet
In the Easter Parade,
For the old is replaced by the new,
And for the smarter men bowlers are made.

For the whole wide world and everybody in it too,
There'll be a true blue new-style bonnet
In the Easter Parade.

[*Interlude*]

In the spring
There'll be a new-style bonnet
In the Easter Parade,
And you'll see
There'll be no ribbons on it
When it's made the American way.
For the WACs wear a hat that is smart and new,
The WAVEs wear a bonnet of Navy blue,
And the Spars come out in a hat that's okay—
There's no original by Lily Daché.
And the men
Will sport a new-style bonnet
In the Easter Parade.
For the Dobbs hat is replaced by a gob's hat,
And for Army men helmets are made.
For the WACs, WAVEs, Spars, WASPs,
Army, Navy, and Marines,
There'll be a true blue new-style bonnet
In the Easter Parade.

[*spoken*] The Spars!

The WASPs!
The Marines!
The WAVES!
The Army Nurse Corps!
And the WAC!

In the spring
There'll be a new-style bonnet
In the Easter Parade.
For the WACs, WAVES, Spars, WASPs,
Army, Navy, and Marines,
There'll be a true blue new-style bonnet
In the Easter Parade.

COME ON, HONEY

Come on, honey, don't say no,
Grab your hat and let us go,
Right down to the USO.
Come on, honey, don't say no—
Fox trots, waltzes, jitterbugs,
They're all down there cutting rugs.
Soldiers, sailors love it so—
Come on, honey, don't say no.
They won't let you get lonesome,
No matter how far you roam.
Remember that the USO
Is your home away from home—so—
Come on, honey, don't say no,
Drop your cares, get in the show.
Come on, honey, don't be slow,
Let's go to the USO.

POOR LONELY MP

Poor lonely MP,
Nobody loves me.
I don't like this state of affairs,
But it seems that nobody cares
For this poor lonely MP.
Lonely little MP,
Nobody loves me.
Couples, couples, everywhere,
But not a soul for me to care for,
Poor lonely MP.

I walk my beat and my heart's keeping beat
To the beat of my feet on the street.
When folks see me coming,
They start in a-running,
So how can I sing
About love in the spring?

Poor lonely MP,
Nobody loves me.
I see a soldier, but who wants to rate
Nothing more than a leftover date?
Poor lonely MP.
[*spoken*] If you smile at him, he thinks you're flirting—
If you don't, he thinks you're an iceberg.
If you let him kiss you, he wishes you were more reserved—
If you don't, he'll seek consolation elsewhere.
If you flatter him, he thinks you're simple—
If you don't, he thinks you don't understand him.

If you talk of love and romance, he thinks you're
  asking him to marry you—
If you don't, he'll go with a girl who will.
If you go out with other fellows, he thinks you're
  fickle—
If you don't, he thinks no one will have you.
[*sung*] I walk my beat and my heart's keeping beat
To the beat of my feet on the street.
When folks see me coming,
They start in a-running,
So how can I sing
About love in the spring?

Poor lonely MP,
Nobody loves me
I see a soldier, but who wants to rate
Nothing more than a leftover date?
Poor lonely MP.

LOST IN A CLOUD OF BLUE

Lost in a cloud of blue,
Adrift in a sea of moonlight,
Lost in a reverie,
I hear my heart calling where you are.
Sometimes I see your face;
Your eyes are the stars above me.
Your lips are inviting,
But when I reach out, you fade into space.
My fate is ever to be alone;
My heart I never can call my own.
If I could be with you
And feel your arms around me,
Then I would never be lonely
And lost in a cloud of blue.

THE WAC HYMN

Music and lyrics by Frank Loesser. Published. Copyrighted May 19, 1944.

We march beside our men of battle
To any shore where the flag must fly.
We march beside our men of battle;
Our step is firm and our courage high.
To share that world of peace tomorrow,
We share the fortunes of war,
As we march beside our men of battle,
The Women's Army Corps.

In freedom's name we serve the colors
And proudly march where they fly above.
In freedom's name we serve the colors
And pledge our strength to the land we love.
To see the dawn of peace tomorrow,
We face the long night of war,
As in freedom's name we serve the colors,
The Women's Army Corps.

OKAY U.S.A.

Music and lyrics by Frank Loesser. Premiere: School for Personnel Services, Lexington, Virginia, in January 1945. Additional song: "Brooklyn Cantata," lyrics by Mike Stratton, music by George Kleinsinger. Production, staging, and cast information unavailable. Nothing is known about who introduced the songs.

A TRIP ROUND THE USA

REFRAIN 1

Hurry, hurry, all aboard,
It's a trip round the USA.
San Francisco and Philadelphia,
Baton Rouge or the Chesapeake Bay—
Hurry, hurry, see the sights
That you knew in a bygone day.
Ashtabula and Pensacola
And old Altoona, PA,
It's a trip round the USA.

INTERLUDE

Now you've read the Army guidebooks
That describe those far-off places:
How to say "good day" in Algiers,
How to smile at Persian faces,
How to make a date in Paris,
How to travel in Brazil,
How to hail a cab in Tunis—
Yes, they've put you through the mill.
It's been so long since you started out to roam
That we thought we'd reacquaint you
With your home sweet home, so—

REFRAIN 2

Hurry, hurry, board the bus,
For a trip round the USA.

Old Chicago and Cincinnati and
Even Brooklyn we'll cover today.
Hurry, hurry, see the sights,
From Seattle to old Broadway.
Lose your dogtags, drop your barracks bags,
Throw your guidebooks away—
It's a trip round the USA!

WAY DOWN TEXAS WAY

VERSE

Oh, the sight of a horse
Fills my heart with remorse,
And I long to be back on the trail.
Yes, I'm hungerin' now
For the smell of a cow
And the sight of a bow-legged male.
Wanna feel my face get leathery and tan,
Wanna feel a saddle underneath my
Can't you see me—

REFRAIN 1

Where the mountains rise and where the bison play,
Where the bars stay open twenty hours a day,
Where they ain't yet recognized the USA,
Way down Texas way,
Yippee-ki-ay-i-ay.

Where a tenderfoot is just an Eastern spy,
Where the men are men but couldn't say just why,
Where a snake bites man, the snake is sure to die,
Way down Texas way,
Yippee-ki-ay-i-ay.

Texas, dear old Texas,
You've been just like a mom.
A right good place to visit
But a better place to be from.

You can hear the croakin' of the thirsty frogs
As they pray for rain a-settin' on their logs,
'Cause it's so durn dry where the trees chase dogs,
Way down Texas way,
Yippee-ki-ay-i-ay.

REFRAIN 2

Where the rancher's daughter has a shape like this,
But remember, pardner, when you steal a kiss
That her pappy's rifle ain't been known to miss,
Way down Texas way,
Yippee-ki-ay-i-ay.

Once a wife sued husband there for quick divorce,
Said he didn't love her, acted mean and cross,
And the correspondent was his saddle horse,
Way down Texas way,
Yippee-ki-ay-i-ay.

Way out on the prairie
I long to lay my haid.
Yes, bury me in Texas,
But be gol-durned sure that I'm daid.

Where you gotta ride a hundred miles or more
Just to court the cutie that you're yearnin' for,
But you're too darned tired when you reach her
    door,
Way down Texas way,
Yippee-ki-ay-i-ay,
Way down Texas way.

MY CHICAGO

Chicago, Chicago,
My hometown, Chicago.
It's dusty and it's windy,
But it's my Chicago.
Though I've been everywhere,
How I long to be there!

Chicago, Chicago,
My hometown, Chicago.
In ev'ry dream I dream
I seem to sigh "Chicago."
From the loop to the shore
Let me wander once more.

Let me wait on State Street
Till she appears,
Sweet Chicago babe I haven't seen in years.
Let me rush down to Rush Street,
Turn to the right,
Jump into the Aragon and dance all night.

In Chicago, Chicago,
My hometown, Chicago.
I'm sorry that I had to say,
"Goodbye, Chicago."
How I long to be there tonight,
How I long to be there!

MISS AMERICA

Oh you've probably seen Miss America
In the glamorous days of yore.
It was in Atlantic City;
She was charming, she was pretty,
She was wonderful—but then came the war.

Yes, you've probably seen Miss America
In the good old civilian style.
But now Sally, Jane, and Mary
Have gone slightly military,
And they've got the others beat by a mile.
Here they come
Down the aisle:

Miss Infantry!*
Miss Cavalry!
Miss Signal Corps!
Miss Air Corps!
Miss Quartermaster Corps!
Miss Airborne!

TONIGHT IN SAN FRANCISCO

Tonight in San Francisco,
San Francisco by the sea,
A girl sits at her window,
Waiting just for me.
The harbor lights are gleaming
And the moonlight's on the bay,
It's on the bay.

Tonight I know she's dreaming
Dreams of yesterday.
Dream on, sweetheart,
My love is true;
Though we're apart,
My heart is there with you.

Tonight in San Francisco,
San Francisco by the sea,
Beside her at the window
Is where I long to be.

---

* "Bathing beauties" played by soldiers parade to
Irving Berlin's "A Pretty Girl Is Like a Melody."

WHEN HE COMES HOME

Published. Copyrighted February 6, 1945. Intended for
male-female duet.

VERSE

Got a guy, a guy from New Orleans,
I wrote a letter to him today.
Though he's gone, I know how much he means.
Someday he's gonna be bound my way.

REFRAIN 1

When he comes home,
He comes right straight home to me,
Right straight home to me,
Not to Mabel or Marie.
When he comes home,
He comes right straight to my door.
Now he's gone to war,
Ah, but he's been gone before,
And when he comes home,
He comes right straight down the line,
Nine times out of nine,
Into no one's arms but mine.
So I can smile and wait a while,
Though he's far across the sea,
'Cause I know
That when he comes home,
He comes right straight home to me.

REFRAIN 2 (NOT IN SHEET MUSIC VERSION)

When I come home,
I come right straight home to you,
Right straight home to you,
Not to Dotty, Jane, or Sue.
When I come home,
I come right straight to your door.
Now I've gone to war,
Ah, but I've been gone before,
And when I come home,
I come right straight down the line,
Nine times out of nine,
Passing ev'ry detour sign.
So you must smile and wait a while,
Though I'm far across the blue.
'Cause you know
That when I come home,
I come right straight home to you.

ALTERNATE VERSE (SHEET MUSIC VERSION)

I'm the girl the soldier left behind;
Now my heart ought to be much concerned.

Out of sight, they say, is out of mind,
But from experience I have learned:

THE TALL PINES

Earlier title: "Does the Moon Shine Through the Tall Pine?" Lyric originally written for (but unused in) *Northwest Mounted Police* (1940).

When the moon shines
On the tall pines,
And the night wind
Murmurs low,

When the moon shines
On the tall pines,
Let me dream of
Long ago.

Let me see the tribal fires,
Let me feel the wild desires,
Let me hear the tom-toms of the Navajo,

When the moon shines
On the tall pines,
And the night wind murmurs low,
And the night wind murmurs low.

YOU'RE OK, USA!

Paris in spring
Don't mean a thing;
'Tain't like the guidebooks say.
I crave the dark
In Central Park—
You're OK, USA!

London has fogs
Not fit for dogs;
Can't see a foot away.
Just give me Maine
In pouring rain—
You're OK, USA!

I've been to New Guinea
And Guadalcanal;
They're quaint,
But they ain't very gay.
You name the town,

We'll settle down;
Promise we'll never stray.
Though some may sing
Of traveling,
We found it doesn't pay—
You're OK, USA!

Visited Nome,
Nome isn't home;
Eskimo girls won't play.
I'll take my snow
In Kokomo—
You're OK, USA!

Sailing the sea
Isn't for me;
Lead me to Frisco Bay.
A ferry line
Would suit me fine—
You're OK, USA!

My rear is so weary
From steering a jeep;
I go for a slow Chevrolet.
Guam and Bengal,
I've seen 'em all;
Don't want 'em on a tray.
I'll drop my shoes
In Syracuse
Or Phil-a-del-phi-ay—
You're OK, USA!

ANIMAL SONGS

These songs were written in 1945 and offered to Paramount, which elected not to publish them.

THE BEE

Registered for copyright as an unpublished song July 6, 1948. Registered for copyright as an unpublished song under the alternate title "The Peculiar Bee" May 4, 1981.

Once there was a bee,
A most peculiar little bee,
Who was in love with only one delicious flower.
He said, "My name is mud
If I don't kiss that pretty bud
Ev'ry week, ev'ry day, ev'ry hour."

So the story goes,
Until he found his blushing rose
In what you'd call a very compromising setting:
Another little bee
Had sort of wandered in for tea—
What a sweet double cross he'd been getting.

He thought that he'd go crazy,
Till he met a gentle daisy,
Who was good to him, though not exactly young.
And soon, of course, she wilted
And was subsequently jilted—
Ah, those gentle daisies always do get stung.

So now the little bee
Decided he had best agree
With all the other bees who buzz around the
      bower:
That it's a lot of fun
To kiss a new and diff'rent one
Ev'ry week, ev'ry day, ev'ry hour.

THE DOG

Registered for copyright as an unpublished song under the alternate title "A Dachshund in a Dusenberg" May 4, 1981.

A dachshund in a Dusenberg,
However blue-blooded and rich,
To that ignorant slut
Of a street-corner mutt,
Is a bow-legged
Son of a bitch.

THE DUCK

Registered for copyright as an unpublished song under the alternate title "The Central Park Duck" May 4, 1981.

"I love New York," said the Central Park duck,
With a terrible cold in her beak.
"Just love New York," said the Central Park duck,
Though she hadn't slept well in a week.

"I love New York," said the Central Park duck,
"And they tell me I'm losin' mah drawl.
Ah, the charm and urbanity,

Pace and profanity—
I'm so in love with ya all
That I'll never fly south in the fall."

"I love New York," said the Central Park duck,
Who subsisted on old cracker crumbs.
"Just love New York," said the Central Park duck
To the rest of her shivering chums.

"I love New York," said the Central Park duck,
Still deluding herself on that score.
"Ah, the not-so-respectable,
Somehow delectable
Hustle and bustle and roar—
Guess I'll never fly south anymore."

"I love New York," said the Central Park duck,
As the cold in her beak turned to flu.
"Just love New York," said the Central Park duck,
And the crumbs that she found were too few.

"I love New York," said the Central Park duck,
Very shortly before she was dead.
"It's so gay and artistic,
It seems a sophisticate
Couldn't live elsewhere instead."
And she really believed what she said—
Little ducks are so easily led.

THE FISH

Registered for copyright as an unpublished song under the alternate title "The Trout Who Wouldn't Bite" May 4, 1981.

"Ev'rything's got a hook in it,"
Said the trout who simply wouldn't bite.
"That's a very suspicious looking fly up there,
And that worm doesn't seem quite right."

" 'Ev'rything's got a hook in it,'
I'll repeat that till my dying breath."
So said the trout with a sickly pout
As he slowly starved to death.

THE HORSE

Registered for copyright as an unpublished song May 4, 1981.

There's a three-toed Eocene horse
In a great museum, of course,
And he just cannot understand,
Though he often has heard it told,
That he's nineteen million seven thousand
A hundred and four years old.

He's a three-toed Eocene horse,
Mostly reconstructed, of course,
And he just cannot understand,
With his view of the park below,
Why the fillies on the bridle path
Never bother to nod hello.

THE MOUSE

Registered for copyright as an unpublished song May 4, 1981. Alternate title: "The Indignant Mouse."

"We have people," said the mouse,
"We have people in the house—
Just listen, just listen and you'll hear.
We have people round the place—
Just imagine the disgrace!
Just listen, oh dear, oh dear, oh dear!"

"I had no notion at all,
When we moved into this wall,
Every room would be a human breeding cell.
We have people round the house,
And if I weren't such a mouse,
I'd call up and give
The landlord hell!"

THE OWL

Alternate title: "The Wise Old Owl."

There's a wise old owl
Who's a wise old fowl
On the top floor of City Hall.
Oh, his life is cream and peaches,

For the party writes his speeches,
And on Decoration Day he gives his all.

He's a wise old owl
With a silver trowel
For the cornerstones he lays.
Oh, he's dignified and solemn,
And there is no gossip column
That can point a sordid finger at his ways.

Only once in a while he cautiously hoots
Or very benignly blinks.
And the rest of the time, since nineteen-oh-five,
He thinks and thinks and thinks.

He's a wise old fowl,
Is this wise old owl,
For he's still up there on his rafter.
And unless he gets run over
Or he's chewed to bits by Rover,
He will probably live happy ever after.

THE SEAL

Registered for copyright as an unpublished song May 4, 1981.

She sits on a rock
In such dignified repose,
Disdaining to balance
The ball upon her nose.
No loud raucous barking,
No diving, no tricks;
She's got the crowd remarking,
"She's too cute to mix."

She sits on a rock,
Supercilious and cool,
While you do your flip-flops
And I go round the pool.
Let's tell the herring tosser,
This creature must go!
The dirty double-crosser
Is stealing the show.

THE WORM

Registered for copyright as an unpublished song under the alternate title "Oliver the Bookworm" May 4, 1981.

Oliver lived in *Richard the Third*,
Which no one had opened for years.
He stolidly nibbled
What Shakespeare had scribbled
Without even cocking his ears.
Then somebody opened the book
And gave a significant look,
Profoundly recited a line,
And shouted, "Immortal, divine!"

Now Oliver lives in *Richard the Third*
Absorbing a page at a gulp.
With diligent juices he madly reduces
Each quotable passage to pulp.
For though he can't read it, alas!
He's learned that the stuff has got class.
So if you should open the book,
Just listen a bit as you look.

There's Oliver deep in *Richard the Third*,
His appetite strangely ambitious,
And though it's a term rather bright for a worm,
You can hear him exclaiming, "Delicious!"

IT'S THE GOODS

A musical comedy for the Quartermaster Corps. Copyrighted November 21, 1945. Book by Frank Provo and John Pickard. Lyrics by Frank Loesser, Frank Provo, John Pickard, and David (Dave) Mann. Music by Mann and Loesser. Additional songs included "Montage" and "Service Spiritual," lyrics by Frank Provo and John Pickard, music by David Mann.

Available evidence indicates that this show was never performed.

CIVVY IN A FORK LIFT TRUCK

I'm just a civvy in a fork lift truck,
I'm just a civvy in a fork lift truck.
The fellows in the uniforms

Have gone and passed me by.
The tanks are on the battlefields;
The planes are in the sky.
The men are in the foxholes, ah!
But where the hell am I?
Back home like a dumb cluck,
A little civvy in a fork lift truck.

I'm just a civvy in a fork lift truck—
It's time they drafted me and changed my luck.
The fellows with the ribbons
Have been fighting ev'ryplace;
They've been right in the struggle
For each jungle island base.
The only struggle I've been in
Is with a packing case.
Ain't no shrapnel to duck
When you're a civvy in a fork lift truck.

Yes, I'm a civvy in a fork lift truck,
They've got me in the mood to run amok.
Someday I'll be the father
Of a bright and bouncing kid;
Someday I'll have to tell that kid
Exactly what I did:
There was a rugged war on,
But the gov'ment had me hid.
Eighteen years and still stuck,
Frozen like a snowdrift,
I was the hero of the swing shift,
A little civvy in a fork lift truck.

IS THIS BY CHANCE ROMANCE?

Music and lyrics by Frank Loesser and David Mann.

VERSE

It's time to own up
That now we're grown up,
Not kids anymore.
Something new has been added,
Suddenly you're the one I adore.

REFRAIN

I look at you,
You look at me;
It's not the kind of look
That it used to be—
Oh, is this by chance romance?

You talk to me,
I talk to you;
It's not the baby-talkin'
We used to do—
Oh, is this by chance romance?

Seems that we were schoolkids
Only yesterday;
How'd we get this way?
I'm a little bit surprised
To hear myself say:

My heart is yours,
Your heart is mine;
It's more than just a phrase
From a Valentine—
Oh, is this by some strange chance
That grown-up thing they call romance?

HEROES

Music and lyrics by Frank Provo, John Pickard, David Mann, and Frank Loesser.

VERSE 1

The Infantry, it moves ahead,
And that's my favorite dream:
To be a rugged rifleman,
My combat medal agleam,
My combat medal agleam.

REFRAIN

Heroes, heroes,
This is a day of heroes.
This is a world that needs
Young men who will set it free—
Maybe they need a man like me.

Heroes, heroes,
This is a job for heroes.
This is a world that needs
Young men that are brave and true—
Brother, they need a man like you.

VERSE 2

The bombardiers they fly aloft;
The Japs are getting no rest.
And oh, to be a bombardier,
The flying cross on my chest,
The flying cross on my chest!

REPEAT REFRAIN

VERSE 3

The tanks are full of heroes too;
I'll bet the feeling is grand.
Oh, roll me off an LST
Upon the enemy land,
With Patton shaking my hand!

REPEAT REFRAIN

WHAT MIGHT HAVE BEEN

Music and lyrics by Frank Provo, John Pickard, and Frank Loesser.

VERSE

Tomorrow, tomorrow,
It seemed so young and alive;
Tomorrow for us will never arrive.

REFRAIN

Oh, my darling, what might have been,
What might have been!
My dreams will all be dreams
Of what might have been.
I'll see you close beside me,
No matter where I go.
I'll see you close beside me, though I know
That it's merely what might have been
Had fate been kind,
That journey into life our two hearts designed.
The time has come for leaving
This wonderland we're in,
The cottage small,
The fireplace,
The cozy chair,
Your warm embrace,
And all those things that might have been.

ALL THE WAY

All the way, all the way
Goes the Quartermaster Corps,
Right out there in the thick of it.
If the goods need defending, say no more,
We'll go any night, any day,

And you'll hear our rifles roar,
Fighting all the way, all the way,
That's the Quartermaster Corps.

WHAT A WAY TO WIN A WAR

Music and lyrics by Frank Provo, John Pickard, Dave Mann, and Frank Loesser.

VERSE 1

We'll be pushing along in the big push,
In the big push for enemy ground.
We'll be pushing,
Yes, pushing,
Pushing supplies around.

REFRAIN

What a way to win a war,
What a way to win a war,
What a way to win a—
What a way to win a war!
What a way to win a war,
What a way to win a war,
What a way to win a—
What a way to win a war!

VERSE 2

We'll be driving along in the big drive;
We'll contribute to Tojo's hard luck.
We'll be driving,
Yes, driving,
Driving a laundry truck.

REPEAT REFRAIN

VERSE 3

We'll be moving along in the big move
When the Army moves in for the kill.
We'll be moving,
Yes, moving,
Moving a mule uphill.

REPEAT REFRAIN

VERSE 4

We will face each peril bravely;
We will never know defeat.
Neither sunburn nor mosquitoes
Can make us sound retreat.

But when a deadly booby trap
Lays low our stalwart buddy,
We must confess we think that war
Is definitely bloody.

[*Soldiers carry off wounded comrade while singing last six lines.*]

We can't help wond'ring,
What the dickens are we for?
We can't help complaining,
What a way to win a war!
What a way to, what a way to, what a way to,
What a way to win a war!

LET'S MAKE IT FOREVER

Music and lyrics by Frank Provo, John Pickard, David Mann, and Frank Loesser.

VERSE

Our hearts can keep on dancing,
Our eyes can still be bright,
Although the music's over for tonight.
Our hearts can keep on dancing,
Although the band is through,
Yes, dancing on for possibly a century or two.

REFRAIN

Let's make it forever,
Forever and a day.
Let's wake up ev'ry morning to find
Love is here to stay.
Let's make it forever,
A lifetime love affair.
Forever isn't any too long
For the way we care.

IT'S THE GOODS

Music and lyrics by Frank Provo, John Pickard, David Mann, and Frank Loesser.

VERSE

Ask any guy in the first wave
What he needs to see him through,
You'll hear that guy in the first wave

Give the QMC its due.
Can't make the grade on the beachhead
Till they push those goods along.
From the shirt upon my back
To the rations in my pack,
It's the goods that make me strong.

REFRAIN

What keeps 'em rollin'
When they've up and hit the shore?
It's the goods, it's the goods.
What's right behind 'em
With enough and plenty more?
It's the goods, it's the goods.
It's the food, it's the clothes,
It's the fuel and the stuff
That will keep a soldier tough
When the going's rough.
And with pride he'll confide that
What has seen him through the woods
Is the good old goods,
Is the good old goods.

MISCELLANEOUS SONGS OF 1944–45

LEAVE US FACE IT (WE'RE IN LOVE)

Published. Copyrighted January 14, 1944. "Lyrics, Words and Malady wrote by 'Archie' of Duffy's Tavern aided and indebted by Abe Burrows and Frank Loesser" (quoted from cover of sheet music). Loesser and Burrows wrote this for Ed Gardner, who played the character of Archie on the radio comedy show *Duffy's Tavern*. Burrows was the show's head writer from 1941 to 1944.

VERSE

I stand here at good old Duffy's,
Where the elite meet t' eat.
Me red corpsuckles racin',
I await for you, my sweet.
In me hand is a diamond unfurled;
We should holler it out to the world:

REFRAIN

Leave us no longer pretend
That you are merely a friend,
For it is wrote in the stars above;
Though we have tried to act cold,
Suddenly lo and get hold,
Leave us face it, we're in love.

Leave us not blush with no shame
If people bandage our name;
Shoes and old rice are worth dreaming of.
Stories like in our two eyes
Could win the Putziller Prize.
Leave us face it, we're in love.

In some other life
We was once a man and wife;
In an old French chapeau we was mated.
Now mine love for thine,
Just as thine love for mine,
Has been reincarcerated.

So I plight me troth at your feet;
Don't leave me life uncomplete—
I'm like a turtle without a dove.
Love light ain't meant to be hid—
No, no, no, perish forbid!
Leave us face it, we're in love.

THE ONE-PIP WONDER

Published. Copyrighted March 20, 1944. Song of the Canadian Armored Corps.

VERSE

You'll know us when you see us,
Anywhere, anytime.
You'll know us when you see us
By the grease and the grime.

REFRAIN

We come rolling over the hills of Canada,
We're the cream of Canada's finest crop,
With the Troop-Troop-Trooper at the bottom of
    the Ram
And the One-Pip Wonder at the top.
We come rolling over the fields of Canada,
We're the team that nothing on earth can stop,

With the Drive-Drive-Driver catching all the hell
    and damn*
From the One-Pip Wonder at the top.

So call for the man in the black beret
When you call for a man of war;
Call the Canadian,
Call the Canadian,
Call the Canadian Armored Corps,
And we'll come rolling over the fields of
    Canada,
Singing "Clang-a-rattle-de-bang-bang-pop!"
With the Troop-Troop-Trooper at the bottom of
    the Ram
And the One-Pip Wonder at the top.

THE SAD BOMBARDIER

Published. Copyrighted March 20, 1944.

VERSE

A sad bombardier am I today,
A sad bombardier without a shack.
And if you'd care to know
The cause of all my woe,
It's the stupid son of a bitch behind my back.

REFRAIN 1

Oh, the pilot had his head up,
His head up, his head up—
He put me at the foot of the class.
For the pilot had his head up,
His head up, his head up,
The pilot had his head up his ass.

REFRAIN 2

Bet your life I had my head down,
My head down, my head down,
A-staring at the hairs through the glass.
But the pilot had his head up,
His head up, his head up,
The pilot had his head up his ass.

REFRAIN 3

When I asked him for a level,
He banked like the devil—

---

* *Sheet music version indicates polite version:*
    . . . taking orders like a lamb

The run was just a plain waste of gas.
For the pilot had his head up,
His head up, his head up,
The pilot had his head up his ass.

REFRAIN 4

Oh, I could have hit the barrel,
The old pickle barrel—
I could have hit a small demitasse.
But the pilot had his head up,
His head up, his head up,
The pilot had his head up his ass.

REFRAIN 5

So if I become a private,
An old busted private,
I'll blame it on the snake in the grass:
The guy who had his head up,
His head up, his head up,
The guy who had his head up his ass.

REFRAIN 6

But the hero of my story
Will fly on to glory—
You'll know him by his hat made of brass.
That's in case he gets his head up,
His head up, his head up,
In case he gets his head up his ass.

ONE LITTLE WAC

Published. Copyrighted April 10, 1944. Music by Eddie
Dunstedter.

REFRAIN

One little WAC,
A khaki-covered cutie,
One little WAC
Released a man for duty.
One little man,
He flew through the flak
To Berlin and back
With bombs in his rack.
And one little bomb
He dropped upon the city,
One little bomb,
He aimed so true and pretty.
That was the bomb
That broke Hitler's back,

A score for the Yanks,
Thanks to one little WAC.

INTERLUDE

The Women's Army Corps, the Double-U–A–C,
The Women's Army Corps, the Double-U–A–C,
The Women's Army Corps, the Double-U–A–C.
You wanna win this war?
Well, Double-U–A–C spells—

REPEAT REFRAIN

SALUTE TO THE ARMY SERVICE FORCES

Published. Copyrighted October 31, 1944. In an interview published in *Yank* magazine (November 16, 1945),
Loesser referred to this as "the Army song to end all
Army songs. . . . It said 'hurray' . . . for 32 pages. It was
like making love to a telephone book."

When the guns of war are silent,
When the days of war are through,
When the fighting men march home again
Proudly passing in review,
When the time has come for cheering
That the victory is won,
Hail the Army Service Forces
For a job well done!

Hail the Medics! Hail the Ordnance!
Hail the Signal Corps marching back!
Hail the Chaplains, Transportation,
Special Services and the WAC!
Hail the Nurses and the MPs
And the brave and true Engineers!
They're the Army Service Forces—
Give 'em your cheers!

VOICE 1: I drive a truck for the QMC*
VOICE 2: I repair the heavy tanks.
VOICE 3: I load cargo day and night.
    ALL: And then we pick up our rifles and we
          fight.
VOICE 4: I build big bridges and roads.
VOICE 5: I'm the guy that brings the food.
VOICE 6: I keep traffic running right.

———————
* *Earlier:*
    I drive a truck full of supplies.

    ALL: And then we pick up our rifles and we
          fight.
VOICE 7: I string long telephone lines.
VOICE 8: I'm the guy who pays the men.
VOICE 9: I guard pris'ners through the night.
    ALL: And then we pick up our rifles and we
          fight.
VOICE 1: I'm from the Adjutant General's Office.
VOICE 2: I'm from Chemical Warfare.
VOICE 3: Morale Services Division.
VOICE 4: I'm from the Judge Advocates Department.
VOICE 5: I work in the Personal Affairs Branch.
VOICE 6: I'm from the Inspector General's
          Department.
VOICE 7: I run a PX on a little Pacific isle.
  VOICE: But you hear that? [*music cue*]
          That means I pick up my rifle and I
          fight.
          We all pick up our rifles and fight.

BUY A BOND (WHAT HAVE YOU GOT TO LOSE?)

Music by Lou Alter. Probably early 1944.

You save a little nickel
And then you save a dime,
And you'll have eighteen dollars plus
In just a little time.
Hi-ho, buy a bond,
What have you got to lose?

At Kiska and Salerno,
They really did their share—
Be glad to do your fighting here
Instead of over there.
Hi-ho, buy that bond,
What have you got to lose?

Hi-diddle-diddle, that's a tune,
A tune to croon both night and noon.
Hi-ho, you'd better buy it soon
And never mind the new shoes.

And sometime in the future
When interest comes in,
Well, you can show your children
How you really helped to win.
Hi-ho, buy that bond,
What have you got to,
What have you got to,
What have you got to lose?

RODGER YOUNG

Published. Copyrighted February 19, 1945. Recorded by Burl Ives (Decca) and Nelson Eddy (Columbia), among others.

Next to "Praise the Lord and Pass the Ammunition," this was Loesser's most famous World War II song. Susan Loesser related this story of its origins in *A Most Remarkable Fella*:

> The infantry kept after my father for a "proper" infantry song. Finally he decided to write a ballad about a Medal of Honor recipient and got hold of a list of World War II "winners" to search for a name that would scan. He came upon the name Rodger Young, liked the sound of it, and thus was born one of the most memorable songs of World War II.
>
> The infantry loved the ballad enough to put together a public relations campaign to promote it, and the campaign director asked my father for some background. This presented him with a problem, since you can't very well say you went through a list of Medal of Honor recipients until you came to a name you thought would sing well. As it happened, my parents' friend Larry Adler had just returned from entertaining the troops in the South Pacific. Larry is probably the world's best-known harmonica player, and Rodger Young was a harmonica player, so Larry was asked if he could have told my father about a brave, harmonica-playing soldier who was killed on the island of New Georgia in the Solomons. Larry allowed as how he *could* have, and the story was made official.
>
> My mother told me that my father always felt rather guilty about the cold-blooded reality of the evolution of the song as well as its packaging. But the song itself is surely moving and Rodger Young was a genuine hero despite the fact that he was immortalized while hundreds of other war heroes remained unsung because their names didn't scan well.

Oh, they've got no time for glory in the Infantry,
Oh, they've got no use for praises loudly sung,
But in ev'ry soldier's heart in all the Infantry
Shines the name, shines the name of Rodger
   Young.

Shines the name Rodger Young,
Fought and died for the men he marched among.
To the everlasting glory of the Infantry
Lives the story of Private Rodger Young.

Caught in ambush lay a company of riflemen,
Just grenades against machine guns in the gloom.

Caught in ambush till this one of twenty riflemen
Volunteered, volunteered to meet his doom.

Volunteered Rodger Young,
Fought and died for the men he marched among.
In the everlasting annals of the Infantry
Glows the last deed of Private Rodger Young.

It was he who drew the fire of the enemy,
That a company of men might live to fight.
And before the deadly fire of the enemy
Stood the man, stood the man we hail tonight.

Stood the man Rodger Young,
Fought and died for the men he marched among.
Like the everlasting courage of the Infantry
Was the courage of Private Rodger Young.

On the island of New Georgia in the Solomons
Stands a simple wooden cross alone to tell
That beneath the silent coral of the Solomons
Sleeps a man, sleeps a man remembered well.

Sleeps a man Rodger Young,
Fought and died for the men he marched among.
In the everlasting spirit of the Infantry
Breathes the spirit of Private Rodger Young.

No, they've got no time for glory in the Infantry,
No, they've got no use for praises loudly sung.
But in ev'ry soldier's heart in all the Infantry
Shines the name, shines the name of Rodger
   Young.

Shines the name Rodger Young,
Fought and died for the men he marched among.
To the everlasting glory of the Infantry
Lives the story of Private Rodger Young.

TWO BEAUTIFUL THINGS

Probably early 1945.

VERSE

I saw her walking gaily by
As I came down the stairs.
She made that ancient phrase apply
That "good things come in pairs."

REFRAIN

'Cause she had two beautiful things,
Two beautiful things,

Two beautiful things to drive a guy crazy,
Two heavenly bundles she just couldn't hide.
I walked by her side;
My eyes opened wide
To see those two beautiful things,
Two beautiful things.
She was one of nature's fortunate mammals,
I mean mammals.
But the way that she displayed them got my goat;
Oh, she should have kept them covered with her
   coat.
Two beautiful things:
Kleenex and Camels!

WAVE TO ME, MY LADY

Published. Copyrighted December 10, 1945. Music and lyrics by William Stein and Frank Loesser. Recorded by the Dinning Sisters (Capitol), Gene Autry (Columbia), and Art Kassel (Vogue).

Just took a job in the railroad yard,
Pay me good, work me hard.
Just took a job in the railroad yard
And now I'm doin' fine;
So won't you wave to me, my lady,
Wave to me, my lady,
Wave to me, my lady,
As I roll down the line?
Oh, won't you wave to me, my lady,
Wave to me, my lady,
Wave to me, my lady, down the line?

Just took a job on a railroad freight,
Tote that sack, lift that crate.
Just took a job on a railroad freight
And now I'm doing fine;
So won't you
Wave to me, my lady,
Wave to me, my lady,
Wave to me, my lady,
As I roll down the line?
Oh, won't you wave to me, my lady,
Wave to me, my lady,
Wave to me, my lady, down the line?

Just took a job on a railroad switch,
Won't go broke, can't get rich.
Just took a job on a railroad switch
And now I'm doin' fine;
So ain't you
Proud of me, my lady,
Proud of me, my lady,

THE COMPLETE LYRICS OF FRANK LOESSER

Proud of me, my lady,
As I roll down the line?
Oh, ain't you proud of me, my lady,
Proud of me, my lady,
Proud of me, my lady, down the line?

Just took a job on a railroad brake,
Daily bread, Sunday cake.
Just took a job on a railroad brake
And now I'm doin' fine;
So won't you
Say to me, my lady,
Say to me, my lady,
Say to me, my lady,
As I roll down the line—
Oh, won't you say to me, my lady,
Say to me, my lady,
Say to me, my lady, you'll be mine?

PORT BATTALIONS ON PARADE

From undated ozalid. Probably early 1945.

VERSE

Did you ever stop and wonder
When our guns are making thunder
Who brings our guns overseas?
Well, it's the old TCPBs.

REFRAIN

We load it off and we load it on,
At night, and noon, and in the chilly dawn.
We move it out, and we move it in,
That ammunition that'll hit Berlin.

We don't get any glory like the rest of them,
But we've been under fire with the best of them,
As we swing it aft and we swing it fore,
The Port Battalions of the Transportation Corps.

Spike Jones and Mary Hatcher in Variety Girl.
Inset: *Betty Hutton in the film* Perils of Pauline

Songs of 1946–1947

THE DAY BEFORE SPRING

Unproduced MGM feature film based on Alan Jay Lerner and Frederick Loewe's musical *The Day Before Spring*, which opened in New York on November 22, 1945, and ran 165 performances. Although the songs bear the credit "By Johnny Green and Frank Loesser," it is assumed that Loesser wrote the lyrics and Green the music. Green (1908–1989) composer, arranger, pianist, and conductor wrote the music for "Body and Soul," "I Cover the Waterfront," "Easy Come, Easy Go," and many other hits.

IT'S TIME FOR THE LOVE SCENE

Registered for copyright as an unpublished song November 20, 1946.

It's time for the love scene
For you and me,
It's time for the love scene
That had to be.
The light in your eyes
Once promised me this moment supreme,
And I've rehearsed
The lover's part in ev'ry dream.
So let there be moonlight and violins:
We met in the moonlight,
The scene begins,
And now as I hold you close,
That breathless moment arrives.
Let's make it the love scene
Of our lives!

WHO COULD FORGET YOU?

Registered for copyright as an unpublished song November 20, 1946.

Who could forget you,
Love you
And then take his heart back again

And forget you?
Who could smile and dismiss you?
Gaily and strong go through life
Without longing to kiss you?
Who could forget
He was yours one wonderful day,
Foolishly throw such a dream away?
Oh! How could he let you
Linger behind,
Out of sight, out of mind
And forget you?
Darling, who could?
In a thousand years
Not I.

BING BANG

Registered for copyright as an unpublished song December 9, 1946. Melody and countermelody sung first separately and then together.

MELODY

Bing! Bang! Cling! Clang!
That was the song your father sang
For Harrison long ago!
Bang! Bing! Clang! Cling!
Gentlemen, let your voices ring,
For Harrison again meets the foe!
And let them look to their laurels when they hear
Da-ra-ra-ra the mighty cheer
Of the school we hold so dear!
Give a Harrison Bing! Bang! Cling! Clang!
That was the song your father sang
When Harrison won the fray!
Razzle-dazzle-dee!
Bang! Bing! Clang! Cling!
Gentlemen, give them ev'rything,
We win again today!

COUNTERMELODY

Behold this noble institution
Of higher learning.
Behold the beacon light of culture so brightly
  burning.
And hearken to the proud alumni
At length returning,
Bearing pearls of wonderful wisdom.
Pearls of wisdom such as Bing! Bang! Bing!
A razzle-dazzle and a Cling! Clang! Cling!
For this they need a big university!
Behold the bankers and the lawyers
In marching column—

Oh! hear their voices wise and solemn!
Razzle-dazzle-dee!
Four years of Greek and economics and calculus
  and—
All that remains in these powerful brains
Is the Bing! Bang! Bing! Bang! Hahahahaha!

MY SENTIMENTAL NATURE

Registered for copyright as an unpublished song December 9, 1946.

REFRAIN 1

It might have been my sentimental nature
That made me sing
A crazy little song of love
All spring.
Remember that hummable thing?
It might have been my sentimental nature
That made me sigh
When happy couples arm in arm
Strolled by.
Remember that moon in the sky?
April came around and soon I found
My heart melting away.
Funny how that feeling started on the day we met.
And yet it merely might have been my sentimental
  nature;
I wish I knew:
Was I in love with love
Or was it you?

REFRAIN 2

It might have been my sentimental nature
That made me sing
A tender little song of love
All spring.
Remember the hummable thing?
It might have been my sentimental nature
That made me sigh
And wonder after all these years
Just why
The tune still refuses to die.
April came around and soon I found
My heart melting away.
Funny how that music started on the day we met.
And yet it merely might have been my sentimental
  nature;
I wish I knew:
Was I in love with love
Or was it you?

YOU'RE SO RELIABLE

Registered for copyright as an unpublished song December 9, 1946.

VERSE 1

HE: My life grows more beautiful
With each passing day,
And you keep it beautiful
In one very gratifying way.
You're so—how shall I say?—
You're so, you're so—

REFRAIN 1

You're so reliable,
But so reliable,
But such a true blue type,
The most dependable, highly commendable
Lady who lights my pipe.
You're an angel at breakfast;
That's when I love you the most.
Yes, down at the office
I very proudly boast,
"She never burns the toast!"
You're so reliable,
But so reliable,
You win the Nobel Prize!
An unassailable, always available
Talent for tying bow ties!
Though you may be no siren
Draped in a flowered sarong,
It's undeniable that you're reliable
As the day is long.

REFRAIN 2

SHE: You're so reliable,
But so reliable,
But such a level head,
The most dependable, highly commendable
Husband a girl could wed.
You're an angel at breakfast;
That's when I'm carried away.
Yes, down at the beauty shop
I've been known to say,
"He kissed my cheek today!"
You've got integrity,
Yes, sir, integrity,
Yes, sir, and that's what counts!
I dream at night of it,
Oh, the delight of it,
Knowing that your checks don't bounce!
Though you may be no Gable
Playing a passionate scene,

It's undeniable that you're reliable
As the nine-fifteen.

VERSE 2

HE: That sweet simple mind of yours,
I've harnessed its power.
I count on that mind of yours
To change ev'ry hour on the hour.
You're so—how shall I say?—
You're so, you're so—

REFRAIN 3

You're so reliable,
But so reliable.
Darling, when I feel ill,
You have the prettiest,
Warmest and wittiest
Manner of keeping still.
You were heaven by moonlight
Touring the Rockies last year:
Yes, driving along on a night so bright and clear,
You never stripped a gear.
You're such a capable,
But such a capable hostess to all the boys.
And though they drink to you,
Who'd slip the wink to you,
Darling, you've got such great poise!
Though you may be no bombshell,
Painted and sinfully blond,
It's undeniable that you're reliable
As a Fed'ral Bond!

IBBEDY BIBBEDY SIBBEDY SAB

Registered for copyright as an unpublished song December 23, 1946.

VERSE

Ibbedy Bibbedy Sibbedy Sab!
If I wrote songs, there's a title I'd grab!
Ibbedy Bibbedy Sibbedy Sab!
Canal Boat!!

Ibbedy Bibbedy Sibbedy Sab!
It should be carved on a mah-harble slab.
Ibbedy Bibbedy Sibbedy Sab!
Canal Boat!!

REFRAIN

Boowah! Sound the trumpets!
Boowah! Boowah! What a day!
Boowah! Pass the crumpets!
Patrick Henry never said it this way—
"Give me Ibbedy Bibbedy Sibbedy Sab!"
I'm almost through, someone call me a cab!
Ibbedy Bibbedy Sibbedy Sab!
I love you!

THE PERILS OF PAULINE

A Paramount Picture produced by Sol C. Siegel. Music and lyrics by Frank Loesser. Released in July 1947. Directed by George Marshall. Cast featured Betty Hutton, John Lund, Billy De Wolfe, William Demarest, and Constance Collier. "Poor Pauline," lyrics by Charles McCarron, music by Raymond Walker, was also part of the score.

THE SEWING MACHINE

Published. Copyrighted April 10, 1947. Introduced by Betty Hutton. Recorded by Betty Hutton (Capitol).

VERSE (NOT SUNG IN FILM)

She sits there in the workshop
With the great big circles neath her eyes.
She sits there in the workshop
And she sighs—

REFRAIN 1*

Oh, the sewing machine, the sewing machine,
A girl's best friend.
If I didn't have my sewing machine,
I'd come to no good end.
But I bobbin the bobbin, and pedal the pedal,
And wheel the wheel by day,
So by night I feel so weary
That I never get out to play.

* *Sheet music note for singer says: "Irish and sarcastic."*

REFRAIN 2 (NOT SUNG IN FILM)

Oh, the sewing machine, the sewing machine,
A pal so dear.
If I didn't have my sewing machine,
I'd try a stage career.
But I bobbin the bobbin, and pedal the pedal,
Till amateur night comes by,
But by then I feel so weary
That I haven't the strength to try.

REFRAIN 3

Oh, the sewing machine, the sewing machine,
A friend in need.
If I didn't have my sewing machine,
A wicked life I'd lead.
But I bobbin the bobbin, and pedal the pedal,
And dream about romance,
So by night I feel so weary
That I never get out to dance.

REFRAIN 4

Oh, the sewing machine, the sewing machine,
A helping hand.
If I didn't have my sewing machine,
I'd drink to beat the band.
But I bobbin the bobbin, and pedal the pedal,
As busy as a bug,
So by night I feel so weary
That I hardly can lift a mug.

REFRAIN 5

Oh, the sewing machine, the sewing machine,
My pride and joy.
If I didn't have my sewing machine,
I'd marry James McCoy.
But I bobbin the bobbin, and pedal the pedal,
And that's the end of Jim,
'Cause by night I get so weary
I don't even look good to him!

REFRAIN 6

Oh, have I got a boss, he looks like a hoss.
His name's Joe Gurt.
I'm willing to bet the wages I get
That face of his must hurt.
While I bobbin the bobbin, and pedal the pedal,
He keeps his eyes on me,
Oh, I've never had a nightmare where
I didn't meet Mr. G.

TAG (NOT SUNG IN FILM)

Oh, the sewing machine, the sewing machine,
A girl's best friend,
This is the end!

RUMBLE, RUMBLE, RUMBLE

Published. Copyrighted March 14, 1947. Introduced by Betty Hutton. Recorded by Betty Hutton (Capitol), the Murphy Sisters (Apollo), and Madeline Kahn (Painted Smiles).

VERSE

I gotta move,
I gotta move.
That's what I tell my landlord,
"Landlord, I gotta move,"
'Cause there's a man lives right upstairs from me
Making a nightmare of some melody.
This is a situation not likely to improve.

REFRAIN 1

He goes a-rumble, rumble, rumble on the left
   hand,
He goes a-tinkle, tinkle, tinkle on the right,
Rumble, rumble, rumble,
Tinkle, tinkle, tinkle,
Plays piano all night.

He goes a-rumble, rumble, rumble on the bottom,
He goes a-tinkle, tinkle, tinkle on the top,
Rumble, rumble, rumble,
Tinkle, tinkle, tinkle,
Positively won't stop.

I tried a-knocking, knocking, knocking on the
   ceiling,
I tried a-knocking, knocking, knocking on the
   wall.
He takes a breather—
No, he doesn't, either;
Just when I figure that's all—

He goes a-rumble, rumble, rumble on the black
   keys,
He goes a-tinkle, tinkle, tinkle on the white,
Rumble, rumble, rumble,
Tinkle, tinkle, tinkle,
Plays piano all right,
But he plays piano all night,

INTERLUDE

Instead of cooking himself a quiet kettle of tea
   up there,
Or maybe getting himself a girl and taking her out
   somewhere,
Instead of sitting around, reading the jokes,
Washing his socks, writing his folks,
Taking a pill, sleeping the night through,

What does he do?
[spoken] What does he do?

REFRAIN 2

He goes a-rumble, rumble, rumble,
Look at the whole building crumble.
Tinkle, tinkle, tinkle,
Look at the wallpaper wrinkle.

Rumble, rumble, rumble
Tinkle, tinkle, tinkle.
He could give insomnia to Rip Van Winkle
With that rumble, rumble, rumble,
I've got a good right to grumble,
Tinkle, tinkle, tinkle,
I'm gonna raise quite a—[spoken] stop it,
   will ya?!
Rumble—
Tinkle—
Police! Somebody, break his lease!

I tried to hammer, hammer, hammer on the steam
   pipe,
I tried to holler, holler, holler down the hall.
I've got a feelin' he'll come through the ceilin',
Big foot, piano, and all!!

He goes a-fumbaly, fumble, fumbling with his left
   hand,
He goes a grope-grope-gropin' with his right.
He goes a-fumbaly-fum-grope,
A-fumbaly-fum-grope, a-fumbaly-grope,
Fumbles till he gets it right.
But he plays piano—
Plays piano all night!

I WISH I DIDN'T LOVE YOU SO

Published. Copyrighted April 10, 1947. Introduced by Betty Hutton. Leading recordings by Vaughn Monroe and His Orchestra (RCA Victor), Dinah Shore (Columbia), Betty Hutton (Capitol), Dick Haymes (Decca), and Dick Farney (Majestic). Other recordings include Aretha Franklin (Columbia), Ray Charles (Tangerine), and Peggy Lee (Capitol). Nominated for an Academy Award as Best Song of the Year.

VERSE (NOT SUNG IN FILM)

After all this time without you,
After all this time I find

That it's still no use to say to myself:
"Out of sight, out of mind."

REFRAIN

I wish I didn't love you so.
My love for you
Should have faded long ago.
I wish I didn't need your kiss;
Why must your kiss
Torture me as long as this?
I might be smiling by now
With some new tender friend,
Smiling by now
With my heart on the mend.
But when I try,
Something in that heart says no—
You're still there;
I wish I didn't love you so.

POPPA, DON'T PREACH TO ME

Published. Copyrighted March 12, 1947. Introduced by Betty Hutton and ensemble. Recorded by Betty Hutton (Capitol), Phil Harris (RCA Victor), Lena Horne (Charter), and Dinah Shore (Columbia).

VERSE

HUTTON: On a Paris boulevard
I picked up a postal card
Someone had forgotten (how you say?)
to mail.
Seems as though some tourist had
Meant for it to reach her dad,
For it told a typical tale.
Nat'rally I read what she wrote.
This is what she said, and I quote:

REFRAIN 1

I came to Paris to buy me a gown,
To Paris, to Paris,
And oh, what a town!
The lights were shining,
The music was gay;
I bought me my gown
And decided to stay.
Now Poppa, don't preach to me, preach to me,
Poppa, don't preach to me—
Let my heart break while it's young.
Now Poppa, don't preach to me, preach to me,

Poppa, don't preach to me—
Let me fling till my fling is all flung!

REFRAIN 2

I danced in Paris last night with Pierre;
That X marks my room,
But I'm seldom up there.*
I strolled through Paris
Today with Maurice.
The Rue de la Paix
Means the Street of the Peace.
Now Poppa, don't preach to me, preach to me,
Poppa, don't preach to me—
Let my heart break if it must.
Now Poppa, don't preach to me, preach to me,
Poppa, don't preach to me—
And don't cut off my guarantee trust!

[Dance]

REFRAIN 3

HUTTON: I'm here in Paris since early in May;
My gown got all worn out, but I'm still okay.
BOYS: You're made for Paris.
HUTTON: I'm finding that out.
I still have no past,
But my future's in doubt.
Now Poppa, don't preach to me, preach to me,
Poppa, don't preach to me—
Let my heart break, let it roam.
BOYS: Let it roam.
HUTTON: Now Poppa, don't preach to me, preach to me,
ALL: Poppa, don't preach to me,
Or I'll never, no never, come—
HUTTON: Preach to me, preach to me—
ALL: Or I'll never, no, never come home!
BOYS: Poppa!
HUTTON: Poppa!
BOYS: Poppa!
HUTTON: Hey, Pop!
Poppa, don't preach to me, preach to me,
Poppa, don't preach to me—
ALL: Or I'll never, no, never come home.

Phil Harris's recorded version of the refrains made the following changes:

REFRAIN 1, LINES 1–7:

I came to Paris to buy me a hat.
To Paris, to Paris,

* Sheet music version:
But I'm never up there.

And that's where I'm at.
The lights were shining,
The music was gay;
I bought me my hat
And decided to stay.

REFRAIN 2, LINES 1–5:

I'm fond of Fifi, I'm crazy for Claire;
That X marks my room,
But I'm seldom there.
I danced with Mimi
And dined with Bernice.

REFRAIN 3, LINE 2:

My hat got blown off, but I'm still OK.

THE FIREMEN'S BALL

Manuscript dated January 9, 1946. Not used in film. Also considered for *Variety Girl*. Song returned to Loesser by Paramount per agreement dated October 20, 1947.

VERSE

From Hook and Ladder Number One
To Hook and Ladder Number Two
To Hook and Ladder Number Three
Go I.
At Hook and Ladder Number One
And Hook and Ladder Number Two
And Hook and Ladder Number Three
I wait
And I sigh,
And here's why:

REFRAIN

I met my love at the Firemen's Ball,
Firemen's Ball,
Firemen's Ball.
I met my love at the Firemen's Ball,
One Saturday evening last June.

Gaily he waltzed me all over the hall,
Over the hall,
Over the hall.
He was so handsome, so young, and so tall,
But he left the party too soon.

For a big three-alarm rang out that night
And away dashed my dashing prince.

Oh, he must have had quite a blaze to fight,
For he never returned to hold me tight,
And I haven't located him since.

Oh, where is my love from the Firemen's Ball?
Sadly I call,
Sadly I call.
He was my treasure, my life, and my all,
But I never did catch his name.
Oh, where is my love from the Firemen's Ball
Who set my heart aflame?

PATTER

His suspenders are red like the curls on his head,
And his muscles are harder than rocks.
Oh, he's ready and rough, which I know well
    enough,
For he told me he sleeps in his socks.

In his eyes was a shine when they looked into mine,
And his voice was so sweet when he spoke.
And I fondly recall, when we danced at the ball,
That his mustache smelled faintly of smoke.

Oh, I'd leap from nine stories or ten
Just to land in his arms again.

VARIETY GIRL

A Paramount Picture produced by Daniel Dare. Released in October 1947. Music and lyrics by Frank Loesser. Screenplay by Edmund Hartmann, Frank Tashlin, Robert Walsh, and Monte Brice. Directed by George Marshall. Choreography by Billy Daniels and Bernard Pearce. Cast featured Mary Hatcher, Olga San Juan, and DeForest Kelley with cameo appearances by Bob Hope, Bing Crosby, Gary Cooper, Ray Milland, Alan Ladd, Barbara Stanwyck, Paulette Goddard, Dorothy Lamour, Veronica Lake, Pearl Bailey, Spike Jones and His City Slickers, and other stars. The songs for this film also included "Harmony," lyrics by Johnny Burke, music by James Van Heusen, and "Tired," lyrics and music by Allan Roberts and Doris Fisher.

YOUR HEART CALLING MINE

Published. Copyrighted August 27, 1947. Introduced by Mary Hatcher with Spike Jones and His City Slickers. Hatcher performed the song in a straightforward manner while Jones and his orchestra tried to unnerve her.

In the call of the thrush on the blossoming bough,
I hear your heart calling mine.
In the sigh of the breeze that caresses me now,
I hear your heart calling mine.
There is laughter in the woodland stream
As it hurries on its way.
May the laughter of the woodland stream
Tell me, darling, of the joy that I'm feeling today.
For the call of the thrush on a blossoming bough
Brings a song so divine;
I hear your heart calling mine.

TALLAHASSEE

Published. Copyrighted April 15, 1947. Introduced by Alan Ladd and Dorothy Lamour with ensemble. Leading recordings by Bing Crosby and the Andrews Sisters (Decca) and Dinah Shore and Woody Herman (Columbia). Other recordings include Johnny Mercer (Capitol) and Vaughn Monroe (RCA Victor). A recording by Frank Loesser and Abe Burrows from a 1947 radio broadcast is on the compact disc *Frank Sings Loesser* (Koch).

VERSE

Oh, won't you listen, all you people on the
    southbound train,
Oh, won't you listen to my friendly advice?
About a quarter after seven we'll be pulling into
    paradise.

REFRAIN (DUET)

1ST VOICE: When you see land
2ND VOICE: Out of the window of a train
1ST VOICE: Kinda green and grassy,
2ND VOICE: How in the world can you complain?
1ST VOICE: Beneath a moon
2ND VOICE: You ought to see the way it shines,
1ST VOICE: Bright beyond compare,
2ND VOICE: The way it shines upon the pines.
    BOTH: When you hear blue jays
        Chirping high and sassy,

1ST VOICE: And catch one sniff of southern
        cooking
        Hanging on the evening air.
2ND VOICE: Supper's waiting on the table!
1ST VOICE: When you see folks
2ND VOICE: Having their after-dinner chats,
1ST VOICE: All polite and classy,
2ND VOICE: Gentlemen all remove their hats,
1ST VOICE: And ev'ry smile,
2ND VOICE: Perfect harmony and peace,
1ST VOICE: Bids you stay and rest,
2ND VOICE: Hand the porter your valise—
1ST VOICE: Get off that train—
2ND VOICE: Sit down and rest your chassis:
    BOTH: You're in Tallahassee,
2ND VOICE: The capital city of Florida
    BOTH: And the Southland at its best—
2ND VOICE: But Dixie at its very best!

REFRAIN (SOLO)

When you see land
Kinda green and grassy
Beneath a moon
Bright beyond compare,
When you hear blue jays
Chirping high and sassy
And catch one sniff of southern cooking
Hanging on the ev'ning air,
When you see folks
All polite and classy
And ev'ry smile
Bids you stay and rest—
Get off that train,
You're in Tallahassee,
The Southland at its best.

HE CAN WALTZ

Published. Copyrighted July 16, 1947. Introduced by Olga San Juan lip-synching to the voice of Mary Hatcher.

VERSE (SHEET MUSIC VERSION)

He is so diff'rent, he is so rare;
He's not the kind that you'll find ev'rywhere.

REFRAIN

He can waltz,
He can waltz.
With the grace of an angel
He sways me up to the blue.

He can waltz,
He can waltz.
But there isn't much else in this world
He knows how to do.
Helpless at polo,*
Hopeless at tea,
Harmless alone in the moonlight with me.
But for all of his faults,
When there's music in three-quarter time there,
And I'm there, he's wonderful,
For he can waltz.

FILM VERSES

The guy that I adore is diff'rent,
The guy that I adore is rare.
He's got a beat to his dancing,
A beat you don't find ev'rywhere.
So when the band plays the customary
Doodle-da-doy, doodle-da-doy-doy, doodle-da-doy-
    vout,
You'll always find him sitting one out.

The guy that I adore is diff'rent,
And as I said before, he's strange.
He wants a style to his music,
That most arrangers don't arrange.
So when the band plays the customary
Toydle-oy-doy, rah-dah-dat, rip-rip-die-die-die-reet,
You'll never find him up on his feet.
He never comes to life till the music is soft and sweet.

IMPOSSIBLE THINGS

Introduced by offscreen choir, which sang only the last
two lines of the refrain at the end of the finale during
the closing credits.

VERSE

This is more than just a pleasure,
It's a night I'll always treasure,
For it's you I've been longing to meet.
Now my life is incredibly sweet.

REFRAIN

I promised myself such impossible things,
Impossible things about you.*
I started believing a crazy daydream
That hadn't a chance to come true.
I promised myself that my heart would have wings
And music to which it could dance;
A walk in the starlight with you beside me,†
A moment of magic romance.

Impossible things, and yet at last we've met,
And here in the starry light you're mine tonight.
I'm hearing that music, my heart's on those wings,
The daydream has really come true.
Of all the impossible things, it happened,
This moment of moments with you.

WE FRENCH, WE GET SO EXCITED

Used instrumentally only. Also considered for *The Perils of Pauline.*

VERSE

Welcome to Paree, Miss Peoria.
Welcome to Paree, Miss Fort Worth.
Welcome to the fastest town on earth.
And when I say fast,
I do not mean
Those taxicabs you see.
It's the bon vivant, the gay young blade,
Who make Paree Paree.
That's me!

REFRAIN 1

I greet you on the boulevard,
The very day you land,
And it isn't enough we're side by side,
I've gotta be hand in hand.
For we French, we get so excited,
We French, we are so easily ignited.
Oh, we French, we get so excited,
And just so I won't create a scene,
You fall for that hand-in-hand routine.

REFRAIN 2

I walk you down the boulevard—
I swear I mean no harm—
But it isn't enough we're hand in hand,
I've gotta be arm in arm.
For we French, we get so excited,
The French are friends, and they must not be
    slighted.
Oh, we French, we get so excited,
And although at first you disagree,
You're soon walking arm in arm with me.

REFRAIN 3

I stop along the boulevard
At Café Montparnasse,
'Cause it isn't enough we're arm in arm,
I've gotta be glass to glass.
We sit there by the boulevard,
I say, "You're magnifique."
But it isn't enough we're glass to glass;
I've gotta be cheek to cheek.

REFRAIN 4

Then stars fall on the boulevard
From L'Opéra to Montmartre.
It's a dangerous thing, this cheek to cheek,
We're suddenly heart to heart.
(For we French, we get so excited,
We French, we are so easily ignited.
Oh, we French, we get so excited.)*

REFRAIN 5

So when you sail back to your home state
And meet your old boyfriend at the gate,
When he asks you,
[*spoken*] Where did you go, baby?
What did you see, baby?
What did you—
[*sung*] Do?
Tell him we French, we get so excited
That you kinda got excited too.

---

* *Film version:*
    Helpless at tennis,

---

* *Earlier version:*
    Impossible things that I'd do.

† *Earlier version:*
    A walk on the highway of fame and glamour.

---

* *Lines in parentheses are sung in French.*

THE FRENCH, THEY GET SO EXCITED

Earlier version of "We French, We Get So Excited." From Paramount censorship file dated February 7, 1946.

VERSE

Welcome to Paree, Miss Peoria,
Welcome to Paree, Miss Fort Worth—
Welcome to the fastest town on earth!
And when I say fast
I do not mean
Those taxicabs you see.
It's the bon vivant, the gay young blade,
Who make Paree Paree.

REFRAIN 1

He greets you on the boulevard
The very day you land,
And it isn't enough you're side by side,
He's gotta be hand in hand.
For the French, they get so excited,
The French, they are so easily ignited.
Oh, the French, they get so excited,
And just so he won't create a scene,
You fall for that hand-in-hand routine.

REFRAIN 2

He walks you down the boulevard—
He swears he means no harm—
But it isn't enough you're hand in hand,
He's gotta be arm in arm.
For the French, they get so excited,
The French are friends, and they must not be
    slighted.
Oh, the French they get so excited,
So merely to satisfy his whim,
You're soon walking arm in arm with him.

REFRAIN 3

You stop along the boulevard
At Café Montparnasse,
'Cause it isn't enough you're arm in arm,
He's gotta be glass to glass.
And the French, they get so excited,
The French, they are so easily ignited.
The French, they get so excited,
And you wouldn't want to get him sore,
So you drink just one, and then one more.

REFRAIN 4

You sit there by the boulevard;
He says, "You're magnifique."
But it isn't enough you're glass to glass,
He's gotta be cheek to cheek.
Oh, the French, they get so excited;
The French go mad when love is unrequited.
Oh, the French, they get so excited,
And you feel so foolish and so gay,
So you say, in perfect French, "Okay."

REFRAIN 5

Then stars fall on the boulevard,
Your heart goes click, click, click.
It's a dangerous thing, this cheek to cheek,
You've gotta run right home quick.
But the French, they get so excited,
Oh, the French, they are so easily ignited.
Oh, the French, they get so excited
That he takes it for a sign of love
When you accidentally drop your glove.

REFRAIN 6

You hurry down the boulevard;
He follows through the throng,
'Cause it isn't enough you run home quick,
He's gotta come right along.
Now the French, they get so excited,
The French move in before they are invited.
Oh, the French, they get so excited,
And that's where he goes a bit too far,
'Cause that's where he meets your ma and pa.

And that's how you marry in the spring,
And that's when you learn one certain thing,
A thing that you maybe never knew:
That you kinda got excited too.
Yes, the French, they get so excited
That you kinda get excited too.

(I MUST HAVE BEEN) MADLY IN LOVE

Not used in film. From Paramount censorship files dated October 3, 1946, and November 12, 1946.

I guess I must have been madly in love at the time.
[spoken] Mmm.
[sung] Guess I treated my friends like they weren't
    worth a dime.

[spoken] And I don't usually act like that.
[sung] They say I couldn't be reached by phone.
I was a stranger they'd never known.
They say I brushed the old crowd
As up to my cloud I'd climb,
[spoken] Too high.

[sung] I guess I must have been madly in love with
    that kid.
[spoken] Well, I'd say he was a man about thirty.
[sung] That kid who told me he never would leave,
    but he did.
[spoken] Last night.
[sung] Oh, please forgive me, my good, good
    friends—
As of this morning the whole thing ends.
And if there's any excuse for my antisocial crime,
[spoken] Well, there just isn't any excuse.

[sung] It was weak,
It was selfish,
It was aww . . .
It was sensational.
I guess I must have been madly in love at the time.

I WANT MY MONEY BACK

Registered for copyright as an unpublished song February 16, 1948. Intended for Betty Hutton. Not used in film. A performance of the song by Betty Garrett was filmed for *Neptune's Daughter* but was not included.

VERSE 1

I've been reading all those advertisements
In the very latest magazines,
Advertisements selling poor defenseless girls
Everything from soap to artificial pearls
And claiming if they'll only take a chance,
That such-and-such a product brings romance.
In every advertisement, there's a dainty little
    miss,
And underneath her picture, the endorsement
    reads like this:

[spoken] After using Kornbloom's Kornplasters for
    three weeks, my feet felt so good that I was able
    to take my boyfriend Harry for a walk in the
    country to see my rich uncle's oil well. It was
    on that walk that he asked me to marry him.
    He said he loved me because of my healthy
    feet. Thank you, Kornbloom's Kornplasters!
    Or there's the one that goes like this: Before

taking Bull Moose Reduce Juice,* I was a big fat slob. Now, thanks to Bull Moose Reduce Juice, my boyfriend Jack says he loves me because I'm thin as a beanstalk.

[*sung*] Who are these dames, who sign their names,
To all these false and fantastic claims?
If they want a testimonial,
Why doesn't somebody ask me?
I'd tell them a thing or two—or three:

[*spoken*] Ah, ah! Smooth-o, the Lotion of Devotion.

[*sung*] I tried your famous lotion
Just to see if you were right.
I rubbed it in my fingers
Till all twelve were soft and white.
And when John held my hand,
Did he propose to me last night?
No!

REFRAIN 1

I want my money back, money back, hey!
I want my money back, money back, ho!
I want my money back
Or I'm suing the company!

I don't care what it did
For that fortunate kid
In your advertisement—
It did positively nothing for me.

I want my money back, money back, hey!
I want my money back, money back, ho!
I want my money back—

[*spoken*] Oh-oh! Glammo, the Royal Mounted Perfume. It always gets its man.

VERSE 2

[*sung*] I've used your brand of perfume
Ev'ry night throughout the year.
I never fail to put
A half a pint behind each ear.
And when he gets a whiff of me,
Does Harold say "Come here"?
No!

REFRAIN 2

I want my money back, money back, fast!
I want my money back, money back, now!
I want my money back
Or I'm suing the company!

Though your product may click
For that cute little chick
In your advertisement,
It smells—! [*grimaces as if smelling it*] Absolutely awful on me!

I want my money back, money back, fast!
I want my money back, money back, now!
I want my money back—
[*spoken*] Hmmmmmm. Hungerdunger's Cooking Academy.

VERSE 3

[*sung*] I signed up with your cooking school;
I had the cash to spare.
There's nothing like good food, you said,
To make a fellow care.
Now when the stars shine down, does he get
   [*pause*]
Hungry as a bear?
Yeah!

REFRAIN 3

I want my money back, money back, hey!
I want my money back, money back, see!
I want my money back
Or I'm suing the company!

If you taught her to fry,
And it got her a guy
In your advertisement,
How come nothing is a-cooking with me?

I tried a hunk of your junk
And found your junk was the bunk.
I took enough of your stuff
To know your stuff was a bluff.
I had a slew of your goo
And all your goo wouldn't do.
Though you claimed you had the old know-how,
I want my money back
Right now!

---

* *Originally Blue Goose Reduce Juice. Louis Lipstone, the Paramount censor, found this line "objectionable," and insisted Loesser write a replacement.*

MISCELLANEOUS SONGS OF 1947

PINDY FENDY

Written for unproduced Paramount Picture *Lady from Lariat Loop*. Lyric from undated demo recording by Lynn Loesser and an unidentified performer, who chants American Indian–style to a tom-tom accompaniment. The song starts out as a "translation" of what the "Indian" is chanting (indicated in brackets). Another Loesser song, "Batten Down Her Hatches," was written for the picture, but no lyrics or music have been found.

[*Chanting*]

He says:
A long, long time ago
There was a big chief,
And his name was Dog Eyes.
And he had a daughter,
Gosh, oh gosh, was she beautiful!
Along came a brave hunter:
[Indy Fendy] Pindy Fendy!
[Indy Fendy] Pindy Fendy!
[Indy Fendy] Pindy Fendy!
[Indy Fendy] Pindy Fendy!
That was his name.

He wanted to get married
In the very worst way,
The very worst way.
He took one look at her
And . . . [*rapid exuberant chanting*]
THAT is how he felt.

So he said to the chief's daughter,
"Chief's daughter, will you marry me?"
She said, "Get me a live eagle,
A live eagle, and then your bride I'll be."

So he went into the hills
Where the eagles liked to fly,
And for seventeen days
He kept looking at the sky.
And for seventeen nights
He kept a-climbin' up the trees,
A stubbin' at his toes
And a scrapin' on his knees.
Seventeen eagles got away,
But he tangled with one

And caught him one day.
Seventeen miles he dragged the bird.
They saw him coming down the road
And spread the word:
[Indy Fendy] Pindy Fendy!
[Indy Fendy] Pindy Fendy!
[Indy Fendy] Pindy Fendy!
[Indy Fendy] Pindy Fendy!
That was his name.

He came in draggin'
With his head bent low,
With scratches all over
From head to toe.
But the big chief's daughter
Was standin' by the door.
He gave her the bird, but she wanted more.
She said to Pindy Fendy, "Pindy Fendy,
That eagle won't do.
Bring me a live wildcat,
A live wildcat,
And then I'll marry you."

So he went into the woods
Where the wildcats roam,
And for twenty-nine days he was away from home.
And for twenty-nine nights
He kept a lookin' for the varmints,
A-bumpin' into rocks
And a-tearin' up his garments.
Twenty-nine wildcats got away,
But he found one wildcat
That happened to stray.
Well, he rassled and he rassled,
And he got that critter down,
And the people all hollered
When they dragged him into town:
[Indy Fendy] Pindy Fendy!
[Indy Fendy] Pindy Fendy!
[Indy Fendy] Pindy Fendy!
[Indy Fendy] Pindy Fendy!
Like I told you.

He came in weary and far from fit;
He couldn't find a place
Where he hadn't been bit.
To the big chief's daughter
He gave the cat,
But I guess she wanted more than that.
She said to Pindy Fendy, "Pindy Fendy,
That wildcat won't do—
Bring me a live buffalo,
A live buffalo,
And then I'll marry you."

So he went out on the plains
Where the buffalo run,
Waited forty-four days in the boiling hot sun,

Waited forty-four nights on the lone prairie,
And did you see a buffalo?
Neither did he.
Well, he ran out of food,
And the time came to pass
He had to chew roots
And he had to nibble grass.
He ran out of grass,
And he had to eat dirt;
He swallowed his moccasins for dessert.
And he waited and he waited, day and night,
Till finally a buffalo came in sight.
Well, he swung his rope around the buffalo's neck—
That's a pretty hard job for a physical wreck.
The buffalo didn't like his plan,
So he rushed right in and butted that man.
He butted him and butted him, buffalo-style,
And every time he butted him, he flew about a mile.
He butted him at day and he butted him at night,
And still Pindy Fendy held the lasso tight.
He butted him up and he butted him down,
And that's how Pindy Fendy got
Butted back to town.
The people saw him come,
Rolling through the clover,
Broken down, baggy eyes, bruises all over.
[Indy Fendy] Pindy Fendy!
[Indy Fendy] Pindy Fendy!
[Indy Fendy] Pindy Fendy!
[Indy Fendy] Pindy Fendy!
He was thinking of changing his name.

He brought the buffalo to his lady friend,
And he fell at her feet, saying, "This is the end."
And the big chief's daughter, she stood right
    there,
Stars in her eyes and braids in her hair,
And she said to all the people
As she stood there in the dawn,
"Get me a live Indian—
This one here is plum gone!"
[Indy Fendy
Indy Fendy
Indy Fendy
Indy Fendy
Indy Fendy]
Ha!

BLOOP, BLEEP!

Published. Copyrighted June 11, 1947. Leading recordings by Alvino Rey and His Orchestra, vocal by Rocky Coluccio (Capitol); Danny Kaye, accompanied by Billy May and His Orchestra (Decca); and Frank Loesser (Mercury). Another Loesser performance of this song,

from Abe Burrows's radio show, is on the compact disc *Frank Sings Loesser* (Koch). The song became a surprise hit, and received the following notice in the July 21, 1947, *Time* magazine in a brief article entitled "Drip Song":

> Seeping in from the West Coast, a jangling jingle known as "Bloop, Bleep," the song of the leaky faucet, was beginning to inundate the nation. Modeled on the ancient Chinese water torture, it had a similar effect on its hearers. Half a dozen bands had already rushed to market with recordings of it. . . . The creator of this latter day Water Music is a short, jumpy Tin Pan Alleytite named Frank Loesser, who has a remarkable talent for tunes that at first attract and then nauseate.

The Merchant Plumbers Association of Los Angeles made Loesser an honorary member "for his outstanding contribution to the plumbing industry by having composed the ode to the leaky faucet, 'Bloop, Bleep' "— quoted from certificate presented to Loesser and signed by W. H. Nothoff, president of the Merchant Plumbers Association of Los Angeles.

Bloop, bleep, bloop, bleep, bloop, bleep,
The faucet keeps a-dripping and I can't sleep.
Bleep, bloop, bleep, bloop, bleep, bloop,
I guess I never should have ordered clam soup.

Bloop, bleep, bloop, bleep, bloop, bleep,
I wonder where to go to buy a car cheap.
Bleep, bloop, bleep, bloop, bleep, bloop,
What is it with the babe next door?

What is it she does to me?
What mad kind of thrill do I find,
Looking at her walking, just walking by?
Don't know I'm alive, and she's driving me out of
    my
Bloop, bleep, bloop, bleep, bloop, bleep,
The faucet keeps a-dripping and I just can't sleep!

WHAT ARE YOU DOING NEW YEAR'S EVE

Published. Copyrighted July 11, 1947. Leading recording by Margaret Whiting (Capitol). Other recordings include Ella Fitzgerald (Verve), Mel Tormé (Musicraft), Dick Haymes (Decca), Harry Connick Jr. (Columbia), Lou Rawls (Capitol), and Steve Lawrence and Eydie Gorme (Columbia).

VERSE

When the bells all ring, and the horns all blow,
And the couples we know are fondly kissing,
Will I be with you, or will I be among the missing?

REFRAIN

Maybe it's much too early in the game,
Ah, but I thought I'd ask you just the same,
What are you doing New Year's, New Year's Eve?
Wonder whose arms will hold you good and tight
When it's exactly twelve o'clock at night,
Welcoming in the new year, New Year's Eve?
Maybe I'm crazy to suppose
I'd ever be the one you chose
Out of the thousand invitations you'll receive.
Ah, but in case I stand one little chance,
Here comes the jackpot question in advance:
What are you doing New Year's,
New Year's Eve?

KEEP YOUR EYE ON THE SKY

Registered for copyright as an unpublished song July 19, 1947.

REFRAIN

Keep your eye on the sky,
Follow the bright silver wings of the Air Force.
Keep your eye on the sky,
Never you worry, never you weep,
Never you worry, long as you keep
Them there, in the air,
Roaring a strong freedom song high above.
Keep your eye on the blue, blue sky,
Over the land you love.

INTERLUDE

Bet on the man with the brass wing and prop upon
  his collar,
Bet on the plane with the bright star agleam upon
  her wings,
Bet on the team, it's the bet that should get your
  bottom dollar,
Bet on the team that will face whatever tomorrow
  brings.

A TUNE FOR HUMMING

Published. Copyright October 20, 1947. Recorded by Eddy Howard and His Orchestra (Majestic) and Bob Houston (MGM).

This is a tune for humming

[*Hum melody.*]

Or maybe for whist'ling

[*Whistle melody.*]

But never for talking.
If you're weary of the words,
The foolish little words
You find in ev'ry song,
Look what I brought along.
Simply a tune for humming

[*Hum melody.*]

Or maybe for whist'ling.

[*Whistle melody.*]

WHERE'S
CHARLEY?
1948

WHERE'S CHARLEY?

Tryout: World premiere: Forrest Theatre, Philadelphia, September 13–October 2, 1948. New York premiere: St. James Theatre, October 11, 1948. 792 performances. London premiere: Palace Theatre, February 20, 1958. 489 performances. Musical comedy based on Brandon Thomas's play *Charley's Aunt.* New York production presented by Cy Feuer and Ernest H. Martin in association with Gwen Rickard. Book by George Abbott. Music and lyrics by Frank Loesser. Production directed by George Abbott. Dances directed by George Balanchine, assisted by Fred Danieli. Sets, lighting, and costumes by David Ffolkes. Vocal arrangements by Gerry Dolin. Orchestrations by Ted Royal, Hans Spialek, and Phil Lang. Musical director, Max Goberman. Cast starred Ray Bolger (Charley) and featured Allyn Ann (billed as Allyn) McLerie (Amy), Byron Palmer (Jack), Doretta Morrow (Kitty), Horace Cooper (Mr. Spettigue), Jane Lawrence (Donna Lucia), and Paul England (Sir Francis). Cast also included John Lynds (Brassett), Edgar Kent (Wilkinson), Jack Friend (Professor), James Lane (Photographer), Marie Foster (Patricia), and Douglas Deane (Reggie).

Loesser was originally hired to write lyrics to Harold Arlen's score. Before work on the show began, Arlen withdrew from the project. After much lobbying by director George Abbott and producer Cy Feuer, the show's star, Ray Bolger, gave his consent, and Loesser became composer and lyricist.

A film version of *Where's Charley?* was produced by Warner Bros. and released in July 1952. Music and lyrics by Frank Loesser. Screenplay by John Monks Jr., adapted from the musical play *Where's Charley?* by Frank Loesser and George Abbott. Directed by David Butler. Choreography by Michael Kidd. Cast again starred Ray Bolger and featured Allyn Ann McLerie and Horace Cooper in their original roles, along with Robert Shackleton, Mary Germaine, and Margaretta Scott.

Owing to a musicians' strike there is no cast album of the original New York production. Two recordings were made by original cast members on Decca: Ray Bolger and Allyn Ann McLerie (two-sided ten-inch 78 rpm singles). The 1958 London production cast album, with Norman Wisdom as Charley, was originally on British Columbia.

Ray Bolger and cast members of Where's Charley?
Inset: *Ray Bolger*

THE YEARS BEFORE US

Published as part of vocal score. Copyrighted July 9, 1964. Previously registered for copyright as an unpublished song July 6, 1948. Introduced by male chorus (students).

Now take my heartfelt hand clasp,
Now sigh the farewell sigh,*
And may the years before us be
As sweet as the years gone by.

In all the years before us,
Though fortune part our ways,
How fond the recollection of
These merry salad days.

[*Repeat first four lines.*]

Now join the farewell chorus,
Now drain the goblet dry,
And may the years before us be
As sweet as the years gone by.

BETTER GET OUT OF HERE

Published as part of vocal score. Copyrighted July 9, 1964. Previously registered for copyright as an unpublished song July 6, 1948. Introduced by Allyn Ann McLerie (Amy), Doretta Morrow (Kitty), Ray Bolger (Charley), and Byron Palmer (Jack).

AMY: [*spoken*] Suppose we stay?
[*sung*] Wouldn't it be daring,
And wouldn't it be fun?
KITTY: We just can't stay.
See the way they're staring—
It isn't being done.
AMY: Ah, but mine is a perfect gentleman,
And yours is the noble type.
KITTY: And for ev'ry perfect gentleman
Comes a time.
AMY: Comes a time.
KITTY: And the time—
AMY: And the time—
KITTY: May be ripe.
AMY: [*spoken*] Oh, no!

———
* *Earlier version:*
  Say the brave goodbye,

[*sung*] He wouldn't dream of trying to
kiss me—
It's not the sort of thing he has
planned.
KITTY: He wouldn't dream of trying to kiss me
Or even gently holding my hand.
BOTH: They wouldn't dream of trying to kiss us,
For after all they're civilized too.
KITTY: But Amy, just to be on the safe side—
BOTH: We'd better get out of here before
they do!

[*Dance*]

CHARLEY: Suppose they stay?
Wouldn't it be daring,
And wouldn't it be fun?
JACK: They just can't stay.
Don't be overbearing—
It isn't being done.
CHARLEY: Ah, but we're known as perfect
gentlemen,
The stiff-upper Oxford type.
JACK: And for ev'ry perfect gentleman
Comes a time.
CHARLEY: Comes a time.
JACK: And the time—
CHARLEY: And the time—
JACK: May be ripe.
CHARLEY: [*spoken*] Oh, no!
JACK: [*sung*] I wouldn't dream of trying to
kiss her,
There's nothing more remote from my
mind.
CHARLEY: I wouldn't dream of closing that door
there;
I wouldn't dream of drawing that blind.
BOTH: We wouldn't dream of trying to kiss
them,
For after all we're civilized too.
But just to be a bit on the safe side,
They'd better get out of here before
we do!

[*Dance*]

AMY: He wouldn't dream of singing those
rude songs,
The sort of things all college boys chant.
KITTY: He wouldn't dream of telling me stories
That he could not repeat to his aunt.
BOTH: They wouldn't dream of even suggesting
That we should have a brandy or two.
KITTY: But Amy, just to be on the safe side—
BOTH: We'd better get out of here before
they do!

[*Dance*]

137

BOTH: They wouldn't dream of trying to kiss us,
For after all they're civilized too.
KITTY: But Amy, just to be on the safe side—
AMY: [*spoken*] Come along.

Unused introduction

AMY: It strikes me that he likes me,
That he likes me rather well.
And here we are alone
Without the chaperone,
But he's a gentleman, I can tell.
KITTY: It strikes me that he likes me
That he likes me very much.
And here we are alone
Without the chaperone—
I'm sure he knows that we mustn't touch.
AMY: And though he might be on the very brink,
he wouldn't—
KITTY: At least, I very confidently think he
wouldn't—

THE NEW ASHMOLEAN MARCHING SOCIETY AND STUDENTS' CONSERVATORY BAND

Published. Copyrighted May 4, 1950. Published as part of vocal score. Copyrighted July 9, 1964. Previously registered for copyright as an unpublished song August 23, 1948. Introduced by Byron Palmer (Jack), Doretta Morrow (Kitty), Allyn Ann McLerie (Amy), Bobby Harrell, and ensemble (students and young ladies). Recorded by Johnny Mercer (Capitol), Bing Crosby (RCA Victor), and the Modernaires (Decca), among others.

JACK: Here they come with the sunlight on
the trumpets,
Here they come with the banners
flying high.
KITTY: In my throat I've a lumpy sort of
feeling.
AMY: And the bright gleam of pride is in
my eye.
Here they come with the clarinets
a-wailing,
Here they come rather bravely up the
square.
CHORUS: And I know in a moment I'll be
cheering
And my best Sunday hat will be high
in the air

For the New Ashmolean Marching
Society and Students' Conservatory
Band.
Yes, the New Ashmolean could have
whipped Napoleon,
With all those deadly instruments in
hand.
JACK: There are those who favor the
philharmonic flavor,
But to me the finest in the land—
CHORUS: Is the New Ashmolean Marching
Society and Students' Conservatory
Band.

JACK: Though they march only slightly out
of tempo—
1ST MAN: Though they play just a trifle out of
tune—
GIRLS: Though there's just a suggestion in
the oboe
Of the sound of a hound beneath the
moon—
CHORUS: Though the trombone's a little
independent
And the drummer is not exactly
choice,
Still the old college spirit is upon me
And I shout ev'ry time at the top of
my voice

For the New Ashmolean Marching
Society and Students' Conservatory
Band.
If you're analytical, sensitive, or
critical,
You'll like it more the farther back you
stand.
JACK: But to me it's bully, it satisfies me
fully,
When I hear that thunder close at
hand—
CHORUS: From the New Ashmolean Marching
Society and Students' Conservatory
Band.

[*Dance*]

ENSEMBLE: [*spoken*] By George—
[*sung*] What a band!

Unused lyrics

Here he comes with his mighty, mighty tuba,
Here he comes like a badly wounded steer,
And the old college spirit is upon me,
And I shout and I cheer as he brings up the rear
For the New Ashmolean Marching Society and
Students' Conservatory Band.

Let the tuba blast a piece
Of some classical masterpiece,
And watch this loyal chest of mine expand.
And though Bach and Handel
Might call the man a vandal,
It's a tune that I can understand
By the New Ashmolean Marching Society and
Students' Conservatory Band.

MY DARLING, MY DARLING

Published. Copyrighted September 7, 1948. Published as part of vocal score. Copyrighted July 9, 1964. Previously registered for copyright as an unpublished song July 6, 1948. Introduced by Byron Palmer (Jack) and Doretta Morrow (Kitty). The top recording, number one on the popular music charts, was by Jo Stafford and Gordon MacRae with the Starlighters (Capitol). Other leading recordings were by Doris Day and Buddy Clark (Columbia), Peter Lind Hayes with the Stardusters (Decca), and Sarah Vaughan (Mercury).

JACK: Till a moment ago we were "Mister" and
"Miss,"
Discussing the weather, avoiding each
other's eye,
Till a moment ago when we happened to
kiss,
And we kissed the "Mister" and "Miss"
goodbye.
Now at last I can sigh—

My darling, my darling,
I've wanted to call you my darling
For many and many a day.
My darling, my darling,
I fluttered and fled like a starling,
My courage just melted away.
Now all at once you've kissed me
And there's not a thing I'm sane enough
to say
Except my darling, my darling,
Get used to that name of my darling,
It's here to stay.

KITTY: Till a moment ago we were "Kitty" and
"Jack,"
So distant, so proper, the meaningless
repartee.
But a moment ago I was taken aback
When you swept the "Kitty" and "Jack"
away.
In reply, let me say:

My darling, my darling,
I've wanted to call you my darling
For many and many a day.
My darling, my darling,
I fluttered and fled like a starling,
My courage just melted away.
Now all at once you've kissed me
And there's not a thing I'm sane enough
    to say,
Except my darling, my darling,
Get used to that name of my darling,
It's here to stay.

MAKE A MIRACLE

Published. Copyrighted March 30, 1949. Published as part of vocal score. Copyrighted July 9, 1964. Previously registered for copyright as unpublished song July 6, 1948, under the title "Someday." Introduced by Allyn Ann McLerie (Amy) and Ray Bolger (Charley). Recorded by Ray Bolger and Allyn Ann McLerie (Decca) and Frank and Lynn Loesser (Mercury). A private recording by Frank and Lynn Loesser is on the compact disc *Frank Sings Loesser* (Koch).

AMY: Our future will be marvelously exciting.
CHARLEY: [*spoken*] Exciting!
AMY: [*sung*] For progress is a thing there's no use fighting.
CHARLEY: [*spoken*] Progress!
AMY: [*sung*] They say it will seem like emerging into the light
From a dismal penitentiary.
CHARLEY: [*spoken*] What are you talking about?
AMY: [*spoken*] The twentieth century!
CHARLEY: [*spoken*] Amy, don't change the subject!
AMY: [*sung*] I've just read a book on what's to be expected—
They'll have wireless telegraphy perfected,
Electric lights and fountain pens,
And machines by which a lie can be detected!
CHARLEY: [*spoken*] Amy, what about us?
AMY: [*sung*] Horseless carriages on the road,
Breakfast cereals that explode—
CHARLEY: [*spoken*] Yes, I know, I know, I know, I know, I know.

[*sung*] Someday they'll have horseless carriages that fly.
AMY: Horseless carriages that fly.

CHARLEY: Horseless carriages and someday
They'll be roaring all about the sky.
AMY: Spelling out slogans—"Buy a beer at Hogan's."
CHARLEY: But who knows when that age of miracles will come to be?
So meanwhile, darling, make a miracle and marry me.
AMY: Horseless carriages! I can't believe it— no, I can't.
CHARLEY: Someday they'll have stereopticons that move—
AMY: Stereopticons that move.
CHARLEY: Stereopticons appearing in cathedrals larger than the Louvre.
AMY: How romantic!
CHARLEY: Colossal!
AMY: Gigantic!
CHARLEY: But who knows when that great, great cultural event will shine?
So, meanwhile, darling, make a miracle and say you're mine.
AMY: Stereopticons! I can't believe it—no, I can't.

CHARLEY: And I will see the wonders of the future in your eyes,
Brightly gleaming,
Wonders that I challenge modern science to devise.
Oh yes, I know that
Someday, after we've grown very, very old—
AMY: Oh, so very, very old!
CHARLEY: Old enough to bury,
Someone, rather bright, will cure the common cold.
AMY: Not the British! [*sniff*] Never the British!
CHARLEY: And someday just a small white pill will feed a family.
But meanwhile, let's have steak and kidney pie,
And meanwhile—
AMY: [*spoken*] What a future!
CHARLEY: [*sung*] Let's be sure our feet are dry,
And meanwhile—
AMY: [*spoken*] What a future!
CHARLEY: [*sung*] Darling, make a miracle and marry me.
AMY: Horseless carriages! I can't believe it, no, I—
Stereopticons! I can't believe it, no, I—

CHARLEY: [*spoken*] Someday—
[*sung*] They'll be wearing skirts way up to here.
AMY: [*spoken*] Daring skirts way up to here.

CHARLEY: [*sung*] Wearing skirts way up to—
Someday, with a neckline equally sincere.
AMY: Ah, the future, to peer into the future!
CHARLEY: A vision that, alas, I may not be alive to see—
So meanwhile, darling, make a miracle and marry me.
AMY: Wearing skirts way up to—can't believe it—no, I can't.
CHARLEY: Someday life will be one sweet domestic dream.
AMY: Be one sweet domestic dream.
CHARLEY: On that sweet domestic,
Someday, they'll be heating cottages with steam.
AMY: Not the British! [*sniff*]
CHARLEY: Never the British!
AMY: Never the British!
CHARLEY: But somehow, can't you warm this heart
Until that dream comes true?
Yes, meanwhile, darling, make a miracle and say "I do."
AMY: Heating cottages! I can't believe it—no, I can't.

CHARLEY: And I will see the wonders of the future in your eyes,
Brightly gleaming,
Wonders that I challenge modern science to devise.
Oh yes, I know that
Someday, when your mind keeps harboring a grouch—
AMY: Ouch!
CHARLEY: Someday Doctor Bones will place you on a couch
And listen to your sad, sad story for a handsome fee.
But meanwhile, let's get one big Morris chair,
And meanwhile—
AMY: [*spoken*] What a future!
CHARLEY: [*sung*] Tell me all your troubles there—
And meanwhile—
AMY: [*spoken*] What a future!
CHARLEY: [*sung*] Darling, make a miracle and marry me.
AMY: Stereopticons! I can't believe it— No, I can't believe it.
CHARLEY: Marry me.
AMY: No, I—
Heating cottages! I can't believe it, No, I—
Wearing skirts way up to—
CHARLEY: [*spoken*] Marry me.

SERENADE WITH ASIDES

Published as part of vocal score. Copyrighted July 9, 1964. Previously registered for copyright as an unpublished song July 6, 1948. Introduced by Horace Cooper (Mr. Spettigue).

If there's one thing that I hate,
It's the thought of acquiring a mate.
Especially one with a face like a hatchet,
A voice like a duck, and a figure to match it!

Short of sight and long of tooth,
With a walk that's decidedly funny—
And yet, and yet,
If there's one thing I love, it's money!
And since she has oh so much of it,
I'm all for the golden touch of it.*

Lucia, Lucia,
You stand at your window and smile.
Lucia, Lucia,
Oh, please ask me in for a while.
Lucia, Lucia,
Tonight to your side I must dash,
To be close to the warmth of your lips and your
    arms
[spoken] And your cool twenty million in cash!
[sung] Lucia, Lucia,
Oh, precious one, show me a sign
That you're willing to make my life thrilling.

LOVELIER THAN EVER

Published. Copyrighted November 17, 1948. Published as part of vocal score. Copyrighted July 9, 1964. Previously registered for copyright as an unpublished song August 13, 1948. Introduced by Paul England (Sir Francis) and Jane Lawrence (Donna Lucia) with ensemble. Recordings include the Ray Charles Singers (MGM) and Mal Fitch (Mercury).

SIR FRANCIS: 'Twas a bright blue sky
    And a lark sang high
    On a bough that was blossom-laden,
    And I had my eye on a certain
        pretty maiden.
DONNA LUCIA: 'Twas a perfect day

_____
* Alternate version:
    I'm off for the golden touch of it.

In the month of May
And the sun was a blazing yellow,
And I had my eye on a certain
    handsome fellow.
SIR FRANCIS: The lady they call Springtime
    All but swept me off my feet.
DONNA LUCIA: She filled my heart with promises
    Extravagant and sweet.
BOTH: And now, again, we meet.
SIR FRANCIS: [spoken] She hasn't changed a bit.
DONNA LUCIA: [spoken] I don't know how she
    manages it.

[sung] Springtime,
You're looking lovelier than ever,
Lovelier than ever before,
Still irresistible in the same old
    gown of green,
Still irresistible as that lilac-scented
    scene
When I was seventeen.
Springtime,
You haven't changed your way of
    whisp'ring,
Whisp'ring that romance lies in
    store.
Springtime,
You're being devastatingly clever
And lovelier than ever before.

SIR FRANCIS: Springtime,
    You're looking lovelier than ever—
SIR FRANCIS
AND CHORUS: Lovelier than ever before,
    Still irresistible in the same old
        gown of green,
    Still irresistible as that lilac-scented
        scene—
DONNA LUCIA: When—
DONNA LUCIA
AND WOMEN: —I was seventeen.
ALL: Springtime,
    You haven't changed your way of
        whisp'ring,
    Whisp'ring that romance lies in
        store.
DONNA LUCIA: Springtime,
ALL: You're being devastatingly clever
    And lovelier than ever before.
BOTH: Springtime,
    You're being devastatingly clever
    And lovelier than ever before.

THE WOMAN IN HIS ROOM

Published as part of vocal score. Copyrighted July 9, 1964. Previously registered for copyright as an unpublished song July 6, 1948. Introduced by Allyn Ann McLerie (Amy).

Charley's a nice boy, a dear boy,
A sweet boy, a fine boy,
A good boy, through and through.

Charley's a nice boy, a sweet boy,
A fine boy, a good boy,
So loyal and so true.

I am his one girl, the one girl,
The one girl, the one girl,
No other can replace.

So when my Charley's far from me,
I'm content as I can be
Just to close my eyes
And picture his face
And picture his face
And picture—
[spoken] Picture!

[sung] That picture, that picture,
That picture of that woman,
That picture of that woman
On the piano in his room!

That picture, that picture,
That picture of that woman
Wearing tights
And a vulgar ostrich plume!

That woman, that woman,
That hussy of a woman,
That woman in the picture,
That woman in his room!
Oh, the shock of it,
A woman in his room!

That woman, that woman,
I wonder if he's kissed her,
I wonder if he's kissed her?
[spoken] Of course, of course I'm such a fool.
[sung] She's probably his sister,
Just a photograph taken at a masquerade—
What a terrible, terrible mistake I've made!

Charley's a nice boy, a dear boy,
A sweet boy, a fine boy,
A good boy, through and through.

Charley's a nice boy, a sweet boy,
A fine boy, a good boy,
So loyal and so true.

I am his one girl, the one girl,
The one girl, the one girl
No other can replace.

[spoken] No other living relative—
That's exactly what he said.
No other living relative, except his aunt!
[sung] For all the rest are dead!
[spoken] He has no sister!
Then exactly who is
[sung] That woman, that woman,
That woman in the picture,
That woman in the picture
On the piano in his room?

That woman, that woman,
That woman who, I have no doubt,
Is drenched in a hideous French perfume!

That woman, that woman,
That gaudy, bawdy Venus,
That woman's come between us,
That woman in his room.

Oh, the gall of him!
A woman in his room!
That woman, that woman,
For this he'll have to answer,
For this he'll have to answer.

[spoken] Oh, why am I so suspicious?
[sung] She's probably some dancer,
Just a lady my Charley doesn't even know.
Just the cover of the program
Of some London show.

Charley's a nice boy, a dear boy,
A sweet boy, a fine boy,
A good boy, through and through.

I shall be patiently waiting
When Charley returns from that urgent
Rendezvous.
[spoken] A French word.
I've seen it in a novel.
Rendezvous—meaning—
[sung] That woman, that woman,
I know he's with that woman,
I'm sure he's with that woman
On the piano in his room.
That woman, that woman,
That monster of a woman
Cast a spell over my intended groom.

It's ended, all ended—
They're up there sweetly sighing,
And I thought love undying
Had just begun to bloom.
Oh, the shame of it!
A woman in his room!

PERNAMBUCO

Published. Copyrighted September 7, 1948. Published as part of vocal score. Copyrighted July 9, 1964. Previously registered for copyright as an unpublished song July 13, 1948. Introduced by Ray Bolger (Charley), Allyn Ann McLerie (Amy), and chorus ("Pernambucans"). Recorded by the Four Lads (Columbia).

WOMEN: Pernambuco—
MEN: Pernambuco—
ALL: Unbelievable town,
Where the crops go to seed
And the bank is in need of financing,
Still the people keep dancing.

WOMEN: Pernambuco—
MEN: Pernambuco—
ALL: Unbelievable town,
Where the farmers all play the guitar
And they're perfectly charming,
But there's nobody farming.

The starlight is in their eyes
And blossoms are in their hair
And this tune's ev'rywhere.

Pernambuco,
Unbelievable town,
Where they hum and they strum
And they drum till the feeling is frantic
By the shiny Atlantic.

Where they hum and they strum
And they drum till the feeling is frantic,
And they call it romantic,
And so do I.

[Dance]

WHERE'S CHARLEY?

Published. Copyrighted September 7, 1948. Published as part of vocal score. Copyrighted July 9, 1964. Previously registered for copyright as an unpublished song July 6, 1948. Introduced by Byron Palmer (Jack), Cornell McNeil, Stowe Phelps, and other members of the ensemble. Recorded by the Four Lads (Columbia).

1ST BOY: Where's Charley?
2ND BOY: How's Charley?
3RD BOY: Why did he ever roam?
ENSEMBLE: Where's Charley?
How's Charley?
When's Charley coming home?
JACK: From this most auspicious day,
Gentlemen, we embark
On the stormy sea of life to voyage,
Each of us determined to make his mark.
Strong and upright,
Stalwart men and true,
The glorious class of ninety-two!
CHORUS: [spoken] Hip, hip, hooray!
Hip, hip, hooray!
Hip, hip, hooray!
4TH BOY: [sung] They will say of Freddie Smith,
"There goes the great tycoon."
They'll be writing odes in praise of
Humbolt,
Governor Gen'ral of Rangoon.
Twombley will be the subject of a play.
As for Wykeham, they merely say—

ENSEMBLE: Where's Charley? How's Charley?
When's Charley coming home?
Where's Charley? How's Charley?
Why did he ever roam—
JACK: From a life so lovely?
ENSEMBLE: Does Charley
Still nip the barley?
How many beaches can he comb?
Where's Charley? How's Charley?
When's Charley coming?
When's Charley coming?
When's Charley coming home?
3RD BOY: I can see his anxious bride,
Poor little darling dear.
I can see her waiting at the altar,
Waiting for our boy to appear.
I can hear each wedding guest point out
The usual state of doubt.

ENSEMBLE: Where's Charley? How's Charley?
When's Charley coming home?*
Where's Charley? How's Charley?
Why did he ever roam†
From a life so lovely?
Where is it
He goes to visit?
Hong Kong, Baluchistan, or Nome?
Where's Charley? How's Charley?
When's Charley coming?
When's Charley coming?
When's Charley coming home?

Where's Charley? How's Charley?
When's Charley coming home?
Where's Charley? How's Charley?
Why did he ever roam
From a life so lovely?
Does Charley
Still nip the barley?
How many beaches can he comb?

Where's Charley? How's Charley?
When's Charley coming,
When's Charley coming,
When's Charley coming home?
Where's Charley? How's Charley?
When's Charley coming?
When's Charley coming?
When's Charley coming . . . home?

Additional verse in sheet music

I can see his vacant cage
Down at the Bankers Trust.
I can see his desk piled high with papers,
Papers that are gathering dust.
I can hear each fellow employee
As usual asking me—

Unused refrain

Where's Charley? How's Charley?
Why did he ever roam
From a girl so pretty?
Where is he? Who keeps him busy
Just as the gloaming stands to gloam?
Where's Charley? How's Charley?
When's Charley coming?
When's Charley coming?
When's Charley coming home?

---

* *Earlier version:*
  When's Charley coming back?

† *Earlier version:*
  What made him jump the track

ONCE IN LOVE WITH AMY

Published. Copyrighted September 27, 1948. Published as part of vocal score. Copyrighted July 9, 1964. Previously registered for copyright as unpublished song July 6, 1948. Introduced by Ray Bolger (Charley). Recordings by Frank Sinatra (Capitol), Ray Bolger (Decca), and Perry Como (RCA Victor), among others. A private recording by Frank Loesser is on the compact disc *Frank Sings Loesser* (Koch).

As Susan Loesser recalled, the song was actually written six years earlier when Frank Loesser, Peter Lind Hayes, and Hayes's wife, Mary Healy, were working for the Army's Radio Productions Unit in California:

> Always an early riser, he [Loesser] would already be pounding away on the muted keyboard when Mary came downstairs at 6:00 a.m. She would bring him coffee, which he appreciated so much that he wrote a song for her: "Once in Love with Mary." Six years later it became Ray Bolger's show-stopper.

I caught you, sir,
Having a look at her
As she went strolling by.
Now, didn't your heart go
Boom, boom, boom, boom, boom?
Now, didn't you sigh a sigh?

I warn you, sir,
Don't start to dream of her,
Just bid such thoughts be gone,
Or it will be boom, boom,
Boom, boom, boom, boom, boom,
Boom, boom, boom, boom
From then on—

For once in love with Amy,
Always in love with Amy,
Ever and ever fascinated by her,
Sets your heart afire to stay.
Once you're kissed by Amy,
Tear up your list, it's Amy,
Ply her with bonbons, poetry, and flowers,*
Moon a million hours away.

You might be quite the fickle-hearted rover,
So carefree and bold,
Who loves a girl and later thinks it over†
And just quits cold.

---

* *Earlier version:*
  Slick down your hair and send the lady flowers,

† *Earlier version:*
  Who tells himself it's over, and it's over

Ah, but once in love with Amy,
Always in love with Amy.
Ever and ever
Sweetly you'll romance her.
Trouble is, the answer will be
[*spoken*] Ha, ha, ha, ha,
[*sung*] That Amy'd rather stay in love with me!

THE GOSSIPS

Published as part of vocal score. Copyrighted July 9, 1964. Previously registered for copyright as an unpublished song October 19, 1948. Introduced by female ensemble members Jane Judge, Marie Foster, Rae Abruzzo, Betty Oakes, Katherine Reeves, Gloria Sullivan, Eleanor Parker, Mary Alice Bingham, Irene Weston, Ruth McVane, and Geraldine Delaney.

1ST GIRL: A pity.
2ND GIRL: A pity.
1ST GIRL: Poor Amy.
2ND GIRL: Poor Kitty.
1ST GIRL: But of course you've all heard?
OTHERS: No, tell us, tell us, tell us.
1ST GIRL: No, I promised I'd never breathe a word.
OTHERS: [*spoken*] Oh!
1ST GIRL: [*spoken*] However—
[*sung*] It seems that two young ladies
Went visiting two chaps.
OTHERS: Went visiting two chaps!
1ST GIRL: Went visiting perhaps.
2ND GIRL: Behaving in a manner
That can hardly be ondoned—
Unchaperoned!
OTHERS: [*spoken*] Oh!
2ND GIRL: Unchaperoned!
1ST GIRL: Unchaperoned!
2ND GIRL: Unchaperoned!
1ST GIRL: Unchaperoned!
2ND GIRL: Unchaperoned!
1ST GIRL: Unchaperoned!
2ND GIRL: Unchaperoned!
OTHERS: [*spoken*] What a shame. Would you imagine it in all your life of those well-brought-up girls?!
1ST GIRL: [*spoken*] And suddenly—

[*sung*] Old Spettigue, their guardian,
Arrived upon the scene—
OTHERS: Arrived upon the scene!
1ST GIRL: So crafty and so mean!
2ND GIRL: But standing there to greet him

Like a potted rubber plant—
OTHERS: Who?
2ND GIRL: Charley's aunt!
1ST GIRL: Who's Charley's aunt?
2ND GIRL: Who's Charley's aunt?
1ST GIRL: Who's Charley's aunt?
2ND GIRL: Who's Charley's aunt?
1ST GIRL: Who's Charley's aunt?
2ND GIRL: Who's Charley's aunt?
OTHERS: [spoken] I don't know. I never heard of
her in all my life. I wonder who she
means.
3RD GIRL: [spoken] I know! I know!

[sung] It's Charley Wykeham's aunt,
Lucia,
Slightly off her track.
Those chaps the girls went visiting
today
Were Charley and Jack!
OTHERS: Oh, tell us, tell us, tell us!
3RD GIRL: No, I swore that my silence wouldn't
crack.
[spoken] Oh, well.
[sung] Charley Wykeham's aunt was
there
To act as chaperone,
But somehow she went wandering
away
And left them alone.
2ND GIRL: I know, I know, I saw him, I saw
him—
OTHERS: [spoken] Who?
2ND GIRL: [sung] Spettigue!
OTHERS: Spettigue? Where?
2ND GIRL: Under the window, singing.
OTHERS: Singing?

2ND GIRL: "Lucia, Lucia,
You stand at your window and smile,
Lucia, Lucia,
Oh, please ask me in for a while.
Lucia, Lucia."
4TH AND
5TH GIRLS: We saw Jack proposing to Kitty!
OTHERS: They saw Jack proposing to Kitty.
What did he say to her?
What did she answer?

4TH AND
5TH GIRLS: "My darling, my darling,
I fluttered and fled like a starling,
My courage just melted away."
6TH GIRL: [spoken] I remember now!
OTHERS: [spoken] What?
6TH GIRL: [spoken] Just this afternoon
[sung] We heard Charley—

OTHERS: [spoken] Charley?
6TH GIRL: [sung] Saying this to Amy:

"Marry me—"
7TH GIRL: "Make a miracle—I—"
6TH GIRL: "Marry me—"
7TH GIRL: "Horseless carriages, I—"
6TH GIRL: "Marry me—"
7TH GIRL: "Can't believe it, no, I—"
6TH GIRL: "Marry me—"
7TH GIRL: "Stereopticons, I—"
6TH GIRL: "Marry me—"
7TH GIRL: "Heating cottages, I—"
6TH GIRL: "Marry me—"
7TH GIRL: Can't believe it.
1ST GIRL: A pity, a pity,
2ND GIRL: Poor Amy, poor Kitty,
But of course you've all heard—
OTHERS: No, tell us, tell us, tell us!
2ND GIRL: [spoken] Well,
[sung] I promised I'd never say a
word.
OTHERS: [spoken] Oh!
2ND GIRL: [spoken] Well, it's old Spettigue—

[sung] He'll never let them marry,
Their money's in his hands.
OTHERS: Their money's in his hands.
2ND GIRL: And that's the way it stands:
He loses all their money
If they take the marriage vow.
OTHERS: [spoken] Shh!
[sung] Here they come,
Here they come.
Shh!
Here they come now!

AT THE RED ROSE COTILLION

Published as part of vocal score. Copyrighted July 9,
1964. Previously registered for copyright as unpublished
song July 13, 1948. Introduced by Byron Palmer (Jack),
Doretta Morrow (Kitty), and ensemble (Guests). Danced
by Ray Bolger (Charley) and Allyn Ann McLerie (Amy).

When they see me waltzing with you
At the Red Rose Cotillion,
They will know the bouquet that you're wearing
Means you care and you'll never stop caring.
When they see me waltzing with you
On the moon-bright pavilion,

There'll be hearts full of envy about you,
But they'll just have to live life without you—
For I'll not let you out of my sight*
At the Red Rose Cotillion tonight.

CUT AND UNUSED SONGS

CULTURE AND BREEDING

Dropped prior to New York opening. Earlier title: "The
Argument." Introduced in Act I, scene 1, following
"Better Get Out of Here," by Ray Bolger (Charley play-
ing his aunt) and Horace Cooper (Mr. Spettigue).

AUNT: When I was a girl, as most women are,
Especially when they're aged three,
I very distinctly remember
My mother explaining to me
That a man of culture and breeding
May be tall or short or slim or fat,
But a man of culture and breeding
Always removes his hat.
Take off that hat!
Take off that hat!
SPETTIGUE: Don't shout like that.
AUNT: Do as you're told.
SPETTIGUE: I've a cold.
AUNT: Take it off.
SPETTIGUE: I've a cough.
AUNT: You may sneeze, you may wheeze,
You may choke if you please,
But as long as you're here for a chat—
SPETTIGUE: You old bat.
AUNT: Take off your hat!

When I was a child, as most people
are,
Especially when they're quite young,
How well I recall the polite little
notions
To which Mother clung,
That a man of culture and breeding
May be old or young or strong or
weak,

_____
*Earlier version:
For I promise I'll cling to you tight

But a man of culture and breeding
Rises when ladies speak.
Out of that chair!
Out of that chair!
SPETTIGUE: This is unfair.
AUNT: Stand when I speak.
SPETTIGUE: I'm feeling weak.
AUNT: Straighten out.
SPETTIGUE: I've the gout.
AUNT: I don't burn with concern
That your stomach may turn
Or your spine is in need of repose.
SPETTIGUE: You're no rose.
AUNT: Up on your toes!

When I was a babe, as most babies are,
Especially when they're just born,
I still recollect the wise words of my
    mother,
Who told me one morn
That a man of culture and breeding
May be ill or well or rich or broke,
But a man of culture and breeding
Asks if he please may smoke.
Drop that cigar!
SPETTIGUE: Don't go too far.
AUNT: Instantly cease.
SPETTIGUE: Thruppence apiece.
AUNT: What a stench!
SPETTIGUE: You old wench!
AUNT: Shall I try to reply
Or just spit in his eye,
Or perhaps a demure upper cut?
SPETTIGUE: You old slut!
AUNT: Put out that butt!
Take off that hat!
SPETTIGUE: Don't shout like that.
AUNT: Do as you're told.
SPETTIGUE: I've a cold.
AUNT: Take it off.
SPETTIGUE: I've a terrible cough.
AUNT: Out of that chair!
SPETTIGUE: This is unfair.
AUNT: Stand when I speak.
SPETTIGUE: I'm feeling weak.
AUNT: Straighten out.
SPETTIGUE: I've terrible gout.
AUNT: Drop that cigar!
MAN: Don't go too far.
AUNT: Instantly cease.
SPETTIGUE: Thruppence apiece.
AUNT: What a smell!
SPETTIGUE: Go to hell!
AUNT: So to hell!

SAUNTER AWAY

Registered for copyright as an unpublished song July 6, 1948. Dropped during pre-Broadway tryout prior to New York opening. Introduced by Paul England (Sir Francis) and Jane Lawrence (Donna Lucia) in Act II, following "The Gossips," in a scene deleted from the show.

We'll be so poor,
Poor but so proud,
No one'll know as we saunter through the crowd,
No one'll know there's a dark, dark cloud.

We'll saunter by the elegant inns
And look at their food and wipe our chins,
Saunter by the elegant inns
And sniff at the mutton they're carving,
And saunter away, fiddle-de-day,
And no one'll know that we're starving.

We'll saunter into gentlemen's shops
And pick at cravats and riding crops,
Saunter into gentlemen's shops
And keep our manner convincing,
And saunter away, fiddle-de-day,
And no one will know how we're wincing.

We'll saunter past the opera house,
The opening night of *Fledermaus*,
Saunter past the opera house
And learn if they liked it or hissed it,
And saunter away, fiddle-de-day,
And no one'll know that we missed it.

We'll saunter through the beautiful parks,
A couple of merry meadowlarks,
Saunter through the beautiful parks,
For buttonhole flowers are cheap there,
And saunter away, fiddle-de-day,
And no one'll know that we sleep there.

No one'll know.
No one'll know.
No one'll know as we saunter and we grin,
No one'll know what a fix we're in.

We'll saunter by the best of hotels;
We'll order a suite and ring some bells—
Saunter by the best of hotels
And trot our imperious tone out,
And saunter away, fiddle-de-day,
And no one'll know we'd been thrown out.

We'll saunter by the bar of a pub
And linger and let our elbows rub,
Saunter by the bar of a pub

And chat with the manager's daughter,
And stagger away, fiddle-de-day,
And no one'll know it was water.

We'll saunter through a masquerade ball
And capture the prize as Best of All,
Saunter through a masquerade ball
All ragged and weary and drooling,
And saunter away, fiddle-de-day,
And no one'll know we weren't fooling.

We'll saunter past the frivolous girls
And look at their curly, curly curls,
Saunter past the frivolous girls
And never admit they're enchanting,
And saunter away, fiddle-de-day,
And no one'll know how we're panting.

No one'll know,
No one'll know,
No one'll know as we saunter fit and fine,
No one'll know how our trousers shine.

Alternate first verse

We'll saunter by the elegant inns
And jig to their distant violins;
We'll saunter by the elegant inns
And envy the wealthy a-sleeping,
And saunter away, fiddle-de-day,
And hide that inside we are weeping.

Verses cut prior to production

We'll saunter by the Buckingham wall
Whenever they hold a royal ball,
Saunter by the Buckingham wall
And mingle among the invited,
And saunter away, fiddle-de-day,
And no one will know we were slighted.

We'll saunter over meadow and lane
And scoff at the toff who rides a train;
"We're nature lovers," we will explain,
"And few are the carriages we take,"
And saunter away, fiddle-de-day,
And no one will know how our feet ache.

We'll saunter by the gentlemen's clubs,
Returning their gentlemanly snubs;
We'll saunter by the gentlemen's clubs
For seventy freezing Novembers,
And saunter away, fiddle-de-day,
And no one will know we're not members.

YOUR OWN COLLEGE BAND

Registered for copyright as an unpublished song July 6, 1948. Replaced prior to production by "The New Ashmolean Marching Society and Students' Conservatory Band."

When it's your own college band,
Isn't it great, isn't it grand?
What if they play far from sweet?
There is a chill, thrill down to your feet.
And as they march round the square,
There goes your hat, high in the air.
The godforsaken battery of trumpets
Should evermore be stuffed to the brim with
    crumpets.*
But isn't it great, isn't it grand
When it's your own college band?

On Friday night you venture forth
To hear a symphony play,
And then you come away
With highly critical,
Analytical
Things to say:

"The interpretation wasn't quite inspired;
The performance left a lot to be desired.
The second movement could stand improvement,
And it hurt so
To hear the scherzo
Done dirt so
By the percussion,
Which was just a bit too vehemently—Russian!"

---

* *Alternate version of lines 7–8:*
    The tuba player, blowing solemn strains out,
    Would bless the music world if he blew his brains
        out.

On Tuesday night you go to hear
A chamber music soiree.
Again you come away
With highly critical,
Analytical
Things to say.
You're a perfectionist of classical persuasion.
Yes, except on one particular occasion—

When it's your own college band,
Isn't it great, isn't it grand?
What if they flat ev'ry note—
Feel the immense, tense
Lump in your throat?
And as they come marching by,
There is a proud gleam in your eye.
The dismal din of drum and cymbal crashes
Might just as well be somebody hauling ashes.
But isn't it great, isn't it grand?
When it's your own college band?

THE TRAIN THAT BROUGHT YOU TO TOWN

Unused. Registered for copyrighted as an unpublished song July 6, 1948.

VERSE

Here's to Donna Lucia d'Alvadorez,
Gracious lady, you've come to save the day!
But while I'm saluting you,
May I please include a few
Of the noble men who sped you on your way?

REFRAIN

They ought to strike off a shiny, shiny medal,
A medal for the engineer.
They ought to carve out the conductor's name
In eternal marble for the hall of fame.
They ought to pension and honorably mention
That porter Ambercrombie Brown,
Of the train, the train, the holiday train,
The train that brought you to town.

DON'T INTRODUCE ME TO THAT ANGEL

Unused. Registered for copyrighted as an unpublished song July 6, 1948. Later used with slight lyric changes as "Jenny Kissed Me" in the 1974 London stage production *Hans Andersen*, which was an adaptation of the film *Hans Christian Andersen*.

Don't introduce me to that angel,
To that angel over there.
Why tempt my heart? She's much too divine.
Why let it start? She'd never be mine.
To know her and hopelessly to need her
Would be more than I could bear.
So don't introduce me to that angel,
To that angel over there.

Songs of
1948 – 1950

ON OUR MERRY WAY

Produced by Benedict Bogeaus and Burgess Meredith for United Artists. Released in June 1948. Directed by King Vidor and Leslie Fenton. Screenplay by Laurence Stallings and Lou Breslow, based on a story by Arch Oboler and John O'Hara. Cast starred Paulette Goddard, Burgess Meredith, James Stewart, Henry Fonda, Harry James, Dorothy Lamour, Victor Moore, and Fred MacMurray. Earlier title: *A Miracle Can Happen*.

THE QUEEN OF THE HOLLYWOOD ISLANDS

Published. Copyrighted February 13, 1948. Introduced by Dorothy Lamour.

LAMOUR: She was born in New Orleans,
Ran an elevator in Chicago,
But she got to California somehow.
So farewell to New Orleans
And goodbye to Chicago,
'Cause look what she's a native of now.

She's the Queen of the Hollywood Islands
Since they photographed her wearing a sarong.
She's never even seen Tahiti,
Still she's the big Tahitian sweetie
From wearing her shirt short and her lashes long.

She's the star of those tropical pictures,
And she's strictly for the monkeys when she smiles.
She couldn't even sing Aloha,
They had to get a guy to show her,
The Queen of the Hollywood Isles.

Oh, they spray her with oil to make her shiny,

So she'll look like she has swum in some lagoon.
The electrical guys
Light the stars in the skies
And the wind machine starts blowing the typhoon.
There's a treadmill for her to run away on
And she always runs into the leading man.
He's a muscular Joe,
Six foot five and a schmoe—
Takes a gallon and a half to paint him tan.

STAGEHAND: [*spoken*] Now?
LAMOUR: [*spoken*] No. Not now. Not—cue!
LEADING MAN: [*spoken*] Mooi, do you love me?
LAMOUR: [*spoken*]No, Pooi, it is forbidden.
LEADING MAN: [*spoken*] Kiss me, Mooi. Kiss me, Mooi. Mooi. Mooi.

LAMOUR: [*spoken*] Pooi.
Hooga dooga booga fish poi.
Hooga dooga booga poi fish.
[*Repeat three times.*]

[*sung*] She's the Queen of the Hollywood Islands*
Since they photographed her wearing a sarong.
She's never even seen Tahiti,
Still she's the big Tahitian sweetie
From wearing her shirt short and her lashes long.

She's the belle of those Hollywood jungles
In that same old plot they dig up from the files.
But never judge her by her chassis,
She's ev'ry bit as smart as Lassie,
The Queen of the Hollywood Isles.

From the film Neptune's Daughter
Top: *Ricardo Montalban and Esther Williams.*
Bottom: *Red Skelton and Betty Garrett*

* *Stanza not sung in film.*

NEPTUNE'S DAUGHTER

Produced by Jack Cummings for Metro-Goldwyn-Mayer. Released in June 1949. Music and lyrics by Frank Loesser. Screenplay by Dorothy Kingsley. Directed by Edward Buzzell. Cast featured Esther Williams, Red Skelton, Ricardo Montalban, Betty Garrett, Keenan Wynn, and Xavier Cugat and His Orchestra. The song "Baby, It's Cold Outside" received the Academy Award for Best Song of 1949. For the song "I Want My Money Back," see page 132.

I LOVE THOSE MEN

Copyrighted April 28, 1948, and June 10, 1948. Introduced by Betty Garrett and Red Skelton with Xavier Cugat and His Orchestra.

VERSE*

With the brokers and the bankers, it's the same old itch;
They're going money, money, money all the day.
With the stokers on the tankers, it's the same old pitch;
I mean they shovel, shovel, shovel it away.
From the guy who runs the Follies
To the guy who runs the trolleys,
Ev'ryone has quite a fascinating gimmick with his hands—
But the guys who drive me crazy are musicians in the Latin bands.

REFRAIN

I love those men who go
[*Imitating guitar*] Brroom
[*Imitating claves*] Click, click
[*Imitating maracas*] Ka chick a chick
[*Imitating guitar*] Brroom
[*Imitating claves*] Click, click
[*Imitating maracas*] Ka chick a chick
[*Imitating guitar*] Brroom
[*Imitating claves*] Click, click
[*Imitating maracas*] Ka chick a chick
[*Whistling à la flute*] Whistle
[*Imitating timpani*] Ta-boom

* *Verse not sung in film.*

[*Imitating guitar*] Brroom
[*Imitating claves*] Click, click
[*Imitating bass*] Dm dm dm dm
[*Imitating scratcher*] Scrr scrr
[*Imitating cymbal*] Pah
[*Imitating guitar*] Brroom
[*Imitating maracas*] Chick a chick a bom chick
[*Imitating drums and maracas*] A bom chick
[*Imitating pizzicato violin*] Ning ning ning
Ning ning ning ning—

[SKELETON *throws sticks at timpani.*]

Boom!
Give me a South American drummer
And keep your butcher and your plumber.
Or let me hear the fabulous fracas of the maracas.
Give me the guy who strums the guitar
A cinco quatro to the bar.
I'll even take the yokel
From Buenos Aires Musicians' Local
Who does the vocal.

I love the men who go
[*Imitating guitar*] Brroom
[*Scratcher*]
[*Maracas*]
[*Bongos*]
[*Brazilian shaker*]
They've warned me time and again
[*Claves*]
But oh, how I love those men,
Those men,
Those men—
[*Maracas*]
[*Claves*]
[*Trumpet*]
[*Trombone*]
[*Drums*]
[*Cymbals*]
[*Bass*]
[*Tom-tom*]
[*Violin*]

I love those men who go—
[*Maracas*]
[*Guiro*]
[*Bass*]
[*Claves*]
[*Maracas*]
[*Guiro*]
[*Bass*]
[*Claves*]
[*Maracas*]
[*Guiro*]
[*Bass*]
[*Claves*]
[*Maracas*]

[*Guiro*]
[*Bass*]
[*Claves*]

[*Instrumental interlude with dance sequence*]

But oh, how I love those men!

ON A SLOW BOAT TO CHINA

Published. Copyrighted September 7, 1948. Previously registered for copyright as an unpublished song May 7, 1948. This song is played instrumentally in *Neptune's Daughter* during a swimsuit fashion show. Esther Williams told film historian Miles Kreuger she originally sang this number, but the censors had it removed because the lyrics suggest an "immoral liaison." Recordings include Kay Kyser and His Orchestra, vocal by Harry Babbitt and Gloria Wood (Columbia); Freddy Martin and His Orchestra, vocal by Glen Hughes (RCA Victor); Eddy Howard and His Orchestra (Mercury); Art Lund (MGM); Snooky Lanson (Mercury); Larry Clinton and His Orchestra, vocal by Helen Lee and the Dipsy Doodlers (Decca); Benny Goodman and His Orchestra, vocal by Al Hendrickson (Capitol); Bing Crosby and Peggy Lee (United Artists); Liza Minnelli (A&M); Ella Fitzgerald (Pablo); and Sammy Davis Jr. (Decca).

REFRAIN

I'd love to get you
On a slow boat to China,
All to myself, alone.
Get you and keep you
In my arms evermore,
Leave all your lovers
Weeping on the faraway shore.
Out on the briny
With a moon big and shiny,
Melting your heart of stone.
I'd love to get you
On a slow boat to China,
All to myself alone.

INTERLUDE

There is no verse to this song,
'Cause I don't want to wait a moment too long
To say that—

REPEAT REFRAIN

MY HEART BEATS FASTER

Published. Copyrighted May 11, 1949. Introduced by Ricardo Montalban. Recorded by Ricardo Montalban (MGM) and Tony Martin (RCA Victor).

My heat beats faster, faster,
Faster and faster at the sight of you.
My heart beats faster, faster,
Faster than I have ever felt it do.
You bring me madness, madness,
Beautiful madness ev'ry little while,
When you pass by and you smile.

My heart beats faster, faster,
Not its own master, when I hear your voice,
My heart hears music, music,
Music for dancing and it has no choice.
And if I never kiss you,
Tell me what can my poor heart do
But just beat faster and faster
Until it breaks in two.

BABY, IT'S COLD OUTSIDE

Published. Copyrighted April 25, 1949. Previously registered for copyright as an unpublished song April 5, 1948. Introduced by Esther Williams and Ricardo Montalban and by Betty Garrett and Red Skelton. The leading recordings were by Margaret Whiting and Johnny Mercer (Capitol) and by Dinah Shore and Buddy Clark with Ted Dale's Orchestra (Columbia). Other recordings are by Frank and Lynn Loesser (Mercury), Ella Fitzgerald and Louis Jordan (Decca), Louis Armstrong and Velma Middleton (Decca), Sammy Kaye and His Orchestra with vocals by Donn Dornell and Laura Leslie (RCA Victor), and Homer and Jethro (Henry Haynes and Kenneth Burns) (RCA Victor). A private recording of the song by Frank and Lynn Loesser is on the compact disc *Frank Sings Loesser* (Koch). The song won Loesser his only Academy Award.

Susan Loesser notes the song's history prior to its film release:

My father had written "Baby, It's Cold Outside" in 1944, in New York. Shortly after my parents moved into the Navarro Hotel, they decided to give themselves a housewarming party, including the requisite performances. When their turn came, Lynn and Frank went to the piano and introduced "Baby, It's Cold Outside" to their friends.

Well, the room just fell apart [my mother remembered]. I don't think either of us realized the impact of what we'd sung. We had to do it over and over again and we became instant parlor room stars. We got invited to all the best parties for years on the basis of "Baby." It was our ticket to caviar and truffles. Parties were built around our being the closing act.

For several years my father held on to the song, which he and my mother performed regularly at parties on both coasts. They would sit together at the piano and act out the lyrics with great charm. They even made a recording of it—then, as now, a collector's item.

My mother treasured that song. She loved performing it. She loved the fact that it was theirs alone to perform for adoring audiences. Then, in 1948, my father decided to sell it to MGM for the film *Neptune's Daughter*, starring Esther Williams and Ricardo Montalban.

I felt as betrayed as if I'd caught him in bed with another woman. I kept saying "Esther Williams and Ricardo Montalban!!!" He finally sat me down and said, "If I don't let go of 'Baby' I'll begin to think I can never write another song as good as I think this one is." He had to let go of it.

The song is sung with the last word of each line overlapping the first word of the next.

MOUSE: I really can't stay.
WOLF: But baby, it's cold outside!
MOUSE: I've got to go 'way.
WOLF: But baby, it's cold outside!
MOUSE: This evening has been—
WOLF: Been hoping that you'd drop in!
MOUSE: So very nice.
WOLF: I'll hold your hands, they're just like ice.
MOUSE: My mother will start to worry—
WOLF: Beautiful, what's your hurry?
MOUSE: And Father will be pacing the floor.
WOLF: Listen to the fireplace roar!
MOUSE: So really I'd better scurry.
WOLF: Beautiful, please, don't hurry.
MOUSE: Well, maybe just a half a drink more.
WOLF: Put some records on while I pour.
MOUSE: The neighbors might think—
WOLF: But baby, it's bad out there.
MOUSE: Say, what's in this drink?
WOLF: No cabs to be had out there.
MOUSE: I wish I knew how—
WOLF: Your eyes are like starlight now.
MOUSE: To break the spell.
WOLF: I'll take your hat. Your hair looks swell.
MOUSE: I ought to say, "No, no, no, sir!"

WOLF: Mind if I move in closer?
MOUSE: At least I'm gonna say that I tried.
WOLF: What's the sense of hurting my pride?
MOUSE: I really can't stay.
WOLF: Oh, baby, don't hold out.
MOUSE: Ah, but it's—
WOLF: Baby, it's—
BOTH: Cold outside.

MOUSE: I simply must go!
WOLF: But baby, it's cold outside!
MOUSE: The answer is no!
WOLF: But baby, it's cold outside!
MOUSE: The welcome has been—
WOLF: How lucky that you dropped in!
MOUSE: So very nice and warm.
WOLF: Look out the window at that storm.
MOUSE: My sister will be suspicious.
WOLF: Gosh, your lips look delicious.
MOUSE: My brother will be there at the door.
WOLF: Waves upon a tropical shore!
MOUSE: My maiden aunt's mind is vicious.
WOLF: Gosh, your lips are delicious.
MOUSE: Well, maybe just a cigarette more.
WOLF: Never such a blizzard before.
MOUSE: I've got to get home.
WOLF: But baby, you'd freeze out there.
MOUSE: Say, lend me a comb.
WOLF: It's up to your knees out there.
MOUSE: You've really been grand—
WOLF: I thrill when you touch my hand.
MOUSE: But don't you see—
WOLF: How can you do this thing to me?
MOUSE: There's bound to be talk tomorrow?
WOLF: Think of my lifelong sorrow—
MOUSE: At least there will be plenty implied.
WOLF: If you caught pneumonia and died.
MOUSE: I really can't stay.
WOLF: Get over that old doubt.
MOUSE: Ah, but it's—
WOLF: Baby, it's—
BOTH: Cold outside.

NEPTUNE'S DAUGHTER

Registered for copyright as an unpublished song March 1, 1948. Not used in film.

Neptune's daughter,
The girl in the scanty bathing suit,
Poor, sad victim of censorship's law.
Why oh why is her costume a thing of wicked repute
When her character hasn't a flaw?

Ev'ry season without reason
Righteous citizens call the cops.
Cranks and biddies
Hide their kiddies
Till she stops
Driving ev'rybody crazy.

Neptune's daughter,
The girl in the scanty bathing suit,
Bright, bright stars of the summery skies.
Oh, they pester
And arrest her,
But they'd see what an innocent thing she was
If they ever would bother to look
In her eyes.

ROSEANNA MCCOY

Produced by Samuel Goldwyn for RKO/Samuel Goldwyn. Released in October 1949. Screenplay by John Collier based on a novel by Alberta Hannum. Directed by Irving Reis. Cast starred Farley Granger, Charles Bickford, Raymond Massey, Richard Basehart, and Joan Evans.

ROSEANNA

Published. Copyrighted June 13, 1949. Sung under opening credits by unidentified singers. Recorded by Freddy Martin Orchestra, vocal by Merv Griffin (RCA Victor), and John Laurenz (Mercury). Loesser wrote this song when Samuel Goldwyn rejected "More I Cannot Wish You," which was used the following year in *Guys and Dolls*.

Roseanna, Roseanna,
The wind sings her name.
And all night through, all chilly night through,
She sets my heart aflame.

Roseanna, Roseanna,*
The moon smiles her smile.
And where I walk, wherever I walk,
She follows all the while.

---

* *Lines 5–8 not sung in film.*

Little did I know, little did I care,
When I met her dancing at the fair,
Little did I crave, little did I cry,
Little did I dream I'd be haunted by

Roseanna, Roseanna,
I love her alone.
And now I'll need, I'll evermore need
Roseanna for my very own.

RED, HOT AND BLUE

Produced by Robert Fellows for Paramount Pictures.
Released in October 1949. Screenplay by John Farrow
and Hagar Wilde, based on a story by Charles Lederer.
The title of film is from Cole Porter's 1936 Broadway
musical, but no Porter songs are used and there is no
other relationship to the 1936 stage musical. Directed by
John Farrow. Choreography by Billy Daniels. Cast
starred Betty Hutton and Victor Mature and featured
William Demarest, June Havoc, and Frank Loesser (in
his only film role, as a gangster named "Hair-Do
Lempke").

I WAKE UP IN THE MORNING FEELING FINE

Published. Copyrighted June 15, 1949. Introduced by
Betty Hutton. Recorded by Betty Hutton (Capitol) and
Gordon Jenkins (Decca).

I get to bed about a half past three;
That's not supposed to be so good for me—
Still, I wake up in the mornin' feeling fine.
I never bother with the coffee blend,
The blend all the famous doctors recommend—
Still, I wake up in the morning feeling fine.

It must be 'cause you kiss me good night ev'ry night,
Next day I rise king-size with my eyes ashine—
I'm healthier than Hercules.
I haven't got one of those blankets with the wires
    inside,
I like my potatoes and I like 'em fried—
Still, I wake up in the morning feeling fine,
Feelin' fine
Since you're mine!

I'm in fine fettle, steamin' like a kettle.
I could climb up Popocatepetl.
Feel my pulse, test my mettle,
Superior to Superman.
I never rub the goose grease on my skin,
I open up the windows
And let the smog roll in—
Still, I wake up in the mornin' feeling fine,
Feeling fine
Since you're mine.

THAT'S LOYALTY

Published. Copyrighted July 8, 1949. Introduced by
Betty Hutton. Recorded by Betty Hutton (Capitol).

VERSE

I love a feller and he loves me,
But his mind has got a very strange twist;
I hesitate to introduce him to my friends.
In fact I'm thinking of introducing him
To a psychoanalyst.

REFRAIN

He keeps telling me he doesn't like my hat—
The brim's a little grim,
The crown's a little flat.
But just let anybody else mention that
And he'll yell and he'll holler
And he'll double up his fist,
Break your arm, black your eye, knock you down;
And for seven miles around you can hear the man
    insist
It's the prettiest hat in town.

He keeps telling me my dancing's out of whack—
My waltz is full of faults,
My rumba's off the track.
But just let anybody else make a crack
And he'll yell and he'll holler
And he'll double up his fist,
Break your arm, black your eye, knock you down;
And for seven miles around you can hear the man
    insist
It's the fanciest dancin' in town.

That's loyalty.
A little peculiar,
But it's loyalty.
He figures it this way:
He can treat me like dirt,
But you'd better treat me like royalty

And it really is immense
How he comes to my defense
If you even so much as frown.
I keep telling him I'm doing the best I can,
But he's got me on the pan,
Saying my girdle shows
And "powder your nose"
And "straighten your hose"
And heaven only knows.

He'll yell and he'll holler
I'm a doll, a drool, a daisy, a dream,
A ding-dong delicacy, a moment supreme,
According to him!
I'm just the loveliest gal in town.

HAMLET

Registered for copyright as an unpublished song July 1,
1949. Introduced by Betty Hutton and ensemble. Re-
corded by Betty Hutton (Capitol), Bibi Osterwald
(Painted Smiles), and Debbie Shapiro Gravitte (Varese
Sarabande). The lyric that follows was transcribed from
Betty Hutton's recording for Capitol Records.

This is the story of *Hamlet*,
William Shakespeare's most notable play,
A magnificent dignified work of art.
But for you, buster,
I guess I oughta tell it this way:

Hamlet was the prince of a spot called Denmark.
There never was such a frantic guy
Either before or since.
(He was a dream boy.)
And like a hole in the head
Denmark needed that prince.

He bumped off his uncle
And he Mickey Finned his mother
And he drove his girl to suicide
And stabbed her big brother
'Cause he didn't want nobody else
But himself should live.
He was whatcha might call
Un-co-operative.

Hamlet had a lady friend named Ophelia.
She was a cool put-together chick
That made men thrill.
But Hamlet, he thought
She was from Uglyville.
[*spoken*] He didn't seem to get the message.

He chopped down her father
Just to teach the girl a lesson.
Yes, he cut him up in slices
Like a pound of delicatessen.
'Cause murder was one thing
Hamlet sure did enjoy.
Sure did enjoy.
He was what you might call
Quite the mischievous boy.

Ophelia, overcome with such grief and sorrow,
She went and flipped her lid,
She popped her cork,
She jumped the track.
And her intelligent mind
Developed a permanent crack.
[*spoken*] Things went black!

Ophelia had a six-and-a-half-foot brother.
He thought that Hamlet had been
A trifle too impolite.
So in the third act
He challenged him to a fight.
What a night!
It was dog eat dog eat dog in Denmark.
Yes, it was dog eat dog eat dog in Denmark.
The moral of my story is very plain—
You better get a muzzle if you've got a great Dane.
And the name of this omelette is Hamlet.

(WHERE ARE YOU) NOW THAT I NEED YOU

Published. Copyrighted May 4, 1949. Introduced by Betty Hutton. Leading recordings by Betty Hutton (Capitol), Doris Day (Columbia) and Frankie Laine (Mercury). Additional recordings by Kay Thompson (Decca) and Petula Clark (Liberty).

VERSE (NOT SUNG IN FILM)

I called you on the phone last night,
And baby, you were not there.
I tried your doorbell umpteen times,
Then walked away in despair.
Then finally I sat me down
And wrote you quite a long note.
And baby, baby, baby,
Here's the heartbroken note I wrote:

REFRAIN

Where are you
Now that I need you?

Now that I want you
So badly I could cry?
Where are you?
Where did fate lead you?
Funny how I dreamed
You'd still be standing by.
I had you at my beck and call;
I called you any time at all.
I guess I took too much for granted;
I never thought I'd lie awake and sigh,
Where are you
Now that I need you?
Now that I love you so madly
I could die.

LET'S DANCE

Produced by Robert Fellows for Paramount Pictures. Released in November 1950. Music and lyrics by Frank Loesser. Screenplay by Allan Scott and Dane Lussier, adapted from the story "Little Boy Blue" by Maurice Zolotow. Directed by Norman Z. McLeod. Cast starred Betty Hutton and Fred Astaire and featured Roland Young, Ruth Warrick, Lucille Watson, and Gregory Moffett. Milton DeLugg makes a brief appearance.

CAN'T STOP TALKING

Published. Copyrighted May 22, 1950. Introduced by Betty Hutton and Fred Astaire. Recorded by Betty Hutton (RCA Victor).

VERSE (NOT PUBLISHED)

His eyes, his nose,
His fingers, his toes,
His smile when he says "Please,"
And when he sneezes—his sneeze.
His arms and chest
And coat and vest,
His ev'rything is sweeter than sweet.
I try and try, but honest to Pete—

REFRAIN

I can't stop talking about him,
And talking about him, and talking about him,
I can't stop talking about
The man that I adore.
Oh, no, I can't stop talking about him,

And talking about him, and talking about him,
I can't stop talking about him,
And though I seem a bore,
I simply can't stop telling about him,
And yelling about him, and telling about him.
I can't stop hollering over the moment that we
     met—
He had a pin-striped whaddeyacallit,
A beautiful smile and a barrel of money.
I can't stop talking about him yet.
He kissed me and a bell went bong,
A whistle went woooo,
A trapdoor opened
And I flipped right through,
And now I can't stop talking about him,
And talking about him, and talking about him,
And if he was yours, well, neither would you—

Additional lyrics sung in film

Stop talking about him, and talking about him,
And talking about him, and talking about him
Until your face turned blue,
Just from talking about him, and talking about
     him,
And talking about him, and talking about him
All day through.

JACK AND THE BEANSTALK

Registered for copyright as an unpublished song July 31, 1950. Introduced by Fred Astaire, with Gregory Moffett.

ASTAIRE: [*spoken*] Jack and the Beanstalk, now
          who was he?
          Jack and the Beanstalk, now let me see.
          Jack and the Beanstalk—oh, I
             remember now:
          The boy who took the beans from the
             family cow.

          [*sung*] Yes, Jack was a boy of financial
             immaturity;
          Jack was a big mess of mortgages and
             liens.
          Jack was a kid whose collateral
             security
          Amounted to a handful of beans.
          They called him Jack and the
             Beanstalk,
          Jack with the get-rich talk,
          Jack and the Beanstalk,

A story with exactly this to preface
    it—
A deficit.

Well, Jack took the beans and he
    started to manipulate
Deep in debentures and promissory
    notes.
Jack made the grade, and by this I
    mean to stipulate
The feller knew his beans from his
    oats,
For he was Jack and the Beanstalk.
Jack made the darn thing rise
High in the blue, blue skies.
[spoken] And what exactly did he do
    for credit?

MOFFETT: [spoken] You said it.
ASTAIRE: [sung] Our hero Jack climbed the
    beanstalk.
Jack beat the bankruptcy;
Up to the top went he.
And standing there so ugly and
    defiant—
[spoken] was a mammoth structure
    complete with accumulated
    dividends and interlocking
    directorate—the giant!
[sung] Well, Jack took a poke at the
    giant's corporation,
For Jack had the nerve and the
    courage and the crust.
Jack ran away with the capitalization—
Yes, the little guy had busted the trust.
And then he flew down the beanstalk,
Flew like a rocket plane,
Blew with the capital gain.
And why exactly did the giant follow
    him?

MOFFETT: To swallow him?
ASTAIRE: But he was Jack and the Beanstalk,
Jack with the billion bob.
Jack showed the Wall Street mob
A deal that positively couldn't fail.
And as the monkey said when he
    backed into the cactus,
That's the end of my tail.

OH, THEM DUDES

Published. Copyrighted May 22, 1950. Introduced by Fred Astaire and Betty Hutton.

ASTAIRE: Oh, them dudes—
HUTTON: Oh, them dudes—
ASTAIRE: They're a-doin' our dance.
HUTTON: They're a-doin' our dance.
ASTAIRE: Them city dudes—
HUTTON: Them city dudes—
ASTAIRE: They're a-doin' our dance.
HUTTON: They're a-doin' our dance.
ASTAIRE: Down in the nightclubs, look what I
    found—
    Do-si-do and all-hands-round.
BOTH: Them dudes, them dudes,
    Them big-city dudes, they're a-doin'
    our dance.
    Oh, them rustlers—
HUTTON: Oh, them dudes—
ASTAIRE: Oh, them dudes—
HUTTON: They're a-stealin' our stuff.
ASTAIRE: They're a-stealin' our stuff.
HUTTON: Them city dudes—
ASTAIRE: Them city dudes—
HUTTON: They're a-treatin' us rough.
ASTAIRE: They're a-treatin' us rough.
HUTTON: Down in the nightclubs, what did I
    hear
    But a jug and a fiddle they was playin'
    by ear!
BOTH: Them dudes, them dudes,
    Them big-city dudes, they're a-stealin'
    our stuff.
    Oh, the coyotes!
    Saddle up old Flossie,
    Call out all the posse,
    This here kind of thievin's got to stop.
    We'll give them fair warnin'
    If they don't stop by mornin'
    We'll retaliate by takin' up—
HUTTON: Beep—
ASTAIRE: Boop—
HUTTON: Bop.
ASTAIRE: On account of them dudes—
HUTTON: Oh, them dudes—
ASTAIRE: They're a-doin' our dance.
HUTTON: They're a doin' our dance.
ASTAIRE: Them city dudes—
HUTTON: Them city dudes—
ASTAIRE: And their uncles and aunts.
HUTTON: And their uncles and aunts.
ASTAIRE: Down in nightclubs, look at them go,
    All hands round and do-si-do.
HUTTON: Playin' gittar and musical saw,

Jumpin' our claim on the "Turkey in
    the Straw."
ASTAIRE: Look at them varmints—
BOTH: Wearin' our garments
    Down to the Levi pants.
    Oh, them dudes, them dudes,
    Them big-city dudes, they're a-doin'
    our dance!

[Interlude—twelve bars]

ASTAIRE: Oh, them dudes—*
HUTTON: Oh, them dudes—
ASTAIRE: They're a-doin' us dirt.
HUTTON: They're a-doin' us dirt.
ASTAIRE: Them city dudes—
HUTTON: Them city dudes—
ASTAIRE: They're a-gonna get hurt.
HUTTON: Don't nobody move!
ASTAIRE: Down in the nightclubs, look at that
    group—
HUTTON: All hands round with a holler and a
    whoop—
ASTAIRE: Stompin' a foot and yellin' out "Yippee!"
HUTTON: That b'longs west of the Mississippi.
ASTAIRE: Matter of pride—
BOTH: Tonight we ride
    Or the West don't stand a chance.
    Oh, them dudes, them dudes,
    Them big-city dudes, they're a-doin'
    our dance!

WHY FIGHT THE FEELING?

Published. Copyrighted May 22, 1950. Introduced by Betty Hutton. Recorded by Vaughn Monroe and His Orchestra (RCA Victor).

VERSE (NOT SUNG IN FILM)

You, with your attitude superior,
Me, with my very cool exterior—
Never before has a moonlit scene been drearier.
So forgive me if I unmask,
Put my arms around you and ask:

REFRAIN

Why fight the feeling,
The feeling, the fabulous feeling?
Why fight the feeling?

* Remainder of lyrics unpublished.

We're face to face with romance.
Why miss the magic,
The magic, the moment of magic?
Why miss the magic?
Relax and give it a chance.
We're right on the very brink
Of kiss number one.
There's no time to stop and think,
It's too late to run,
The beguine has begun.
So, why fight the feeling,
The feeling that started us reeling?
Why fight the feeling
That says: "Tonight is the night"?
Why fight the feeling
When it's oh so right?

THE HYACINTH

Published. Copyrighted May 22, 1950. Tune played on music box; lyrics not used in film. Danced by Fred Astaire and Lucie Watson.

Ah, to be a hyacinth
By your garden gate!
Ah, to be a hyacinth,
Ah, the glorious fate!

I should bloom there patiently
Till my day came due,
Then languish in your flower vase,
But die content to know I was
The hyacinth picked by you.

TUNNEL OF LOVE

Published. Copyrighted April 17, 1950. Previously registered for copyright as unpublished song February 16, 1948. Introduced by Fred Astaire and Betty Hutton. Recorded by Nat "King" Cole (Capitol), the Mills Brothers (Decca), and Dinah Shore and Jack Smith (Columbia). Also considered for *Variety Girl*.

HUTTON: I should have known, I should have known.
I wasted my time till I got him all alone

In the tunnel of love, the tunnel of love.
One more ride through the tunnel of love

And he's mine.
ASTAIRE: I've started in to weaken,
And I'm on the right track.
The couple in back
Last time round told me,
"Stick with it, mac, you'll do fine."
HUTTON: Hey! It's quarter to eleven, so before—
BOTH: So before they go and close the old
amusement park,
I gotta have another session in the dark,
A session in the dark
Where I can set those eyes ashine.
HUTTON: A pair of tickets, mister—
BOTH: To the tunnel of love, the tunnel of love.
One more ride through the tunnel of love,
One more ride through the tunnel of love,
One more ride through the tunnel of love
And he's [she's] mine.

ASTAIRE: I bought her a frozen custard.
HUTTON: For I was a special date.
ASTAIRE: I fed her a dog with mustard.
HUTTON: And then he let a feller guess my weight.
ASTAIRE: We rode on the roller coaster.
HUTTON: And also the carousel.
ASTAIRE: She won an electric toaster.
HUTTON: I swung the hammer and rang the bell.
ASTAIRE: But I was getting nowhere fast
In matters of romance
Until we found a place at last
Where I stood ev'ry chance.
HUTTON: Frozen custard, dog with mustard,
Roller coaster, 'lectric toaster,
I should have known in advance.
ASTAIRE: About what?
HUTTON: About the tunnel of love, the tunnel of love.
BOTH: One more ride on the tunnel of love,
One more ride on the tunnel of love,
One more ride on the tunnel of love
And he's [she's] mine.

THE MING TOY NOODLE COMPANY

Not used in film. Intended for Betty Hutton.

INTRODUCTION

[*Spoken*]

HUTTON: Yeow!!
WAITER: What's wrong, missee, what's wrong?

HUTTON: It says here, "He who love you is he
who you love" . . . signed by the
Ming Toy Noodle Company.
WAITER: Who he?
HUTTON: Who he? He who loves me. Don't you
know who he?
WAITER: Sure, missee, he who is who he.
HUTTON: Oh, that's not hooey, that's on the
level. He loves me.

VERSE

HUTTON: [*sung*] Ho ho, am I bouncin'!
Hee hee, am I beamin'!
I'm high as a worm-fed lark.
Got hip to who is my true love,
And I'm no longer in the dark.
My boyfriend may arrive for dinner late,
But though the chow mein's gettin' cold,
I'll wait
For my date
'Cause the news is great.

REFRAIN

HUTTON: Oh, the Ming Toy Noodle Company says
he loves me,
And the Ming Toy Noodle Company's
always right.
Yes, I broke a rice cake open
And the hope that I was hopin'
Was a-written on the ticket
In black and white!
Now the Ming Toy Noodle Buddha has
smiled above me,
So you'll pardon me for breakin' right
into song;
'Cause the Ming Toy Noodle Company
says he loves me
And the Ming Toy Noodle
Company—never has been wrong!
WAITER: Ah so lichee oh rumaki noodle foodle
yung
Oh ho socki yocki poo naga sack.
HUTTON: No!!
In the nineties, Admiral Dewey
Dropped around for a load of chop suey,
Gave the Ming Toy message a look.
And it said he'd take Manila,
And Manila he took.

[*Dance interlude*]

Mister Gallup of the Gallup Poll
Dropped in for foo yung bung egg roll,
Picked a ticket and away he went
Knowin' who was gonna be president.
[*wink*]

WAITER: Hopalongee sing chow yee subgum
Yucca mucca ma he foo . . . you all.
HUTTON: [spoken] Suh!
[sung] Kentucky colonels eat here
To get the name of the Derby winner
for next year.
Winchell comes to Ming Toy for inside
dope;
Crosby drew a ticket and it said—
Hope!
And now my turn has come to learn
my fate
And though the chow mein's gettin'
cold, I'll wait
For my date
'Cause the news is great.

Oh, the Ming Toy Noodle Buddha has
smiled above me,
So you'll pardon me for breakin' right
into
Wata nabi wana sabi oolia koo
Chica like ooka nooka wang pie,
'Cause the Ming Toy Noodle Company
says he loves me
And the Ming Toy Noodle Company . . .
better not be wrong!
Hah!

MISCELLANEOUS SONGS OF 1948–1950

THE LAST THING I WANT IS YOUR PITY

Published. Copyrighted January 6, 1948. Leading recordings by Red Foley (Decca) and the Dinning Sisters (Capitol).

VERSE

I can tell it's over,
I can tell we're through;
Darling, say the word and you're free.
Don't get tender-hearted
Ling'ring in my arms
Just because you're sorry for me.

REFRAIN

Oh, the last thing I want is your pity,
Never mind how forlorn I feel.
If it's time that we part,
Go ahead, break my heart—
Why pretend that your love is still real?
Though I cry bitter tears as you leave me,
Don't turn back out of sympathy,
'Cause the last thing I want is your pity
If you no longer care for me.

THE FEATHERY FEELING

Published. Copyrighted January 20, 1948. Recorded by Hoagy Carmichael (Decca), Helen Forrest (MGM), Vic Damone (Mercury), and Sam Browne (London Gramophone), among others.

VERSE

Got a covey of quail
Flyin' round my noggin,
Got a covey of quail
In frantic flight.
I'm a little bit pale
And my eyes keep a-foggin'
Since the covey of quail
Flew in last night.

REFRAIN

Came home with the feathery feelin'
Under my sombrero,
Came home with the feathery feelin'
Up and down my spine,
Came home and I really was reelin'
Under my sombrero,
Came home with the feathery feelin'
'Bout that gal of mine.

Slipped out to serenade 'er
And the night was a velvety black.
And oh, the tune I played 'er
With my gittar
Slung behind my back!
Came home with the feathery feelin'
Under my sombrero,
Came home with the feathery feelin'
Up and down my spine,
The feathery feelin'
'Bout that gal of mine.

DOWN THE STAIRS, OUT THE DOOR WENT MY BABY

Registered for copyright as an unpublished song May 7, 1948. Frank Loesser's demo of this song appears on the compact disc *Frank Sings Loesser* (Koch).

Down the stairs, out the door,
To the station and far away
Went my baby.
Down the stairs, out the door,
To the station and gone from me.
Did I sigh, did I cry?
No, I smiled when I said goodbye
To my baby,
Let her go, let her blow,
Let her hurry out fancy free.

But now, oh, how a room can get gloomy!
Oh, how a room can get bare!
Oh, how a room can get much too roomy
When the love is gone from there!

Down the stairs, out the door,
To the station and far away
Went my baby.
Down the stairs, out the door,
Bag and baggage and gone was she.
Now I sigh and I cry
And I pray for the day I say,
"Here comes baby,
Up the stairs, in the door,
And forevermore home to me."

HOOP-DEE-DOO

Music by Milton DeLugg (b. 1918). Published. Copyrighted April 3, 1950. The recording by Perry Como (RCA Victor) was number one on the popular music charts, and the Kay Starr (Capitol) recording was number two. Other recordings by Doris Day (Columbia), Russ Morgan (Decca), and Milton DeLugg King. Milton DeLugg was an accordianist, composer, arranger, and conductor. He also wrote the hit song "Orange Colored Sky" with William Stein and conducted for *The Abe Burrows Show*, *The Tonight Show*, and other radio and television productions.

Hoop-dee-doo,
Hoop-dee-doo,
I hear a polka and my troubles are through.

Hoop-dee-doo,
Hoop-dee-dee,
This kind of music is like heaven to me.
Hoop-dee-doo,
Hoop-dee-doo,
It's got me higher than a kite.

Hand me down my soup and fish,
I am gonna get my wish
Hoop-dee-dooin' it tonight.
When there's a trombone playin' rah-ta dah-dah-
    dah,

I get a thrill,
I always will.
When there's a concertina stretchin' out a mile,
I always smile,
'Cause that's my style.
When there's a fiddle in the middle and he*
Plays the tune so sweet,
Plays the tune so sweet that I could die,

---

* *Alternate lines:*
    When there's a fiddle in the middle,
    Oh it really is a riddle how he

Lead me to the floor
And hear me yell for more,
'Cause I'm a hoop-dee-dooin' kind of guy.

CODA

I'm in clover, I'm in bloom,
When I'm dancin', give me room.
Hoop-dee-dooin' it with all of my might.
Rain may fall and snow may come,
Nothin's gonna stop me from
Hoop-dee-dooin' it tonight.

GUYS AND DOLLS | 1950

GUYS AND DOLLS

Tryout: Shubert Theatre, Philadelphia, October 14–28, 1950, then transferred to the Erlanger Theatre and resumed tryout, October 31–November 18. New York premiere: Forty-sixth Street Theatre, November 24, 1950. 1,194 performances. London premiere: London Coliseum, May 28, 1953. 555 performances. Musical fable based on the short story "The Idyll of Miss Sarah Brown" by Damon Runyon. New York production presented by Cy Feuer and Ernest H. Martin. Book by Jo Swerling and Abe Burrows. Music and lyrics by Frank Loesser. Production directed by George S. Kaufman. Dances and musical numbers staged by Michael Kidd. Settings by Jo Mielziner. Musical director: Irving Actman. Orchestral arrangements by George Bassman and Ted Royal. Vocal arrangements and direction by Herbert Greene. Costumes by Alvin Colt. Cast featured Robert Alda (Sky Masterson), Vivian Blaine (Miss Adelaide), Sam Levene (Nathan Detroit), Isabel Bigley (Sarah) and Pat Rooney Sr. (Arvide Abernathy), with B. S. Pully (Big Jule), Stubby Kaye (Nicely-Nicely Johnson), Tom Pedi (Harry the Horse), Johnny Silver (Benny Southstreet), Paul Reed (Lt. Brannigan), Douglas Deane (Rusty Charlie), and Netta Packer (General Cartwright). Major New York revivals include the New York City Center in 1966, an all-black Broadway production in 1976, and another Broadway revival in 1992.

Loesser tersely summarized his role in the show's origins during a 1959 radio interview: "My association with *Guys and Dolls* starts with a phone call from my friends Feuer and Martin, the producers. So when I heard Feuer's voice on the phone and he said the magic word 'Runyon,' I said let's have a meeting and that was it." Loesser's role was in fact a bit more complicated. His songs incorporated the Runyon characters but were written before even the first scenes of a libretto were complete. When the initial bookwriter Jo Swerling left the project, Abe Burrows wrote a new libretto around Loesser's songs. None of Swerling's work was retained; however, the language of his contract is responsible for the credit "Book by Jo Swerling and Abe Burrows."

A film version was produced by Samuel Goldwyn and released in November 1955. Music and lyrics by Frank Loesser. Screenplay by Joseph L. Mankiewicz, adapted from the musical *Guys and Dolls* by Jo Swerling, Abe Burrows, and Frank Loesser. Directed by Joseph L. Mankiewicz. Choreographed by Michael Kidd. Cast featured Marlon Brando (Sky Masterson), Jean Simmons (Sarah Brown), Frank Sinatra (Nathan Detroit), and Vivian Blaine (Miss Adelaide), Stubby Kaye (Nicely-Nicely Johnson), Robert Keith (Lt. Brannigan), B. S. Pully (Big

Stubby Kaye, B. S. Pulley, Robert Alda (center), Johnny Silver, Sam Levene, and members of the ensemble in the 1950 New York production of Guys and Dolls

Jule), Johnny Silver (Benny Southstreet), Regis Toomey (Arvide Abernathy), Sheldon Leonard (Harry the Horse), Dan Dayton (Rusty Charlie), Veda Ann Borg (Laverne), Kathryn Givney (General Cartwright), and the Goldwyn Girls.

Recordings: Original cast (Decca), 1976 revival (Motown), London 1982 revival (Chrysalis), 1992 revival (RCA Victor). The Marlon Brando and Jean Simmons songs from the 1955 film soundtrack were released by Decca. An all-star recording of most of the songs was made on Reprise in 1964 with Frank Sinatra, Dean Martin, Bing Crosby, Jo Stafford, Dinah Shore, Sammy Davis Jr., and others. Frank Loesser's demo recordings of eight *Guys and Dolls* songs are on the compact disc *An Evening with Frank Loesser* (DRG). A two-CD complete recording of the stage score plus the three film songs and "Traveling Light" was released in 1996 (Jay) with Loesser's daughter Emily singing the role of Sarah Brown.

FUGUE FOR TINHORNS

Published. Copyrighted December 28, 1950. Previously registered for copyright as an unpublished song August 29, 1950. Published as part of *Guys and Dolls* vocal score, September 3, 1953. Introduced by Stubby Kaye (Nicely), Johnny Silver (Benny), and Douglas Deane (Rusty Charlie). Performed as a round. Recorded by the Andrews Sisters (Decca); Frank Sinatra, Bing Crosby, and Dean Martin (Reprise); Sonny Burke and His Orchestra (Decca); and Barry Manilow (Arista), among others. Frank Loesser's demo recording is on the compact disc *An Evening with Frank Loesser* (DRG).

NICELY: I got the horse right here,
The name is Paul Revere,
And here's a guy that says if the weather's clear,
Can do, can do.
This guy says the horse can do.
If he says the horse can do,
Can do, can do.

For Paul Revere I'll bite,
I hear his foot's all right.
Of course it all depends if it rained last night.
Likes mud, likes mud.
This "X" means the horse likes mud.
If that means the horse likes mud,
Likes mud, likes mud.

I tell you Paul Revere,
Now this is no bum steer,
It's from a handicapper that's real sincere.

Can do, can do,
This guy says the horse can do.
If he says the horse can do,
Can do, can do.
Paul Revere,
I got the horse right here.

BENNY: I'm pickin' Valentine,
'Cause on the morning line
The guy has got him figured at five to nine.
Has chance, has chance,
This guy says the horse has chance,
If he says the horse has chance,
Has chance, has chance.

I know it's Valentine,
The morning works look fine.
Besides, the jockey's brother's a friend of mine.
Needs race, needs race,
This guy says the horse needs race.
If he says the horse needs race,
Needs race, needs race.

I go for Valentine,
'Cause on the morning line
The guy has got him figured at five to nine.
Has chance, has chance,
This guy says the horse has chance.
Valentine!
I got the horse right here.

RUSTY
CHARLIE: But look at Epitaph.
He wins it by a half,
According to this here in the *Telegraph.*
Big threat, big threat,
This guy calls the horse big threat.
If he calls the horse big threat,
Big threat, big threat.

And just a minute, boys,
I got the feed box noise.
It says the great-grandfather was Equipoise.
Shows class, shows class,
This guy says the horse shows class,
If he says the horse shows class,
Shows class, shows class.

So make it Epitaph,
He wins it by half,
According to this here in the *Telegraph.*
Epitaph!
I got the horse right here!

FOLLOW THE FOLD

Published. Copyrighted October 2, 1950. Previously registered for copyright as an unpublished song August 14, 1950. Touring version revised February 27, 1952. Published as part of *Guys and Dolls* vocal score, September 3, 1953. Introduced by Isabel Bigley (Sarah), Pat Rooney Sr. (Arvide), and the Mission Band.

SARAH AND
MISSION
BAND: Follow the fold and stray no more,
Stray no more, stray no more.
Put down the bottle and we'll say no more;
Follow, follow the fold.
SARAH: Before you take another swallow.
ALL: Follow the fold and stray no more,
Stray no more, stray no more.
Tear up your poker deck and play no more;
Follow, follow the fold.
To the meadows where the sun shines,
Out of the darkness and the cold.
SARAH: And the sin and shame in which you
wallow.
ALL: Follow the fold and stray no more,
Stray no more, stray no more.
If you're a sinner and you pray no more,
Follow, follow the fold.

Touring version

SARAH AND
MISSION
BAND: Follow the fold and stray no more,
Stray no more, stray no more.
Live by the gospel and we'll say no more;
Follow, follow the fold.
SARAH: And fill your heart that once was hollow.
ALL: Follow the fold and stray no more,
Stray no more, stray no more.
Walk in your aimless godless way no more;
Follow, follow the fold.
To the meadow where the sun shines
Out of the darkness and the cold.
SARAH: And the sin and shame in which you
wallow.
ALL: Follow the fold and stray no more,
Stray no more, stray no more.
If you're a sinner and you pray no more,
Follow, follow the fold.

Drawing by Al Hirshfield. From left to right: Douglas Deane, Tom Pedi, Stubby Kaye, Johnny Silver, Robert Alda, Sam Levene, B. S. Pulley, Vivian Blaine, Pat Rooney, and Isabel Bigley.

THE OLDEST ESTABLISHED

Published. Copyrighted December 28, 1950. Previously registered for copyright as an unpublished song November 24, 1950. Published as part of *Guys and Dolls* vocal score, September 3, 1953. Introduced by Stubby Kaye (Nicely), Johnny Silver (Benny), Sam Levene (Nathan), and ensemble. Recorded by Frank Sinatra, Bing Crosby, and Dean Martin (Reprise).

NICELY: The Biltmore garage wants a grand.
BENNY: But we ain't got a grand on hand.
NATHAN: And they've now got a lock on the
door
Of the gym at Public School
Eighty-four.
NICELY: There's the stockroom behind
McClosky's Bar.
BENNY: But Missus McClosky ain't a good
scout.
NATHAN: And things being how they are,
The back of the police station is
out.
NICELY: So the Biltmore garage is the spot—
ALL: But the one thousand bucks we ain't
got!
CRAP
SHOOTER: Why, it's good old reliable Nathan.
CRAP
SHOOTERS: Nathan, Nathan, Nathan Detroit.
If you're looking for action, he'll
furnish the spot.
Even when the heat is on it's never
too hot.
Not for good old reliable Nathan,
For it's always just a short walk
To the oldest established permanent
floating
Crap game in New York.

There are well-heeled shooters
ev'rywhere, ev'rywhere,
There are well-heeled shooters
ev'rywhere,
And an awful lot of lettuce
For the fella who can get us there.
NICELY,
BENNY
AND NATHAN: If we only had a lousy little grand,
We could be a millionaire.
ALL: That's good old reliable Nathan,
Nathan, Nathan, Nathan Detroit.
If the size of your bundle you want
to increase,
He'll arrange that you go broke in
quiet and peace,

In a hideout provided by Nathan,
Where there are no neighbors to
squawk.
It's the oldest established permanent
floating
Crap game in New York.
Where's the action? Where's the
game?
NICELY,
BENNY
AND NATHAN: Gotta have the game or we'll die
from shame.
ALL: It's the oldest established permanent
floating
Crap game in New York.

I'LL KNOW

Published. Copyrighted September 15, 1950. Previously registered for copyright as an unpublished song August 14, 1950. Published as part of *Guys and Dolls* vocal score, September 3, 1953. Introduced by Isabel Bigley (Sarah) and Robert Alda (Sky). Recorded by Tommy Dorsey (RCA Victor), Sarah Vaughan (Columbia), Harry James (Columbia), Nancy Wilson (Capitol), Jo Stafford (Reprise), Sammy Davis Jr. (Decca), and Billy Eckstine (MGM), among others. Frank Loesser's demo recording is on the compact disc *An Evening with Frank Loesser* (DRG).

VERSE 1

SARAH: For I've imagined every bit of him,
From his strong moral fiber to the wisdom
in his head,
To the homey aroma of his pipe.
SKY: You have wished yourself a Scarsdale
Galahad
The breakfast-eating Brooks Brothers
type!
SARAH: [spoken] Yes.
[sung] And I shall meet him when the time
is ripe.

REFRAIN

SARAH: I'll know when my love comes along,
I won't take a chance.
For oh, he'll be just what I need,
Not some fly-by-night Broadway romance.
SKY: And you'll know at a glance
By the two pair of pants.
SARAH: I'll know by the calm steady voice,
Those feet on the ground.

I'll know as I run to his arms
That at last I've come home safe and
    sound.
And till then, I shall wait,
And till then, I'll be strong,
For I'll know when my love comes along.

VERSE 2

SKY: Mine will come as a surprise to me.
    Mine I leave to chance, and chemistry.
SARAH: [spoken] Chemistry?
SKY: [spoken] Yeah, chemistry.

REFRAIN

SKY: [sung] Suddenly I'll know when my love
        comes along
    I'll know then and there.
    I'll know at the sight of her face
    How I care, how I care, how I care!
    And I'll stop and I'll stare
    And I'll know, long before we can speak,
    I'll know in my heart.
    I'll know, and I won't ever ask,
    "Am I right? Am I wise? Am I smart?"
    But I'll stop
    And I'll stare
    At that face in the throng.
    Yes, I'll know—
BOTH: When my love comes along.

[SKY exits.]

SARAH: I won't take a chance—
    My love will be just what I need
    Not some fly-by-night Broadway romance.
    And till then I shall wait
    And till then I'll be strong,
    For I'll know when my love comes along.

A BUSHEL AND A PECK

Published. Copyrighted September 15, 1950. Previously registered for copyright as an unpublished song August 14, 1950. Published as part of **Guys and Dolls** vocal score, September 3, 1953. Introduced by Vivian Blaine (Adelaide) and ensemble (The Hot Box Girls). The top recordings were by Perry Como and Betty Hutton (RCA Victor) and by Margaret Whiting and Jimmy Wakely (Capitol). Also recorded by Doris Day (Columbia), the Andrews Sisters (Decca), Johnny Desmond (MGM), and the McGuire Sisters (Reprise).

In a 1984 radio interview with Ezio Petersen, Lynn Loesser gave this version of how the song came about:

This was written before *Guys and Dolls* was even thought of. It had come about because I had read a book by Truman Capote called *Other Voices, Other Rooms*, a collection of short stories that came out as he was just breaking on the literary scene. I insisted that Frank read it. I was getting ready for bed one evening and Frank came tearing upstairs hollering, "You've got to come down, I've just found something." So I went down to the piano and he'd found a passage in Capote's book that quoted on old nursery rhyme that went "I love you a bushel and a peck and a hug around the neck." He quickly wrote the whole song based on that line.

After he'd written it I asked him if maybe he should talk to Capote and ask if it was alright to use the line. Frank brushed it off as being obviously in the public domain since it was quoted as a nursery rhyme or saying. When *Guys and Dolls* came along, Frank pulled it out of the trunk and that was that.

I met Capote a year or so later and he said he'd almost sued Frank but decided at the last minute that it wasn't worth it.

GIRLS: He loves me, he loves me not.
    He loves me, he loves me not.
ADELAIDE: I love you
    A bushel and a peck,
    A bushel and a peck
    And a hug around the neck.
    Hug around the neck
    And a barrel and a heap,
    Barrel and a heap
    And I'm talking in my sleep
    About you.
GIRLS: [spoken] About you?
ADELAIDE: [sung] About you.
GIRLS: [spoken] My heart is leapin',
    Havin' trouble sleepin'.
ADELAIDE: [sung] 'Cause I love you
    A bushel and a peck.
    You bet your pretty neck I do.

ALL: Doodle, oodle, oodle,
    Doodle, oodle, oodle,
    Doodle, oodle, oodle-oo.
GIRLS: Doodle, oodle, oodle,
    Doodle, oodle, oodle,
    Doodle, oodle, oodle-oo.

ALL: I love you
    A bushel and a peck,
    A bushel and a peck
    Though it beats me all to heck.

ADELAIDE: Beats me all to heck
    How I'll
    Ever tend the farm,
    Ever tend the farm,
    When I want to keep my arm
    About you.
GIRLS: [spoken] About you?
ADELAIDE: [sung] About you.
GIRLS: [spoken] The cows and chickens
    Are going to the dickens.
ADELAIDE: [sung] 'Cause I love you
    A bushel and a peck.
    You bet your pretty neck I do.

ALL: Doodle, oodle, oodle,
    Doodle, oodle, oodle,
    Doodle, oodle, oodle-oo.
    [spoken] G'bye now.
    [sung] Doodle, oodle, oodle,
    Doodle, oodle, oodle,
    Doodle, oodle, oodle-oo.

ADELAIDE'S LAMENT

Published. Copyrighted December 28, 1950. Previously registered for copyright as an unpublished song August 14, 1950. Published as part of **Guys and Dolls** vocal score, September 3, 1953. Introduced by Vivian Blaine (Adelaide). Recorded by Carol Burnett (Decca), Debbie Reynolds (Reprise), and Barbra Streisand (Columbia), among others.

Originally written for a stripper who caught cold due to exposure, the song was revised after Abe Burrows's book for *Guys and Dolls* was completed. Vivian Blaine, who originated the role, nearly turned it down. "I almost walked out," she recalled in a 1959 radio interview. "But before I could finish the line 'Thanks a lot, Frank—' he said, 'Wait a minute, I want you to hear something.' He then sat down and played 'Adelaide's Lament.'"

VERSE 1

[spoken] It says here:
[sung as she reads] "The av'rage unmarried
    female,
Basically insecure,
Due to some long frustration, may react
With psychosomatic symptoms,
Difficult to endure.
Affecting the upper respiratory tract."
In other words, just from waiting around
For that plain little band of gold,
A person can develop a cold.
You can spray her wherever you figure

The streptococci lurk;
You can give her a shot
For whatever she's got,
But it just won't work.
If she's tired of getting the fish eye
From the hotel clerk,
A person can develop a cold.

VERSE 2

"The female remaining single,
Just in the legal sense,
Shows a neurotic tendency. See note."
[*spoken*] Note:
[*sung*] "Chronic, organic syndromes,
Toxic or hypertense,
Involving the eye,
The ear and the nose and the throat."
In other words, just from worrying whether
The wedding is on or off,
A person can develop a cough.
You can feed her all day with the vitamin A
And the Bromo Fizz,
But the medicine never gets anywhere near
Where the trouble is.
If she's getting a kind of name for herself
And the name ain't his,
A person can develop a cough.
And furthermore,
Just from stalling and stalling
And stalling the wedding trip,
A person can develop la grippe.
When they get on the train for Niag'ra,
And she can hear church bells chime,
The compartment is air conditioned
And the mood sublime,
Then they get off at Saratoga
For the fourteenth time,
A person can develop la grippe. [*clears throat*]
La grippe,
La postnasal drip,
With the wheezes and the sneezes,
And a sinus that's really a pip!
From a lack of community property
And a feeling she's getting too old,
A person can develop a bad, bad cold.

GUYS AND DOLLS

Published. Copyrighted September 15, 1950. Previously registered for copyright as an unpublished song August 14, 1950. Cut lyrics from script draft dated September 11, 1950. Published as part of *Guys and Dolls* vocal score, September 3, 1953. Introduced by Stubby

Kaye (Nicely) and Johnny Silver (Benny). Danced by Peter Gennaro and Beverly Larsen. Recorded by Frank Sinatra and Dean Martin (Reprise), Bobby Darin (Atco), Ella Fitzgerald (Verve), Johnny Mathis (Columbia), and Harry James (Columbia), among others.

VERSE

NICELY: What's playing at the Roxy?
I'll tell you what's playing at the Roxy:
A picture about a Minnesota man
So in love with a Mississippi girl
That he sacrifices everything
And moves all the way to Biloxi.
That's what's playing at the Roxy.
BENNY: What's in the *Daily News*?
I'll tell you what's in the *Daily News:*
Story about a guy who bought his wife a
small ruby
With what otherwise would have been his
union dues.
That's what's in the *Daily News.*
NICELY: What's happening all over?
I'll tell you what's happening all over:
Guy's sitting home by a television set who
once
Used to be something of a rover.
BOTH: That's what's happening all over.
Love is the thing that has licked 'em,
And it looks like Nathan's just another
victim.

REFRAIN 1

NICELY: [*spoken*] Yes sir.
[*sung*] When you see a guy
Reach for stars in the sky,
You can bet
That he's doing it for some doll.
BENNY: When you spot a John waiting out in the
rain,
Chances are he's insane as only a John
Can be for a Jane.
NICELY: When you meet a gent
Paying all kinds of rent
For a flat
That could flatten the Taj Mahal—
BOTH: Call it sad, call it funny,
But it's better than even money
That the guy's only doing it for some doll.

REFRAIN 2

BENNY: When you see a Joe
Saving half of his dough,
You can bet
There'll be mink in it for some doll.

NICELY: When a bum buys wine like a bum can't
afford,
It's a cinch that the bum is under the
thumb
Of some little broad.
BENNY: When you meet a mug
Lately out on the jug
And he's still lifting platinum folderol,
BOTH: Call it hell, call it heaven,
It's probable twelve to seven
That the guy's only doing it for some doll.

REFRAIN 3

BENNY: When you see a sport
And his cash has run short,
Make a bet
That he's banking it with some doll.
NICELY: When a guy wears tails with the front
gleaming white,
Who the hell do you think he's tickling
pink
On Saturday night?
BENNY: When a lazy slob
Takes a good steady job
And he smells from Vitalis and
Barbasol—
BOTH: Call it dumb, call it clever,
Ah, but you can give odds forever
That the guy's only doing it
For some doll, some doll,
The guy's only doing it for some doll!

Additional lyrics in sheet music

The following lyrics were intended for Adelaide and the dolls, as the number was originally written as a duet between Nathan and Adelaide with backing from the ensemble.

ADELAIDE: When you see a dame
Change the shape of her frame,
You can bet
She's reducing it for some guy.
When you find a doll with her diamond
in hock,
Rest assured that the rock has gone to
restock
Some gentleman jock.
When you see a mouse
Hurry out of the house
And she runs twenty blocks for cigars
and rye,
Call it dumb, call it clever,
Ah, but you can give odds forever
That the doll's only doing it for some guy.

Cut lyrics

DOLLS: That's more than a somewhat wrong
   point of view.
  Hey, Adelaide, tell 'em a thing or two.

ADELAIDE: When you see a skirt
  Busy starching a shirt,
  Make a bet that she's doing it for some
   guy.
  When you see his mate
  And she says, "I feel great,"
  But she's still got the supersuds in her
   eye,
  Call it sad, call it funny,
  But it's better than even money
  That the doll's only doing it for some
   guy.

IF I WERE A BELL

Published. Copyrighted September 15, 1950. Previously registered for copyright as an unpublished song August 14, 1950. Cut lyrics from script draft dated September 11, 1950. Published as part of **Guys and Dolls** vocal score, September 3, 1953. Introduced by Isabel Bigley (Sarah). Recorded by Dinah Shore (Reprise), Doris Day (Columbia), Ella Fitzgerald (Verve), Carmen McRae (Decca), and Sarah Vaughan and Joe Williams (Roulette), among others.

SARAH: Ask me how do I feel,
  Ask me now that we're cozy and clinging.
  Well, sir, all I can say is,
  If I were a bell I'd be ringing.
  From the moment we kissed tonight,
  That's the way I've just got to behave.
  Boy, if I were a lamp I'd light,
  And if I were a banner I'd wave.
  Ask me how do I feel,
  Little me with my quiet upbringing.
  Well, sir, all I can say is,
  If I were a gate I'd be swinging.
  And if I were a watch I'd start
  Popping my spring.
  Or if I were a bell I'd go
  Ding, dong, ding, dong, ding.

  Ask me how do I feel
  From this chemistry lesson I'm learning.
SKY: [spoken] Chemistry?
SARAH: [spoken] Yeah, chemistry.
SARAH: [sung] Well, sir, all I can say is,
  If I were a bridge I'd be burning.

Yes, I knew my morale would crack
From the wonderful way that you looked.
Boy, if I were a duck I'd quack
Or if I were a goose I'd be cooked.
Ask me how do I feel,
Ask me now that we're fondly caressing.
Pal, if I were a salad
I know I'd be splashing my dressing.
Ask me how to describe*
This whole beautiful thing.
Well, if I were a bell I'd go
Ding, dong, ding, dong, ding.

Cut lyrics

Ask me how do I feel
And my answer is perfectly candid.
Yes, if I were a fish, I'd be hooked,
I'd be hauled, I'd be landed.
In addition, may I announce,
It's a feeling that simply won't stop.
Boy, if I were a ball I'd bounce,
Or if I were a bubble I'd pop.
Ask me how do I feel,
Little me with the weak solar plexus.
Man, if I were a state, I'd be grand,
I'd be great, I'd be Texas.
Ask me how to describe
This whole beautiful thing.
Well, if I were a bell I'd go
Ding, dong, ding, dong, ding.

MY TIME OF DAY

Published. Copyrighted October 2, 1950. Previously registered for copyright as an unpublished song August 14, 1950. Published as part of **Guys and Dolls** vocal score, September 3, 1953. Introduced by Robert Alda (Sky). Recorded by Mel Tormé (Atlantic), Carmen Cavallero (Decca), and Jo Sullivan Loesser and Don Stephenson (DRG), among others.

My time of day is the dark time:
A couple of deals before dawn,
When the street belongs to the cop
And the janitor with the mop,
And the grocery clerks are all gone,
When the smell of the rain-washed pavement

---

* *Sheet music lyrics:*
 Or if I were a season
 I'd surely be spring.

Comes up clean and fresh and cold,
And the street lamplight
Fills the gutter with gold.
That's my time of day,
My time of day,
And you're the only doll I've ever wanted
To share it with me.

I'VE NEVER BEEN IN LOVE BEFORE

Published. Copyrighted September 15, 1950. Previously registered for copyright as an unpublished song August 14, 1950. Cut lyrics from script draft dated September 11, 1950. Published as part of **Guys and Dolls** vocal score, September 3, 1953. Introduced by Robert Alda (Sky) and Isabel Bigley (Sarah). Recorded by Frank Sinatra (Reprise), Mel Tormé (Polydor), and Doris Day (Columbia), among others. Frank Loesser's demo recording is on the compact disc *An Evening with Frank Loesser* (DRG).

I've never been in love before;
Now all at once it's you,
It's you forevermore.
I've never been in love before.
I thought my heart was safe.
I thought I knew the score.
But this is wine
That's all too strange and strong.
I'm full of foolish song
And out my song must pour.
So please forgive
This helpless haze I'm in;
I've really never been
In love before.

[*Repeated as follows: Lines 1–10 sung by* SARAH; *lines 11–14 sung by* SARAH *and* SKY.]

Cut lyrics

CODA (SUNG TO "MY TIME OF DAY")

SARAH: Your time of day can never be mine
  We're wrong for each other.

SKY: My time of day,
  My time of day,
  And you're the only doll I've ever wanted
  To share it with me.

The following lyrics were intended as a bridge between "My Time of Day" and "I've Never Been in Love Before." The bracketed insertions are Loesser's.

I guess I've never been in love before;
Now all at once . . . [*interrupting himself*]
Did you happen to hear what I said?
Someone ought to examine my head.
I've never been in love before. [*à la Henry Aldrich*]
My routines were so clever and bright
Now it's suddenly amateur night.
I've never been in love before. [*à la Pinza, laughing at himself*]
Guess I sound like a songwriter pouring it on,
About miracles out of the blue.
But the terrible, wonderful thing is
That it's true.
I've never been in love before . . .

After the lyrics above were cut, Abe Burrows wrote the following dialogue segue between the two songs:

SKY: Obediah!
SARAH: Obediah! What's that?
SARAH: Obediah Masterson. That's my real name. You're the first person I've ever told it to.

"I said to Frank, 'That's the best love scene I ever wrote,'" Burrows recalled. "And Frank just wanted to hit me . . . he wanted room for a musical saying of it."

TAKE BACK YOUR MINK

Published. Copyrighted December 28, 1950. Previously registered for copyright as an unpublished song November 24, 1950. Published as part of *Guys and Dolls* vocal score, September 3, 1953. Introduced by Vivian Blaine (Adelaide) and The Hot Box Girls. Recorded by Pearl Bailey (Roulette), Debbie Reynolds (Reprise), Julie London (Liberty), and Dorothy Shay (Columbia), among others.

Choreographer Michael Kidd, in a 1990 interview with Steve Nelson, recalled how this song was added to the show just prior to its New York opening:

"Take Back Your Mink" was added on the last night we were in Philadelphia. The second act used to start with "A Bushel and a Peck." Abe [Burrows] had the idea of going to the Hot Box earlier, moving Bushel to the first act and coming

up with a new number for Act 2. Frank had a number in the trunk all the time, and figured we could do it as a strip.

Now this was a week or so before we left Philly. Alvin Colt was excited and began working on costumes and props that could be easily taken off, pearl bracelets with bicycle clips, things like that. He went back to New York and we continued to work, laid out the whole number with rehearsal props and makeshift minks. The costumes arrived the morning of our last day, with only a few hours before a matinee. The show started, but there was still no music for the number. Near the end of the first act, the music arrived—the smell of ammonia from the copiers nearly knocked us over when the package was opened.

Irving Actman got the orchestra together at intermission and gave them their parts, quickly talking everyone through the material they would have to play cold for the first time in a few minutes. They ran through the fingering as Actman gave them tempos and cues. The costumes, music, everything was happening for the first time. And it literally stopped the show. Like in the movies, only for real.

ADELAIDE: He bought me the fur thing five winters ago
And the gown the following fall.
Then the necklace, the bag, the gloves, and the hat—
That was late 'forty-eight, I recall.*
Then last night in his apartment
He tried to remove them all!
And I said as I ran down the hall:

"Take back your mink,
Take back your pearls—
What made you think
That I was one of those girls?
Take back the gown,
The shoes, and the hat.
I may be down,
But I'm not flat as all that!

"I thought that each expensive gift you'd arrange
Was a token of your esteem.
Now when I think of what you want in exchange,
It all seems a horrible dream.
So take back your mink
To from whence it came,

---

* In film:
Oh, what generous gifts I recall!
And go shorten the sleeves.

And tell them to Hollanderize it*
For some other dame!"

ADELAIDE
AND GIRLS: "Take back your mink,
Take back your pearls—
What made you think
That I was one of those girls?"
I'm screaming,
"Take back the gown,
Take back the hat—
I may be down
But I'm not flat as all that!

"I thought that each expensive gift you'd arranged
Was a token of your esteem.
But when I think of what you want in exchange,
It all seems a horrible dream—eek!
Take back your mink,
Those old worn-out pelts,
And go shorten the sleeves
For somebody else."

ALTERNATE LYRICS

ADELAIDE: He bought me the fur thing five winters ago,
And the gown the following fall.
Then the necklace, the bag, the gloves, and the hat—
Oh, what generous gifts I recall!
But I found he had a motive,
A motive not nice at all.
What I said could be heard in the hall:

"Take back your mink,
Take back your pearls—
What made you think
That I was like other girls?
Take back the gloves, the hat, and the shoes;
Your evening gown is one I choose to refuse.
I thought that each expensive gift you'd arranged
Was a token of your esteem.
Now when I think of how you suddenly changed,
It all seems a horrible dream.

---

* The phrase "Hollanderize it" refers to a process by which inexpensive coats were streaked to resemble sable and other more exotic furs. The Hollander Company was then one of the more prominent firms providing this service.

So take back your mink
To from whence it came,
And tell them to shorten the sleeves
For some other dame."

ADELAIDE'S SECOND LAMENT

Introduced by Vivian Blaine (Adelaide). Recorded by
Kim Criswell on Jay Records by John Yap in 1996.

In other words, just from sitting alone
At a table reserved for two,
A person can develop the flu.
You can bundle her up in her woolies,
And I mean the warmest brand;
You can wrap her in sweaters and coats
Till it's more than her frame can stand—
If she still gets the feeling she's naked,
From looking at her left hand,
A person can develop the flu.
Huh! The flu,
A hundred and three point two!
So much virus inside
That her microscope slide
Looks like a day at the zoo!
Just from wanting her mem'ries in writing,
And a story her folks can be told,
A person can develop a cold.

MORE I CANNOT WISH YOU

Published. Copyrighted December 4, 1950. Previously
registered for copyright as an unpublished song March 21,
1949. Published as part of *Guys and Dolls* vocal score,
September 3, 1953. Originally written for, but not used
in, the film *Roseanna McCoy*. Introduced by Pat
Rooney Sr. (Arvide). Recorded by Bing Crosby (Decca),
Mabel Mercer (Atlantic), Jo Sullivan Loesser (DRG),
and Ed Ames (RCA Victor), among others.

In a letter (quoted in Susan Loesser's *A Most Remarkable Fella*) responding to a question about the phrase
"the sheep's eye and the lickerish tooth," Loesser went on
to discuss his use of the phrase and the song's origins:

"Sheep's eye" is, just as you suspect, descriptive of
amorous longing. I suppose the exact expression is
"making sheep's eyes at." The color and sound of

this was enough for me. . . . Now we come to
"lickerish tooth. . . ." So I consulted Roget (grudgingly, because usually I know more than he does)
to find that "covetous" (which was the key meaning in my mind) could be described as "lecherous." I then looked up lecherous for variations less
appalling in sound to the modern ear. This I did
by way of the *Oxford English Dictionary* (the big
twelve-volume one) and found to my great delight
two archaic spellings: one was licorice (somehow
combining the literal sense of "sweet tooth" with
the fundamental meaning of the word)—and the
other "lickerish" which had a much more satisfying adjective suffix. In the exemplary material on
these words I found "lickerish tooth," which fitted
neatly with the notes in hand, and even more
neatly with my sense of what the old man's mischief should sound like in the scene.

I correct myself. It was not the old man originally
but the older brother of the young lady Roseanna
McCoy, heroine and title character of a Sam Goldwyn movie. It was for a scene in which she sits beside
her brother in the seat of a wagon. She is 16 and she
is being taken to her first fair. . . . Sam Goldwyn neither liked nor understood the song and asked me for
another. This turned out to be "Roseanna" which
gained certain broad approval and was quite right for
the picture. I held on to the original and found quite
proper use for it in *Guys and Dolls*.

Velvet I can wish you
For the collar of your coat,
And fortune smiling all along your way.
But more I cannot wish you
Than to wish you find your love,
Your own true love, this day.

Mansions I can wish you,
Seven footmen all in red,
And calling cards upon a silver tray.
But more I cannot wish you
Than to wish you find your love,
Your own true love, this day.

Standing there
Gazing at you
Full of the bloom of youth.
Standing there
Gazing at you
With the sheep's eye
And the lickerish tooth.

Music I can wish you,
Merry music while you're young,
And wisdom when your hair has turned to gray.
But more I cannot wish you
Than to wish you find your love,

Your own true love, this day,
With the sheep's eye
And the lickerish tooth
And the strong arms to carry you away.

LUCK BE A LADY

Published. Copyrighted October 10, 1950. Previously
registered for copyright as an unpublished song August 14, 1950. Published as part of *Guys and Dolls* vocal
score, September 3, 1953. Introduced by Robert Alda
(Sky) and craps shooters. Recorded by Frank Sinatra
(Reprise), Sammy Davis Jr. (Decca), Vic Damone (Columbia), and Cy Coleman (Capitol), among others.
Frank Loesser's demo recording is on the compact disc
An Evening with Frank Loesser (DRG).

VERSE

SKY: They call you Lady Luck,
But there is room for doubt.
At times you have a very unladylike
way of running out.
You're on this date with me,
The pickings have been lush;
And yet before this evening is over
You might give me the brush.
You might forget your manners;
You might refuse to stay.
And so the best that I can do is pray.

REFRAIN

SKY: Luck, be a lady tonight.
Luck be a lady tonight.
Luck, if you've ever been a lady to
begin with,
Luck be a lady tonight.

Luck, let a gentleman see
How nice a dame you can be.
I know the way you've treated other
guys you've been with—
Luck be a lady with me.

A lady doesn't leave her escort;
It isn't fair, it isn't nice.
A lady doesn't wander all over the
room
And blow on some other guy's dice.

So let's keep the party polite.
Never get out of my sight.
Stick with me, baby, I'm the fellow you

came in with,
Luck be a lady,
Luck be a lady,
Luck be a lady tonight.

CRAP-
SHOOTERS: Luck be a lady tonight.
Luck be a lady tonight.
Luck, if you've ever been a lady to
begin with,
Luck be a lady tonight.

SKY: Luck, let a gentleman see—
CRAP-
SHOOTERS: Luck, let a gentleman see—
SKY: How nice a dame you can be.
CRAP-
SHOOTERS: How nice a dame you can be.
SKY: I know the way you've treated other
guys you've been with.
CRAP-
SHOOTERS: Luck be a lady, a lady, be a lady with me.
SKY: Luck be a lady with me.

SKY: A lady wouldn't flirt with strangers;
She'd have a heart, she'd have a soul.
A lady wouldn't make little snake eyes
at me—
CRAP-
SHOOTERS: Roll 'em, roll 'em, roll 'em, snake eyes—
SKY: When I've bet my life on this roll.
CRAP-
SHOOTERS: Roll 'em, roll 'em, roll 'em.
SKY: So let's keep the party polite.
CRAP-
SHOOTERS: So let's keep the party polite.
SKY: Never get out of my sight.
CRAP-
SHOOTERS: Never get out of my sight.
Stick here, baby, stick here, baby.
SKY: Stick with me, baby, I'm the fellow you
came in with,
Luck be a lady—
CRAP-
SHOOTERS: Luck be a lady—
SKY: Luck be a lady—
CRAP-
SHOOTERS: Luck be a lady,
Roll, will ya—roll, will ya—
What's the matter? Roll the dice!
SKY: Luck, be a lady tonight.
CRAP-
SHOOTERS: Comin' out, comin' out,
Comin' out, comin' out right.
SKY AND
CRAP-
SHOOTERS : Ha!

SUE ME

Published. Copyrighted November 27, 1950. Previously registered for copyright as an unpublished song August 14, 1950. Cut lyrics from script draft dated September 11, 1950. Published as part of *Guys and Dolls* vocal score, September 3, 1953. Introduced by Vivian Blaine (Adelaide) and Sam Levene (Nathan). Recorded by Debbie Reynolds and Allan Sherman (Reprise) and Carmen Cavallero (Decca), among others. Frank Loesser's demo recording is on the compact disc *An Evening with Frank Loesser* (DRG).

VERSE (FOR SOLO VERSION)

So you're all the time right and I'm all the time
wrong.
So my character's weak and your character's
strong.
So your brow is so high and my brow is so low.
So brow, shmow,
I'm close to you now,
And all I can tell you is oh, go—

REFRAIN (LINES 1–3 SUNG IN FILM ONLY)

ADELAIDE: You promise me this,
You promise me that,
You promise me anything under the
sun,
Then you give me a kiss
And you're grabbin' your hat
And you're off to the races again.
When I think of the time gone by—
NATHAN: Adelaide! Adelaide!
ADELAIDE: And I think of the way I try—
NATHAN: Adelaide!
ADELAIDE: I could honestly die.

NATHAN: Call a lawyer and sue me, sue me,
What can you do me?
I love you.
Give a holler and hate me, hate me,
Go ahead, hate me,
I love you.
ADELAIDE: The best years of my life I was a fool to
give to you.
NATHAN: Alright already, I'm just a nogoodnik.
Alright already, it's true, so nu?
So sue me, sue me,
What can you do me?
I love you.

ADELAIDE: You gamble it here,
You gamble it there,

You gamble on everything, all
except me,
And I'm sick of you keeping me up in
the air
Till you're back in the money again.
When I think of the time gone by—
NATHAN: Adelaide! Adelaide!
ADELAIDE: And I think of the way I try—
NATHAN: Adelaide!
ADELAIDE: I could honestly die.

NATHAN: Serve a paper and sue me, sue me,
What can you do me?
I love you.
Give a holler and hate me, hate me,
Go ahead, hate me,
I love you.
ADELAIDE: When you wind up in jail, don't come
to me to bail you out.
NATHAN: Alright already, so call a policeman.
Alright already, it's true, so nu?
So sue me, sue me,
What can you do me?
I love you.

ADELAIDE: You're at it again;
You're running the game,
I'm not gonna play second fiddle to
that.
And I'm sick and I'm tired of stalling
around.
And I'm telling you now that we're
through.
When I think of the time gone by—
NATHAN: Adelaide! Adelaide!
ADELAIDE: And I think of the way I try—
NATHAN: Adelaide!
ADELAIDE: I could honestly die.
NATHAN: Sue me, sue me,
Shoot bullets through me.
I love you.

CUT LYRICS

ADELAIDE: You tell me I'm yours,
You tell me you're mine,
You tell me whatever comes into your
head.
And I'm tired of stalling and waiting
around,
And I'm telling you now that we're
through.

SIT DOWN YOU'RE ROCKIN' THE BOAT

Published. Copyrighted October 10, 1950. Published as part of *Guys and Dolls* vocal score, September 3, 1953. Introduced by Stubby Kaye (Nicely) and ensemble. Recorded by Louis Armstrong (Decca), Sammy Davis Jr. (Reprise), Carmen Cavallero (Decca), and Don Henley (MCA), among others. Frank Loesser's demo recording is on the compact disc *An Evening with Frank Loesser* (DRG).

VERSE 1

NICELY: I dreamed last night
I got on a boat to heaven
And by some chance
I had brought my dice along.
And there I stood
And I hollered, "Someone fade me,"
But the passengers, they knew right
    from wrong.

REFRAIN 1

For the people all said, "Sit down,
Sit down, you're rockin' the boat."
ENSEMBLE: People all said, "Sit down,
Sit down, you're rockin' the boat."
NICELY: "And the devil will drag you under
By the sharp lapel of your checkered
    coat.
Sit down, sit down, sit down, sit down."
ENSEMBLE: "Sit down, you're rockin' the boat."

VERSE 2

NICELY: I sailed away
On that little boat to heaven,
And by some chance
Found a bottle in my fist.
NICELY: And there I stood—
NICELY: Nicely passin' out the whiskey,
But the passengers were bound to
    resist.

REFRAIN 2

NICELY: For the people all said, "Beware,
You're on a heavenly trip."
ENSEMBLE: People all said, "Beware, beware—"
NICELY: People all said, "Beware,
Beware, you'll scuttle the ship—"
ENSEMBLE: People all said, "Beware—"
NICELY: "And the devil will drag you under—"
ENSEMBLE: "Sit down—"

NICELY: "By the fancy tie round your
    wicked throat.
Sit down, sit down, sit down, sit
    down."
ENSEMBLE: "Sit down, sit down."
NICELY: "Sit down, you're rockin' the boat."
ENSEMBLE: "Sit down, you're rockin' the boat—
    down—"

VERSE 3

NICELY: And as I laughed
At those passengers to heaven,
A great big wave
Came and washed me overboard.
NICELY: And as I sank—
NICELY: And I hollered, "Someone save me!"
That's the moment I woke up—
NICELY: Thank the Lord.
ENSEMBLE: Thank the Lord, thank the Lord.

REFRAIN 3

NICELY: And I said to myself, "Sit down,
Sit down, you're rockin' the boat."
ENSEMBLE: Said to himself, "Sit down, sit down."
NICELY: Said to myself, "Sit down,
Sit down, you're rockin' the boat."
ENSEMBLE: Said to himself, "Sit down."
NICELY: "And the devil will drag you under
With a soul so heavy you'd never float.
Sit down, sit down, sit down, sit
    down—"
ENSEMBLE: "Sit down, you're rockin' the boat."

NICELY AND
ENSEMBLE: "Sit down, you're rockin',
Sit down, sit down,
Sit down, you're rockin' the boat.
Sit down, you're rockin',
Sit down, sit down,
Sit down, you're rockin' the boat.
Sit down, you're rockin' the boat!"

ADELAIDE MEETS SARAH

Published as part of *Guys and Dolls* vocal score. Copyrighted September 3, 1953. Previously registered for copyright as an unpublished dramatic work April 3, 1951. Introduced by Vivian Blaine (Adelaide) and Isabel Bigley (Sarah). Recorded by Emily Loesser and Kim Criswell on Jay Records in 1996.

SARAH: So please forgive—
ADELAIDE: "Keep the Vick's on your chest
And get plenty of rest,"
You can wisely warn her.
SARAH: This helpless haze I'm in—
ADELAIDE: But in spite of the quiet,
Massages and diet,
She's still a goner.
SARAH: I've never really been—
ADELAIDE: Once she gets the idea that the little
    church—
SARAH: In love—
ADELAIDE: Will always be around the corner—
SARAH: Before—
ADELAIDE: A person can develop a cold.

MARRY THE MAN TODAY

Published. Copyrighted September 7, 1951. Previously registered for copyright as an unpublished song December 4, 1950. Published as part of *Guys and Dolls* vocal score, September 3, 1953. Introduced by Vivian Blaine (Adelaide) and Isabel Bigley (Sarah).

ADELAIDE: [*spoken*] At Wanamaker's and Saks and
    Klein's
[*sung*] A lesson I've been taught:
You can't get alterations on a dress you
    haven't bought.
SARAH: At any veg'table market from Borneo
    to Nome,
You mustn't squeeze a melon till you
    get the melon home.
ADELAIDE: You've simply got to gamble.
SARAH: You get no guarantee.
ADELAIDE: Now doesn't that kind of apply to you
    and I?
SARAH: You and me.
ADELAIDE: [*spoken*] Why not?
SARAH: [*spoken*] Why not what?

ADELAIDE: [*sung*] Marry the man today,
Trouble though he may be,
Much as he loves to play,
Crazy and wild and free.
BOTH: Marry the man today,
Rather than sigh and sorrow.
ADELAIDE: Marry the man today
And change his ways tomorrow.
SARAH: Marry the man today.
ADELAIDE: Marry the man today,
SARAH: Maybe he's leaving town.
ADELAIDE: Maybe he's leaving town.

SARAH: Don't let him get away.

ADELAIDE: Don't let him get away.

SARAH: Hurry and track him down.

ADELAIDE: Counterattack him and—

BOTH: Marry the man today,
Give him the girlish laughter.

SARAH: Give him your hand today
And save the fist for after.

ADELAIDE: Slowly introduce him to the better
things,
Respectable, conservative, and clean.

SARAH: *Reader's Digest!*

ADELAIDE: Guy Lombardo!

SARAH: Rogers Peet!

ADELAIDE: [*spoken*] Golf!

SARAH: [*spoken*] Galoshes!

ADELAIDE: [*sung*] Ovaltine!

BOTH: But marry the man today,
Handle it meek and gently.

ADELAIDE: Marry the man today and train him
subsequently.

SARAH: Carefully expose him to domestic life,
And if he ever tries to stray from you,
Have a pot roast.

ADELAIDE: Have a headache.

SARAH: Have a baby.

ADELAIDE: Have two!

SARAH: [*spoken*] Six!

ADELAIDE: [*spoken*] Nine!

SARAH: [*spoken*] Stop!

BOTH: [*sung*] Marry the man today
Rather than sigh and sorrow.
Marry the man today
And change his ways,
And change his ways,
And change his ways
Tomorrow!

CUT AND UNUSED SONGS

SHANGO

Registered for copyright as an unpublished song August 14, 1950. Intended for the Havana scene. Dropped prior to New York opening.

Anybody roun' here wanna shango?
Anybody roun' here wanna shango?
Gimme six bits, mister, we go crazy all night.
Anybody roun' here wanna shango?
No more money for whiskey,
No more money for rum;
I buy lottery number,
Goddam number don't come.
Anybody roun' here wanna shango?
Everybody sometime gotta shango.

Anybody roun' here wanna shango?
Anybody roun' here wanna shango?
Gimme six bits, mister, dance, get drunk, have
good time.
Anybody roun' here wanna shango?
I go dance in Havana,
I get put in the jail;
Then I swear, "Judge, Your Honor,
No more shango for sale."
Anybody roun' here wanna shango?
Everybody sometime gotta shango.

TRAVELING LIGHT

Registered for copyright as an unpublished song August 14, 1950. Intended for Sky Masterson and Nathan Detroit. Dropped prior to New York opening although listed in opening-night program. Cut verse from script draft dated September 11, 1950. Frank Loesser's demo recording is on the compact disc *An Evening with Frank Loesser* (DRG). Also recorded by Gregg Edelman (Sky) and Tim Flavin (Nathan) on Jay Records in 1996.

Sam Levene, who originated the role of Nathan Detroit, later explained that his vocal talent was not what got him the part:

> I went to Mr. Loesser's house and he sat down at the piano and said, "Let me hear you sing. What do you know?" I said " 'Pony Boy,' " he said, "I don't believe it. That's ALL you know? Don't you know 'The Star-Spangled Banner'?" and I said, "Not enough of it," so he told me to sing "Pony Boy." I sing it and he sits there for a second and comes over to me. "This is impossible. Do it the right way." "This IS the right way," I tell him. "I don't know any other way." He fell down laughing and I got the job.

In addition to cutting most of his solo and duet singing opportunities, Loesser instructed Levene to mouth the words during chorus numbers so as not to throw off the other vocalists.

VERSE

Most guys buy themselves houses
And promptly box themselves in
With the stove and the wife,
A subscription to *Life*,
And the sound of Junior practicing violin.
And they no longer dream about places they'll
go;
They just brood about places they've been.
Well, thank you very much,
Though the joys be many,
Thank you very much,
I'm not having any.

REFRAIN

I'm traveling light;
No one's weighing me down—
Got my ticket in my pocket and
I'm ready to blow town.
Ticket in my pocket and
I'm ready to blow town.

I'm traveling light,
Mister, see what I mean?
Got my ticket in my pocket if
I don't like your routine.
Ticket in my pocket and
I'm ready to break clean.

And I'm damned if your mortgage I'll carry,
Though your proposition's a beaut.
And I'm damned if your sister I'll marry—
Guess I left my heart in my other suit.

And I'm traveling light;
No one's weighing me down—
Got my ticket in my pocket,
For the minute the gods frown,
Ticket in my pocket and
I'm ready to blow town.

CUT VERSE

Some guys march to the altar
And promptly lose all their chums,
'Cause their moxie turns mush
And they'll drop a straight flush
To go home to their dear ever-lovin' when twelve
o'clock comes.
And they no longer feast on tomorrow's peach pie;
They just nibble on yesterday's crumbs.
Well, listen to me, boy,
You can do without it;
Listen to me, boy,
While I tell about it.

NATHAN'S PROBLEM

Unfinished lyric. Intended for Nathan Detroit. No music known to exist.

I wanted to be a cop
When I was a boy of nine,
I shudder and shrink
Whenever I think
Of that childhood perversion of mine.

I wanted to be a cop,
An ugly abnormal streak:
When my father found out,
He gave me a clout,
And said, "No cigarettes for a week."

I come from a family of artists;
Regard their illustrious lives:
My grandpa was Max the Engraver—
Such beautiful singles and fives!

My aunt was a fashion designer;
Her name was on everyone's lips.
This woman invented the falsies,
The brassiere stuffed with policy slips.

IT FEELS LIKE FOREVER

From undated typescript with note "Incomplete." This title was listed on the cover of early publications of *Guys and Dolls* sheet music. Abe Burrows recalled hearing Loesser play the song some months before Burrows was hired to write the show's book.

REFRAIN

Forever, forever, it feels like forever.
That great love the last time
Was merely a pastime.
But now this is it,
This is everything,
This is all.
Forever, forever, it feels like forever,
Ev'ry time you fall.

VERSE 1

Yesterday's romance was only in fun,
Yesterday's romance that's over and done.

Now that your starlight tonight has begun,
Yesterday's romance was only in fun.

[*Repeat refrain lines 4–8 after each verse.*]

VERSE 2

Yesterday's starlight was tinsel and glue,
Stuck to the ceiling an hour or two.
Now that your love boat has sailed into view,
Yesterday's starlight was tinsel and glue.

VERSE 3

Yesterday's love boat was papier-mâché,
Yesterday's love boat that drifted away.
Now from your dreamhouse you casually say,
Yesterday's love boat was papier-mâché.

VERSE 4

Yesterday's dreamhouse was built upon sand,
Yesterday's dreamhouse has crumbled, as
    planned.
Now that pure heaven is really at hand,
Yesterday's dreamhouse was built upon sand.

VERSE 5

Yesterday's heaven you willingly fled,
Yesterday's heaven that's deader than dead.
Now with each new love that goes to your head,
Yesterday's heaven was only a bed.

I COME A-RUNNING

From undated piano-vocal sheet. Frank Loesser noted on a review of his catalogue in the early 1960s that the song was "left over from *Guys and Dolls*." A private recording of the song by Loesser is on the compact disc *Frank Sings Loesser* (Koch).

I come a-running
When you call my name.
I come a-running
To get set aflame,

Lost all my cunning
And all sense of shame.
I come a-running
When you call my name.

Oh, snap your fingers or whistle
When I come round.
No hide and seek,
No hare and hound.

So why go a-gunning
For wild, wary game?
I come a-running,
I get in touch
When you so much
As call my name.

THREE-CORNERED TUNE
(Based on "Fugue for Tinhorns")

Published. Copyrighted April 17, 1951. Music previously copyrighted as "Fugue for Tinhorns." Recorded by Dinah Shore (RCA Victor), Blossom Dearie (Painted Smiles), and Sarah Brightman (Polygram). Performed as a round.

It has a tender sound, this little tune I found,
I don't know why it's following me around,
La da,
La da,
La da-dya da da-da da,
La da-dya da da-da da,
La da, la da.

I heard it all begin above the Broadway din
And it was so appealing I joined right in,
La da,
La da,
La da-dya-da da-da da,
La da-dya-da da-da da,
La da,
La da.

And now I walk along among the Broadway
    throng
Inviting everybody to sing my song,
La da,
La da,
La da-dya-da da-da da,
La da-dya-da da-da da,
La da,
La da.

GUYS AND DOLLS (FILM)

PET ME, POPPA

Published. Copyrighted October 3, 1955. Previously registered for copyright as an unpublished song February 7, 1955. Introduced by Vivian Blaine (Adelaide) and The Hot Box Girls. Recorded by Rosemary Clooney (Columbia), Carmen Cavallero (Decca), and Micki Marlo (Capitol), among others.

INTRODUCTION

GIRLS: One meow, two meow, three meow, scat!
　　　What's the initial of my pet tomcat?
　　　Is it ABCDEFG? Is it H or J or LMNOP?
　　　Is it LMNOPQRST? No, it's U!
　　　You're the cat for me!
　　　Meow!

VERSE

ADELAIDE: You know you've been mean to me,
　　　　　And you know when you're mean to me
　　　　　How it always makes me want to roam.
　　　　　And you know there's a danger
　　　　　That some gentle stranger
　　　　　Might pick me up and make me feel at
　　　　　　home.
　　　　　So—

REFRAIN

ADELAIDE: Pet me, Poppa,
　　　　　Poppa, pet me nice.
GIRLS: Meow. Meow.
ADELAIDE: Pet me, Poppa,
　　　　　Poppa, melt the ice.
GIRLS: And you know how.
ADELAIDE: If you don't want me out roaming the
　　　　　　city,
　　　　　Talk to me pretty,
　　　　　"Here, kitty, kitty,"
　　　　　And pet me, Poppa,
　　　　　Poppa, pet me nice.
　　　　　Pet me, Poppa,
　　　　　Poppa, pet me good.
GIRLS: Meow. Meow.
ADELAIDE: Pet me, Poppa,
　　　　　Proper like you should.

GIRLS: As you know how.
ADELAIDE: If you care to keep me home by the
　　　　　　fire,
　　　　　Specially when it's time to retire—
ALL: Then pet me, Poppa,
　　　Poppa, pet me good.
ADELAIDE: Warm up my saucer of milk
　　　　　And maybe I'll purr.
　　　　　Lay out my cushion of silk;
　　　　　Don't rumple my fur.
　　　　　Just reach over and—
ALL: Pet me, Poppa,
　　　Poppa, pet me nice.
GIRLS: Tasty little mouse,
　　　　Meet me on the roof
　　　　And we'll have one on the house!
ALL: Pet me, Poppa,
　　　Poppa, melt the ice.
ADELAIDE: If you don't want me out roaming the
　　　　　　city—
ALL: Talk to me pretty,
　　　"Here, kitty, kitty,"
　　　And pet me, Poppa,
　　　That's my good advice.
　　　Pet me, Poppa, meow!
　　　Pet me, Poppa, rrrow!
　　　Pet me, Poppa,
　　　Poppa, pet me—
　　　That'll get me—
　　　Pet me, Poppa,
　　　Poppa, pet me nice!

ADELAIDE

Published. Copyrighted October 3, 1955. Previously registered for copyright as unpublished song March 1, 1955. Introduced by Frank Sinatra (Nathan). Recorded by Sammy Davis Jr. (Decca), Steve Lawrence (Coral), and Jerry Vale (Columbia), among others. Frank Loesser's demo recording is on the compact disc *An Evening with Frank Loesser* (DRG).

VERSE

Unaccustomed as I am to gettin' married,
I am takin' this occasion here to say
That me and Adelaide are finally namin' the day.
Though she knows deep in her heart
I'm a phony and I'm a fake,
She wants five children to start—
Five's a difficult point to make!

REFRAIN

But Adelaide, Adelaide,
Ever-lovin' Adelaide
Is takin' a chance on me.
Takin' a chance I'll be respectable and nice,
Give up cards and dice
And go for shoes and rice!
So, gentlemen, deal me out,
Do not try to feel me out,
I got no more evenings free
Since Adelaide, Adelaide,
Ever-lovin' Adelaide
Is taking a chance
(Talk about your long shots),
Taking a chance on me!

A WOMAN IN LOVE

Published. Copyrighted October 3, 1955. Previously registered for copyright as an unpublished song February 3, 1955. Introduced (in Spanish) by Ruben de Fuentes, the Los Amigos Trio, and Rene Renor. Danced by Marlon Brando and Jean Simmons. Reprised by Marlon Brando (Sky) and Jean Simmons (Sarah). Recorded by Marlon Brando and Jean Simmons (Decca), Frankie Laine (Columbia) and Gordon MacRae (Capitol), among others.

SKY: Your eyes are the eyes of a woman in love,
　　　And oh, how they give you away!
　　　Why try to deny you're a woman in love
　　　When I know very well what I say?
　　　I say no moon in the sky ever lent such a
　　　　glow;
　　　Some flame deep within made them shine.
　　　Those eyes are the eyes of a woman in love,
　　　And may they gaze evermore into mine,
　　　Tenderly gaze evermore into mine.

SARAH: And what about you?
　　　　It's got you, too.

　　　　Your eyes are the eyes of a man who's in love.
SKY: That same flame deep within made them
　　　shine.
SARAH: Those eyes are the eyes of a man who's in
　　　　love—
SKY: Woman in love—
BOTH: And may they gaze evermore into mine,
　　　Lazily gaze evermore into mine.

Hans Christian Andersen

and the dancer

Suddenly your heart is winging to song...and lilting to dances that are indescribably beautiful...and glowing to the glorious story of the greatest storyteller of them all.

Yes, something wonderful *really* happens when you see Samuel Goldwyn's multi-million dollar Technicolor musical "Hans Christian Andersen"!

COLOR BY TECHNICOLOR

8 WONDERFUL SONG HITS!
"No Two People", "Anywhere I Wander", "Thumbelina", "Wonderful Copenhagen" ...and more

HANS CHRISTIAN ANDERSEN | 1952

HANS CHRISTIAN ANDERSEN

Produced by Samuel Goldwyn. Released by RKO Radio in November 1952. Music and lyrics by Frank Loesser. Screenplay by Moss Hart, based on a story by Myles Connolly. Directed by Charles Vidor. Choreography by Roland Petit. Musical direction by Walter Scharf. Cast starred Danny Kaye, Farley Granger, and Zizi Jeanmaire (billed as Jeannmaire) and featured Erik Bruhn, John Brown, John Qualen, Jeanne Lafayette, Robert Malcolm, Peter Votrian, and Roland Petit.

Samuel Goldwyn first assigned writers to work on the project in 1938. By the time Moss Hart and Loesser completed the script and songs, Goldwyn owned thirty-two different versions of the show. Farley Granger summarized the plot as "Boy meets girl; boy loses girl; boy gets boy."

Recordings: Danny Kaye's studio versions of the eight songs from the film were released on Decca. Frank and Lynn Loesser recorded "The Ugly Duckling," "The Inch Worm," and "The King's New Clothes" for MGM Records. The Kaye and Loesser recordings appeared at the time of the film's release. Frank Loesser's private performances of "Wonderful Copenhagen" and "No Two People" (with Lynn Loesser) are on the compact disc *Frank Sings Loesser* (Koch).

THE KING'S NEW CLOTHES

Published. Copyrighted September 20, 1952. Previously registered for copyright as an unpublished song October 3, 1951. Introduced by Danny Kaye with children's chorus. Recorded by Danny Kaye (Decca) and Frank Loesser (MGM), among others. Loesser's private recording is on the compact disc *Frank Sings Loesser* (Koch).

Loesser was aware that purists might resent his changing "Emperor's" to "King's": "When you get home tonight," he told the *Boston Herald* prior to the film's release, "you try to make up a song with the word emperor in it, and then you'll see why I had to use the word king instead. I'll probably start a couple of wars when the picture opens, but I just couldn't do it the other way."

VERSE 1

KAYE: [*spoken*] Once there was a king who was very fond of wearing new clothes.* One day, two swindlers came to see the king to sell him what they *said* was a magic suit of clothes. Now the king was very fond of

---
* *Opening sentence not used in film.*

new clothes, so he said, "Well, let me see it."
But there wasn't any suit of clothes. You see, the swindlers held up their hands like this [*gestures*] and said, "Your Majesty, this is a *magic suit*. And since you're very wise and intelligent, you can see how beautiful it is, but to a fool, it is absolutely invisible!"
Well, he said, "I see," and not wanting to appear a fool, he added, "Yes indeed, I see it perfectly. It's beautiful!"

REFRAIN 1

KAYE: "Isn't it grand! Isn't it fine!
Look at the cut, the style, the line!
[*sung*] The suit of clothes is altogether,
But altogether, it's altogether
The most remarkable suit of clothes
That I have ever seen.
These eyes of mine at once determine
The sleeves are velvet, the cape is ermine,
The hose are blue, and the doublet is
A lovely shade of green."
CHORUS: A lovely shade of green.
KAYE: "Somebody send for the queen!"

VERSE 2

KAYE: [*spoken*] The queen came, and she was told very quickly how all the wise people could see the—
CHORUS: Magic suit.
KAYE: And naturally, not wanting to appear a fool, she said—

REFRAIN 2

KAYE: "Isn't it great! Isn't it rich!
Look at the charm of ev'ry stitch!
[*sung*] The suit of clothes is altogether,
But altogether, it's altogether
The most remarkable suit of clothes
That I have ever seen.
These eyes of mine at once determine
The sleeves are velvet, the cape is ermine,
The hose are blue, and the doublet is
A lovely shade of green."
CHORUS: A lovely shade of green.
KAYE: "Summon the court to convene!"

VERSE 3

KAYE: And all the court came. The ministers came. The ambassadors came. And naturally, not wanting to

seem like fools, they quickly agreed with the—
CHORUS: King and queen.

REFRAIN 3 (NOT SUNG IN FILM)

KAYE: "Isn't it [*whisper*] oh!
Isn't it [*whisper*] ah!
Isn't it absolutely [*whistle*]!
The suit of clothes is altogether,
But altogether, it's altogether
The most remarkable suit of clothes,
As you've already said.
These eyes of ours at once determine
The sleeves are velvet, the cape is ermine,
The hose are blue, and the doublet is
A lovely shade of red."
CHORUS: [*shouted*] Green!
KAYE: [*sung*] "Oh, yes, green!
How could we think it was red?"

VERSE 4

KAYE: [*spoken*] And the king issued a proclamation as follows:

REFRAIN 4

KAYE: [*sung*] The suit of clothes is altogether,
But altogether, it's altogether
The most remarkable suit of clothes
A tailor ever made.
Now quickly put it all together
With gloves of leather
And hat and feather—
It's altogether
The thing to wear in Saturday's parade.
CHORUS: Saturday's parade.
KAYE: Leading the Royal Brigade!

VERSE 5

KAYE: [*spoken*] Well, by this time everybody had heard about the king's new clothes, and that he was going to wear them in the parade. The people lined the streets as

The Artillery came by,
And the Infantry came by,
And the Cavalry came by,
And the Fife and Drum Corps,
And the Royal Guard,
And finally, the king!
And everybody cheered:
ALL: Hooray!
KAYE: Because nobody wanted to appear a fool. Nobody, that is, except one little boy, who for some strange reason hadn't

heard about the king's new magic suit, and didn't know what he was *supposed* to see. Well, he took one look, turned a little pale, and said:

REFRAIN 5

KAYE: "Look at the king! Look at the king!
Look at the king, the king, the king!
[*sung*] The king is in the altogether,
But altogether, the altogether.
He's altogether as naked as
The day that he was born.
The king is in the altogether,
But altogether, the altogether—
It's altogether the very least
The king has ever worn.
Call the court physician!
Call an intermission!
His Majesty is wide open to ridicule and
    scorn.
The king is in the altogether,
But altogether, the altogether.
He's altogether as naked as
The day that he was born.
And it's altogether too chilly a morn!"

THE INCH WORM

Published. Copyrighted September 17, 1952. Previously registered for copyright as an unpublished song September 24, 1951. Introduced by Danny Kaye and children's chorus. Recorded by Danny Kaye (Decca), John Coltrane (MCA), Doris Day (Columbia), and Frank and Lynn Loesser (MGM), among others. The Loesser's private recording is on the compact disc *Frank Sings Loesser* (Koch).

Loesser's affection for this song was recalled by his daughter Susan in *A Most Remarkable Fella:*

It was his favorite song in the movie, and so, in June 1953, he was delighted to receive a letter, dated "Now," with no return address, and handwritten in a peculiar curvy, loopy, caterpillian script:

Dear Loesser your song Inchworm makes me very happy; not only from an inchwormitarian point of view (I know you must realize that people will not be so repelled by us after this) but from the aspect of downright beauty. It is conceivable that if Robert Burns and the god Pan, and Antoine de St. Exupery, and Euclid had gotten together for three days and three nights they might have been able to write almost equally good words, but as I see it no

group of musicians nor any other one musician could have written the beautiful music. It is simple, yet it is so intricate, the harmony is perfect and the counterpoint—well it just gives me a headache when I think of what it would be like to try to write it tho I suppose for you it was easy.

I'd like to send you a leaf or something in appreciation of the delight your song has given me, but since that probably wouldn't be the correct thing to do, I'll close by promising you that after this I'll try to admire the marigolds. Respectfully, a Kansas inchworm. (Please excuse the writing. It is not a customary practice, and besides, my back has been aching a little today. Have been following my hunches a little too often lately.)

My father noted that the letter was postmarked Lawrence, Kansas. He had his secretary find the local newspaper with the biggest readership, then placed a five-inch-square ad in the *Daily Journal World:*

<pre>
        H   W
  I   C   O   M
    N   R
</pre>

F.L. SAYS

THANKS FOR

THE LETTER

Happily, the inchworm could read as well as write. It telegraphed "GRATITUDE GRATEFULLY AND HAPPILY RECEIVED" and wrote to explain that its name was Emily Preyer, a kindergarten teacher and the daughter of a piano teacher. "I have always made up stories for the children, so when I knew I had to write you about 'Inchworm' I just made up a story for you. Your 'thanks' in our paper was one of the nicest things that ever happened to me."

VERSE (NOT SUNG IN FILM)

Two and two are four,
Four and four are eight.
That's all you have on your bus'nesslike mind.
Two and two are four,
Four and four are eight.
How can you be so blind?

REFRAIN

CHILDREN: Two and two *are* four,
Four and four *are* eight,
Eight and eight *are* sixteen,
Sixteen and six*teen* are thirty-two.

[CHILDREN *repeat refrain and continue it beneath the following lines:*]

KAYE: Inchworm, inchworm,
Measuring the marigolds—
You and your arithmetic,
You'll probably go far.

Inchworm, inchworm,
Measuring the marigolds—
Seems to me you'd stop and see
How beautiful they are.

I'M HANS CHRISTIAN ANDERSEN

Published. Copyrighted September 17, 1952. Previously registered for copyright as an unpublished song November 30, 1951. Introduced by Danny Kaye. Recorded by Danny Kaye (Decca), Tommy Steele (Marble Arch), and Bernard Cribbins (MFP), among others.

KAYE: I'm Hans Christian Andersen,
I've many a tale to tell,
And though I'm a cobbler,
I'd say I tell them rather well.
I'll mend your shoes and I'll fix your boots
When I have a moment free,
When I'm not otherwise occupied
As a purple duck, or a mountainside,
Or a quarter after three.
I'm Hans Christian Andersen,
That's me!

I'm Hans Christian Andersen,
And this is an April day.
It's full of the magic
I need to speed me on my way.
My pocketbook has an empty look;
I limp on a lumpy shoe.
So I turn into a flying fish
Or a millionaire
With a rocking chair
And a dumpling in my stew.
I'm Hans Christian Andersen,
Andersen, that's who.

I'm Hans Christian Andersen,
The pride of the cobbler's trade.
Permit me to show you a great
    discovery I've made.
A shoe goes squeak and a shoe goes
    squawk,

A squeakiddy-squawk all day.
And though you'd figure a shoe can't
   talk,
If you listen close to the squeak and
   squawk,
You can plainly hear it say,
"Let Hans Christian Andersen
Fix me right away."

In Hans Christian Andersen
Your feet have a loyal friend,
The sort of a doctor, I'm sure, your
   toes would recommend.
I work all night if a shoe's too tight
To see where the pinch comes from.
I raise my hammer and shut one eye,
And I sometimes hit on the reason why,
And sometimes I hit my thumb.

POLICEMAN: [spoken] What's your name?
KAYE: [sung] I'm Hans Christian Andersen.
POLICEMAN: [spoken] Thank you, you're under
   arrest.

KAYE: I'm Hans Christian Andersen
   That fortune has smiled upon.
   Although I'm a duckling today,
   Tomorrow I'm a swan.
   A tale I told
   And it turned to gold,
   As gold as a tale can be.
   I laugh "ha ha," but I blush a bit,
   For I realize while I'm reading it
   That it's also reading me.
   "By Hans Christian Andersen"—
   I am a swan!

   I write myself a note each day
   And I place it in my hat.
   The wind comes by, the hat blows
      high,
   But that's not the end of that.
   For round and round the world it
      goes;
   It lands here right behind myself.
   I pick it up, and I read the note,
   Which is merely to remind myself
   I'm Hans Christian Andersen.
   Andersen.

   I'm Hans Christian Andersen,
   I bring you a fable rare.
   There once was a table
   Who said, "Oh, how I'd love a chair."
   And then and there came a sweet
      young chair
   All dressed in a bridal gown.
   He said to her in a voice so true,

"Now I did not say I would marry
   you,
But I would like to sit down."
I'm Hans Christian Andersen,
Andersen's in town.

Unused verses

I'm Hans Christian Andersen;
I see what I wish to see.
That you are a rosebud, madam,
Is very clear to me.
It seems that I am a butterfly,
And over to you I flit.
I kiss you once and I kiss you twice,
And it's awfully good, and it's rather nice,
And you don't mind me a bit.
I'm Hans Christian Andersen—
Andersen!
That's it!

I'm Hans Christian Andersen;
My pen's like a babbling brook.
Permit me to show you,
Dear sir, my very latest book.
Now here's a tale of a simple fool;
Just glance at a page or two.
You laugh "ha ha," but you blush a bit,
For you realize while you're reading it
That it's also reading you.
I'm Hans Christian Andersen.
How do!

I'm Hans Christian Andersen
And this is an April day.
And speaking of April,
I've heard she hates her sister May.
Her sister May leads a life so gay;
Oh my, what a thoughtless brat.
While April sits having crying fits,
Little thanks she gets making violets
For her sister's Sunday hat.

I'm Hans Christian Andersen,
The man with the shop on wheels.
And I have a little story, kind souls,
To set upon your heels.
There once were two little Army boots;
Whenever they'd march they'd fight.
The right one said he was always left;
He was left bereft by the tough old left,
Who insisted he was right.
And Hans Christian Andersen
Brought the case to light.

WONDERFUL COPENHAGEN

Published. Copyrighted September 17, 1952. Previously registered for copyright as an unpublished song September 24, 1951. Introduced by George Chandler (Farmer, dubbed by Ray Linn) and male ensemble, with Danny Kaye and Joey Walsh (Peter) joining in on repeated refrain. Recorded by Danny Kaye (Decca), Guy Lombardo (Decca), and Frank and Lynn Loesser (Koch), among others.

VERSE

FARMER: I sail up the Skaggerak and sail down
   the Kattegat,
   Through the harbor and up to the quay,
   And there she stands, waiting for me,
   With a welcome so warm and so gay!

REFRAIN

FARMER: Wonderful, wonderful Copenhagen,
   Friendly old girl of a town,
   Neath her tavern light*
   On this merry night—
ALL: Let us clink and drink one down—
FARMER: To wonderful, wonderful Copenhagen,
ALL: Salty old queen of the sea!
FARMER: Once I sailed away,
   But I'm home today—
ALL: Singing, "Copenhagen,
   Wonderful, wonderful
   Copenhagen for me!"

STREET VOICES

Registered for copyright as an unpublished song December 26, 1951. Introduced by ensemble.

---

* When Frank Loesser was asked to remove references to alcohol for a 1955 choral arrangement, he complied and submitted the new lyric with the following caveat: "I have found that alcohol is one of the few things that make group singing bearable." Special lyrics for refrain, lines 3–6, Fred Waring choral arrangement, 1955:
   With her harbor light
   That she wears at night
   Like a golden, golden crown—
   Oh, wonderful, wonderful Copenhagen,

NEWSPAPER BOY: *Copenhagen Weekly Gazette*—get your *Weekly Gazette*!

MATCH GIRL: Matches! Matches! Please buy my matches!

BRIC-A-BRAC MAN: Bric-a-brac! Bric-a-brac! Bric-a-brac!

FLOWER GIRL: Nice fresh roses! Nice fresh roses!

MILKMAN: Milkman—milkman!

POTS-AND-PANS MAN: Pots and pans! Pots and pans!

CHIMNEY SWEEP: Chimney sweep, sweep your chimney!

FISH WOMAN: Bass! Bass! Buy a bass!

CLAM WOMAN: Nice fresh clams!

FISH MAN: Fresh fish!

RHUBARB WOMAN: Buy rhubarb—rhubarb— buy rhubarb!

SAUSAGE MAN: Sau-sa-ges! Sau-sa-ges!

FLOWER GIRL: Pretty flowers!

CHEESE SELLER: Cheese—buy it here!

BERTHA THE BAKER: Buy your bread from Bertha the baker!

THUMBELINA

Published. Copyrighted September 17, 1952. Previously registered for copyright as an unpublished song September 24, 1951. Introduced by Danny Kaye. Recorded by Danny Kaye (Decca) and Guy Lombardo (Decca), among others. It was nominated for an Academy Award as Best Song of the Year, but lost out to the title song from *High Noon*.

Susan Loesser recalled that her father had little regard for the song and "referred to 'Thumbelina' as an insignificant little ditty, not a real song. Whenever he wanted to make a point about a cheap song, his own or someone else's, he would mention 'Thumbelina.' He never gave himself credit for writing exactly what the scene required: a charming 'little ditty' meant to entertain a small child."

VERSE 1

Though you're no bigger than my thumb,
Than my thumb,
Than my thumb,
Sweet Thumbelina, don't be glum.
Now, now, now!
Ah, ah, ah!
Come, come, come!

REFRAIN

Thumbelina, Thumbelina, tiny little thing.
Thumbelina, dance! Thumbelina, sing!
Oh, Thumbelina, what's the diff'rence
If you're very small?
When your heart is full of love,
You're nine feet tall.

VERSE 2 (NOT SUNG IN FILM)

Though you're no bigger than my toe,
Than my toe,
Than my toe,
Sweet Thumbelina, keep that glow.
And you'll grow,
And you'll grow,
And you'll grow!

REPEAT REFRAIN

THE UGLY DUCKLING

Published. Copyrighted September 17, 1952. Previously registered for copyright as an unpublished song December 17, 1951. Introduced by Danny Kaye. Recorded by Danny Kaye (Decca), Mitch Miller (Golden), and Frank Loesser (MGM).

There once was an ugly duckling
With feathers all stubby and brown,
And the other birds,
In so many words, said,
"(Quack!) Get out of town.
(Quack!) Get out,
(Quack! Quack!) Get out,
(Quack! Quack!) Get out of town."
And he went with a quack
And a waddle and a quack
In a flurry of eiderdown.

That poor little ugly duckling
Went wandering far and near,
But at ev'ry place,
They said to his face,
"(Quack!) Get out of here.
(Quack!) Get out,
(Quack! Quack!) Get out,
(Quack! Quack!) Get out of here."
And he went with a quack
And a waddle and a quack
And a very unhappy tear.

All through the wintertime he hid himself away,
Ashamed to show his face,
Afraid of what others might say.
All through the winter in his lonely clump of weed,
Till a flock of swans spied him there and very soon agreed,
"You're a very fine swan indeed!"

[*spoken*] "Swan? Me a swan? Aw, go on!"
"Yes, you're a swan!
Take a look at yourself in the lake and you'll see!"
And he looked and he saw, and he said:
"I *AM* a swan! Whee!"

[*sung*] "I'm not such an ugly duckling,
No feathers all stubby and brown.
For in fact these birds,
In so many words,
Said, 'Tsk!* The best in town.
Tsk! The best,
Tsk! Tsk! The best,
Tsk! Tsk! The best in town!' "

Not a quack, not a quack,
Not a waddle or a quack,
But a glide and a whistle and a snowy white back
And a head so noble and high!
"Say, who's an ugly duckling?
Not I!"

ANYWHERE I WANDER

Published. Copyrighted September 17, 1952. Previously registered for copyright as an unpublished song September 24, 1951. Introduced by Danny Kaye. Recorded by Danny Kaye (Decca), Julius LaRosa (Cadence), Jan Peerce (RCA), Mel Tormé (Capitol), and Tony Bennett (Columbia), among others.

VERSE 1

Her arms were warm as they welcomed me;
Her eyes were fire bright.
And then I knew that my path must be
Through the ever-haunted night, for—

REFRAIN

Anywhere I wander,
Anywhere I roam,
Till I'm in the arms of my darling again

* *Alternately, an admiring whistle.*

My heart will find no home—
Anywhere I wander,
Anywhere I roam.

VERSE 2 (NOT SUNG IN FILM)

Her voice was, oh, such a soft caress;
Of love it gently told.*
And in her smile was the tenderness
I may never more behold, but—

REPEAT REFRAIN

VERSE 3 (NOT SUNG IN FILM)

Her tears were silver as morning dew
As she bade me goodbye.
And ev'ry tear was a promise true
That her love would never die, so—

REPEAT REFRAIN

NO TWO PEOPLE

Published. Copyrighted September 17, 1952. Previously registered for copyright as an unpublished song October 8, 1951. Introduced by Zizi Jeanmaire and Danny Kaye. Recorded by Doris Day and Donald O'Connor (Columbia), Dinah Shore and Jack Smith (Capitol), Danny Kaye and Jane Wyman (Decca), Steve Lawrence and Eydie Gorme (Decca), and Frank Loesser and Lynn Loesser's private recording (Koch).

JEANMAIRE: Never before and never again could
Anything more romantic and
beautiful be!
KAYE: Never before and never again,
No two people have ever been so in
love—
JEANMAIRE: Been so in love—
KAYE: Been so in love—
JEANMAIRE: Been so in love—
KAYE: Been so in love.
JEANMAIRE: It's incredible.
No two people have ever been so in
love—
KAYE: Been so in love—
BOTH: As my lovey dove and I.
JEANMAIRE: This is unique,
The positive peak,

*Alternate line:
Her hair was moon-bright gold.

Oh, we are the most unusual couple
on earth!
KAYE: No two people have ever mooned such
a moon—
JEANMAIRE: Mooned such a moon—
KAYE: Juned such a June—
JEANMAIRE: Juned such a June—
KAYE: Spooned such a spoon.
JEANMAIRE: What he means is that
No two people have ever been so in
tune—
KAYE: Been so in tune—
BOTH: As my macaroon and I.
KAYE: And when we kiss—
JEANMAIRE: And when we kiss—
KAYE: And when we kiss—
JEANMAIRE: Well, it's like this.
KAYE: Well, it's historical,
It's hysterical—
JEANMAIRE: Let me tell it.
KAYE: Well, certainly, darling.
JEANMAIRE: No two people have ever been so in
love—
KAYE: Been so in love—
JEANMAIRE: Been so in love—
KAYE: Been so in love—
JEANMAIRE: Been so in love—
KAYE: It's impossible.
No two people have ever been so in
love—
JEANMAIRE: Been so—
BOTH: As my lovey dove and I.
JEANMAIRE: This is the cream, the very
extreme,
The sort of a dream you couldn't
imagine at all.
KAYE: Well, anyway,
No two people have ever been so in
love—
JEANMAIRE: Been so—
BOTH: As my lovey dove and I.

THE SHOE SONG

Registered for copyright as an unpublished song September 24, 1951. Intended for Danny Kaye. Not used in film.

VERSE 1

Do your shoes go squeak?
Do your shoes go squawk?
Do your shoes go squeak, squawk
When you walk?

REFRAIN

Well, wood or leather, leather or wood,
I fix your shoes and I fix 'em good.

VERSE 2

Do your toes go ooh?
Do your toes go ow?
Do your toes go ooh, ow
Right now?

REPEAT REFRAIN

VERSE 3

Do your soles go flap?
Do your soles go flip?
Do your soles go flap, flip
Every trip?

REPEAT REFRAIN

GIVE YOUR LOVE TO ME

From undated typed lyric sheet. No music is known to survive.

VERSE

I do not ask for treasure
To make all my dreams come true.
I'd have wealth beyond all measure;
Just one thing I need from you.

REFRAIN

Give your love to me,
All your love to me,
And the love you give will live deep in my
heart.
While we're close like this,
Share my burning kiss;
Give your love to me and swear we'll never part.
Let your heart beat fast;
Make this moment last—
Say that mine and mine alone you'll always be.
From the thrilling spell of you
I'll never be free.
My darling, give your love to me.

SECOND FANTASY

From undated typed lyric sheet. Intended for Danny Kaye and Zizi Jeanmaire.

KAYE: Come away with me,
Come away with me,
Come away to the warm and tender
    land
Of my heart.
Come away with me.
JEANMAIRE: I must dance,
I must dance,
I must dance . . .
KAYE: Come away with me.
JEANMAIRE: No! I must dance,
I must dance,
I must dance.

[*Interlude*]

JEANMAIRE: Don't follow me, please.
KAYE: I'll follow you everywhere.
JEANMAIRE: Please beware.
BOTH: My love.

SO YOU WANT TO BE A FIREMAN?

From undated typed lyric sheet. Written as a party number during work on *Hans Christian Andersen*. Not in film. No music known to survive.

So you want to be a fireman
And wear a big red hat?
Or maybe join the circus
And leap like an acrobat!
Or maybe a policeman
With a badge new and shiny;
Or maybe a deep-sea diver
Who lives down in the briny?
Or maybe a doctor
Who helps make people better;
Or maybe the friendly postman
Who loves to bring a letter!
Or maybe the busy farmer
Who mows the fields of hay?
Or maybe a famous movie star
And sing like Danny Kaye!

THE MOST
HAPPY FELLA
1956

THE MOST HAPPY FELLA

Tryouts: Shubert Theatre, Boston, March 13–28, 1956, and Shubert Theatre, Philadelphia, April 10–28, 1956. New York premiere: May 3, 1956, Imperial Theatre. 676 performances. London premiere: April 21, 1960, London Coliseum. 288 performances. New York production presented by Kermit Bloomgarden and Lynn Loesser. Book, music, and lyrics by Frank Loesser, based on Sidney Howard's play *They Knew What They Wanted.* Directed by Joseph Anthony. Scenery and lighting by Jo Mielziner. Costumes by Motley. Choreography by Dania Krupska. Orchestrations by Don Walker. Orchestral and choral direction by Herbert Greene. Cast featured Robert Weede (Tony), Jo Sullivan (Rosabella/Amy), Art Lund (Joe), Susan Johnson (Cleo), Shorty Long (Herman), and Mona Paulee (Marie), with Arthur Rubin (Giuseppe), Rico Froehlich (Pasquale), John Henson (Jake/Ciccio), Keith Kaldenberg (Doctor), and Lee Cass (Cashier/Postman). Revived in New York in 1979 and 1992.

Nearly five years in the making, *The Most Happy Fella* was Loesser's one-man attempt (libretto, lyrics, and music) to create a sung-through work such as Broadway had not seen since Gershwin's *Porgy and Bess* in 1935. "Actually it's not opera," Loesser told an interviewer shortly before the show's opening. "It just has a great frequency of songs."

Cast recordings: Original cast (Columbia); London cast (HMV); 1991 Broadway revival (two-piano version)—(RCA). A 1953 private demo of an early version of Act I, scene 1 is on the compact disc *An Evening with Frank Loesser* (DRG). Instrumental selections from the show were recorded by Percy Faith (Columbia). In 2000 a complete recording (including many cut songs) was released, featuring Louis Quilico and Emily Loesser (Jay).

OOH! MY FEET!

Published as part of the piano-vocal score and libretto. Copyrighted March 5, 1956. Previously registered for copyright as part of the unpublished vocal score and libretto January 10, 1956. Introduced by Susan Johnson (Cleo). A private demo recording of this song by Maxene Andrews is on the compact disc *An Evening with Frank Loesser* (DRG). The song was originally intended

Robert Weede (in wheelchair), Jo Sullivan (fainting) and cast members in the 1956 New York production of The Most Happy Fella. *Inset: Jo Sullivan and Susan Johnson*

for *Guys and Dolls,* to be sung by a weary cop on the beat. When the character was transformed into vice-chasing Lieutenant Brannigan, the number was dropped and Loesser rewrote it here for a waitress.

Ooh! My feet!
My poor, poor feet!
Betcha your life
A waitress earns her pay.
I've been on my feet,
My poor, poor feet,
All day long today.

Ooh! My toes!
My poor, poor toes!
How can I give
The service with a smile
When I'm on my toes,
My poor, poor toes,
Mile after mile, after mile,
After mile, after mile?

This little piggy's only broken,
This little piggy's on the bum,
This little piggy's in the middle,
Consequently absolutely numb.

This little piggy feels the weight of the plate,
Though the freight's just an order of Melba toast.
And this little piggy is the littlest little piggy,
But the big son of a bitch hurts the most!

Ooh! My feet!
My poor, poor feet!
Betcha your life
A waitress earns her pay.
I've been on my feet,
My poor, poor feet,
All day long today
Doing my blue-plate-special ballet!

I KNOW HOW IT IS and SEVEN MILLION CRUMBS and I DON'T KNOW and MAYBE HE'S KIND OF CRAZY

Published as part of the piano-vocal score and libretto. Copyrighted March 5, 1956. Previously registered for copyright as part of the unpublished vocal score and libretto January 10, 1956. Introduced by Jo Sullivan (Rosa-

bella) and Susan Johnson (Cleo). A private demo recording of "I Know How It Is" and "Seven Million Crumbs" is on the compact disc *An Evening with Frank Loesser* (DRG).

I Know How It Is

ROSABELLA: [*spoken*] Cleo, I don't care if he fires me! I'm not going out with that slimy . . . slob.
CLEO: [*sung*] I know how it is,
Don't tell me, I know how it is—
When you're number twenty-seven on the list,
Being kissed is not exactly being . . .
ROSABELLA: [*spoken*] I guess I've helped a few fellas prove they were fellas, but they were guys I liked and they thought I was something special . . .
CLEO: [*sung*] I know how it is—
ROSABELLA: [*spoken*] . . . and they asked me nice.
CLEO: [*sung*] Don't tell me, I know how it is.
But when you're just twenty-seven in his book,
Getting took out is much more like getting took!

Seven Million Crumbs

ROSABELLA: Cleo! Cleo!
What do you think a customer left me?
Cleo!

[CLEO *is obviously occupied with her feet.*]

What do you think a customer left me?
CLEO: I know how it is
Don't tell me, I know how it is.
ROSABELLA: [*spoken*] What do you think he left?
CLEO: [*sung*] Seven million crumbs and a gravy spot,
Teaspoon stuck in the mustard pot,
Napkin on the floor,
Ashes in the cup,
And one Canadian dime.
So you pick it up
With the seven million crumbs and the—
ROSABELLA: It's jewelry!

[*Dialogue:* ROSABELLA *discovers the note left along with the tie pin.*]

I Don't Know

ROSABELLA: [*spoken*] Listen. It says:
[*sung*] "My dear Rosabella—"

CLEO: [*spoken*] Rosabella?

ROSABELLA: [*spoken*] I guess that's me!
[*sung*] "I call you Rosabella because I don' no your name,
And I am too a-scared to ask you."

CLEO: [*spoken*] That's what this place has always needed, a bashful customer.

ROSABELLA: [*sung*] "I canno leave you money on the table you look too nice.
And so I leave you my genuin amotist tie pin."

CLEO: [*spoken*] I wonder if it *is* real. Say, if it is, maybe a hock shop would give you a hundred dollars for it. Did you ever see a hundred-dollar bill? Back home in Dallas they're known as Texas callin' cards.

ROSABELLA: [*spoken*] Cleo, it doesn't matter if the stone is real. . . . *This* is real. I shouldn't have made fun of it. . . . It's a real love letter!
[*spoken*] Listen to what he says:
[*sung*] "I don no not'ing about you,
Where you ever go,
Wat you ever done
I don no not'ing about you.
I don wanna no,
I don gotta no.
Wat I see is kind of yung lady
I want to get marry."

CLEO: [*spoken*] Lemme see that!
[*sung*] "I don't know nothing about you,
Where you ever go,
What you ever done.
What I see is kind of young lady
I want to get marry!"

Maybe He's Kind of Crazy

ROSABELLA: Maybe he's kinda crazy.
This young fella, this young fella.
But I'm gonna send him his postcard saying:
"Thank you, Yours sincerely, Rosabella."

CLEO: He could be some kind of Rasputin
Or a small-town Jack the Ripper!
To start with
He's a lunatic of a tipper.
[*spoken*] Now how about going home?

ROSABELLA: [*spoken*] We've been going home every night, kinda *wanting* something . . . but wanting what, Cleo.

CLEO: [*spoken*] *Wanting* to soak my feet!
Come on, dream girl.

ROSABELLA: [*sung*] Wanting to be wanted.
Needing to be needed.
That's what it is.
That's what it is.
Now I'm lucky that—

[*Segue into "Somebody Somewhere."*]

SOMEBODY, SOMEWHERE

Published. Copyrighted March 9, 1956. Previously registered for copyright as part of the piano-vocal score and libretto March 5, 1956, and as part of the unpublished vocal score and libretto January 10, 1956. Introduced by Jo Sullivan (Rosabella). Recorded by Doris Day (Columbia), Ella Fitzgerald (Verve), and Jo Sullivan Loesser (DRG), among others.

Somebody, somewhere
Wants me and needs me;
That's very wonderful to know.
Somebody lonely
Wants me to care,
Wants me of all people
To notice him there.
Well, I want to be wanted,
Need to be needed,
And I'll admit I'm all aglow,
'Cause somebody, somewhere
Wants me and needs me,
Wants lonely me to smile
And say hello.
Somebody, somewhere
Wants me and needs me
And that's very wonderful to know.

PRELUDE TO "THE MOST HAPPY FELLA"

Published as part of the piano-vocal score and libretto. Copyrighted March 5, 1956. Previously registered for copyright as part of the unpublished vocal score and libretto January 10, 1956. Introduced by Lee Cass (Postman), Robert Weede (Tony), and ensemble.

POSTMAN: [*sung*] Come a-runnin'!

TOWNSPEOPLE: The mail is in!
The mail is in,
The mail is in,
The mail is in!

POSTMAN: Farnsworth!

FARNSWORTH: [*spoken*] Here I am!

POSTMAN: [*sung*] Your uncle's all right!
Johnson!

JOHNSON: [*spoken*] Yep!

POSTMAN: [*sung*] Better pay the gas and light!
Sullivan!

SULLIVAN: [*spoken*] That's me!

POSTMAN: [*sung*] You're here, thank the Lord!
'Cause Sullivan, you're breakin' my back with Montgomery Ward.
Van Pelt!
Your sister had a baby girl.
Greene!

GREENE: [*spoken*] Herbie Greene?

POSTMAN: [*spoken*] Say! Who's Pearl?
Esposito!

TOWNSPEOPLE: [*sung*] That's for Tony!
That's for Tony!
That's for Tony!

w/POSTMAN: Where's Tony Esposito?

TOWNSPEOPLE: The mail-order love affair,
The mail-order love affair.
Ev'rybody's followin'
The mail-order love affair
Of Tony Esposito!

TONY: [*spoken*] Aspetta un momento!
[*sung*] 'At's-a me!
[*spoken*] Che bellezza! È bella come un colpo di cannone! Che bella faccia!

TOWNSPEOPLE: [*sung*] What did she write ya?
What did she write ya?
What did she write ya now?

[*Segue into "The Most Happy Fella."*]

THE MOST HAPPY FELLA

Published. Copyrighted March 9, 1956. Previously registered for copyright as part of the vocal piano-score and libretto March 5, 1956, and as part of the unpublished vocal score and libretto January 10, 1956. Introduced by Robert Weede (Tony) and ensemble. Recorded by Johnny Desmond (Coral) and Frankie Laine (Decca), among others.

TONY: Hey!
Omma the most happy fella

In the whole Napa Valley,
In the whole Napa Valley,
The most happy man—
'At's me!
Look-a my Rosabella.
TOWNSPEOPLE: He's the most happy fella.
TONY: Look-a my Rosabella.
TOWNSPEOPLE: Look-a his Rosabella.
TONY: She was-a send me her
photograph,
And she was ask-a me for mine.
TOWNSPEOPLE: Ooh, fine, that's-a fine,
That's-a fine, that's-a fine.
Look at the most happy fella—
TONY: You wait an' you see!
TOWNSPEOPLE: In the whole Napa Valley.
TONY: She gonna marry me!
TOWNSPEOPLE: Good luck to you, Tony Esposito!
VOICES: [*spoken*] Hey, Tony, how did it all
get started?
Yeah. Tell us about it, Tony. etc.
TONY: [*spoken*] You wait an' I will-a tell
you.
[*sung*] In da winter time from
Frisco
She was-a write to me one
postcard.
Then I was-a write, then she was-a
write.
Then I was-a write, then she was-a
write,
Then me, then she, then me, then
she, and
Now she's-a make da springtime
come so fast!
She's-a make da green come on the
vine!
She was-a send me her photograph
And she was ask-a me for mine!*
TOWNSPEOPLE: That's-a fine, that's-a fine, that's-a
fine.

---

* *Cut sequence below followed "ask-a me for mine":*
HERMAN: *May the trains all hurry!*
GERMAN: *May the stamps all stick!*
HERMAN: *May the postman's whistle*
Sound like a beautiful song! [*Postman's*
whistle]
TOWNSPEOPLE: *And may the mail-order love affair*
Keep coming along!
For the most happy fella—
TONY: *Grazie! Grazie! Grazie!*
TOWNSPEOPLE: *In the whole Napa Valley—*
ALL: *In the whole Napa Valley*
The most happy man.
TOWNSPEOPLE: *Most happy, most happy, most*
happy man!
TONY: *That's me!*

Look at the most happy fella—
TONY: Grazie!
TOWNSPEOPLE: In the whole Napa
Valley.
TONY: Marona! Marona!
So much omma holler,
I bet you a dollar
I bust-a my collar,
You take-a one look-a my face an'-
a wha'd'ya see?
TOWNSPEOPLE: The most happy fella,
The most—
TONY: At's-a me!
TOWNSPEOPLE: Happy man!

A LONG TIME AGO

Published as part of the piano-vocal score and libretto. Copyrighted March 5, 1956. Previously registered for copyright as part of the unpublished vocal score and libretto January 10, 1956. Introduced by Mona Paulee (Marie) and Robert Weede (Tony).

MARIE: [*spoken*] What do you really know about
her?
TONY: [*sung*] I don' know not'ing about her,
Where she ever go, what she ever done,
I don' know not'ing about her,
I don' wanna know, I don' gotta know.
What I was-a see is kind o' young lady
I want to get marry!
MARIE: [*spoken*] Married?
TONY: [*spoken*] Yeah.
MARIE: [*spoken*] Tony!
[*sung*] A long time ago in the old country
Mamma looked at me right before she
died
And with her poor tired eyes she was
sayin':
"Marie, take care of Tony,
Marie, take care of your dumb,
Funny-lookin' big brother Tony."
And ever since then—
TONY: [*spoken*] Marie . . .
MARIE: [*sung*] I tried.
TONY: What I was-a see is kind o' young lady
I want to get marry.

STANDING ON THE CORNER

Published. Copyrighted March 9, 1956. Previously registered for copyright as part of the piano-vocal score and libretto March 5, 1956, and as part of the unpublished vocal score and libretto January 10, 1956. Introduced by Shorty Long (Herman), John Henson (Jake), Alan Gilbert (Clem), and Roy Lazarus (Al). Recorded by Dean Martin (Capitol), the Mills Brothers (Decca), Frankie Avalon (Chancellor), and Andy Griffith (Capitol), among others.

ALL: Standing on the corner,
Watching all the girls go by.
Standing on the corner,
Watching all the girls go by.
HERMAN: Brother, you don't know a nicer
occupation!
Matter of fact, neither do I—
ALL: Than standing on the corner,
Watching all the girls,
Watching all the girls,
Watching all the girls go by.
HERMAN: I'm the cat that got the cream.
Haven't got a girl, but I can
dream.
Haven't got a girl, but I can wish,
So I take me down to Main Street,
And that's where I select my
imaginary dish!
ALL: Standing on the corner,
Watching all the girls go by.
Standing on the corner,
Giving all the girls the eye.
HERMAN: Brother, if you've got a rich
imagination,
Give it a whirl, give it a try.
ALL: Try standing on the corner,
Watching all the girls,
Watching all the girls,
Watching all the girls go by.
HERMAN: Saturday, and I'm so broke,
Couldn't buy a girl a nickel Coke.
Still I'm living like a millionaire,
When I take me down to Main
Street
And I review the harem parading
for me there!
ALL: Standing on the corner,
Watching all the girls go by.
Standing on the corner
Underneath a springtime sky.
HERMAN: Brother, you can't go to jail
For what you're thinking

Or for the "Ooooh" look in your
eye.
ALL: You're only standing on the corner,
Watching all the girls
Watching all the girls,
Watching all the girls go by.

JOEY, JOEY, JOEY

Published. Copyrighted March 9, 1956. Previously registered for copyright as part of the piano-vocal score and libretto March 5, 1956, and as part of the unpublished vocal score and libretto January 10, 1956. Introduced by Art Lund (Joe). Recorded by Art Lund (Columbia), Peggy Lee (Decca), and Billy Eckstine (RCA Victor), among others.

Like a perfumed woman,
The wind blows in the bunkhouse.
Like a perfumed woman,
Smellin' of where she's been.
Smellin' of Oregon cherries
Or maybe Texas avocado
Or maybe Arizona sugar beet.
The wind blows in
And she sings to me,
'Cause I'm one of her ramblin' kin.

She sings:
"Joey, Joey, Joey.
Joey, Joey, Joe.
You've been too long in one place
And it's time to go, time to go!
Joey, Joey, Joey.
Joey, travel on.
You've been too long in one town
And the harvest time's come and gone."

That's what the wind
Sings to me—
When the bunk I've been bunkin' in
Gets to feelin' too soft and cozy,
When the grub they've been cookin' me
Gets to tastin' too good,
When I've had all I want
Of the ladies in the neighborhood—

She sings:
"Joey, Joey, Joey.
Joey, Joey, Joe.
You've been too long in one place
And it's time to go, time to go!
Joey, Joey, Joe!"

SOON YOU GONNA LEAVE ME, JOE

Published as part of the vocal score and libretto. Copyrighted March 5, 1956. Previously registered for copyright as part of the unpublished vocal score and libretto January 10, 1956. Introduced by Robert Weede (Tony) and Art Lund (Joe).

TONY: Soon you gonna leave me, Joe,
Soon you gonna leave me, Joe,
And pick somebody else's crop, far away.
JOE: [spoken] What's got into you, boss? Ain't that kind of sentimental talk?
BOTH: [sung] Soon, you gonna leave me Joe.
TONY: Ma, ev'ry mornin' when omma wake up
I wanna see a pitch',
A pitch' o' da best damn foreman ever come to work for me.
JOE: [spoken] You want a picture of me?
TONY: [sung] My Joe, young handsome Joe,
Da best damn foreman ever come to work for me.
JOE: [spoken] Why sure, Tony, I don't mind.
TONY: [spoken] At's-a good. Hey, Max.
[sung] Hurry him up and take his pitch'.
Hurry him up, Max.
[spoken] Mamma, mamma, I know it's-a wrong . . . Rosabella to come-a here and get-a marry.

ROSABELLA

Published as part of the piano-vocal score and libretto. Copyrighted March 5, 1956. Previously registered for copyright as part of the unpublished vocal score and libretto January 10, 1956. Introduced by Robert Weede (Tony).

She t'ink maybe omma young man wit' a handsome kind-a face.
'At's-a why omma gotta do what omma do.
She t'ink maybe omma young man wit' a handsome kind-a face.
An' me, I don' wanna show her what's true.
Oh, my beautiful

Rosabella, sweet like a flower.
Rosabella, look! my heart he's in you power.
Rosabella, young like a baby.
Rosabella, say someday you love me, maybe.

Omma scared to look in you eye
And shake-a you hand hello.
Omma scared you slap-a my face an' you go.
Oh, my beautiful

Rosabella, sweet like a flower.
Rosabella, look! my heart he's in you power.
Rosabella, omma love you so!

ABBONDANZA

Published as part of the piano-vocal score and libretto. Copyrighted March 5, 1956. Previously registered for copyright as part of the unpublished vocal score and libretto January 10, 1956. Introduced by Rico Froehlich (Pasquale), Arthur Rubin (Giuseppe), and John Henson (Ciccio). Reprised in Act III. Recorded by the Abbondanza Boys (Columbia).

PASQUALE: La frutta!
GIUSEPPE: La frutta!
CICCIO: La frutta!
PASQUALE: La torta!
GIUSEPPE: La torta!
CICCIO: La torta!
ALL: Abbondanza, abbondanza, abbondanza,
P'ognipanza!
Abbondanza, abbondanza, abbondanza,
P'ognipanza!

PASQUALE: I fiori!
GIUSEPPE: I fiori!
CICCIO: I fiori!
PASQUALE: Formaggio!
GIUSEPPE: Formaggio!
CICCIO: Formaggio!
ALL: Abbondanza, abbondanza, abbondanza,
Pien di fragranza!
Abbondanza, abbondanza, abbondanza,
Pien di fragranza!

PASQUALE: Ventagli!
GIUSEPPE: Ventagli!
CICCIO: Ventagli!
PASQUALE: Regali!
GIUSEPPE: Regali!
CICCIO: Regali!
ALL: Abbondanza, abbondanza, abbondanza,
Quant' eleganza!
Abbondanza, abbondanza, abbondanza,
Quant' eleganza!!

PASQUALE: La luce!

GIUSEPPE: La luce!

CICCIO: La luce!

PASQUALE: Andiamo!

GIUSEPPE: Andiamo!

CICCIO: Andiamo!

ALL: Abbondanza, abbondanza, abbondanza,
Che stravaganza!
Abbondanza, abbondanza, abbondanza,
Che stravaganza!

PLENTY BAMBINI

Published as part of the piano-vocal score and libretto. Copyrighted March 5, 1956. Previously registered for copyright as part of the unpublished vocal score and libretto January 10, 1956. Introduced by Robert Weede (Tony).

'At's what I want,
'At's what's gonna be.
Plenty bambini, plenty bambini,
Plenty bambini like a step, step, step.
Alfonso, Fiorello, Matilda, Giusepp'!
Plenty bambini, roun' my place,
Wit' a face like my wife's purty face,
Plenty bambini roun' my place.

SPOSALIZIO

Published as part of the piano-vocal score and libretto. Copyrighted March 5, 1956. Previously registered for copyright as part of the unpublished vocal score and libretto January 10, 1956. Introduced by Rico Froehlich (Pasquale), Arthur Rubin (Giuseppe), John Henson (Ciccio), and ensemble.

PASQUALE: Sposalizio!

GIUSEPPE: Sposalizio!

CICCIO: Sposalizio!

TOWNSPEOPLE: Hey! Look at the lights, look at the food, look at the flowers.
Hey! Look at the wine, look at the place!

I like a great big Italian sposalizio.
Set it up and I'll be there
With the lanterns glowing

And the vino flowing
And the good strong smell of mozzarella in the air!

MEN: Mozzarella!

WOMEN: Smell of—

ALL: Mozzarella in the air!
Great big Italian sposalizio.
Lay it out and count me in!

MEN: I'm the kind of fella—

WOMEN: Love to go out—

MEN: Likes a tarantella—

WOMEN: To a blowout—

ALL: To the fine, fine music of a mellow mandolin!

MEN: Mandolin! Mandolin!

WOMEN: Music of a mellow—

ALL: Mandolin!
With all the neighbors
And all the neighbors' neighbors
All the friends and all of their friends
And the mangia, mangia, mangia never ends—
Never ends!

I like a great big Italian sposalizio.
Set it up and I'll be there
With the lanterns glowing—
Look at 'em over your head—
And the vino flowing,
Malaga, Malaga red,
And the good, strong smell of mozzarella in the air!
Set it up—

MEN: Set it up, set it up—

ALL: And I'll be there!

[*Interlude—tarantella*]

ALL: With all the neighbors
And all the neighbors' neighbors,
All the friends and all of their friends,
And the mangia, mangia, mangia never ends,
Never ends.
I like a great big Italian sposalizio,
Set it up and I'll be there,
With the lanterns glowing
And the vino flowing
And the good strong smell of mozzarella in the air!
Set it up—

MEN: Set it up, set it up—

ALL: And I'll be there!

I SEEN HER AT THE STATION

Published as part of the piano-vocal score and libretto. Copyrighted March 5, 1956. Previously registered for copyright as part of the unpublished vocal score and libretto January 10, 1956. Introduced by Lee Cass (Postman) and Art Lund (Joe). The program refers to this number as "Special Delivery (I Seen Her at the Station)."

POSTMAN: I seen her at the station with her straw suitcase
And a kind of sad and disappointed look on her face.
So I put her in my buggy and I took her for a ride,
Special delivery, one bride!

JOE: [*spoken*] I'm sorry nobody got there in time.

POSTMAN: [*spoken*] Yep,
[*sung*] I seen her at the station, so I hauled her free
With the compliments of Route Eleven RFD.
Here she is in fair condition with a slightly damaged pride,
Special delivery, one bride!

BENVENUTA

Published as part of the piano-vocal score and libretto. Copyrighted March 5, 1956. Previously registered for copyright as part of the unpublished vocal score and libretto January 10, 1956. Introduced by Rico Froehlich (Pasquale), Arthur Rubin (Giuseppe), John Henson (Ciccio), and Art Lund (Joe).

PASQUALE: La signora padrona!

PASQUALE AND CICCIO: Signora padrona!

PASQUALE, CICCIO, AND GIUSEPPE: Signora padrona!

PASQUALE: Benvenuta, cara sposa!

CICCIO: Benvenuta, cara, cara bella sposa.

GIUSEPPE: Benvenuta in casa vostra—

ALL THREE: Casa vostra che sarà più luminosa, luminosa, luminosa.

PASQUALE: Benvenuta!

GIUSEPPE AND CICCIO: Benvenuta!

JOE: [spoken] That means
welcome.
PASQUALE: [sung] Cara sposa.
GIUSEPPE AND CICCIO: Cara sposa.
JOE: [spoken] Dear bride.
PASQUALE: [sung] Benvenuta cara, cara
bella sposa.
GIUSEPPE AND CICCIO: Bella sposa.
JOE: [spoken] Pretty bride.
GIUSEPPE: [sung] Benvenuta in casa
vostra—
ALL: Casa vostra che sarà più
luminosa, luminosa,
luminosa.
PASQUALE: Ecco i fiori.
CICCIO: Volete bere?
PASQUALE: Ecco i fiori.
GIUSEPPE: Famm'o favore.
ALL: S'accommodi, s'accommodi,
s'accommodi.
PASQUALE: Benvenuta—
GIUSEPPE AND CICCIO: Benvenuta—
PASQUALE: Cara sposa.
GIUSEPPE AND CICCIO: Cara sposa.
PASQUALE: Benvenuta, cara, cara bella
sposa.
GIUSEPPE AND CICCIO: Bella sposa.
GIUSEPPE: Benvenuta in casa vostra—
ALL: Casa vostra che sarà più
luminosa, luminosa!
PASQUALE: Luminosa, luminosa!
CICCIO: Luminosa, luminosa!
GIUSEPPE: Luminosa, luminosa!
ALL: Luminosa, luminosa,
luminosa, luminosa!
Luminosa, luminosa,
luminosa, luminosa!
Luminosa!

AREN'T YOU GLAD

Published as part of the piano-vocal score and libretto. Copyrighted March 5, 1956. Previously registered for copyright as part of the unpublished vocal score and libretto January 10, 1956. Introduced by Jo Sullivan (Rosabella) and Art Lund (Joe).

ROSABELLA: Such friendly faces, all around me!
Here I am, and look what I found me,
Friendly faces all around.
I'm sorry I got mad, I'm sorry I got sore.
You see, I've never been a mail-order
bride before.

But now I'm happy I'm who I am,
And I'm happy you're who you are,
And I'm happy today is today.
Gosh! Haven't you got something to
say?
I mean, glad I'm here?
I mean, here beside you, dear?
That is, aren't you glad,
I mean, glad I came?
I mean, came to share your name?

I thought I'd be settling
For a place to hang my hat,
For three square meals a day,
Some good fresh air, and that was
that.
But this is much nicer and sweeter
and warmer.
Tell me, aren't you glad?
I mean, glad I'm here?
You know, here beside you,
Tony dear.
JOE: [spoken] Tony? I'm not Tony! I'm Joe.
ROSABELLA: [spoken] You're not Tony?
JOE: [spoken] No! I'm Joe.

NO HOME, NO JOB

Published as part of the piano-vocal score and libretto. Copyrighted March 5, 1956. Previously registered for copyright as part of the unpublished vocal score and libretto January 10, 1956. Introduced by Jo Sullivan (Rosabella).

No home, no job,
Not even mad money.
Just that old man, that old man,
People will be laughing, it's so funny!
Laughing at me for coming down here to
That old man,
That old man,
People will be laughing, it's so funny.
Specially him, whatever his name is.
Him with the pink shirt
And the know-it-all smile.

DON'T CRY

Published. Copyrighted May 9, 1956. Previously registered for copyright as part of the piano-vocal score and libretto March 5, 1956, and as part of the unpublished vocal score and libretto January 10, 1956. Introduced by Art Lund (Joe) and Jo Sullivan (Rosabella). Recorded by Eddy Arnold and Chet Atkins (RCA Victor) and Frankie Laine (Columbia).

JOE: Don't cry, don't cry.
Come on back in the house and don't
cry.
Come on back in the house
And get out from under that old cold
sky.

Don't weep, don't weep.
Come on back in the house, little
sheep.
Come on back in the house
For a smile of welcome and go to
sleep.

Guess I know how you feel.
It's that wild runaway feeling in your
heart
When you've had the wrong dream
And you wake with a start!

Well, don't cry, don't cry.
Come on back in the house and don't
cry.
Come on back in the house
And get out from under that old cold
sky.
Guess I know how you feel . . .
ROSABELLA: [spoken] Yes, you know how I feel!
Well, don't you worry! I went
through with it, didn't I? I said I'd
marry him. . . . Well, I married
him.
JOE: [spoken] And you'll never be sorry.
ROSABELLA: [spoken] Take your hands off me!
JOE: [spoken] You know I had nothing to do
with that photograph.
ROSABELLA: [spoken] No, but you're laughing
about it.
JOE: [spoken] No, kid, no.
ROSABELLA: [spoken] Inside you're laughing about
how I got myself stuck with a—
[brief pause]
Take your hands off of me.
JOE: [sung] Tony sure is a fine feller—
ROSABELLA: [spoken] Leave me alone!

JOE: [*sung*] With the strength of a giant
And the soul of a saint.
ROSABELLA: He's an old man, an old man,
I don't want him leaning all over
me!
JOE: With the strength of a giant
And the smile of a baby.
ROSABELLA: Strength of a giant!
But an old man, an old man.
I don't want him breathing all
over me!

JOE: Don't cry, don't cry.
Come on back in the house and
don't cry.
Come on back in the house
And get out from under that old
cold sky.

[*End Act I*]

FRESNO BEAUTIES and COLD AND DEAD

Published as part of the piano-vocal score and libretto. Copyrighted March 5, 1956. Previously registered for copyright as part of the unpublished vocal score and libretto January 10, 1956. Introduced by ensemble, Art Lund (Joe), and Jo Sullivan (Rosabella).

Fresno Beauties

VINEYARD
WORKERS: Comin' home
When the summer is over,
Comin' home,
Pretty woman o' mine.

Comin' home
With the money, with the money
From the Fresno Beauties,
The Fresno Beauties,
The Fresno Beauties.

Don't you cry,
Don't you call me a rover.
Don't you cry,
Little bucket o' brine.

Comin' home
With the money, with the money
From the Fresno Beauties,
Round and ripe and fine.

Comin' home
When the summer is over,
Comin' home,
Pretty woman o' mine.
Comin' home
With the money, wi—

[*Segue immediately to "Cold and Dead."*]

Cold and Dead

JOE: There she is—
ROSABELLA: Here he comes—
JOE: There she is,
Ev'ry day for a week now—
ROSABELLA: Here he comes, ev'ry day since a week
ago—
JOE: And the best we can do—
ROSABELLA: And the best we can do—
BOTH: Is nod good morning.
JOE: I'll never know why I grabbed her.
ROSABELLA: I'll never know how.
JOE: It didn't matter then.
ROSABELLA: It doesn't matter now.
BOTH: It's cold, cold,
Cold and dead,
Dead and buried.
Buried and gone.
JOE: Gone, forgotten—
ROSABELLA: Gone, forgotten—
JOE: Far away—
ROSABELLA: Far away—
BOTH: Cold and dead,
And now ev'ry day
The best we can do
Is nod good morning.

[*Cut back to "Fresno Beauties."*]

VINEYARD
WORKERS: Pickin' Fresno Beauties,*
Gettin' ten cents a box,
Pickin' Fresno Beauties
Ain't no better than choppin' rocks.
So I tell my woman,
"Don't you worry over me,"
But the Fresno Beauties
Got her crazy with jealousy.
I'm comin' home.

[*Cut immediately to "Fresno Beauties (reprise)."*]

---

* *The following sequence came immediately after "Cold and Dead." Cut prior to New York opening.*

Fresno Beauties (reprise)

VINEYARD
WORKERS: —With the money from the Fresno
Beauties,
The Fresno Beauties,
The Fresno Beauties.
Don't you cry,
Don't you call me a rover.
Don't you cry,
Little bucket o' brine.
Comin' home,
With the money, with the money
From the Fresno Beauties,
Round and ripe and fine.

LOVE AND KINDNESS

Published as part of the piano-vocal score and libretto. Copyrighted March 5, 1956. Previously registered for copyright as part of the unpublished vocal score and libretto January 10, 1956. Introduced by Robert Weede (Tony) and Keith Kaldenberg (Doc).

TONY: [*spoken*] Twelve weeks in da chair!
Gimme da medicine, gimme da
pills! Hurry up quick!
DOC: [*spoken*] Easy now, easy, Tony, easy, easy.
[*sung*] Take medicine. Take tonic. Take
pills.
But none of them will cure an old grouch
of his ills.
If you've got to take something,
Take a prescription that's old as the hills.
TONY: [*spoken*] What omma take, Doc, what omma
take?
DOC: [*sung*] Take love and kindness,
Love and kindness,
Love and kindness from the nurse,
The good-looking nurse.
Take love and kindness,
Love and kindness,
And you will never, ever
TONY: [*spoken*] Ma porca miseria.
DOC: [*sung*] Take a turn for the worse.
She's good for what ails you
When you feel ready to holler and curse—

Take love and kindness,
Love and kindness,
Love and kindness from the nurse,
The good-looking nurse.
TONY: [*spoken*] Ma maybe she don' wanna—

DOC: [*sung*] She's good for what ails you
 When you feel ready to holler and curse.
 Take love and kindness,
 Love and kindness,
 Love and kindness
 From the nurse,
 The good-looking nurse,
 The nurse, the nurse.

HAPPY TO MAKE YOUR ACQUAINTANCE

Published as part of the piano-vocal score and libretto. Copyrighted March 5, 1956. Previously registered for copyright as part of the unpublished vocal score and libretto January 10, 1956. Introduced by Jo Sullivan (Rosabella), Robert Weede (Tony), and Susan Johnson (Cleo). Recorded by Sammy Davis and Carmen McRae (Decca).

ROSABELLA: When you meet somebody for the first time,
 There are special things you're supposed to say,
 Which you may not mean,
 But they sound polite as can be.
 Would you like to learn them?
TONY: [*spoken*] Oh, sì.
ROSABELLA: [*sung*] Well, then repeat after me:
 Happy to make your acquaintance.
TONY: 'Appy to make you acquaintance.
ROSABELLA: Thank you so much, I feel fine.
TONY: T'ank you so much, omma feel fine.
ROSABELLA: Happy to make your acquaintance.
TONY: Acquaintance.
ROSABELLA: And let me say the pleasure—
TONY: Da pleasure—
ROSABELLA: Is mine.
TONY: Da pleasure's a-mine.
ROSABELLA: How do you do?
 Pleased to know you.
TONY: 'Ow do you do?
 Pleased to know you.
ROSABELLA: And though my English is poor.
TONY: My English is-a goddamn poor!
BOTH: Happy to make your acquaintance.
ROSABELLA: Now won't you please say
 Likewise.
TONY: Looka-wise,
ROSABELLA: No, likewise.
TONY: Like-a-ways.
ROSABELLA: No, likewise.

TONY: Oh, like-a-wise—
BOTH: I'm sure.

[CLEO *enters. Dialogue; then:*]

CLEO: [*spoken*] How are you?
TONY: [*spoken*] How I am?
 [*sung*] 'Appy to make you acquaintance.
CLEO: [*spoken*] Feeling better after the accident?
TONY: [*sung*] T'ank you so much. Omma feel fine.
CLEO: [*spoken*] Certainly nice to meet you.
TONY: [*sung*] 'Appy to make you acquaintance.
CLEO: [*spoken*] It's a pleasure.
TONY: [*sung*] An' let me say da pleasure, she's-a mine.
CLEO: [*spoken*] He's cute.
TONY: [*sung*] 'Ow do you do? Pleased to know you.
CLEO: [*spoken*] And so polite, too.
TONY: [*sung*] An' do' my English he's poor,
CLEO: [*spoken*] Your English suits me fine.
CLEO
AND TONY: [*sung*] Happy to make your acquaintance.
ROSABELLA: Now won't you please say Likewise.
TONY: Looka-wise.
ROSABELLA: No, likewise.
TONY: Like-a-ways.
ROSABELLA: No, likewise.
TONY: Oh, likewise—
ALL THREE: I'm sure.

[*Dialogue;* CLEO *exits. Then:*]

ROSABELLA
AND TONY: How do you do?
 Pleased to know you.
 And though my English is poor,
 Happy to make your acquaintance.
ROSABELLA: Now won't you please say Likewise.
TONY: Looka-wise.
ROSABELLA: No, likewise.
TONY: Like-a-ways.
ROSABELLA: No, likewise.
TONY: Oh, likewise—
BOTH: I'm sure.

I DON'T LIKE THIS DAME

Published as part of the piano-vocal score and libretto. Copyrighted March 5, 1956. Previously registered for copyright as part of the unpublished vocal score and libretto January 10, 1956. Introduced by Mona Paulee (Marie) and Susan Johnson (Cleo).

MARIE: [*spoken*] Oh, Cleo! I gotta talk to you.
 I know I can talk to you.
 [*sung*] You're her friend and he's my brother.
 You understand, we can talk to one another,
 You understand.
CLEO: I understand.
MARIE: You understand.
CLEO: I understand.
MARIE: When the girl's too young for the man,
 You understand.
CLEO: I understand.
MARIE: You understand.
CLEO: I understand.
MARIE: She got her ways,
 He got his.
 The only trouble is when they get married,
 Little by little
 From the diff'rence in their ages
 Comes the trouble, all the trouble.
 A million kinds of trouble,
 Trouble, trouble, trouble . . .

CLEO: [*aside*] I don't like this dame.
 No, I don't like her one bit.
 But since I'm company
 Right now, into her eye I can't exactly—
MARIE: You understand.
CLEO: I understand.
MARIE: You understand.
CLEO: I understand.
MARIE: She gets restless,
 He gets sick.
 And it's a dirty trick on both of them
 When little by little
 From the diff'rence in their ages
 Comes the trouble, all the trouble,
 A million kinds of trouble,
 Trouble, trouble, trouble . . .
CLEO: [*aside*] I don't like this dame,
 I'm getting pains in my head.
 But since I'm company,
 Right now I guess I can't suggest her dropping—
MARIE: You understand.
CLEO: I understand.

MARIE: You understand.

CLEO: I understand.

[*spoken*] I'll be a goddamn son-of-a-bitch!

BIG D

Published. Copyrighted March 9, 1956. Previously registered for copyright as part of the piano-vocal score and libretto March 5, 1956, and as part of the unpublished vocal score and libretto January 10, 1956. Introduced by Susan Johnson (Cleo), Shorty Long (Herman), and ensemble (Vineyard Workers). Recorded by Jo Stafford (Columbia), Julie Andrews and Carol Burnett (Columbia), and Eddy Arnold and Chet Atkins (RCA Victor), among others.

HERMAN: [*spoken*] Ev'nin', ma'am!

CLEO: [*sung*] Would you mind sayin' that again?

HERMAN: I said "Ev'nin', ma'am!"

CLEO: "Ev'nin', ma'am!"
Mister, you've got a way of sayin'
"Ev'nin', ma'am"
That puts me in a friendly state of mind.

HERMAN: Would you mind sayin' that again?
I mean "friendly state."

CLEO: "Friendly state."

HERMAN: Sister, you've got a way of sayin'
"friendly state"
That gives me the impression you're my kind.

CLEO: Would you mind sayin' "crazy crystals"?

HERMAN: "Crazy crystals."
Would you mind sayin' "Neiman Marcus"?

CLEO: "Neiman Marcus."

HERMAN: [*spoken*] Wait a minute! Wait a minute!

[*sung*] You're from big D,
I can guess,
By the way you drawl
And the way you dress,
You're from big D!

BOTH: My, oh yes,
I mean big D, little A, double L, A, S.
And that spells Dallas, my darlin',
darlin' Dallas.

HERMAN: Don't it give you pleasure to confess
That you're from big D?

BOTH: My, oh yes,
I mean big D, little A, double L, A,
Big D, little A, double L, A,
Big D, little A, double L, A, S.
And that spells Dallas,

Where ev'ry home's a palace—

HERMAN: 'Cause the settlers settle for no less.
Hooray for big D!

BOTH: My, oh yes,
I mean big D, little A, double L, A,
Big D, little A, double L, A,
Big D, little A, double L, A, S.

CLEO: You're from big D,
I can guess,
By the way you drawl
And the way you dress,
You're from big D!

BOTH: My, oh yes,
I mean big D, little A, double L, A, S.
And that spells Dallas,

CLEO: Just dig a toe in Dallas
And there's oil all over your address,
Back home in big D.

BOTH: My, oh yes,
I mean big D, little A, double L, A,
Big D, little A, double L, A,
Big D, little A, double L, A, S.
And that spells Dallas,
I mean it with no malice—

CLEO: But the rest of Texas looks a mess
When you're from big D.

BOTH: My, oh yes,
I mean big D, little A, double L, A,
Big D, little A, double L, A,
Big D, little A, double L, A, S.

WORKERS: Big D, big D,
People from big D, big D,
Talkin' 'bout big D, big D.

VOICE: [*spoken*] Big what?

WORKERS: [*sung*] D!

[*Dance interlude*]

WORKERS: [*spoken*] Oil oil oil!
[*sung*] Cattle, cattle, cattle
My, oh Dallas, Dallas, Dallas, Dallas,
Big D! Little A, double L, A, S!

CLEO,
HERMAN,
AND
WORKERS: [*sung*] And that spells Dallas,
My darlin', darlin' Dallas.
Don't it give you pleasure to confess
That you're from big D.
My, oh yes,
I mean, big D, little A, double L, A,
Big D, little A, double L, A,
Big D, little A, double L, A, S!

HOW BEAUTIFUL THE DAYS

Published as part of the piano-vocal score and libretto. Copyrighted March 5, 1956. Previously registered for copyright as part of the unpublished vocal score and libretto January 10, 1956. Introduced by Robert Weede (Tony), Jo Sullivan (Rosabella), Art Lund (Joe), and Mona Paulee (Marie).

TONY: How beautiful da days!
Dey come an' go.
Lunedi,

ROSABELLA: Lunedi,

TONY: Martedi,

ROSABELLA: Martedi,

TONY: Lunedi,

ROSABELLA: Lunedi,

TONY: Martedi,

BOTH: How beautiful the days!
They come and go.

TONY: Lunedi,

ROSABELLA: Lunedi,

TONY: Martedi,

ROSABELLA: Martedi,

TONY: Lunedi,

ROSABELLA: Lunedi,

TONY: Martedi—

BOTH: How beautiful the days!
They come and go.
Lunedi,
Lunedi,
Martedi,
How beautiful the days!
They come and go.

MARIE: Those two,
They make me feel so lonesome
And sad.
Martedi,
I don't know why—
But I feel left out.

TONY: Lunedi, Martedi . . .

ROSABELLA: Lunedi . . .

ALL THREE: How beautiful the days—

MARIE: Could be without her—

TONY AND
ROSABELLA: They come and go.

MARIE: Around the place—

ALL THREE: How beautiful the days!

JOE: The wind sings, "Joey, Joe,
Ya never been to New Mexico."
I want to look at New Mexico
And see

MARIE: I'm lonely rememb'ring.

ALL: How beautiful the days,
They come and go.

JOE AND
MARIE: Why should I feel so restless and
      lonely,
      So restless all the time?
TONY AND
ROSABELLA: Lunedi,
          Martedi,
          Lunedi,
          Martedi . . .
TONY AND
ROSABELLA: How beautiful the days!
          They come and go.

YOUNG PEOPLE

Published as part of the piano-vocal score and libretto. Copyrighted March 5, 1956. Previously registered for copyright as part of the unpublished vocal score and libretto January 10, 1956. Introduced by Mona Paulee (Marie) and Robert Weede (Tony).

MARIE: Young people gotta dance, dance, dance.
      Young people kinda natur'lly want their
      chance
      To get out in the sun and be free.
TONY: [spoken] Ma shu, last-a year da whole crop
      was-a late ficause I was-a teach 'em da
      Charleston.
MARIE: [sung] Young people gotta dance, dance,
      dance!
      Why should they bother with you and me?
TONY: [spoken] Ficause dey like us.
MARIE: [spoken] You mean they're sorry for old
      people. And for people who can't get
      around.
TONY: [spoken] Ma, da doc was-a tol' only t'ree
      more weeks in da chair.
MARIE: [sung] Young people gotta dance, dance,
      dance.
      Old people oughta keep in mind.
TONY: [spoken] Old people? Keep in da mind?
      What, Marie?
MARIE: [sung] That young people gotta dance,
      dance, dance.
      Old people gotta get left behind.

[Segue into "Warm All Over."]

WARM ALL OVER

Published. Copyrighted May 9, 1956. Previously registered for copyright as part of the piano-vocal score and libretto March 5, 1956, and as part of the unpublished vocal score and libretto January 10, 1956. Introduced by Jo Sullivan (Rosabella). Recorded by Jo Stafford (Columbia), Hazel Scott (Decca), Ella Fitzgerald (Verve), and Andy Williams (Columbia), among others.

Where's that smile?
Where's that glow?
Where's that happy face
That I depend on so?
Or didn't you know?
It makes me feel
Warm all over,
Warm all over.
Ev'ry time you smile you get me
Warm all over.
Sometimes I feel kind of out in the cold,
But then I touch your hand and I'm home,
Home again and
Warm all over,
Warm all over.
Gone are all the clouds that used to
Swarm all over.*
Please always let me keep feeling the way I do,
So warm all over
With a tender love for you.

OLD PEOPLE GOTTA

Published as part of the piano-vocal score and libretto. Copyrighted March 5, 1956. Previously registered for copyright as part of the unpublished vocal score and libretto January 10, 1956. Introduced by Robert Weede (Tony).

Young people gotta dance, dance, dance.
Old people gotta sit dere an' watch, watch, watch
Wit' da make-believe smile in da eye.
Young people gotta live, live, live.
Old people gotta sit dere an' die.

---

* Earlier Version:
  Safe and sound and happy with the
  Storm all over.

I LIKE EV'RYBODY

Published. Copyrighted June 15, 1956. Previously registered for copyright as part of the piano-vocal score and libretto March 5, 1956, and as part of the unpublished vocal score and libretto January 10, 1956. Introduced by Susan Johnson (Cleo) and Shorty Long (Herman).

CLEO: [spoken] Ooh! Smile, smile, smile!
      [sung] That's all you do is smile,
      You tell the whole damn' world
      To step right up and take advantage.
HERMAN: Oh, I don't mind.
CLEO: You don't mind!

HERMAN: I like ev'rybody
        That I've ever met.
        I never met anybody
        That got me upset.
        No chip on my shoulder,
        Hate in my heart,
        Or green in my eye.
        And as I get older
        I find that more and more

        I like ev'rybody;
        That's my kind of fun.
        And though I strike ev'rybody
        As chump number one,
        No robber can rob
        This good-natured slob
        Of his private sky of blue.
        I like ev'rybody
        And extra-specially
        I like you,
        I like you,
        I like you.

I LOVE HIM

Published as part of the piano-vocal score and libretto. Copyrighted March 5, 1956. Previously registered for copyright as part of the unpublished vocal score and libretto January 10, 1956. Introduced by Jo Sullivan (Rosabella) and Susan Johnson (Cleo).

ROSABELLA: I love him, I love him,
          But he treats me like a baby.
          He doesn't seem to understand.
          I love him,
          And he treats me like a kid.

CLEO: I know how it is.
Don't tell me, I know how it is!
All that modesty and shyness at the start
Kind of worked their way into your little heart.

ROSABELLA: [*spoken*] He doesn't act like we were married or anything. He's my husband, isn't he?

CLEO: [*sung*] I know how it is!
Don't tell me, I know how it is!
All his bashful ways that seemed so very right,
They turned out to be the things you've got to fight.

ROSABELLA: I love him,
Yes, I love the way he looks and smells and feels

CLEO: Don't tell me, kid—
Tell him.
Tell him exactly how!
And like they say in a musical comedy!
[*spoken*] Here he comes now!

[*As* DOC *coaches,* TONY *tries, haltingly, to walk on-stage.* CLEO *quickly takes* DOC *offstage as* TONY *collapses dejectedly into the wheelchair. He turns to notice* ROSABELLA, *who advances on him with great determination. Immediate segue to "Like a Woman Loves a Man."*]

LIKE A WOMAN LOVES A MAN

Published as part of the piano-vocal score and libretto. Copyrighted March 5, 1956. Previously registered for copyright as part of the unpublished vocal score and libretto January 10, 1956. Introduced by Jo Sullivan (Rosabella) and Robert Weede (Tony). Recorded by Rosemary Clooney and Perez Prado (RCA Victor) and Chris Connor (Atlantic).

ROSABELLA: I love you, I love you—
TONY: [*spoken*] 'At's-a nice.
ROSABELLA: [*sung*] And you treat me like a baby,
You just don't seem to understand.
TONY: [*spoken*] What, Rosabella, what?
ROSABELLA: [*sung*] Like a woman loves a man,
That's how I love you.
TONY: Rosabella, nunja say what you no mean.

ROSABELLA: Like a woman needs a man,
Darling, I need you.
TONY: [*spoken*] Ma, omma old enough to be you papa.
ROSABELLA: [*sung*] I'm no baby, I know what I want.
I want holding you very close to me,
Just as close to me as I possibly can.
TONY: Rosabella!
ROSABELLA: Not like a child but
Like a woman holds a man,
That's how I'll hold you.
Wouldn't blame you if you ran
Now that I've told you.
TONY: Carissima!
ROSABELLA: I'm no baby. I know what I know,
And I know it's my plan
Just to love you
Like a woman loves a wonderful man.
TONY: Rosabella, Rosabella!

MY HEART IS SO FULL OF YOU

Published. Copyrighted May 9, 1956. Previously registered for copyright as part of the piano-vocal score and libretto March 5, 1956, and as part of the unpublished vocal score and libretto January 10, 1956. Introduced by Robert Weede (Tony) and Jo Sullivan (Rosabella). Recorded by Chris Connor (Atlantic) and Sammy Davis Jr. (Decca).

TONY: My heart he's so full of you,
So full of you,
He's got no room for anyt'ing more in dere.
Rosabella, you make me a man
Crazy on fire!
Crazy wit' love!
Crazy wit' love!
Ah, sono contento,
Sono contento!
Tu mi stai a cuor!

ROSABELLA: My heart is so full of you,
So full of you,
There is no room for anything more.
What other wish can I wish?
What other plan can I plan?
What other dream can I dream?
And what for? Whatever for?
BOTH: When my heart is so full of you,
So full of you,
There is [He's got] no room,

No room in my heart
For anything more.

TONY: [*spoken*] Carissima! I wanna tell everybody. Everybody in da whole beautiful world! Tonight we give-a big party. Da sposalizio! Everybody was-a miss da sposalizio ficause I was-a have accident. Now, tonight, we gonna have it. Then omma gonna get up an' make a speech. A speech like-a dis:
[*sung*] Ladies an' gentlemen,
Omma t'row-a dis party today
To make big announcement—

My wife, she's-a love me now!
My wife, she's-a love me now!
My wife she's-a fall
In love wit' me!
ROSABELLA: What other wish can I wish?
What other plan can I plan?
What other dream can I dream?
And what for, whatever for?
BOTH: When my heart is so full of you, so full of you—
ROSABELLA: There is no room,
No room in my heart—
TONY: Now my young new heart ain' got no more room—
BOTH: For anything more.

MAMMA, MAMMA

Published as part of the piano-vocal score and libretto. Copyrighted March 5, 1956. Previously registered for copyright as part of the unpublished vocal score and libretto January 10, 1956. Introduced by Robert Weede (Tony).

Mamma, Mamma, up in heaven,
How you like my girl?
How you like da simpatica smile on da face,
Mamma, da face?
Like da sun,
She's-a light up my place!
Mamma, Mamma, up in heaven,
How you like you dumb, funny-lookin' boy?
He was wait-a so long.
He's a find-a such joy,
He's a find-a such joy!

In Palermo, Mamma,
When I was a young man,

In Palermo, Mamma,
You was used to say:
"Bring home nice young lady, Tony,
Bring home nice young lady."
Look, Mamma, she's here,
She's here today!

An' I'm feel-a so young,
An' I'm feel-a so strong,
An' I'm feel-a so smart!
Tell-a me,
Mamma, Mamma, up in heaven,
How ya like-a my sweetheart?
How ya like-a my sweetheart?

[*End Act II*]

GOODBYE, DARLIN'

Published as part of the piano-vocal score and libretto. Copyrighted March 5, 1956. Previously registered for copyright as part of the unpublished vocal score and libretto January 10, 1956. Introduced by Susan Johnson (Cleo) and Shorty Long (Herman).

CLEO: Supposin' I should have to say goodbye,
    darlin'.
    What would you say, darlin'?
HERMAN: I'd say "Goodbye, darlin'."
CLEO: That's not what I mean!
    Supposin' I just packed my bag and
    went, darlin'.
    How would you feel, darlin'?
HERMAN: I'd feel content!
CLEO: Content?
HERMAN: Content that you'd be back pretty soon
    From wherever it was you went.
CLEO: I'm gonna give you one more chance.
    I may be leavin' in a little while, darlin'—
    How can you smile, darlin'?
HERMAN: Smilin's my style, darlin'!

[*Segue into "I Like Ev'rybody (Duet)."*]

I LIKE EV'RYBODY (DUET)

Published as part of the vocal score and libretto. Copyrighted March 5, 1956. Previously registered for copyright as part of the unpublished vocal score and libretto

January 10, 1956. Introduced by Susan Johnson (Cleo) and Shorty Long (Herman). Herman and Cleo parts are sung in counterpoint.

HERMAN: I like everybody
    That I've ever met.
    I never met anybody
    That got me upset.
    No chip on my shoulder,
    Hate in my heart,
    Or green in my eye,
    And as I get older,
    I find that more and more
    I like everybody;
    That's my kind of fun,
    And though I strike ev'rybody
    As chump number one,
    No robber can rob
    This good-natured slob
    Of his private sky of blue.
    I like ev'rybody
    And extra-specially I like you!

CLEO: Smile, smile, smile—
    That's all you do is smile.
    You wouldn't shed one tear
    If I went miles, miles, miles
    From here.
    Goodbye,
    Farewell,
    So long,
    We're through!
    I'm tired
    Of watching you
    Smile, smile, smile—
    That's all you do is smile.
    You don't get mad or sad
    Or just feel bad
    To hear me say
    Goodbye,
    Farewell,
    So long,
    We're through!
CLEO: [*spoken*] Oh, go away!
HERMAN: [*spoken*] All right, darlin'! See you later!
CLEO: [*sung*] And extra-specially I like you.

SONG OF A SUMMER NIGHT

Published as part of the piano-vocal score and libretto. Copyrighted March 5, 1956. Previously registered for copyright as part of the unpublished vocal score and li-

bretto January 10, 1956. Introduced by Keith Kaldenberg (Doc) and ensemble.

DOC: All nature seems to know
    There are two lovers tonight,
    There are two lovers tonight
    Hereabouts.
    All nature seems to know
    And sing her song,
    Her tender song
    That all is well
    And all is right.
    [*spoken*] Listen!

    [*sung*] Do you hear what I hear?
ENSEMBLE: Do you hear what I hear?
    Song of a summer night,
    Song of a summer night,
    Song of a thousand voices
    Full of a rare delight.
    I hear it in the air.
    It's a kind of lover's music,
    Kind of music for the happy, happy
      pair.
    Listen, listen to the
    Song of the cricket call,
    Song of the lazy breeze,
    Song of a blossom falling
    Down from the 'cacia trees!
    I hear it ev'rywhere.
    It's a kind of lovers' music,
    Kind of music for the happy lovers.
    Listen! Listen to it!

    Look, here comes the blushing,
      blushing bride.
    Ah, look, here comes the happy, happy
      groom.
    Let's all leave them standing side by side!
    Let's, let's!
    Ah, yes, they wanna be alone,
    They wanna be alone, alone, alone.
    Leave 'em alone, alone, alone.
    Leave 'em alone to hear the—

    Song of a summer night!
    Song of a summer night!
    Song of a thousand voices
    Full of a rare delight.
    I hear it in the air.
    It's a kind of lovers' music,
    Kind of music for the happy, happy pair.
    Softly, gently playing.
    Leave them, let's leave them,
    Leave them, let's leave them
    There.

PLEASE LET ME TELL YOU

Published as part of the piano-vocal score and libretto. Copyrighted March 5, 1956. Previously registered for copyright as part of the unpublished vocal score and libretto January 10, 1956. Introduced by Jo Sullivan (Rosabella).

Please let me tell you that I love you.
Just one more time before I go.
Please let me tell you that I love you,
'Cause it happens to be so.
How I hurt you,
And how you must hate me,
I know, oh God, I know!
But let me tell you that I love you.
That's all, and now I'll go.

TELL TONY AND ROSABELLA GOODBYE FOR ME

Published as part of the piano-vocal score and libretto. Copyrighted March 5, 1956. Previously registered for copyright as part of the unpublished vocal score and libretto January 10, 1956. Introduced by Art Lund (Joe), Norris Greer (Brakeman), Alan Gilbert (Clem), John Henson (Jake), and Roy Lazarus (Al).

JOE: I've been too long in one place
And it's time to go, time to go.
CLEM: [*spoken*] Where you gonna go?
JOE: [*spoken*] Santa Fe. Santa Fe, New Mexico.
CLEM: [*spoken*] Santa Fe!
JOE: [*sung*] Will ya tell
Tony and Rosabella goodbye for me?
Tell 'em goodbye for me.
Tell 'em it smelled like the day
I ought to be on my lonesome way.
And will ya tell—
BRAKEMAN: [*spoken*] All aboard!
JOE: [*sung*] Tony and Rosabella goodbye?
CLEM: [*spoken*] Sure.
JOE: [*spoken*] This is for them.
CLEM: [*spoken*] Hey! It's candy for the party!
JOE: [*sung*] Tell 'em goodbye for me.
JAKE, CLEM,
AND ALL: So long, Joey.
So long, Joe.

So long, so long, so long, so long, so long.

SHE'S GONNA COME HOME WIT' ME and NOBODY'S EVER GONNA LOVE YOU (TRIO)

Published as part of the vocal score and libretto. Copyrighted March 5, 1956. Previously registered for copyright as part of the unpublished vocal score and libretto January 10, 1956. Introduced by Robert Weede (Tony), Mona Paulee (Marie), and Susan Johnson (Cleo).

She's Gonna Come Home wit' Me

TONY: She ain't got no place to go.
No money, no food to eat.
Soon she gonna have da baby
In da street,
In da street.
It's no good! It's no good! It's wrong!
I don' care what she was-a do!
She maybe gon' die alone an' me too!
[*spoken*] She could-a run away an' tell me not'ing. She could-a just run away an' let me feel like a no-good, ugly old wop!
[*sung*] It's no good! It's no good! It's wrong!
She gonna come home wit' me.
She gonna come home wit' me.
My Rosabella.
She gonna come home again wit' me!
She gonna come home wit' me,
She gonna come home wit' me,
My Rosabella.
She gonna come home again wit' me!

Nobody's Ever Gonna Love You (Trio)

MARIE: Tony, Tony,
I don't know what's been going on.
But whatever's been going on,
Please, please, please
Let her go if she wants to go,
Let her go if she wants to go.
Remember,
Nobody's ever
Gonna love you like I love you.
Nobody's ever gonna have in the heart
What's in my heart.
Nobody's ever
Gonna love you like I love you—

TONY: She's gonna come home wit' me,
My Rosabella,
My Rosabella.
Now
She's gonna come home,
My Rosabella.
MARIE: Worry like I worry,
Bother like I bother.
CLEO: He's all you've got
And you don't want to lose him,
But he's wise to you now,
He's got your number.
He's all you've got
And you don't want to lose him,
But he's wise to you now,
He's got your number, sister.
He's all you've got
But you don't stand a chance anymore,
Not a chance
Anymore!
MARIE: Nobody's ever gonna love you like I love you,
Nobody's ever gonna have in the heart.
Nobody's ever gonna love you like I love you,
Worry like I worry,
Bother like me!
TONY: She's gonna come home wit' me,
My Rosabella, my Rosabella, now
She's gonna come home,
My Rosabella, my Rosabella!
MARIE: You ain't young no more!
TONY: [*spoken*] No!
MARIE: [*sung*] And you ain't good-looking!
TONY: No.
MARIE: And you ain't smart!
TONY: [*spoken*] No! In da head omma no smart, Ma, in da heart! Marie, in da heart!

[*With sudden desperation,* MARIE *snatches the cane from* TONY's *hand and retreats with it.* TONY *totters and almost falls but* CLEO *catches him. Now both face* MARIE. TONY, *calm, powerful*]

TONY: Gimme my cane, Marie.

[MARIE *stands there.*]

CLEO: [*deadly earnest*] Give him his cane!

[*As* MARIE *refuses,* CLEO *leaves* TONY *to lunge at* MARIE. *The two women struggle violently for the cane.* PASQUALE *enters and watches the scene, as* CLEO *finally grabs the cane and quickly hands it to the staggering* TONY, *who now uses it to walk off behind the bus. The enraged* MARIE *advances on* CLEO *and the fight continues, featuring hair-pulling, biting, and screaming.* PASQUALE *steps in to separate the two tigresses and manages to push them apart. A glance toward the bus tells* MARIE *that she is defeated and she exits* D.S.L. *in tears. But* CLEO *is sprawled on the ground, having been shoved a little too roughly by* PASQUALE. HERMAN *has entered* U.S.L. *during the struggle and sees the push* PASQUALE *has given* CLEO *leaving her sprawled on the ground.* HERMAN'S *usual smiling face has an unusually dark and angry expression. He runs to* PASQUALE *and hauls off and slugs him.* PASQUALE *falls to the ground.* HERMAN *stands over him threateningly as* PASQUALE *beats a dazed and frightened retreat off* D.S.L. *With growing wonder,* CLEO *has been watching. Now she looks at* HERMAN'S *still brandished fist and a look of surprise and admiration comes over her face.*]

CLEO: Herman!

[*Segue immediately into "I Made A Fist."*]

I MADE A FIST

Published as part of the piano-vocal score and libretto. Copyrighted March 5, 1956. Previously registered for copyright as part of the unpublished vocal score and libretto January 10, 1956. Introduced by Shorty Long (Herman) and Susan Johnson (Cleo).

HERMAN: [*spoken*] Look!
CLEO: [*spoken*] I'm lookin'.
HERMAN: [*spoken*] Look!
    [*sung*] I made a fist!
    I made a fist!
    I folded up the fingers of my left hand
    And there it was
    Exactly at the end of my wrist!
CLEO: Herman, my hero,
    Herman, my hero!
HERMAN: I made a frown.
    I made a frown.
    It started with a pucker in my
      eyebrows—
    I got so mad the corners of my mouth
      turned down.
CLEO: Herman, my hero!
HERMAN: And I can lick anybody in town
    Since I made a fist and a frown!
CLEO: Herman, my hero,
    Herman, my hero,
    Herman, my hero,
    Herman, my hero!

FINALE

Published as part of the piano-vocal score and libretto. Copyrighted March 5, 1956. Previously registered for copyright as part of the unpublished vocal score and libretto January 10, 1956. Introduced by Robert Weede (Tony), Jo Sullivan (Rosabella), and ensemble.

TONY: I canno leave you money on da table,
    You look too nice.
    An' so I give you my genuine amotist
      tie pin.
ROSABELLA: [*spoken*] How can you be so good to
      me? How can you be so kind? So
      kind, after what I—
TONY: [*sung*] I don't know not'ing about
      you,
    Where you ever go,
    What you ever done—
ROSABELLA: [*spoken*] After what I did?
TONY: [*sung*] I don't know not'ing about
      you—
ROSABELLA: [*spoken*] Tony!
TONY: [*sung*] I don' wanna know!
ROSABELLA: [*spoken*] Tony!
TONY: [*sung*] I don' gotta know!
ROSABELLA: [*spoken*] You wonderful Tony!
TONY: [*sung*] What I see is kind of young
      lady
    I wanna get marry!
    [*spoken*] Hey! You late for da big
      party! Come on, ev'rybody, up
      to da house!
CROWD: [*spoken*] Hooray! [*etc.*]
TONY: [*spoken*] Ma, before we start . . . in
      case you was-a worry . . . ficause
      me an' Rosabella was-a have li'l
      argumente . . . I wanna make big
      announcement . . .
    [*sung*] My wife, she's-a love me now!
ROSABELLA: What other wish can I wish—
TONY: My wife, she's-a love me now!
ROSABELLA: What other plan can I plan—
TONY: My wife she's-a fall—
ROSABELLA: What other dream can I dream?
TONY: In love—
ROSABELLA: And what for?
TONY: Wit' me!
ROSABELLA: Whatever for?
BOTH: When, my heart is so full of you,
    So full of you,
    There is no room,
    No room in my heart
    For anything more!
ENSEMBLE: Most happy, most happy, most
      happy man

In the whole Napa Valley,
    The most happy, most happy,
    Happy, happy, happy, happy man!
TONY: 'At's-a me!

[*Curtain*]

CUT AND UNUSED SONGS

HOW'S ABOUT TONIGHT?
(Part 1)

Intended for Amy (Rosabella), the cashier, and another waitress in Act I, scene 1. Cut prior to rehearsals. A private demo recording of this scene (including Maxene Andrews as Cleo and Lee Cass as the cashier) is on the compact disc *An Evening with Frank Loesser* (DRG).

CASHIER: How's about tonight?
WAITRESS: Oh gosh, got a date.
CASHIER: Can't you drop it for tonight?
WAITRESS: Oh gosh, no I can't,
    'Cause it's a steady date.
CASHIER: What the hell.
    Some night, you and me.
WAITRESS: Sure, Al, sure.
CASHIER: Some night, you and me.
WAITRESS: Sure thing.

[*Interlude*]

CASHIER: How's about tonight?
AMY: No thanks, not tonight.
CASHIER: What's the matter with tonight?
AMY: No thanks, not tonight, or any other
      night.
CASHIER: There you go—
    [*mockingly*] "No thanks, not tonight.
    No thanks, not tonight."
AMY: [*spoken*] That's right!
CASHIER: [*sung*] Why give me such a bad time?
    Don't I rate, honey?
    Don't I dress nice?
    Don't I spend money?
    Say, there's lots of waitresses laying
      off
    All over town

That a man like me
Don't have to ask twice.
How's about tonight?

AMY: No thanks, not tonight.

CASHIER: What's the matter with tonight?

AMY: No thanks, not tonight or any other
night.

CASHIER: What the hell.
[*spoken*] Okay, okay, okay!
[*sung*] Go home to your cheap little
furnished room
And let your arteries harden!
Go home to your cheap little furnished
room
With your copy of *House and
Garden*!

[*Segue into "House and Garden."*]

HOUSE AND GARDEN

Intended for Rosabella in Act 1, scene 1. Cut prior to
New York opening. A private demo recording of this
song (singer currently unknown) is on the compact disc
An Evening with Frank Loesser (DRG).

So home I go to my cheap little furnished room
With my copy of *House and Garden*.
House and Garden.
Now those are two very faraway,
Safe and sound, ladylike words.
You know, mine's American colonial,
With a brass-plated knocker,
And a chintz-covered rocker,
And there's a view of a pretty green maple tree,
Busy with birds.
And there I sit in the middle of it all,
A-rocking in the rocker, crocheting on a shawl,
And the ladies and gentlemen who come to call
Say "please" and "I beg your pardon."
Ah, but it's just in my dear old,
Dog-eared, year-old
Copy of *House and Garden*.

[*Segue into "How's About Tonight (Part 2)"*]

HOW'S ABOUT TONIGHT?
(Part 2)

Intended for Cleo, the cashier, and another waitress in
Act I, scene 1. Cut prior to start of rehearsals. A private
demo recording of this song (with Maxene Andrews as
Cleo and Lee Cass as the cashier) is on the compact disc
An Evening with Frank Loesser (DRG).

CLEO: Look, there goes lover boy, fast on the
outside.

CASHIER: How's about tonight?

WAITRESS: Why, sure, I'm with you.

CASHIER: Baby, I could treat you right.

WAITRESS: Me, too. Ah, but first
I want to heist a few.

CASHIER: Wait for me. Outside.

WAITRESS: Meet you there.

CASHIER: Outside.

WAITRESS: Meet you there.

CASHIER: All right, all right. Closing time.
Get your tables cleaned up and get out
of here.
Closing time!

LOVE LETTER

Intended for trio of waitresses in Act I, scene 1. Cut
prior to start of rehearsals. A private demo recording of
this song (singers unknown) is on the compact disc *An
Evening with Frank Loesser* (DRG).

GIRL 1: Love letter.

GIRLS 2
AND 3: Love letter.

GIRL 1: She got a love letter.

GIRL 2: Love letter on a menu,
Love letter on a menu.

GIRL 1: A girl should know better—

GIRL 3: Love letter.

GIRL 1: Than believe what it says in a—

GIRL 3: Love letter, love letter.

GIRL 2: Now where will that get her?

GIRL 3: Love letter, love letter.

SO BUSY

Intended for Rosabella and waitresses in Act I, scene 1.
A private demo recording of this song is on the
compact disc *An Evening with Frank Loesser* (DRG).
Except for Maxene Andrews as Cleo, the singers are
unknown.

HILDA: [*spoken sarcastically*] Well, what do
you know!

[HARRIET *and the other waitresses laugh and chatter
scornfully.*]

CLEO: [*shouting*] Quiet!
[*sung*] Let her read it!

HARRIET: All right, so let her read it!

ROSABELLA: "My dear Rosabella—"

OTHERS: Rosabella?

ROSABELLA: "I call you Rosabella because I don't
know your name—"

OTHERS: Rosabella?

ROSABELLA: "I am too afraid to ask you."

HARRIET: What did he look like?

[ROSABELLA *shrugs helplessly.*]

HILDA: What did he look like?

ROSABELLA: [*puzzled*] I don't know.

HAZEL: Didn't you see him?

HARRIET: Didn't he talk to you?

ROSABELLA: [*spoken*] No!
[*sung*] Tonight the customers had me
dizzy.
Tonight the place was so busy, but so
busy!
And I never notice a face
Or listen to a voice—
I just hand them the menu
And let them take their choice.
Now he might be the tongue and
spinach

[*She is trying to remember.*]

Or he might be the Friday special
Or the meatballs and—

[*Now she gasps.*]

That's who he is!
The meatballs and macaroni!

[*Now she reconsiders.*]

Or is he?

[*She shrugs again.*]

> Tonight the place was so busy, but so
>   busy!
> And I never notice a face
> Or listen to a voice—
> I just hand them the menu
> And let them take their choice.

[*Add eight measures for babble of waitresses and dismissal by* CLEO.]

CLEO: [*spoken*] Shut up! Why don't you go
   home?
   [*To* ROSABELLA] Go ahead, kid.
ROSABELLA: [*sung*] "I cannot leave you money on
   the table,
   You look too nice.
   And so I leave you my genuine
   amethyst tie pin."
HARRIET: [*spoken*] Is it real?
HILDA: [*spoken*] Amethyst? Is it really real?
HARRIET: [*spoken*] Probably made of glass. If a
   hockshop was open you could find
   out. Is it really real?

[*Segue to "Is it Really Real?"*]

IS IT REALLY REAL? and WANTING TO BE WANTED

Intended for waitresses, Cleo, and Rosabella in Act I, scene 1. "Is It Really Real" cut prior to start of rehearsals. "Wanting to Be Wanted" cut prior to New York openings. Private demo recordings of these songs are on the compact disc *An Evening with Frank Loesser* (DRG). (Except for Maxene Andrews as Cleo, singers are unknown.) "Wanting to Be Wanted" also recorded by Jo Sullivan Loesser (DRG).

Is It Really Real?

GIRLS: Is it real?
   Is it real?
   Is it really real?
   Is it really real?
   Is it really real?
   Is it really real?
   Is it glass?
   Is it glass?
   Is it made of glass?
   Is it made of glass?

A GIRL: If a hockshop was open
   This time of night,
   She could find out—
GIRLS: Is it real?
   Is it real?
   Is it really real?
A GIRL: And make herself a deal.
GIRLS: It is it real?
   Is it real?
   Is it really real?
   Can you tell?
   Can you tell?
   Can you really tell?
   Do you know?
   Do you see?
   Do you think?
   Do you feel?
   Is it really, really, really real?
ROSABELLA: [*sung*] It doesn't matter if the stone
   is real—
   This is real, very real!
   [*spoken*] Listen to what he says:
   [*spoken*] "I don't know nothing about
   you,
   Where you ever go,
   What you ever done,
   I don't wanna know,
   What I see is kind of young lady
   I want to get marry."
CLEO: [*spoken*] Lemme see that!

[ROSABELLA *hands* CLEO *the menu.*]

   [*sung*] "I don't know nothing about
   you,
   Where you ever go,
   What you ever done . . .
   What I see is kind of young lady
   I want to get marry"!
   [*spoken*] Yeah!

[CLEO *hands the menu back to* ROSABELLA, *who resumes reading note.*]

ROSABELLA: [*sung*] "Please send me a postcard,
   Just a little card,
   Just to say hello,
   And you make me very happy.
   Yours truly, Tony."

[CLEO *takes the menu and licks a bit of gravy from it.*]

CLEO: The meatballs and macaroni!
ROSABELLA: Maybe he's kinda crazy,
   This young fella, this young fella,
   But I'm gonna send him a postcard
   saying:

"Thank you, Yours sincerely,
   Rosabella."
CLEO: He could be some kinda Rasputin
   Or a small-town Jack the Ripper!*
   To start with—

[*She looks at the tie pin.*]

He's a lunatic of a tipper!
   Come on, let's get out of here!
ROSABELLA: [*dreamily*] I'm gonna send him a
   postcard saying:
   "Thank you, Yours sincerely,
   Rosabella."
   'Cause it feels nice
   When somebody thinks you're special.
   An' he thinks I'm special.
   It's nice when somebody thinks
   you're special.
CLEO: [*interrupting; impatiently*] I know how
   it is,
   But, come on, kid, it's getting late!
ROSABELLA: [*still dreamily fixed on the subject*] After
   all,
   I'm just like anybody else I know.
   We all walk around kind of wanting
   something,
   Whether we admit it or not.
   Kind of wanting something,
   But wanting what, Cleo?
   Wanting what?
CLEO: Wanting to go home and soak my feet,
   While the water is still running hot!

Wanting to Be Wanted

ROSABELLA: Wanting to be wanted.
   Needing to be needed.
   That's what it is.
   That's what it is.

   Wanting to be wanted,
   Needing to be needed.
   So many people go through life that
   way,
   Kinda desp'rately
   Wanting to be wanted,
   Needing to be needed.
   That's how it was with me until today.
   Suddenly I'm necessary to someone.
   It's a feeling I've never known,
   I'm necessary to someone
   Who cried for me, for me alone,
   When I was
   Wanting to be wanted,

---
* *Earlier version:*
   Or a jerky Jack the Ripper!

Needing to be needed.
So many people go through life that
way.
I'm very proud and happy I can say
Somebody wants me today.

JOE'S ENTRANCE

Lead-in to "Joey, Joey, Joey." Intended for Herman and Joe in Act I, scene 2. Cut prior to New York opening.

HERMAN: Hey, fellas! Look at Joe!
Hey, Joe! Whatcha doin'?
How come you're buyin' a duffle bag, Joe?
Are you leavin' town?
Are you leavin' town?
JOE: Yes, and I should have gone long ago!
HERMAN: Does Tony know you're leavin' him?
Does Tony know his foreman is leavin' him?
JOE: He knows, he knows!
I told him I heard that voice of the wind in the night
When I drop into my bunk
And I blow out the light! [*He blows.*]

EVERYBODY IS TALKING
("Rosabella," Part 1)

Intended for Tony and Marie in Act I, scene 2. Cut prior to New York opening. Recorded by Louis Quilico and Nancy Shade under the title "Tony and Marie Duet" (Jay).

TONY: Rosabella,
Sweet like a flower,
Rosabella, look, my heart he's in your power.
Rosabella,
Young like a baby,
Rosabella, say someday you love me maybe.
MARIE: Tony, Tony,
Ev'rybody is talking, talking,
Ev'rybody is saying how you're out of your head
For that chippie from Frisco.
TONY: She's-a no chip!
She's-a my Rosabella—
MARIE: Tony, Tony, what would Mamma say—
TONY: Sweet like a flower.

MARIE: If our mamma was alive today?
Tony, Tony, please—
TONY: Rosabella, look,
My heart he's in you power!
MARIE: Please listen to me what I'm telling you!
After all,
What do you know about her?
What do you know about her?

NOBODY'S EVER GONNA LOVE YOU

Intended for Marie in Act I, scene 2. Cut prior to New York opening. Recorded by Nancy Shade (Jay).

Nobody's ever gonna love you like I love you!
Nobody's ever gonna have in the heart
What's in my heart!
Nobody's ever gonna love you like I love you,
Worry like I worry,
Bother like I bother.
'Cause you ain't young no more!
And you ain't good-looking!
And you ain't smart!

Nobody's ever gonna love you like me,
Your sister, Marie!
Me, that reads you the papers out loud after supper,
Me, that chases the salesmen away,
When they come around selling you junk.
Me, that cooks when you're hungry,
Me, that drives when you're drunk,
Me, that knows where's your bathrobe,
Me, that tells you what's true,
Me, that never got married
Just to stay home and take care of you!

No, no, nobody's ever gonna love you like I love you!
Nobody's ever gonna have in the heart
What's in my heart!
Nobody's ever gonna love you like I love you,
Worry like I worry,
Bother like I bother,
'Cause you ain't young no more!
And you ain't good-looking!
And you ain't smart!

Somebody's maybe gonna give you a smile
Now and then,
Here and there,
But nobody's ever gonna care like I care!

I'M-A NO WANNA

Intended for Tony in Act I, scene 2. Cut prior to New York opening.

I'm-a scared to look in you eyes
And shake-a you hand hello,
I'm-a scared you slappa my face and you go.
[*spoken*] Mamma. Look, Mamma,
It's-a no good, Mamma. No, I'm-a wanna take-a no pitch'.
[*sung*] I'm-a no look good.
I'm-a just look rich.
No.
I'm-a no wanna take-a no pitch'.
I'm-a no wanna take-a photograph.
I'm-a no wanna.
It's-a no make love;
It's-a just make laugh.
No.
I'm-a no wanna photograph.

COLLAR INCIDENT

Registered for copyright as part of the unpublished vocal score and libretto January 10, 1956. Intended for Tony in Act 1, scene 3. Cut prior to New York opening.

Stu colletto!
Stu colletto!
Stu fettente colletto!

[*He asks the servants to fix his collar.*]

Akoonchialo!
Akoonchialo!
Famo favore!

[*All three servants rush and surround* TONY. MARIE *re-enters. One by one she brushes the servants aside. With a twist of the wrist, she fixes the collar.* TONY *grins and gratefully kisses her.* PRIEST, ALTAR BOY, *and* FLOWER GIRL *enter.*]

TONY: [*spoken*] Hello, Douglas Fairbanks.
Hello, Mary Pickford!
All dressed up for my wedding, huh?

SIX O'CLOCK TRAIN

Intended for Tony in Act 1, scene 3. Cut prior to New York opening.

When you hear
Choo-ga-da, choo-ga-da,
Ding-a, ding-a,
Choo-ga-da, choo-ga-da,
Ding-a, ding-a,
Choo-ga-da, choo-ga-da,
Ding-a, ding-a, woooo,
Far away,
Dat's mean she's come-a to Napa to marry me
On da six o'clock train today,
On da six o'clock train,
Choo-ga-da, choo-ga-da,
Ding, ding-a.

MARIE AND DOC

Intended for Marie and Doc in Act 1, scene 4. Cut prior to New York opening.

DOC: And what's the matter with you, Marie?
　　 Smile, Marie!
　　 It's your brother's wedding day!
MARIE: It ain't me, Doc, it's Tony.
　　 Doc, I'm worried about him,
　　 I'm worried about him,
　　 I can't help it, I'm worried about him, I—
DOC: I know, Marie, I know.
MARIE: It ain't that I mind getting thrown out of
　　　 my own house
　　 And taking a furnished room with the
　　　 neighbors.
　　 It's Tony, Doc. I'm worried about him.
　　 I'm worried about him, I can't help it,
　　 I'm worried about him, I—
DOC: I know, Marie, I know.
MARIE: Will she love him enough?
　　 Will she love him enough?
　　 Will she understand what he's talking
　　　 about?
　　 Will he like her coffee?
　　 Will he need me—
　　 Will he, for godsakes, need me?
　　 Oh! What's the matter with you, Marie?
　　 Smile, Marie,
　　 It's your brother's wedding day!

AREN'T YOU GLAD—TAG

Intended for Rosabella and Joe in Act 1, scene 4. Cut prior to New York opening.

ROSABELLA: [sung] Well, thank you very much!
　　　 It's been a charming visit!
　　　 But if this isn't you,
　　　 Who is it?

[JOE looks at the picture, laughs, etc.]

JOE: It's me, all right!
　　 Yep, it's me, all right!
　　 I guess he sent you my picture
　　 Instead of his!
　　 Why, the foxy grandpa!
ROSABELLA: [spoken] Foxy what?
JOE: [sung] The foxy grandpa!
ROSABELLA: He's an old man,
　　　 An old man.
　　　 Isn't he an old man?
JOE: Tony's a fine feller,
　　 Honest, he is a fine feller.
　　 Wait'll you see.

MAD MONEY

Earlier version of "No Home, No Job." Intended for Rosabella in Act 1, scene 4. Cut prior to New York opening.

Where do I think I'm going?
What street? What number?
What door? What room?
What room all ready for the
Foolish young lady's returning?
Cool white sheets,
Milk and cookie,
And a lamp left burning.
Mad money! One, two, three, four, five.
Taxi, taxi, get me away from here.
Drive, driver, drive.

EYES LIKE A STRANGER

Intended for Marie in Act 1, scene 4. Cut prior to New York opening. Reinstated in 1992 New York revival. Recorded by Nancy Shade (Jay).

He looked at me
With eyes like a stranger,
My big baby looked at me
With eyes like a stranger,
Strong and proud like they'd
Never cry tears no more.

He talked to me
With words like a stranger,
My big baby talked to me
With words like a stranger,
Words that said there was
Nothing he'd need me for.

He used to cry,
"Marie, Marie, take me home,
Make me coffee.
Marie, Marie, take me home,
Make me coffee,
Marie, same like all the time.
I was wrong, you was right.
Marie, Marie, take me home,
Make me coffee tonight."

And just now he looked at me
With eyes like a stranger,
Strong and proud like they'd
Never cry tears no more,
Little boy tears no more.

SUCH A PRETTY PICTURE

This number extended "No Home, No Job" and segued to earlier version of "Don't Cry." Intended for Rosabella and Joe in Act 1, scene 4. Cut prior to New York opening.

ROSABELLA: Such a pretty picture!
　　　 Oh, such a pretty picture
　　　 I painted of what was going to be.
　　　 And here it hung in a nice neat frame
　　　 In my foolish, lonely mind,
　　　 And ah, but it was pretty to see.
　　　 So now what have I got?
　　　 No home, no job,
　　　 Not even mad money tucked in my
　　　　 shoe!
　　　 Just a pretty picture I painted of me.
JOE: [spoken] Rosabella!
ROSABELLA: [sung] And you!
JOE: [spoken] Rosabella!
　　 [sung] Come on back in the house,
　　 Come on back in the house.
　　 Don't cry,
　　 Don't cry!

ROSABELLA: [*spoken*] Leave me alone.
JOE: [*sung*] I had nothing to do with that
　　　photograph,
　　Honest,
　　Honest, kid.
　　Don't cry,
　　Don't cry.
ROSABELLA: [*spoken*] Take your hands off me!
JOE: [*sung*] Tony's a fine feller,
　　Honest, he is a fine feller,
　　Wait'll you see.
　　Don't run away,
　　Give him a chance, will ya?
　　Tony's a fine feller!
　　With the strength of a giant
　　And the soul of a saint!
ROSABELLA: He's an old man, an old man!
　　I don't want him leaning all over me!
JOE: But the Arrow Collar Man he ain't.
ROSABELLA: Why'd he fool me? Why?
JOE: With the strength of a giant
　　And the smile—
ROSABELLA: The strength of a giant—
JOE: —of a baby!
ROSABELLA: But an old man, an old man!
　　I don't want him breathing all over me!
JOE: Come back in the house!
　　Come on back in the house.
ROSABELLA: Don't you worry.
JOE: [*spoken*] Atta girl.
ROSABELLA: [*sung*] I'm goin' through with it.
　　That's what I'm here for.
　　I'm gonna marry him.
　　I'm goin' through with it.
　　Goin' through with it.
JOE: Don't cry, don't cry.
　　I had nothing to do with that
　　　photograph,
　　Honest, honest, kid.
　　Don't cry, don't cry.

DOCTORS DON'T TELL YOU EVERYTHING

Intended for Marie and Tony in Act II, scene 3. Cut prior to New York opening.

MARIE: Is it fair?
　　Is it fair to a nice young girl like her over
　　　there?
TONY: What's-a no fair?
MARIE: Is it fair she should spend her life
　　The wife of a sick old man?
TONY: Sick? Who's-a sick?

[*Dialogue*]

MARIE: Doctors don't tell you ev'rything,
　　Not ev'rything they know.
　　Oh, no, not ev'rything they know.
　　'Specially old people,
　　They wanna keep 'em happy.
TONY: [*spoken, shocked and hurt*] Old people?
MARIE: [*spoken*] How do you know you'll ever be a
　　real man again? How do you know
　　you'll ever get up out of that chair? The
　　priest was telling me, you ain't really
　　married. You ain't living like husband
　　and wife yet. Besides, you was married
　　in the house, not in the church. You
　　could get what they call "annulled."
TONY: [*spoken, pained*] Dat's mean like divorce?
　　Marie! No! No! Nunja tell me dat.
MARIE: [*spoken*] I ain't telling you, Tony, I'm just
　　asking—
　　[*sung*] Is it fair?
　　Is it fair to a nice young girl like her over
　　　there?
　　Give her a chance!
　　After all, young people gotta dance,
　　Young people gotta dance.

[MARIE *exits.* TONY *again slumps into despair.*]

THEY'RE THROWING A PARTY TODAY

Intended for workers and neighbors in Act II, scene 5. Cut prior to New York opening. Sung as a round with three voices. The Rosabella and Cleo section was later converted to dialogue.

ENSEMBLE: They're throwing a party today,*
　　Oh, hey!
　　I heard them say
　　They're throwing a party today,*
　　Oh, hey!
　　I heard them say
　　They're throwing a party today,*
　　Oh, hey!

[*Interlude*]

ROSABELLA: What am I gonna do, Cleo?
　　What am I gonna do?

____

* Originally:
　They're getting married, married today,

CLEO: I don't know how it is;
　　Don't ask me.
ROSABELLA: A baby!
CLEO: I don't know how it is.
　　I don't know.
ROSABELLA: [*spoken*] Oh my God. A baby!

LOVERS' QUARREL

Intended for workers, neighbors, and Doc in Act III, scene 2. Cut prior to New York opening. Recorded by William Burden as Doc (Jay).

GROUP 1: What's the matter?
GROUP 2: I don't know!
GROUP 1: What's the matter?
GROUP 2: I don't know!
GROUP 1: What's the matter?
GROUP 2: I don't know!
GROUP 1: What's the matter?
GROUP 2: I don't know!
DOC: It's only a fam'ly quarrel,
　　It'll be over in a minute.
BOTH
GROUPS: Only a fam'ly quarrel,
　　Why stick our lovable noses in it?
　　It'll be over in a minute.
　　In the meantime,
　　In the meantime,
　　In the meantime . . .

I'LL BUY EV'RYBODY A BEER

Intended for Doc and ensemble in Act III, scene 2. Cut prior to New York opening. Recorded by William Burden (Doc) and ensemble on Jay Records in 2000.

DOC: I'll buy ev'rybody a beer!
WOMEN: Whadee say?
　　Whadee say?
　　Whadee say, huh?
MEN: He said he'll buy beer.
DOC: I'll buy ev'rybody a beer!
MEN: Come on, come on.
WOMEN: Beer!
DOC: Come on over to Clancy's.
　　Can't you hear me volunteer?
MEN: Come on, come on now, gals.
DOC: I'll buy ev'rybody a round here.
　　A beer!
ALL: Hey, come on, come on—beer!

DREAM PEOPLE | 1957
and Other Songs of 1951–1961

DREAM PEOPLE

Based on *A Touch of the Moon*, an unproduced Garson Kanin play. Except where noted, all lyrics are from Frank Loesser's first-draft script of September 28, 1957. The last script revisions were dated October 21, 1957. The music survives in the form of a manuscript score dated between September 1956 and August 1957.

Kanin and Loesser had talked for many years about collaborating on a musical before they settled on this project. Loesser began to rewrite Kanin's script for *A Touch of the Moon*, which concerned a young woman with a very vivid mental picture of her ideal love. Doris, the principal character in Loesser's adaptation, has elements of Adelaide and Sarah from *Guys and Dolls* and Rosabella from *The Most Happy Fella* in her dreamy imaginings of romantic bliss.

The story is an odd mix of ethereal stage effects and conventional musical comedy romance. Unhappy with the reworking of the play and tired of seeing the piece pushed to the background as other projects came up, Kanin and Loesser abandoned it for good in 1959.

Loesser was taken with the more mystical qualities of *A Touch of the Moon*, a penchant that lead him to B. J. Chute's novel *Greenwillow* less than a year after abandoning *Dream People*.

In addition to Doris, the characters include her roommate, Eva; Ted, the ideal love Doris imagines; Butch, one of several imagined children of Doris and Ted; Crandall, a private detective who follows Ted; and Roy, her real would-be boyfriend.

DREAM PEOPLE (OPENING)

Act I opening. Intended for ensemble. Loesser's stage directions describe the ensemble as "an assortment of wandering human figures. They do not seem to walk, but rather to glide—weaving slowly among each other.... The galaxy of strange, weirdly illuminated wanderers now seem to glide forward and address the audience."

We are dream people
Waiting in the blue,
Dream people
Begging to come true.
Each one the creation
Of somebody's eager imagination,
Each one the love ideal

Frank Loesser (at piano) and campers at Camp Hiawatha, Kezar Falls, Maine

Somebody wishes
Were really real.
We are dream people
Waiting in the blue,
Begging to come true.

IMAGINING

Act I, scene 1. Intended for Doris and Eva.

DORIS: Any man I meet,
          If he wants to steal a kiss,
          Let him steal it—
          I just won't feel it.

          Any man I know,
          If he wants to pet my hand,
          Let him pet it—
          I just don't get it.

          That's how I've been
          And that's how I'll be
          On ev'ry date
          Till the right thing happens.
EVA: [*spoken*] You'll wait for godsakes what?
DORIS: [*sung*] I'll wait.
EVA: [*spoken*] You're going to be thirty years old soon!
DORIS: [*sung*] I'll wait for the one—
EVA: [*spoken*] The what?
DORIS: [*sung*] The one—
EVA: [*spoken*] The new briefcase—
DORIS: [*sung*] The one I keep imagining;
          The someone I'm going to love.
EVA: [*spoken*]—with the casaba melon.
DORIS: [*sung*] The one I designed
          Up here in my mind,
          The one for a lifetime,
          The one of a kind.
EVA: [*spoken*] Oh my God!
DORIS: [*sung*] I'm having the fun, the fun,
          The fun of just imagining
          How perfect he's going to be
          And dreaming the one, the one,
          The one I keep imagining
          Is somewhere, imagining me.
EVA: [*spoken*] But who? Where?
DORIS: [*sung*] Out there somewhere
          Imagining me!

Act II Partial Reprise of "Imagining"

Loesser wrote a scene in Act II in which the following portion of the "Imagining" lyric was to be reprised by Ted (Doris's imagined perfect lover) and Crandall (a private detective who is following Ted). Loesser intended this scene as a dance ("in soft shoe tempo, slow enough for Ted to walk to, in a dreamy semi-dance pattern") in which the two characters perform a "me-and-my-shadow routine, covered by a follow spot." While Ted sings, Crandall shadows him and writes down the words on a notepad. After Ted exits, Crandall reprises the lyric.

The one I designed,
Up here in my mind.
The one for a lifetime,
The one of a kind.

DREAM PEOPLE
(Part II)

Act I. Intended for Doris, Eva, and ensemble.

ENSEMBLE: [*sung*] We are dream people,
           Waiting in the blue.
DORIS: [*spoken*] A whole world of them.
              Mine's out there.
ENSEMBLE: [*sung*] Dream people,
           Begging to come true.
EVA: [*spoken*] That's for high-school kids.
ENSEMBLE: [*sung*] Each one the creation
           Of somebody's eager imagination.
           Each one the love ideal
           Somebody wishes
           Were really real.
DORIS: [*spoken*] I'm going to wait till I meet mine.
EVA: [*spoken*] But Doris, baby, like I keep saying—you're
              twenty-eight and Roy makes a good living.
ENSEMBLE: [*sung*] But when life makes you
           Practical and smart—
DORIS: [*spoken*] I know.
ENSEMBLE: [*sung*] Dream people
           Vanish from your heart.
           Listen, dreamer, listen—
           Tonight you may hear one cry.
SOLOIST: If I am your dream,
           If I am your dream,
           If I am,
           If I am,
           If I am your dream—

197

ENSEMBLE: Please don't let me die.
TED: If I am your dream,
Please don't let me die.
ENSEMBLE: [sung] Dream people,
Waiting in the blue.
DORIS: [spoken] I think I know how his voice is
going to sound. Kind of a dopey
romantic baritone. Baritone is nice.
So is dopey. I mean *lovable* dopey.
EVA: [spoken] Oh, stop now!
DORIS: [sung] I'm having the fun, the fun,
The fun of just imagining
How perfect he's going to be
And dreaming the one, the one,
The one I keep imagining
Is somewhere, imagining me—
Out there somewhere, imagining me!

AT THE HOME APPLIANCE SHOW

Act I. Intended for Roy.

I got her in the mood for marrying me
At the Home Appliance Show.
Oh boy, I'm glad I said, "Let's go
To the Home Appliance Show."
I had her dreaming dreams of settling down
In a well-run bungalow.
I'd been a bashful Romeo
Till the Home Appliance Show.

But then she saw some things that opened her
eyes—
Electric blankets, the double size,
Alarm clocks playing "Oh, Promise Me,"
And that pink transformer
On the baby-bottle warmer
Got her in the mood for marrying me.
And though my progress had been slow,
I got her in the mood
For breakfast food,
For staying home nights
And raising a brood,
Without saying one thing forward or crude.
I set her little heart aglow
At the Home Sweet Home Appliance Show.

MARSHMALLOW MAGIC

Act I. Intended for Doris and Ted.

DORIS: Ooh, you marshmallow magic,
You choc'late and strawberry flame.
TED: Ooh, you carmel pecan mystery,
You flavor I can't quite name,
But I can taste it.
DORIS: Ooh! you marshmallow magic,
Whoever you happen to be,
TED: Please keep happening again and again,
Please keep happening to me.

[Dialogue]

TED: Dextrose, fructose, glucose,
I can take them or leave them
Till the day that I die,
For you are my lifelong sugar supply.
DORIS: Ooh, you marshmallow magic,
You pure maraschino supreme.
TED: Ooh, you carbohydrate symphony,
You sweeter-than-sweet sweet dream.

[Burp offstage.]

I keep repeating:
Ooh, you marshmallow magic,
Whoever you happen to be,
BOTH: Please keep happening again and again;
Please keep happening to me.

WE HARMONIZE

Act I. Intended for Doris and Ted.

VERSE

DORIS: Ha ha ha!
BOTH: Ha ha ha!
TED: Ho ho ho!
BOTH: Ho ho ho!
Oh, how compatible are we—
TED: Compared to the rest of the so-called
Lovey-dovey little lovebirds
That we see.
BOTH: Tee hee hee.

REFRAIN

BOTH: You and I, we harmonize,
Harmonize, harmonize,
While other dolls and other guys,
They clash! clash!
Give each other a nervous rash!

You and I, we harmonize,
Harmonize, harmonize.
It must be love, or otherwise
We'd screech! scratch!
Bug each other and never match!

Peaches and cream may turn sour,
Purple and gold may fail to blend,
Longines may fight with Wittnauer
But ours is a love without end.

For you and I, we harmonize,
Harmonize, harmonize,
Yes, you and I, we harmonize
All the day long,
And life is one beautiful song—[discord]
[spoken] Wrong!
[sung] Life is one beautiful song.

WON'TCHA SETTLE FOR ME?

Act I. Intended for three unnamed couples. Reprised near end of Act I by Roy.

THIRD BOY: I guess I'm dull.
SECOND BOY: I know I'm square.
FIRST BOY: I'm not very dashing—
SECOND BOY: Or debonaire.
THIRD BOY: I'm not the super-perfect, magic
lover
A girl imagines someday may appear.
THREE BOYS: But this is now
And I am here.
And this is your crucial twenty-
ninth year.

THREE GIRLS: [spoken] Oh, dear.
FIRST BOY: [sung] Won'tcha settle for me—
SECOND BOY: Though I don't seem to be your
dream come true—
THIRD BOY: Settle for my undying love for you?
FIRST GIRL: [spoken] Marlon!
SECOND GIRL: [spoken] Tyrone!
THIRD GIRL: [spoken] Elvis!

FIRST BOY: [*sung*] Won't you settle for this—
        [*producing ring*]
SECOND BOY: Solid engagement ring upon your hand.
THIRD BOY: Might as well know exactly how you
        stand.
FIRST GIRL: [*spoken*] Marlon!
SECOND GIRL: [*spoken*] Tyrone!
THIRD GIRL: [*spoken*] Elvis!
THREE BOYS: [*sung*] I'm the ordinary male
        With the ordinary mind,
        The muscles and the morals
        Of the ordinary kind.
        And my ordinary question is,
        How much better can you do?
FIRST GIRL: [*spoken in whispered terror*] Marlon!
SECOND GIRL: [*same*] Tyrone!
THIRD GIRL: [*same*] Elvis!
THREE BOYS: [*sung*] Won't you settle for me?
        Though I don't seem to be your
          dream come true,
        Settle for my undying love
        For you?

AMATEUR PSYCHIATRIST

Act II. Intended for Doris and ensemble. Performed in "calypso like accents." Loesser's stage directions for this scene indicate that Doris "wears a bizarre 'native' costume of voodoo persuasion. Upstage of her stand witch doctors somewhat resembling psychiatrists, chanting the ostinato-like phrase—"

ENSEMBLE: Free-floating anxiety,
        Free-floating anxiety,
        Free-floating anxiety,
        Free-floating anxiety.
DORIS: Ev'rybody amateur psychiatrist,
        Amateur psychiatrist.
        They describe my malady,
        Free-floating anxiety.

        Amateur psychiatrist,
        All my friends cannot resist
        Advising the couch instead
        Of the nice warm double bed.

        Well, I love you, me baby—
        Do you love me?
        That is all I got in my mind
        Continually.

        Well, I love you, me baby—
        Do you love me?

You alone are my
Free-floating anxiety.

But ev'rybody amateur psychiatrist,
Woman friend, she head the list.
Three divorce, but very sure
I'm the one that's insecure.

Amateur psychiatrist,
There is nothing they have missed,
Except maybe to enjoy
Playing doctor when small boy.

Well, I love you, me baby,
Do you love me?
That is all I got in my mind
Continually.

Well, I love you, me baby,
Do you love me?
You alone are my
Free-floating anxiety.

But ev'rybody amateur psychiatrist,
Ev'rywhere this type exist.
Amateur psychiatrist
At each other shake the fist,
Violently disagree
Over *my* hostility.

FOR THE FAM'LY ALBUM

Act II. Intended for ensemble and Butch. The scene involves a photo session for the imagined family of Ted and Doris. The character Butch is "a younger son."

ENSEMBLE: Let's have one for the fam'ly album—
        Ev'rybody watch the birdie.
        Let's have one for the fam'ly album
        To remember this very fine day.

        Let's have one for the fam'ly album—
        Ev'rybody watch the birdie.
        Let's have one to be bound in leather
        With the rest of the fam'ly display.
BUTCH: Smile!
        As you never before have smiled!
        Gather behind the old folks
        Holding the great-great-grandchild.
ENSEMBLE: Let's have one for the fam'ly album—
        Ev'rybody watch the birdie.
        Let's have one for the fam'ly album,
        Kind of corny but ever so gay,
        To remember this very fine day.

THE GREEN-EYED MONSTER

From undated piano-vocal sheet. Considered for show but never in script. Possibly an unused lyric from the early 1930s.

VERSE 1

The green-eyed monster of jealousy
Came by my bed and he said to me,
"You kissed your gal goodnight around the
    downstairs door,
But how's about that boarder on the second floor?"
It was the—

REFRAIN

Green-eyed monster, the green-eyed monster,
The green-eyed monster sang me that song,
It was the green-eyed monster made me do
    wrong.

VERSE 2

I jumped right up and I laced my shoes;
He whispered, "Son, there's no time to lose;
Remember when she kinda raised her eyes a bit?
Well, she was lookin' if the boarder's light was lit!"
It was the—

REPEAT REFRAIN

VERSE 3

As I went hurrying out my door,
He stopped me cold by my bureau drawer.
I never thought of homicide in all my life,
But now I know who made me take along that
    knife.

Then I got hold of my tortured self
And put that knife back upon the shelf,
But once again I seemed to hear that demon's
    voice
Say, "Put it in your pocket, son, you got no choice."
It was the—

REPEAT REFRAIN

VERSE 4

I rushed right over to my gal's place,
And now I'm hiding my shameful face;
She met me on the stairway full of righteous
    tears—
They hadn't had a boarder there in fifteen years!

And so, Your Honor, my only plea
Is blame those green eyes of jealousy;
I really didn't do it; I was just misled
In cutting up that harmless little feather bed.
It was the—

REPEAT REFRAIN

TAKE ME NOW

From undated piano vocal sheet. Considered for show
but never in script.

VERSE

Take me now, while I'm blind,
While I'm slightly out of mind;
Take me now, while it's new,
All this dazzling splendor of you.

REFRAIN

Take me now, as we meet,
While this whole thing's wondrously sweet.
Before I see that you're wearing your lashes too long,
Before I sense that you're wearing your perfume
    too strong,
Before I learn you're a little short of refined,
Take me now, while I'm blind.

Take me now, while you seem
All I've longed for, dream after dream.
Before the chemistry there on your lips fails to catch,
Before I notice our senses of humor don't match,
Before I leave all my tender illusions behind,
Take me now, while I'm blind.

OTHER SONGS OF 1951–1961

MEET ME AT THE COLLEGE BOWL

Music by George Bassman (1914–1997). Registered for
copyright as an unpublished song March 2, 1951. Better
known as an arranger, Bassman wrote "I'm Getting Sentimental with You" with lyricist Ned Washington; it became
Tommy Dorsey's theme song. This song was written for
The College Bowl, a television program aired on Monday
nights on ABC from October 2, 1950, to March 26, 1951.
Not to be confused with *The G.E. College Bowl*
(1959–1970), this show starred Chico Marx as the propri-
etor of the College Bowl, a campus soda fountain at a
small-town university. It spotlighted young talent, with
Andy Williams among the performers who appeared.

Meet me at the College Bowl.
You need no diploma to rock and roll.
Freshman, Junior, Sophomore,
Come over to the campus
And into our door.

No! It isn't quite the Ritz,
But these banana splits
Will kick you for a goal.
So if there's music in your soul,
Meet us at the College Bowl.

WE'RE IN LOVE WITH THOSE WONDERFUL GUYS

From an undated lyric sheet. To be sung to the tune of
Richard Rodgers and Oscar Hammerstein II's "A Wonderful Guy" from *South Pacific*. Performed by Diosa
Costello and William Tabbert in "A Tribute to Rodgers
and Hammerstein by Show Business," July 9, 1951, at
the Stork Club, New York City.

I'll take tickets a year from next August;
I don't care if I hang from the flies.
Not the Old Vic, I mean Oscar and Dick,
I'm in love with those wonderful guys.

I have worn out a roomful of albums;
Five *Oklahoma*s and six *King and I*'s.
And you will note I can quote what they wrote,
'Cause I dote on those wonderful guys.

I sit there while the Met's doing *Tosca*,
But something by Oscar I crave.
I sit there while they root for the Dodgers
And think about Rodgers and rave!

I'll take tickets a year from next August;
I don't care if I hang from the flies.
I think it's quite clear, I'm like anyone here—
I'm in love, I'm in love, I'm in love, I'm in love,
I'm in love with those wonderful guys!

GIRLS' SCHOOL ALMA MATER

Music by Franz Waxman and Frank Loesser. From Paramount censorship file dated July 31, 1951. Intended for
the 1952 Paramount Picture *My Son John*. Not used in
film. Music not known to survive.

Alma Mater, proudly we will hail
Thy glory evermore.
May thy spirit guide us through the path
Of life that lies before.
May chapel bells a-tolling
Fondly to our hearts recall.
Alma Mater, proudly we will hail
Thy glory evermore.
May your spirit guide us through the path
Of life that lies before.
Alma Mater, Alma Mater dear!

STONE WALLS

From manuscript dated November 1952. Registered for
copyright as an unpublished song June 3, 1965. In the
early 1950s, at the suggestion of his attorney Harold Orenstein, Loesser began to explore composing popular songs
in the country music idiom. He had previously dabbled in
the genre with such songs as "Jingle, Jangle, Jingle" and
"Have I Stayed Away Too Long?" and his work with Jule
Styne for the Judy Canova films. "Big D" for *The Most
Happy Fella* was also written during this period.

REFRAIN

Stone walls do not a prison make, nor iron bars a
   cage—
I'm locked in jail, but oh my soul is free.
I left a heartless woman in my blind and helpless
   rage;
Our loveless home was worse than jail to me.*

VERSE 1

In the cold blue steel of her eyes love was dead,
In the mean, mean tone of her voice.
If I don't go home, it's desertion, they said,
And I'm glad now that I've made my choice.

REPEAT REFRAIN

VERSE 2

In the cold blue steel of her eyes love was dead,
In the hard, hard look of her face.
It's a two-year term for desertion, they said,
But I'm not going back to that place.

REPEAT REFRAIN

VERSE 3

In the cold blue steel of her eyes love was dead,
In her grim, grim step on the stair.
What I'm guilty of is desertion, they said,
But I'd rather be here than be there.

REPEAT REFRAIN

MAKES ME FEEL GOOD ALL OVER

From manuscript dated November 2, 1952. Music not
known to survive.

Makes me feel good all over when I've prayed,
Makes me feel good all over when I've prayed.
Makes me feel good like after walking in the
   sunshine,
Feel good all over when I've prayed.

---

* *Alternate version of refrain, lines 3 and 4:*
   The loveless home from which I ran in blind and
      helpless rage,
   That loveless home was more like jail to me.

Makes me feel good all over when I've prayed,
Makes me feel good all over when I've prayed.
Makes me feel good like after washing in the
   river,
Makes me feel good all over when I've prayed.

When I've been on my knees to the Lord
And I've said all my thanks to the Lord,
Well, then the Lord sends me down my reward:
He makes me feel good all over when I've prayed.

Makes me feel good all over when I've prayed,
Makes me feel good like walking in the sunshine,
Feel good all over when I've prayed.

NO SWALLERIN' PLACE

Music and lyrics by June Carter (1929–2003) and Frank
Loesser. Published. Copyrighted May 8, 1953. Previously registered for copyright as an unpublished song
January 16, 1953. Pencil manuscript of melody and
lyrics dated October 1952. A demo recording by Shorty
Long appears on the compact disc *Frank Sings Loesser*
(Koch). Country music singer and legend June Carter
wrote and performed many Nashville standards. She
later married Johnny Cash, and they wrote one of his
biggest hits, "Ring of Fire."

I got a song, it's a pretty good song,
Only one thing wrong with the pretty good song,
'Cuz the pretty good song goes along and along
   and along . . .

[*Repeat "and along" till almost winded.*]

Till it gits me red in the face.
Whew! Gulp! 'Cuz it ain't got . . . no swallerin'
   place.

Here's that tune, it's a pretty nice tune,
But I just ain't built like a rubber balloon.
It's a pretty nice tune, but I croon and I croon and
   I croon . . .

[*Repeat "And I croon" till almost winded.*]

Till I can't keep up with the pace.
Gulp! 'Cuz it ain't got . . . no swallerin' place.

Now I can finish a sack of Crackerjack
In fifteen seconds flat
And still keep conversation runnin' fair.
When I kiss my darlin' sweetheart,

I can hold it half an hour,
And I ain't half dead when I come up for air.
But durn this song, it's a pretty good song,
Only one thing wrong with the pretty good song,
'Cuz the pretty good song goes along and along
   and along . . .

[*Repeat "and along" till almost winded.*]

Like a doggone marathon race.
Gulp! 'Cuz it ain't got no swallerin' place.

BENNY TO HELEN TO CHANCE

Music and lyrics by Frank Loesser and Milton DeLugg.
Registered for copyright as an unpublished song
April 16, 1953. Introduced by Benny Goodman and
Helen Ward. Loesser wrote this number for a television
special as a favor to Goodman, who was one of the first
bandleaders to perform Loesser's songs in the early
1930s. The title refers to the famous Chicago Cubs in-
field of "Tinkers to Evers to Chance."

"He wrote 'Junk Man' with Joseph Meyer in 1932,"
Goodman later recalled. "Mildred Bailey sang it—so did
Johnny Mercer and Jack Teagarden. Before I ever knew
him, I played his songs—because they were great. He
was inventive, alive. I can remember looking up from the
bandstand and seeing that face . . . how *could* you feel
about a guy with a face like that?"

BENNY: Well now, a good band has got to have a
      "girl noise"—
      You can't play the music with just boys.
      A good band has got to make "girl noise"
      Ev'ry once in a while.
      And so I looked in the file
      For someone just the right style
      And I picked out the biggest "girl noise"
      I ever welcomed aboard,
      Miss Helen Ward!

[*After applause, music out*]

BENNY: [*spoken*] Yes, Helen is back and I'll tell you
      how it all happened. I dialed her on the
      phone. It was long distance. [*Phone
      rings.*] And she answered.
VOICE: [*spoken*] Hello, who's this?

[*Clarinet riff*]

[spoken] This is Benny?

[Clarinet riff]

[spoken] Benny Goodman?

[Clarinet]

[spoken] I can feel the ray, what do ya say, hey?

[Clarinet]

[spoken] Come back to Benny?

[Clarinet]

[spoken] Say pretty please.

[Clarinet]

[spoken] He never even had to ask me twice.

[Segue to HELEN WARD's first number.]

JUST ANOTHER POLKA

Words and music by Frank Loesser and Milton DeLugg. Copyrighted April 30, 1953. Previously registered for copyright as an unpublished song April 9, 1953. Recordings include Jo Stafford (Columbia), Guy Lombardo (Decca), and Eddie Fisher (RCA Victor), among others.

This is just another polka, just another polka,
But oh, what a girl in my arms!
Am I in heaven since we met?
Is this the Philharmonic playing *Romeo and Juliet*?

[spoken] No!

[sung] Just another polka like any other polka,
But somehow the music has charms.
This is just another polka, but holy schmolka—
Oh, what a girl in my arms!

I'm dancing with an angel,
With an angel, an angel, an angel.
Oh yes, I'm dancing with an angel,

That's why the band is sounding better
From the moment that I met her,*
'Cause I'm dancing with an angel,
With an angel, an angel, an angel,
She's got me dancing like I never thought I could,
Oh, Arthur Murray never had it so good.

This is just another polka, just another polka,
But oh, what a girl in my arms!
Am I in heaven since we met?
Is this the Philharmonic playing *Romeo and Juliet*?

[spoken] No!

[sung] Just another polka like any other polka,
But somehow music has charms.
This is just another polka, but holy schmolka—
Oh, what a girl in my (play it again!),
Oh, what a girl in my arms!

ALL IS FORGIVEN (AND ALL IS FORGOTTEN)

Published. Copyrighted September 2, 1953. Pencil manuscript dated October 1952. A recording by Frank and Lynn Loesser is on the compact disc *Frank Sings Loesser* (Koch).

I look through the newspapers morning and night
For a message to come shining through
Saying, "All is forgiven and all is forgotten,"
And calling me home to you.

I read ev'ry name while I'm searching for mine
And I envy those fortunate men
Finding all is forgiven and all is forgotten,
And hurrying home again.

Oh, I know you were right and I know I was wrong,
Still I can't come and beg at your door,
But oh, darling, if you only knew how I long
For a sign that you want me once more!

So I look through the newspapers morning and night
For the message to come shining through
Saying, "All is forgiven and all is forgotten,"
And calling me home to you.

---

* If sung by a woman, these lines read:
    And there is heaven in the rhythm
    Ev'ry minute that I'm with 'im.

CRYING POLKA

Music and lyrics by Frank Loesser and Milton DeLugg. Published. Copyrighted March 22, 1954. Previously registered for copyright as an unpublished song January 8, 1954.

VERSE 1

Boo hoo hoo hoo, listen to her cry,
Boo hoo hoo hoo, as she dances by,
Boo hoo hoo hoo, for her lost romance.
Oh, don't request this number
If you take her out to dance.

REFRAIN

She goes dancing ev'ry Wednesday night,
And twenty diff'rent fellows hold her mighty tight.
Now twenty diff'rent fellows should make the lady gay,
But she's in tears
When she hears
The band begin to play
Her sentimental polka.
She can't get over that.
The tune reminds her of
Her one and only love,
Her one and only love
Who left her flat.

VERSE 2

Boo hoo hoo hoo, listen to her cry,
Boo hoo hoo hoo, as she dances by.
Boo hoo hoo hoo, she just can't forget,
And ev'ry dancing partner
Gets his shoulder soaking wet—

REPEAT REFRAIN

VERSE 3

From all the boo hoo hoo hoo, listen to her cry,
Boo hoo hoo hoo, as she dances by,
Boo hoo hoo hoo, for her lost romance.
Oh, don't request this number
If you take her out to dance.

REPEAT REFRAIN

WARM AND WILLING

Registered for copyright as an unpublished song September 30, 1958. Copyist piano-vocal sheet dated January 18, 1955. Loesser manuscript of melody, entitled "Aphro," dated November 1954.

Now you come here, you,
Come here to me,
Warm and willing and, ooh,
Near to me.
[*spoken*] That's good.

You know tonight is the night,
It's in the book.
I've been a-watching' how you walk,
Looking how you look.

Now you come here, you,
Come here to me.
Warm and willing and, ooh,
Tenderly.
[*spoken*] That's better.

You know we're long overdue,
Time's gone to waste.
I want to feel how you feel,
Taste how you taste.
Now you come here, you,
Come here to me,
Warm and willing and, ooh,
Frequently.
[*spoken*] That's the best.

You've been a-running around the room
Begging me to quit,
Put on a fine little show
Of fighting it.

Now you come here, you.
[*spoken*] Mmm!

DON'T SEND LUCY TO THE STORE

Lyric for Mrs. Harold (Lucy) Orenstein. From undated handwritten lyric, probably 1955. Harold Orenstein was Frank Loesser's attorney. No music is known to exist.

Don't send Lucy to the store, Harold.
Oh, don't send Lucy to the store.
For she just got back from Europe
And her dander must be sure up.
It would only insecure up your rapport.
(That's a French word.)

Don't send Lucy to Gristede's, Harold;
By this time shopping is a bore.
Let her struggle with valises,
Open windows, rinse chemises,
But don't send Lucy to the store.
(It's probably raining.)
Don't send Lucy to the store.

PIELS BEER COMMERCIAL

Registered for copyright as an unpublished song May 20, 1958.

FALSETTO: Cool-brewed, cool-brewed,
Cool-brewed, cool-brewed—
1ST VOICE: Piels!
2ND VOICE: The beer with the barrel of flavor.
FALSETTO: Cool-brewed, cool-brewed—
1ST VOICE: Piels!
2ND VOICE: The beer with the barrel of flavor.
FALSETTO: Cool-brewed, cool-brewed—
1ST VOICE: Piels!
2ND VOICE: The beer with the barrel of flavor.
1ST AND
2ND VOICES: Do yourself a favor.
FALSETTO: Cool-brewed—
ALL: Piels!

ANALYST'S WIFE

From an undated handwritten lyric sheet. Sung to the tune of Richard Rodgers and Oscar Hammerstein II's "Oh, What a Beautiful Morning!" Performed by Lucille Stein at the New York Psychoanalytic Association Winter Dinner, 1961.

Oh, what a mis'rable morning,
Oh, what a constraint in my life!
Hark to my song of subjection,
I am an analyst's wife.

Oh, the family are standing like statues,
Very guilty repressed little statues.
My once gay apartment's a sad catacomb
Since my husband started to practice at home.

Oh, what a mis'rable morning—[*dog barks*]
Rover, lie down and play dead! [*children's high
voices: "Mama," etc.*]
Children, stop romping and laughing—
Father is shrinking a head.

Oh, the patient in there must think deeper,
So my maid can't start using the sweeper.
A door must not slam and a phone must not ring,
And the analyst's wife can but quietly sing:

Oh, what a mis'rable morning,
Oh, what a frustrating day!
I have a paranoid feeling
Nothing is going my way.

It's a quarter to ten and he's free now—
Maybe he'll have some coffee with *me* now.
I'll wait till he's out of the bathroom, and then—
[*buzzer*]
There's a female neurotic arriving at ten!

Oh, what a mis'rable morning!
Pardon my functional pain.
Why not put me on the couch, dear?
I'm the one going insane! [*shriek*]
I'm the one going INSANE!

GREENWILLOW | 1960

GREENWILLOW

Tryout: Shubert Theatre, Philadelphia, January 30–February 27, 1960. New York premiere: March 8, 1960, Alvin Theatre. 97 performances. Book by Lesser Samuels and Frank Loesser based on the novel by B. J. Chute. Produced by Robert A. Willey in association with Frank Productions. Directed by George Roy Hill. Choreography by Joe Layton. Orchestrations by Don Walker. Musical direction by Abba Bogin. Sets by Peter Larkin. Costumes by Alvin Colt. Lighting by Feder. Cast starred Anthony Perkins (Gideon Briggs) and featured Cecil Kellaway (Reverend Birdsong), Pert Kelton (Gramma Briggs), Ellen McCown (Dorrie Whitbred), William Chapman (Reverend Lapp), Lee Cass (Thomas Clegg), Bruce MacKay (Amos Briggs), Grover Dale (Andrew), Elaine Swann (Maidy), Lynn Brinker (Martha Briggs), Saralou Cooper (Emma), and Dortha Duckworth (Clara Clegg).

Recordings: Original Broadway cast album (RCA Victor).

A DAY BORROWED FROM HEAVEN

Registered for copyright as an unpublished song February 29, 1960. Introduced by Maggie Task (Mrs. Hasty), Marie Foster (Mrs. Lunny), Jordan Howard (Preebs), William Chapman (Lapp), Anthony Perkins (Gideon), and ensemble.

MRS. HASTY: 'Twill be a day borrowed from heaven.
MRS. HASTY,
MRS. LUNNY,
AND PREEBS: 'Twill have a sky wonderous blue.
ENSEMBLE: 'Twill be a day borrowed from heaven.
Woke up this morning and somehow I knew.
MRS. HASTY: I turned my neck and the crick was gone.
PREEBS: I heard a dove at the break of dawn.
MRS. LUNNY: Slept on my left side and lived the night.
ENSEMBLE: How can the weather be other than bright?
'Twill be a joy seven till seven.
Know it for sure, know it for true.
Twill be a day borrowed from heaven.

Cecil Kellaway, Anthony Perkins (center), and cast members

Woke up this morning and somehow I knew.

[REVEREND LAPP *enters.*]

LAPP: [*spoken*] Rain.
ENSEMBLE: [*spoken*] Rain?
MRS. HASTY: [*spoken*] I'd thought so.
ENSEMBLE: [*spoken*] Rain!
LAPP: 'Twill be a day glummer than gloomy.
'Twill have a sky grayer than smoke.
ENSEMBLE: 'Twill be a day glummer than gloomy.
Knew it this morning the moment I woke.
MRS. HASTY: I turned my neck and the crick was there.
PREEBS: I heard a groan on the cellar stair.
MRS. LUNNY: Dreamed of a pleasure and woke in pain.
ENSEMBLE: How can the weather be other than rain?
MRS. CLEGG: [*spoken*] Perhaps we'd best ponder tomorrow.
ENSEMBLE: [*spoken*] Tomorrow.

MRS. LUNNY: 'Twill be a day borrowed from heaven.
'Twill have a sky—
ENSEMBLE: Wonderous blue.
'Twill be a day borrowed from heaven.
Wake up tomorrow and see it come true.

GIDEON: 'Twill be a day borrowed from heaven.
'Twill have a sky wonderous blue.
'Twill be a day borrowed from heaven.
Woke up this morning and somehow I knew.

Stamp on the weed and then do the charm.
Be there a traveler, he'll bring no harm.
Stamp on the weed, then make the sign.
How can I feel any feeling but fine?

'Twill be a joy seven till seven.
Know it for sure, know it for true.
'Twill be a day borrowed from heaven.
Woke up this morning and somehow I knew.

DORRIE'S WISH

Registered for copyright as an unpublished song January 13, 1960. Introduced by Ellen McCown (Dorrie).

Nesting dove or flying lark,
I wish me Gideon, day and dark.
Flying lark or nesting dove,
I wish me Gideon for love.

A-TANGLE, A-DANGLE

Registered for copyright as an unpublished song January 20, 1960. Introduced by Lynn Brinker (Martha), Pert Kelton (Gramma), Ian Tucker (Micah), and Brenda Harris (Sheby).

MARTHA: There comes my dearest love,
Climbing the hill.
GRAMMA: Shame, oh, shame—
Oh, look at your hair in a tangle,
A smudge on your nose,
And your apron a-dangle!
Shame to greet a good man looking so
A-tangle, a-dangle, head to toe,
Tangle, a-dangle, agape and akimbo.
There comes my boy, my boy;
Can't hide my tears of joy.
MARTHA,
MICAH,
AND SHEBY: Shame, oh, shame,
Oh, look at your hair in a tangle,
A smudge on your nose,
And your apron a-dangle!
Shame to greet a good man looking so
A-tangle, a-dangle, head to toe
Tangle, a-dangle, agape—

AMOS LONG ENTRANCE

Unused. Originally with "A-Tousle." From typed lyric sheet dated February 1960. Intended for Amos.

Haul the hawser,
Stroke the oar,
Hitch-o,
Heave-o,

I'm home
Once more.

THE MUSIC OF HOME

Published. Copyrighted February 16, 1960. Previously registered for copyright as an unpublished song December 2, 1959. Introduced by Anthony Perkins (Gideon), Bruce MacKay (Amos), and ensemble. Reprised by ensemble in Act II. Recorded by Bing Crosby (RCA Victor) and Kate Smith (Tops).

VERSE 1

GIDEON: Just hear the teakettle sing,
"Away, awee. Away, awee"—
AMOS: And Clegg's old cow
Moo in the meadow.
And hear the morning chimes
Down in the village clear as clear.
GIDEON: Clear as clear.
In tune with the robin on the roof—
AMOS: And the neighbor's chopping axe
Ringing on a maple—
GIDEON: In tune with the laughing of the young ones
Having at a game.
AMOS: And the voice of one I dearly love
Calling my name.

REFRAIN

GIDEON: 'Tis the music of home,
The music of home,
Full of wonder as angel song.
All the music of home,
The music of home,
Singing, "Home is where I belong."
Singing, "Home is where I belong."
GIDEON
AND AMOS: Home is where I belong.

VERSE 2

AMOS: In tune with the crickets in the grass—
GIDEON: And the old oak meadow gate singing on her hinges—
AMOS: In tune with the crackle of the hearth
Aflicker and aflame.
ENSEMBLE: Welcome to you, Amos—
Greetings, Amos, again.
AMOS: And the voices of the folk I love
Calling my name.

ENSEMBLE: Amos, we welcome you,
Welcome you, welcome you.

REFRAIN

AMOS AND
ENSEMBLE: 'Tis the music of home,
The music of home,
Full of wonder as angel song.
All the music of home,
The music of home,
Singing, "Home is where I belong,
Home is where I belong."

GIDEON BRIGGS, I LOVE YOU

Published. Copyrighted January 27, 1960. Previously registered for copyright as an unpublished song December 8, 1959. Introduced by Anthony Perkins (Gideon) and Ellen McCown (Dorrie).

GIDEON: [spoken] It's been waiting inside me like a long hunger.

[DORRIE holds basket out to him.]

'Tis another kind of hunger. It makes me want to shout!
[sung] Shout!
And to sing it out
And to leave you no doubt when I say,
"Dorrie, I dearly love you, love you."
There it is, plain as daylight.
I love you, love you,
Love you with all my heart.

[Dialogue]

DORRIE: Gideon Briggs, I . . .
[spoken] . . . believe your shirt needs a mend. I'll sew it.
GIDEON: What's that to do with love?
DORRIE: 'Tis a way of showing it.
GIDEON: [sung] I'll not spell it in fancy embroidery
Nor bake it into a bilberry tart.
Dorrie, I dearly love you, love you,
Love you with all my heart.
DORRIE: Gideon Briggs, I . . .
Gideon Briggs, I . . .
GIDEON: [spoken] Kissing will give me the answer.

SUMMERTIME LOVE

Published. Copyrighted January 27, 1960. Previously registered for copyright as an unpublished song December 2, 1959. Introduced by Anthony Perkins (Gideon) and ensemble. Recorded by Rosemary Clooney (RCA Victor), Eddie Fisher (Ramrod), and Harry Belafonte (RCA Victor), among others.

VERSE

GIDEON: I've been told, I've been told
By the wise and the old
Something good I'm supposed to remember.*
If my first love I've found in the warm of July,
It'll cool in the nip of September.

Now they point to the skies,
Do the old and the wise,
And they speak of a chill in the air.
And they wink while they're nudging me over to
The pretty little ladies in the square.
But I don't care, for—

REFRAIN

Still I love my summertime love;
Still I love the kissing and the courting.
Still I love my summertime love,
With a heart still summertime true.
ENSEMBLE: Ooh, aah, oh, ay, ee, ooh.†
GIDEON: Still I love my summertime love;
Still I want her walking close beside me.
Still I love my summertime love,
Let the seasons change as they do.
ENSEMBLE: Ooh, aah, oh, ay, ee, ooh.
GIDEON: Let the chilly autumn wind blow in my window—
ENSEMBLE: Ooh . . .
GIDEON: Chilly autumn wind blow in my door—
ENSEMBLE: Ooh. . . .
GIDEON: Chilly autumn wind blow down my chimney

---

* Original line:
Something good for a boy to remember.

† Originally:
Fly in the face of providence,
He'll fly in the face of providence,
One little love for Gideon.

And up through the crack in the floor.
ENSEMBLE: Let it roar,
And still he loves his summertime love.
GIDEON: I love you, love you—
ENSEMBLE: Still he loves the kissing and the courting.
GIDEON: There it is plain as daylight—
ENSEMBLE: Still he loves his summertime love—
GIDEON: With a heart still summertime true—
ENSEMBLE: Ooh, aah, oh, ay, ee, ooh.
GIDEON: Heart still summertime true—
ENSEMBLE: Heart still summertime true.

BLASPHEMY

Introduced by Anthony Perkins (Gideon).

Come one and all to church today
And hear our God-earnest minister
Clear his throat,
Squint like a goat,
Clutch at his coat
And say . . .

[*spoken, burlesquing* REVEREND LAPP'*s pulpit mannerisms and voice*]

"I publish the banns of marriage between Gideon Briggs and Dorrie Whitbred."

WALKING AWAY WHISTLING

Published. Copyrighted January 27, 1960. Previously registered for copyright as an unpublished song December 2, 1959. Introduced by Ellen McCown (Dorrie). Recorded by Ethel Smith (Decca).

He'll be walking away whistling,
Whistling, whistling,
Walking away whistling,
Whistling, come dawn.
I could give him an ocean of loving,
I could give him a mountain of care;
But a wandering man is a wandering man,
And there's oceans and mountains out there.

He'll be walking away whistling,
Whistling, whistling,
Walking away whistling,
Whistling, come dawn.

I could lay him a table of plenty,
I could spread him a bed of down;
But a wandering man is a wandering man,
And he'd never rest easy in town.

He'll be walking away whistling,
Whistling, whistling,
Walking away whistling,
Whistling, and gone.

THE SERMON

Registered for copyright as an unpublished song February 19, 1960, under the title "The Sermon." Alternate title "The Coming of Winter." Original manuscript title "Double Sermon." Introduced by William Chapman (Lapp) and Cecil Kellaway (Birdsong). Lapp and Birdsong sing their lyrics together, with Birdsong beginning after Lapp's first line.

LAPP: The coming of winter, the coming of winter,
The coming of wretched cold, cold winter
Is a warning,
A warning to repent.
Repent, repent,
Repent, repent, repent.
Give heed, lest wild storms kill your trees,
Kill your trees.
For your sins God will punish you.
Trees will die, branches fall.
Let sinners all beware,
Beware, beware,
Beware, beware, beware.
You should know
From Genesis Six: Five,
God saw
That the wickedness of man was great.
Wickedness,
Wickedness.
And so repent.
Repent, repent
Repent, repent,

BIRDSONG: The coming of winter,
Blessed old winter,
Nights of long deep
Featherbed sleep
And a hot plum porridge in the morning.
Rejoice,
Rejoice,
Rejoice, rejoice.
The merry white snowdrifts,
Nippy breeze calling,
"Dance, dance, dance, there's wind in the sky."
So there's good, good firewood for all.
Be glad,
Be glad,
Be glad, be glad.
Of course you know
From Genesis One: Thirty-one,
God saw everything that he had made,
And behold, it was very good;
Behold it was very good.
Rejoice,
Rejoice,
Rejoice.
LAPP: Ay-men!
BIRDSONG: Ah-men!
LAPP: [*spoken*] I prefer "Ay-men!"
BIRDSONG: [*spoken*] Oh, "Ay-men."
LAPP: [*spoken*] Long as we're of one mind about things.
BIRDSONG: [*spoken*] So be it.
BOTH: [*sung*] Ay-men!

COULD'VE BEEN A RING

Registered for copyright as an unpublished song January 13, 1960. Originally titled "But We Never." Introduced by Lee Cass (Clegg) and Pert Kelton (Gramma).

CLEGG: 'Twas the lilac bushes where I spied you
Getting altogether dry
From your altogether dip in the brook.
For the lilac bushes couldn't hide you,
Couldn't hide you from the look,
From that ever-longing look that I took.
Now there was a good thing
For a single young man.
GRAMMA: And speaking of good things,
'Tis a good thing I ran.
BOTH: Oh yes, there
Could've been a ring,
Could've been a ring-ding,
Could've been a ring-ding-dee.
CLEGG: Could've been a hurry-up laying of the plans—

GRAMMA: Wagging of the tongues—
CLEGG: Crying of the banns.
BOTH: Could've been a ring,
Could've been a ring-ding
For you and me.
CLEGG: But we never—
GRAMMA: No, we never—
CLEGG: We came mighty near to nearly—
GRAMMA: But—
CLEGG: We never.
You were cautious.
GRAMMA: I were clever.
BOTH: We came mighty near to nearly,
But we never.
Oh yes, there
Could've been a ring,
Could've been a ring-ding,
Could've been a ring-ding-dee.
CLEGG: Could've been a hurry-up saying of the
vows—
GRAMMA: Building of the crib—
CLEGG: Raising of the brows.
BOTH: Could've been a ring,
Could've been a ring-ding
For you and me.
CLEGG: But we never—
GRAMMA: No, we never—
CLEGG: We came cozy close to mostly—
GRAMMA: But—
CLEGG: We never.
You were cautious.
GRAMMA: I were clever.
BOTH: We came cozy close to mostly,
But we never.
Oh yes, there
Could've been a ring,
Could've been a ring-ding,
Could've been a ring-ding-dee.
CLEGG: Could've been a written-down on the
Bible page—
GRAMMA: Telling 'bout his name—
CLEGG: Lying 'bout his age.
BOTH: Could've been a ring,
Could've been a ring-ding
For you and me.
CLEGG: But we never—
GRAMMA: No, we never—
CLEGG: We came to the brink distinctly—
GRAMMA: But—
CLEGG: We never.
You were cautious.
GRAMMA: I were clever.
BOTH: We came to the brink distinctly,
Cozy close to mostly,
Mighty near to nearly,
But we never.

[Dialogue]

GRAMMA: Praise God,
There's never been a thing,
Never been a one thing
Twixt you and me.
BOTH: To the brink distinctly,
Cozy close to mostly,
Might near to nearly,
But we never.

GIDEON BRIGGS, I LOVE YOU
(Solo)

Published. Copyrighted January 27, 1960. Introduced by Ellen McCown (Dorrie). This solo for Dorrie reprises some lyrics (lines 9–16) introduced by Gideon in the earlier version of "Gideon Briggs, I Love You" (page 207).

Oh, I wish I were brazen and bold
Instead of so ladylike shy,
For then as we meet
I'd not gape at my feet
But I'd look at him straight in the eye.
And I'd shout!
And I'd sing it out!
And I'd leave him no doubt when I say,
"Gideon Briggs, I love you, love you."
There it is, plain as daylight.
I love you, love you,
Love you with all my heart.
I'll not spell it in fancy embroidery
Nor bake it into a bilberry tart.
Gideon Briggs, I love you, love you,
Love you with all my heart.
Oh, I wish I were brazen and bold
Instead of so ladylike shy. . . ! [exits]

Unused preamble

Down deep in his heart there's a crying need
Beneath that angry frown that he wears.
A lost little boy with a crying need,
A need to feel sure there is someone who cares,
Evermore truly cares.

And I am that someone who waits in his path
All ready to fall like a round bottom skittle?
Oh, how can he want it so much
And trust it so little?

NEVER WILL I MARRY

Published. Copyrighted January 27, 1960. Previously registered for copyright as an unpublished song December 8, 1959. Previously titled "Never Never." Introduced by Anthony Perkins (Gideon). Recorded by Vic Damone (Columbia), Sheena Easton (MCA), Nancy Wilson and Cannonball Adderley (Capitol), Judy Garland and Liza Minnelli (Capitol), and Barbra Streisand (Columbia), among others.

VERSE

Any flimsy-dimsy looking for true love
Better smile me no "good dearie, good day."
Any flimsy-dimsy looking for true love
Better look her looking some other way.

For my kiss can be no evermore promise,
But a fancy-dancy fiddle-and-free.*
Any flimsy-dimsy looking for true love
Better waste no time, no time on me.

REFRAIN

Never, never will I marry,
Never, never will I wed.
Born to wander solitary,
Wide my world, narrow my bed.
Never, never, never will I marry,
Born to wander till I'm dead.

No burdens to bear,
No conscience nor care,
No mem'ries to mourn,
No turning, for I was

Born to wander solitary,
Wide my world, narrow my bed.
Never, never, never will I marry,
Born to wander till I'm dead.

---

* Earlier version of lines 5–6:
Tender fond though now it be
Kissing flitting fancy-dancy free,

GREENWILLOW CHRISTMAS

Published. Copyrighted May 13, 1960. Previously registered for copyright as an unpublished song December 8, 1959. Introduced by Lynn Brinker (Martha) and ensemble. Recorded by the Browns (RCA Victor) and George Beverly Shea (RCA Victor).

ENSEMBLE: Come see the star,
Come hear the bells,
Come learn the tale
This night forever tells.*
Come one and all
From far and wide,
Come know the joy,
The joy,
The joy,
Come know the joy
Of Christmastide.
MARTHA: Three wise men followed a star one
night
To where glad bells were pealing,
And soon beheld the Holy Child
And all the shepherds kneeling.
ENSEMBLE: Come see the star,
Come hear the bells,
Come learn the tale
This night forever tells.
Come one and all
From far and wide,
Come know the joy,
The joy,
The joy,
Come know the joy
Of Christmastide.

ADDITIONAL VERSE (IN SHEET MUSIC)

'Twas long ago in Bethlehem,
Yet ever live the glory,
And hearts all glow and voices rise
A-caroling the story.

---

* *Earlier version of lines 1–4:*
  Come see the star
  Bright gleaming high above;
  Come hear the bells proclaiming
  A time of peace and love.

FARAWAY BOY

Published. Copyrighted January 27, 1960. Previously registered for copyright as an unpublished song December 2, 1959. Introduced by Ellen McCown (Dorrie). Recorded by Della Reese (RCA Victor).

Kind sir, I'm sure I love you
A very merry much.
I know it by the tingle
The moment that we touch.

Oh, sir, 'tis not a new thing.
This feeling of joy.
Well, sir, 'tis all because of
Some faraway boy.

Some faraway boy
With a name past recall
And a face I'd not likely
Remember at all.

Some faraway boy
Who first wakened my heart;
If there's love there for you, sir,
He made it all start.

Some faraway boy
With a long-ago kiss;
Else I'd never have learned, sir,
To love you like this.

Forgive me if my
Secret tale should annoy,
And be grateful, kind sir,
To that faraway boy.

CLANG DANG THE BELL

Registered for copyright as an unpublished song January 13, 1960. Introduced by Anthony Perkins (Gideon), Pert Kelton (Gramma), Lynn Brinker (Martha), Ian Tucker (Micah), Brenda Harris (Sheby), and John Megna (Jabez).

GIDEON, GRAMMA,
MARTHA, MICAH,
SHEBY, AND JABEZ: Clang dang the bell,
Gather by the well.
Sprinkle joy on baby boy
So's he'll not go to hell.

Flap flop the broom,
Give the rev'rend room.
Wash the sins off babykins
And save a soul from doom.
MICAH: Let's give him the name of
Nebuchadnezzar,
He was a Bible king.
GIDEON: Let's ponder the name of David,
'Tis easier to sing.
SHEBY: Let's give him the name of
'Lijah the prophet,
Eli or Elihu.
JABEZ: Let's give him the name of
blasphemy
For that's in the Bible too.
ALL: Clang dang the bell,
Gather by the well.
Sprinkle joy on baby boy
So's he'll not go to hell.
Hell, hell, hell, hell, hell . . .

WHAT A BLESSING

Registered for copyright as an unpublished song January 13, 1960. Previously titled "Blessing Song." Introduced by Cecil Kellaway (Birdsong).

Oh, I know it's the devil who tempts me to crime
And to sin and corruption, and worse.
But I find in resisting him time after time
That I can't quite believe he's a curse.
For in fact, I believe . . . the reverse.

What a blessing to know there's a devil
And that I'm but a pawn in his game;
That my impulse to sin
Doesn't come from within,
And so I'm not exactly to blame.

What a blessing to know there's a devil
Ever leading me into some vice.
And though easily led,
I can hold up my head
Knowing I'm fundamentally nice.

What relief, oh what blessed relief
That a thief is by nature no thief,
And a liar is merely the innocent buyer

Or lies from the liar-in-chief,*
So of course the remorse may be brief.

What a blessing to know there's a devil
And that I'm but a pawn in his game,
For I never do wrong
Until he comes along,
And so I'm not exactly the one
Who's to blame.

[*spoken*] Hand in pockets, the hungry wretch walks
    in the crowd
For supper too poor, and for begging too proud.
Hands in pockets till trapped in a devilish plot,
For the hands are his own
But the pockets are not.
Then it comes to him, like a shot—

[*sung*] What a blessing to know there's a devil
In these devil-crazed moments of crime.
With a now lucid brain
I can stoutly maintain
That I wasn't exactly myself
At the time.

[*spoken*] Oh, the poor lonely widower mourns his
    late wife
And regrets being nasty to her during life.
But he soon is aware
That he's been made a goat
As they loosen his fingers from her dear dead
    throat.
From the gallows . . . this last note (quote):

[*sung*] What a blessing to know there's a devil
Who has made me this mischievous elf.
Being decent, I daren't
Accuse either parent
And certainly never myself.

It's a fact, it's a comforting fact,
That the soul remains whole and intact,
Facing fraud and deceit, a forbidden sweetmeat,
Or some game in which cards have been stacked,
With this thought, for when caught in the act:

What a blessing to know there's a devil
And that we're not exactly to blame
For all guile and all greed
And each rotten misdeed
Which might blacken sweet mankind's good name.

What a blessing to know there's a devil
Or we'd all simply die of shame!

---

* *Original version of lines 18–19:*
    That the flames of hell's fire, inspire a liar
    To say things beyond all belief.

REPRISE (SUNG BY BIRDSONG IN ACT II, SCENE 4)

What a blessing to know there's a devil
When I hear myself utter a lie
That it wasn't my fib
But just popped out ad lib
By a glibber old fibber than I.

Cut verses

What a blessing to know there's a devil
When I'm tipsy from strong barley malt
That my elbow he bent
Quite without my consent
And I'm staggering home having spent all the rent
And that I'm not exactly at fault.

A blessing to know there's a devil
When I hear myself telling some lie.
His ventriloquist voice
Hardly leaves me a choice
And that makes him more guilty than I.

What a blessing to know there's a devil
When some truth I attempt to impart.
If I happen to fib,
That's the devil's ad lib,
And it couldn't have come from the heart.

What a blessing to know there's a devil.
Let us name the old villain by name,
For we never do wrong
Until he comes along—
What a pleasant relief from my shame.

What a blessing to know there's a devil
Who incites me to riot and brawl.
When I'm caught in the act,
It's a comforting fact
That I'm not really bad after all.

Like the rasping of a bow
On an otherwise mellow-toned fiddle,
Or a tiny little tack
On an otherwise comfortable chair,
Like the painful pang of gas
In an otherwise well-nourished middle,
Comes the devil to corrupt
Every otherwise innocent soul everywhere,
Bringing sin, degradation, and grief,
Ah, but also such blessed relief.

What a blessing to know there's a devil
And I answer at his beck and call.
What relief when I'm caught
To resort to the thought
That I'm not really rotten at all!

HE DIED GOOD

Registered for copyright as an unpublished song January 13, 1960. Introduced by Marie Foster (Mrs. Lunny), Maggie Task (Mrs. Hasty), Jordon Howard (Preebs), and ensemble.

ENSEMBLE: He died good. He died good.
MRS. LUNNY: Come his dying moment—
ENSEMBLE: He died good.
MRS. HASTY: How nice for the widow—
ENSEMBLE: In her widowhood.
MRS. HASTY: The comfort of knowing—
ENSEMBLE: He died good.
PREEBS: Saved by the Rev'rend—
ENSEMBLE: Saved by the Rev'rend—
PREEBS: Who loosened up Satan's control.
ENSEMBLE: Saved by the Rev'rend—
PREEBS: Who sent him to heaven with a
ENSEMBLE: Tender sweet soul.
MRS. HASTY: Hog mean.
MRS. LUNNY: Pinchpenny.
ENSEMBLE: Hog mean, pinchpenny,
    Tender sweet soul.
MRS. HASTY: Spiteful.
MRS. LUNNY: Hateful.
ENSEMBLE: Spiteful, hateful,
    Hog mean, pinchpenny.
PREEBS: Blaspheming.
MRS. HASTY: Poison tongue.
ENSEMBLE: Blaspheming, poison tongue,
    Spiteful, hateful,
    Hog mean, pinchpenny.
VILLAGER: Flint-hearted.
MRS. HASTY: Evil-eyed.
ENSEMBLE: Flint-hearted, evil-eyed,
    Blaspheming, poison tongue,
    Spiteful, hateful,
    Hog mean, pinchpenny,
    Tender sweet soul.
MRS. LUNNY: A lifetime of living—
ENSEMBLE: As no human should—
MRS. HASTY: And wonder of wonders—
ENSEMBLE: He died good.

THE MUSIC OF HOME

(Finale)

Published. Copyrighted January 17, 1960. Previously registered for copyright as an unpublished song December 2, 1959. Introduced by Anthony Perkins (Gideon), Ellen McCown (Dorrie), and ensemble. Recorded by Bing Crosby (RCA Victor) and Kate Smith (Tops).

GIDEON: I hear the teakettle sing,
"Away, awee, Away, awee,"
And Clegg's cow
Moo in the meadow.
I hear the morning chimes,
Down in the village clear as clear,
In tune with the robin on the roof,
And the neighbor's chopping axe
Ringing on a maple
In tune with the laughing of the young ones
Having at a game—
DORRIE: [*spoken*] Gideon?
GIDEON: [*sung*] And the voice of one I dearly love calling my name.
DORRIE [*spoken*] Gideon . . .
GIDEON: [*sung*] Calling my name.
DORRIE: Gideon Briggs, I love you, love you.
GIDEON: There it is, plain as daylight.
ENSEMBLE: 'Tis the music of home,
The music of home,
Full of wonder as angel song.
All the music of home,
The music of home, singing,
"Home is where I belong,
Home is where I belong."

CUT AND UNUSED SONGS

RIDDLEWEED

Manuscript dated February 20, 1960. Intended for Gideon, Gramma, and ensemble. This was the show's original opening number. Dropped from show prior to New York premiere. Additional lyrics from manuscripts dated March 1959 and June 1959.

GIDEON: Go round, go round, go riddle, go round.
ALL: Go riddle, go straddle.
GIDEON: Go spit a little and away.
MAIDY, EMMA, AND GRAMMA: Spit a little and away—
GIDEON: Trav'ler, bring me no harm today.
ALL: Trav'ler, bring me no harm today—
Hwak! [*They spit.*]
Too!

ADDITIONAL LYRICS

GRAMMA: Traveler, be you a bug, bite me not.
ENSEMBLE: Big bug.
GRAMMA: Traveler, be you a bird, bite me not.
ENSEMBLE: Black bird.
GRAMMA: Sing me no evil song.
ENSEMBLE: Sweet bird.
ALL: Be you a human, do me no wrong.

MY BEAUTY

Registered for copyright as an unpublished song February 19, 1960. Originally intended for Anthony Perkins (Gideon) to sing to his pregnant cow to open Act I. Dropped prior to New York opening. Susan Loesser recalled in *A Most Remarkable Fella* the circumstances of the song's creation and demise:

"My Beauty" had the same tune as "Riddleweed," but it was a love song for Gideon to sing to his pregnant cow. My father proudly performed his new opening number for the musical director [Abba Bogin], orchestrator, rehearsal pianists, stage manager, company manager, and producers—who met it with embarrassed silence.

"Well, if you don't like it, say so!" he said. "Tell me you hate the fucking thing! I'll throw it out the window. Tell me *something*. Don't just sit there!" Pause. "God dammit." And back he went to work. This was now the second week in Philadelphia. Everyone was staying at the same hotel. Around 4:00 a.m., Abba Bogin's phone rang:

In a fog, I say "hello." This wide-awake voice says, "You sleeping or fucking? . . . In that case, get your ass down here. I've got something to show you. And what do you want for breakfast? We're just ordering." So I get dressed and go to his room. Jimmy Leon, the rehearsal pianist, is there. So Jimmy plays an introduction and Frank starts to sing "A Day Borrowed from Heaven." It's sensational.

GIDEON: My very own sweet cow,
My very own sweet cow,
I've but to close my eyes
And I can see her now.
She is my beauty, my beauty, my round-belly beauty,
My round-belly, brown-eyed, heaven-smelling beauty.
There purple gold in the twilight she stands,
There by my barn she stands,
And I count me rich feeling her tail switch
At the loving touch of my hands.
None but my hands may touch my beauty.
CHORUS: Beauty.
GIDEON: My beauty—
CHORUS: Beauty.
GIDEON: My round-belly beauty—
CHORUS: Beauty.
GIDEON: My round-belly, brown-eyed—
ALL: Heaven-smelling beauty.
GIDEON: Warm bedded down though the wind cry strong,
Warm bedded all night long.

I'm a man of means,
Feeling how she leans
To my tender lullaby song.
None but my song may bed my beauty,
My beauty, my round-belly beauty,
My round-belly, brown-eyed, heaven-smelling beauty.
My very own sweet cow,
My very own sweet cow.
She's to be mine someday—
No telling when nor how
I'll own my beauty.
CHORUS: Beauty.
GIDEON: My beauty—
CHORUS: Beauty.
GIDEON: My round-belly beauty—
CHORUS: Beauty.
GIDEON: My round-belly, brown-eyed—
ALL: Heaven-smelling beauty.
GIDEON: There purple gold in the twilight she stands,
There by my barn she stands,
And I count me rich feeling her tail switch
At the loving touch of my hands,
None but my hands.

ALL A-TOUSLE

Unused. Earlier version of "A-Tangle, A-Dangle." From typed lyric sheet dated "Nov." Intended for Martha, Gramma, Micah, Sheby, and Amos. A still earlier version, from typescript, is dated "10/59."

MARTHA: Amos.
GRAMMA ET AL.: Fling off your apron.
MARTHA: Amos.
GRAMMA: Tie your bow.
MARTHA: Amos.
GRAMMA ET AL.: Lest he turn and go
From a scarecrow
All a-tousle
Head to toe.
All a-tousle,
Jelly and akimbo—
Never let him see you so
All a-tousle,
Jelly and akimbo.
GRAMMA: Oh, there comes my boy
Climbing the hill.
MARTHA ET AL.: Look at you now,
All a-tousle
Head to toe.
All a-tousle,
Jelly and akimbo—
Never let him see you so
All a-tousle,
Jelly and akimbo.
GRAMMA: He brings me tears of joy;
He always will.
MARTHA ET AL.: Look at you now,
All a-tousle
Head to toe.
All a-tousle,
Jelly and akimbo—
Never let him see you so
All a-tousle,
Jelly and akimbo.
MICAH: Oh, there comes Pa.
SHEBY: 'Tis Pa come home.
MICAH: Oh, Pa.
SHEBY: Pa!
MICAH: Pa!
MICAH AND SHEBY: There's your pa.
GRAMMA AND MARTHA: All a-tousle
Head to toe.
All a-tousle,
Jelly and akimbo—
Never let him see you so
All a-tousle,
Jelly and akimbo.
AMOS'S VOICE: [offstage, spoken] One more haul on the hawser—

QUINTET: [sung] All a-tousle,
Jelly and akimbo.
AMOS'S VOICE: [spoken] One more stroke of the oar—
QUINTET: [sung] All a-tousle,
Jelly and akimbo.
AMOS'S VOICE: [spoken] One more hitch
And one more heave—
QUINTET: [sung] All a-tousle,
Jelly and akimbo.
AMOS: [spoken] And I'm home forevermore.
QUINTET: [sung] Oh!

Earlier version
(intended for Gramma and children)

GRAMMA: Easy there,
Easy there,
Cool and calm,
Run a comb through your hair.
Never greet a man
All a-tousle,
All a-tousle,
Jelly and akimbo.
Easy there,
Easy there.

Look now,
Look now,
Look now,
There he comes
Up the hill.
Oh my heart,
Do settle still.

There he comes;
There's my boy.
Just no stopping my
Tears of joy.

1ST CHILD: There comes Pa.
Yonder, trudging strong and fast.
Oh Pa! Oh Pa!
Home to us at long last.
2ND CHILD: Where?
Oh Pa!
Oh Pa!
We have him home again!

THE CALL

Registered for copyright as an unpublished song February 19, 1960. Unused.

AMOS: [spoken] The devil *did* take me as ever he does. One night his call comes and there's no hushing it when it strikes. [sung] All of a sudden out of nowhere
Like a thunderbolt inside my head—
'Tis a warning!
For I know that comes another day . . .
willing or no, I'll wander off . . .
And all of that night the spell grows and soon I'm heeding no word nor glance nor beckon.
Then next—
The devil's tune comes to my lips in a whistle.
That whistle!
And there's no conscience or care left in me to stop it.
For my ears fill with the wild hissing of ocean spray
Alone with the ever-moaning and crying wind
And the echo of faraway thunder,
And out of it all come the voices—
VOICES: [spoken] Amos. Amos. Amos.
AMOS: [spoken] Voices calling my name—
VOICES: [spoken] Amos. Amos. Amos.
AMOS: [spoken] Calling me to come away,
Away from the peace and love of home,
And go wandering into hell—
And be glad of it.

A HEAD ON HER SHOULDERS

Registered for copyright as an unpublished song January 13, 1960. Dropped from show prior to New York opening.

LAPP: From this day
Ev'ryone will say
In a great admiration, "Now
There's one young lady with a head on her shoulders.
There's one young lady who's the envy of all.

There's one young lady who will live to a
hundred,
With not one foolishness of heart to
regret."

DORRIE: No heart—
BOTH: To recall.
LAPP: "Yes,
There's one young lady with a head on
her shoulders.
There's one young lady no young man
can upset.
There's one young lady who will live to a
hundred,
With not one starry-eyed mistake to
regret."
DORRIE: No heart—
BOTH: No regret.
LAPP: Never once the sentimental dunce.
DORRIE: Never once.
LAPP: Come what may, neither dizzy nor carried
away.
DORRIE: Never once.
LAPP: Never once the victim of some fling.
DORRIE: Never once.
LAPP: No bird of spring—
DORRIE: Never once.
LAPP: With a broken wing.
DORRIE: Not a tail feather missing.
LAPP: There's one young lady—
BOTH: With a head on her shoulders.
There's one young lady who's the envy
of all.
There's one young lady who will live to
be a hundred,
With not one foolishness of heart to
recall,
No heart to recall.

Listen to the church bell,
Hark now.
Listen to the church bell,
Hark now.
A buzz a buzz a
Busy buzz.
MAIDY
AND EMMA: Just hear the village
A buzz a buzz buzz.
ENSEMBLE: Want to see the bride.
Ah, ah,
Such a pretty bride!
Glad, I'm so
Glad I came
Down to the wedding now,
April wedding,
An April wedding,
An April wedding today.
EMMA: All full of joy over the wedding.
MAIDY: There's nothing quite as sweet as an
April wedding.
MARTHA: Just hear the bride's old ma
Weeping a flood of happy tears—
MAIDY: In tune with the singing of the
choir—
EMMA: And the far-off rat-a-tat raising of a
new barn.
MAIDY
AND EMMA: In tune with the sentimental chiming
of a wedding bell.
ENSEMBLE: Happy couple, happy couple!
MAIDY
AND EMMA: 'Tis a joyful sound all Greenwillow
round
Wishing them well.
ALL: 'Tis the . . .

[*Segue to "The Music of Home."*]

I shall wait to meet my mate.
I shall wait for some quieter day
To meet my Davey
Dipping bread in gravy,
To meet my Billy
Riding on a sleigh,
To meet my Charley
Roaming through the barley,
To meet my Harry
Lying in the hay.

I shall wait for a quieter day
To speak to the matter, to come to the point
Without all the clatter.
Of somebody's nose out of joint.

HEART OF STONE

Manuscript dated April 1959. Unused. Recorded by
Emily Loesser (DRG).

I wish I had a heart of stone.
So cool as to feel no caring,
Feel no caring.

I wish I had a heart of stone,
Cool, chilly cool, chilly pass-him-by cool.
Then I'd not want him for my own,
Cool, chilly cool, chilly pass-him-by cool.
I'd feel no more this care I've known,
Poor silly fool, silly tagalong fool.
Wish I had a heart of stone,
Cool, chilly cool, chilly pass-him-by cool.

BUZZ A BUZZ

Intended as Act II vocal opening. Manuscript dated September 1959. Unused.

ENSEMBLE: Buzz a buzz a
Buzz a buzz a
Buzz a buzz a
Busy buzz.
I love a wedding,
I love a wedding,
I love a day in
April for a wedding day.

PERCUSSION BALLAD

Accompanied by rhythmic hammering, sawing, banging,
and the falling debris of a barn building. From manuscripts dated June 1959 and July 1959. Unused. Intended
for Dorrie.

Davey, Johnny, Charley, Harry,
Which will I marry?
Calmly I must ponder
Before I rightly know
And so . . .

DOWN IN THE BARLEY

Manuscript dated February 1958. Unused.

All tangle tall
Down in the barley,
Down in the barley
Where shadows fall.
I just don't know
Johnny from Joe,
And I can't tell
Joe from Charley.

HOW TO SUCCEED IN BUSINESS WITHOUT REALLY TRYING | 1961
LEOCADIA | 1962

HOW TO SUCCEED IN BUSINESS WITHOUT REALLY TRYING

Tryout: Shubert Theatre, Philadelphia, September 4–October 7, 1961. New York premiere: Forty-sixth Street Theatre, October 14, 1961. 1,417 performances. Presented by Cy Feuer and Ernest Martin in association with Frank Productions. Book by Abe Burrows, Jack Weinstock, and Willie Gilbert, based on the novel by Shepherd Mead. Music and lyrics by Frank Loesser. Production directed by Abe Burrows. Musical staging by Bob Fosse. Choreography by Hugh Lambert. Costumes by Robert Fletcher. Scenery and lighting by Robert Randolph. Orchestrations by Robert Ginzler. Musical direction by Elliot Lawrence. Cast featured Robert Morse (Finch) and Rudy Vallee (Biggley), with Bonnie Scott (Rosemary), Virginia Martin (Hedy), Charles Nelson Reilly (Frump), Claudette Sutherland (Smitty), Ray Mason (Gatch, Toynbee) Sammy Smith (Twimble, Womper), Paul Reed (Bratt), and Ruth Kobart (Miss Jones). Revived in New York in 1995 with Matthew Broderick and Megan Mullally.

A film version, produced and directed by David Swift, was released by United Artists in 1967. Screenplay by David Swift. Choreographed by Dale Moreda. Cast starred Robert Morse (Finch), and Rudy Vallee (Biggley), and featured Michele Lee (Rosemary), Robert Q. Lewis (Tackaberry), Kay Reynolds (Smitty), Anthony Teague (Bud Frump), Maureen Arthur (Hedy), Sammy Smith (Twimble, Womper), and Ruth Kobart (Miss Jones).

Recordings: Original cast (RCA Victor), 1995 revival (RCA Victor), film soundtrack (United Artists). Frank Loesser's demo recording of ten songs from the score is on the compact disc *An Evening with Frank Loesser* (DRG).

Loesser and Burrows came to this project reluctantly. When Shepherd Mead's satiric corporate how-to was published in paperback in 1956, an agent sent Abe Burrows a copy with a note saying it would make a great musical. "I told him he was crazy," Burrows recalled in his autobiography, *Honest, Abe*. "Who would want to see a show about Big Business? And who would want to write a musical about Big Business? Besides, even though the book was funny, there was no plot, no story to build on. So I passed it up."

Some years later Jack Weinstock and Willie Gilbert wrote a straight play based on Mead's book and sent it to Cy Feuer and Ernest Martin in 1959. Feuer saw musical

---

Robert Morse in the 1962 New York production of How to Succeed in Business Without Really Trying

possibilities and lobbied Burrows to write the libretto and direct. Burrows still hesitated. "I have learned to be wary of other people's enthusiasm. It's contagious, and sometimes fatal."

The clincher for Burrows was Feuer's choice of Robert Morse for the role of Finch. "I jumped at the idea. After [directing him in] *Say, Darling*, I knew what Bobby Morse could do. . . . I had the same lucky break with Sam Levene in *Guys and Dolls* and Lauren Bacall in *Cactus Flower* [1965] . . . I knew the rhythm of their speech and it helped make the dialogue sound sharper and more real."

Initially, Loesser was even more unsure of the project than Burrows. "I've done my wise guy show," he said flatly. "How the hell can you do a musical without a love story? How could people sing and dance in a business office?" But Burrows knew him well. Loesser's business and satiric instincts were equally formidable. He adhered to the great critic and satirist Max Beerbohm's notion that, "satire should be based on a *qualified* love for the original." For Burrows, that was the key:

> As I thought about all this, I realized I had found one of Frank's soft spots. He, too, had a "qualified" love for the Big Business I wanted to satirize. After all, by this time he was president of his own music company, called Frank Music. I went to see him and spoke about my funny experiences in the business world, and he loosened up . . . and began to laugh with me. Finally, he agreed, grudgingly, that it could be a very funny show, but could it be a musical?

Burrows and Loesser were close, but they needed to know how key elements and musical situations would be realized. When do office workers sing and dance? An idea by Loesser gave them the answer:

> We knew that during a coffee break everyone in the office relaxes. . . . Then Frank, who was a coffee addict, said, "Hey, how about if somebody goofed and there's no coffee in the machine?" Then he came up with a sad song written in an appropriately Latin rhythm that said something like "If I can't take my coffee break, something inside me dies." It was a helluva number and suddenly we saw daylight.

HOW TO SUCCEED IN BUSINESS WITHOUT REALLY TRYING

Published. Copyrighted August 30, 1961. Also published as part of the piano-vocal score. Copyrighted October 18, 1962. Previously registered for copyright as an unpublished song July 25, 1961. Introduced by Robert Morse (Finch) and ensemble.

FINCH: How to apply for a job,
How to advance from the mail room,
How to sit down at a desk,
How to dictate memorandums,
How to develop executive style,
How to commute in a three-button suit
With that weary executive smile—
This book is all that I need,
How to, how to succeed.

How to observe personnel,
How to select whom to lunch with,
How to avoid petty friends,
How to begin making contacts,
How to walk into a conference room*
With an idea,
Brilliant business idea,
That will make your expense account
    zoom—
This book is all that I need,
How to, how to succeed.

HAPPY TO KEEP HIS DINNER WARM

Published. Copyrighted October 13, 1961. Also published as part of the piano-vocal score. Copyrighted October 18, 1962. Previously registered for copyright as an unpublished song August 3, 1961. Introduced by Bonnie Scott (Rosemary) and Claudette Sutherland (Smitty). Frank Loesser's demo recording of the song is on the compact disc *An Evening with Frank Loesser* (DRG).

ROSEMARY: New Rochelle . . .
   SMITTY: [*spoken*] What are you talking about?
ROSEMARY: [*sung*] New Rochelle . . .
   SMITTY: [*spoken*] What about it?

---

* *Lines 14–17 appear in sheet music version only.*

ROSEMARY: [sung] That's the place where the
    mansion will be,
    For me and the darling, bright
      young man
    I've picked out for marrying me.
    He'll do well, I can tell,
    So it isn't a moment too soon
    To plan on my life in New Rochelle;
    The wife of my darling tycoon.*

SMITTY: [spoken] The future Mrs. Finch is in
    for some lonely nights.
ROSEMARY: [spoken] I'm prepared for exactly that
    sort of thing.
    [sung] I'll be so happy to keep his
      dinner warm
    While he goes onward and upward.
    Happy to keep his dinner warm
    Till he comes wearily home from
      downtown.
    I'll be there waiting until his mind is
      clear,
    While he looks through me, right
      through me;
    Waiting to say, "Good evening, dear,
    I'm pregnant; what's new with you
      from downtown?"

    Oh, to be loved
    By a man I respect,
    To bask in the glow
    Of his perfectly understandable
      neglect!

    Oh, to belong in the aura
    Of his frown, darling busy frown!
    Such heaven,
    Wearing the wifely uniform
    While he goes onward and upward.
    Happy to keep his dinner warm
    Till he comes wearily home from
      downtown.

---

* Cut lyrics: ten lines following "darling tycoon"
    I'll be so happy
    In the cool suburban night
    With our dinner candles gleaming
    And our table sparkling bright.
    Happy at the close of every day
    With the roast done to perfection,
    Plus his favorite soufflè.
    Happy as the clock strikes seven,
    The clock strikes eight,
    Then nine, ten, eleven . . .

Act II reprise

ROSEMARY: Oh, to be loved by a man with a goal,
    To watch as he climbs
    With a purpose in life and purity of soul.
    Oh, to be there in a corner of his mind,
    Darling, absent mind . . .
    Such heaven
    Wearing the wifely uniform
    While he goes onward and upward.
    Happy to keep his dinner warm
    Till he comes wearily home from
      downtown.

COFFEE BREAK

Published as part of the piano-vocal score. Copyrighted October 18, 1962. Previously registered for copyright as an unpublished song August 3, 1961. Introduced by Charles Nelson Reilly (Frump), Claudette Sutherland (Smitty), and chorus (office staff). Frank Loesser's demo recording of the song is on the compact disc *An Evening with Frank Loesser* (DRG).

FRUMP: [spoken] There's no coffee!
CHORUS: [spoken] No coffee? Oh!!

FRUMP: [sung] If I can't take my coffee break,
    My coffee break, my coffee break,
    If I can't take my coffee break,
    Something within me dies . . .
CHORUS: Lies down and something within me
    dies!

SMITTY: If I can't make three daily trips
    Where shining shrine benignly drips,
    And taste cardboard between my lips,
    Something within me dies . . .
CHORUS: Lies down and something within me
    dies!

VARIOUS
VOICES: No coffee, no coffee, no coffee, no
    coffee,
    No coffee, no coffee,
    No coffee, no coffee!
SMITTY: That office light doesn't have to be
    fluorescent,
    I'll get no pains in the head.
    That office chair doesn't have to be
    foam rubber,
    So if I spread, so I spread.
    But only one chemical substance
    Gets out the lead!

CHORUS: Like she said!
    If I can't take my coffee break,
    My coffee break, my coffee break,
    My coffee break, my coffee break—
FRUMP AND
SMITTY: Gone is the sense of enterprise—
CHORUS: All gone, and something within me
    dies.
    [spoken] No coffee, no coffee, no
    coffee, no coffee,
    No coffee, no coffee,
    No coffee, no coffee, no coffee!

[CHORUS *screams.*]

    [sung] If I can't take my coffee
      break—
SMITTY: Somehow the soul no longer ries.
CHORUS: Coffee, coffee . . .
FRUMP: Somehow I don't metabolize.
CHORUS: Coffee, coffee . . .
FRUMP AND
SMITTY: Something within me—
CHORUS: Coffee or otherwise, coffee or otherwise,
    Coffee or otherwise,
    Something inside of me—
ALL: Dies!

Cut lyrics (followed first seven lines):

Like man, I'm hooked, like a mackerel,
Like man, all right, call me wrong,
But cut me no cream and sugar,
Give me my fix, black and strong,
Or like I crash out of my orbit,
Before too long.

My mind goes numb, I'm half awake,
My typing's dumb, my filing's fake.
If I can't take my coffee break,
Gone is my sense of enterprise.

THE COMPANY WAY

Published as part of the piano-vocal score. Copyrighted October 18, 1962. Previously registered for copyright as an unpublished song August 3, 1961. Introduced by Sammy Smith (Twimble) and Robert Morse (Finch). Reprise by Charles Nelson Reilly (Frump), Sammy Smith (Twimble), and ensemble.

TWIMBLE: When I joined this firm
    As a brash young man,

Well, I said to myself,
"Now, brash young man,
Don't get any ideas."
Well, I stuck to that
And I haven't had one in years!

FINCH: [*spoken*] You play it safe!

TWIMBLE: [*sung*] I play it the company way;
Wherever the company puts me,
There I'll stay.
FINCH: But what is your point of—?
TWIMBLE: I have no point of view.
FINCH: Supposing the company thinks—
TWIMBLE: I think so too!
FINCH: [*spoken*] What would you say if—
TWIMBLE: [*spoken*] I wouldn't say!
FINCH: [*sung*] Your face is a company face.
TWIMBLE: It smiles at executives,
Then goes back in place.
FINCH: The company furniture?
TWIMBLE: Oh, it suits me fine.
FINCH: The company letterhead is—
TWIMBLE: A Valentine!
FINCH: [*spoken*] Is there anything you're
against?
TWIMBLE: [*spoken*] Unemployment!
FINCH: [*sung*] When they want brilliant
thinking
From employees—
TWIMBLE: That is no concern of mine.
FINCH: Suppose a man of genius
Makes suggestions—
TWIMBLE: Watch that genius get
Suggested to resign!
FINCH: So you play it the company way.
TWIMBLE: All company policy is by me okay!
FINCH: You'll never rise to the—
TWIMBLE: But there's one thing clear;
Whoever the company fires,
I will still be here!
FINCH: [*spoken*] You certainly found a home!
TWIMBLE: [*spoken*] It's cozy!

FINCH: [*sung*] Your brain is a company brain.
TWIMBLE: The company washed it and now
I can't complain.
FINCH: The company magazine?
TWIMBLE: Boy, what style, what punch!
FINCH: The company restaurant?
TWIMBLE: Ev'ry day same lunch!
[*spoken*] Their haddock sandwich, it's
delicious!
FINCH: [*spoken*] I must try it.
TWIMBLE: [*spoken*] Early in the week!
FINCH: [*sung*] Do you have any hobbies?
TWIMBLE: I've a hobby;
I play gin with Mister Bratt.

FINCH: And do you play it nicely?
TWIMBLE: Play it nicely . . .
Still, he blitzes me in ev'ry game, like
that!
FINCH: [*spoken*] Why?
TWIMBLE: [*sung*] 'Cause I play it the company
way,
Executive policy is by me okay!
FINCH: How can you get anywhere—?
TWIMBLE: Junior, have no fear;
Whoever the company fires,
I will still be here.
FINCH: You will still be here.
TWIMBLE: Year after year after fiscal,
BOTH: Never-take-a-risk all year!

REPRISE

FRUMP: I'll play it the company way;
Wherever the company puts me there
I'll stay.
ALL: Whatever the company tells him, that
he'll do.
FRUMP: Whatever my uncle may think, I think
so too.
ALL: Oo-oo-ooh,
He's beaming with company pride.
FRUMP: I've conquered that overambitious rat
inside.
TWIMBLE: Old Bud is no longer the Frump he
used to be.
FRUMP: I pledge to the company sweet
conformity.
ALL: Hooray! Hooray!
FRUMP: I will someday earn my medal:
Twenty-five-year employee.
I'll see to it that the medal
Is the only thing they'll ever pin on me.
ALL: The Frump way is the company way;
Executive policy is by him okay!
FRUMP: I'll never be president but there's one
thing clear;
As long as my uncle can stand me,
I will still be here.
ALL: We know the company may like or
lump any man—
FRUMP: [*spoken*] I'm so proud!
ALL: [*sung*] And if they choose to, the
company may dump any man—
FRUMP: [*spoken*] I'm happy!
ALL: [*sung*] But they will never dump
Frump, the company man,
Frump will play it the company,
Frump will play it the company,
Frump will play it the company way—
Frump!

Finale

Published as part of the *How to Succeed in Business*
piano-vocal score. Copyrighted October 18, 1962. Introduced by ensemble.

ALL: We play it the company way.
Executive policy is by us okay.
Though for the departed we shed a mournful
tear,
Whoever the company fires,
We will still be here!

Cut lyrics (from pre-rehearsal manuscript dated July 31, 1961)

I play it the company way;
Wherever the company puts me, there I stay,
Whatever the company tells me, that I do,
Whatever the company thinks, I think so too.
What am I, a radical?
My mood is the company mood,
The company restaurant serves my fav'rite food,
The annual company dance is just my crowd;
I cheer for the company bowling team out loud
And the right people hear me!
When great genius is requested,
That is no concern of mine—
'Cause when genius is requested,
It is frequently requested to resign.
So I play it the company way;
Executive policy is by me okay.
I'll never be wonderful,
But there's one thing clear:
Whoever the company fires,
I will still be here.

A SECRETARY IS NOT A TOY

Published as part of the piano-vocal score. Copyrighted
October 18, 1962. Previously registered for copyright as
an unpublished song August 3, 1961. Introduced by
Paul Reed (Bratt), Robert Kaliban (Jenkins), Charles
Nelson Reilly (Frump), Mari Landi (Miss Krumholtz),
and ensemble. Frank Loesser's demo recording of the
song is on the compact disc *An Evening with Frank
Loesser* (DRG).

BRATT: [*spoken*] Gentlemen!
[*sung*] A secretary is not a toy,
No, my boy, not a toy
To fondle and dandle

And playfully handle
In search of some puerile joy.
No, a secretary is not,
Definitely not, a toy.

JENKINS: [*spoken*] You're absolutely right,
Mr. Bratt.

FRUMP: [*spoken*] We wouldn't have it any
other way, Mr. Bratt.

JENKINS: [*spoken*] It's a company rule, Mr.
Bratt.

BOYS: [*sung*] A secretary is not a toy,
No, my boy, not a toy.
So do not go jumping for joy,
Boy.
A secretary is not,
A secretary is not,
A secretary is not
A toy!

GIRLS: A secretary is not to be
Used for play therapy.

ALL: Be good to the girl you employ,
Boy.
Remember, no matter what
Neurotic trouble you've got,
A secretary is not
A toy.
She's a highly specialized key
component
Of operational unity,
A fine and sensitive mechanism
To serve the office community.

ALL: With a mother at home she
supports,

FRUMP: And you'll find nothing like her
At F.A.O. Schwartz!

MISS KRUMHOLTZ: A secretary is not a pet,
Nor an Erector Set.

MISS KRUMHOLTZ
AND BOYS: It happened to Charlie McCoy,
Boy.
They fired him like a shot
The day the fellow forgot
A secretary is not
A toy.

[*Interlude*]

ALL: A secretary is not a toy.

BOYS: And when you put her to use,
Observe, when you put her
to use—

FRUMP: That you don't find the name
"Lionel" on her caboose.

GIRLS: A secretary is not a thing
Wound by key, pulled by string.
Her pad is to write in

And not spend the night in.
If that's what you plan to
enjoy—
No!

ALL: The secretary y'got
Is definitely not
Employed to do a gavotte
Or you know what.
Before you jump for joy,
Remember this, my boy—
A secretary is not
A Tinker Toy!

Earlier version

Lyrics from private demo recording by Frank Loesser,
available on the compact disc *An Evening with Frank
Loesser* (DRG).

VERSE

Gentlemen, gentlemen, please!
When something of value is placed in your hands,
You treat it maturely, with infinite care,
You don't make paper boats out of money,
You don't toss a fine watch in the air,
So you certainly should be aware—

REFRAIN

That a secretary is not a toy,
No, my boy, not a toy
To fondle and dandle
And playfully handle
In search of some puerile joy.
No, a secretary is not,
Definitely not, a toy.

A secretary is not to be
Used for play therapy.
If that's what you're doing,
You're quite misconstruing
Her function while in your employ.
No, a secretary is not,
Definitely not, a toy.

She's a highly specialized key component
Of operational unity,
A fine and sensitive mechanism
That serves the office community.
With a mother at home she supports,
A mother at home she supports.

Do not tamper, do not tinker—
He who does so is truly a stinker
Who could learn the plain truth from his
shrinker

Or find out
At F.A.O. Schwartz

That a secretary is not a small
Version of volleyball.
If you're feeling eager,
Run down to Davega
And there you can grab the McCoy.
No, a secretary is not,
Definitely not, a toy.

A secretary is not a pet
Nor an Erector Set,
To juggle and jingle
Like something Kris Kringle
Had left for small hands to destroy.
No, a secretary is not,
Definitely not, a toy.

Gentlemen, to recap:
She's a highly specialized key component
Of operational unity,
A fine and sensitive mechanism
That serves the office community.
Please observe, when you put her to use,
Observe when you put her to use—

She's not metal, she's not plastic,
Run by motor or springs or elastic,
And you won't find a name so fantastic
As "Lionel" on her caboose.
For a secretary is not a thing,
Wound by key, pulled by string.
Her pad is to write in
And not spend the night in,
If that's what you plan to enjoy—
No, a secretary is not,
Definitely not, a toy.

First version

From lyric manuscript dated January 9, 1961.

VERSE

Do you ever stop in the middle of dictation
For a tender look at your secretary's build*
Does she bring to mind with a juvenile elation
Little images of your childhood—
Frolicsome, cuddly, and pleasure-filled?†

---

* *Or:*
 form

† *Or:*
 Fun-loving, frolicsome, and warm?

The whirligig you spun around,
The teddy bear you took to bed,
The toy balloons that squealed when you'd
    squeeze,
Do you recollect with that juvenile elation
As you sneak a look at your secretary's knees?
Well, remember this if you please—

REFRAIN

A secretary is not at all
Just a tall
Basketball
For dribbling and tossing*
And quite double-crossing†
Her function while in your employ.

[*Lyric breaks off unfinished.*]

BEEN A LONG DAY

Published as part of the piano-vocal score. Copyrighted October 18, 1962. Previously registered for copyright as an unpublished song August 3, 1961. Introduced by Claudette Sutherland (Smitty), Bonnie Scott (Rosemary), and Robert Morse (Finch). Reprise introduced by Charles Nelson Reilly (Frump), Rudy Vallee (Biggley), and Virginia Martin (Hedy). Frank Loesser's demo recording of the song is on the compact disc *An Evening with Frank Loesser* (DRG).

SMITTY: Well, here it is five p.m.,
    The finish of a long day's work,
    And there they are, both of them,
    The secretary and the clerk—
    Not very well acquainted,
    Not very much to say,
    But I can hear those two little minds
    Ticking away.

SMITTY: Now she's thinking:
ROSEMARY: I wonder if we take the same bus . . .
SMITTY: And he's thinking:
FINCH: There could be quite a thing between
    us . . .
SMITTY: Now she's thinking:
ROSEMARY: He really is a dear.

---

* *Or:*
  bouncing

† *Or:*
  thus mispronouncing

SMITTY: And he's thinking:
FINCH: But what of my career?
SMITTY: Then she says:
ROSEMARY: [*yawn*]
SMITTY: And he says:
FINCH: [*spoken*] Er, uh, well, it's been a long day.
ALL: [*sung*] Well, it's been a long,
    Been a long,
    Been a long,
    Been a long
    Day.

SMITTY: Now she's thinking:
ROSEMARY: I wish that he were more of a flirt.
SMITTY: And he's thinking:
FINCH: I guess a little flirting won't hurt.
SMITTY: Now she's thinking:
ROSEMARY: For dinner we could meet.
SMITTY: And he's thinking:
FINCH: We both have got to eat.
SMITTY: Then she says:
ROSEMARY: [*spoken*] Achoo!
SMITTY: [*sung*] And he says:
FINCH: [*spoken*] Gesundheit!
ROSEMARY [*spoken*] Thank you!
FINCH: [*sung*] Well, it's been a long day.
ALL: Well, it's been a long,
    Been a long,
    Been a long,
    Been a long
    Day.

SMITTY: Hey! There's a yummy Friday Special
    at Stouffer's:
    It's a dollar-ninety veg'table plate.
    And on the bottom of the ad . . .
    Not bad . . .
    "Service for two,
    Three fifty-eight;
    To make a bargain,
    Make a date."
ROSEMARY: Wonderful!
FINCH: It's fate!

SMITTY: Now, she's thinking:
ROSEMARY: What female kind of trap could I
    spring?
SMITTY: And he's thinking:
FINCH: I might as well forget the whole thing.
SMITTY: Now, she's thinking:
ROSEMARY: Suppose I take his arm . . .
SMITTY: And he's thinking:
FINCH: Well, really, what's the harm?
SMITTY: Then, she says:
ROSEMARY: [*spoken*] Hungry?
SMITTY: [*sung*] And he says:
FINCH: [*spoken*] Yeah!

ROSEMARY: [*spoken*] Yeah!
SMITTY: [*spoken*] Yeah!
ALL: [*sung*] Well, it's been a long day.
    Well, it's been a long,
    Been a long,
    Been a long,
    Been a long
    Day.
    Well, it's been a long day.
    Well, it's been a long,
    Been a long,
    Been a long,
    Been a long
    Day.

REPRISE

FRUMP: Now he's thinking:
BIGGLEY: The kid could really put me through
    hell!
FRUMP: And she's thinking:
HEDY: The kid could even name the hotel.
FRUMP: Now he's thinking:
BIGGLEY: I wonder if he'd dare . . .
FRUMP: And she's thinking:
HEDY: There's blackmail in the air.
FRUMP: And he says:
BIGGLEY: It's a holdup!
FRUMP: And she says:
HEDY: Down?
BIGGLEY: [*spoken*] Wait a minute! Okay, you're
    promoted.
ALL: [*sung*] Well, it's been a long,
    Been a long,
    Been a long,
    Been a long
    Day.
FRUMP: Well, it's been a long,
    Been a long,
    Been a long,
    Been a long
    Day.
    Ha!

GRAND OLD IVY

Published. Copyrighted September 1, 1961. Also published as part of the piano-vocal score. Copyrighted October 18, 1962. Previously registered for copyright as an unpublished song August 3, 1961. Introduced by Rudy Vallee (Biggley) and Robert Morse (Finch). Frank Loesser's demo recording of the song is on the compact disc *An Evening with Frank Loesser* (DRG).

BIGGLEY: Grr-r-r-r-roundhog!
FINCH: Grr-r-r-r-roundhog!
BIGGLEY: Stand, Old Ivy,
Stand firm and strong.
Grand Old Ivy,
Hear the cheering throng.
BOTH: Stand, Old Ivy,
And never yield.
Rrr-rip! Rrr-rip! Rrr-rip the Chipmunk
Off the field!

FINCH: When you fall on the ball—
BIGGLEY: And you're down there at the bottom of
the heap—
FINCH: Down at the bottom of the heap—
BIGGLEY: Where the mud is oh so very, very
deep—
FINCH: Down in the cruddy, muddy deep—
BIGGLEY: Don't forget, boy—
BOTH: That's why they call us,
They call us Grr-roundhog!
Grr-roundhog!

FINCH: Stand, Old Ivy—
BIGGLEY: Grr-roundhog! Grr-roundhog!
FINCH: Stand firm and strong.
BIGGLEY: Rrr-rip! Rrr-rip! Rrr-rip the Chipmunk!
BOTH: Grand Old Ivy,
Hear the cheering throng.
BIGGLEY: Grr-roundhog!
FINCH: Stand, Old Ivy—
BIGGLEY: Grr-roundhog!
[spoken] God bless you . . .
BOTH: [sung] And never yield.
Rrr-rip! Rrr-rip! Rrr-rip the Chipmunk
Off the field!

PARIS ORIGINAL

Published. Copyrighted August 30, 1961. Also published as part of the piano-vocal score. Copyrighted October 18, 1962. Previously registered for copyright as an unpublished song August 9, 1961. Introduced by Bonnie Scott (Rosemary), Claudette Sutherland (Smitty), Ruth Kobart (Miss Jones), and girls. Frank Loesser's demo recording of the song is on the compact disc *An Evening with Frank Loesser* (DRG).

ROSEMARY: I slipped out this afternoon
And bought some love insurance,
A most exclusive dress from Gay Paree.
It's sleek and chic and magnifique,
With sex beyond endurance.
It's me!
It's me!
It's absolutely me!
And why?
One guy!

This irresistible Paris original
I'm wearing tonight,
I'm wearing tonight
Specially for him.
This irresistible Paris original's
All paid for and mine.
I must look divine
Specially for him.

Suddenly he will see me
And suddenly he'll go dreamy
And blame it all
On his own masculine whim . . .
Never knowing that

This irresistible Paris original,
So temptingly tight,
I'm wearing tonight
Specially for him . . .
For him . . .
For him.

[*Interlude. Two other women enter wearing the same dress.*]

For him . . .
For him . . .
This irresistible Paris original,
I'm wearing tonight . . .
She's wearing tonight
And I could spit!

Some irresponsible dress
manufacturer

Just didn't play fair:
I'm one of a pair—
ROSEMARY AND
FIRST GIRL: And I could . . .
[spoken] Oh, no!
SECOND GIRL: [sung] This irresistible Paris
original,
All slinky with sin . . .
Already slunk in,
And I could die!
ROSEMARY, FIRST
AND SECOND GIRL: And I could [spoken] kill her.
[sung] And I could—
SMITTY: This irresistible Paris original,
Très sexy, n'est-ce pas?
Goddammit, voilà!
And I could spit!
ALL: [spoken] Oh!
[sung] Thirty-nine bucks I hand
out
For something to make me
stand out,
And suddenly I've gone
Into mimeograph . . .
MISS JONES: [spoken] Some laugh!
ALL: [sung] This irresistible Paris
original,
This mass-produced crime,
I'm wearing tonight
For the very last time!

ROSEMARY

Published as part of the piano-vocal score. Copyrighted October 18, 1962. Previously registered for copyright as an unpublished song August 3, 1961. Introduced by Robert Morse (Finch), and Bonnie Scott (Rosemary). Frank Loesser's demo recording of the song is on the compact disc *An Evening with Frank Loesser* (DRG).

FINCH: [sung] Suddenly there is music
In the sound of your name . . .
Rosemary,
Rosemary, was the melody locked
inside me,
Till at last out it came . . .
Rosemary!
Rosemary, just imagine if we kissed,
What a crescendo,
Not to be missed!
As for the rest of my lifetime
program,
Give me more of the same . . .

Rosemary.
Rosemary, there is wonderful music
In the very sound of your name.
Suddenly there is music in the
    sound of your name . . .

ROSEMARY: [*spoken*] I can't hear a thing.
FINCH: [*sung*] Rosemary . . .
[*spoken*] Just listen, it's all around me
    like a beautiful pink sky . . .
ROSEMARY: [*spoken*] Now look here, J. Pierrepont
    Finch, have you lost your mind?
FINCH: [*spoken*] Rosemary, darling, will you
    marry J. Pierrepont Finch?
ROSEMARY: [*spoken*] Now I hear it! I hear it! I
    hear it!
[*sung*] Suddenly there is music in the
    sound of your name . . .
J. Pierrepont . . .
FINCH: Rosemary, just imagine if we kissed,
    What a crescendo. . . !

INTERLUDE

BOTH: Not to be missed.
FINCH: As for the rest of my lifetime
    program,
    Give me more of the same . . .
FINCH: Rosemary . . .
ROSEMARY: J. Pierrepont, J. Pierrepont . . .
FINCH: Rosemary . . .
ROSEMARY: J. Pierrepont . . .
BOTH: There is wonderful music in the very
    sound
    Of your name!

FINALE, ACT ONE

Published as part of the piano-vocal score. Copyrighted October 18, 1962. Introduced by Robert Morse (Finch), Bonnie Scott (Rosemary), and Charles Nelson Reilly (Frump). Referred to in program as "Finaletto."

FINCH: [*spoken*] This is Mr. Finch . . . I want my
    name on my door . . . in . . . gold leaf!
[*spoken*] J. Pierrepont Finch . . .
[*sung*] J. Pierrepont!
ROSEMARY: Suddenly there is music—
FINCH: [*spoken*] All capitals!
ROSEMARY: [*sung*] In the sound of my name . . .
FINCH: [*spoken*] Yes, block letters!
[*sung*] J. Pierrepont!
ROSEMARY: Rosemary . . .
FINCH: Vice President—

FRUMP: Vice President!
FINCH: In Charge of Advertising.
ROSEMARY: Rosemary . . .
FRUMP: There must be a way to stop him,
    There must be!
FINCH: F-I-N-C-H.
ROSEMARY: All of my lifetime program
    Will be more of the same.
FINCH: [*spoken*] The usual spelling.
[*sung*] J.—
FRUMP: J. Pierrepont—
FINCH: Pierrepont—
FRUMP: J. Pierrepont—
ROSEMARY: Remember me, Rosemary?
FRUMP: [*spoken*] I can't stand it!
ROSEMARY: [*sung*] Whatever happened to Rose—
FINCH: [*spoken*] Boy, when you see it on your
    own door . . .
ROSEMARY: [*sung*] —mary?
ROSEMARY
AND FINCH: There is wonderful music in the very
    sound
    Of your name.
FRUMP: I will return!

CINDERELLA, DARLING

Published as part of the piano-vocal score. Copyrighted October 18, 1962. Previously registered for copyright as an unpublished song August 3, 1961. Introduced by Claudette Sutherland (Smitty), Bonnie Scott (Rosemary), and girls.

SMITTY: How often does it happen
    That a secretary's boss
    Wants to marry 'er?
GIRLS: Hallelujah!
SMITTY: How often does the dream come true
    Without a sign of conflict
    Or barrier?
GIRLS: Hallelujah!
SMITTY: Why treat the man like he was a
    typhoid carrier?
    How often can you fly
    From this land of carbon paper
    To the land of flowered chintz?
GIRLS: Hallelujah!
SMITTY: How often does Cinderella
    Get a crack at the Prince?
GIRLS: Cinderella and the Prince!
SMITTY: [*spoken*] Don't you realize . . .
[*sung*] You're a real live fairy tale,
    A symbol divine.

So, if not for your own sake,
    Please, darling, for mine—
GIRLS: And mine,
    And mine,
    And mine,

Don't, don't, don't,
    Cinderella, darling,
    Don't turn down the Prince!
SMITTY: Don't rewrite your story;
    You're the legend,
    The folklore,
    The working girl's dream of glory!
ALL: We were raised on you, darling,
    And we've loved you ever since.
    Don't mess up a major miracle,
    Don't, Cinderella,
    Don't turn down the Prince.
SMITTY: Oh, let us live it with you,
    Each hour of each day.
1ST GIRL: On from Bergdorf Goodman—
2ND GIRL: To Elizabeth Arden—
3RD GIRL: In the station wagon—
4TH GIRL: Hurry from '21'—
5TH GIRL: To the Tarrytown PTA.
ROSEMARY: [*spoken*] No, New Rochelle!
ALL: [*sung*] New Rochelle PTA,
    Please!
SMITTY: Oh, do not leave us minus—
GIRLS: Please!
SMITTY: Our vicarious bonus—
GIRLS: Please!
SMITTY: We want to see His Highness—
GIRLS: Please!
SMITTY: Married to Your Lowness!
GIRLS: Ah.
SMITTY: On you, Cinderella, sits the onus.
GIRLS: Ah.
SMITTY: So when you name the happy day,
    Please phone us.
ALL: Phone us!
    But
    Don't, don't, don't
    Cinderella, darling,
    Don't turn down the Prince!
SMITTY: Why spoil our enjoyment?
    You're the fable,
    The symbol
    Of glorified unemployment!
ALL: We were raised on you, darling,
    And we've loved you ever since.
    Don't louse up our fav'rite fairy tale;
    Don't, Cinderella,
    Don't, don't, don't,
    Don't, Cinderella,
    Don't, don't, don't,
    Don't, Cinderella,
    Don't! Don't turn down the Prince!

ROSEMARY: [*spoken*] All right, I'll give him one
more chance.
ALL: [*sung*] Hallelujah!

LOVE FROM A HEART OF GOLD

Published. Copyrighted August 30, 1961. Also published as part of the piano-vocal score. Copyrighted October 18, 1962. Previously registered for copyright as an unpublished song August 9, 1961. Introduced by Rudy Vallee (Biggley) and Virginia Martin (Hedy). Frank Loesser's demo recording of the song is on the compact disc *An Evening with Frank Loesser* (DRG).

BIGGLEY: Where will I find a treasure
Like the love from a heart of gold?
Ever trusting and sweet
And awaiting my pleasure,
Rain or shine,
Hot or cold?
Wealth far beyond all measure
Maybe here in my hands I hold.
Ah, but where will I find
That one treasure of treasures,
The love from a heart of gold?

HEDY: Where will I find a treasure
Like the love from a heart of gold?
Ever trusting and sweet
And awaiting my pleasure,
Rain or shine—
BIGGLEY: Rain or shine—
HEDY: Hot or cold?
BIGGLEY: Hot or cold?
HEDY: Wealth far beyond all measure
Maybe soon in my hands I'll hold.
Ah, but where will I find that one
treasure of treasures—
BOTH: The love from a heart of gold?

I BELIEVE IN YOU

Published. Copyrighted August 30, 1961. Also published as part of the piano-vocal score. Copyrighted October 18, 1962. Previously registered for copyright as an unpublished song August 9, 1961. Introduced by Robert Morse (Finch) and male ensemble. Reprised by Bonnie Scott (Rosemary). Recorded by Peggy Lee (Capitol), Bobby Darin (Atlantic), Nancy Wilson (Capitol), Frank Sinatra and Count Basie (Reprise), and Michele Lee (Columbia), among others. Frank Loesser's demo recording of the song is on the compact disc *An Evening with Frank Loesser* (DRG).

This song was originally written as a conventional love song for Rosemary to sing to Finch. Librettist and director Abe Burrows had other plans for it: "When I came up with the idea of his singing it to himself in the mirror . . . he [Loesser] looked at me for a moment and said, 'I ought to hit you,' and then he laughed and that's how we did the number." Finch sang the song to himself in the washroom as kazoos in the orchestra approximated the sound of the electric razors wielded by the male chorus.

MEN: Gotta stop that man,
I gotta stop that man
Cold . . .
Or he'll stop me.
Big deal, big rocket,
Thinks he has the world in his pocket.
Gotta stop,
Gotta stop,
Gotta stop that man,
That man.

FINCH: Now, there you are,
Yes, there's that face,
That face that somehow I trust.
It may embarrass you to hear me say it,
But say it I must,
Say it I must!

You have the cool, clear eyes
Of a seeker of wisdom and truth;
Yet there's that upturned chin
And the grin of impetuous youth.
Oh, I believe in you,
I believe in you.

I hear the sound of good
Solid judgment whenever you talk;
Yet there's the bold, brave spring
Of the tiger that quickens your walk.
Oh, I believe in you,
I believe in you.

And when my faith in my fellow man
All but falls apart,
I've but to feel your hand grasping mine
And I take heart, I take heart . . .

To see the cool, clear eyes
Of a seeker of wisdom and truth,
Yet with the slam, bang, tang
Reminiscent of gin and vermouth.
Oh, I believe in you,
I believe in you.

MEN: Gotta stop that man,
Gotta stop that man . . .
Or he'll stop me.
Big wheel, big beaver,
Boiling hot with front-office fever . . .
Gotta stop, gotta stop, gotta stop that man.
FINCH: Oh, I believe in you.
MEN: Don't let him be such a hero.
FINCH: I believe in you . . .
MEN: Stop that man, gotta stop him.
FINCH: You . . .
MEN: Stop that man, gotta stop him.
FINCH: You . . .
MEN: Stop that man,
Gotta stop that man.

BROTHERHOOD OF MAN

Published. Copyrighted September 1, 1961. Also published as part of the piano-vocal score. Copyrighted October 18, 1962. Previously registered for copyright as an unpublished song August 3, 1961. Introduced by Robert Morse (Finch), Rudy Vallee (Biggley), Sammy Smith (Wally Womper), Ruth Kobart (Miss Jones), and ensemble. Recorded by Liza Minnelli and Judy Garland (Capitol), Al Hirt (RCA Victor), and Oscar Peterson (Ampex), among others.

FINCH: Now, you may join the Elks, my
friend,
And I may join the Shriners;
And other men may carry cards
As members of the Diners.
Still others wear a golden key
Or small Greek letter pin.
But I have learned there's one great
club
That all of us are in.

There is a brotherhood of man,
A benevolent brotherhood of man,

A noble tie that binds
All human hearts and minds
Into one brotherhood of man.
Your lifelong membership is free.
Keep a-giving each brother all you can.
Oh, aren't you proud to be
In that fraternity,
The great, big brotherhood of man?

[*spoken*] So, Wally, I want you to
 remember that before you
 consider firing Mr. Biggley.
BIGGLEY: [*spoken*] Who's considering this?
FINCH: [*spoken*] You see, Wally, I know what's
 on your mind. You'd like to clear
 out the whole crowd from top to
 bottom. But stop and think . . .

[*sung*] One man may seem
 incompetent,
Another not make sense,
While others look like quite a waste
Of company expense.
They need a brother's leadership,
So please don't do them in;
Remember, mediocrity is not a
 mortal sin.
MEN: We're in the brotherhood of man,
 Dedicated to giving all we can.
FINCH: Oh, aren't you proud to be
 In that fraternity—
MEN: The great big brotherhood of man?

WOMPER: [*spoken*] No kidding!
 [*sung*] Is there really a brotherhood—
MEN: Yes, you're a brother.
WOMPER: Of man?
MEN: You are a brother!
WOMPER: On the level,
 A brotherhood of man?
MEN: Oh yes, oh yes.
 A noble tie that binds
 All human hearts and minds—
WOMPER: Into one brotherhood of man.
MEN: Oh, yes,
 Your lifelong membership is free;
 Keep a-givin' each brother all you
 can.
 Oh, aren't you proud to be—
MISS JONES: You . . . you got me—
MEN: In that fraternity—
MISS JONES: Me . . . I got you-oo—
MEN: The great big brotherhood of man?
MISS JONES: You-oo!

Oh, that noble feeling,
Feels like bells are pealing—
Down with double dealing!

Oh, brother,
You . . . you got me,
Me . . . I got you-oo, you-oo.
Oh, that noble feeling,
Feels like bells are pealing—
Down with double dealing!
Oh, brother,
You . . . you got me,
Me . . . I got you-oo, you-oo.

MEN: Oh, that noble feeling,
 Feels like bells are pealing—
 Down with double dealing!
 Oh, brother,
 You . . . you got me,
 Me . . . I got you-oo, you-oo.
ALL: Your lifelong membership is free;
 Keep a-giving each brother all you
 can.
 Oh, aren't you proud to be
 In that fraternity,
 The great big brotherhood of man?

CUT AND UNUSED SONGS

STATUS

Registered for copyright as an unpublished song August 3, 1961. Introduced during the Philadelphia tryout by Virginia Martin (Hedy). Cut prior to New York opening.

VERSE

The time will come when my phone stops jingling;
The time will come when the men stop tingling.
So I want to be ready
With something dignified and steady
So nobody will wonder
Whatever did become of poor li'l old Hedy:

REFRAIN

Status, status,
I'm seeking that thing called status.
I want to be someone with position,
The girl that's got it made,
The girl who doesn't panic
When her good looks start to fade.

She's already got status, status,
A woman exec, top status.

I want to go push a lot of buttons
And sign a lot of deals
And swing my horn-rimmed glasses
With my fellow business wheels
And nevermore depend upon
The customary female apparatus.
You see what I mean?

Well, that'll take status,
And I want to be up there making the scene.
I'll have me a big box at the op'ra,
A small box at the Chase,
Controlling stock in twenty corporations, just in
 case.
Then when I like a fella,
I can well afford to give the weekend gratis.
You see what I mean?

Well, that'll take status,
And I want to be up there making the scene.
Just imagine my status, status,
Behind a big desk, real status.
I'm there on the intercom dictating,
I'm coming over strong,
I smoke Du Mauriers
And keep my hat on all day long
While *Fortune* magazine's outside
Just waiting for an interview hiatus.
You see what I mean?

Well, that'll take status,
And I want to be up there making the scene.
You see what I mean?
Well, that'll take status.
And I want to be up there making the scene.

I WORRY ABOUT YOU

Registered for copyright as an unpublished song August 3, 1961. Introduced during Philadelphia tryout by Bonnie Scott (Rosemary). Cut prior to New York opening.

I worry about you,
I can't help it;
I worry if you're all right.
I'm going my way without you very nicely,
But worry about you day and night.
I worry about you,
I can't help it;
I worry if you're okay.

I'm going my way without you very nicely,
But somehow I doubt you know your way.

Are you lying sick and dying in the gutter?
Have you pawned your cuff links and your overcoat?
Are you down to dry saltines and peanut butter?
Are you writing your farewell note?

What do I care?
Hey! What do I care?
Hey! What do I care?

I care, that's my trouble;
I worry if you feel well.
I'm going my way without you very nicely,
But I have no doubt you go through hell.
Are you dressing warm enough for chilly weather?
Did those Bellevue interns treat you viciously?*
Are you too far gone to pull yourself together?
Do I hear you crying for—

What do I care?
Hey! What do I care?
Hey! What do I care?
Hey, Ponty!

ORGANIZATION MAN

Earlier version of "The Company Way." Lyrics from private demo recording by Frank Loesser, available on the compact disc *An Evening with Frank Loesser* (DRG). Music is different from that used in "Company Way."

When I joined this firm
As a brash young man,
Well, I said to myself,
"Now, brash young man,
Don't get any ideas."
Well, I stuck to that
And I haven't had one in years!

I'm an organization man;
I do things the organization way.
Wherever the organization puts me,
I stay.

In the organization plan
My name's marked "reliable employee,"
'Cause I've learned the organization's bigger
Than me.

---

* *Alternate line from manuscript dated August 14, 1961:*
   Are you in some barroom drinking heavily?

And if I don't get comical and step out of line,
I'll retire with benefits at eighty-nine!
I'm an organization man;
I do things the organization way,
And that's why the organization loves me
And needs me.

Let me tell you something:
Long ago, when the word came down to vote for
   Landon,
I voted for Landon with abandon.
After that when the word came down
The plant might have to shut,
I waived my vacation
And I gladly took the salary cut—
I'm no radical,
I'm no nut!

I'm an organization man;
I do things the organization way,
And that's why the organization loves me
And needs me.

And I'm going to tell you another thing:
When my wife broke her leg I had to pay the
   doctor—
Four hundred in cash the doctor socked her!
Well, sir, here at the organization they paid it right
   away:
Against my two Flatbush lots and only nine
   percent to pay!
I got credit here!
I'm okay!

I'm an organization man;
I do things the organization way.
And that's why the organization loves me,
And needs me, and wants me,
Day after day after Womper
Organization day!

COMPANY MAN

Another earlier version of "The Company Way." From lyric manuscript dated December 9, 1960.

I'm a company man;
I've got company loyalty.
Life can't stump any man
Who is fundamentally an employee.
I know the firm can like or lump any man,
And if they choose to, they may dump any man;
But they will never dump a company man.

Maybe you,
But never me.

For
I'm a company man,
And the company knows that's true.
On the company plan
I'll retire, with benefits, at ninety-two.
I know the firm can like or lump any man,
And if they choose to, they may dump any man;
But they will never dump a company man—
Never me,
But maybe you.

Long ago when the word came down to vote for
   Landon,
I voted for Landon with abandon.
After that, when the word came down the plant
   might have to shut,
I waived my vacation
And gladly took the salary cut—
I'm no fly-by-night,
I'm no nut.

When my wife broke a leg, I had to pay the
   doctor—
Four hundred in cash the doctor socked her.
Well, sir, here at the company they paid it right
   away:
Against my two Flatbush lots and only nine
   percent to pay!
I've got credit here!
I'm okay!

KNIT PRETTY

Intended for Rudy Vallee (Biggley). From manuscript dated September 1, 1961. Unused.

Busy little fingers, knit, pretty, pretty, pretty knit.
Busy little fingers make ev'ry worry flitter-flit.
See my needles dancing,
See me smiling now—
Oh, I knit, quite a bit, quite a pretty little bit,
But never knit my brow.

Knit, pretty, pretty, pretty.
Knit, pretty, pretty, pretty.
Knit, pretty, pretty, pretty.
Purl two.
Knit, pretty, pretty, pretty.
Something a very pretty periwinkle blue.

WORLD WIDE WICKET

Intended for ensemble. From manuscript dated July 14, 1961. Unused.

World Wide Wicket
We hail with pride.
World Wide Wicket
O'er the world so wide.
World Wide Wicket
Banner unfurled.
World Wide Wicket
For a wider world.

WHITE-COLLAR WORLD

Earlier version of Act I opening. Intended for Robert Morse (Finch) and ensemble. From manuscript dated February 2, 1961. Unused.

FINCH: I will rise
In the white-collar world;
I will rise,
Wait and see.
On the top
Of that white-collar world,
Watch for me!
WINDOW
WASHERS: It's a white-collar world
Where a plain guy like you never fits.
FINCH: I will rise!
WASHERS: They don't do nothing real for a living;
They're just living strictly by their wits.
2ND WASHER: Never hold a nail and hammer—
3RD WASHER: Never hold a pick and shovel—
1ST WASHER: Never hold a thread and needle—
ALL THREE: In their mitts!
WASHERS: It's a white-collar world,
That's what it's!
FINCH: I will start
Pure in heart,
With the gleam of achievement
In my eyes.
I will rise
And my ties
Will be Brooks Brothers ties.

WASHERS: It's a white-collar world
That a plain guy like you just ain't from.

FINCH: I will rise.
WASHERS: They don't do anything real in an office.
In an office
You're a well-dressed bum.
2ND WASHER: Gotta be a trifle crooked—
3RD WASHER: Gotta be at least a nephew—
1ST WASHER: Gotta be a special genius—
ALL THREE: And you're dumb, dumb Memorandum.
1ST WASHER: Memorandum, memorandum—
2ND WASHER: Paper clip—
1ST WASHER: Memorandum, memorandum—
FINCH: I will rise.
2ND WASHER: Paper clip—
1ST WASHER: Memorandum, memorandum—
2ND WASHER: Paper clip—
3RD WASHER: Carbon copy—
1ST WASHER: Memorandum, memorandum—
2ND WASHER: Paper clip—
3RD WASHER: Carbon copy—
1ST WASHER: Memorandum, memorandum—
2ND WASHER: Paper clip—
3RD WASHER: Carbon copy—
4TH WASHER: IBM—
3RD WASHER: Carbon copy!

BLESS THIS DAY

From manuscript dated October 1960. Unused. Frank Loesser note: "Buoyant ballad!"

Bless this day that melted me away,
This day I fell in love.
Bless the stars that now at last I see;
Bless the girl who turned them on for me;
Bless the race, the nice warm human race
I'm now a member of,
Since I broke through my shell
And sighed, "Oh, what the hell,"
And slipped and fell in love.
Oh yes, oh,
Bless this day that melted me away,
This day I fell in love.

LASHES

From manuscript dated October 1960. Also known as "Long Long Lashes." Unused.

Never let me feel your long, long lashes
Brush against my oh so sensitive cheek.
If you let me feel those long, long lashes,
There'll be so much more of you that I seek.
Soon your eyes will blaze with angry flashes,
Warding off my mad, impulsive technique,
Till your frail young form divinely crashes
Up against my somewhat stronger physique
And then,
And then,

With my lovelorn soul reduced to ashes
I'll become your slave, all maudlin and weak.
There'll be raised eyebrows and twirled moustaches
Over my career that slipped from its peak.
They will say I can't tell dots from dashes;
That I'm just an unemployable freak.
They will see my wrists all marked from slashes
And observe that love sent me up the creek.
And then,
And then,

From a trembling hand my brandy splashes
On the soiled white suit within which I reek
As I brush the flies off jungle rashes
Ending my last days in far Mozambique.
There before your eyes the picture flashes
Of a life that one wrong move made so bleak,
When you let me feel your long, long lashes
Brush against my oh so sensitive cheek.

THE BUSINESS MAN'S SHUFFLE

From manuscripts dated October 1960 and January 12, 1961. Unused.

VERSE

When a busy executive invites you to dance,
Don't be fooled into thinking his mind's on romance.
Don't expect to be thrilled by some technique fresh and new,

'Cause there's only one step he's ever learned how
    to do,
Only one step
The poor schlepp
Can do.
It's called the—

REFRAIN 1

Business man's shuffle,
The business man's shuffle.
He hates to dance,
But it's his chance
To walk around and think,
To think about business,
And while he thinks business
The girl supplies
The exercise
To keep him in the pink.

REFRAIN 2

Oh, the business man's shuffle,
The business man's shuffle.
When it suits him,
He gets a whim;
He wants to table-hop.
I feel my feet flitting
Where some tycoon's sitting
And soon we're there,
The table where
It's opportune to stop.

[*Dance interlude*]

Oh, the business man's shuffle,
The business man's shuffle.
He hates to dance,
But it's his chance
To walk around and scheme.
The business man's shuffle is
The death of love's young dream.

BUMPER TO BUMPER

From manuscript dated July 13, 1961. Frank Loesser note
on manuscript: "Too much coffee. Don't use." Not used.

I like it bumper to bumper, bumper to bumper,
Far as the eye can see.
Notice the red Chevrolet in the middle
Evr'y weekend, that's me.

Bumper to bumper, bumper to bumper,
Snuggled among old friends.
Bumper to bumper, bumper to bumper
At the beach the journey ends.

But by the time I get hit with a medicine ball
And the rain comes pouring down,
And my girl gives me the frown,
It's time to drive back to town—

To the honking of horns, the stripping of gears,
The music of crashing chrome.
Bumper to bumper, bumper to bumper,
All the way home.

REACTION TO HEDY

From manuscript dated November 1960. Unused.

BOYS: I took one look
    At what walked in today.
    I took one look
    And all I've got to say
    Is oooooh,
    Oooooh.
GIRLS: Took one look
    At what walked in today.
    I took one look
    And all I've got to say
    Is feh.

MARVELOUS MIND

From manuscript dated April 7, 1961. Unused. Intended for Hedy.

I've got a marvelous mind;
That's what my mother dear used to say.
Simply got a marvelous mind;
That's what my mother dear used to say.
Ah, but the way things developed,
Men don't quite see it that way.

I've got a marvelous mind;
Teachers in school said I would not fail.
I've got a marvelous mind;
Teachers in school said I would not fail.
Then when the time came for college,
Why did they recommend Yale?

I tell a fella:
Try me on my Latin,
Try me on my Greek,
Try me on my calculus
And see how good I speak.
I tell him:
Try me on my method for
Improving the Univac.
But what does he want to try me on?
My back.

Okay, so he's in the mood.
Okay, so I'll be a real good scout.
Okay, so he's in the mood.
That's what my problem is all about.

I've got a marvelous mind;
Why is it nobody wants to find out?
[*spoken*] Ask me questions!
[*sung*] Nobody wants to find out.
[*spoken*] Antidisestablishmentarian!
[*sung*] Nobody wants to find out.
[*spoken*] Dr. Brothers!
[*sung*] Nobody wants to find out.

LEOCADIA

Based on *Time Remembered* by Jean Anouilh. Abandoned project, March–August 1962.
    Following Harry Kurnitz's suggestion in early 1962
that it would make a good musical, Loesser read *Time
Remembered* and began drafting a story outline and the
beginnings of several songs before Anouilh declined
permission for an adaptation. The song order is based
on Loesser's notes and outlines for the piece.

ONLY THE RICH

From undated lyric manuscript. No music is known to
exist.

Only the rich may be peculiar,
But only the terribly rich.
Family wealth entitles one [them]
To the lunatic mind and congenital twitch.
Only the rich may dine on orchids
Or sleep in a sequined toupee (don't try it),

For only the rich may be peculiar*
Without being put away,
Put away, put away,
Gently but firmly
Put away.

Only the rich may be eccentric,
But only the very rich.
Family wealth entitles one [them]
To have girlfriend and boyfriend, plus options to
    switch.†
But only the rich need no attorneys
To prove they are harmlessly gay (don't try it),
For only the rich may be eccentric
Without being put away.

YOU LIVE IN MY HEART

From undated lyric manuscript. Music manuscripts dated
July 1962. Alternate title: "She Lives in My Heart."

You live in my heart,
Radiant and beautiful;
Yes, you live in my heart,
Close to me, still close to me,
While I walk in a world
Shimmering with memories.
From my own exquisite world
Why should I ever depart
When forever
And forever
You live in my heart?

———
* *Alternate line reads:*
    For only the rich may be erratic [demented]

† *Alternate line:*
    To give in to a kleptomaniacal itch.

I AM A JOLLY PEASANT

From undated lyric manuscript. No music is known to
exist.

———

I am a jolly peasant;
I stand around and smile.
Though basic'lly unpleasant
And full of rotten guile,
I'm unemployed at present;
Please buy my wooden shoe.
I am a jolly peasant
And I love to jolly you.*

SPEAK TO ME

From undated lyric manuscript. Music manuscripts
dated July 1962.

———

Speak to me, speak to me,
Dazzling one, speak to me—
Say something gay and outrageously chic to me.
Fill the air with your cleverest multilingual quips;

Let me hear the ping of pearls
As they fall from your lips.
Speak to me, speak to me,
Show [devote] your technique to me—
Quote some remote bit of Cyprian Greek to me.

———
* *Alternate line:*
    And so I jolly you.

Fill the air of my otherwise bored and lonely
    silent day
With the babbling, babbling music
Of nothing at all to say.

Choral version

From typescript dated August 9, 1962. Music manuscripts dated July 1962.

MALE
CHORUS: Speak to me, speak to me,
    Oh charming one, speak to me—
    Say something gay and outrageously chic
        to me.
    Fill the air with your cleverest quips;
    Let me hear the crescendo of pearls
    As they fall from your lips.
    Speak to me, speak to me,
    Apply your technique to me;
    Quote some remote anecdote that is
        Greek to me.
    Fill the air of my desolate day
    With the super-superfluous
    Music of nothing to say.

FEMALE
CHORUS: Speak to me, speak to me,
    O charming one, speak to me;
    Say some cliché that is très romantique
        to me.
    Fill the air with a flattering tale;
    Let me hear the extravagant words
    Of the amorous male.
    Speak to me, speak to me,
    Apply your technique to me,
    Sly innuendo that's clear as Lalique
        to me.
    Fill the air of my desolate day
    With the super-superfluous
    Music of nothing to say.

PLEASURES AND PALACES | 1965

PLEASURES AND PALACES

Tryout: Opened March 11, 1965, at the Fisher Theatre, Detroit. Closed at the Fisher on April 10, 1965, without opening in New York. Presented by Allen B. Whitehead in association with Frank Productions, Inc. Book by Sam Spewack and Frank Loesser, based on a play by Sam Spewack. Music and lyrics by Frank Loesser. Directed and choreographed by Bob Fosse. Scenery and lighting by Robert Randolph. Costumes by Freddy Wittop. Orchestrations by Philip J. Lang. Musical direction by Fred Werner. Cast starred Alfred Marks (Potemkin) (succeeded by Jack Cassidy), Phyllis Newman (Sura), Hy Hazell (Catherine) and John McMartin (John Paul Jones), and featured Leon Janney (Bureyev), Mort Marshall (Kollenovitch), Eric Brotherson (Radbury), Sammy Smith (Von Siegen), Woody Romoff (Polgunov), John Anania (Captain Pasha), Burt Bier (Suslovski), and Michael Quinn (Father Feddor and Villager).

Adapted from a comedy that folded in one night, Spewack's *Once There Was a Russian, Pleasures and Palaces* was originally titled *Holy Russia!* Based on a hypothetical encounter between John Paul Jones and Catherine the Great, the show vacillated between its costume operetta love story and a burlesque of American-Russian relations. After much revision out of town, and against the urging of director and choreographer Bob Fosse, who felt the show could be saved, Loesser closed the production.

I HEAR BELLS

Registered for copyright as an unpublished song February 8, 1965. Introduced by Alfred Marks (Potemkin) and ensemble.

POTEMKIN: Oh, I am more than merely
    magnificent;
    Oh, I am monumentally alive.
    For I have found on taking count
      of all my senses
    So many more than just the
      customary five.
    I close my eyes, and my great
      Russian destiny appears.

Bob Fosse and dancers rehearsing

[*spoken*] Accompanied by what
    physicians have erroneously and
    jealously referred to as a ringing
    in the ears. Nonsense!

[*sung*] I hear bells,
Great bronze bells,
The bells of Saint Petersburg
Calling me to power.*
I see lights,
Big bright lights,
The lights of Saint Petersburg
Signaling my hour.†
I feel fate,
My great fate,
The throne of Saint Petersburg
Over which I'll tower.
I hear bells,
Great bronze bells,
The bells of Saint Petersburg
Calling me to power.
For I am holy Russia's finest flower.

POLICEMEN: You hear bells,
Great bronze bells,
The bells of Saint Petersburg
Calling you to power.
You see lights,
Big bright lights,
The lights of Saint Petersburg
Signaling your hour.
You feel fate,
Your great fate,
The throne of Saint Petersburg
Over which you'll tower.
You hear bells.

POTEMKIN: I hear bells—
POLICEMEN: Great bronze bells—
POTEMKIN: Great bronze bells—
POLICEMEN: The bells of Saint Petersburg
Calling you to power.
POTEMKIN: For I am holy Russia's finest flower.
POLICEMEN: Holy Russia's finest flower.
You hear bells,
Great bronze bells,
The bells of Saint Petersburg—

POTEMKIN: [*spoken*] Our story starts in the Royal
    Palace, Saint Petersburg . . . I am
    in a little trouble . . .
POLICEMEN: [*sung*] Calling you to power,
Calling you to power.

---

* *Earlier version:*
   Singing of my fabulous fame.

† *Earlier version:*
   Spelling out my marvelous name.

Opening

From script dated January 25, 1965. To be sung by Potemkin to open the show and segue into "I Hear Bells." Unused.

The moment I was born
I dismissed the little midwife,
Congratulated Mother,
And cooked the morning meal;
Predicted local weather,
Translated that to Spanish,
And later on that evening
Invented the wheel.

Additional unused lyrics (from manuscript dated October 28, 1964)

To be a genius is to be very lonely,
A stately mansion above the tiny huts,
A giant walking among the little pygmies,
A luscious fruitcake surrounded by mere nuts.

[*spoken*] You. [*snap*]
When is Egypt?
Name two polar bears.
No coaching!
[*sung*] Nowhere but nowhere can I find
Persons of my perceptive kind,
Who feel what I feel,
Who sense what I sense in my uncanny mind.
No wonder I shall leave them all behind.

To be a genius is to be very lonely,
A brilliant diamond among dull bits of glass;
In all this whole herd of stumbling mules and
    donkeys,
In all this whole herd, the single perfect ass.

MY LOVER IS A SCOUNDREL

Registered for copyright as an unpublished song January 29, 1965. Introduced by Hy Hazell (Catherine), Leon Janney (Bureyev), and ensemble.

CATHERINE: He is far from noble,
    Far from clever,
    Far from perfect in any endeavor,
    Far from being the prince he
      would be;
    Yet I weep when, alas,
    He is far from me.
    A scoundrel?
    Yes, I agree.

My lover is a scoundrel,
My lover is a brute.
Yes, my lover is what everyone says—
Extremely bad for my repute.
My lover is a scoundrel,
A liar and a cad;
But my lover is a lover
Such as very few women have had.
My lover is a lover
As good for me as he is bad.*

BUREYEV: [spoken] The man's insanely ambitious.
CATHERINE: [sung] He is out for power,
   Out for plunder,
   Out to be an historical wonder.
   Out, the mad boy, to capture my crown.
   Yet I weep when, alas, he is out of town.
   A scoundrel,
   Yes—and a clown.

   My lover is a scoundrel,
   A liar and a cad;
   But my lover is a lover
   Such as very few women have had.
   My lover is a lover
   As good for me as he is bad.

Unused addendum (from manuscript dated August 1964)

CATHERINE: It's quite easy to criticize
   His political thinking,
   His occasional drinking,
   And his devious dealings.
   Oh, it's easy to analyze
   His ambition so reckless and blind.
   Ah, but gentlemen, please keep in mind
   My womanly feelings.

---

* The following sixteen lines were cut prior to the start of rehearsals. From manuscript dated October 18, 1964.
CATHERINE: So tomorrow I sail away
   Down the Volga to Karkinitzy Bay,
   There to pledge him my heart and hand
   And proclaim it to all throughout the land.
MINISTERS: God save our land
   When your lover takes command!
CATHERINE: My lover is a—
MINISTERS: Scoundrel.
CATHERINE: My lover is a—
MINISTERS: Brute.
CATHERINE: Yes, my lover is what everyone says—
MINISTERS: Extremely bad for your repute.
CATHERINE: My lover is a—
MINISTERS: Scoundrel!
   Liar!
   Cad!

Potemkin Is a Scoundrel, unused ministers' version (from manuscript dated August 1964)

BUREYEV: Potemkin is a scoundrel;
   Potemkin is a fraud.
   Yes, Potemkin is the treacherous fiend
   Who has the Empress overawed.
   Potemkin is a scoundrel
   And power is his aim,
   But Potemkin is her lover
   And she will not extinguish that flame.
   And so, gentlemen, the best we can do
   Is continue to blacken the name.
OTHER
MINISTERS: Blacken the name, blacken the name.
ALL
MINISTERS: Potemkin is a scoundrel;
   Potemkin is a beast.
SUSLOVSKI: Potemkin is what everyone says: a—
BUREYEV: [covering] To say the very least.
ALL
MINISTERS: Potemkin is a scoundrel,
   A liar and a cur.
BUREYEV: But Potemkin is her lover,
   And we just cannot reason with her.
ALL
MINISTERS: Her!
   Her!
   Damn her!

TO MARRY

Registered for copyright as an unpublished song January 29, 1965. Introduced by John McMartin (John Paul Jones).

I am glad to say as I travel abroad
And I hear of a lawful marriage
That my mind's relieved over alien folk
Whom I normally would disparage.
In a foreign land, when a wedding's planned
In an hon'rable forthright way,
I detect the fast-growing influence of the U.S.A.

It is somehow so American
To marry,
So unflinchingly American
When two hearts,
With benefit of clergy, unite.
While it smacks of the Bohemian
To tarry,
And it's quite la vie Parisienne
To spar and parry,
It is somehow so Connecticut,

So Tom Jefferson,
So cash-and-carry,
So American to marry.
[spoken] Mrs. Martha Washington!
Mrs. Molly Pitcher!
Mrs. Dolly Madison!
Mrs. Betsy Ross!
Dear ladies, I salute you;
Your message has come across!
[sung] It is somehow so July the Fourth,
So Niag'ra Falls,
So sanitary,
So American to marry!

HAIL, MAJESTY

Registered for copyright as an unpublished song January 29, 1965. Introduced by ensemble.

ENSEMBLE: Hail, Majesty!
   Hail, Imperial Majesty!
   Hail, Majesty!
   Hail, Imperial Majesty!
MEN: Mother of us all!
WOMEN: Behold our prospering houses
   Beneath our shining blue sky,
MEN: Behold the bounty of our fields
   As you sail graciously by.
WOMEN: Behold the joy in our faces
   And hands in happy acclaim—
MEN: That speak of our abundant land—
ENSEMBLE: And praise your radiant name.
   Hail, Majesty!
   Hail, Imperial Majesty!
   Hail, Majesty!
   Hail, Imperial Majesty!
   Mother of us all!*

Unused vocal dance interlude (from manuscript dated January 9, 1965)

See the village baker and the bread he bakes—
Bread is for the pigs because we all eat cake.
Never will you notice
Anybody hungry and thin,
For here in our well-fed village
Nothing of the kind ever has been.

See the village magistrate who wears a frown—
He's the only disappointed man in town.

---

* Alternate line:
 Radiant, radiant mother of us all!

See the way he searches,
Looking for a criminal case;
But here in our honest village
Nothing of the kind ever takes place.

See the village maiden lying in the hay;
See the handsome village youth come by her way.
See the angry parents
Separating Mary from John.
Here in our decent village
Nothing of the kind ever goes on.

THUNDER AND LIGHTNING

Registered for copyright as an unpublished song January 29, 1965. Introduced by Phyllis Newman (Sura) and Alfred Marks (Potemkin). Recorded by Carol Ventura (Prestige).

SURA: You are thunder and lightning,
Coming to ravish my primitive soul.
You are thunder and lightning;
You are a tempest beyond all control.
You are thunder and lightning,
Heaven and hell with your arms about me tight'ning,
And it is oh so voluptuously fright'ning
That I cannot tell the chill from the warm.
You are thunder and lightning,
And I love being caught in the storm.

POTEMKIN: I am thunder and lightning,
Coming to ravish your primitive soul.
I am thunder and lightning;
I am a tempest beyond all control.
I am thunder—
SURA: Thunder and lightning.
POTEMKIN: And lightning.
SURA: Oh, you are both heaven and hell
With your arms about me tight'ning.
And it is oh so voluptuously fright'ning
That I cannot tell the chill from the warm.
POTEMKIN: I am thunder—
SURA: You are.
POTEMKIN: And lightning.
SURA: Yes, you are, and I love being caught in the storm.

Unused verse (from manuscript dated May 25, 1964)

SURA: When we so much as touch,
You seem to waken within me all the furies.
Yet you have such a touch
That it can make out of me
The houriest of houris.
You are an elemental force;
I would not dream of changing your course.

What are you?
What are you,
Unholy stranger,
That when you come near me
You awaken all the furies?
Yet somehow you make me
The houriest of houris!
As we kiss,
What is this
Delicious danger?
Who are you?
What are you,
Unholy stranger?

TO YOUR HEALTH

Registered for copyright as an unpublished song January 29, 1965. Introduced by Sammy Smith (Von Siegen) and Eric Brotherson (Radbury).

VON SIEGEN: My dear Rear Admiral,
After so many dangerous cruises
What remarkable physical shape you're in,
With no scars, and no wounds, and no bruises.
RADBURY: [*spoken*] You noticed?
VON SIEGEN: [*spoken*] Aber ja! Tell me, what is your special strategy?
RADBURY: [*spoken*] The very careful timing of shore leave.
VON SIEGEN: [*spoken*] Wunderbar!
RADBURY: [*sung*] You nice Vice Admiral,
It is likewise with pleasure I witness
How decidedly well you've preserved your skin;
You're the picture of physical fitness.
VON SIEGEN: [*spoken*] Many thanks.
RADBURY: [*spoken*] Not at all. Tell me, during hand-to-hand combat, what is your special strength?
VON SIEGEN: [*spoken*] Extremely powerful— binoculars.

RADBURY: [*spoken*] Ah, yes. Well—
VON SIEGEN: [*spoken*] Prosit!
RADBURY: [*spoken*] Cheerio!
VON SIEGEN: [*sung*] To your health, to your health,
May it ever continue the best!
To your health, to your health,
May it never be put to the test!
May your drive to survive
Keep you far from the firing line.
May your belly get shot
Full of nothing stronger
Than fine Rhine wine!
BOTH: Fine Rhine wine,
Fine Rhine wine!
RADBURY: Let us quench our thirst for adventure
With fine Rhine wine.

To your health, to your health,
May it ever continue the best!
To your health, to your health,
May it never be put to the test!
May no strife mar your life;
May no swordplay cut short its design.
May your throat feel the tickle
Of nothing sharper
Than fine Rhine wine!
BOTH: May your ship make no trip
Which would dunk you down under the brine.
May you founder and founder
In nothing deeper
Than fine Rhine wine,
Fine Rhine wine,
Fine Rhine wine!
VON SIEGEN: Oh, it's not so salty like water,
This fine Rhine wine.

RADBURY: To your health, to your health,
May it ever continue the best!
To your health, to your health,
May it never be put to the test!
May your craft, fore and aft,
Sail a course uneventful as mine.
May your poop feel the burning of nothing hotter
Than fine Rhine wine!
BOTH: Fine Rhine wine,
Fine Rhine wine!
Here's to peaceful warfare and plenty,
This fine Rhine wine!
VON SIEGEN: [*spoken*] Ach du lieber—
BOTH: [*sung*] Rhine—
RADBURY: [*spoken*] Jolly good—
BOTH: [*sung*] Wine!

NEITHER THE TIME NOR THE PLACE

Registered for copyright as an unpublished song February 18, 1965. Introduced by Alfred Marks (Potemkin) and Hy Hazell (Catherine). Replaced after opening by "I Desire You." Frank Loesser's manuscript note of August 16, 1964, labels this number a "Sex Fandango."

[POTEMKIN, *maneuvering* CATHERINE *toward the bedroom door, does not realize* KOLLENOVITCH *is upstage standing at attention.*]

POTEMKIN: This, my darling, is it!
CATHERINE: Is what?
POTEMKIN: Is *it*—the uncontrollable moment
Of animal truth, as we embrace!
CATHERINE: But this, my darling, alas—
POTEMKIN: A what?
CATHERINE: Alas—is neither the time nor the place.

[CATHERINE *indicates the presence of* KOLLENOVITCH. POTEMKIN *turns and signals for him to disappear. He exits.* POTEMKIN *resumes his approach.*]

POTEMKIN: This, my darling, is fate!
CATHERINE: Is what?
POTEMKIN: Is fate—the wild, impetuous,
Beautiful, breathless, and hot end of
the chase.
CATHERINE: But this, my darling, dommage—
POTEMKIN: Do what?
CATHERINE: Too bad—is neither the time nor
the place.
POTEMKIN: [*spoken*] At least let me show you
my bedchamber. I have had it
especially decorated for you—
your favorite colors.
CATHERINE: [*spoken*] No, Potemkin.
POTEMKIN: [*spoken*] What's that?
CATHERINE: [*spoken*] What's what?
POTEMKIN: [*spoken*] I heard a cry—
CATHERINE: [*spoken*] I heard nothing.
POTEMKIN: [*spoken*] A woman's agonized scream!
CATHERINE: [*spoken*] It's your disordered
imagination.
[*sung*] After we are married—
POTEMKIN: Darling, don't be such a little
peasant.
CATHERINE: After we are wed—
POTEMKIN: For a man, the waiting's quite
unpleasant.
CATHERINE: After we are married—
POTEMKIN: [*spoken*] Please, Katushka, I shall
remain here. Go in alone.

CATHERINE: [*sung*] You may rush me off into
where you said.
POTEMKIN: I said now.
CATHERINE: But I said after we are married.
After we are married.
POTEMKIN: [*spoken*] At least peek through the
keyhole—peek.
CATHERINE: [*sung*] Ah, the nightly bliss!
Promise me you will always be in a
hurry like this.
BOTH: Like this?
CATHERINE: Yes.
This, my darling, is it.
POTEMKIN: Is it?
CATHERINE: Is it.
POTEMKIN: Ah.
CATHERINE: The inconvenient moment of
practical fact
That we must face,
That this, darling, I'm sure—
POTEMKIN: You're sure.
CATHERINE: Quite sure.
BOTH: Is neither the time nor the place.

[POTEMKIN *tries to open door, realizes it's locked, looks for key, kicks door.*]

CATHERINE: [*spoken*] What are you doing?
POTEMKIN: [*spoken*] I am punishing this door.
It has offended me.

[*He kicks it as* CATHERINE *comes over.*]

I wish to break it down! Destroy it.

[CATHERINE *gently takes him away. He looks back piteously as they cross together.*]

CATHERINE: [*spoken*] Silly boy. Don't you realize—?
[*sung*] This, my darling, was it.
POTEMKIN: Was what?
CATHERINE: Was *it*—the mad and marvelous
passion we had to erase.
For this, my darling, alas—
POTEMKIN: A what?
CATHERINE: Alas—
BOTH: Was neither the time nor the place.

I DESIRE YOU

From typescript dated March 23, 1965. Added after opening to replace "Neither the Time nor the Place." Introduced by Hy Hazell (Catherine) and Alfred Marks (Potemkin).

CATHERINE: He is fond of me no more. I wonder
why?
POTEMKIN: She must not go in that door. I'd
sooner die.
CATHERINE: Where's his eagerness of yore?
The passion hot?
POTEMKIN: She must not go in that door, no
matter what!
CATHERINE: I must warm the old rapport and
leave no doubt.
POTEMKIN: As I've mentioned twice before—
she must keep out!
CATHERINE: A woman's doubt—
POTEMKIN: Out!
CATHERINE: [*spoken*] Ready.
POTEMKIN: [*spoken*] Steady.
CATHERINE: [*sung*] I desire you,
Desperately desire you.
Come to my arms while
shamelessly I declare
That
I desire you,
Passionately desire you.
Take me and make my ecstasy yours
to share.
Sing me no song of tomorrow;
We'll get together
Somewhere, somehow—
No!
I desire you,
Desperately desire you;
And when I say desire you,
I mean here and now!

[*Dialogue. Later, same scene:*]

CATHERINE: Why the sudden change of mood?
He's quite complex!
POTEMKIN: Watch me switch from pious prude
to pot of sex.
CATHERINE: All at once the sultry gaze that
spells boudoir.
POTEMKIN: Soon her soul will be ablaze and
there we are.
CATHERINE: Just a little while before, he wouldn't
sin.
POTEMKIN: There's a pretty little door to take
her in!

CATHERINE: I cannot win.
POTEMKIN: In!
[*spoken*] Ready.
CATHERINE: [*spoken*] Steady.
POTEMKIN: [*sung*] I desire you,
Desperately desire you.
Come to my arms while shamelessly I
declare
That
I desire you,
Passionately desire you.
Take me and make my ecstasy
yours to share.
Sing me no song of tomorrow;
We'll get together
Somewhere, somehow—
No!
I desire you,
Desperately desire you;
And when I say desire you,
I mean here and now!
CATHERINE: [*spoken*] Remember, Potemkin, I have
a reputation—not to maintain, but
to establish!

IN YOUR EYES

Published. Copyrighted March 2, 1965. Introduced by
Phyllis Newman (Sura) and John McMartin (John Paul
Jones).

SURA: Let me kindle the flame of desire
In your eyes.
JONES: Young lady, I decline.
SURA: In your eyes.
JONES: Young lady, not in mine.
SURA: Let me bring out the bestial fire
In your eyes.
JONES: Oh, I do not deny the feelings I feel
In such a situation.
Ah, but I am strong.
SURA: [*spoken*] Yes, you are strong, so strong.
JONES: [*sung*] Strong, in the face of temptation.

[*Dialogue*]

SURA: [*sung*] Let me kindle the flame of desire—
JONES: [*spoken*] Desire?
SURA: [*sung*] In your eyes.
JONES: [*spoken*] My one desire is to get dressed.
SURA: [*sung*] Let me bring out the bestial fire
In your eyes.
JONES: [*spoken*] It is gone! Believe me, I have

conquered temptation. Look at
me. You see?

[*Dialogue*]

SURA: [*sung*] All at once I feel shame, merely
looking
In your eyes.

[*Dialogue*]

JONES: [*spoken*] Perhaps you have seen the light.
SURA: [*spoken*] Yes, the light. Yes! The light—
[*sung*] In your eyes.
JONES: [*spoken*] Really, miss, my eyes are just—
SURA: [*spoken*] In your eyes.
JONES: [*spoken*] —ordinary typical Scotch-Irish
blue.
SURA: [*sung*] In your eyes I have seen the light.
JONES: That is kind of you.
SURA: The light of goodness—
JONES: Ah, but no!
SURA: And truth divine.
JONES: It is God's truth and not mine.
SURA: In your eyes I have seen the glow—
JONES: Merely candlelight—
SURA: Of something pure—
JONES: And the warmth—
SURA: And strong—
JONES: Of this occasion—
SURA: And fine—
JONES: Or some strange inner warning of hell's fire.
SURA: Through the years
In my wanton way—
JONES: Poor young thing.
SURA: I roamed the darkness—
JONES: Poor thing!
SURA: Of lust and lies.
JONES: I sincerely hope all that is past.
SURA: Now at last I have touched the stars!
JONES: Thank the Lord!
SURA: I have found my soul!
JONES: You can be saved!
SURA: I have seen the light—
JONES: Praises to heaven!
SURA: In your eyes.
JONES: Praises to heaven.

[*Dialogue.* JONES *exits.*]

SURA: Through the years
In my wanton way
I roamed the darkness
Of lust and lies.
Now at last I have touched the stars,
I have found my soul,
I have seen the light
In his eyes.

Sheet music version

In your eyes I have seen the light,
The light of goodness and truth divine.
In your eyes I have seen the glow
Of something pure and strong and fine.

Through the years in my wanton way
I roamed the darkness of lust and lies.
Now at last I have touched the stars,
I have found my soul,
I have seen the light
In your eyes.

TRULY LOVED

Registered for copyright as an unpublished song January 28, 1965. Introduced by Hy Hazell (Catherine) and
ensemble. Recorded by Tommy Steele (Marble Arch),
Joanne Browne (Silverline), and Bernard Cribbins (EMI).

CATHERINE: Do I appear to glow?
Is there a kind of bloom?
Have I an air of radiant confidence
and poise
As I enter a room?
If I appear to glow
Full of a pride supreme,
That is because I have
The one happiness of heart
Of which all women dream.

I know that I am truly loved
And that ev'ry moment
The man is all mine.
I know that I am truly loved,
And the very knowing
Makes ev'ry moment shine.

So if my bearing is proud
And my smile serene,
I do not mean to proclaim
That I am a queen.
I'm just a woman, but
I know that I am truly loved
And that ev'ry moment
The man is all mine,
And that makes ev'ry moment shine.
MEN: His one beloved—
WOMEN: His one beloved—
CATHERINE: And that makes ev'ry moment shine.
MEN AND
WOMEN: Radiant mother of us all.

SINS OF SURA

Registered for copyright as an unpublished song March 2, 1965. Introduced by Phyllis Newman (Sura) and ensemble.

SURA: [*spoken*] It was in the year 1777 that I first became a wretched sinner in order to amuse myself on the wealthy but lonely estate of my family.
[*sung*] I committed a
Sin!
With a farmer's boy
'Mongst the thorns and the brambles like a peasant
And then, sin!

ENSEMBLE: Sin!

SURA: With a coachman's boy
In the backseat the going was more pleasant.
Sin!
Till my parents called me the vilest and wickedest of creatures
And packed me off to a finishing school, where I soon finished off all my teachers.

ENSEMBLE: Sin!

SURA: [*spoken*] There is more.

ENSEMBLE: [*sung*] Sin!

SURA: [*spoken*] So much more . . .
[*sung*] I have only begun to begin.

ENSEMBLE: Yes? Yes? Yes?

SURA: [*spoken*] In 1778, no longer satisfied with young boys and puny schoolteachers, I ran away into the *real* world. After all, I was no longer twelve.
[*sung*] So I started to—
Sin!
After lunch one day,
Poor and proud, how else could I tip the waiter?
And next, sin!

ENSEMBLE: Sin!

SURA: In a mattress shop
Where I worked briefly as a demonstrator.
Sin!
With a baritone,
During which he would bellow fondly to me,
And then that man from an acrobat troupe and his partner, to whom (oops!) he threw me.

ENSEMBLE: Sin!

SURA: [*spoken*] I am bad.

ENSEMBLE: [*sung*] Sin!

SURA: [*spoken*] I've been had
[*sung*] All the way from Smolensk to Harbin.

ENSEMBLE: Yes? Yes? Yes?

SURA: [*spoken*] In 1779, I appeared in the Court of Nobles, charged with conduct unbecoming a lady. The elderly Chief Justice acquitted me on the basis of habeas corpus, which he explained means in Latin "have the body"— which is precisely the offer I made him.
[*sung*] I was living in—
Sin!
With that old, old judge,
Till he caught me and punished me for cheating.
And then, sin!

ENSEMBLE: Sin!

SURA: With the big blond brute
He sent in to administer the beating.
Sin!
Till the judge fixed me with
A chastity belt and iron tether.
And then there just wasn't any more sin.
Till the locksmith and I got together.

ENSEMBLE: Sin!

SURA: What a past!

ENSEMBLE: Sin!

SURA: What a cast!
What a medal on me you could pin!

ENSEMBLE: Yes? Yes? Yes?

SURA: [*spoken*] In 1780—

MAN: [*spoken*] Why, that's this year!

SURA: [*spoken*] I finally became a selective sinner. I now met intellectuals. People with whom one could converse—afterward.

BUREYEV: [*spoken*] Young lady, let us be slightly more contemporary. What happened lately?

SURA: [*sung*] I am—

[*Freeze, as* POTEMKIN *steps forward to audience.*]

POTEMKIN: [*spoken*] You just can't trust a woman. She must always *tell* someone. The intimate, the most fragrant of memories—bandied about in public! How tactless! How tasteless! And damn dangerous. These are the times that try men's souls. And these are the times that call forth the best in me. Observe!

[*Unfreeze, as song continues.*]

[SURA *stands over trapdoor.* POTEMKIN *works his way to lever. As he approaches it, she moves forward. Then back. Then forward.*]

SURA: [*sung*] —guilty of
Sin! I can hear the din
Down in hell, when I'm belle of all the season.
For I have sinned an imperial sin
With a swine who combined lust and treason.

ENSEMBLE: Treason!

SURA: Sin!

ENSEMBLE: What's his name?

SURA: Sin!

ENSEMBLE: What's his name?

SURA: You are looking at Jezebel's twin.

ENSEMBLE: His name! The name of your partner in sin.

CATHERINE: [*spoken*] Yes, what is the name of your partner in sin?

SURA: [*sung*] His name is Po—

POTEMKIN: [*simultaneously; spoken*] My heart! . . . A doctor a . . . doctor!
The strain—an uncle's anguish—a doctor!

[*He falls on lever as he pulls it. All turn to him and do not see* SURA *plummet straight down as she reaches her vocal climax. When all, including* CATHERINE *and* BUREYEV, *turn back, the girl has disappeared, the trapdoor is closed.*]

[*Act I curtain*]

Unused lyrics

ADDITIONAL REFRAINS (FROM UNDATED TYPESCRIPT)

Sin! With that old, old judge
Who suspected I'd been a reckless rover.
And then sin! With his lifelong friend,
The physician he'd asked to look me over.

Sin! In the diamond vault
Of a jew'ler with tendencies to barter.
Some more sin! With an English knight
Who was far more than knight of any garter.

Sin! I can hear the din
Down in hell, when I'm belle of all the season.
For I have just sinned a king-sized sin
Which combines homicide, lust, and treason!

ENSEMBLE REFRAINS (FROM MANUSCRIPT DATED NOVEMBER 5, 1964)

ENSEMBLE: Sin, sin,
Tell us about each sin.
Pray do begin,
Tell us about ev'ry sin
You have been in.
SURA: When I started to sin!
ENSEMBLE: Tell us more.
SURA: Sin!
ENSEMBLE: Tell us more.
SURA: I am full of remorse and chagrin—
ENSEMBLE: Tell us more.
SURA: From the sin—
ENSEMBLE: Yes? Yes?
SURA: I have been—
ENSEMBLE: Yes? Yes?
SURA: In. [*talk*]

FINALE WITH ENSEMBLE (FROM TYPESCRIPT DATED DECEMBER 6, 1964)

ENSEMBLE: Well? More! More!
What was next?
Don't stop!
It's delightful, exciting!
Delicious!
More!
Please! Rest of story?
Yes!
Next piece of tale!
It's a story too vile to be yours;
It's a story too low to be mine.
All that sex would make you so revolting,
All those details would brand me a swine.
But in anyone else's autobiography,
ENSEMBLE AND SURA: Sin!
Is simply divine.

HOORAH FOR JONES

Registered for copyright as an unpublished song February 4, 1965. Introduced by ensemble.

ENSEMBLE: Hoorah for Jones,
For John Paul Jones!
Proclaim that name in joyful tones.*

* *Alternate line:*
Proclaim that name in loud clear tones.

Jones, the hero,
American hero,
Hero.
Hoorah for Jones,
For John Paul Jones!
Proclaim that name in joyful tones.*
Hoorah for Jones.
Who sank the Turk.
SOLO VOICE: A miracle no Russian ever could work.
ENSEMBLE: Hoorah, hoorah,
Jones! Jones! Jones!

PROPAGANDA

Registered for copyright as an unpublished song February 4, 1965. Introduced by Mort Marshall (Kollenovitch), John McMartin (John Paul Jones), and ensemble.

KOLLENOVITCH: [*spoken*] A foreigner! Jones. They're all the same.
[*sung*] Now why is all the world so full of foreigners,
Delib'rately unlovable and strange,
With languages, and manners, and complexions
Which they do not have the decency to change?
[*spoken*] Their very names offend the human ear
[*sung*] With syllables too short to be sincere.
For example, the heathen Chinese: Lee-Kwo-Chang.
Or the vicious Germans: Hans-Kurt-Schmidt.
And now, the latest interloper:* John-Paul-Jones.
ENSEMBLE: Jones? Jones.
KOLLENOVITCH: The name of Jones.
ENSEMBLE: The name Jones. The name Jones.
KOLLENOVITCH: The very sound of it distinctly chills the bones.†
ENSEMBLE: Chills the bones.
KOLLENOVITCH: The sound of Jones.
ENSEMBLE: Strange.

* *Earlier version (dated May 22, 1964):*
Or the present alien interloper:

† *Earlier version (dated April 27, 1964):*
The sound of it resembles crunching bones.

Weird,
Such a name!
KOLLENOVITCH: It makes one itch.
ENSEMBLE: Itch.
The name gives one the itch.
Brrr, Jones.
KOLLENOVITCH: Now why not plain, simple Vladimir Ivanov Sonavitch?
JONES: [*spoken*] This is an outrage! Has a person no rights in your country? People! Kind decent citizens! I appeal to you. I am John Paul Jones of the—

[*The* ENSEMBLE, *turning up to listen, is now interrupted by* KOLLENOVITCH.]

KOLLENOVITCH: [*spoken*] Ha! You hear that?
[*sung*] The name of John.
ENSEMBLE: John!
JONES: [*spoken*] Russian people! I quote you our American Declaration of Independence. "When in the course of human events—"
KOLLENOVITCH: [*sung*] And also Paul.
ENSEMBLE: Paul.
JONES: [*spoken*] "—it becomes necessary for one people—"
KOLLENOVITCH: [*sung*] They use the names of foreign saints
To mock us all!
JONES: [*spoken*] "We hold these truths to be self-evident—"
KOLLENOVITCH: [*sung*] There's something snide—
ENSEMBLE: Snide.
JONES: [*spoken*] "—that all men are created equal—that they are—"
KOLLENOVITCH: [*sung*] I can't abide—
ENSEMBLE: Can't abide—
KOLLENOVITCH: About the leering—
ENSEMBLE: Leering—
KOLLENOVITCH: Sneering—
ENSEMBLE: Sneering—
KOLLENOVITCH: Hostile undertones.
ENSEMBLE: [*spoken*] Foreigner!
JONES: [*spoken*] "—that among these are life, liberty, and the pursuit of happiness—"

[*At this point the* POLICEMEN *throw a gunnysack over* JONES *and start to lift him up horizontally. From now on* JONES*'s speeches are from inside the sack.*]

ENSEMBLE: [*sung*] Jones! Jones! Jones! Jones!

[*The* POLICEMEN *exit with* JONES, *along with some of the* ENSEMBLE, *leaving enough of a group to sing the finale. Light has faded on the* ENSEMBLE *and is quite bright on* KOLLENOVITCH, *who, satisfied with his work, takes a pleased, vaudeville stance.*]

KOLLENOVITCH: [*spoken*] Ta-ra-ra!

FOREIGNERS

Earlier version of "Propaganda." Typescript dated September 1963. Intended for a proposed Ben Franklin character. Never appeared in final script.

FRENCH AND
FRANKLIN: Foreigners,
I do not like foreigners.
Oh, why is the world full of foreign,
foreign foreigners?
FRENCH: And why do they not reform their
queer manner of living
FRANKLIN: And why do they all pursue their
strange culture and custom?
FRENCH AND
FRANKLIN: When they don't adopt mine?
FRENCH: And how can one trust 'em?
FRANKLIN: Now how can one like 'em?
FRENCH: [*spoken*] Americans take baths—
foreigners!
FRANKLIN: [*spoken*] The French are so Gallic—
foreigners!
FRENCH: [*sung*] Mysterious foreigners!
FRANKLIN: [*sung*] Those ignorant foreigners!
FRENCH: Those obstinate people who
perversely choose to be—
FRANKLIN: Oh, why don't they have the common
courtesy to be—
FRENCH: To be—well, to be different—
FRANKLIN: To be—well, to be sensible—
FRENCH: Suspiciously different—
FRANKLIN: And quite comprehensible—
FRENCH: From plain, simple huitième
arrondissement—
FRANKLIN: Like plain, simple early American—
ALL: Me.

BARABANCHIK

Registered for copyright as an unpublished song January 29, 1965. Registered with additional words and music as an unpublished song February 8, 1965. Introduced by Alfred Marks (Potemkin), Mort Marshall (Kollenovitch), and ensemble. Recorded by the Four Lads (United Artists).

POTEMKIN: There sleeps within my heart a little
drummer boy.
I waken him when enemies appear.
And soon I am inspired by my
drummer boy,
For when he plays, I have no fear.

Barabanchik (chik chik), Barabanchik
(chik chik),
Beat the drum and put courage in my
heart.
Barabanchik (chik chik), Barabanchik
(chik chik),
Beat the drum as for battle I depart.
Barabanchik (chik chik), Barabanchik
(chik chik),
Drummer boy, play it loud and clear
and strong.
Barabanchik (chik chik), Barabanchik
(chik chik),
As I march along.

[*spoken*] Barabanchik,
Chik.
Paradiddle flim flam,
Boom chang chang,
Tickety boo, tickety bam,
Rim-shot Korsakov,
Anachronism,
Hmm?

[*Repeat lines 5–12.*]

Ensemble version

POTEMKIN: Barabanchik—
POLICE: [*mark time*] Chik chik.
POTEMKIN: Barabanchik—
POLICE: Chik chik.
ALL: Beat the drum and put courage in my
heart.
POLICE: Chik chik, chik chik.
POTEMKIN: Barabanchik—
POLICE: Chik chik.
ALL: Beat the drum as for battle I depart.
POLICE: Chik chik, chik chik,
Chik chik, chik chik.

ALL: Barabanchik, Barabanchik,
Drummer boy, play it loud and clear
and strong.
Barabanchik, Barabanchik,
As I march along.
POLICE: And who are we?
POTEMKIN: Barabanchik.
POLICE: By now it ought to be—
POTEMKIN: Barabanchik.
POLICE: Quite obvious that we
Are the great Potemkin's police.
Note—
POTEMKIN: Barabanchik.
POLICE: We're never too remote—
POTEMKIN: Barabanchik.
POLICE: To add a choral note
By the great Potemkin's police.
Barabanchik, play, play, play, play.
POTEMKIN: Beat the drum and put courage in my
heart.
POLICE: Exalted Highness, you are indeed
magnificent.
POTEMKIN: Thank you very much.
ALL: Beat the drum as for battle I depart.
POLICE: What a heart, what a sweet heart!
ALL: Barabanchik, Barabanchik,
Drummer boy, play it loud and clear
and strong—
POTEMKIN: Barabanchik—
POLICE: Deep in the heart of Potemkin—
POTEMKIN: Barabanchik, as I march along.
POLICE: The great Potemkin,
Barabanchik, barabanchik,
barabanchik,
Barabanchalong, march along.

WHAT IS LIFE?

Registered for copyright as an unpublished song January 28, 1965. Introduced by Mort Marshall (Kollenovitch) and Leon Janney (Bureyev). The duet was replaced by a solo version shortly after the show opened. From typescript dated January 12, 1965, and conductor's score dated March 20, 1965.

KOLLENOVITCH: What is life?
BUREYEV: Life is a basket.
KOLLENOVITCH: What is in the basket?
BUREYEV: Look and see.
KOLLENOVITCH: Sticks and stones, but also ripe
peaches.
BUREYEV: So before your little hand
reaches,

KOLLENOVITCH: Ask yourself, if life is a basket,
Not what is in it, but—
What is in it for me?

BUREYEV: [*spoken*] Correct.

KOLLENOVITCH: [*spoken*] On the other hand, life
may not be a mere basket. Life
involves agreements and
decisions.

BUREYEV: [*spoken*] Exactly. If one follows
the wrong leadership—

KOLLENOVITCH: [*spoken*] Please. Put it in a
nutshell.
[*sung*] What is life?

BUREYEV: Life is a contract.

KOLLENOVITCH: What is in the contract?

BUREYEV: Look and see.

KOLLENOVITCH: What I get, and what I am giving.

BUREYEV: So, in case you wish to keep
living,
Ask yourself, if life is a contract,
Not what is in it, but—

KOLLENOVITCH: What is in it for me?

BUREYEV: [*spoken*] Correct.
[*sung*] Not for Vladimir,
Not for Casimir,
Not for Misha,
Not for Grisha—

KOLLENOVITCH: Just for me.

BUREYEV: You're learning nicely.

KOLLENOVITCH: This includes Potemk—

BUREYEV: Precisely.

BOTH: Ask yourself, if life is a contract,
Not what is in it, but—
What is in it for me?

Solo version for Kollenovitch

My dear old grandfather was a man of wisdom.
He gave me knowledge; he gave me truth.
And now tonight I recall the way he taught me
Back in the days of my early youth.
To my appeals he was never, never deaf,
As I would ask of him in the treble clef:

What is life?
Life is a basket.
What is in the basket?
Look and see.
Sticks and stones, but also ripe peaches.
So, before your little hand reaches,
Ask yourself, if life is a basket,
Not what is in it, but—
What is in it for me?
Not for Vladimir,
Not for Casimir,
Not for Misha,
Not for Grisha—

Ask yourself, if life is a basket,
Not what is in it, but—
What is in it for me?

What is life?
Life is a river.
What is in the river?
Look and see.
Weeds and mud, but also fresh trout there.
Ask yourself, if life is a river,
Not what is in it, but—
What is in it for me?
Not for Vladimir,
Not for Casimir,
Not for Misha,
Not for Grisha.
Ask yourself, if life is a river,
Not what is in it, but—
What is in it for me?

What is life?
Life is a lady.
What is in the lady?
Look and see.
Curves, and smiles, but also fine jew'lry.
So, before you start the tomfool'ry,
Ask yourself, if life is a lady,
Not what is in it, but—
What is in it for me?
Not for Vladimir,
Not for Casimir,
Not for Misha,
Not for Grisha,
Just for me
And none other.
This includes your sweet old mother.
Ask yourself, if life is—whatever—
Not what is in it, but—
What is in it for me?

AH, TO BE HOME AGAIN

Registered for copyright as an unpublished song February 8, 1965. Introduced by John McMartin (John Paul Jones), Michael Davis (Second Prisoner), Howard Kahl (Third Prisoner), and Walter Hook (Fourth Prisoner). Recorded by Jan Peerce (United Artists).

JONES: Many a time I've come ashore
On many a foreign strand,
And many a new and dazzling sight,
And many a startling sound of night,
Has made my adventure grand.

Yet ever my heart cries out
For its own sweet land.

JONES AND
PRISONERS: Ah, to be home again,
All my voyaging done and ended.
Ah, to be home again,
So cries my heart.

Home with countrymen,
Ever welcome and warm befriended.
Ah, to be home again,
So cries my heart.

Bold is my venture
And proud shine my eyes,
But soon comes the yearning
Neath strange darkling skies, and

Ah, to be home again,
All my voyaging done and ended.
Ah, to be home again,
So cries my heart.

PRISONER 1: Why should I journey anywhere?

PRISONER 2: I don't understand them.

PRISONER 3: Somehow I can't.

PRISONERS: And they don't even
Try to understand me.

ALL: Home with my countrymen
Ever welcome and warm befriended.
Ah, to be home again,
So cries my heart.

PRISONERS: Cries my heart.

JONES: Bold is my venture
And proud shine my eyes,
But soon comes the yearning
Neath strange and darkling skies, and

ALL: Ah, to be home again,
All my voyaging done and ended.
Ah, to be home again,
So cries my heart.

PLEASURES AND PALACES

Registered for copyright as an unpublished song February 23, 1965. Introduced by Phyllis Newman (Sura). Recorded by Pearl Bailey (Roulette) and Lena Horne (United Artists).

It has been said that it be ever so humble,
There's no place like home.
But I'm afraid if mine were humble, I would
grumble,
For way down deep within my ev'ry chromosome—

I was made for
Chic and sheer negligees,
Cream on my caviar,
Sable rugs wall to wall,
And my prince lying there
Drinking wine from my slipper,
Drenched in gold
From a thousand candelabra above.
Oh yes, pleasures and palaces
Are what I really do love.

I was born for
Fresh rose leaves in my bath,
String quartet while I dress,
Silk peignoir made in France
For my prince to remove.
Velvet couch in the gardens
Just in case during August
Moonlight madness might strike.
Oh yes, pleasures and palaces
Are what I very much like.

I've a taste for
Poodle dogs wearing pearls,
Parakeets talking French,
Foot massage by my maids,
All the rest by the prince.
Pink champagne from the fountains
As we dance a mazurka to an exquisite score.
[spoken] We commission Mozart.
[sung] Pleasures and palaces
Are what I frankly adore.

With mornings for slumber
And evenings for splendor
And nights for the making of
Absolutely superb and luxurious love.

Unused verses (from typed lyric sheets dated February 18, 1965)

And a little
Hundred-room hunting lodge
On my own mountain range
Decorated with quaint
Picturesque peasant folk.
Entourage, all amusing;
Bodyguard—that's His Highness,
Guarding it with such zest.
Ah yes, pleasures and palaces
Fit my temperament best.

I should have a
Private convent, of course,
Built nearby my estate,
Where the dear little nuns
Sew my lace tablecloths.
Young French monks in the cellar

All devoted to making
Brandy that is divine.
Ah yes, pleasures and palaces
Suit my character just fine.

TEARS OF JOY

Registered for copyright as an unpublished song January 28, 1965. Part II registered for copyright as an unpublished song February 5, 1965. Introduced by Alfred Marks (Potemkin), Hy Hazell (Catherine), Woody Romoff (Polgunov), and ensemble.

POTEMKIN: It is true, my beloved,
I am weeping happy tears
Without a trace of shame
Since the moment you hinted
That Your Majesty and I
Might share each other's name.
Just the mention of wedding bells
Has me bleating like a lamb,
Sentimental Slav that I am.
CATHERINE: [spoken] Cry, Gregory, cry! Cry!
POTEMKIN: [sung] Tears of joy,
Tears of joy,
Moments of happiness bring me
Tears of joy.
Young sweethearts in lovers' lane,
Or a puppy dog at play,
Or a new moon,
Or a birthday,
They all affect me this way.

Speak of tragedy,
I don't cry.
Watch me at funerals
As I smile bye-bye.
But show me some little child
With a shiny Christmas toy,
And I'll show you tears,
Tears of joy.
CATHERINE: [spoken] You are sentiment itself.
POTEMKIN: [spoken] You are—Helen of Troy. So
beautiful!
CATHERINE: [spoken] Oh, Gregory, you *make*
me beautiful. [*She begins to sob.*]
POTEMKIN: [spoken] My darling!
CATHERINE: [spoken] I am weeping from sheer
bliss. It must be contagious,
these—these—
[sung] Tears of joy,
Tears of joy—
Moments of happiness bring me

Tears of joy.
Just your hand caressing mine,
Or your very tender kiss,
Or a nosegay,
Or a poem,
They all affect me like this.

When you criticize,
I don't cry.
Hurt me and punish me,
Yet these eyes are dry.
But tell me I'm beautiful,
Like a Helen of Troy,
And I'll show you tears,
Tears of joy.
POTEMKIN: [*blubbering; spoken*] Shall we announce
our betrothal?
CATHERINE: [spoken] Yes!
POTEMKIN: [*shouting off*; spoken] Polgunov!

[CATHERINE *gives a sob.*]

POTEMKIN: [spoken] Control yourself, my
beautiful darling.
CATHERINE: [*between sobs; spoken*] I am trying to.
POTEMKIN: [spoken] So am I.

[POLGUNOV *enters, still in chains. Two guards bring in a huge cake.*]

CATHERINE: [spoken] How lovely! For me? Our
wedding cake! For this alone I
would free you, Polgunov! In any
case, I proclaim a general amnesty.
POLGUNOV: [spoken] Oh, Your Majesty, wedding
cake—this wedding cake—[sobs]
[sung] Chain and torture me;
I'm like oak.
Mention Siberia,
And I get the joke.
But show me a wedding cake
With a Cupid,
Pink and coy—
ALL THREE: And I'll show you tears,
Tears of joy.

Unused lyrics (from manuscript dated "late March 1964")

Tears of joy, tears of joy!
Yes, my beloved, these are tears of joy.
Yes, my beloved, as once more we meet,
Mine is a happiness complete, complete with
Tears of joy, joy of heart.
Heart overflowing, knowing we'll not part!
Weep, my beloved, with your long-lost boy!
Weep, my beloved, unashamed tears of joy!

FAR, FAR, FAR AWAY

Registered for copyright as an unpublished song January 28, 1965. Introduced by Alfred Marks (Potemkin) and Hy Hazell (Catherine).

POTEMKIN: Along she came and away she went,
Passion's pleasure, and damn tomorrow!
But now I know she was my true love,
Or else why this undignified sorrow?

Far, far, far away
Sails my love tonight.
Far, far, far away
All my heart's delight.
Cold, cold, cold this room,
Long each hour's flight, while
Far, far, far away
Sails my one true love
Tonight.
CATHERINE: Evermore, evermore—
POTEMKIN: Far, far, far away—
CATHERINE: They will see me smiling—
POTEMKIN: Sails my love tonight—
CATHERINE: Smiling gaily or perhaps wisely, but
Evermore, evermore—
POTEMKIN: Far, far, far away—
CATHERINE: I will be aloof and apart—
POTEMKIN: Sails my one true love—
CATHERINE: Nevermore, nevermore—
POTEMKIN: Tonight.
CATHERINE: To smile from the heart.

CUT AND UNUSED SONGS

CATHERINE THE GREAT

Intended for Potemkin, Kollenovitch, Polgunov, Radbury, Von Siegen, and ensemble. Typescripts dated March 27 and 30, 1965. Not used in show. Except for the lines "Catherine the Great" and "Little Mother Catherine," the lyrics are spoken.

POTEMKIN: Catherine the Great!
You hear the name?
Catherine the Great!
Immortal!
Catherine the Great!
Powerful—
Catherine the Great!
—but dignified.
Catherine the Great!
No suggestion—
Catherine the Great!
—of sex—
Catherine the Great!
—or scandal.
Catherine the Great!
That's my name for Catherine.
Mull it over.
Catherine the Great.

KOLLENOVITCH
AND POLGUNOV: Unforgettable.
POTEMKIN: Catherine the Great!
KOLLENOVITCH
AND POLGUNOV: What a sound!
POTEMKIN: Catherine the Great!
KOLLENOVITCH
AND POLGUNOV: Like a melody—
POTEMKIN: Catherine the Great!
KOLLENOVITCH
AND POLGUNOV: Going round—
Catherine the Great!
POTEMKIN: They'll be calling her—
KOLLENOVITCH
AND POLGUNOV: Catherine the Great!
POTEMKIN: Just you wait.
KOLLENOVITCH
AND POLGUNOV: Catherine the Great!
POTEMKIN: Only genius—
KOLLENOVITCH
AND POLGUNOV: Catherine the Great!
POTEMKIN: Could create—
ALL THREE: Such a name for Catherine,
Catherine the Great!
POTEMKIN: She deserves me.
ALL THREE: Catherine the Great!
RADBURY: Unforgettable.
KOLLENOVITCH,
POLGUNOV,
AND POTEMKIN: Catherine the Great!
RADBURY: What a name!
KOLLENOVITCH,
POLGUNOV,
AND POTEMKIN: Catherine the Great!
RADBURY: Irresistible.
KOLLENOVITCH,
POLGUNOV,
AND POTEMKIN: Catherine the Great!
RADBURY: Future fame.
KOLLENOVITCH,
POLGUNOV,
AND POTEMKIN: Catherine the Great!

VON SIEGEN: What's so great about—
KOLLENOVITCH,
POLGUNOV,
AND POTEMKIN: Catherine the Great?
RADBURY: I forget.
KOLLENOVITCH,
POLGUNOV,
AND POTEMKIN: Catherine the Great!
VON SIEGEN: What'd she ever do?
KOLLENOVITCH,
POLGUNOV,
AND POTEMKIN: Catherine the Great!
RADBURY: Nothing yet.
ALL: Still the name fits Catherine,
Catherine the Great! Yeah!
POTEMKIN: Tell the whole world.
ENSEMBLE: Catherine the Great!
POTEMKIN: Mary Queen of Scots—
ENSEMBLE: Catherine the Great!
POTEMKIN: Joan of Arc—
ENSEMBLE: Catherine the Great!
POTEMKIN: Minor characters—
ENSEMBLE: Catherine the Great!
POTEMKIN: In the dark.
WOMEN: Catherine the Great [*vocal extension*]!
MEN: Catherine the Great [*vocal extension*]!
ENSEMBLE: Catherine the Great!
POTEMKIN: What a wedding gift—
ENSEMBLE: Catherine the Great!
POTEMKIN: For my mate—
ALL: Little Mother Catherine,
Catherine the Great!

POTEMKIN'S SOLO (A WONDERFUL HUSBAND IS HE)

Intended for Potemkin. From typescript dated March 18, 1965. Frank Loesser's note: "Preceded by endless dialogue for the purpose of nailing down the point of view which provides the song. The lyrics themselves are far from final. There is at this point no music. It cannot be lively or gangy." Not used in show.

A wonderful husband is he;
From her side he never strays far.
Always punctual in the dining room
As well as in the boudoir.

A wonderful husband is he,
Always there to pet or to flog.
Such a fine domestic convenience
That she's never needed a dog.

A great reader—see him reading!
Reading her instructions what to wear.
A great thinker—see him thinking!
Thinking what to give her for her birthday.

A wonderful husband is he;
With respect his name one recalls:
So renowned for banquets he's held for her,
So famed for giving her balls.

A wonderful husband is he—
Such a husband I never will be!

THE FRUIT

Intended for Polgunov. From typescript dated March 16, 1965. Not used in show.

VERSE

I am not like most other men
And I thank the Lord.
Men indulge one animal taste
That I can't afford.
I am referring to women.
The entire world of males
So deeply long for them
That they constantly choose females
That are wrong for them.

I am not like most other men,
Yet I reach for Nirvana
In my passion for an exotic,
Succulent African temptress—

[Opens drawer and retrieves one banana]

She is called the banana.

REFRAIN

The shape
Of banana,
The feel
Of banana,
The more-than-feminine
Tenderness under the peel
Of banana.

The indescribable pleasure
Of slowly undressing her,

[He starts to peel.]

Then nibble by nibble by nibble
Caressing her,
Blessing her.

The taste
Of banana,
The touch
Of banana,
And half a dozen a night
Is not too much
Of banana.
Let man pursue every flavor of woman
Till boredom, exhaustion, or doom.
My love
Is banana, banana, banana!
Such texture! Such warmth! Such perfume!
And so safe
To bring up to one's room.

PEACEFUL HARBOR

Manuscript dated November 19, 1964. Frank Loesser's note: "This is crap on purpose. Approach scoring with *some* sophistication." Not used in show.

How I would love to gaze across a peaceful harbor
And in my sweet contentment watch the little
    white sails
And feel the comfort of the sand beneath my
    sandals
And idly listen to some quaint old fisherman's
    tales.
A man of my importance with such a busy mind
Is absolutely forced to leave all thought of rest
    behind.
There's not an idle moment to rest my busy brain.
It truly is a wonder I don't crack beneath the
    strain.
How I would love to see no more of wild horizons
And flashing storms that bid my star to rise or to
    fall.
But simply sit and gaze upon a peaceful harbor
And be just no one, no one at all.

PARTIAL MARTIAL

Intended for John Paul Jones. From typescript dated October 30, 1964, and undated manuscript. Not used in show.

You just
Bet you can trust
American know-how
For anything from a rebellion
To the milking of a cow.
So, ma'am, ready I am
To furnish a fierce fight.
At bloody and murderous battle
My technique has reached its height.
So, providing it's morally right,
Call on me now
For American know-how.

RODYINA

From typescript dated October 7, 1964. Intended for Potemkin. Frank Loesser note of September 1964: "For not too subtle madness. To be sung (generally) with maniacal calm except for a few explosions, erratic purges, etc." Not used in show.

VERSE

I was born much too magnificent
To be contained by you,
Rodyina, sweet native land.
It is I who should contain you
Here in the palm of my hand.
Rodyina,
Rodyina, please understand.

REFRAIN

Rodyina, Rodyina,
Rodyina, let me possess you.
Rodyina, Rodyina,
Rodyina, do not refuse.
Be mine to fondle,
Be mine to trample,
Mine to charm,
To chain,
To love as I may choose.

Rodyina, Rodyina,
There you lie, ripe to be taken,
Beautiful, bountiful,
Innocent, savage, and free.

Let me possess you;
I must possess you,
As this madd'ning love of you
Possesses me.

AT THE VICTORY BALL

Intended for Polgunov. From typescript dated September 2, 1964. Frank Loesser note: "This would be pretty much the introduction to the victory ball scene. It should deliver both Polgunov's enthusiasm for his metier as a producer of spectacles and illusions—as well as a chance for the gathered or gathering ensemble to join him." Not used in show.

At the victory ball,
When the war is at an end,
At the victory ball,
Oh, my brave and loyal friend,
I hug you,
I kiss you,
I bless you
And all your issue,
I crush you
To thank you
For being so brave through it all—
Not the victory,
But the victory ball!

KAT

Manuscript dated August 1963. Intended for Potemkin in Act I, scene 1. Not used in show.

I call her
My Katushka,
Which I whisper
Soft and low.

I call her
My Katushka,
Not "my darling,"
Not "my dove."

Katushka,
My Katushka,
And she melts
Like April snow.

But Katushka,
Just Katushka,
And she comes to
Me with love.

AS A MAN OF HIGH IMPORTANCE

From undated manuscript. Intended for Bureyev, Kollenovitch, Polgunov, and a priest. Not used in show.

BUREYEV: As a man of high importance,
I've an overburdened brain.
It truly is a wonder
I don't crack beneath the strain.
KOLLENOVITCH: As a man of earned position,
I keep painfully alert
To windfalls that may help me
And pitfalls that may hurt.
POLGUNOV: As a man of proven talent,
I can't loll around and dream.
My life is so exciting,
I could absolutely scream.
PRIEST: For a man of new distinction,
Every day the pressure grows.
When I seem to be upon my knees,
I'm really on my toes.
ALL: Oh, how I envy you,
You lucky, lucky man
Without one intricate scheme,
Without one devious plan.
Oh, how I envy you

Retiring at your age—
The years of indolent calm,
The fun of being offstage!

SONG FOR BOBBY

From undated manuscript. For Bob Fosse. Not intended for show.

VERSE

It's the di——rector's delight,
It's the choreographer's heaven,
On the basis of a theory ancient and profound
That the only way to sing is to sing moving
    around.

REFRAIN

I'm walking down the street [*boulevard, avenue*]
Bouncing a ball,
Bouncing a ball,
Bouncing a ball.
I'm walking down the street
Bouncing a ball,
But that's not all.

I'm walking down the street
Flying a kite,
Flying a kite,
Flying a kite.
I'm walking down the street
Flying a kite.

Raise the derby,
Swing the butt—
That's the part that'll never get cut.
Integrated? I should say!
Just listen how the number
Is a function of the play!

To a tune there's no forgetting
And a beat by which you just know the setting
Is a Bronx [*Bump the lights up.*]
Dance [*Push the drummer.*]
Hall [*Hold the freeze.*]

SEÑOR DISCRETION HIMSELF
1965–1968

SEÑOR DISCRETION HIMSELF

Also titled *Tepancingo*. Book, music, and lyrics by Frank Loesser. Based on a short story by Budd Schulberg entitled "Señor Discretion Himself." Loesser began work on this project in December 1965 and abandoned it in March 1968. The song titles, sequence, character names, most of the lyrics, and Loesser's commentary are from his only completed draft of the libretto, dated February 23, 1967. (Except where noted, the Loesser quotes are from this typescript.) As was the case with his attempts to musicalize Garson Kanin's *A Touch of the Moon* in 1957 and Jean Anouilh's *Time Remembered* in 1962, Loesser was attracted to the more ephemeral qualities of the material. In his introduction to the first draft of *Señor Discretion*, he wrote: "To my mind, this show has a *mystique* to it. I say it that way for want of a Mexican word. The mystique is not announced or heralded, as in the 'once upon a time' opener for a fairy tale. Nevertheless some magic things are going to happen as the play goes on. . . ."

PADRE, I HAVE SINNED

Registered for copyright as an unpublished song April 10, 1985. Intended for Manuel and Francisco, two Franciscan priests, and four of their parishioners ("First," "Second," etc.). The scene takes place in the confessional chamber of a church in the fictional Mexican village of Tepancingo.

FIRST: Padre, I have sinned.
   I have cursed at my little burro.
MANUEL: [*spoken*] You repent?
FIRST: [*sung*] I repent.
MANUEL: [*spoken*] Ten Ave Marias. [*calls offstage*] Francisco! Please!
FRANCISCO: [*offstage; spoken*] I come, I come.
SECOND: [*sung*] Padre, I have sinned.
   I have slapped in the face my wife.
MANUEL: [*spoken*] You repent?
SECOND: [*sung*] I repent.
MANUEL: [*spoken*] Five Ave Marias.
   [*spoken*] Francisco!

Frank Loesser, 1968

FRANCISCO: [*spoken*] I am not finished feeding the migratory birds. Also for the love of God. But what is it, my brother?
MANUEL: [*spoken*] I think I will die of boredom. Listen to these quaint little confessions.
THIRD: [*sung*] Padre, I have sinned.
   I ate hamburger steak last Friday.*
MANUEL: [*spoken*] You repent?
THIRD: [*spoken*] I repent.
MANUEL: [*spoken*] Twenty Mea Culpa. Francisco, I beg you take over.
FRANCISCO: [*spoken*] But I was on duty yesterday.
FOURTH: [*sung*] Padre, I have sinned.
   I came two minutes late for mass.†
MANUEL: [*spoken*] You repent?
FOURTH: [*sung*] I repent.
MANUEL: [*spoken*] Five Credo, five Rosarios.

TO SEE HER

Registered for copyright as an unpublished song April 10, 1985. Intended for Hilario and Francisco. Loesser described the character of Hilario:

Hilario is middle-aged, tall, robust and wide-eyed with uncanny mischief but not villainy. He can be Mastroianni, he can be Cesar Romero with eyes like Robert Newton. Or George Irving or possibly Terry-Thomas, or a large Leo Carillo. Or have you ever met Vernon Duke? Judging from his make-up, carriage and manner of speech he thinks himself both handsome and dashing. His mind darts from subject to subject, without benefit of sequitur. In short, he is a nut, if not a complete madman. Nevertheless there is no doubt that he is masculine. He also better be one hell of a baritone.

HILARIO: The blue-black hair
   Cascading over mango-flavored shoulders;
   The form which moves
   Like jelly of the guava flowing by—
   For me, to see her
   Is to want her,
   And to want her and never to have her
   Is to die.

---

* *Earlier version, December 26, 1965:*
   I ate hot dogs on Friday.

† *Earlier version, December 26, 1965:*
   I did not come to mass.

FRANCISCO: [*spoken*] She is single?
HILARIO: [*sung*] For she is only fifteen.
FRANCISCO: [*spoken*] Ay!
HILARIO: [*sung*] Fifteen.
FRANCISCO: [*spoken*] Qué calamidad!
HILARIO: [*sung*] Fifteen.
FRANCISCO: [*spoken*] You are sure?
HILARIO: [*spoken*] I do not quote the dress size.
   [*sung*] Fifteen,
   Fifteen,
   Fifteen.
FRANCISCO: [*spoken*] Anyone we know?
HILARIO: [*spoken*] Lupita.
   [*sung*] Fifteen,
   Fifteen,
   Fifteen.
FRANCISCO: [*spoken*] Lupita Hernandez? Lupita Delgado?
HILARIO: [*sung*] Fifteen,
   Fifteen,
   Fifteen.
FRANCISCO: [*spoken*] We got a lot of Lupitas.
HILARIO: [*spoken*] Not like this one.
   [*sung*] The soft young throat
   Descends into a blouse full of mere promise.
   The red lips glow
   Where just the kiss of bubble gum has been,
   And yet to see her
   Is to want her
   And to want her—oh, heaven forgive me—
   Is a sin.
BOTH: For she is only fifteen, fifteen, fifteen, Fifteen, fifteen, fifteen.
FRANCISCO: [*carried away; spoken*] One more time!
BOTH: [*sung*] Fifteen, fifteen, fifteen.
FRANCISCO: [*entranced; spoken*] Everybody!
BOTH: [*sung*] Fifteen, fifteen, fifteen.
FRANCISCO: [*spoken*] You must pray, my son.

[*Dialogue intervenes. For this final refrain,* HILARIO *is watching* LUPITA *through binoculars.*]

HILARIO: [*sung*] For me to see her
   Is to want her,
   And to want her
   And never to have her
   Is to die.

Earlier version (manuscript dated December 7, 1965)

She has the blue-black hair
Cascading over weary, sensual shoulders
Above a shape that moves

As I have rarely seen.
She has the sultry eyes
That easily could melt granite boulders
And she is only—God help us—fifteen.

But to see her is to want her;
Just to see her merely strolling along.
To see her is to want her, and want her,
And want her,
And to want her, I know, I know, I know
Is wrong.

She has the warm young neck
Just begging to be fondled and bitten.
She has the full red lips
That promise something wild.
She has a way she walks,
Concerning which the book could be written.
And she is only—oh, Jesus—a child.

But to see her is to want her,
And that brings me to the end of my song.
For to see her is to want her,
And want her, and want her,
And to want her, I know, I know,
I know is wrong.

To see her,
Just merely to see her,
To see her
Stroll deliciously by,
To see her
Is insanely to want her,
And to want her
But not have her
Is to die.

To see the blue-black hair
Cascading over young gleaming shoulders,
To see the form which moves
Like music from a siren [sex-mad] song
As she strolls along,
To see her
Is insanely to want her,
And to want her—
Oh God help me—
Is wrong.

PAN PAN PAN

Registered for copyright as an unpublished song April 10,
1985. Intended for trio. Frank Loesser envisioned this as
an elaborate production number:

The following is the basic refrain. The action will
involve not only the exhortations of the trio, but
the giving away of free samples and the happy acceptance of the crowd of shoppers—in part no
doubt choreographic. The lyrics will include the
fact that this is closing time for the day, so that by
the end of the number the bread counters will
have been withdrawn and shutters pulled over the
bakery front.

Ay, the pan, pan, pan,
Try the pan, pan, pan
From the Pan-, Pan-, Panadería Gomez.
Up in Mazatlán,
Down in Yucatán,
It's the nasch, nasch, national delicatez.
Everybody swallowing
The pan, pan, pan,
Plus the Wrap Saran,
Plus the ring-ding singing commercial which says:
Ay, the pan, pan, pan,
Try the pan, pan, pan
From the Pan-, Pan-, Panadería Gomez.

Unused lyrics (based on the Winston cigarette jingle)

Gomez tastes good
Like a [clap clap]
Loaf of bread should.

PAPA, COME HOME

Registered for copyright as an unpublished song April 10,
1985. Intended for Carolina and ensemble. Loesser saw
Carolina as "still under thirty and not bad looking.
There is a sweet comic weariness about her and although
she is dumb, she is profoundly realistic."

ENSEMBLE: Poor Carolina,
Every day outside the cantina.
Oh, it brings a teardrop to the eye
When I hear the daughter of a
drinking man
Bravely cry and cry.
CAROLINA: Papa, come home, I make you coffee.
Papa, come home, I rub your head.
Papa, come home, I make you coffee;
I take your shoes off;
I dump you into your bed.
ENSEMBLE: Poor Carolina,
She was once bonita y fina.
Ah, but who would want her for a wife?

She will be the daughter of a
drinking man
All her life, her life.
CAROLINA: Papa, come home, I make you coffee,
Or maybe soup or maybe tea.
Papa, come, I make you coffee;
I play you checkers;
I turn on color TV.
ENSEMBLE: Poor Carolina.
CAROLINA: Papa, come home, I make you coffee.
Papa, come home from this bad place.
Papa, come home, I make you coffee;
I press your trousers;
I wash your sweet, dirty face.
ENSEMBLE: Poor Carolina,
Everyday outside the cantina.

[CAROLINA gives up and starts to walk away sadly.]

ENSEMBLE: Oh, it brings a teardrop to the eye
When I hear the daughter of a
drinking man
Bravely cry and cry.

[CAROLINA exits.]

ENSEMBLE: Papa, come home, I make you coffee.
Papa, come home.
Papa, come home.
Papa, come home.

PANCITO'S SONG

Registered for copyright as an unpublished song April 10,
1985. Intended for Pancito and bartender. Loesser wrote
of Pancito:

I see Pancito as a rather small, slight man somewhere in his fifties. He is dressed in the grave
clothing of a shabby but proud businessman in
these parts. . . . Pancito's manner is one of built-
in defensive indignation. He is not drunk enough
for any physical faltering at this point, but we will
see a sort of sag to him—alternating with a quick
assumption of a rigid and huffy attitude whenever he imagines his austerity is under attack. Instant umbrage plus lordosis.

PANCITO: So the taste of you goes away
For the pleasure to spit back
The insult of every day.

"Pancito," she would call me.
"Pancito," she would sigh.

"Pancito, I will love you
Until the day I die."
"Pancito"—little bread man—
My nickname was her song.
"Pancito" spoken gently,
So gently, kept me strong.
And I never heard of dignity or grand
    esteem.
Life was warm then,
Warm and sure,
And I never for one moment knew
Of the fact that I was poor,
Ignorante, small and poor.
"Pancito," she would call me.
"Pancito," she would sigh.
"Pancito, I will love you
Until the day I die."
But the day came!
Ay, that day came
And they put her in the ground.
Providencia, mi amor.
And when she died,
Then I also died
And Pancito was no more,
That Pancito was no more.
"Pancito," she would call me.
"Pancito," she would sigh.
"Pancito, I will love you
Until the day I die."

BARTENDER: [spoken] Hey, Pancito, come on back
    in. I fill everybody up again. What
    do you drink?
PANCITO: [spoken] What do I drink? What I
    drink is none of your business, is
    what I drink.
    [sung] I drink dignity,
    I drink pride,
    To fill up the feeling of nothing
        inside.
BARTENDER: [spoken] Pancito! Come on! It's your
    deal. You'll catch cold out there,
    Pancito.
PANCITO: [sung] "Pancito," now they call me,
    "Pancito," with a sneer,
    "Pancito, you are nothing
    But wind from your last beer."
BARTENDER: [spoken] Come on, Pancito.
PANCITO: [spoken] Do not whistle at me in the
    streets. I am not a dog.
BARTENDER: [spoken] I am sorry. Excuse me.
PANCITO: [sung] "Pancito," she would call me.
    "Pancito," she would sigh.
    "Pancito, I will love you
    Until the day I die."

WORLD PEACE

Registered for copyright as an unpublished song April 10, 1985. Intended for Martin, the schoolteacher, whom Loesser saw as "a sweet, sloppy, absent-minded professor of twenty-seven years, with shaggy hair that has not been combed in a week. . . . Martin speaks at all times in a gentle and patient voice, which goes along with his manner of seeking to please people."

I think about world peace, the end of human
    strife.
The problem of world peace, it occupies my
    life.
And while I am concentrating
Sometimes I forget to comb my hair;
I trip on my shoelaces
And spill soup on what I wear—
In favor of world peace, and hoping it comes
    true—
And speaking of world peace, it might occur to
    you
That dopey old butterfinger, absent-minded
Slob though I may be,
The man who drops the bomb
Will make a lousier mess than me.

IF YOU LOVE ME, YOU'LL FORGIVE ME

Earlier version of Martin's song; replaced by "World Peace." Manuscript dated February 21, 1966.

Today is Monday—
Or is it maybe Friday?
Hey, look, my socks don't match,
And I cannot find my glasses.
I forgot to wind the clock,
But anyhow it is broken.
So what the hell?—
The company is pleasant
And the friendship is sweet
And if you love me, you'll forgive me
That I am not neat.

Alternate version (from undated manuscript)

If you love me, you forgive me
That I seldom comb my hair;
That I cannot find my glasses,

Which I know I put somewhere;
That my necktie always tells you
What I lately had to eat—
If you love me, you forgive me
That I am not neat.

YOU UNDERSTAND ME

Registered for copyright as an unpublished song April 10, 1985. Intended for Hilario, to be sung to Pancito. Frank Loesser notes: "This is a complete refrain of the piece. Maybe it will be worth more. Possibly there is a contribution by Pancito. Anyway, during the song we should be able to observe Pancito's growing comfort with the acceptance of his new friend." A recording by Jo Sullivan Loesser and Emily Loesser is on the compact disc *Loesser by Loesser* (DRG).

You understand me.
You understand me,
Though you and I have points of view
Great oceans apart.
You understand me
As nature planned me;
You see my faults with open mind
And generous heart.

How did I find you,
Sweet gentle kind you,
In all this world of heedless hearts
Where sadly I dwell?
You do not strand me
Nor reprimand me;
You understand me
So very well.

HEAVEN SMILES ON TEPANCINGO

Registered for copyright as an unpublished song April 10, 1985. Martin's sequence (lines 13–17) registered for copyright as an unpublished song April 10, 1985, under the title "Lowenbrau to Heaven Smiles." Intended for Pancito, Martin, Hilario, and ensemble.

PANCITO: If there has come some kind of
    blessing,
    It is not meant only for me.

I seem to find heaven caressing
Ev'ry face I see.

Heaven smiles on Tepancingo,
Little town of little fame.
Little town of Tepancingo,
But the angels know the name.
Heaven smiles on Tepancingo
And with hearts full of content,
Tepancingo smiles at heaven
To return the compliment.

[ENSEMBLE *reprises lines 5–12, followed by dialogue interlude.*]

MARTIN: He was an angry man
Day after loveless day,
But now the anger has faded,
Faded, faded
Away.
ENSEMBLE: Little town of Tepancingo,
But the angels know the name.
HILARIO: [*spoken*] Pancito, I cannot be seen like this. Is there a nearby tailor-haberdasher?
PANCITO: [*spoken*] The very finest. My dear friend the neighbor Negrin.
ENSEMBLE: [*sung*] Heaven smiles on Tepancingo.
HILARIO: [*spoken*] You must advise me what to wear. I am a trifle too flamboyant.
PANCITO: [*spoken*] I like it.
HILARIO: [*spoken*] See Carolina? He gives me courage! Perhaps, Pancito, you might select for yourself, something—
PANCITO: [*spoken*] Yes—a little less dignified.
HILARIO: [*spoken*] And afterward we go somewhere and have a drink. A toast to this occasion, which I wish always to remember!
PANCITO: [*spoken*] But—I no longer drink.
ENSEMBLE: [*sung*] Heaven smiles at Tepancingo,
And with hearts full of content—
PANCITO: [*spoken*] I too wish to remember.
ENSEMBLE: [*sung*] Tepancingo smiles at heaven
To return the compliment.

Earlier version

Tepancingo, Tepancingo,
Little town of no great fame.
If you come to Tepancingo,
Tepancingo is glad you came.
Heaven smiles on Tepancingo;
See how sweetly and content
Tepancingo smiles at heaven
To return the compliment.

I LOVE HIM, I THINK

Registered for copyright as an unpublished song April 10, 1985. Intended for Lupita, whom Loesser described as an underage version of *How to Succeed*'s Hedy LaRue: "Lupita . . . presents quite a precocious image despite her schoolgirl clothing . . . perhaps a sultry way of swinging her school books from their strap, but when she starts to cross [the stage] she confirms a great many of Hilario's wild impressions." Loesser's treatment of this scene harks back to his days at the Hollywood studios.

I love him, I think;
I am not sure.
I only think;
I think I want him a lot.
Also I think
I know for what.
In many old, old películas I see
Late, late at night on the screen of my tee-vee:
[*spoken*] Produced by Warner Brothers.

[*sung*] There is this girl who is too young for the man,
But in her heart is a great romantic plan.
[*spoken*] Music by Max Steiner.

[*sung*] For three long years, he and she are thrown together.
First on a steamboat in very stormy weather,
Then on a small island where they dance the hula,
Then in her grandmother's house in Ashtabula.
[*spoken*] Montages by Slavko Vorkapich.

[*sung*] Three years have passed and then at last
One night they stand very close to one another.
He kisses her like he never kissed his mother.
[*spoken*] Music by Max Steiner!!

[*sung*] He says, "I love you."
She says, "I love you."
[*spoken*] Additional dialog by George Oppenheimer.

[*sung*] And that is always the ending of the play.
So maybe I should be planning things that way,
Because—
I love him, I think;
I am not sure;
I only think;
I think I want him a lot.
Also I think
I know for what.
The same like Doris Day,

The same like Alice Faye
Or even Martha Raye.
I will wait and see.
For if I love him, I think
That in the ending,
He's got to love me.

Unused lyrics (from manuscript dated December 18, 1966)

There is a man and a girl who meet by chance,
And she is crazy about him at one glance.
[*spoken*] Directed by Raoul Walsh.

[*sung*] But he is not even dreaming of romance.
He is the prince. She is the maid.
She wants to love. He is afraid.
He is the boss. She is the clerk.
She is all heart. He is all jerk.
[*spoken*] Screenplay by Panama and Frank.
[*sung*] But all at once he and she are thrown together
Upon the high seas in very stormy weather.

Earlier version (manuscript dated September 16, 1966)

I love him [you], I think.
I don't know, but I think
I want you close by.
I don't know, really, why
I feel you in my heart.
I don't know, but maybe,
If I love you, I think,
Maybe sometime you are going to love me.

VERSE

Suddenly very hungry,
They grab each other,
And he kisses her
Like he never kissed his mother.

COMPAÑEROS

Registered for copyright as an unpublished song April 10, 1985. Intended for Hilario and Pancito.

We are henceforth and forever
Compañeros, compañeros
In whatever we endeavor,
Compañeros, you and I.
Arm in arm we will walk,

Heart to heart we will talk,
Eye to eye we will see—
What a team,
What a team we will be!
Like a big and little brother,
Compañeros, compañeros,
A companion for each other,
Plus a partner, plus a friend.
Compañeros—and to the end.

JULIO'S FIRST SONG

Typescript December 5, 1966. Intended for Julio, who is about Lupita's age.

She acts so cold and strange
And she is my heart's choice.
I wish that things would change,
Especially my voice.

MEXICO CITY

Registered for copyright as an unpublished song April 10, 1985. Intended for Martin, Hilario, and Carolina.

MARTIN: Mexico City,
Mexico City,
Mexico City,
Mexico City.
That is my scheme,
That is my goal,
That is the dream
Deep in my soul—
Mexico City.
HILARIO: Lupita.
MARTIN: Mexico City.
CAROLINA: Hilario.
MARTIN: Mexico City.
CAROLINA: Hilario.
MARTIN: Mexico City.
ALL THREE: That is my scheme,
That is my goal,
That is the dream
Deep in my soul.
MARTIN: [spoken] Well, good night.
HILARIO: [spoken] Good night.
CAROLINA: [spoken] Good night.
MARTIN: [sung] Mexico City.

HILARIO: Lupita.
MARTIN: Mexico City.
CAROLINA: Hilario.
HILARIO: Lupita.
CAROLINA: Hilario.
CAROLINA
AND HILARIO: That is my scheme,
That is my goal,
That is the dream
Deep in my soul.
CAROLINA: [spoken] Goodnight, Hilario.
HILARIO: [spoken] Goodnight.
CAROLINA: [sung] Hilario.
HILARIO: Lupita.
CAROLINA: Hilario.
HILARIO: Lupita.
CAROLINA: Hilario.
HILARIO: Lupita, Lupita.

[HILARIO *is doused with water.*]

HILARIO: Brrrr.

I ONLY KNOW

Intended for Julio. For this scene, Loesser notes, "Julio is eighteen years old. He has a Beatle haircut. He wears a motorcycle jacket and boots, which make him taller. He is playing a guitar and, of all things, he has a manly non-breaking voice with which he sings—passionato Senza Cervello."

I only know, babe,
I only know;
I only know, babe,
I only know—

I only know, babe,
I only know;
I only know, babe,
I only know—

I only know, babe,
I only know—
Three chords on the guitar.

HASTA LA VISTA

Registered for copyright as an unpublished song April 10, 1985. Intended for ensemble. Frank Loesser wrote the following before the melody was finished:

> However raised your eyebrows, I do not apologize for this exercise in banality. As you will see shortly, it turns out to be the *background for something else.* While these lyrics are not as picturesque as those of "Vaya Con Dios" or "Aloha Oe" or "Till We Meet Again"—they form a song that classifies similarly. I have no tune yet. I should only write one as good as one of the three mentioned above, and you would see a joyous Jewish composer! I think this should be with divided voices. It depends on the tune.

Hasta la vista;
I will see you soon again.
Hasta la vista;
God be with you until then.
Hasta la vista;
Though you journey far away,
Hasta la vista
Is a happy thing to say.
Tell me your farewell
With no tears,
Knowing that farewell
Does not mean a thousand years,
But only
Hasta la vista;
I will see you soon again.
Hasta la vista;
God be with you until then.

DON'T DRINK

Intended for Negrin (a townsperson) to sing as a countermelody as the ensemble sings "Hasta la Vista."

ENSEMBLE: Hasta la vista;
NEGRIN: Don't drink the bottled water,
ENSEMBLE: I will see you soon again.
NEGRIN: No matter what you do.
ENSEMBLE: Hasta la vista;
NEGRIN: They boil it and they strain it,
ENSEMBLE: God be with you until then.
NEGRIN: Which is very bad for you.
ENSEMBLE: Hasta la vista;
NEGRIN: Don't drink the bottled water;
ENSEMBLE: Though you journey far away.

NEGRIN: It will thin you out the blood.
ENSEMBLE: Hasta la vista . . .
NEGRIN: No color and no flavor,
ENSEMBLE: Is a happy thing to say.
NEGRIN: And the bottom got no mud.
ENSEMBLE: Tell me your farewell . . .
NEGRIN: In the big town,
ENSEMBLE: With no tears,
NEGRIN: Smoke a lot of strong cigars,
ENSEMBLE: Knowing that farewell . . .
NEGRIN: Fool around with fancy women,
ENSEMBLE: Does not mean a thousand years . . .
NEGRIN: Walk in front of trolley cars.
ENSEMBLE: But only hasta la vista;
NEGRIN: But don't get sanitary,
ENSEMBLE: I will see you soon again.
NEGRIN: Like some gringo from New York.
ENSEMBLE: Hasta la vista;
NEGRIN: Don't drink the bottled water,
ENSEMBLE: God be with you until then.
NEGRIN: Or you're going to need the cork.

GOODBYE AGITATO

Registered for copyright as an unpublished song April 10, 1985. Intended for Lupita, singing to Martin. Loesser was typically particular about how this scene should be played:

The following is delivered in a frenzy of self-enforced preoccupation with little tidyings and packings. In the absence of a sample performance at the moment, I submit that the phrase "I love you" is purposefully delivered en passant with no emphasis, as if Lupita means to say casually that the subject is understood, and that they must get down to the business of his departure.

Goodbye, goodbye, goodbye, I love you,
Have you got the ticket
Safely in your pocket?
Goodbye, goodbye, goodbye, I love you,
Also the umbrella,
Just in case of rain?
Goodbye, goodbye, I think I hear the train—
Goodbye, goodbye, goodbye, goodb—

[Immediate seque into the next song, "I Cannot Let You Go." Loesser notes: "Now she simply cannot resist the pressure of the real emotional point. Without skipping a fraction of a beat it pours out with sincere passion in sequence from what you have just read."]

I CANNOT LET YOU GO

Registered for copyright as an unpublished song April 10, 1985. Intended for Lupita. A recording by Emily Loesser and Don Stephenson is on the compact disc *Loesser by Loesser* (DRG). Loesser notes: "For those musically concerned, it happens that one section of this tune is countermelodic with the others, and so there is a musically kosher duet with which to conclude this love scene." He had a hopeful vision of this conclusion: "This finish is accomplished in a clinch which freezes for predictably wild well-deserved applause."

I cannot let you go.
I cannot let you out of my arms.
Now that your lips are warm upon mine
And eagerly my fingers caress your hair,
I cannot let you go
Without the sudden feeling of doom and despair.
To think of losing you,
Losing you only for a little while
Chills my heart,
And I cannot smile and be brave;
I am both captor and slave.
I say the word goodbye,
But I can hear my soul crying
No!
I cannot,
I cannot ever
Let you go.

Earlier version

To me, the ways of love are new;
My heart is far from clever.
One little day apart from you
Would seem to be forever,
For I am not chic or smart or clever;
So to part with you for a day or a week
Is to me forever.
I say the word "goodbye,"
And yet I hear my soul crying
No!
I cannot,
I cannot ever
Let you go.

GOODBYE AGITATO/ I CANNOT LET YOU GO (Reprise)

Registered for copyright as an unpublished song April 10, 1985. Intended for Lupita and Martin.

LUPITA: Goodbye, goodbye, goodbye.
MARTIN: I love you.
LUPITA: Have you got the ticket
Safely in your pocket?
Goodbye, goodbye, goodbye.
MARTIN: I love you.
LUPITA: Also the umbrella,
Just in case of rain?
Goodbye, goodbye, I think I hear the train—
Goodbye, goodbye,
Goodbye, goodbye,
Goodbye, goodbye,
Goodb—
I say the word goodbye,
But I can hear my soul crying
No!
I cannot,
I cannot ever
Let him go.

THE WISDOM OF THE HEART

Registered for copyright as an unpublished song April 10, 1985. Intended for Lupita. Frank Loesser described the desired effect: "This is one small section of the piece. . . . Shortly Lupita is joined by others on the stage in turn, and the song accumulates a bigness of delivery and insistent pulse. . . . When the total lyric content has been delivered in full once, I visualize the continued use of it as doggerel."

The wisdom of the heart,
The heart inside of you,
It says you what to say,
It does you want to do.
There is no need to be
So very special smart.
The far better wisdom
Is the wisdom of the heart.

Additional lyrics (from manuscript dated February 1, 1967)

The wisdom of the heart
Is very, very real.
It wants you what you want;
It feels you how you feel.
You do not have to be
So clever and so smart
To find inside yourself
The wisdom of the heart.

The wisdom of the heart,
The heart inside of me,
It means me what I mean;
It sees me what I see.
It books you with no book.
It charts you with no chart.
Believe inside yourself
The wisdom of the heart,
The Rimsky corset cover
Wisdom of the heart.
The better wisdom is
The wisdom of the heart.

(from manuscript dated February 2, 1967)

The wisdom of the heart,
It feels you how you feel,
When right is slightly wrong
And false is almost real.
It reads you from no book,
It guides you from no chart.
The far better wisdom is
The wisdom of the heart.

TRAVELING CARNIVAL

Typescript dated February 21, 1966. Registered for copyright as an unpublished song April 10, 1985. Intended for ensemble. Song not included in February 23, 1967, script.

Run, run, run
To the traveling carnival.
Grab your fun
Till the break of the day.
Grab your fun
Before the carnival travels away.

The joys of life,
Like the traveling carnival,
Come around
Only once in a while.

Grab your fun,
Treat your face to a beautiful smile.
All too soon they will pull up stakes,
Roll away, with the canvas furled;
All too soon you are back
In your workaday world, so—

Run, run, run
To the traveling carnival.
Grab your fun
Till the break of the day.
Run, run, run,
Grab your fun
Before the carnival travels away.

GOT TO HAVE A SOMEBODY

Typescript dated February 21, 1966. Registered for copyright as an unpublished song April 10, 1985. Intended for Lupita and ensemble. Song not included in February 23, 1967, script.

I got to have a somebody, somebody
Walking with me,
A caballero very good-looking and tall.
Well, anyway, a somebody, somebody
Walking with me,
Or I will be a nobody,
Nobody at all.

I got to have a somebody all full of masculine charm
To take me for a stroll on the plaza tonight.
Well, anyway, a somebody who I can take by the arm
To show to everybody I
Am doing all right.

Oh, señor, por favor,
Feed a woman's ego.
Dear señor, por favor,
Be a good amigo
And away we go.

I got to have a somebody, somebody
Walking with me,
A caballero very good-looking and tall.
Well, anyway, a somebody, somebody
Walking with me,
Or I will be obliged to feel
Unwanted and small,
Just nobody,
Nobody at all.

Unused lyrics (from undated manuscript)

Hey, look, I got a somebody rich and well-known.
You thought I was a nobody, nobody, nobody much,
And now I got a somebody, somebody.
Yee, hee, hee, hee, hee,
A man of my own.

HILARIO'S HOME-MADE BALLAD

From typescript dated February 21, 1966, and undated manuscript. Intended for Hilario. Song not included in February 23, 1967, script.

I love the color blue;
It looks just like the sky.
It also looks like robin's eggs
And Ricardo Levine's glass eye.
Ricardo Levine?
Ricardo Levine?
I don't think we ever met.

I love the number nine;
It's round and yet it's curly.
It has a smell like fifty-four,
But it happens a lot more early.
Ricardo Levine,
Ricardo Levine,
He died from democracy.

So fight, fight, fight with all your might
While I recall the thrill of it all last night.

I love the color blue;
I love it more than yellow.
I love it more than marble cake
Or that pretty French maid in *Othello*.
Ricardo Levine!
Ricardo Levine!
At last I am in my arms.

AS LONG AS HE IS ONLY A DREAM

Described by Loesser as an "Incomplete Sketch." Typescript dated February 21, 1966. Registered for copyright as an unpublished song April 10, 1985. Intended for Lupita. Song not included in February 23, 1967, script.

As long as he is only a dream,
He might as well be very handsome.
I might as well give him a small black mustache,
A talent for dancing, and plenty of money,
A charming smile,
A purple sports car,
And sex appeal in the extreme.
I might as well make him impossible,
As long as he's only a dream.

NOW I LOVE HER

Manuscript dated December 12, 1965. Song not included in February 23, 1967, script.

Now I love her;
Never before did I love her—
Or did I?
Well, anyway, now I love her,
Now that it's all too late.

THE REAL CURSE OF DRINK

From undated manuscript. Song not included in February 23, 1967, script.

What did I say—last night—what did I say?
Who(m) did I curse, who(m) did I damn?
How many doors did I slam?

How many friends did I meet last night
Who will not be my friends anymore?

How many friends that I spoke to
Now are no longer speaking to me?

The real curse of drink
Is the torture of trying to think.

Last night where was I?
And what da-da-da did I say?
Last night, how many friends did I run into,
Tell me how many,
Who are no longer friends today?

Last night where was I?
Last night, how many friends did I run into
For the purpose of knocking them down?

MARTIN (TO THE PTA)

Undated manuscript. Intended for Martin. Song not included in February 23, 1967, script.

My mother, she is ignorant,
And my father is a clown.
I come from Tepancingo,
Which is not much of a town.

The schoolhouse was a two-by-four;
The teacher's brains were dim—
My parents paid the taxes,
And the taxes paid for him.

So of course I rose above it all;
It's a hard climb to the top.
My mother, she is middle-class;
My father owns a shop.
I come from Cuernavaca,
Where the fast trains never stop.

THE PADRE

Fragment. From undated manuscript. Song not included in February 23, 1967, script.

The Padre connected to the Abbot,
The Abbot connected to the Bishop,
The Bishop connected to the Cardinal;
Now hear the word of the Lord.

From left to right: John Loesser, Hanna Loesser, Frank Loesser, Jo Sullivan Loesser, Susan Loesser

Trunk Songs and Verse
1939–1969

AND THEN WE MET

From an undated piano-vocal sheet. Music by Peter Tinturin (b. 1910). Probably written in the 1940s. Tinturin, who wrote, directed, and produced army shows during World War II, collaborated with lyricist Jack Lawrence on "Foolin' Myself" and "What Will I Tell My Heart?"

Once there was an angel,
A lovely angel who came to me in my dreams
And promised she would reappear,
Maybe some day, maybe some year.
Foolish little notion,
The strange devotion
That made me cling to my dreams.
But suddenly they all came true
The very moment I saw you.

And then we met and so I loved you,
That's all the heart within me knows.
And since we met, I've always loved you,
That's how my simple story goes.
I'd never known a kiss
That made me thrill like this;
I'd never been in love before.
And then we met and so I loved you,
And now I'll give my heart away no more.

I MET YOU

From an undated manuscript. Also called "My Simple Story." Based on "And Then We Met," music by Peter Tinturin. The lyric was considered for *Guys and Dolls* but never included in the score.

I was the wicked wolf last night
And you were the helpless lamb.
Now who's in love?
I'm in love,
Witless wolf that I am.
Now we could try to analyze
The turning of the tables,
And tag my state of mind
With many psychiatric labels,
Or blame it on the starlight
Or on some trick of fate.
But darling, when we tell our kids,
Let's tell it to them straight:

That I met you,
And all at once I loved you,

And that's the way my simple story goes.
I met you,
And all at once I loved you,
And how it happened heaven only knows.
I was proud of my precious freedom,
Glad of my empty heart,
Sure of step on any path I chose;
And then—
I met you,
And all at once I loved you,
And that's the way my simple story goes.

APRIL IN APRIL

This is a Loesser lyric inserted into the E. Y. Harburg and Vernon Duke song "April in Paris." It was to be sung to a portion of George Gershwin's *An American in Paris*. Loesser wrote it in the mid-1940s for his first wife, Lynn, to sing at parties. The musical arrangement for this unusual hybrid is not known to survive. A portion of Yip Harburg's lyric for "April in Paris" is quoted at the end to indicate how Loesser's words were to blend in.

I was blue,
Alone in Paris I was blue,
Far from ev'ry friend I ever knew.
I'd go to Ciro's for an hour
Or climb the Eiffel Tower for the view
And dream of home
All winter through.
Sad,
I'd never been so very sad
Till
I found the thrill I never had.
It was the breaking of the springtime,
The sentimental springtime of Paree.
You'd understand if you could see

[April in Paris,
Chestnuts in blossom, etc.]

ASKING FOR TROUBLE

From an undated typescript labeled "Incomplete." Probably written in the late 1940s or early 1950s. A private recording by Frank Loesser is on the compact disc *Frank Sings Loesser* (Koch).

I'm only asking for trouble
Each time we kiss,

Each time I let the warmth of you melt me down.
I'm like a child walking right into danger,
Taking candy from a stranger
On the wrong side of town.
Why don't I run on the double
From your embrace
And never learn what heartbreak is all about?
I'm only asking for all kinds of trouble,
And you're much too ready to hand it out.

THE BOYCOTT: A WALTZ FOR ANYBODY–1964

From manuscript dated 1964. Loesser note reads: "To be harmonized by a laughing happy white banjo-playing sheriff."

Your sister has the secret hots
For my highly paid educated very black butler
So?
Secede!
Secede!
Secede!
You finks, you stinkers
You Coca-Cola drinkers!
Secede and let the grasses
Grow over your piss poor asses
And swing by your nuts
Till I buy Carolina butts
Or shirts made in Al-abam
Or one stale Virginia ham
And hang by your shriveled tits
Till I go down and spend two bits
On one lousy Mardi Gras
Or one weekend with your Ma!
Secede!
Secede!
Secede!

THE DELICATESSEN OF MY DREAMS

From an undated piano-vocal sheet. Probably mid-1940s. Frank Loesser and his first wife, Lynn, performed this at Hollywood parties.

HE: Join me, my sweet, for a bite to eat
    In the delicatessen of my dreams.

SHE: Tempt me, my prince, with a handmade blintz
    In the land where the Russian dressing gleams,
BOTH: Where salamis are endlessly long and lovely
    And the liverwurst is bursting at the seams.
HE: You will be mine—
SHE: By the kosher sign—
BOTH: In the delicatessen of my dreams!

SHE: Lead me, my love, to that realm above,
    To the delicatessen of my dreams.
HE: Help me, my mate, to a heaping plate,
    Where the celery tonic gently streams,
BOTH: Where the herring are patiently marinating
    As the hot pastrami sits around and steams.
HE: We shall return—
SHE: For one sweet heartburn—
BOTH: To the delicatessen of my dreams!

EVERY LOVE

From an undated piano-vocal sheet.

VERSE 1

Oh, that fiery kiss,
Oh, those haunting eyes,
Oh, that warm and tender hand!
Yes, I'm dreaming of yesterday's loves, my
    darling,
But try to understand,
Try to understand that—

REFRAIN

Ev'ry love I've ever known
Still lingers in my heart;
Ev'ry one a memory
That simply won't depart.
Ev'ry time I'm all alone,
They wander into view;
There's ev'ry love I've ever known,
And ev'ry love is you.

VERSE 2

Oh, that quiet café,
Oh, that masquerade,
Oh, that moonlit autumn sky!

Yes, I'm dreaming of yesterday's loves, my
    darling,
But I have told you why,
I have told you why, for—

REPEAT REFRAIN

FOR GOD AND GIDEON

Manuscript dated October 1968. No music is known to exist.

One of his last lyrics, this is all that survives of Loesser's attempt to musicalize Paddy Chayevsky's play *Gideon*. Jo Sullivan Loesser recalled that, "Paddy didn't really want him to do it. Frank imagined God coming out of the orchestra pit." Loesser's health was failing and the project was quickly abandoned. He died July 28, 1969, of lung cancer.

For God and Gideon,
God and Gideon,
Warriors,
I call warriors.
Come all warriors
To me.

To arms,
I call you to arms,
To battle for
Gideon and God,
Gideon and God,
Gideon
And God.

HELEN TO RICKY
(After Dialogue about Smoking, Drinking, etc.)

From undated manuscript. Probably 1964.

Mommies are wiser than Daddies.
Somehow or other it's true.
Mommies have always told Daddies
Exactly what to say,
Exactly what to do.
Daddies are larger than Mommies.
Daddies play fine volleyball,

But Mommies are wiser than
Doctor Spock or Rod Larocque
Or even Louis Nizer
And Daddies are just little boys grown tall.

I COULD HAVE TOLD YOU

From undated piano-vocal sheet labeled "Basic Version."

I could have told you
That you'd be crying.
I could have told you
How blue you'd feel.
I could have told you
That somebody else's sweetheart
Was strictly to look at,
Not something to steal.

I could have told you
His arms might hold you,
But he would let things
Go just so far.
And that before you get much older,
You'd be crying on my shoulder,
And sure enough, baby, here you are.

LES OEUFS (BALLS)

Lyric from a manuscript dated May 1963. Music from undated manuscript.

You gave hundreds of parties and banquets
That my mind only dimly recalls,
But my heart remembers what I love most:
Balls!

You set fireworks off on my birthday,
But that memory hardly enthralls
Like the madcap, flamboyant way you held your
Balls!

In the winter they dazzled the Waldorf;
In the summer you brought them outdoors.
They were so big,
Ah, but so big.
Of course everyone knew they were yours.

And you tossed them each time in my honor;
In return dear, the least I can do

253

Is to raise up my glass
And propose a toast:
Balls to you!

A MAN CAN BE TALENTED AND ALSO BE NICE

From an undated manuscript. No music is known to
exist.

A woman inspired young Meyerbeer.
She'd often help Meyerbeer buy a beer,
And he in return made it clear once or twice
That a man can be talented and also be nice.

A woman stood right behind César Franck,
Or how could poor César Franck raise a franc?
So he in response to her loyal support
Proved a man can be talented and still be a sport.

A woman paid rent once for Scriabin
Or else how immoral could he a-been?
Sonatas cost money, but fun was still fun.
Yes, a man can be talented in more ways than one.

A woman was there when Scarlatti wrote
And that's why Scarlatti wrote what he wrote.
He always was in when the lady would call.
Yes, a man can be talented and also play ball.

LYRICS FOR A LEADING MAN IN AN UNCONVINCING OPERETTA

From an undated manuscript. Probably written in the
1960s.

This is a poem that says
That I love you—
Says that I love you so much I could die.
This is a poem that says
How I love you—
Love you much better than
Choc'late, vanilla,
Or straw-berry lemon or lime—
Love you much better than

Money or virtue or
Money or distance or time
Or money or reason or rhyme.
This is a poem that swears that I love you.
This is a terrible lie.

MY OPENING SONG

From an undated typed lyric sheet. No music is known
to exist.

This is my opening song,
My opening song.
My agent insisted on an opening song,
A chance to show off my hairdo and my raiment.
It's not to be confused with entertainment,
It's just an opening song,
An opening song.
I promise you faithfully it won't be too long.
Will the waiters all kindly retreat?
Will that couple right there be discreet?
Will the man who's in charge of the mike see that
    nothing goes wrong?
One two three four, one two three four, hello out
    there—
That's the end of my opening song.

NOSTALGIA

From an undated piano-vocal sheet. Loesser wrote this
lyric (probably in the mid-1940s) to a Mexican folk song
for his first wife, Lynn, to sing at parties.

Years have come and years have gone,
And never does a new day dawn
With solace for my melancholy heart.
And never does the twilight fall
But that I find myself recalling you I left
    behind me.

And never can another kiss
Make such a helpless, homeless,
Endless pain as this depart.
Years have come and years have gone,
And never does a new day dawn
With solace for my melancholy heart.

Nostalgia.
I have moments of nostalgia,

Tender moments when my eyes are full
Of longing for the sight of you.
Nostalgia.
Like the wind upon an ember
When a song of love can make my heart
    remember
The delight of you.

Nostalgia.
For that sleepy little village
By the ocean in the starlight that was paradise,
And then,
And then goodbye.
And now these everlasting moments of nostalgia
Tell me there you are
And here am I.

ON THE OTHER SIDE OF THE ROOM

From an undated lyric sheet. No music is known to
exist.

Here am I,
Full of that feeling of gloom,
Lonely, though you're only
On the other side of the room.

Here I sigh,
Suddenly facing my doom.
Clearly you are merely
On the other side of the room.

Just suppose we should really part—
Heaven knows, you could break my heart,

When here am I,
Full of that feeling of gloom,
Lonely, though you're only
On the other side of the room.

ON THE ROAD TO ROMANCE

From an undated lyric sheet. No music is known to exist.

Far from the sorrow and sin, far from the clamor
    and din,

Far from the busy old avenue you're working
    in,
Far from the struggle and strife, out of your
    workaday life,
Lies a most beautiful street
Where lonely hearts may meet.

Go and find the one you love
On the road to romance.
Stars will guide you from above
On the road to romance.
She'll be listening for your song;
Then you'll meet as you stroll along,
And soon two hearts together will dance
On the road to romance!

TELL ME NO TALL, TALL TALE

From an undated piano-vocal sheet.

VERSE

He was building the customary building,
He was lying the customary lie,
He was being the very gay romancer,
And then he got his answer
As she let fly:

REFRAIN

Tell me no tall, tall tale about your love,
Tell me no tall, tall tale about your love,
Tell me no tall, tall tale,
Keep it on a small, small scale,
Tell me no tall, tall tale about your love.

You talk of mountains.
High mountains you would climb for me.
You talk of oceans,
Deep oceans you would swim.
You talk of yearning,
Such yearning all the time for me.
Well, I'm only a whim;
Why go out on a limb, Jim?

Tell me no tall, tall tale about your love,
Tell me no tall, tall tale about your love,
Tell me no tall, tall tale,
Keep it on a small, small scale,
Tell me no tall, tall tale about your love.

THAT WAS MY LOVE I GAVE YOU

From an undated piano-vocal sheet.

That was my love I gave you;
That was no casual kiss in the night.
That was my love I gave you
With young, eager delight.

That was my heart I poured out;
Those were no meaningless words of some song.
That was my heart I poured out
The night you came along.

Not that it matters now, awf'lly much,
Now that we're, shall we say, "out of touch."
Not that it matters now, after all,
But that moment with me, you may vaguely
    recall—

That was my love I gave you
For your collection of small souvenirs.
That was my love I gave you,
And these, these are my tears.

THE WIND BLOWS IN MY WINDOW

From an undated piano-vocal sheet. A slightly altered version of the first four lines was used in "Summertime Love" from *Greenwillow*.

REFRAIN

Oh, the wind blows in my window,
The wind blows in my door,
The wind blows down the chimney
And up through the crack in the floor.
Oh, the wind blows in the nighttime,
The wind blows in the day;
But the way I've sinned,
It'll take more wind
To blow my sins away.

VERSE 1

Wife number one had a ruby-red ring;
She was the wife I shot.
For the ruby-red ring was the genuine thing,
And wife number one was not.

REPEAT REFRAIN

VERSE 2

Wife number two was a very poor cook;
She was the wife I drowned.
'Twas the watery brew of her very own stew
Where wife number two was found.

REPEAT REFRAIN

VERSE 3

Wife number three was a likable gal;
She was the wife I hanged.
For it happened to be that she never liked
    me,
So wife number three be danged.

REPEAT REFRAIN

YESTERDAY'S LOVE

From an undated lyric sheet. No music is known to exist.

Last night we kissed goodbye, and now you're
    gone,
And yet, you're lingering on,
For now the morning light reveals again
The tender scene we played then;
This lonely room contains such bittersweet
    remains.

Two glasses are empty today,
Still fragrant from our last frappé,
Sweet memories of yesterday's love.

And here's that gardenia you wore,
Still begging for one hour more,
Still whispering of yesterday's love.

Poor forlorn souvenirs, they'll disappear
    today.
But not my dreams, not my tears—
They'll be here, here to stay.

Soft voices, and footsteps at night,
Drawn curtains, and warm amber light . . .
These always will be precious to me,
Sweet memories of yesterday's love.

UNTITLED— FOR GORDON JENKINS

From an undated lyric sheet. Frank Loesser note: "These are substitute lyrics for the humming parts." To be sung to the tune of "A Tune for Humming" (page 135).

All day,
All night,
It tells me the world's all right,
This gay little roundelay,
All night,
All day.

Come rain,
Come shine,
It sings in this heart of mine,
Around and around again,
Come shine,
Come rain.

With joy,
With love,
Sing high to the sky above.
Sing out, little girl and boy,
With love,
With joy.

UNTITLED— ON CARDBOARD

Written on the cardboard backing of a sketchpad. Probably 1960s. The underlining and punctuation are Loesser's.

We are
Down to the
Cardboard—
The suck-tooth poor;
And that's what <u>I'm</u>
And that's what <u>you're</u>.

NO SALES SLIP NECESSARY

Typescript dated December 27, 1939. Submitted to *Saturday Evening Post*, but not accepted for publication.

You'll find no red whiskers on me, my friend,
No reindeer and bells all a-jingle.
However, I happen to be, my friend,
That heart-of-gold known as "Miss G," my friend,
Drop up to the sixth floor and see, my friend,
Your honest-to-goodness Kris Kringle.

For I am Miss G of the So and So Store,
In charge of exchanges, north corner, sixth floor.
I'll take back those slippers Aunt Emily sent—
We all know how well your Aunt Emily meant,
But since they don't fit and they're terribly red,
Well, how about three quarts of bourbon instead?
That fine mellow bourbon you hinted about,
Which Santa Claus pointedly left you without!

On Christmas I never appear, old pal—
The heck with the wrapping and packing!
But early the following year, old pal,
I know I'll be seeing you here, old pal,
For all of that holiday cheer, old pal,
That somehow or other was lacking.

For I am Miss G of the So and So Store—
The line will please form to the left of the door—
"Why, certainly that's a returnable lamp,
That holiday horror from Grandma and Gramp—
Providing it hasn't been damaged or frayed,
The twelve ninety-five that the purchaser paid
I cheerfully give you, to right such a wrong,
With maybe those bath towels you've needed so long."

You'll find no red whiskers on me, Madame,
I hang out a practical shingle.
So if you happen to be, Madame,
In need of post-Yuletide esprit, Madame,
Drop up to the sixth floor and see, Madame,
Your honest-to-goodness Kris Kringle,
And get what you really asked Santa Claus for
From good old Miss G of the So and So Store!

NURSERY RHYME FOR CHILD WHO MISSES MOBILE STOLEN FROM NURSERY BY IDIOT WHO THOUGHT IT WAS WORTH SOMETHING BECAUSE IT MOVED

Up the wall
Went Seymour Small,
Up the wall he went!
Down the wall
Came Seymour Small
With a copy of something nobody else would buy.

UNRHYMED IMAGES FOR THE MIND THAT SEEKS NO COMFORT

D-FLAT TO E-FLAT-SEVEN MODULATION
    BY HARMONICA RASCALS
UNMATCHED WALLPAPER ROSES WITH
    COFFEE STAIN
FLAT TIRE ON MONOCYCLE ON FLYPAPER
GIRL WITH THREE TITS, ONE BLUE
CHOPPED LIVER SANDWICH WITH
    MAYONNAISE
MONTROSE LEVY

MOZART'S IN HIDING, NOT DEAD

Lyric found in letter to Samuel Taylor, August 5, 1957. Written in response to Taylor's play *The Happy Time*. Punctuation, emphases, and note are Loesser's. An excerpt from the letter precedes the lyric.

As far as songwriters are concerned, I feel that you have a leaning toward the *exquisite*. I would rather curve this in the direction of *hairy-ass*. There is something wonderful about commercial songwriters and something very sensitive too, as witness Irving Berlin's great renunciation scene called "The Girl That I Marry," or Adler and

Ross's plot transition entitled "Hernando's Hide-away." I am scared of a lyric writer who is such a language stickler and refiner that he can't be ar-gued into writing a hit; or the tune writer who knows all the César Franck chords and none of Walter Donaldson's. My specialty is dragging them up to your knowledgeable, sensitive but wholesome class. I can't guarantee dragging any-body down from Cloud 9. I would like you to trust me on this. You wrote a very solid, understand-able, healthy, robust, real, happy, funny play. I now submit the following envoi:

Bernstein effetely would broil it,
Blitzstein would mention the toilet.
As for Menotti,
He'd do it with spotty
Allusions to God, which would spoil it.

Forrest and Wright would sound shrewish,
Arlen would paint it all bluish,
Further conjecture
That Harburg would lecture
And Rome would compose it in Jewish.

Leave things to me,* like I said.
(Mozart's in hiding, not dead.)

POEM WITH WHICH TO PROCLAIM EXTENT OF ERUDITION AND DRAW CHEERS FROM THOSE WHO LOOKED THE WORDS UP TOO

The mavis clamoring for Meerane, soul aflame,
Toward Melampus, Amythaon, and Eidomine
    pleading,
As if in gentle mercara, shriven.
Plaintive module in time's modillion
Ever the monassir,
Ever the plaintive, striated ixtl-fed mavis.

* *Loesser's note: me, the boy producer*

HOLIDAY FOR JEWS?

From an undated typescript. Loesser's note reads: "To the tune 'Holiday for Strings' by David Rose (Reformed)."

Oy gevalt and vay iz meer,
I dassent nosh or drink a beer.
I couldn't smoke a fine cigar
Or take a bissel halavah.
From my gederum comes a groan,
Already I atone,
Yom Kippur.

DIGGEREL DOGGEREL, MURIEL HOLLANDER

Manuscript dated May 22, 1967.

Diggerel doggerel,
Muriel Hollander.
Interamehutinal
Greetings anon—
Plus, immerwieder, my
Pleniavuncular
"What are we going to
Do about John?"

Poetry, schmoetry,
Muriel Hollander.
Isn't the bubbeleh
Putting us on?
Hark to the clamorous
Ganzemeschpochedich
"What are we going to
Do about John?"

    Characteristic'lly,
    Frank Loesser

A WORD FROM JUNIOR

From typescript dated February 5, 1968. Punctuation and emphasis are Loesser's.

How I hate *both* mother and father!
To hate *one* I'd very much rather.
But I hate *both* father and mother
(Who thru life have adored one another).
Yes my eyes, they stare—
And my nostrils flare—
And my mouth is inclined to foam—
Out of hate for *both* mother and father
I'm the child of an *un*broken home.

MY DOCTOR SAID

Unfinished. From undated manuscript. Probably late 1968.

My doctor said push-ups would kill me,
And swimming would make my feet wet.
So you is the only excuse I get.

My doctor forbid me to pole vault,
It raises too much of a sweat.
So you is the only excuse I get.

Pay no mind,
I'm the stay-at-home kind
And I'm having my setting-up fit.

PLEA TO MY WIFE

Undated manuscript. Written for Jo Sullivan Loesser. Punctuation and emphases are Loesser's.

Be there and <u>cook</u> for me,
Be a big <u>schnook</u> for me,
When I'm lost, <u>look</u> for me,
Jump in the <u>brook</u> for me,
Wallow in <u>gook</u> for me.

For a finale
When I'm on a show,
Up a blind alley
With nowhere to go,

PLEASE WRITE THE <u>BOOK</u> FOR ME!

Index

This is an alphabetical index of song titles and first lines (including first refrains) of Frank Loesser's lyrics. When the first line of a refrain begins with or is identical to the song title, the first line is not included. Alternate titles are listed except where they duplicate first lines. The index also includes individual song copyright information.

The following copyright information should be added to individual notices according to the corresponding number:

(1) Warner Bros. Publications U.S. Inc., Miami, FL 33014.

For all lyrics: International Copyright Secured. All Rights Reserved. Used By Permission.